CAGED BIRD

DAVE RACER

ALETHOS PRESS LLC

⊕ALETHOS PRESS LLC

P.O. Box 600160
St. Paul, Minnesota 55106
651-772-4344
www.alethospress.com

www.cagedbird.net

Book design by Scot Skogerboe Design.
Printed in the United States of America.

ISBN 0-9702509-0-8

10 9 8 7 6 5 4 3 2 1

CONTENTS

INTRODUCTION

I first heard the name Tom Bird in 1989. At the time, I published a political newspaper in Minnesota called *Dave Racer's Minnesota Report* and had run a story about Kathy Greening. Someone murdered her in July of 1982 and the case remained unsolved. Several politicians seemed to be less than enthusiastic about pursuing her killer and I enjoyed writing about lazy and corrupt politicians.

Rev. Kenneth P. Kothe, pastor of Redeemer Lutheran Church in Burnsville, Minnesota, read the Greening murder story and called me. His friend and seminary classmate Tom Bird had been wrongfully convicted of murder, he said. Would I get involved?

All my attention focussed on Minnesota and Ken failed to change my focus. Ten years later, though, he asked me to write a book about Tom. This time I caught on and we plunged ahead on this project. Kothe's fervent and continued pursuit of justice for Tom impressed me; anyone who would stick with a friend that long at least deserved a hearing.

I began writing *Caged Bird* on July 2, 1999, and thought I would finish the project late in the year. I had no idea how huge this job would be. It involved three criminal trials, several appeals, thousands of news stories and even a four hour TV mini-series—*Murder Ordained*.

As I write this introduction, I have expended more than 2,200 hours on this project. I have read nearly 10,000 pages of material. These include trial transcripts, appeals, court decisions, investigative reports, letters, memos, news stories and even Tom's mother's personal journals. I have conducted dozens of interviews and traveled to Kansas' Lansing Correctional Facility eight times.

I set out to do something no one else who ever wrote a word about Tom Bird had done—tell the story from his perspective. Even so, Kothe and I agreed that we would let the evidence take us where it would. If it proved that Tom killed his wife, so be it. If it proved he killed Marty Anderson, we would report it. It took me nearly nine months to finally draw my conclusions about these charges. You will have to read the book to learn them.

This book is filled with names. I did not personally interview them all. In fact, some are now dead and a few have conveniently disappeared. Yet every name that appears in this book is the result of a written record that I allow to speak for itself.

Some men and women found themselves not only caught up in these criminal accusations, but also held up to public exposure and ridicule. In several cases, I have changed those names. They need no further shame. All other names are listed alphabetically at the end of the book to aid you in sorting through all the players in this drama.

The Bird family spent scores of hours with me putting spirit on to the flesh of cold facts. Tom Bird worked very hard under the difficult and frustrating circumstances of incarceration to answer the hundreds of questions I threw at him. At all times he was forthcoming. On a few occasions, his answers didn't square with what I had discovered in written reports. He forthrightly set the record straight.

I resisted requests in this introduction to tell you much about myself. If you want to know more, go to my website: http://www.daveracer.com.

Learn about Alethos Press LLC at http://www.alethospress.com.

Caged Bird has its own website at http://www.cagedbird.net. Several long documents that I chose not to reprint for this book are contained there. You are free to download them.

And to more closely follow Tom Bird's activities, his friends have created a website at http://www.tombird.net.

This is a story about a pastor, a paramour, and a quadrangle murder. Though it is long and complicated, I hope you enjoy reading it as much as I enjoyed writing it.

Dave Racer
The Year of Our Lord, 2000

Updated Information

Tom Bird's case continues to evolve as will this book. I expect to hear from scores of people, not all of them friendly, with their bit of "evidence." If you are one of these, feel free to write. Use e-mail at alethospress@aol.com or write to me at P.O. Box 600160, St. Paul, Minnesota 55106.

It seems likely that updated editions of this book will be published in the future. If you wish to be informed of new publications, send me your name and address.

The ultimate piece of news of course would be Tom Bird's release from prison. If you want to be among the first to know, let me know who you are.

Dave Racer—Author, *Caged Bird*

ACKNOWLEDGEMENTS

Dave Racer and Ken Kothe wish to thank the following people for help in producing *Caged Bird:*

To LaMarr Blecker for transcribing the closing statements and *Murder Ordained;* Jeanne Turner and her staff at the Lyon county Court House for putting up with Dave for 11 days in May, 2000; Charlie Deutschmann for helping to set up Free Tom Bird, Inc.; Dr. Eugene Bunkowske for spiritual guidance; to the Elders of Redeemer-Burnsville: Barry Leaon, Robert Huber, Lyle McCarty, Curt Thompson, Charlie Deutschmann Ron Sprengeler, Richard Williams for encouraging their pastor to go on Freedom Walk in Kansas; Daren and Mary Gangelhoff, Barb Allen, Jody Bown, Shirley Hildebrandt, Kathy Kasten, Vicki Leaon, Clarice Sprengeler, Kristi Zacharis for stuffing and mailing letters; Rev. Herman Otten, for years of faithful service keeping Tom Bird's story alive, and for the many stories about the book in *Christian News;* Ralph and Mark Bird for their hours and hours of interviews, and along with Gloria and Felix Cates, their years of continued love and support for Tom, a son and brother; Virginia Bird, for her 2,100-page daily journal; Richard Johnson, for seeking out financial support; all those who provided financial support for this project, especially our publishing partners; David Racer Sr., the author's father, for hours of proof reading; Rev. Eugene and Mrs. Barz for their hospitality; Rev. and Mrs. David Spaeth for their hospitality; Susan Ewert for her hours of interviews, support and belief in both Tom Bird and our effort; Don and Lois Froelich for revealing their hearts and teaching the author so much about Faith Lutheran Church and faith.

A very special thanks to Katherine Kothe for her 13 years of support and encouragement as Pastor Ken relentlessly pursued this project; for Rosanne Racer who allowed Dave to take hundreds of hours away from the family and for forgoing the financial stability a "real job" brings; for Terry Lyn Bird, an incredible woman who has not only stood with Tom Bird since October of 1983, but continues to work relentlessly for his freedom. These are three very, very special women.

FOREWORD

"Woe to those who acquit the godless for a bribe, and deprive the innocent of his right." Isaiah 5:23

When CBS-TV aired the four-hour mini-series, *Murder Ordained,* in 1987, it purported to tell the true story of a love quadrangle that resulted in a double murder by a Lutheran minister in Emporia, Kansas. As I watched it, I sat stunned—stunned because of the nature of the crime and my personal knowledge of the man whom the movie said did these horrible crimes.

My heart wrenched with emotions as I watched, but my mind needed more facts. Did a seminary classmate murder his wife? Did he conspire to murder the church secretary's husband? The prosecutors said, "yes." The defense said, "no." Two juries found him "guilty" after reviewing the evidence. Or did they?

At the time I believed the juries. We are taught to trust juries to do the right thing. Surely, if they found him guilty he must be guilty, I reasoned. But we shall see in the pages to follow that the prosecutors, the judges, the juries, the lawyers and Tom Bird himself did not have all of the facts at the time of his trials. Even the "facts" they had were weak and circumstantial, but still convicted and caged Bird.

I first met Tom Bird in 1972, at Concordia Theological Seminary, Springfiled, Illinois. Those were days filled with cherished memories. Finished with the movie, I sat back and reflected on those memories.

I remembered a Tom Bird who was considerate, intellectual, and focused—a man filled with compassion and caring for others. I remembered the time when my day-old son Jake faced life-threatening pneumonia at St. Johns Hospital and Tom prayed for him. I remembered Tom as a classmate who studied hard and got good grades so as to follow in the footsteps of his father, Rev. Ralph Bird.

I remembered the dinners we enjoyed with other seminarians and their wives. And I remembered the music of the 60's as we danced the night away atop "the soup" in the recovery room of the seminary clinic where my wife and I lived. And most of all, I remembered Tom and Sandy Bird as a couple in love.

I remembered how Sandy lit up a room as she entered, and her keen intellect. She studied hard to learn the Lutheran faith, and she looked forward to a lifetime of service with Tom.

Those memories formed a barrier for me to Tom's guilt. I wanted to know the truth. I needed answers to questions. Memories are rarely convincing in court and do not sway evidence. But that movie stirred in me other issues of sex, lies and injustice.

I began my search for truth in circumstantial evidence, for an explanation in lies that persuaded the jurors, and for justice in a system that betrayed it's highest principle: truth itself.

I asked to read all the appeals. I talked with Rev. Ralph and Virginia Bird, Tom's brother Mark, his sister Gloria and new wife Terry.

I wrote articles. I begged newspaper reporters to investigate.

I begged numerous people to get involved including Kansas Senator Bob Dole, TV personality Dick Clark, radio-talk host Rush Limbaugh, syndicated columnist Calvin Trillin, presidential candidate Pat Buchanan, Illinois Senator Paul Simon, Chicago attorney Glen Peglau, and actor Wayne Storm. Buchanan, Simon, Peglau, and Storm took interest in the cause. Buchanan was busy running for president of the United States in February of 2000, but said that he might help later. Simon put me into contact with John Podesta, Chief of Staff in the Clinton White House.

Peglau had passion for Tom and even more for justice. He worked for years to win justice for Tom, but he died.

Storm pushed the leads I gave him but the system was greater than an actor wanting to write a screen play and produce a movie. "Ken, as long as Tom Bird is in prison no one will touch him. It's too risky." Time forced Storm out of the picture.

For many years I worked with Herman Otten, editor of *Christian News,* a New Haven, Missouri, weekly newspaper. Otten did his own investigation and concluded that Bird was innocent. Apart from his own family, Otten has done more for Tom Bird than any other single person alive and he continues to do so.

I read in *Christian News* of another murder involving a Lutheran minister, but this was different and justice turned expedient. The man suffocated his wife with a pillow for the love of another woman. He was tried, convicted and sentenced to life in a Texas prison. But an extraordinary turn of events took place.

Some thought it was mercy while others thought it was justice run-a-muck. Just four years into his sentence, the Texas penal system paroled him. It was incompetence at it best and justice at its worst. It was also dangerous, setting free a cold-blooded murderer. Why did Texas set free a murderer who served just fours years of a life sentence? I was curious and angered, so I searched him out.

I discovered him living in Missouri and gave him a call. "Why were you paroled?"

"Two reasons," he said. "One, I was guilty. I admitted it and showed remorse. Two, the Texas prison system was overcrowded and they believed I was rehabilitated and wouldn't murder again. So I was paroled."

The difference in Tom's case is that Tom did not murder his wife. Nor did he conspire to murder the church secretary's husband. This presents a moral dilemma for Tom because he can't admit guilt nor can he show remorse for something he didn't do. If he showed remorse and admited guilt he most likely would be paroled, but if he did so, he would sacrifice the one thing that means the most to him, his integrity.

So many long years passed and little has happened to free Tom. It looked hopeless.

Then I ran into Dave Racer again. We first met in 1989. At that time, I read *Dave Racer's Minnesota Report,* a monthly investigative newspaper, and thought immediately he could help. But Dave was busy with other issues and Emporia injustice was far removed from political corruption in St. Paul. He graciously declined.

But over the years we kept in touch and I kept telling him about Tom. Finally, in July of 1999, he accepted my invitation to write a book about Tom.

I thought that perhaps Dave had the connections to get into the case, and if he could, he would be able to write a book filled with convincing evidence. I felt sure the Kansas judicial system was by now well-protected, and maybe prosecutors and judges were still lurking around to cover themselves.

Was Dave afraid to give it a try? Not at all! Would I help him? You bet I would! I gave him articles, magazines, appeals, and "that movie" *(Murder Ordained,* a movie better named *Murder Framed).* I told him I would ride my bike through Kansas with *Caged Bird* in hand and give it to the Chief Justice of the Kansas State Supreme Court, and to others.

So, the investigation began and the true story of Tom Bird would be told. And now he has finished.

For those who believe Tom Bird is innocent, Caged Bird will be a testimony to their belief; for those who have doubts, it will drive them to call for a new trial. For those who believe he is guilty, fairness will drive them to seek the whole truth in a new trial. And for those interested in justice issues, *Caged Bird* should provide the force behind a demand for a new trial.

What follows is shocking—shocking because it reveals the many blemishes of sinful humanity and the judicial system that sometimes falls prey to it. *Caged Bird* cuts to the heart of the human consciousness.

This much we know: Sandy Bird and Martin Anderson are dead. The murderer(s) run(s) free.

Dave Racer strips bear the lies behind the circumstantial "evidence" and gets to the heart of the matter—Tom Bird was framed.

This, then, is Dave's story.

Rev. Kenneth P. Kothe

DEDICATION

To Reverend Kenneth P. Kothe, Tom Bird's incredible friend and Concordia Seminary classmate without whom this book never would have even gotten started.

SECTION I:

Confusion now hath made his masterpiece!
Most sacrilegious murder hath broke open
The Lord's anointed temple, and stole thence
The life of the building!

Macbeth; William Shakespeare

Sandy Bird's body found

The morning of July 17, 1983, was hot as usual in Emporia, Kansas. Most of the city's 25,000 residents were headed to or from its 51 churches, proud of their reputation as a community of religious people.

The Sunday service at Faith Lutheran Church was full again, just as it had been since 33-year-old Reverend Thomas P. Bird became its pastor early in 1982. This Sunday, however, Pastor Bird missed church. Earlier that morning, he called Lay Minister Don Froelich and asked him to come to his house. He told Froelich that Sandy Bird, his wife, had dropped him off at church the night before and went to Emporia State University to use the school's computer. She did not return at 11:30 as she and Tom planned. She never came home. He asked Froelich to preach the sermon that day.

Froelich saw that Bird looked tired, worried, shaken and vulnerable, not at all the confident, strong leader he came to love and respect over the past 18 months. Froelich told Tom he would be happy to preach the sermon and tell the congregation what was happening.

During worship Froelich prayed for Sandy and Tom. After service many of the church members intended to go home, change clothes and head out to search for the pastor's wife. They loved her as they loved Tom. Her absence could not be good news for them.

Fletcher skipped church, too

About 10:20 a.m., Brian Fletcher and his fiancé parked their car near the Rocky Ford Bridge, just a few miles southeast of Emporia. The old single-lane steel structure resembles a railroad trestle more than a bridge built for auto traffic. It is ugly. The bridge, which has a wooden deck, spans the swift-flowing, muddy Cottonwood River. Fletcher planned to spend the day paddling his canoe down the river.

As he approached the bridge, Fletcher looked down 65 feet to the river. There he spotted a human body. It looked like a woman lying face down in an eddy formed by a small dam made of rocks and mud. He looked again, leaning forward over the bridge and saw the underbelly of a car, partially submerged in the river. She lay in front of the car, trapped by the eddy.

Fletcher knew there was nothing he could do for the woman in the water. He drove south to the mobile home of Mark Gibbons, and they called the police. Then Fletcher and Gibbons raced back to the bridge to await the police officers. Joined by Fletcher's fiancé, the three studied the accident scene.

Charles Smith, a Sergeant with the Kansas Highway Patrol, was the first

2

officer to arrive. It was 10:52 a.m. A minute later, Kansas Highway Patrolman John Rule, an accident specialist, joined Trooper Smith at the bridge.

Rule was a veteran trooper who had responded to more than 750 auto accidents. He immediately saw that this accident was different from the others. He and Smith photographed the accident scene, took measurements and recorded other observations. They knew they had to satisfy the curiosity of many interested parties — family, insurance companies, sheriffs, coroner. Despite his experience and curiosity about the accident, Rule treated it like any other.

More law enforcement and rescue officers drove up to begin their specialized duties as part of the grim task. One of the men in the water got the okay to roll the body over. He looked into the face of a pretty young woman.

A rescue worker found the woman's purse inside the car and took out her billfold. He passed it up to Rule who read the name on the driver's license. It was Sandra Stringer Bird.

Trooper Smith left the accident scene and followed by Emporia Police Officer Scott Cronk, drove to 1005 Henry Street, the Bird's house. Delivering a death message was the hardest thing Smith had to do, but he had done it before. He rehearsed the right words to say.

Waiting for word

Pastor Bird sat fidgeting in his living room near the telephone. Sometimes he'd walk to the picture window, looking up and down the street, hoping at any minute to see Sandy's white Peugeot station wagon turn the corner. He felt his anxiety increase with each passing moment.

He had fed the children their breakfast and, as the morning wore on, sent them to play at a neighbor's. Since just past midnight, he had reviewed in his mind every possible scenario. Sandy got lost. Sandy fell asleep. Sandy drove to her mother's, "no, she would never do that." He told himself. Sandy got mugged. Sandy got kidnapped. "She would have been here with me if I would have just come home with her last night." He tried to be hopeful.

Bird's hope was shattered when he saw the officers walk up the sidewalk. One of them carried Sandy's purse. His heart sank. His long night of worry ended in the worst possible way.

Trooper Smith told Pastor Bird that Sandy died in a single car accident at the Rocky Ford Bridge. They said she apparently lost control of her car and it went over the edge, plunging into the water below. They had few details.

Tom saw things moving in slow motion. He stood stunned, confused and crestfallen, with the officers in front of him, but trying to visualize a bridge, a river, his wife lying next to the wreck, bruised, bloody and dead. He had questions but no answers.

Tom asked them, "What was she doing out there? We never go out there." He paused. "Well, where is it?"

Grim work began

Dr. Thomas Butcher, the coroner declared Sandy Bird dead at the scene. Later that day, Tom identified Sandy's body. Dr. Juan Gabriel did an autopsy on Monday. It took a few days before Tom heard the autopsy report. Gabriel reported Sandy died from a nearly severed left kidney that caused immense internal bleeding. She bled to death, probably within 15-30 minutes of sustaining the injury.

Tom and his family buried Sandy Bird's body on Wednesday, July 20, 1983, in Alexander, in Saline County, a suburb of her hometown of Little Rock, Arkansas. Two days later, Pastor Bird, his mother Virginia and his three children flew back to Emporia. There was a church waiting and ministry to perform. Life must go on.

Tom started the difficult task of rebuilding his life and might have been successful, except for Lyon County Sheriff Dan Andrews and Kansas Highway Patrolman John Rule. The two veteran police officers, aided by a curious gawker, saw some things at the accident scene that bothered them. By the next day, they wondered if Sandy's death had been accident.

The officer's hunch went unheeded until November 4, 1983, when Lorna Anderson's depraved death scheme ended in the cold-blooded, execution-style murder of her husband Martin. Officers from two counties worked the two death investigations as one scheme twisted together. They conceived it as a torrid love affair that turned violent. Journalists, judges, prosecutors and scandal-thirsty Emporia citizens shared their hunch.

In July of 1985, a Lyon County Jury tried Thomas P. Bird for the first-degree murder of Sandy Bird. Unable to prove his innocence, the jury found him guilty.

On August 7, 1985, the State of Kansas sentenced Tom to life in prison.

Enter the judge—1990

"The present crimes and the prior crimes are but equal parts in a scheme. The crimes are so closely connected that their probative value overwhelms their prejudicial effect. This crime did not occur in a vacuum and proof of its commission and the identity of the actor should not be tried in a vacuum."

4

Trial Judge Melvin Gradert,
From a 1990 ruling on a defense motion filed by Thomas P. Bird,
about to stand trial for the murder of Martin K. Anderson

Judge Gradert penned these words before the 1990 trial began. He based his decision on what he already knew and believed about the case. He heard thousands of words of testimony from dozens of witnesses during Geary County's inquisition into Martin Anderson's murder. He reviewed scores of investigative reports. He listened to Steven Opat, Geary County Prosecutor. Perhaps he watched the 1987 CBS TV mini-series *Murder Ordained*. It left no doubt that Tom killed Marty.

Gradert knew much about Tom Bird, too. He knew Tom was no longer a pastor, but a twice-convicted felon. He knew the chief witness, Lorna, was no longer a church secretary, but *also* a twice-convicted felon. He had Lorna's eyewitness account of the murder and her confession at hand. He knew Bird's wife and Anderson's husband were dead. That is all he needed to know: two deaths, same scheme. Let the guilty man stand trial.

November 4, 1983—Martin Anderson Murdered

Martin Anderson, 35, lived with his wife Lorna and their four young daughters, Lori, 8; Julie, 6; and the twins, Jennifer and Janelle, 2, in Emporia, Kansas. He was the chief laboratory technician at Emporia's Newman Memorial Hospital.

Marty also served in the Army Reserves. One weekend each month he reported to either Fort Riley, near Junction City, or to the National Guard Armory in Topeka, to fulfill his military obligation. Each location is a bit more than an hour's drive from Emporia.

On Friday, November 4, 1983, Marty packed a picnic lunch for his family. They left Emporia just after noon and headed to Fort Riley to shop at the Post Exchange and Wal-Mart. Marty wanted to buy a new camouflage jacket before reporting for his scheduled reserve duty two weeks later. Lorna wanted to pick up a good supply of diapers and other family necessities.

When Marty left his house that day, he had no idea that Lorna wanted more than diapers—she wanted him dead, and this was the day her evil scheme would be consummated. Lorna believed that soon she could bank the hundreds of thousands of dollars coming from Marty's life insurance policies. She would finally be free from his beatings. Best of all, she would have the freedom to move in with her latest lovebird.

The family picnicked at Fort Riley before going to the Clothing Exchange to buy the jacket. Because it was quite chilly and rainy that day, they ate their picnic lunch in their Ford conversion van. The children got out and played until the chill sent them scurrying back into the warm van. While she watched the children play, Lorna rehearsed her part in the death drama about to unfold. Marty planned the schedule for the rest of the day. He wanted them to get back to Emporia to play in the co-ed volleyball game that night. He knew that while Lorna was playing volleyball with him, she could not be in the arms of another man.

Next, Marty drove to the PX. The family walked up to the PX door, but Lorna was turned away. She had left her ID card in the van. Lorna returned to the van and waited for Marty. Maybe it was at this time that she passed the .22 caliber Colt Woodsman to the hit man, or maybe she did it earlier, or even the night before. Her purse had served as its holster for a long time, waiting for this day.

Marty drove them to Wal-Mart to buy diapers. During this stop, Marty, who had charge of Jennifer, slipped out the door for a few minutes and left the little girl wandering about by herself. A store clerk found the child and brought her to Lorna. Lorna wondered where Marty had gone and why he left the child behind.

She went out to the parking lot where she spotted Marty, already in the van. As she got in, she alleged that she saw that Marty had a roll of money and had told her, "Someday you'll thank me for this." She told this to police and to her closest friends, raising the possibility that Marty was a drug dealer.

Before getting on the road back to Emporia, Marty took the family to McDonald's for a treat. Everyone said he was good with the girls, even though he had no respect for Lorna. The girls got strawberry sundaes. Lorna sampled them—or at least made it appear as though she did.

Marty looked at his watch. He had just enough time to get back to Emporia to play volleyball. He never got to play that game. In less than an hour he was dead.

Before leaving McDonald's, Lorna complained that she was sick to her stomach and felt like throwing up. Since she was allergic to strawberries, Marty never questioned her sudden attack of nausea.

After she finished in the restroom, she told Marty, "You take care of the kids. I'm driving." She got into the driver's seat. Lorna had to control all their movements from then on for her plan to work. She headed south on Highway 177 toward I-70.

Lorna pulled into a gas station just north of I-70. Marty waited for her to get out, but she did not. This was not the pre-arranged murder site and it was still a little too early.

One of the twins had fallen asleep on Marty's lap. Lorna put the sleeping twin on the folded-down seat in the back of the vehicle, and then pulled the big Ford conversion van back onto Highway 177, and continued heading south. She ignored the I-70 east exit they usually took because her plan required her to stop alongside Highway 177, a two lane concrete road with gravel shoulders that tailed sharply off into the ditches straddling the corn and hay fields on either side of the road.

About three miles south of I-70 Lorna again complained of nausea. She needed to throw up. She saw that the pre-arranged murder site was coming soon and started to slow down. She pulled off the road, but suddenly lurched back on—still not the right place. Then she spotted the marker, a mailbox about a mile south of McDowell Creek Road. She pulled over and stopped. Lorna had her role well memorized.

She turned off the motor, pulled the car keys from the ignition and ran from the van down into the grassy stubble in the ditch by the mown hayfield. It seemed odd to some that she took the keys with her, but she claimed that is what Marty always told her to do. Most importantly, the murder plot depended on it. Marty and the four girls stayed inside to wait for her. Seeing his chance to take control again, he moved over to the driver's seat.

About 40 feet from the road toward the hayfield, Lorna bent over and faked vomiting. She stood just north of the tractor gateway that crossed the highway. A farmhouse and its outbuildings sat empty on the east side of the highway. A clump of trees grew a few hundred feet north. Another farmhouse sat about a half-mile south on the same side of the road. Otherwise, there were no buildings near where she had stopped the van. An occasional car drove by, but the murder would be done down in the ditch, the sight line blocked by the big van.

Done with her fake vomiting, Lorna called out to Marty. "I dropped the keys!" She went to the van. "I dropped the keys down there in the ditch."

Marty got out and went down into the ditch. Lorna stood a little ways off, her heart pounding, as she knew the grim deed was almost done. Marty dug around in the six-inch long grass and stubble. Just then a masked gunman came toward him from the north. The gunman shouted at Marty. Lorna claimed he said, "Give me your wallet!" The gunman put three bullet holes in the back of Marty's head. Marty fell dead. A pool of blood seeped into the muddy dirt beneath his body.

Now all Lorna had to do was wait a few minutes until the hit man got away. She rehearsed her lines again. "He pulled me down into the ditch. He said he was going to shoot me, but his gun didn't fire. He ran south." When the witnesses came, she had to act hysterical, out of control, but she was good at that.

Prosecutors heard it was Tom Bird

On August 30, 1985, nearly two years later, after signing on to a plea agreement of her own, Lorna told police officers and Geary County Attorney Steven Opat, that the hit man who murdered Martin Anderson was Tom Bird, former Pastor of Faith Lutheran Church in Emporia, where she worked as the church secretary. In exchange for her statement, Anderson received a "use immunity" agreement from the prosecutor. By fingering Tom, Lorna improved her own chances for a pardon. She just had to be careful to tell them what they wanted to hear. Nothing she told them could be used against her in court, unless the officers could verify the evidence independently or unless she lied—which she did, repeatedly.

Lorna told investigators that she and Tom Bird had been lovers since the spring of 1983. She said they wanted to spend their lives together. It was the same fantasy she told them and some of her friends before. She said Tom wanted to murder Marty, for the same reason he murdered Sandy, so Tom and Lorna could spend their lives together.

As Lorna made this statement, Tom was serving a 2-7 year prison term because of his July 1984 conviction for trying to hire someone to murder Marty Anderson. He had just started serving a life sentence for the first-degree murder of Sandy Bird. Tom posed no threat to Lorna. She needed to make a deal for her own benefit.

In September of 1985, after giving her statement about Tom Bird, Lorna began serving a 5 to 18-year sentence. She had hammered out a plea agreement with Lyon County Attorney Rodney Symmonds. She pled guilty to two counts of solicitation to commit murder in the death of Marty Anderson. No murderer had yet been charged. She hoped for an early parole and believed Tom would be convicted of Marty's murder. She then could get on with her life.

In May of 1987, once prosecutors determined that her August 1985 statement contained lies, and evidence pointed to her direct involvement in the murder, Geary County charged Lorna with the First Degree murder of Marty Anderson. In 1988, Lorna again pled guilty, this time to a reduced charge of second-degree murder. The county made this agreement in exchange for her cooperation in their upcoming trial of Tom Bird. The State sentenced her to 15 years to life in prison.

These two dead spouses and the lusty, passion-driven plot behind their demise formed the "equal parts in a scheme" about which Judge Gradert wrote in his 1990 decision.

On February 28, 1990, the first-degree murder trial of Tom Bird finally convened, more than six years after Martin Anderson's terrified little daughters had witnessed his murder. The state's star witness, Lorna Anderson, prepared to seal Tom Bird's fate.

Murder Scene Witnesses

Martin Anderson lay dead in the ditch next to a mown hayfield alongside Kansas Highway 177 with three .22 caliber bullet holes in his head. The murderer had fired the deadly shots sometime between 6:00-6:15 p.m. on November 4, 1983. The crime site sat four miles south of Interstate 70, south of Manhattan and east of Junction City, Kansas. Fort Riley lay just a few miles west; Topeka just over 50 miles to the east.

Highway 177 is a regular thoroughfare for people heading to and from work. The time between 4:00-7:00 p.m. on a Friday is very busy with commuter traffic. The weekend had started and people headed to football games, or just out of town.

Lorna Anderson and her accomplice(s) saw this as the perfect spot for a murder that they meant to look like a random highway robbery.

A long line of people drove past the murder site that evening. If someone had set up a video camera tower in the hayfield on the west side of the highway during the time of the murder, they would have taped this scene:

Theron Mayhew eyed a 1972-74 blue or green Chevy Nova parked the wrong way in a driveway just south of the murder scene at 5:45 p.m.

Margaret Wyatt spotted a similar-looking car at McDowell Creek Road at 5:55 p.m., suggesting the car moved to a site with a better vantagepoint. Wyatt remembered the car because it faced the wrong direction, and no one was around. Continuing her drive south, she did not see a van parked alongside the highway.

Sheryll Hoffman, followed a Ford conversion van with the license plate CPT MSC. The van was moving erratically, slowing down, turning left and right, then slowing again. Hoffman swerved to avoid hitting the van when it suddenly pulled off the road.

Joan Johnson noticed the van parked on the west side of the highway just after 6:05 p.m. She slowed down to see if there was something she could do to help, and saw two men talking in front of the van—men she could clearly discern and describe. But she kept on driving since everything looked in order.

Flash from a gun that fired four times at a man kneeling in the grass alongside the hayfield.

Brian Huffman noticed a man walking north, away from the parked van around 6:15 p.m.

Ron Say drove with a light colored car following close behind—maybe a full-sized Ford. It sped up and dropped back. He was sure the car turned around and headed north again.

Kenneth Kemp, Ph.D., a professor from Kansas State University, passed a blue van on the west side of the road about 6:20 p.m. Its flashers were on, but he saw no one near the van, even slowing down just in case someone needed help. He headed home.

With Marty dead, the murder plan Lorna and her accomplice(s) hatched depended on giving the hit man time to get away. They needed 15 minutes, so just after Dr. Kemp drove past, Lorna began her act as a distressed, hysterical wife whose husband lay murdered in the ditch.

Time slows down as evidence gets collected

James Henderson and his wife stopped first. James saw Lorna directly in front of her van waving her arms. She was very upset. "My husband has been shot. Please help him," she said.

James tried to calm her down. "She wasn't crying, but was hysterical, and talked in a loud voice, but she really wasn't screaming or yelling. She didn't appear dirty at all. She looked real clean."

Lorna pointed to the area of the ditch that cradled Marty's body. James turned his red Pinto around to shine its headlights down into the field to break through the darkness that shrouded the ditch. He flagged down Dennis Bayless and his wife. After James told them what he knew, Dennis drove to a house just north of the murder site and called the police. It was 6:27 p.m.

Deborah Bayless, a Registered Nurse, and James went down to the body. Deborah cleared Marty's mouth and started CPR, hoping she could somehow perform a miracle and revive the dead man.

James saw it was hopeless. "There was a lot of blood on his [Marty's] side, tissue on the left side of his head above the left ear. He was lying on his right side. His head was real bloody. Mrs. Bayless checked for a pulse, but couldn't find one. She said he was still warm. We rolled him over on his back so Mrs. Bayless could do CPR. He was whitish blue in color. His skin looked like plastic and was kind of waxy. When she tried CPR, we could hear gurgling noises. I saw vomit on his mouth."

The CPR lasted for 30-45 minutes before the police arrived.

While Dennis was still gone, James waived down John and Becky Leonard. It was now 6:30 p.m. John got out of his Chevy Blazer and spotted Lorna acting hysterical and shouting, "My husband has been shot! Is he going to be alright?"

John pulled his Blazer up on the gateway and angled it toward the ditch to shed more light on Marty's body. Then he went down to the body. It was "discolored and purple."

Becky Leonard tried to console Lorna. Lorna felt the time was right to tell her story, the one she had rehearsed earlier that day. So far, the plan was working.

Lorna said she lost her keys. Marty came to help her search. While Lorna recited her lines, Becky looked down and spotted the leather key case about six feet in front of her. She picked it up and gave the keys to Lorna who reacted by collapsing into Becky's arms. She helped Lorna get into the van with help from one of the Anderson children, and lay Lorna down inside.

Becky turned to the children. "What happened here?"

One of the girls said they had, "been to McDonalds and her mother got sick. Then she saw a man with a mask and a flash."

At that time, a school bus with 27 Clay Center football fans aboard pulled over and stopped. Ten of the bus riders got off and milled around the murder scene, checking out the body and staring at Lorna.

Charron Cales left the bus and went to the van. She and her friend Teresa Speltz got in to help comfort the children. Something about the girls puzzled Charron. She expected them to be hysterical like their mother. "They did not cry or ask any questions." Did Lorna calm them down while she waited for the right time to flag down a car? Did she tell those young impressionable girls what to say?

Charron asked what had happened. "One of the girls said she was 'looking out the window and saw a man with a mask on and then she saw sparks...and her dad was on the ground.' The man told her mother to lie down. And the voice she heard was not her father's." None of the girls recognized the hit man's voice.

Many of the witnesses who saw Lorna at the crime scene said she was overdoing it, as if *acting* hysterical and distressed rather than really being distraught. They were right.

Dark now and cold, law enforcement officers began arriving and were alarmed by what they saw. The gawkers and Good Samaritans who walked around the site trampled down the muddy field and grassy stubble. Marty's body had already been moved at least twice. It was an investigative nightmare. The investigators moved to protect what was left of the murder scene.

By the time Emergency Medical Treatment personnel, police officers, sheriffs, other investigators and the bystanders left that night, Geary County Deputy Sheriff Bill Deppish said as many as 39 people had been there. He hoped that not all the evidence was destroyed. Deppish knew that this murder investigation would be difficult. He heard the story about a robber who just happened to jump out from the bushes hoping to steal some poor stiff's billfold. He knew it was bogus.

A deputy drove Lorna to the hospital in Junction City while investigators collected what evidence they could find that night. Having found little, they set a guard to protect the site, planning to return Saturday morning.

Within hours, Deppish and Kansas Bureau of Investigation Agent Don Winsor began piecing together the puzzle. Within days, they uncovered what looked like the second part of a deadly scheme that began with Sandy Bird's death at Rocky Ford Bridge on July 17, 1983.

Pastor Bird unusually late

Reverend Larry Kalsow, pastor of Messiah Lutheran Church in Emporia, was a seminary classmate of Tom Bird's. He recommended calling Tom as Missions Pastor for the specific purpose of taking on the new ministry at Faith.

While investigators were poking around in the stubble of a ditch trying to find clues to help them solve Marty Anderson's murder, 52 miles east of them Kalsow attended a seminar on church growth at Washburn University in Topeka. Eleven members of Faith also attended, including Tom Bird. Kalsow spotted Tom "about 20 minutes after the [7 p.m.] meeting started." Kalsow said, "there was nothing unusual that would cause me to suspect stress or anxiety." He was, apparently, just a little late.

Several minutes before that, Steve and Beth Hanschu, members of Faith, drove on 17th Street in Topeka, toward Washburn. They saw Pastor Bird in his blue Toyota driving just ahead of them. "I guess we won't be the only ones late," Steve told his wife. They arrived just behind Tom, "around 7:15 or 7:20 p.m." To them, Pastor Bird "seemed normal that night."

During a break in the program around 8 p.m., Kalsow got paged to take a phone call from Mike Pruisner from Emporia. Pruisner was a member of Messiah and a fellow Optimist Club member with Kalsow, Marty Anderson and Tom Bird. Pruisner said he just heard on his police scanner that Marty had been shot. He told Kalsow it was either a robbery attempt or he committed suicide at a motel somewhere out near Junction City. The details were scant.

Kalsow knew Marty and Lorna personally. He introduced Lorna to Tom, and the Andersons had become members of Faith. Kalsow knew that Tom gave instructions to the Andersons, helping them convert to the Lutheran faith. He knew about the special bond between pastors and those whom they help make such a transition. Kalsow knew, too, that just a few months earlier, he strongly cautioned Tom about getting too close to Lorna. This made it harder for Kalsow to tell his friend Tom of the tragedy. He found it even harder on July 25. Kalsow presided at the memorial service for Sandy Bird. Since then, Kalsow saw the stress produced by Tom's personal grief and his problems with adjusting to life without Sandy. But it had to be done.

Kalsow found Tom and eyed him for a moment. He looked normal, chatting with his friends, talking about sports. Even for pastors, as with police officers, telling a friend about the death of someone close is one of the hardest things to do.

Kalsow gave Tom the news, and he reacted with, "Shock. Disbelief." Kalsow said Tom had "normal reactions to the news of death. He took it personally." Tom felt a personal responsibility to get involved and help right away. It was expected of a pastor.

Tom's mind quickly ran through a list of details. The first would be to find out what had happened. There would be funeral arrangements, children to care for and Lorna; oh Lorna would be a tough one, he knew. But that was premature.

Tom started making phone calls. He called Dr. "Mike" Miguelino at Newman Medical Center where Marty worked, to verify what they heard. Mike confirmed that Marty was shot dead, although that was about all he knew.

Tom was desperate for detail and called the Geary County Sheriff's Office. He talked with a dispatcher. "This is Reverend Tom Bird, a pastor, a minister from Emporia and I'm calling from Topeka. I'm pastor to Marty and Lorna Anderson from Emporia. I have gotten word, don't know if it is true or not, that Martin Anderson committed suicide in a motel room there."

"Well, there has been a death and our officers are investigating at this time." The dispatcher did not want to give out information without proof of identity. He measured his words carefully. "Marty Anderson was killed in this...Shot."

Tom's mind went immediately to the safety of Lorna and the children. His heart raced as he asked the dispatcher for more information. "Where is Lorna? Where are the children? Are they alright?"

"We're not allowed to divulge that information over the phone," the dispatcher answered. But he assured Tom that they were all okay.

"Have Lorna's parents, the Slaters from Hutchinson, Loren Slater, have they been notified?"

"Yes and they are on their way up."

Breaking the news

All fall, Tom had wrestled with his feelings. He longed for peace and direction in his life. He loved the ministry, but with Sandy gone and three children to raise along with all his pastoral commitments, he lived on the edge of emotional tolerance. "On the outside I was supposed to be this strong, confident pastor, like my dad, who said, 'Be strong, Tom.' But I didn't feel strong."

It had been more than three months since Sandy's death, and he was still unable to set his life in order. Just a week earlier he was in West Memphis with his best friend from seminary, Rev. Charles Smith, and his wife Carolyn, talking things out. Now he was faced with another bleak tragedy at Faith. More than ever, such news upset the already emotionally vulnerable man.

At the 8:45 p.m. seminar break, Kalsow and Bird gathered together the group that had traveled up from Faith to give them the bad news. Tom was shaken and walked past Kalsow whispering, "I can't tell them."

Kalsow saw that Tom was "very upset, almost in shock. Overwhelmed."

Tom sat down and covered his face with his hands as Kalsow broke the news. Don Froelich watched Tom's reaction. "He acted surprised and with disbelief. I certainly didn't sense that Tom had any foreknowledge."

When told of the shooting, the close-knit church group reacted with shock and tears, and some anger. Sharon Meyer, wife of one of the lay ministers, had told her husband that she thought Lorna and the pastor were too close, and she did not trust Lorna. She snapped, "This is Lorna's doing," but then whispered an apology for saying this.

The shocked church members talked about what to do.

Tom believed the role of a pastor included going to any length to comfort members of his church. His members believed the same way, and if he failed in this duty, he knew he would be judged for it. He wanted to get over to the hospital and comfort Lorna as quickly as he could. As well as they knew Tom, and no matter what their expectations were, the Faith lay ministers also knew the problems Lorna created for him. They had cautioned him about the perception that the two had a special relationship and they were aware of the gossip. They urged him not to go. At least not that night.

Pastor Kalsow agreed. Howard Meyer and Don Froelich said, "It will take over an hour to get there," and, "there's really nothing you can do this late."

Tom listened to them. He pondered their words. Tom's training, coupled with the extensive personal and private counseling he had done with Lorna, made the present situation even more urgent. But the lay ministers prevailed, and he agreed to return home, with Bart Laib riding along.

Still Tom felt he had to do something right away before he could leave for home. He found Rev. Donavan Sprick, a Lutheran pastor from Junction City. At Tom's urging, Sprick agreed to go to the hospital and look in on Lorna. Even if he could not be there, Tom just would not be satisfied with leaving Lorna alone without pastoral care.

Others—police investigators, *Emporia Gazette* writers, Soap Opera-loving Emporia citizens—began to question why Tom Bird was so insistent on getting over to see Lorna that night. They wanted to know why he was late for the meeting. They wanted to know how he reacted to the news that Marty was dead. Their thirst for the latest news and gossip about Tom Bird and licentious Lorna would not be quenched until they constructed a conspiracy around everything he said, did or had done.

Investigators salvage evidence

Al Buskey, a Geary County Deputy Sheriff received a call from his dispatcher at 6:32 p.m. on November 4, 1983. Dennis Bayless had reported a possible homicide on Highway 177 south of I-70. Buskey flipped on his lights and siren and headed directly for the crime scene.

As Buskey raced down the highway he had no problem telling where to stop. He saw a school bus, several vehicles and several police cars. He was relieved that the other officers were already there. It reduced his risk of danger. He counted more than 15 people milling around the area. Leaving his car he walked down into the ditch where he saw Marty's body covered with a blanket. He stood about 50 feet from the road. No matter how many dead bodies he saw, nothing ever prepared him for the next one. Buskey described Marty's body:

> "White male subject possibly mid 30's, black hair, brown eyes, subject was wearing a white sports shirt, gray dress slacks, a blue sport type jacket, appeared to have a black eye (left), and an obvious head wound with bone and brain matter protruding from the head." Buskey noted that Marty's trousers had mud on both knees, puzzling at first because the body was on its back.

Buskey conferred with Deputy John Fink, Deputy (later Sheriff) Bill Deppish and Kansas Highway Patrolman Earl Stackhouse. They told Buskey "that a man with his wife and children had stopped along the side of the road, because the wife had gotten sick and vomited, and lost her car keys out by the vehicle and her husband had gone out to assist her in looking for the keys and that a person unknown had approached [the] victim and shot him." The officers pointed out Lorna to Buskey. He saw an hysterical woman, unable to communicate with the officers. The officers called an ambulance to transport her to the Geary Community Hospital for treatment.

Buskey radioed for a Junction City Crime Scene Technician and a Kansas Bureau of Investigation (KBI) Agent to be dispatched. Tom Lesher, from the Junction City Police Department received the call at 6:55 p.m. The dispatcher told him that Deputy Buskey needed him immediately at the scene of a "possible homicide."

Lesher arrived at 7:28. He spotted the Anderson van parked along the highway and the patrol cars. He parked at the end of the line and walked toward the green conversion van. From there he could see Marty's body lying in the ditch.

Trooper Stackhouse walked up and told what he knew based on the description given by Lori Anderson, Marty's 8-year old daughter. "While the two [Lorna and Marty Anderson] were looking in the field someone appeared, the young girl heard her father talking as if in an argument. She then heard and saw sparks. The girl then said the man made her mother lay down and the man went away."

Lori Anderson described the man. "He had black on his face and was wearing some kind of mask." Lori could not see his eyes. Neither she nor her sisters recognized the man's voice.

Stackhouse told Lesher that at least two individuals had tried CPR. The body had been disturbed. Lesher knew that would make his investigation more difficult. He would have to make assumptions about some things.

KBI Agent Don Winsor arrived. Lesher, Buskey and Winsor began collecting evidence. Geary County Coroner Dr. Alex Scott arrived and officially pronounced Marty dead.

Lesher got floodlights from his service vehicle and installed them around the site. Once he could see better, he noticed a woman's shoe lying in the grass. It was Lorna's.

Lesher looked for footprints. It was hard because of the nearly 40 people who had been walking around the crime scene. He spotted, "two shoe prints a few feet away from the feet of the body leading into the field." This would be in the direction Lorna told them the robber had fled. He followed the footprints, but there were no others on that trail.

Then Lesher spotted "The same style print a few feet away from the head and toward the highway leading away from the body, across the vehicle path between the field and the shallow ditch." This was valuable evidence. "These prints were spaced at what seemed to be a long distance apart and ended by the trail leaving the patch and going into the grass toward the ditch." Lesher knew these might prove someone ran away from the site.

Investigators followed the footprints. They found a spent .22 caliber cartridge next to the far edge of the path.

Satisfied that they had found everything they could that night, without further disturbing the crime scene, they moved Marty's body. Lesher wrote in his report, "there was a large amount of blood on the ground and grass under the head and also in a large area to the right of the head. There was blood on the neck, forehead and hair of the victim and the left eyelid was dark blue. The head was tilted to the right and a puffed up area was found above the left ear toward the back of the head."

Lesher retrieved a silver watch sticking out from under Marty's shoulder. He saw vomit in Marty's mouth and noted that the vomit contained "small pieces of egg." He saw mud on the knees of Marty's trousers but everything else about the clothing looked right. There was mud "smeared on the bottom of both shoes," suggesting he had been walking in the ditch.

KBI Special Agent Scott Teeselink arrived just then. He set up a video camera and taped the investigation. It made for a good training video. Using the headlights from cars parked up on the highway, and the portable floodlights, Teeselink taped the investigators inspecting Marty's body, placing evidence into bags and checking over the body.

KBI Agent Don Winsor arrived during the videotaping. He was the closest resident KBI agent and was permanently assigned to the case.

They continued "to collect the items of evidence starting with the watch under the right shoulder of the victim and then a large sample of the suspected vomit and blood from under the right shoulder also. The victim's hands were bagged and then the body was rolled onto a large plastic sheet from the CSSU van."

They placed the .22 shell casing they had found into a plastic bag. They rolled Marty over and checked his pockets. They "checked for the wallet his wife said he should have. It was not located." If she told the truth, the hit man took the billfold, so not finding it here supported her story. They found nothing in his pockets.

The investigators realized that Lorna's hands should be tested for nitrate traces. Maybe she fired the gun? They radioed David Klamm of the Junction City Police Department and asked him to get over to Geary County Hospital and swab *her* hands. By the time he got there, she had washed them at least once. Light nitrate traces were found on her hands, but a good attorney would insist that could be from fertilizer or some other environmental cause.

The mortician came for the body. While waiting for him to arrive, Lesher made a plaster cast of the best and most distinguishable footprint, "the one leading into the field by the victim's feet."

Marty's body headed to the morgue to await a Saturday date with forensic pathologist Dr. William Eckert. Eckert was the best. He was called the "Quincy of Kansas," and he often claimed the TV character was based on him. Eckert could find what no one else noticed, but Tom Bird discovered a year later, Eckert could find what was not necessarily there as well, once he had his mind made up.

The investigators walked east across Highway 177 to the deserted farm. They searched the yard and outbuildings; they found nothing.

It was too dark now, so Lesher and Buskey posted two deputies at the crime scene, and returned to the Junction City Police Department. There they collected and processed the evidence. They left for home at 2:00 a.m.

Saturday shift

On Saturday morning, at 7:30 a.m., Lesher and Buskey met at the Sheriff's Office. Along with Deputy Deppish and a "large number of deputies and reserve deputies," they set out for the crime scene. They conducted a line search of the field to the west and the shallow ditch on each side of the road. They slowly walked about a half-mile in either direction, looking down for anything out of the ordinary. Lesher took several photographs from many angles, including around where Marty's body had laid. They found nothing new. The search ended.

Lesher and Buskey were not satisfied with the first attempt and researched the area later that day aided by a metal detector. They swung the device back and forth, looking for the missing keys, gun or more shell casings. Again, they found nothing new.

They went to lunch, joining Agent Winsor and Officer Klamm at the Country Kitchen. An emergency call interrupted them at 12:53. The highway patrol apprehended a possible gunman and "reported a hostage situation at 177 and K-4." Even more urgent, the "suspect was reported to be wearing a ski mask and holding others at gun point."

Their hearts pounding and adrenaline levels raised, they sped to the arrest site. Could this be the hit man? These were veteran police officers and did not need a checklist to prepare for what might await them. Yet, all the same, their minds sub-consciously reviewed procedure. They did not want to make a mistake with a killer walking around lose.

Once at the scene, they found Kansas Highway Patrolmen guarding four men who were on their knees "in a felony stop position." One man wore a stocking cap, not a mask—a false alarm. The alleged perpetrator had been target shooting and the others put their hands over their ears blocking out the gun's blasts.

At 5:20 p.m., Buskey learned that the autopsy revealed Marty had been shot three times in the head with either a .22 or .25 caliber weapon. He had three broken ribs.

On Sunday, Buskey talked directly with Dr. Eckert. Eckert said that Marty had been shot "above and behind the left ear, behind the left ear and above the right ear. All the shots had been from behind and downward." He reported that the fractured ribs had occurred prior to death, suggesting the hit man may have kicked Marty, wanting to be sure he was dead before running away.

The picture became clearer; the three bullet holes came from a gun fired from above and behind; Marty had mud stained knees. Lorna said the man stood by the van 50' away and shot him. Hardly. Marty knelt. He was shot at close range. Lorna lied.

Another search, with results

On Monday, November 7, Lesher returned to the crime scene. He brought along the metal detector. Assisted by trainee officers, they searched the crime scene once more.

They found another .22 caliber shell casing just a "couple of feet away from the location of the casing found the night of the shooting…two feet closer to the highway." Several minutes later, they found two more spent .22 caliber shell casings. One lay about a foot farther from the body. The other "almost directly across the path from the first one he located."

In total, they found four spent .22 caliber shell casings. Marty had three bullet holes. Did the hit man miss one time, or was there another explanation? Could the hit man have forced Lorna to fire one round to implicate her in the murder?

While Lesher searched the mud at the crime scene, Agent Winsor followed leads that led to Emporia. He called Lyon County Deputy Sheriff Mack Long for help in his investigation.

Long told Winsor that he had some limited involvement in an investigation about an unusual auto accident just outside of Emporia. A pastor's wife, Sandra Bird, died in the July wreck and it appeared suspicious.

Long said Trooper John Rule, Deputy Gary Eichorn and KBI Agent Vern Humphrey worked on the accident investigation together. During their investigation, the officers heard that the minister, Thomas P. Bird, was having an affair with an unknown person.

Now that Marty was dead, rumors exploded. That morning Long received a tip from an anonymous source. The source told Long that "he was talking to another individual who told him that the Minister was having an affair with his church secretary, who would be Lorna Anderson."

The anonymous caller also told Long that Marty was in serious financial trouble. He said Marty just recently took out "$200,000 insurance coverage." Actually, it was $370,000.

Winsor called Lyon County Sheriff Dan Andrews and Agent Humphrey to verify what Long just told him. Andrews described the wreck and accident scene where Sandy was found. He told Winsor that John Rule questioned "whether the death was caused by accident or other means." Andrews found an "unknown red substance" on the bridge—human blood. No one could explain how the blood got on the bridge.

Humphrey said "they had heard rumors during the investigation that the minister was having an affair with some individual, and the name of the possible woman with whom he was having the affair had been determined to be the church secretary." The church secretary was Lorna. Lorna's promiscuous reputation followed her everywhere. If someone claimed Lorna was sharing intimacies with her minister, to the police it seemed it was likely.

The two jurisdictions—Geary and Lyon County—believed for the first time that Sandy's and Marty's deaths were two parts of the same scheme whose end was to pacify the sex-crazed desires of the town vamp and her preacher-lover. Rumors took over their investigation, and the people of Emporia were more than willing to spread anything they heard.

Looking for witnesses

On Monday evening, Deputy Deppish and two other Geary County Deputy Sheriffs set up a North-South roadblock on highway 177, identified a few possible witnesses. With a list in hand, they closed the roadblock down at 7 p.m. This preliminary list led them to several more witnesses. The investigation was progressing nicely.

On Thursday the 10th, Buskey went back to the crime scene. He searched for places where a gunman could hide at that time of night without being seen. Buskey recorded four possible sites:

"1. Feed pen north of the crime scene at the end of the cultivated field.
2. A cattle loading pen north of the crime scene.
3. The vacant farmstead directly east of the crime scene, across the road.
4. McDowell Creek Road, where witnesses reported seeing a small, blue or blue gray car sitting abandoned."

In the six days following Marty's murder, investigators collected a sizable amount of physical evidence. They identified and questioned several people who were at the murder scene or who drove past that night. They heard rumors about Lorna and Tom.

It was time to talk with the eyewitnesses again. They provided the best evidence, even if the eyewitnesses included an adulterous wife who reportedly was intimate with her pastor, and a little 8-year old girl, the daughter of the deceased.

Lorna and Lori Anderson's first statements

An ambulance carried Lorna to Geary County Hospital. She was still acting hysterical. Meanwhile, her four little girls were left in the van with Charron Cales. It was now nearly 7:30, more than an hour after Marty was murdered. Marty still lay in the ditch, about 50 feet from the van. Deputy Al Buskey finally had a sheriff take the children to a safe place in Junction City.

At 10:27 p.m. that night, Agent Winsor interviewed Lori Anderson, Marty's 8-year old daughter.

Charron, who had been on the school bus, took charge of the children at the murder scene. She was still with them when Winsor arrived at the Sheriff's Office and witnessed the interview with Lori.

Lori told Winsor the family "came to this area sometime after noon, after my mother got off work." Lorna told them that they were going to Fort Riley.

"We all went into a store on the base that had army stuff, and my dad bought a camouflage field jacket. We went to the store together, as a family, and that was all we bought except for some army pins." From there they went to Wal-Mart, but "we did not buy anything there."

"We brought some food with us. We had hard-boiled eggs, pop, chicken, brownies, bananas and apples. We were going to have a picnic outside the van. We had paper plates and tablecloths, but it was too cold, so we ate inside the van. We were at a park area [unknown location]. After we got through eating, me and the kids got out and played at the park."

Lori said that her mom and dad stayed in the van while the children played outside.

After driving around Manhattan, "We went to McDonalds to eat…Me and mom had cherry pie and some pop. The kids had a strawberry sundae. Mom had some of the sundaes."

They left McDonalds to head home. Lori said her Mom drove the van "with my dad in the front seat, and the kids were in the back." She pointed to the right to show where her dad sat—the passenger's seat.

As they drove down the highway, her mom "said that she felt sick and stopped the van. It was dark then, and she stopped. Mom didn't get out of the van. She drove on a little further and stopped the van. Then mommy got out of the driver's side and walked around to the front of the van."

"Where did she go?"

"Away from the road down in the ditch area."

After a few minutes, Lorna "walked back up to the front door. She opened the door and she said that she thought she lost the keys."

Lori thought Lorna had shut the engine off. She did not recall if the headlights were on. She remembered that after her mom "got out of the van, daddy moved over" to the driver's side. When her mother said she lost the keys, Marty got out "and walked across in front of the van."

Then her folks started looking for the keys. "I saw some sparks and heard some sounds. I heard a man's voice. I thought it was daddy." He said "Ow!"

Lori said there was quite a bit of yelling but she could not hear the words. "I think the man came up to the van and talked to mommy or something." Lori thought her Mom said, "I don't know what's happening."

Lori saw her Mom standing by the right rear side of the van. She heard Lorna say something else, but was unsure what it was. "Then the man ran off somewhere behind the van...to the back of the van, and I did not see him again."

Lori was close enough to the shooter to see that "the man either had a mask on, or might have been black." She could not see his eyes. That was "the reason I think he was wearing a mask."

"Can you describe him anymore than that?"

"No."

"Did you recognize his voice?"

"No."

"Were your mom and dad fighting?"

Lori hesitated a moment before she answered. "I don't remember."

"Is there anything else you remember?"

"No." She said nothing about the man pulling her mom down into the grass. That was the story she told at the crime scene.

Did Lorna coach the girls before she waived down James Henderson's car? Evidence strongly suggests that Lorna spent 10-15 minutes alone with the girls before anyone stopped at the scene. Did she tell Lori, a little girl who just saw her Dad murdered, the kinds of answers to give to investigator's questions?

Marty's brother called

Lorna's father Loren Slater had the difficult task of calling family members and telling them that Marty was dead. At about 12:30 a.m., November 5, he called and awakened Stephen Anderson, Marty's brother. Stephen was a professor of music at the University of Kansas in Lawrence.

Loren asked if this was the right *Stephen* Anderson. "Yes Loren, this is the correct one. How are you?"

"I tried to call earlier, but got the wrong Steve Anderson's."

"Yes, there are several in the book. What's the matter?"

Slater sighed. "I have some bad news."

"What's happened?"

Slater told him straight, "It's Marty. He's been killed."

"Oh my God! How? What happened? What about Lorna and the kids?"

"They're all okay. Lorna's in the hospital here in Junction City and the kids are back in Emporia," Slater tried to sound calm and in control. Anderson demanded details. "Marty was shot," was all Slater could say.

"Shot? How? What happened?"

"We don't know. We just don't know. They stopped the van on the road and...we just don't know...but Marty has been shot and he has expired."

"So Lorna was there? She's alright?"

"Yes, she's in shock and they've given her a sedative."

"And the kids were in Emporia?"

"No, they were with them, but they've gone back with friends. They're all okay," Slater assured him.

Stephen pressed for more details. "Oh God, how could this have happened. Why'd they stop?"

"We just don't know anything yet."

"I'll be over as soon as I can."

"There's nothing you can do. There's no point in coming tonight."

"Okay. I'll be there first thing in the morning. Where are you?"

Loren gave him the hospital details and they said good night. Then Anderson called university colleagues to cover his Saturday classes.

His only brother murdered; that was tragic, but he knew Lorna was scatter-brained, and he was worried about her children. How would they all survive without Marty?

Hospital calls
What's a good pastor supposed to do?

Bart Laib rode home from Topeka with Tom Bird the night of November 4. Tom drove his blue Toyota Corolla.

Laib noticed that Tom was deeply troubled. Leaving a grieving widow alone in a hospital went against his grain. A good pastor sets aside his own comfort and immediately heads off to the hospital. He did this for all his church members. It's a pastor's job, but Pastors Kalsow and Sprick, and the Faith lay ministers had persuaded him that there was nothing he could do that night. Loren Slater said the same thing.

So Tom went home. He hoped to get some rest and head out to Junction City early the next morning. After he took care of Lorna he could go back to the conference at Washburn.

Tom got home shortly after 11 p.m. and dismissed the babysitter. He checked on his children. Andrea stirred slightly, said "Night Daddy!" and rolled over asleep. He went into Paul and Aaron's room and found one of them asleep on the floor. He settled the boys back into bed, prayed a nighttime prayer with them, and then whispered another. He wanted his questions about Marty's death answered. He wanted to know why God let Marty die just a few months following Sandy's death? These two deaths, so close together, added to his grief.

Tom had to know more, right now. He called Captain Ray Larson, the Lutheran chaplain at Fort Riley to see if he knew any more about Lorna. Larson was a seminary classmate of Tom's. He told Tom that she was still hysterical, would not accept the fact that Marty was dead, and even with medication she would not calm down. He suggested Lorna was overdoing it and asked, "Is that characteristic of her?"

Tom tried to explain how emotional Lorna was. He visualized his own many, difficult counseling sessions with the manic-depressive woman. "I'm not surprised she is reactionary," Bird responded.

Larson said that Loren and Alta Slater, Lorna's parents, had arrived. Tom wanted to talk to them. As he was waiting, next door neighbor Stephanie Moore came over. The Moores were very close friends with Tom and Sandy, and Stephanie, a member of Faith, had heard the news about Marty. Stephanie waited for Tom to get off the phone.

Loren Slater came on the line and told Tom the Anderson children were okay. They were sent back to Emporia to stay with a family there. But Lorna looked terrible. "She is upset. She's not taking things well. She won't settle down," the worried father said. "I'm afraid she's going to collapse." He explained that even the sedatives doctors gave her were doing no good.

Tom worried about the elder Slaters and urged Loren to make sure they took care of themselves. "Should I come up right now? Would it help?"

"No. There is nothing you can do. Come up in the morning."

Mixed feelings

Tom was very upset and confused. He felt guilty for the times he got angry at Marty for his sometimes-bullish ways. He believed Marty was an alcoholic, and he recalled the times Lorna came to work bruised. Had Marty beaten her? Every time he asked her, she was evasive. Others told him that

Marty beat her. He told her to get help, but she never did. He even loaned her $1,000 for counseling, but she never used it for that.

Sometimes Tom wanted to tell Marty to get out of the church and leave Lorna alone.

Tom also remembered the great times and good fun he had with Marty. Just the previous evening they played basketball together. On other Friday evenings, they would have played co-ed volleyball together. In the summer, they played softball together. Marty could be a fun guy to be around.

Tom turned to talk to Stephanie. She had heard his side of the conversation with Loren Slater. Besides being immediate next door neighbors and members of Faith, Steve and Stephanie Moore had grown close to the Birds. Their children were about the same age and played together every day. Stephanie tried to help Tom cope with the hardships of single parenting since Sandy's death. When she heard about Marty, she knew Tom would need her help again.

Stephanie was close to Lorna, too. The two belonged to Beta Sigma Phi sorority, a social and service sorority for women. "Lorna and I were in the Ritual chapter. Lorna was always scatter brained, but she seemed really nice and liked to have a good time." She did not know either the extent or nature of the "good times" Lorna enjoyed.

While she waited for Tom to get off the phone, Moore reflected that on the previous night, Lorna picked her up to take her to the sorority dinner. On the way, they stopped at Messiah Lutheran Church. Stephanie thought it was strange that Lorna went there to use the copier since Faith had a perfectly good one, but there was something else that troubled her more. "She was maybe a little more scatter brained that night than usual. Because when we got back into the van she couldn't find her purse. She had no clue where it was." Moore never knew her to lose things.

Stephanie also had strong feelings about Marty. "I only knew Marty through Lorna. I didn't really care for him because he was abrupt; not real approachable. He seemed immersed in his work at the hospital and didn't care a whole lot about much else."

When Stephanie saw Tom come home late that Friday night, she came right over. Stephanie told him it would be wise for Steve to drive Tom to Junction City in the morning and then on to Topeka. The steering on Tom's Toyota was acting up. He didn't relish the thought of breaking down on the highway. He told Stephanie he would think about it and she went home.

Tom stepped outside, coatless, into the chilly night air of the quiet city. The street was empty. He looked north and south on the street he used to love so much. He pictured Sandy coming home from ESU in the Peugeot. He looked at the front yard and saw his kids and the neighbors playing whiffle-ball. This was a busy neighborhood alive with children and hard-working parents, but it had its secrets. He saw the Palmer house and knew there was a troubled marriage there. He shrugged. There was so much he knew about the people that lived around him, but he had to keep it all inside. It was one of the heavy burdens of pastoring. Some secrets he would take to his own grave. Many secrets he wished he never knew. He wished there was someone who could understand his own emptiness and fill the void in his own heart. Now Lorna was alone. Marty was murdered. He had questions, but no answers, and he was emotionally drained.

His thoughts turned to Lorna and Marty. So many times he had been afraid that they would destroy each other. They needed counseling badly, or perhaps even a divorce. "A strange mixture of a large dose of compassion leavened by a pinch of passion toward Lorna crossed my mind." Don Froelich and a couple others had said perhaps all these tragedies had happened for God's purpose, and maybe He had a plan for Lorna and Tom. So Tom let himself consider that with Marty dead, perhaps he should take care of Lorna and the Anderson children. But that was a crazy thought. He could hardly take care of his own children, and he knew what an emotional load Lorna could be. But he knew nothing of her promiscuity. He thought her problems were with Marty, not men.

A short, restless night

Tom decided it was wise to have Steve Moore go with him in the morning to see Lorna at the hospital. Then they could go to the Church Growth Seminar and travel back to Emporia together. He walked next door and told Stephanie to get Steve up and ready, and he went home and tried to sleep. It was after 3 a.m. before he finally dozed off, and his alarm rang at 5 a.m.

Within a few minutes, he and Steve Moore were on their way to Junction City. They stopped at Burger King to pick up some breakfast. He ate his previous meal at another Burger King in Topeka less than 12 hours earlier. Five people saw him that night, proving he couldn't have been near Marty's murder scene.

The men made small talk on the 1-hour drive to Junction City. It was hard to know what to say. When they arrived at the hospital, they found that Lorna was on the third floor. It was just a few minutes after 7 a.m. and the hallways were empty.

Steve decided not to go in with Tom and went to the coffee shop to wait.

As he came out of Lorna's room, Loren Slater spotted Tom walking down the hall. "Rev. Bird, Lorna is not doing well," he said, taking Tom back down the corridor away from Lorna's room. He wanted to explain some things to him.

Tom asked "Was she hurt, too?"

"No, she was not shot or anything like that." Loren's voice gave away his deep concern. "She's still in shock. She keeps saying Marty is not dead."

He pleaded with Bird. "You've got to talk with her. If you can, help her snap out of it." He patted the dampness from his forehead with a folded handkerchief.

Tom wanted to sound confident, but inside he felt shook. "I'll talk with her." Before going in he asked Loren about the details of the previous night.

Even though Loren had spent many hours with Lorna since arriving the night before, he knew very little. There were many gaps in his story. Armed with basic details, Tom was ready to talk with Lorna.

Distressed widow

Tom saw that there was only one bed being used in the double-occupancy room and Alta Slater, Lorna's mother sat close up to it. He heard her say, "Now, now Sister, you must rest. Sister, please settle down." Loren and Alta had called her "Sister" since her brother Daryl was born.

Sister helped serve Daryl's needs. Call her "Sister," not Lorna. Tom thought about this before. Lorna suffered from a very low self-image. Pleasing her brother formed a part of her self-image. That day in the hospital, Tom did not yet understand that her low self-image drove her to try to please men—a lot of men.

Alta could not comfort Lorna.

Tom looked directly at the bed and saw Lorna sitting there, legs pulled up, rocking back and forth, disheveled and childlike. Her eyes were sunken and hair all matted. She looked old, and her 5' 6", 110-pound frame seemed almost skeletal. Tom was shocked at the sight. He was used to seeing Lorna dressed neatly. This woman was someone he did not know. What little confidence he had going into the room was shattered seeing her like this.

Tom needed time to get himself together. He turned to Alta. "Hi, Mrs. Slater."

"Oh Rev. Bird, I'm so glad you are here." Alta and Loren knew that Lorna loved her job at Faith, and she spoke highly of this young pastor.

Out of the corner of his eye Tom saw Lorna's hand cover her mouth at the sound of his voice. She was shivering, but not from the cold. Knowing she had to face Tom, who had come to know her mind and spirit so well, frightened her. She found Tom a mystery, a man she could not control.

At the sound of his voice Lorna had a rush of hysteria. "No, Tom, tell me. No. Tell me it isn't so. Oh no, my babies, my girls, where are they. I want my girls. I've got to get out of here. Tom, take me home. What is going on? Please tell me Marty isn't dead. Tom! Daddy! They were helping Marty, a nurse, a man were giving him respiration. Tell me he's alive."

Tom had never seen this kind of behavior before—in anyone. Again he turned to Alta Slater to buy time. "Mrs. Slater, it looks like you need a break. Why don't you let me talk with Lorna?" As he said this Lorna continued her hysterical chatter.

Loren, standing behind her said, "Come on mother, let's step out."

As they left, Alta said to Lorna, "We'll be right out in the hallway, Sister."

Tom watched the two tired and worried parents leave the room. The sad ordeal was taking its toll on them. He wanted to do something about their suffering, but Lorna was his priority.

He turned back toward Lorna. She became silent, her wide-opened eyes stared at him. She said weakly, "Is Marty alive?"

Tom was worried how to answer, not wanting to set off her hysteria again. He looked at his feet. "No."

She protested by chattering on about the nurse and the others who tried to help Marty. Tom said, "I don't know about that, but Marty's dead."

"No!"

He stayed silent, hoping it would calm her down. Finally, Lorna quieted.

Tom wanted to minister to her spirit, to extend grace and comfort. Nothing else mattered until he did this. He had done this before with others, but none in this situation—a husband murdered—and with no one like Lorna. He experienced her depressions several times over the last 11 months. He counseled her about suicide. How he handled this immediate situation with her was critical. Generating as much calmness as he could muster, He said softly but directly, "What has happened is terrible. It may seem like an awful dream but it is real." He looked her directly in the eye when he said "real."

She started to answer, but he waived her off. "It's real. You don't want it to be and that's why you're not accepting it. There is nothing anybody can say to make sense of this or make you feel better and you're not going to remember anything now much at all. You've just got to work through this in your own way, the best way you can. I want you to know and recognize that a lot of people, a lot of us are going to help you and the girls and you are going to make it."

Tom reached out and gently took both her hands in his. "Let's pray."

"Alright," she answered, and offered a weak "Amen." Tom felt her calm down.

Weakly, but quietly she began telling Tom what happened the night before. He saw this as the first step in the process of grief recovery, the same process he had been working through since July.

Stephen Anderson arrived at the hospital just as Tom and Lorna finished talking. Tom and Loren met him in the hallway outside Lorna's room. Tom and Stephen met here for the first time and after introductions, Stephen went in to see his sister-in-law.

Tom found Steve Moore in the coffee shop and they drove over to Topeka.

The next act begins

Lorna was calm when Tom Bird left her room.

Stephen entered a few minutes later and saw her very upset. She acted this way each time another person entered. She cried a great deal, and said virtually nothing except, "What am I going to do?" and "What am I going to tell the kids?"

Stephen left the room to find a pay phone. He called his wife to let her know he was all right and returned to Lorna's room. He sat with her on the bed and held her. During this time, Lorna never discussed the murder with him. Loren told him the details.

Soon after Stephen arrived, the doctor released Lorna from the hospital. Loren, Stephen and Lorna went to the mortuary to sign a paper directing them where to take Marty's body, and then headed to the sheriff's office. As they waited for Winsor to come and talk with them, Stephen noticed that Lorna looked exhausted and appeared to be in an absolute daze, like a drunken stupor.

Winsor came and took Lorna's fingerprints and samples of her hair. He informed them that "return of her clothing and purse was not possible at this time." Then Winsor took them to Gross Wrecker Service to the van. After getting the house keys from the van, Loren and Lorna headed for Emporia.

Stephen stayed behind and was interviewed by Deputy Deppish. Then he went into Lorna's van and gathered the packages the children had bought the day before at Wal-Mart. (These packages perplexed investigators because Lorna and the children had said they never bought anything there. This inconsistency was but one of dozens they would encounter over the next eight years.) Stephen left the van stored at the garage.

After calling his wife, Stephen left for Emporia, driving past the spot where his brother had been murdered just a half-day earlier. He vowed to help Lorna deal with some of her immediate issues. He prepared himself for the worst. If Marty left Lorna and the girls without money, he felt a responsibility to help. The idea did not thrill him, but he was an honorable man and would do the right thing.

Lorna got home long before Stephen got there. She had three immediate goals. She needed to contact someone in Wellington, Kansas, to bury Marty's body. She needed to call the funeral home to set a time to make arrangements. But most of all, she needed to call Chris Kimble, her life insurance agent, to see how long it would take for Marty's policies to pay off.

Kimble heard about Marty's death from Dr. "Mike" the night before. Lorna called him at 12:45 p.m., Saturday, November 5. Kimble understood the insurance business meant handling death claims periodically. The task brought joy and sorrow; joy from helping a distressed widow, sorrow when a good friend had died.

Kimble knew both Marty and Lorna, and he saw in the manner she reported this death something that left him curious. When she called, he heard in her voice that she was not as distraught as the others had been. She wanted to know when to come and do the paperwork. Kimble felt she over-did the distressed widow routine a bit, and described her words as "trashy statements that did not come close to being sincere." Chris Kimble had personal knowledge of the "trashy" side of Lorna.

The van

Agent Winsor and Deputy Deppish showed up at the hospital Saturday morning. They came to see Lorna to get permission to search her van. Given the strange scene they witnessed, and even stranger story she told them the night before, they wanted the van, not her—not yet, at least. Lorna signed a release.

They headed to Gross Wrecker Service in Junction City and took several pictures of the exterior before entering the van. Winsor wrote, "The vehicle is a 3-tone, green, '78 Ford Econoline 150 van, bearing Lyon County personalized Kansas license plate CPT MSC. We were advised this had the meaning of Captain Medical Service Corps. It is a 1984 license plate. There is an approximate 18", horizontal, wood grain painted stripe completely around the approximate middle of the van."

The van was unique and easy to spot. It was well known in and around Emporia.

The investigators wrote, "The vehicle had a set of keys in the ignition, which consisted of a light brown leather key case with numerous keys."

All the interior reading lights worked, but had to be turned on individually.

After doing an inventory of everything in the van, the officers removed several items and took fingerprints. They got three "partial latent lifts from the right side and rear of the vehicle," about where Lori Anderson said her mom and the shooter stood together. They lifted six other prints from the van's exterior.

They found Lorna's other shoe in the van along with a zipper bag attached to the engine cover and some items of clothing. They removed these items and marked them as evidence. Lorna complained later that once the police seize your stuff, they never give it back. She wanted it back. They wanted it as evidence against her.

While they were still working on the van, Lorna and her father drove up and asked for the house key and keys to Marty's file cabinets. Then they left for Emporia.

At about 11:45 a.m., the investigators finished their search. Stephen drove it to a storage garage in town.

While vans can't talk, if this one could have, it would have told investigators a far different story than Lorna's. Evidence *can* "talk," of course, and sometimes it even "screams." But not the evidence found in the van that day. Deppish and his crew only had Lorna's hysterical recitation and what little they could gain from an 8-year old girl.

Stephen answers the sheriff

At 11:12 a.m. on November 5, Deputy Deppish interviewed Stephen at Gross Wrecker Service. Stephen wanted to help all he could, and Deppish needed his help badly. Deppish wrote a report about the meeting:

"Stephen said: He never knew his brother or his brother's family to own any type of guns...

"Stephen said that Lorna, besides being a church secretary, was also a licensed real estate agent.

"The last time he had been with Martin and the family was in April at a funeral in Hutchinson.

"Martin had been married before around 1971 for a 'year or so' and the marriage was not successful, with no children. Following the first marriage Martin had some serious problems and had joined a 'fly by night' religion [sic] group and then when Lorna came along as his new wife she was able to 'straighten him out.'

"His brother described Martin as a 'regular citizen' of Emporia, belonging to the Optimist Club, the Army Reserve, a softball team member, among other things.

"The brother said that he knew that the family 'several times' had financial problems and at one time got rid of all their credit cards or had them taken away. At one time they had traded down in their home because of financial problems. Martin then purchased another house in anticipation of receiving money from his mother's estate but then had to pay two house payments for several months because it took so long to close out the estate and this also caused additional financial problems.

"Martin had taken lab tech training at Hutchinson Jr. College and seemed to do much better in his job than in his personal and family life. According to Stephan it appeared to him that the wife Lorna often had the inability to cope with day to day problems and the husband would often take the lead role. Both seemed to be very dependent on her folks (Mr. & Mrs. Slater).

"Then again, Stephen said, Lorna was the 'strong one' during the dying of Martin's mother. Stephen said that he never knew of any mental problems that Lorna had and seemed surprised that the question was brought up. He said that maybe some people would think that because of the way Lorna talked."

Stephen saw Lorna enough to know how she talked and acted. When demonstrative, she spoke in a childish voice, like a star-struck teenage girl. When seductive, she spoke syrupy and sweet, talking in low, soft tones. When demanding her way, she whined and pouted. When laughing, she laughed loudly and smiled widely. Lorna used her voice and flair for drama to control the men in her life.

The interview ended at 11:40 a.m., but the discourse with Stephen continued for many more years as he, and the investigators, learned more about Marty, Lorna and what really happened alongside Highway 177.

Stephen and Lorna plan the funeral

Stephen left Junction City right after talking with Deppish. He headed to Lorna's house in Emporia, arriving about 3:00 p.m. He saw Lorna dressed in black now. She looked better and had refreshed herself. He saw that Loren and Alta were there, trying their best to help out.

Lorna greeted Stephen. "They tell me I have to make decisions, but I don't even know about what."

"We need to make funeral plans. We need to pick out clothes for him to wear."

Together they chose a burial suit. Stephen insisted they go directly to the funeral home and complete the funeral details. He told Lorna to write down all Marty's vital statistics.

On the way to the funeral home, they agreed to bury Marty in

Wellington, his hometown. Lorna liked that. "That's good. He'll be with his family that way. I don't know how long I'll be in Emporia."

By 5:00 p.m. they were back in the car, headed to Lorna's. They continued talking about details. "I'll take care of picking out the cemetery plot. I'll drive to Wellington and back on Monday and then back to Emporia on Tuesday for the funeral." Stephen offered.

"That's so good of you. Can't you get someone to do that so you don't have to make that trip?" They considered alternatives.

Stephen had some nagging questions. It was time to ask them. "There are some things I need to ask you. Is that okay?"

"Sure, what?"

"First, this is kind of difficult. Do you want me to buy one or two grave plots?"

"Oh, two of course," Lorna answered without hesitation.

"Are you certain? You're very young. You may meet someone else. Many things can change." Stephen had no idea how prophetic his words actually were.

"Oh no, I loved Marty. Someday I'll be there with him."

They talked about Marty's will. He had none. Stephen told her to retain an attorney to work through estate issues. Lorna said she and Marty had intended to talk with Emporia attorney Darrell Meyer about a will. Maybe he would be a good choice to help out now. Lorna did call Meyer. Lack of a will was the least of her problems, and Darrell Meyer would learn that lesson very soon.

Stephen asked more questions. "Now, for my own piece of mind I need to know this. What about insurance? But I want you to know that if there's anything at all that you and the girls need you don't have to worry. We'll take care of you."

"Oh, there's no problem with money. There are several insurance policies. He had $35,000 through the hospital, $35,000 through the reserves, and $400,000 with Chris [Kimble, their life insurance agent]." Lorna called Kimble within minutes of arriving home, like it was almost the first thing she did. "I talked to him today and he says that it's all okay and we'll get it all."

"That's terrific. That's a lot better off than I am. Thank goodness. Their education should be guaranteed if you manage it well. That's really lucky." Luck had nothing to do with it. Lorna made sure Marty was well insured just a few months earlier.

"Oh yes, they're the luckiest little girls in the world."

"Well not exactly. They just lost their father," Stephen answered sadly.

The week following Marty's death, Stephen spent considerable time with Lorna. Something bothered him. He recorded his apprehensions for

33

County Attorney Steven Opat.

"Knowing Lorna's account of the events surrounding the killing of my brother, I was prepared to try to deal with her probable feelings and expressions of guilt for having been sick and having stopped at that site. I was prepared for all the possible 'If only' scenarios, such as: 'If only I hadn't eaten that sundae," or 'If only I had stopped a mile sooner, or later,' etc. Never once in the days that followed the killing did Lorna express any of these possible statements. There was no expression of this sort of responsibility or guilt."

Nor would there ever be. There would be lies, manipulations, false trails and a diabolical plot that was writing itself even as Stephen watched his sister-in-law mourn. It was a mourning that would turn to darkness.

Lorna's Private Communion

Tom Bird arrived at church early on November 6, 1983. Because it was the first Sunday of the month, a communion Sunday, he needed extra time to prepare. Tom enjoyed this time as he anticipated sharing in the Lord's Supper with his people. The preparation for communion and last minute attention to his sermon provided much-needed relief from his own personal grief over Marty Anderson's death just two days earlier.

As Tom led the worship and communion service that morning he noticed that Lorna was missing. "Pray with me as we remember Lorna and her children in their time of grief and loss," he said, adding her dilemma to the other prayers offered that day.

With the service over, Tom headed home for lunch with his children, but his communion duties were not yet complete.

After lunch, Tom headed back to Faith to gather up the extra communion wafers and wine. These he put into his portable "communion kit." He planned to head out to visit church members who were in nursing homes where he would participate in private communion ceremonies with each of them. During the week, Tom often set aside time on his schedule to perform private communion for other people who were unable to attend the Sunday service. As he finished collecting up the extra communion elements that day, Lorna walked into the sanctuary. Tom saw she was visibly upset and crying, just as he expected a recent widow to appear. He had experienced a similar scene many times in his career.

"I'm sorry I missed the service today," she apologized."

"We understand why you weren't here. No need to be upset about that," Tom responded compassionately. His response was genuine, but laced with a need to keep good control of the conversation or he could experience another of Lorna's explosive emotional upheavals.

Lorna knew that it was communion Sunday and that was the purpose of her visit. "Would you serve me communion now, Tom?" She had seen him do this with others.

"Well, I'd rather not." Tom believed, based on his experience with others, that it was Lorna's grief and emotional state that drove her to make this request. He was also mindful of the many stops he had to make that afternoon and his need to return home to care for his children. And it was affection and attention she needed right then, not communion. Marty's death was Lorna's tragedy, but not Lorna's sin. "We could do it another time," he offered.

"I need communion now!" she insisted. "I need God's forgiveness for all the bad things I did to Marty. I want to be assured of forgiveness," she implored him dramatically.

Lorna plainly knew the significance of communion. Tom had taught her and Marty well when they converted to the Lutheran faith. Lorna knew that communion was a sacrament practiced by Christians since the First Century. She knew that during this quiet and somber ceremony, she could confess her sins, receive forgiveness, and amend her sinful life. She knew that by taking the communion elements, she was eating and drinking the very body and blood of Jesus Christ, and in this, she was receiving the forgiveness of her sins. She also knew that if she were unrepentant, it would accrue to her judgement and damnation. But it made no difference to her that afternoon, so desperate was she for relief. She was willing to risk God's punishment by insisting, "I want to he sure God still loves me."

Tom knew he might as well proceed.

When he performed a private communion, it was just the same as the service that he held earlier that morning when the sanctuary was full. He could have intimacy with Christ through communion whether there was 1 or 1,000 people participating. And like many other private communion services, this one was held in front of the altar in the church's sanctuary.

"The communion service is a time for believers to come together to share the Lord's Supper, and I often participate myself," he explained. And he took communion along with Lorna.

During the ceremony, Lorna's conscience was at war with her flesh, knowing the gravity of her sexual sins, and now, the murder of her husband. Seeking forgiveness, she shut out the torment elicited by Tom's words. "Lorna, take, eat. This is the true body of our Lord and Savior Jesus Christ given into death for your sins. Lorna, take, drink, this is the true blood of our Lord and Savior Jesus Christ shed for you for the forgiveness of your sins."

The sheer terror of eternal punishment drove Lorna to the communion rail that day, but this memorial would not offer her the relief she desperately needed. It lacked an honest confession of her vile sin, a confession, had it been given, that would have changed everything for her and Tom in the years ahead.

He watched the pitiful woman as she went through the sacred supper with him. He well knew about *some* of Lorna's sins. He had seen the marks of brutality laid on her which, he had been told, were from Marty's beatings. As her pastor, Tom carried her own suffering in his spirit and he grieved with her, but he had no concept of how deeply rooted in Hell were Lorna's sins against Marty; how the crimson stains of Marty's blood flowed directly from her unrepentant heart of deceit and her extreme promiscuity. Tom did not comprehend the depth of the degradation of her affront to the God of life with whom she was seeking communion that morning. This complete misunderstanding of the true nature of Lorna's fleshly ways lay beyond his comprehension for nearly two more years.

Once the private communion was ended, Lorna left and Tom headed out to fulfill his pastoral duties, hoping there would still be ample time in the afternoon to spend with his children. With Sandy gone, almost all his spare energy was focussed on the children, and what little was left, on the new woman in his life, Terry Smith.

Susan Ewert

Susan Ewert sold real estate in and around Emporia. Fashionable, well educated—degreed in psychology and a trained therapist—aggressive, outgoing and pretty, Susan and her husband Jim were close friends with Marty and Lorna. They met at First Presbyterian Church in Emporia where the Andersons attended until coming to Faith. The four grew close during a protracted heated debate that threatened to divide their church—they all played a central role in the drama. First Presbyterian was home to many prominent Emporians, including District Judge Gary Rulon.

In the early summer of 1982, Lorna called Susan to tell her she discovered a great preschool program at Faith—Lord's Lambs. The Ewert's two sons enrolled along with the Anderson girls in the preschool. Susan met Pastor Tom Bird. His friendliness and the sense of caring that he exuded struck her, but she saw nothing particularly unusual about him. "He was not a charismatic, magnetic person, just very caring."

Once Lorna became a target of the investigators, Ewert paired with Tom to do everything she could to help her maintain her freedom. She, like Tom, saw Lorna as a victim of unscrupulous policemen who dared to besiege a grieving widow. During the on-going investigations, Susan built a strong friendship with Tom. "Lorna and Tom became like a brother and sister to me."

At first, Susan liked Marty Anderson, too, but she saw him change. She began to believe that Marty didn't much like her. "I had gotten tired of Marty. Marty was trashing me... I kept telling Jim I don't like the way he's relating to me. Jim would say 'He's just kidding' and I would say, 'No he's not kidding. He's dead serious' I don't know what the reason was. I was a strong personality, but I don't know." Others close to Marty saw the same kind of change in him, more agitated and nervous, negative and unhappy.

"Marty was always talking about money. We don't know what was true or fiction."

The money issue loomed large. "There may have been some gambling involved. In the end of September, we went to a picnic at First Presbyterian and Herb [a church member] called Marty and Lorna, not knowing they moved their membership to Faith, but he encouraged them to come anyway and they were there. And even at that picnic, something was mentioned about money. After Marty died I was there at the house right in the time frame of when he was killed, and something came; a get-rich quick pyramid scheme came to the house. He was always looking for something."

This puzzled Susan, because "Marty was making good money. They had more money than we did...Their house payment was high, like $750 per month, but he was in the Reserves. It seems like [they earned] $45-50,000 combined."

Susan grew closer to Lorna and Marty resented it. "Maybe I served a purpose as the whipping person when he was away from Lorna. And it really troubled me. Lorna said that Marty beat her, but now I don't know."

On the evening of November 5, 1983, Ewert was out of town when her husband "read me what was in the paper...that Marty was shot. The story left a lot to the imagination."

Knowing that Lorna was in trouble, "We started back home around 7 or so and I called one of the church members who had been in this group of people and she said it just doesn't look good. The two of us went over there to the house then."

Susan walked into Lorna's house and saw the usual mess and clutter. "I cleaned up the house. I picked up his clothes that he had left there. After Marty was killed I cleaned the house three times when it was in disarray. His clothes were out on the chair, and that was a weird feeling, but there was a bill there from an attorney that was on the floor in the bedroom and I picked it up and put it on the dresser. Lorna later volunteered that she had gone to [Emporia attorney Michael] Patton and talked to him about a divorce and that she just wouldn't be able to get enough money to subsist on."

Ewert "...tried to call Tom at church the next morning and later on he talked to me and said he had been in Junction City." Tom told her the story. Ewert wanted to help her emotional friend Lorna and needed to know as much as possible.

After church Susan drove to Lorna's house again. "I decided to take the two older girls home. Jim and I took the kids and did something with the children and I gave the children baths."

Despite her natural curiosity, Ewert tired hard to be sensitive to the trauma experienced by the children just two days earlier. "I hadn't brought anything up about the murder. I figured if they wanted to talk, they would talk. I didn't pump the girls for information.

"Julie was sitting in the bathroom and I was drying her hair—she was 4. She said, 'Do you want to hear about what happened the other night?' I responded, 'If you want to tell me.' Then I think Lori got in on the conversation about the man coming to the car and looking in the window. Like he had a mask on, using her fingers to try to exemplify a mask. And Julie in her four-year old voice said, 'and there were sparkles.'"

The thought of these young children being exposed to such a hideous crime shook Susan. Her training told her the girls would suffer their own emotional problems because of what they saw. She worried about them.

Susan believed that someone did a deadly and evil deed by murdering Marty. She was right about that. That the murder resulted in the suffering of her best friend, Lorna was true, too. She remained intimately involved in all the developments as facts unfolded, and did her best to sustain the spirits of Lorna and Tom later on, when the sparks from sex-laced rumors began to ignite Emporia. And above all else, like Tom, Susan remained devoted to helping Lorna prove her innocence.

Marty's funeral

On Monday, November 7, Rev. Larry Kalsow from Messiah presided at Martin Anderson's funeral service held at Faith, in Emporia. Rev. Tom Bird preached a funeral message and handled the committal service in Wellington. As Tom delivered his message, he saw Lorna and the girls, the Slaters, Stephen Anderson and his family, all of them mourning the senseless and brutal slaughter of Marty. Many of the people at the service in Wellington knew Marty as a child and watched him grow into manhood. They knew him as a Methodist, not as a Lutheran.

Pastor Bird read the text for his sermon to the mourners. It came from Matthew 10:28, "And do not fear those who kill the body but cannot kill the

soul. But rather fear Him who is able to destroy both soul and body in hell."
He emphasized "the Law and the Gospel" in his sermon. He spoke of sin that
damns and grace that forgives. He spoke of those going to hell because of
unrepented sins and he spoke of heaven for those who are forgiven. Some at
the service misunderstood what he said—they thought it odd that he spoke
this way under the circumstances. To the Lutherans, it sounded normal.

Ron and Betty Shepherd, longtime friends of Marty's parents, lived in
Wellington. They barely knew Lorna, even though she occasionally stopped
by their house with Marty and the children. To them Lorna "always seemed
a little quiet and a little bit aloof."

Betty watched Lorna's actions at the graveside. She did not like what she
saw or heard. "Lorna was so worried about Stan Goodhugh not being at the
funeral and talked to several people about that and said she hoped that he
would arrive in time for the graveside services." Goodhugh was an old friend
of the Andersons, but Betty had no idea how close he was to Lorna. She just
saw what she saw, and it puzzled her.

"I didn't even tell my wife about this for a long time," Ron added, about
what he saw Lorna do at the reception in Wellington following the funeral.
"I was standing in a small entryway at the bottom of the stairs of the
Methodist Church where the lunch was to be served after the service... I was
the only one there. Lorna was coming down the stairs along with someone
else, and Lorna was laughing out loud, a very big laugh, until she saw me.
Then the laugh stopped at once. Lorna's looks and actions became very
reserved and solemn." Lorna put on an act. Ron knew it. Ron did not know
the man he spotted, but wondered if it was Rev. Bird.

Tom never went to the Wellington reception. Instead, he and the driver
of the hearse left right after the graveside service and drove back toward
Emporia. On the way they stopped at McDonalds for a bite to eat. Returning
to the hearse, the driver discovered he had locked the keys in the car. "We
had to ask a lady if she had a hanger we could use to unlock the door," Tom
laughed about it. "She wondered if we were really trying to steal the car. She
wanted to know if there was a body inside." Eventuality a police officer
opened the door for them. Tom wondered later how someone who saw a man
with Lorna could imply that *he* was the man. Worse, he was puzzled that
investigators would put any stock in this kind of "evidence." He soon learned
that when it came to him and Lorna, people saw and said a lot of things that
made no sense.

Kenneth and Geraldine Jones, like the Shepherds, were longtime friends
with Marty's parents. They knew Marty and his brother as young boys. They
started a memorial fund for Marty through the Wellington Methodist Church.
Geraldine was upset at Lorna's reaction to their offer to start this fund. "I

asked my husband to write out a check for $25.00 and then after he had made out the check to Lorna Anderson, she had him tear it up and make out a new one to 'The Martin Anderson Memorial Fund.'" When the check finally cleared her bank, though, "it had been endorsed first by Lorna Anderson and then stamped with a deposit stamp by the Faith Lutheran Church in Emporia."

Days later, the Jones visited Marty's gravesite. Lorna did not bother laying a headstone at the grave, not even any flowers. They believed she buried her husband and then forgot him. Geraldine contacted the funeral home and called Stephen Anderson to get a marker placed. "I just don't see how a wife that was to have loved her husband so much could have left this undone."

The Jones agreed with the Shepherds about the way Lorna acted that day. "She did not seem to be a woman in great grief." She witnessed that "when Lorna received the folded flag from Marty's casket, she held it to her chest with crossed arms [but] it seemed very much 'put on,' and she was still holding it that way when she came to the church for the luncheon after the service." Lorna asked Geraldine where the lady's room was and handed her the flag. Returning from the restroom, Lorna "took the flag and held it that way again, almost like she was acting."

The Jones' were not pleased with Rev. Bird either. While they were not sure specifically what it was he said at the funeral and graveside, "it just didn't seem like what should be said for such a loss as the death of Marty." But they added that perhaps the "Lutheran Church does things different than their church." Even so, they "did not feel good about it."

Jane Schalk, also of Wellington, watched Lorna at the funeral and at graveside. She said, "Lorna was only acting out the part of a distressed wife and several people I talked to after the services felt the same way." Schalk's son Larry told her that even before Marty was killed, "Lorna was really a good actress and would use this to get her way with Martin and anyone else."

There were even those who openly questioned why Rev. Bird preached at the funeral, given the rumors floating around Emporia about him and Lorna during the previous few months. Stephanie Moore said those concerns were ridiculous. "Why wouldn't Tom do it? Marty was a member of our church." Steve Moore was a pallbearer, so Stephanie rode with the pallbearers to the graveside service in Wellington. The pallbearers were all men from Faith.

Years later, Lorna claimed that Tom suggested that Darrel Carter serve as a pallbearer. Tom never did that. Carter was an Emporia building contractor, one of a long list of men who later confessed to having sex with Lorna. It would have been a sinister irony if Carter were a pallbearer. Just weeks later, he claimed that Tom Bird tried to get him to find someone to murder Marty Anderson.

KBI Interviews Bird

Investigators are obligated to follow any and all leads that even hint to be legitimate. In Marty Anderson's murder investigation, those leads included escalating rumors about Tom and Lorna. Sheriff Andrews quietly continued to pursue an investigation into Sandy Bird's death. With Marty dead, investigators believed the two spouses' deaths were directly related. They heard the rumors, they saw two dead bodies. The possibility that Tom and Lorna partnered in Marty's murder drove investigators to Bird's doorstep. Even if Tom had nothing to do with Marty's murder, he would have information about the Andersons that was vital to the investigation. Agent Winsor and Deputy Deppish left Junction City and drove to Emporia to interview Tom on November 10.

Winsor saw that Tom was relaxed and confident during the interview. He was relaxed and confident because in his mind, this was about Lorna's loss and finding the murderer. It was not about him. He was a pastor trying to help a church member.

"Pastor Bird said he does not own any firearm and does not like guns. He says he has had a gun in his hands only a few times during his lifetime," Winsor wrote.

About guns, Tom later said:

"I would like to say I never fired a gun but I can't. No guns were ever in our house. We were not hunters."

Rev. Ralph Bird, Tom's father, did not have guns in the house. Tom's brother and sister, Mark and Gloria, never had nor fired a gun. They did not know Tom had a couple of experiences with guns, but not the kind that would qualify him as a murderer.

Tom continued:

"When I was 13 I went dove hunting with a friend with a pellet gun. I shot at a dove in a tree about 20 times and the dove just sat there on the branch. Finally I hit the dove. It fell; we walked up to it. I saw the red blood spot on its breast and the big brown but lifeless eyes. I thought two things: how is this called a sport? And why would anyone enjoy killing creatures like this? I concluded, I would never go hunting again, except with a camera.

"Once when I was 20 I shot a .22 caliber pistol at some bottles with my soon-to-be brothers-in-law at their grandfathers farm in

Ruston, Louisiana.

"I once went skeet shooting with a member of my congregation when I was around 30 years old. The best I did was chip one of the clay pigeons. John Holland just laughed at me, told his son to go fetch the clay pigeon to use again sometime, and said to me 'let's go get some of Mom's pie' (implying that I was better at eating than shooting)."

It struck Tom odd that Winsor would ask *him* about guns. He had no connection whatsoever with Marty's murder. He accounted for his time on November 4. He wondered, though, just like everyone else, who had done such an awful deed. He intended to cooperate fully with investigators who, he believed, work for the people, and they work hard to get it right. He had no reason to fear them. They always got their man, he believed.

Tom pondered the allegations that Lorna had something to do with Marty's murder. He asked himself how they could possibly even *consider* she had anything to do with it? It angered him. He knew a lot about her, but as her pastor, his loyalty was to serve her spiritual needs, not the needs of investigators poking around and causing her even more trouble.

Widow whines—Tom cheers her

Tom presided over and preached at many funerals. He knew that when a funeral is over the pastor's job often gets even harder. No matter the age of the deceased or the circumstances surrounding the death, the survivors need care, comfort and love. Sometimes they need financial assistance, grief counseling and help in relocating. Some refuse to eat or care for their most basic needs. Among those serious about their religious faith, there are serious spiritual questions.

Tom counseled many grieving survivors; none as difficult as Lorna Anderson.

For more than 10 months, Lorna served as Tom's secretary. They had experienced the highs and lows of a pastor's busy, complicated life. Lorna remained by Tom's side as he went through his own grief upon the sudden tragic death of his wife Sandy just a few months earlier. In fact, Lorna showed up unexpectedly time and again, trying to serve Tom's needs and win his favor.

There had been other complications between Tom and Lorna before and after Sandy's death.

Beginning early in 1983 and for several months Tom counseled Lorna, and this caused no end of grief. The lay ministers, individual church members and even Sandy cautioned him about the amount of time he spent counseling Lorna. Gossip that the counseling included a physical relationship began to surface.

Tom strongly believed that his pastoral call meant caring for people who were in the most impossible of situations. They expected him to be strong, to stand against rumor and innuendo. The Lutheran Confessions are very clear about this. The Confessions taught him to put the best construction on everything he heard. He refused to hear rumors. He relied on his own observation and knowledge. This made him a trusted counselor to the members at Faith. They knew that anything they shared with him would stay with him.

Tom saw Lorna as a child of God. He saw her deep emotional and spiritual scars, just as he saw bruises on her body. As her pastor, nothing else needed to be said. Sometimes there was sexual tension, but he understood his humanity. He never acted on these fleshly impulses. He knew it. Lorna knew it. God knew it. He had no personal knowledge of anything Lorna ever said about him, and she had spun some very sordid stories around town.

Lorna's situation provided him with special challenges. At times, Tom and the Lutheran Faith was all she had. Her relying on Tom fed his own sense of self-worth. "I needed to be needed. Lorna needed me."

Lorna knew how to play on his emotions and sense of responsibility — his need to be needed. During the days since Marty's death, she played the role supremely.

Two days following Marty's funeral, Tom stopped at the Anderson house to check on the family. He found Lorna depressed. Already she had heard the police were not treating Marty's death as a chance robbery. In fact, she was a suspect.

"You probably don't need to come back to work." He knew it was useless for her to try to continue working at Faith. Things would be better at church with her gone. Her staying would just create more controversy and gossip.

Driven by her depression, Lorna responded, "I'm going home. No one cares about me. Everyone is turning against me. Now I have the kids alone. I don't know what to do."

"The church is still here. We're here by your side."

"Can you come tomorrow?"

"No, I've got to go to a church conference." She knew Tom had enrolled in a three-day Pastor's Teachers' Conference scheduled from November 10-11, and would be gone until Saturday evening. She had typed the calendar.

"See! You're leaving me, too," she whined.

He assured her he would be back in Emporia on Saturday evening. Tom thought back to his own experience after Sandy died, and the strength he drew from his closest loved ones. He tried to assure her that she would be able to make it through those days. For her it was a bad time for him to go away but he needed to go.

"You don't love me. You don't care for me," She wailed.

Tom failed to comfort her.

He went home to pack. He spotted several greeting cards on the desk, and decided to choose two for Lorna. A wave of grief washed over him as he realized that Sandy had bought these cards the prior spring. He had a good use for them now; Sandy would be pleased.

He pulled out two cards and glanced at them. Though he did not study their verses, they seemed appropriate for Lorna's current dilemma. "These look good."

The first words he saw of the poem's text would do nicely to express the grief that so often welled up and stuck in his own throat as he saw remembrances of Sandy. It read:

"Miss you. miss you, miss you;
Everything I do
Echoes with the laughter
And the voice of you.
You're on every corner,
Every turn and twist,
Every old familiar spot
Whispers how you're missed.

"Miss you, miss you, miss you;
Everywhere I go
There are poignant memories
Dancing in a row,
Silhouette and shadow.
Of your form and face
Substance and reality
Everywhere displace.

"Oh I Miss you, miss you, miss you...
There's a strange, sad silence
'Mid the busy whirl,
Just as tho' the ordinary,
Daily things I do,
Wait with me, expectant,
For a word from you."

Tom had given similar cards to other hurting friends and church members, and it was his practice to personalize them. He wrote a note to Lorna:

"I love you. I am confident of the future and that makes the present OK. Take care of the kids. Love you always, Tom"

He sealed this card in an envelope and wrote "Thursday" on it.

He took the second card in hand. It read:

"If you have a goal in life
that takes a lot of energy,
that incurs a great deal of interest,
and that is a challenge to you—
you will always look
forward to waking up
to see what the new day brings.

"If you find a person in your life
who understands you completely,
who shares your ideas,
and who believes in everything you do,
you will always look
forward to the night
because you will never be lonely."

On this card he wrote:

"You are so very special. I hope time goes very fast until Saturday evening. It should with all the work with the children. I love you so very much and that's forever. Tom"

He sealed it in an envelope wrote "Friday" on it.

He delivered the cards to Lorna and instructed her, "I want you to open this card tomorrow and this one Friday." He hoped this would help her cope during the next few days. Friday would be critical. It was just a week after Marty's murder.

He hurried to leave Emporia because he and Terry Smith, the woman he had been quietly dating since October, planned a date later that night. Tom drove to Wichita for the pastor's conference where Terry helped with registration. Once registration closed, they slipped away for dinner and dancing; the first of many dates during the conference. They dined at The Jammers Club and saw Angie Duensing, the young woman who directed Lord's Lambs. Angie remembered they were, "holding hands and having their arms around each other. It was obvious they were having a date, and this

45

was not just friendship."

While Tom dated Terry, Lorna mourned in Emporia. He never knew whether she ever read the cards he left. Eventually he heard she had placed them in her dresser drawer. Police investigators discovered them there along with a partially completed undated letter she wrote to Tom, but never delivered. Investigators saw the greeting cards—later labeled "love letters" by the media, investigators and prosecutors—as prime evidence that Tom and Lorna were lovers.

Hotline produces hot lead

At about 2 p.m. on November 15, 1983, the phone rang on KBI Agent Don Winsor's desk. A young single Emporia mother called to tell him she was worried about her former bed-partner. She was certain that he was involved in the murder of Marty Anderson. The woman refused to give her name, but said she had information that would prove useful in the Anderson murder case. She was afraid of her former boyfriend and refused to talk on the phone. Winsor agreed to meet her at 7 p.m. that evening at the Travel Lodge Motel on West 6th Street in Emporia.

Winsor was at the motel at 7 p.m., a little early for the appointment. Investigators usually are a cool lot, but his heart was beating a little faster given the potential outcome of this meeting. Gail Wilson's heart beat faster, too, but from fear. After that first meeting, Winsor wrote in his report:

"She identified herself as Gail, and was very reluctant to talk to SA Winsor at first. She stated that she had been living with a man for a couple of months and this person had been receiving a lot of phone calls over the past several months from Lorna Anderson.

"She said that she would answer the phone many many times herself, and whenever she answered the phone, this individual she knew as Lorna, would ask for her boyfriend. Some of the times he was not there and if he was not there to answer the phone she agreed to give him the message to call her, and would hang the phone up rather angrily.

"She had discussed the telephone calls with her boyfriend and her boyfriend had told her that Lorna was wanting to get rid of her husband.

"She said she did not know Marty Anderson very well, and asked why she wanted to do this? Her boyfriend answered, you don't know Marty. He's not what he appears to be, he's a different person,' or words to that affect."

"What were you referring to when you said 'get rid of her husband'?" Winsor asked the frightened woman.

"To kill him," Wilson replied bluntly. "My boyfriend had told me several different times that something bad was going to happen to Marty. I saw the Topeka paper today." She showed Winsor a clipping she cut out of the newspaper that reported on Marty's murder. "I remembered what my boyfriend had said." She still cared for her boyfriend, "but I think Lorna Anderson is still dating him."

Winsor knew he was on to something, a huge break in the case.

Wilson continued. "My boyfriend said that if a certain person calls and gave me some nickname, I was to take a message and contact him. Then I was supposed to forget the person ever called."

"What was that nickname?"

"I don't remember, but if I remember I'll let you know, but the person never called anyway."

More from Winsor's report:

> "Gail said she did not believe that her boyfriend would have killed Martin Anderson, however, believed that he probably contacted someone, or knows who did do so. He also appears to be upset and rather nervous over something and she does not know why.
>
> "She states she, herself, is now scared since Martin Anderson was killed. She said her boyfriend would never, never believe or suspect that she would go to the police."

Wilson asked Winsor, "Are you aware of the drowning of the minister's wife?"

"Yes, why?"

Winsor wrote that she said:

> "She advised she did not know for sure what happened there, did not even know the minister or his wife, however, thinks that this was related somehow to Martin Anderson's death. She said her boyfriend has mentioned several times about the woman drowning, however, did not elaborate or give any details.
>
> "Said that she rides to work in a car pool. Sometimes with a man who drives a van, in company with several other people. This unknown named man owns some land adjoining the bridge where the pastor's wife drowned. She said that she was out in a field in that area taking some photographs and she later showed some of the photographs to her boyfriend, and the bridge where the accident occurred was in the background. She said he asked, 'do you know what happened there?' And she advised, she didn't. He said something

about her drowning, however, again did not elaborate."

Winsor asked, "Why would Lorna Anderson have her husband killed?"
"It was over some money."
"The individual who murdered her was doing it for money?"
She clarified her answer. "I don't know, but Lorna wanted her husband killed so she would get some money. I don't know how." She knew nothing about insurance.

Winsor pulled out a list he carried on a note pad. It contained names of men he had been told were having affairs with Lorna Anderson. As he opened the notebook, Wilson saw the names and said, "You already have my boyfriend's name."
"Oh, which one are you referring to?"
She put her finger on the name Danny Carter.
"Can you describe him?"
"Sure, he's 35, about 5' 9", maybe 155-160 pounds. He's got thinning, curly brown hair and sharp features. I don't know his address, but he lives in a beige-colored house, a two-story house, apartment number 4."
"What kind of car does he drive?"
"An old white color Buick and an old, older white colored Pontiac."
Gail and Danny met at work. She was a secretary for Davis Electrical and he welded for them at the Wolf Creek Nuclear Plant.

Winsor thanked her for her help and let her know they would need to talk again.

The next day, November 16, Winsor called Gail at Davis Electrical to ask more questions. "How long have you known Mr. Carter?"
"Since January of 1983. I lived with him for about two months in the apartment behind the Presbyterian Church." She moved out around the first of September. They were still friends. She rode to work with him every day. "This weekend I'm getting some teeth pulled and he's going to baby-sit for me."
"Who does he know at Wolf Creek? Who does he hang out with?"
"I really don't know, but he's got a lot of friends in Emporia."
"What are their names?"
"I don't know."
More from Winsor's report:

> "She said the Sunday after the homicide she had talked to Danny Carter, or tried to. He told her, 'we don't talk about it, why does it bother you?'
>
> "She said she accused him of being involved in the homicide and he got mad at her but didn't answer. Sometime about this time he made

the statement, 'You are going to try to pin this on me, are you?' This was when he got mad and left on Sunday.

"She said that when she lived with Danny, she received phone calls every week and several times on Saturday from Lorna Anderson, asking for Danny Carter."

Gail Wilson was terrified. To protect herself she eventually moved out of Kansas. Her mail was forwarded to her parent's home in North Carolina and she simply disappeared.

The Geary County investigators finally had their big break. Their first real target was Danny Carter, the divorced Emporia native—the playboy ex-hairdresser, lover of Lorna Anderson, Gail Wilson and several other area women and the younger brother of Darrel Carter.

Danny confesses

Daniel R. Carter, 5' 9" tall with brown hair and weighing about 165 pounds, grew up in Emporia.

On November 17, 1983, Danny lived with another in a long line of girlfriends at an apartment on 8th Avenue and Mechanic Street in a building owned by his brother Darrel. At about 6:40 p.m. he heard a knock at the door. He opened it to find Deputy Sheriffs Deppish and Buskey and Lyon County Deputy Sheriff David Samuels. Danny said, "I was expecting you."

Since Marty's death, Danny knew eventually the police would catch up to him. The question begged answering; had he and those he knew prepared for that eventuality? Did it give them all time to make up a good cover story? Though no police record ever indicated as such, the question needed to be asked whether Danny or others had found a way to meet with Lorna to make sure that all stories lined up so that any risk to Danny might be minimized.

Deppish and Buskey said they wanted to ask him some questions about Marty's murder. He agreed to talk with them, but only at the Lyon County Sheriff's Office. The sheriffs asked to search his apartment but he refused. The idea of a search frightened him. He told the sheriffs he grew marijuana in his apartment—something he had just started doing—and was afraid they would get the wrong idea. Without a search warrant in hand, they had no choice but to wait until later.

The deputies waited on the porch while Danny disappeared behind the closed door for a few minutes. He joined them on the porch but told them they needed to wait until Darrel arrived. It was about 7:15 p.m. When Darrel arrived, he told the investigators that he needed to wait at the apartment until someone from the water department showed up to turn the water back on. He said it was turned off earlier that day. Darrel stayed alone at the apartment while Samuels drove the rest of them to the sheriff's office. Samuels returned minutes later to keep an eye on the place.

Danny only did hairstyling for the women who slept with him. Otherwise, he worked as a welder for Davis Electric, one of the subcontractors at Wolf Creek nuclear power plant. The men who worked at Wolf Creek were a rough bunch and included among their ranks many itinerant workers, specialists who would finish at one place and follow the jobs to similar sites across the country.

Carter had worked as a hairdresser at "Mr. & Ms. Place" on Commercial Street in Emporia. He met Lorna there.

Danny told the investigators that in June of 1982 during the time he worked as Lorna's hairdresser, she invited him over to her house. Marty was away at summer camp. Lorna told Danny not to worry about fooling around with her because Marty had a girlfriend in Topeka. Carter said, "From then on we just had a little thing going," until late in 1982 when he said the physical relationship ended. Danny said Lorna was "just getting too serious—more than I could handle at the time." Lorna wanted a different husband. Danny had no interest in the assignment.

Danny said that Lorna and Marty talked about getting a divorce and Lorna wanted to marry him. He said Marty pretty much lived in the basement. For Danny, sex with Lorna was one thing, but marriage was out of the question. (While this affair between Lorna and Danny was reaching its peak, Lorna and Marty were taking instruction in the Lutheran church from Tom Bird. Then they joined Faith.)

Carter told the sheriffs he "would see her at her home two or three times a week and more during summer camp. Once in a while she would come to his house." Danny had sex with Lorna at the Anderson house when Marty was out of town even though her four young girls were home. He stayed overnight several times as well.

One day while Danny was visiting Lorna, Marty came home unexpectedly. Lorna was naked, sitting in the tub taking a bath. Danny sat fully clothed on the toilet next to the tub talking with her. Marty walked in on the couple, noted their presence and simply turned and walked out again.

Danny and Lorna were really not very discreet about their dating, quite often going to the Paragon Club and other places together.

Lorna claimed that Danny was a small-time drug dealer, supplying the itinerant workers at Wolf Creek. She and Danny would smoke pot together. Lorna said he grew marijuana at his parent's place. She said he showed her where he hid the stuff at his apartment, in a place up inside the chimney.

Danny and his ex-wife Linda had moved to Colorado several years earlier. They had one son named Casey, who was born in 1970. While in Colorado, Linda threw Danny out of the house for having an affair with one of her girlfriends. He moved in with another woman. In trouble once again, his brother Darrel collected him and brought him back to Emporia. Darrel had a long history of bailing out his brother.

Linda and Danny were divorced on May 20, 1982. Emporian Attorney Mike Patton represented Danny in this matter.

Darrel Carter, the older brother, was a building contractor. He also lived in Emporia and Mike Patton was also his attorney.

Together, Darrel and Danny operated two firecracker stands—"Carter's Crackers."

Besides owning the Emporia house were Danny lived now, Darrel also owned the converted garage in which Danny used to live before it burned down. About the fire, Lorna claimed that one day Darrel told Danny to remove his possessions from the apartment, located across the ally from First Presbyterian Church. Once his personal goods were out, the brothers burned it down. The insurance company paid the claim. They were disinterested in pursuing an investigation. Lorna was their alibi, claiming that the brothers were working at Crackers while the fire burned. A powerful bond between the three of them was established.

Darrel also had sex with Lorna.

From July to September, 1983, Danny's live-in girlfriend was North Carolina native Gail Wilson. Wilson became afraid after Marty's murder because she knew of Danny's involvement with Lorna. Not only was there a prior sexual relationship, Wilson knew that Lorna placed numerous phone calls to Carter during the fall of 1983. She also knew they met together that summer, although she says Carter told her not to worry, "Lorna says she's dating a preacher."

Wilson's call to the Kansas Bureau of Investigation led the sheriffs to Danny's door that night.

As Deppish and Buskey interviewed Carter, one or the other would step out of the room. Later, Agent Winsor joined in the good cop/bad cop game. He stepped in while the two sheriffs took a break.

The deputies asked Danny about his last contact with Lorna, and whether he had firearms. Deppish records this:

"Question: 'Did she [Lorna] ever ask if you knew of someone that would kill her husband?' Answer, 'No.' At this time subject Dan Carter appeared to become more nervous. [I] talked to him in reference to the laws in regards to conspiracy. Dan listened with much concern and interest."

Closing the deal

At this point, Buskey called Deppish out of the interrogation room and Agent Winsor went in. He wanted to talk to Danny alone. Within five minutes, Winsor called them back to the room. "I think that Dan wants to tell us what really happened."

Danny confessed, but before he went too far he wanted to know, "What's in it for me?" The investigators said they could not promise anything, but would tell the county attorney how cooperative and truthful he was.

Danny wrote his statement out on two sheets of tablet paper.

"I Daniel R. Carter, 16 East 8th, #4, working for Davis Electric, give the following statement.

"On or about the month of Sept. was contacted by Lorna Anderson about finding someone or helping her kill her husband Marty Anderson. She said she was tired of being beat and watching her children beat by Marty, her husband. After trying to talk her out of doing it, I told her I would try to find someone that might do it. I knew it was wrong to do it but she kept begging me. I wouldn't have said I would find someone if it hadn't been for Marty beating the children.

"I ask [sic] a man at work if he knew of anyone that was in the business of killing people. He said he knew someone that might do it. He later contacted me (about a week later) and said he had found a man that would do it for $5,000. He needed information about the man. What he did for a living. What he drove. What he looked like. And his schedule. I contacted Lorna and told her what was needed to be done.

"About three days later she brought me an envelope and said everything was there that they needed. I delivered the envelope to Greg Curry, a man I worked with. He said he would give it to someone he had contacted.

"After that I told him I didn't want to know anything more about what happened. After about a week Lorna called on the phone and wanted to know what was going on. I said I didn't know but would try to find out. I contacted Greg. He said he would call the man he gave all the information to and would let me know. This went on for some time, Lorna calling wanting to know what was going on because Marty was still alive.

"Greg kept telling me he called the man but never would give me a straight answer. Finally he quit his job around four weeks be for [sic] Marty was killed. I called him the day he quit and asked him what was going on and that I wanted the money Lorna had given him back because I didn't want to have anymore to do with it. He said he would send it when he got to where [he] was going and would tell the man the deal was off.

"After about a week Lorna called and I told her I was trying to get her money back and to stop calling me. I haven't heard from her since around the first of October, or heard from the man that I gave the envelope to.

"I don't know to this day who killed Marty. I have had no contact with either Lorna or Greg since then. The envelope to the best of my knowledge contained $5,000, a type written letter [sic] describing Marty, what he drove, where he worked, and where he would be on different dates. I think it might have had some pictures also, but couldn't be sure."

Danny and Agent Winsor both signed the handwritten statement at 10:17 p.m. that night. While a deputy typed his statement, Carter told Deppish and Buskey he knew they would eventually question him. Danny said, "I'm a prime suspect." Danny told his story without an attorney or his brother Darrel present.

Guarding the Carter home

While Danny was being interrogated, Deputy Samuels drove back to his apartment. He intended to keep an eye on the place until officers returned with a search warrant. This is Samuels's report from that night:

"At 7:22 p.m., this officer returned to the above apartment to secure it until such time as the Geary County investigators would be able to obtain a search warrant for the apartment of Danny Carter. Upon arrival at the apartment, this officer noticed movement inside the apartment of Danny Carter. The lights to the apartment had been left on. Within 10 seconds, Darrel Carter walked out of the south entranceway to the building and proceeded to walk east down the sidewalk to the intersection..."

Samuels described how Darrel looked. He wore a pullover sweater and blue denim jeans. What did Darrel Carter carry under his sweater, if anything? Samuels saw nothing, but it would be easy to hide any number of things from view. Samuels followed Darrel around the corner, but he was gone.

Samuels returned to his post to watch the building. At 7:50 p.m. someone from the city water department arrived but left immediately "as no one was there to meet with him." No proof exists that the water was turned off by the city.

Samuels next recorded:

"Approx. 8 p.m., a yellow early 1970s model Pontiac or Oldsmobile pulled into the driveway into the apartment building and turned off its lights. After aprx. 5 minutes, Darrel Carter exited the vehicle, this time wearing a lt. colored button up short sleeve shirt and blue denim jeans." [He discarded the pullover sweater he wore earlier.]

Samuels talked to Darrel in front of the apartment building for a few minutes. Darrel said he was the one inside Danny's apartment. Danny was his brother and besides, he owned the building.

After Danny signed his confession, investigators drove back to his house with a search warrant in hand. They found .22-caliber shells. The shells proved to be exactly the same make as the four shell casings found in the grass next to Marty's body. Investigators found no gun. They found a jeans jacket and a baseball cap that resembled what some of the Junction City witnesses saw worn by a man at the murder site. They also found "grow lights," the kind used by drug dealers to produce a marijuana crop, but these lights held no interest to them. They wanted a killer, not a drug dealer.

Danny mentioned one other name in his formal statement—Greg Curry. The cold investigative trail just got hot, and they wasted no time tracking down the elusive Mr. Curry.

Danny never mentioned Tom Bird. He didn't know him. They never met. Lorna never spoke his name to Danny. Anything he knew about Lorna's "boyfriend" she had told him and she didn't tell him much.

Darrel attended a soccer meeting that evening and then headed over to the jail to talk with Danny. He got angry when he heard Danny had spilled his guts without an attorney present. Darrel called Mike Patton who came over right away. Patton had served as Lyon County prosecutor and as a general practice attorney in Emporia.

At 4 a.m., Patton and Darrel left the jail and talked for a time in the parking lot before they left for home, to meet later that day and plot a strategy to save Danny from his foolishness.

Curry confesses

Greg Curry was a 6' tall, 167 pound blond 20-year old with a reputation as a braggart. He worked as a welding supervisor at Wolf Creek Nuclear Power Plant, moving into the Emporia area in March of 1983. On July 29,

Curry transferred to the Electrical Supports section at Wolf Creek. Here he met Danny Carter, a welder. Greg inspected Carter's work and claimed, "He is the best welder out there."

Greg, originally from Corinth, Mississippi, lived in a temporary apartment in Emporia with his pregnant wife. He quit Wolf Creek abruptly on October 20, and moved out of Emporia the next day. From Emporia he drove to his hometown of Corinth, Mississippi. Then he headed to Painesville, Ohio. He reported to work on the 27th at the Perry Project, another nuclear power plant.

Deputy Deppish and Agent Winsor went to Painesville on November 20, 1983, to arrest Greg. First they had to get him to talk. When they arrived at his apartment, his wife greeted them at the door. She said Greg was sleeping. The officers insisted on talking to him. Once awakened Greg agreed to go to the Lake County Sheriff's Office to be questioned.

The official report of the interview is lengthy. Greg verbally danced around their questions. He did not want to implicate himself. Then the investigators took off the gloves. Deppish wrote, "We had talked to a lot of individuals during this investigation and had a lot of information prior to talking to him. He was told to think very carefully about the question I was going to ask him. He was asked if he had ever been told by Danny Carter, or asked by Danny Carter, if he knew of anyone who could take care of somebody."

Greg got the picture. He gave the following statement:

"During an inspection I was doing for Dan Carter we had discussed many various subjects. Danny Carter asked if I knew someone who could help one of his friends in a delicate situation.

"From what I gathered, a certain man was brutally abusing his wife and children and she wanted someone to scare him into getting a divorce, and/or leaving her alone. After some days, Carter assured me that he was serious about the situation, for me to find someone. I told him that I would find someone to help the lady, and he said, just have him call me, so we agreed on the name Letterman to be used so Carter would know who was calling. That was around the 1st or 2nd week of September.

"I contacted Johnny Bingham to see if he knew anyone who could handle such a job. He said he knew someone who might be able to do something about someone like the supposed wife and child beater, so I told Carter I had found someone.

"On September 8th or 9th, Carter was going to South Carolina to pick up his girlfriend's child and he stopped by my apartment to give me the package with all the details about who it was and his whereabouts for the next 3 or 4 weeks.

"The package contained several pictures, all of which I didn't see, and $5,000 in cash. The money was to be in two (2) installments, $2,500 for before and $2,500 when Carter told me to finish the payment.

"On September the 10th, I gave the entire package to Bingham because I didn't want anything to do with a divorce suit or testifying in court, if he were to find out who roughed him up.

"Several weeks after my vacation, Carter told me to call the whole thing off because the couple was getting a divorce, so I contacted Johnny's landlady and she had Johnny to call me so he did. I told Johnny that Carter said the couple was getting a divorce, to call the whole thing off and Johnny said, okay but he wouldn't get any money back.

"A few days later I told Carter what Johnny said and he said that was fine because he wasn't worried about the money, he didn't want anything to do with it.

"I never heard anything else until tonight when Officer Winsor told me the man had been killed. I am still not sure it was even the same man because I never knew his name or what he looked like. This is all I know about the arrangements that Dan Carter and I had."

Several months later Greg clarified his story. "We [he and Danny Carter] were just havin' a conversation….and I asked him about a tattoo he had on his arm and he had a pair of barber scissors on his arm and that led into who he cuts hair for and everything like that and he told me that he only cut hair for his girlfriends. And the conversation just led up to what I said…what a sad situation one of his girlfriends was in…She was bein' brutally abused and beaten by her husband, their children were bein' beaten by the father and that one point that he had held a shotgun on her all night one night to keep her from callin' the police."

Greg took $2,500 of the cash with him to work on September 8, before leaving for Mississippi. He flashed it around to impress his co-workers, and he placed a bet with Bev Lnu, another worker at Wolf Creek, a bet he eventually won. He always insisted, though, that he gave the entire $5,000 to Bingham, a fact that investigators never could confirm.

Why ask this guy?

Why did Danny ask a 20-year old nomadic worker to find someone to rough up or murder Marty? Danny said he heard Greg brag about knowing tough guys. Danny said their first conversation about "his girlfriend" was on August 22. He never mentioned the intended victim's name to Greg until money changed hands.

Carter's and Curry's stories disagreed in several significant ways. They did agree that Lorna wanted her husband murdered and paid someone $5,000 to do the job.

Greg said he told Danny that he had talked to Johnny Bingham of Corinth, Mississippi. Bingham came from Chicago where he had a well-earned reputation as a tough guy. Greg claimed Danny and Bingham directly negotiated the $5,000 price tag. Danny said he never talked to Bingham, and that Greg negotiated the deal.

Danny said he took the $5,000 Lorna gave him and went directly to Greg's apartment. Greg and Danny disagreed on some of the details of how the money was handled during this exchange, but they both agreed that the exchange took place. They both agreed the money was to pay a killer.

On the weekend following the exchange, Greg sped off to Corinth with his wife for a vacation. He drove out to see Johnny Bingham. Greg said he handed off the entire $5,000. He wanted to be out of the loop.

Following his confession, Greg Curry was arrested and returned to Kansas. The investigators felt confident about their ability to bring a quick closure to this crime. They had talked to two suspects and got two confessions, and did it before the suspects demanded their right to have an attorney present.

Deputy Deppish and Agent Winsor next went to Corinth to question Johnny Bingham, an investigation that had its own strange turns and twists and ended suddenly without resolution. Johnny would spoil their perfect record of confessions.

Nervous Lorna

With Danny's arrest the previous evening, Lorna feared she was next. She confided her fear to the two people closest to her—Tom Bird and Susan Ewert—but she could not tell them why she was afraid. They believed she was an innocent victim, a widow left with four children. The idea that police suspected Lorna put them on the defense.

On Friday, Lorna was depressed and anxious. She called Tom who, just as before, came to try and talk her through her depression. He had counseled Lorna several times in the past. He desperately wanted to avoid a scene where she became whiney and hysterical. He wanted to help her calm down, just like in the hospital.

Marty's brother Stephen arrived at Lorna's about mid-afternoon. He brought back her van. When he arrive he saw Lorna dressed in black. She was "despondent." Tom sat next to her on the couch.

Absorbed in their own thoughts and conversation, neither Tom nor Lorna much acknowledged Stephen. Lorna did tell Stephen, "They arrested a man last night."

"Really? Who? Where?"

"He's Danny Carter from here in Emporia."

"Are you serious? Do you know him?"

In an understatement laced with lies that characterized Lorna she answered, "Yes, he used to do my hair. Lori's, too, but I haven't seen him in months. I don't know why they'd arrest him, but they're talking conspiracy."

"Conspiracy? What...who?"

Lorna's face dropped. "With me, uh, there was a news conference and everything and I was named."

That shocked Stephen. He thought out loud, "Well, maybe they do have something on this guy or they wouldn't have arrested him." To Lorna, "But I'll bet to take the heat off himself he's just pointing the finger at you."

Stephen was duped just like Tom and Susan. He never suspected his own brother's wife until much later. Though she had sex with dozens of area men, he knew nothing of this either, just like the folks at Faith.

In retrospect, Stephen was confused by how Tom and Lorna spoke together that afternoon, in quiet hushed tones, as if they did not want him to hear. While he pondered this, it never occurred to him that pastors normally try to limit counseling conversations to only those involved.

Caught in the middle

Tom again was tangled in Lorna's deep and, this time, understandable depression. He had no idea what she knew about what really happened to Marty. She said she was innocent and a victim. This belief drew him in deeper. He just wanted to help her and the girls work through yet another crisis.

Stephen paced the floor or answered phone calls all afternoon. He wanted to spare Lorna exposure to inquiring friends and media. He, too, tried to protect her.

At one point Lorna blurted, "Maybe I should go turn myself in."

"Heavens no. If they have anything on you they'll come and get you. My bet is that they don't have anything or they'd be here already," Stephen counseled.

The November 18 *Emporia Gazette* arrived around 4:40 p.m. and the Danny arrest story was on the front page. Lorna was named a co-conspirator in the murder. Wanting to save Lorna's parents from the shock of hearing the news from others, Stephen called Loren Slater at work to give him the news. "Loren, I have some news. Are you alone?"

"Yes, I can talk. What is it?"

"Well, there's been an arrest in the case. Some guy named Daniel Carter from Emporia has been charged with conspiracy."

"From Emporia?"

"Yes, and there's more." How do you tell a father news like this? "The warrant for his arrest names Lorna as a co-conspirator."

Loren jumped at that. "I knew it. I knew it. I knew she knew something about this. I knew there were other guys involved in this deal. Where is she? I want to talk to her."

Stephen answered the angry father, "Now Loren, let's don't jump to any conclusions. I figure maybe this guy does know something but is trying to divert attention from himself by pointing the finger at Lorna. We just don't know."

"Where is she? I want to talk to her," Loren demanded.

Trying to defend his "victimized" sister-in-law from her own father, Stephen answered incredibly, "She really doesn't want to talk to anyone right now."

"This will just kill her mother. Where is she?" Loren refused to quit.

Lorna walked up to Stephen and agreed to talk to her dad. Stephen heard her say, "No, no, Daddy. I don't know. No, daddy, no." She handed the phone back to Stephen and he finished the conversation with Loren, the two agreeing that they would talk later when more was known.

In her state of mind, Lorna could not be left alone. Susan came over to stay with her. They all agreed it would be best for the children to go back to Stephen's house in Lawrence, in case Lorna was arrested in the days ahead. They wanted to spare the children.

Nobody knows what Lorna did that weekend while she was alone.

On Monday, Lorna's hopes were revived somewhat. Darrell Meyer, her attorney, told her what was going on. Meyer also served as the attorney for Faith, and he was a close friend of Tom's. Meyer said the police did not have enough evidence to arrest her.

She called Stephen. "I've got great news. They don't have enough evidence so they're not going to arrest me."

"That is good news. How did you find this out?"

"Darrell [Meyer] has been on the phone all day. Anyhow, I'm going to come up and get the kids. I just talked to daddy, too, and he doesn't want me to drive up there today so I'll come tomorrow."

"That's OK, but why don't you leave them through Wednesday?

They're all just fine and Lori and Julie are at Ann's school and are really looking forward to the Thanksgiving feast there on Wednesday noon. Besides, you could use the time to just relax a bit."

"Are you sure? They won't be too much trouble?"

"No, not at all," he assured her. "We're having a terrific time."

"Well, okay. Why don't I call you tomorrow? I'm going to my grandmother's in Topeka and I want to do some shopping."

They talked about insurance matters. Lorna said, "I've talked to Chris [Kimble, her life insurance agent] again. He says the insurance will pay with no problem. We don't even have to wait on a death certificate." But as in most other aspects of Lorna's fantasy, the payment of insurance proceeds was a huge problem that ended up in federal court. And she never got a dime.

Little Lori changes her story

On November 22, Agent Winsor headed out to Lawrence to Stephen Anderson's home. Lori Anderson, Winsor, Stephen and his wife all sat together in the living room while Winsor interviewed the little girl. Lori added a few details to her first interview, and changed others.

She remembered that Marty drove the van to McDonald's and that Lorna drove when they left. She added that her mother "felt sick so she stopped. We stopped first at a gas station, pulled into the gas station but nobody got any gas."

"Did anyone get out of the van?" Winsor asked.

"No." After stopping, they drove down Highway 177.

She remembered it was dark when the van stopped and she saw no one outside the van. "All the girls were in the back of the van."

When Lorna went down into the ditch to vomit, Marty sternly told the girls "not to stare at their mother," but Lori did not understand why he said that.

"After mommy told daddy she lost the keys, daddy got out and he and mommy went down into the ditch to search." It was then that, "Somebody came. Maybe from behind the van." Her eyes lit up as she recalled, "I saw some sparks."

"Where did you see the sparks?"

"Kind of far away from the van, around where mommy was standing."

"What happened next?"

"Then the man came up and talked to my mom."

"Are you sure they talked?"

"I think they did, I think I saw them." Lorna told investigators that the man shot Marty and ran away from the van, toward the south. She never said

60

anything about talking to the man.

"What did he look like?" Winsor continued.

"He was about as tall as my dad."

"Did your mother talk to you about what to say to the police?"

"No. She never said to say or not say anything to you," Lori claimed. Winsor could never be sure this was true.

"Do you know a man named Danny Carter?" Winsor changed his line of questioning.

"He usually cuts my hair, Julie's hair, and mommy's hair."

"Where did he do this?"

"At the place he used to work. He also pierced my ears."

Feeling she knew more about Danny, Winsor asked, "Did Danny Carter ever come to your house?"

Lori paused before answering, as though she was not sure she should say anything. "Twice he came over at night with his son, and one other time in daylight with his son." She paused again and then added, "Another time he came in the day without his son."

"Did you ever see Danny and your mother kissing?"

"No." Strange since Danny admitted to a sexual relationship with Lorna that included visits to her house.

"Can you think of any other time they might have been alone together?"

"One time mommy went over to his apartment and I stayed in the van and took care of Julie while mommy was in the apartment."

Winsor asked her about Tom Bird. Lori said, "That's Pastor Bird. He has a daughter, Andrea, who is six-years old and goes to Village Elementary School with me." She mentioned Paul and Aaron, the other two Bird children.

"Have you ever seen your mother and Pastor Bird kissing?"

"Yes, two times."

"When?"

"One time after Bible study." She described the event. "My sisters were downstairs and I was in the bathroom one time and was in the kitchen the other time when I saw them kissing."

"Was anyone else home?"

"No."

"What did you see?"

"Pastor was kissing mommy on the mouth." Stephen and his wife had never heard anything like this before.

"Where was your dad when this happened?"

"One time he was out jogging or playing racket ball. He wasn't there either time."

Tom Bird remembered kissing Lorna, too. He remembered that Lori and Julie saw them, but the instance bore little resemblance to Lori's story.

"The only time I remember was the day that we finished the instruction class for membership in the church and we were with another couple and one single individual. The class that particular afternoon was at the Anderson's home. We finished the class and everyone was up and positive.

"Marty and Lorna and the others committed to joining the church. I shook Marty's hand, he gave me a slap on the shoulder and he headed for the kitchen to serve punch or whatever. I turned to hug Lorna and she gave me a celebrative, exaggerated kiss on the cheek saying, 'This is so wonderful!'

"The two kids—Lori and Julie—giggled at the kiss and Lorna went on to serve the refreshments. Julie said, 'Mom kissed Pastor Bird,' and giggled some more. I said something to the girls like 'You all are being silly.' I went on to talk to the other three class members. It was nothing romantic or clandestine." This happened late in 1982.

Lori was an eye-witness to her father's murder just 17 days earlier. On that night she heard the shooter talking to Lorna and yelling. She never changed that story. She also said she didn't recognize the hit man's voice. As the daughter of the Faith church secretary, enrolled in school with and frequent play-friends of Tom Bird's children, and attending services on a reqular basis, Lori recognized Tom Bird's voice just as readilly as her own father's. But Lori did not recognize the hit man's voice.

Lori's testimony about kissing loomed large in the months and years ahead, but her lack of recognition of the shooter's voice faded away in significance. Her testimony about the kiss changed in later months and it was once again different under oath.

Winsor asked if Lori knew Greg Curry. She did not.

Lori's description of the events of November 4, were materially different from those of Lorna. Either the little girl was confused or Lorna was lying. Little girls have big imaginations, but investigators welcomed her testimony, as long as it supported their mounting suspicions about Lorna Anderson and Tom Bird.

Sorrowful Thanksgiving

The first holiday, birthday or anniversary after a loved one dies can be extra tough. This is especially true in a family like the Bird's that traditionally celebrates big and small things. Thanksgiving had been such a day for Tom and Sandy Bird.

In 1983, Thanksgiving fell on the 24th. Tom packed his children in the car on the 22nd and headed off to Fort Worth, responding to Jane Grismer's demands that he join them for the holiday. Jane Grismer was Sandy's mother. She had divorced Randall Stringer—Sandy's father—several year's earlier and married Little Rock Doctor Jerry Grismer.

Tom had always been frustrated by the way Jane tried to control the lives of others, and he had no desire to be with her at this time of his grief, but he went anyway.

Unbeknownst to Tom, his leaving town that day set off alarms with the men investigating Marty's murder. Lorna, too, had left town that day. Someone reportedly saw them together in the morning, and they worried that the two were fleeing the state to avoid prosecution.

Tom and his children were not the only ones grieving Sandy's death. Her mother Jane Grismer and her extended family, many of whom had helped raise Sandy, were all hurting.

Tom said, "Jane talked me into coming to Fort Worth to meet with the family—sisters, cousins, and others. I went with the kids. While I was there the family kind of ganged up on me to move back to the Little Rock, Arkansas, area." "Mama" Jane lived in Little Rock.

"I felt pressure. They also pressured me about having the kids down at Little Rock for Christmas. Jane would not take no for an answer, putting a lot of guilt upon me about pulling the kids away from them."

Despite this pressure, Tom was pleased that Jane "gave me her blessing on getting married again." He and Terry Smith had been dating for several weeks, and it was going well.

The time with the Grismer family would have been tense under normal circumstances. Given the nagging questions about how Sandy died simply intensified the drama. Of his state of mind during that family visit Tom said, "I did not know everything about Sandy's death. I felt guilt at her death and I felt anger at Sandy for her death; based on the idea that she might have been driving somewhere at 2:00 or 3:00 in the morning. I didn't know."

He had meditated on these sentiments many times during the proceeding months. His natural grief, anger and frustration became intensified because he was a pastor; "pastor's are supposed to be immune to these human pressures." His family and church urged him to be strong, but he had times of immense weakness and loneliness. And just like many others close to Sandy, he sometimes got angry with God for her death.

Being with other family members who had been suffering in the same way, and who had spent countless hours speculating about what really happened at Rocky Ford Bridge, added to the tension. It was a hard time to be together. Little things became big irritants.

On Saturday an issue arose over haircuts. "Before I went out to play football with the cousins, Jane said she wanted one of the nieces to cut the kids hair. I told her she could cut Andrea's because Andrea wanted it done. I told her not to cut the boys' hair because a member of my church, Dennis Kasten cut their hair and Aaron was a handful."

This provoked a mild argument. "Jane said that the boys' hair was a mess and needed cutting. I said no." He headed outside to join the football game.

When he came back in the house a little later, he "found Aaron on a stool crying hysterically, surrounded by five aunts and nieces having his hair cut. I went off!"

Tom stomped out of the room and began packing the family's clothes to leave immediately. Jane followed him into the bedroom where there was an angry exchange.

Tom held intense negative feelings about Jane's strong, controlling personality. She was a determined and driven woman. Some of her ways had rubbed off on Sandy. Over the months, as Tom had pondered Sandy's accident, he felt that her strong will contributed to her death because she insisted on going back to ESU late that Saturday night, rather than heading home. If Sandy drove home, she would still be alive.

"Jane called me aside to a bedroom where we argued and cried; both of us upset. I told her that she tried to run Sandy's life before and she wasn't going to run ours. She was afraid of losing contact with the children. We were both sad and angry about Sandy's death and in that context I said if Sandy was not so stubborn and independent as Jane and her sisters that maybe she would be alive today."

The remark greatly offended Jane. Investigators and others believed it was a veiled confession that Sandy's belligerence triggered Tom into a violent and fatal outburst from which Sandy died.

Tom said, "she [Jane] held that against me" from then on. So did others. This, to them, was just more evidence that Tom was hot-tempered and wanted to deflect any serious discussion of what may have really happened to Sandy.

Lorna arrested

Stephen Anderson cared for Lorna's children during the days leading up to Thanksgiving. This gave Lorna time and space to plan her next move, which she had told Tom, was to move back to Hutchinson, close to her parents. "She wanted to be where folks wouldn't recognize her so easily, giving her some room to get on with her life," Tom said.

She took time to drive to Topeka, about an hour north of Emporia, to spend time with one of her grandmothers.

Unbeknownst to her, investigators had secured a search warrant for her house. Deputies Buskey and Deppish, as well as Agents Humphrey and Winsor drove to the Anderson house at about 1:30 p.m. on Tuesday, November 22, 1983. They found the house empty. Securing a locksmith to open the door, they entered the house at 3:10 p.m. and began an extensive search.

As thorough was their search, they found no "evidence" of any crime. No gun. No bullets. No scribbled notes or pieces of clothing left behind by Danny or any other of Lorna's boyfriends. No black mask.

Deputy Deppish searched Lorna's bedroom. While rifling through her lingerie drawer, next to her most intimate apparel, he found and seized "...two *love letters* to Mrs. Anderson from a subject named Tom. One letter was found to the subject 'Tom' written by Mrs. Anderson, this was seized also." [Emphasis added]

Deppish thought to himself that he held in his hand the corroborating evidence to prove Lorna and Tom were secret lovers. Investigators had followed the gossip for months, but had no "hard evidence." Now he held two cards from Tom and a partially written, undated and never sent letter from Lorna to Tom. The cards were in two envelopes marked "Thursday" and "Friday" and bore the kinds of greetings commonly sent to a friend who was undergoing a stressful time, or to reaffirm love and devotion to that person. Tom's handwritten notes on the cards caught his eye. Deppish saw the notes as an admission that the widower pastor had more than spiritual intentions toward the new widow.

The discovery of this "evidence" blazed a trail for the officers. It provided a motive for Marty's murder. For the first time, the officers believed they had a strong, evidentiary lead that could draw Tom into their loop. Some, like Trooper John Rule, found even more significance in the "love letters," having believed since July that Bird had something to do with his wife's death.

Agent Winsor executed a second search warrant the same day to seize all of Marty and Lorna's bank records at the Lyon County State Bank. Winsor added these bank records to the "love letters" to help build a case against both Lorna and Tom.

With Danny Carter's and Greg Curry's confessions now on file, with the "love letters" in hand, the officers prepared to arrest Lorna, but they worried that she and Tom slipped through their hands that very day. Lorna's neighbor told them that the two were seen together that morning, and both had left town. Try as they could all that night and the next morning they could not locate Tom (he was in Fort Worth with Sandy's extended family).

Stephen Anderson informed the nervous officers that Lorna had gone to her grandmothers in Topeka to celebrate Thanksgiving. He had no idea where Tom was.

At 11:35 a.m. on November 23, 1983, Deppish, Winsor and a Topeka Police Detective arrested Lorna at her grandmother's house and charged her in Geary County "on Probable Cause for Conspiracy to commit 1st degree Murder [sic]."

Buskey wrote, "The decision was made to arrest Mrs. Anderson at this time after it was learned she had just taken out a bank loan on the 15th of November, 1983 for a little over $12,000.00." Marty and Lorna had tried in vain to find a bank that would lend them money just months earlier. Their credit was no good. Did Lorna promise to pay from the generous life insurance benefits due her from Marty's untimely death?

The officers felt confident that all they lacked was the actual hit man. With Lorna, Danny and Greg reeled in, they focused on the killer. They believed that Lorna would quickly see the advantage of confessing her role in the drama, as had the other two, and name the hit man.

The deputies took Lorna to the Geary County Sheriff's Office for processing and then to the Junction City Jail. Buskey talked with Lorna's attorney Darrell Meyer. Meyer believed the investigators were giving him the runaround, trying to get her to talk without him being present. They did this before, with Danny Carter and Greg Curry. He, like Tom Bird and Susan Ewert, believed the distraught widow told him the truth.

Lorna spent Thanksgiving in jail, and was released on a $50,000 bond on Friday. Don Froelich, the lay minister from Faith, called Tom in Fort Worth on Friday and informed him of her arrest.

When Tom returned to Emporia on Saturday, besides preparing for Sunday services, he needed to plan and preside at two funerals. With Lorna under arrest, he knew trouble lay ahead and hours more of his time would be sucked up by her latest predicament.

The timing and method of Lorna's arrest made Tom suspicious of the tactics of the investigators. He perceived that they were trying to take advantage of her and talk her into a concocted confession, just to remove the pressure on them. The next time Tom met the investigators, he decided to be careful, to protect Lorna. Had he known they would use his gesture of caring—two greeting cards—to tie him into a murder plot, he never would have met them again without an attorney present. Investigators began questioning members at Faith, the level of gossip ratcheted up, Lorna leaned on him for even more support and Tom still had to perform his official acts. He knew he had been caught in a vicious circle, but believed in time he would be freed to re-build his life. Instead tempest increased.

Johnny of Corinth

Greg Curry and Danny Carter both pointed to Johnny Bingham of Corinth, Mississippi, as the prime suspect in Marty Anderson's murder. Danny claimed Greg gave him Johnny's name, and Greg claimed he gave $5,000 to Johnny to kill Marty. Greg insisted that Johnny and Danny negotiated the price directly.

Johnny stood 6' 1", a 200-pounder with curly blond hair and a moustache. Given the different stories Danny and Greg had told about him, he could have easily resolved the conflict, but instead claimed he had no knowledge of any of it.

Agent Winsor and Deputy Deppish traveled to Corinth on December 2, 1983. Corinth is a rough, dingy and downtrodden town in Alcorn County, located just Southwest of Memphis, Tennessee. The Kansas investigators asked for help from local police authorities in finding and questioning Johnny, and were assigned Chief Deputy Sheriff Terry Doles. An investigator from the District Attorney's office, Kenneth Marlar helped them prepare and secure a search warrant for Johnny's mobile home.

They found Johnny at home with his wife Teresa, and asked him if he would be willing to go to the sheriff's office to answer questions. "This has to do with some things that happened in Kansas that you might know some thing about," Winsor told him, not wanting to tip his hat. Johnny agreed to go with them.

While Winsor and Doles questioned Johnny, Deppish and another Alcorn County sheriff conducted a search of his mobile home.

Winsor noticed that Johnny was very nervous during the interview. Johnny worked as a self-employed farmer for Mr. Suitor, harvesting and trucking milo. "I work from dawn to dusk when there's work to do, but I get time off when I got things to do, when the crops don't need to be collected."

"Mr. Bingham, I'm an agent with the Kansas Bureau of Investigation. I'm investigating a recent homicide there," Winsor began.

"Where's Kansas?" Johnny asked.

"Huh?"

"You mean Kansas City? I ain't never been there in my life. I don't even know where Kansas is." Johnny said he had to repeat ninth grade twice, and then dropped out of school.

Winsor showed him on a map where to find Kansas.

"Do you know anyone in Emporia, Kansas?" Winsor continued.

"No sir."

"Have you ever spoken to anyone in Emporia, either by phone or in person?"

"No sir."

"Mr. Bingham, do you own any firearms?"

"Yes sir. I've got a 30-30 rifle, and a .22 cal browning rifle, a Marlin .22 caliber rifle, a 12 gauge shotgun, 8 mm Magnum rifle, an FIE Brand .25 automatic pistol."

"Is that all you own?"

"Yes sir."

"I saw a .22 caliber Ruger revolver in a holster hanging in your bedroom while we were there," Winsor reminded him.

"Oh yea, I forgot. I don't shoot that one anymore because it hurts my ears."

"Have you ever owned or borrowed any other .22 caliber handguns?"

"No sir."

"Mr. Bingham, where do you do your banking?"

"I don't use no bank. I don't have no checking or savings account."

"How do you make money?"

"Just by farming. I get paid weekly in the spring and summer months."

"About how much do you make?"

"$300 a week or so, plus at the end of the year I get a percentage of the crop."

Winsor changed directions. "Do you know a Danny Carter from Emporia?"

"No sir."

"Have you ever heard the name?"

"Well, there's a Danny Carter in Corinth, but not from Kansas. No sir."

"How about a Mr. Letterman?" Letterman was a code-name Greg said Johnny would use if he called Danny.

"Who? No sir. I don't know that name."

"Have you ever spoken to Danny Carter from Emporia either in person or on the telephone?"

"No sir. I don't know him."

"Well, do you know the name Lorna Anderson?"

"No sir."

"Have you ever spoken to Lorna Anderson either in person or on the phone?"

"No. I don't know her."

"Johnny, do you know a man named Greg Curry?"

"Yea. I know his dad and him both." Johnny forgot to mention that he also knew Greg's uncle with whom he had had an auto accident during the past September. The accident looked suspicious, and authorities wondered if it was a staged accident. Records found later showed that Johnny pocketed $2,900 from that mishap.

"I ain't seen Greg since back in the spring or summer, though. Maybe June or July, maybe at Gerald's, his dad's," Johnny continued. "I normally see him when I go see my brother. It might have been a year since I've seen him. I would say I saw him at my brother's house. I'm pretty sure that's where it was at."

"He ever been to your house?"

"If he's been to my house, I can't remember it."

"Curry ever give you anything? A package or any object at all in the last several months?"

"No sir, nothing."

"What kind of cars do you drive, Johnny?"

"I got a tan '74 Chevy Blazer and a blue '72 Chevy Camaro, with a white stripe on it. My wife drives the Camaro." Witnesses saw a small blue or gray car facing the wrong way on McDowell Creek Road minutes before Marty's murder.

"Johnny, do you have any nicknames that people call you?"

"No sir."

"How about Jim Beam?" This served as an alternative code word, according to Greg Curry.

"No. Folks always call me Johnny. That's all."

Winsor decided to bore in. "Johnny, have you ever been asked by anyone in Kansas to either injure or scare someone in the state of Kansas?"

"No sir."

"Have you ever been contacted to take care of, or to kill anyone in Kansas?"

"No sir."

"Would you be willing to take a lie detector test and answer these questions?" Winsor told him how the test worked.

Johnny hesitated before answering, but finally said, "Sure, I suppose I'd take the test if you asked me to."

"Where were you on November 4, 1983?"

"Let me think. I was pretty much around the house, I think. I was tryin' to figure out when deer season opens. I go hunting in Natchez Trace in Tennessee. I'm gonna have to ask Teresa to see if she can remember." Then he added, "I will find out about my alibi."

(Why did Johnny have to check with someone about his *alibi?* Wouldn't most people have said, "I need to check to see where I was, or what I was doing?")

"Do you have any objection to our looking in your residence for physical evidence or checking your farm property and vehicles?" (Deputy Deppish was already searching his mobile home.)

"I don't care. I also rent a barn at my place near my house. I keep my horses in it. Mr. Suitor lets me use it without paying rent."

"When's the last time you fired a handgun?"

"I don't like much to fire handguns 'cause I got a inner ear problem. Shooting a handgun messes up my balance."

"Wouldn't an 8 mm rifle shot cause you the same problem? It's just as loud or louder?"

"Ah, no. When I fire it I'm usually concentrating on something, like when I'm hunting. It doesn't cause me any trouble."

Johnny said he used to live in Cicero, Illinois and had two children, one by his former wife and a little three year old girl with Teresa. He had lived in Corinth for about 11 years.

"You know, I think the hunting season in Tennessee was about the first of November. I think maybe I was hunting," Johnny added.

Winsor informed him that deputies were searching his property at that very moment, and the interview ended. They all drove back to Johnny's place.

Deppish found $2,830 in cash in $100 bills in the master bedroom stuck in a closet drawer. He seized the money as potential evidence, and handed a receipt to Johnny. Deppish also found a loaded handgun.

Johnny told Winsor the cash was his "milo money," money he had earned hauling milo to the grain company.

"When were you paid this money?"

"About two or three months ago." Then he changed his story. "No wait, that money was insurance money I got from my auto accident. I got about $2,900 from State Farm three weeks ago."

There was nothing found during this initial interview and investigation of Johnny that should have dissuaded the officers from further pursuing him as a prime suspect. The officers headed back to Kansas to talk again with Danny Carter and Greg Curry.

Rumors run amok

Tom Bird's orthodox Lutheran theological training coupled with his own value system compelled him to disdain rumors; to refuse to even hear them. And it was totally out of character for him to spread rumors. Joyce Rosenboom, a member at Faith said, "Oh he never believed rumors. If he couldn't personally experience something or know something, to him it wasn't a fact. He refused to have anything to do with rumors."

Furthermore, his religious training dictated that he put the "best construction" on everything. He believed instinctively what people told him unless he learned otherwise. When someone related a negative story to him, he would attempt to turn it to a positive. He reflexively looked for good in what people plainly said, and not to their motives, especially evil motives. He presumed innocence, not guilt.

Since Sandy's death, Tom, a young well-educated eligible widower, became more susceptible to rumors. At least one female member of his church approached him about considering a long-term relationship, and by turning away her advances, he left her angry. The lay ministers wisely recognized the potential for danger, and cautioned him about even a perception of evil.

The rumors about him and Lorna were the most frequent and vicious. Joyce Rosenboom put these in perspective. "Tom Bird never cared what people thought as long as *he* knew what was the truth." As best he could, Tom ignored the rumors and kept following his call.

Following Marty's murder, the intensity and frequency of the rumors about Tom and Lorna increased. Tom said as much to Agent Winsor and Deputy Deppish during a November 10 interview.

Winsor wrote:

> "Pastor Bird was very calm and relaxed and cooperative throughout the interview.
>
> "He stated he [Bird], himself, had been confronted by other people, and knew there were all kinds of rumors flying around the community, however, [he] was thinking that hopefully these had been laid to rest. He stated that his involvement with Lorna Anderson is strictly an emotional one and one of counseling, and there is no other relationship at all. He stated that I and other pastors are very vulnerable to such gossip, especially since the death of his own wife. He said, we are really together a lot, however, that is as far as it goes."

Tom's statements were consistent with his own disclaimers to Sandy in the spring, to Angie Duensing during the summer and to Sharon Meyer, the wife of one of the lay ministers, in the fall. They all talked to Tom about the perception of impropriety his closeness to Lorna presented. With each of them he had maintained that the relationship was professional and pastoral— nothing more.

Still, with the rumor-mill spinning at an ever-increasing intensity, Tom reached the breaking point. On November 29, Susan Ewert called Tom and told him she had learned that Darrel Carter was the person fanning the flames. The rumors were salacious and, added to the effect of police investigators who were conducting investigations with Faith members, greatly disturbed Tom. He determined to put a stop to them.

Tom knew that his neighbor three doors south of him, a young mother named Julie Palmer, had been sleeping with Darrel Carter. He knew this for a long time, but he kept his mouth shut just as he had been trained to do. (He learned later that Darrel Carter also shared Lorna's bed.)

The idea of imposing himself into someone else's business weighed on him, and he hated confrontation. Tom decided he would send a strong message to Darrel through Palmer. He naively thought that simply threatening to expose this affair would cause a family man like Darrel to stop the rumors. He planned on saying something like, "Julie, you need to give a message to Darrel. Tell him that I know what you and him are doing, and that rumors can cut both ways. I want the rumors stopped."

On December 1, a nervous Tom Bird walked to the Palmer house to confront her. This whole idea rubbed him wrong and he grew guiltier about doing it. She had small children, and though what she did was wrong, he really did not want to create trouble for her. Julie opened the door to his knock and it caught him off guard. Because it was cold, Tom entered. Julie, who suffered a nervous breakdown after all this became public, later testified by deposition about this meeting. Julie was spared appearing in open court where she could be aggressively cross-examined. (The following is taken from that deposition.)

"What if anything did the defendant [Bird] say after he stepped inside your home in the entry way?"

"It seemed to be double talk. He said sometimes we know things we wish we didn't know and do things we wish we didn't do. He seemed to be trying to get to a point but started out that way."

She didn't respond to Tom's confused statement. Trying to avoid being too direct or confrontational, he believed that she knew exactly what he meant, and the mere fact that he knew and the not-so-subtle threat that he might publicly reveal this affair would be motivation enough for her to do what he was asking.

"He wanted to know if I would give a message to Darrel Carter and..."

"Did you make a response to his request that you give a message to Darrel Carter?"

"Yes, I did. I said I didn't know when I would see him or if I would but that I would give him a message that he wanted to talk with him."

"Did the defendant indicate to you why it was that he wanted to visit with Darrel Carter?"

"Yes. He said he wanted to reaffirm a trust some business they had talked about, he and Darrel."

Julie asked Tom why he didn't just pick up the phone and call Darrel himself. Tom said, "No, no phones."

Once Tom left her house, Julie wasted no time. That same day, she drove to the building site where Darrel was working, near the school that one of her sons attended. She told him that Tom wanted to talk with him, but she never again talked with Tom.

"Did Darrel ever visit with you concerning any meeting which he may have had with the defendant?"

"Yes."

"What if anything did he tell you concerning that meeting?"

"Well, at one time he mentioned that his youth group or some group at the church might want to sell fire works and that he, I assume, had a meeting."

The prosecutors continued to probe the sexual relationship between Darrel and Julie, to which she admitted. Both of them were married at the time.

During the same time period that Tom was trying to warn Darrel that he would publicly expose his infidelity, Darrel was meeting with Mike Patton, criminal attorney for Danny Carter. Patton, the two Carters, investigators and Steven Opat the Geary County Attorney, for several days had pounded out an agreement that would eventually spare Danny from serving a single day in prison. To help his younger brother, Darrel agreed to bait Tom into making a confession about what he claimed had taken place at a meeting that they had months earlier at Faith. By making this deal, prosecutors accomplished two goals. First, they had levers on Danny to make sure he would testify against Lorna. And, Darrel helped them press their budding case against Tom.

Tom knew nothing about the deal Danny and Darrel cut with Opat, and he never suspected investigators would try to trap him into a confession for a crime that he never committed.

Danny dealt a winning hand

Once Danny got tied to the Marty Anderson murder, Darrel came to the rescue. He brought along his attorney, Mike Patton.

Patton wrote a series of letters to Opat laying out the terms of his client's cooperation in the case. He demanded a reduction in the charges to a class "D" felony of solicitation to commit murder. (Solicitation is a result of someone simply asking another to commit a crime, a serious offense if offered seriously.) Danny, however, had already confessed to taking money from Lorna and giving it to Greg Curry for the expressed and explicit purpose of hiring a hit man to kill Marty. Furthermore, someone actually did the job.

The charge of conspiracy to commit murder is very serious. Investigators, though, believed that Danny's passing money to hire a murderer was not related to the actual murder. This was quite a leap in logic considering that as yet, they had not ruled out Mississippian Johnny Bingham as the hit man. Greg said he gave Danny's money to Johnny to do the murder. They still questioned Johnny as late as March 23, 1984, months after Opat made this deal with Danny.

Danny claimed he withdrew the offer when he told Greg to call off the hit in late October. Generally, when one withdraws such an offer, it clears them of the crime (although this standard was never applied to Tom Bird). If Danny could have fought this on the grounds that he withdrew the offer, then why would he plead guilty to any crime?

Furthermore, Patton demanded that the state trade parole for Danny's cooperation, and if the state reneged on this detail, Patton wrote in a letter to Opat that Danny would renege on the plea agreement.

Despite all the loose ends in the criminal investigation, Opat accepted it. He may have already decided who did the murder and thought this was the quickest route to his door—or pulpit. He wrote his reasons for accepting Danny's plea demands on a yellow legal pad. They are reproduced verbatim (note: clarifying comments are in parentheses):

"1. Carter's life was already in danger because he talked. A snitch doesn't last long in prison. (Why should Opat care?)

"2. No immunity, will not give unless no other alternative—his conviction and probation will allow controls. (He wanted to withhold immunity from prosecution, but Patton insisted on it as a condition of the agreement.)

"3. Plead to a legal ruling of solicitation, not conspiracy. This potential defense of withdrawal available—some evidence substantiates that affirmative defense (PIK) withdrawal is available— if believed, could create reasonable doubt leading to Carter's acquittal which is not desirable from State's standpoint. (By calling off the hit, Danny could claim he was guilty of nothing. Opat feared he might do so and then there would be not conviction at all. He believed the plea agreement assured some sort of punishment.)

"4. Carter immediately confessed when interrogated— cooperated fully in disclosing his involvement, Gregory Curry's and what he knows about Lorna Anderson's—cooperated fully in providing info. About activities others who maybe [sic] involved, at considerable risk to himself and his member [sic] of his family. (He gave Danny credit for 'fessin up right away, but this does not mean that Danny's confession was true.)

"5. Evidence indicates and corroborates the extent of Carter's participation, and lack of involvement in further activities which led to M.A.'s death." (The investigation had barely begun at this time. Many crime scene witnesses came forward months after the murder.)

"6. Without Carter, would not have Curry or Lorna Anderson, others who may be involved in M.A. killing. (Opat saw Danny's cooperation as essential in convicting Lorna.)

"7. While could choose to proceed against Carter alone, responsibility to weigh certain things in interests of society—a totality test has led me to believe that more at stake than Dan Carter alone. (Opat believed Danny was a small bird, and he aimed to fry a larger Bird.)

"8. Duty not only to convict but to do justice which in this case requires that I make best use of what evidence I have available— although it may be personally distasteful because of the consequences of conduct of all parties involved in the events which led to M.A.'s death, must use Dan Carter and to do that must protect him—to use and protect him has led to the conclusion must agree to his probation in this case—if was convinced that he hadn't made an effort to withdraw, which could be a compete defense to crime charged, if wasn't convinced he's told truth and cooperated fully to pain of potential danger to himself and family, if was convinced was evidence about further involvement, would not engage in this agreement.

"Must do some things in job which may personally disagree with, are repugnant, are hard to swallow, but must in this case because of everything which has to be considered."

(Opat, like many prosecutors, believes it is better to let a confessed criminal walk free if it will enhance their ability to convict someone else. This paradox of the justice system always results in a miscarriage of justice. It places the state in the position of sanctioning some criminals at the expense of others. It leaves unanswered questions: Do guilty people walk free for telling a prosecutor what he wants to hear? Do innocent people get convicted based on the false testimony of guilty persons who have made plea agreements? Do some guilty people get better treatment than others who commit the same crime, but get off simply because they made the prosecutor's job easier?)

Patton eventually won more than just a reduction to solicitation for his client. Opat agreed not to charge Danny with the actual murder, a steep price to pay unless Opat believed he had the real killer in his sights.

The state dragged out Danny's sentencing until March 8, 1984. They had a reason. The others still under investigation felt the pressure of not knowing what Danny might say. Danny had to stay clean and tell the truth, at least a version that proved the prosecution's case. As long as Opat kept him hanging in the breeze he felt confident Danny would cooperate. Lyon County prosecutors did the same to Lorna, refusing to settle her criminal case until Tom Bird was caged. Swift justice has little to do with time when it serves the prosecutor to drag things out.

When Danny was finally sentenced, the conviction said it was for "the offense of Criminal Solicitation, a class "D" felony, contrary to K.S.A. 21-3303, 1982 Supplement..." The penalty would normally be an "indeterminate term of imprisonment, the minimum of which shall be not less than two (2) years and the maximum of which shall be not more than five (5) years in the care, custody and control of the Secretary of Corrections." But Danny served no time, except for the first night in jail. Instead, "The court further suspends imposition of the sentence and places the defendant on four (4) years supervised probation ..." and then it laid out the conditions of the probation: he had to remain law abiding, get a regular job, pay a fine of $1,000 and pay $114 in court costs within 16 months. Danny won the game and got off with barely a slap on the wrist. The stories told by him and his brother were woven together, under the safety net of a settled plea agreement, to build a legal cage for Tom Bird.

(Plea agreements create their own legal proverb. The criminal who knows an attorney who knows how to deal with criminals make quick pleas and cause no pain for prosecutors. They walk away with a slap on the hand. Innocent people who refuse plea agreements and go to trial, if they lose, do prison time, even for the same crime.)

Confronting Curry

Kansas investigators went to talk again with Greg Curry. If Greg had told them the truth, Johnny Bingham looked like the prime suspect as Marty's murderer.

Opat offered to reduce charges against Greg to one count of solicitation to commit murder, a class D felony, same as the charge against Danny. On December 16, Greg accepted Opat's offer. He agreed to cooperate with the investigation and to take a polygraph test. His attorney, Ralph De Zago, insisted on a provision prohibiting the state from further prosecuting Greg in the murder, "provided the defendant is truthful in any subsequent testimony or statements given with reference to the events and circumstances for which he is charged in the amended Complaint/Information."

On December 4, Deputies Buskey and Deppish interviewed Greg. He gave mostly the same answers as in earlier statements, but added a few new wrinkles.

"What was the denomination of the bills you received from Carter?"

"I'm not sure if they were all 100s or 50s. There may have been some 20s even."

"Did you make any long distance calls to Bingham at any time from your home in Emporia, Kansas?"

"I called Bingham's landlady and left a message for him to call me collect."

"Did you make only the one call?"

"Yes."

"What was the landlady's name?"

"Suitor. I don't know the first name."

"Would you go over your conversation with Carter again?"

"Yes. Carter asked me where the money was and why nothing had happened. Carter also told me a date and time Anderson was going to be in Topeka. Johnny Bingham got ahold of me and I passed on the time and date."

"Do you remember the date?"

"No. Carter contacted me and asked me to call it off and try to get the lady's money back. Carter said the lady wanted it called off because her husband had agreed to a divorce after all. This was about two weeks before I moved. I discussed this with Johnny in person while I was home on a weekend."

"Tell us about the delivery of the money and pictures and typed information sheet you say Carter delivered."

"Carter brought the envelope to my apartment. It was the only time he came to my apartment. When Carter arrived, my minister from the Westside Baptist Church in Emporia, was at my door.

"Carter came in and I told the minister to excuse me, I had company. The minister left. Carter opened the envelope, it was about 8" x 10" and inside was a white business size envelope with the money in it. Also there was pictures of a house, car (Volari station wagon) and a van (green Ford), and pictures of a guy. I told Carter I didn't want to see that stuff.

"Carter told me I was to pay Johnny two separate payments of $2,500 each. Carter then counted the money into two envelopes. I then marked each envelope 'Wizard #1' and 'Wizard #2.' Carter told me to have Johnny contact him and ask for Mr. Letterman."

"Did Carter know Johnny and did he ever contact him?"

"I don't know if he ever contacted him. All Carter knew was Johnny. But Johnny had Carter's number. Johnny used the code name 'Jim Beam' when he called me. Carter was the one who told me it was going to cost $5,000, so I guess Johnny told Carter the cost directly, because I didn't know.

"When Carter was talking about calling it off, he was scared and told me, 'They were going to kill Anderson and Lorna's new boyfriend did the same thing to his wife.' Carter was scared and wanted the whole thing called off."

Greg never said anything about Lorna's "new boyfriend" in earlier statements. The deputies had heard and were following the rumors about Lorna's boyfriend (how they could ever know which boyfriend fit the definition of "new" is hard to comprehend, given the number of men Lorna dated). They had "love letters" from her lingerie drawer. Jan Mead told them Lorna and Tom were in love and wanted their spouses out of the way.

The deputies were pleased with the new information they heard that day.

By this time, Darrel Carter was deeply involved in the legal negotiations with his brother Danny. Did the two plot a strategy to remove themselves from suspicion? Did they talk with Greg about their plan? Within a few days, Darrel would provide investigators with "evidence" that directly tied Tom Bird to two murders.

Nervous parents

Six days later, Greg's mother and father contacted Deputy Deppish. They had just visited their son in jail and wanted to know more about his case.

They met at Stacy's Café in Junction City. Deppish told them about the plea agreement offer made to Greg. Gerald Curry, his father, said he was concerned about "Gregory's safety," adding that, "it may not be too safe for him to be out right now." (Who scared Greg?)

The Currys knew Johnny Bingham. They told Deppish that he was not "the kind of guy that would do something like that. Maybe he got someone else or maybe just kept the money." They never heard of Johnny being in trouble.

Deppish used this meeting to check on Greg's claims about visiting Johnny while he was in town during the past months. They confirmed these visits, but Mrs. Curry added that Greg, "wanted to borrow $1,200 from Johnny for his move to Ohio." Later, Greg borrowed the money from a bank.

Deppish asked for all of Greg's phone records and told the Currys that he was hoping Greg would cooperate in the case. Greg had told them "that he knew he had done wrong, but just felt sorry for the woman." Both parents believed he would tell the truth.

Deppish hoped so, but which version of the truth should he believe? He must have thought many times that there were far better solutions for domestic violence than murdering one's husband.

Spinning a tale

Tom and Lorna's long distance phone bills skyrocketed after she moved to Hutchinson. During the time she had worked for Tom, and during her numerous marital and personal crises, they had burned thousands of minutes of phone time. Now the calls were long distance and expensive, but it made no difference. They often talked multiple times a day trying to keep on top of developments in the case.

(This pattern of frequent phone calls continued long after Tom's first incarceration where, even from his jail cell, he still tried to help Lorna. She had him convinced she was innocent of any crimes, and needed to know what investigators were up to, and what people were saying. She had access to some police reports not available to him and, likewise, he had information she did not have. They used each other to find out the latest developments in their cases.)

Early in the investigation, Lorna had no access to police reports and had to rely on gossip and rumor. All this added to her normal paranoid anxiety and when Lorna was anxious, she was *very* demanding and difficult. Wanting to help her, Tom felt he needed to know as much as possible about the actions of the investigators.

Tom also wanted to avoid getting caught in any backwash generated by the scurrilous rumors that continued to float around town, rumors that had increased since Marty's death; rumors that made it very hard to be a dad and a preacher; rumors fanned by Darrel Carter.

On December 10, late in the afternoon, as Tom played ball with the kids in the neighborhood, he saw Darrel backing away from Julie Palmer's house. Tom watched Darrel's car creep up the street and stop in front of him. Darrel reached his hand out the window and handed Tom a note.

Tom remembered the note. "He wanted to talk to me sometime about this thing his brother was involved in. I threw it away and did not intend to meet with him. I had successfully made my point." But Darrel had not made *his* point nor had he fulfilled his obligation to investigators who had made a deal with his brother Danny.

After Danny had been arrested and charged with conspiracy to commit murder, the Carters saw that Danny could be a prime suspect as the hit man. On December 10, Darrel told Agent Humphrey that Tom, at a May-meeting at Faith arranged by Lorna, had asked him to find someone to murder Marty.

Even more ominous for Tom, Darrel said one of the methods they had discussed was to get Marty drugged or drunk and run him off a bridge in a remote area of town. Darrel claimed that Tom described the bridge as having a 50-foot drop. Humphrey immediately saw the connection with Sandy Bird's death on July 16, at the Rocky Ford Bridge. His "finding" seemed to support some of the investigative work done by amateur homicide detective Trooper John Rule. Darrel Carter linked the two together. Police found their "smoking gun." It gave them an A-B-C theory.

> A. Tom and Lorna asked Darrel to find a murderer. That's conspiracy to commit murder.
>
> B. Sandy Bird died in a suspicious auto accident. That's murder number one.
>
> C. Marty Anderson was shot. That's murder number two.

To tape a murder plot

On December 12, Darrel called Tom at the church and asked to meet. After some discussion, Tom suggested the parking lot at the bowling alley on 6th Street. Tom dreaded a direct confrontation with Darrel, but he hoped the meeting could gain him more information. He could directly confront Darrel about the rumors he was spreading.

The noose had closed tighter on his good friend Lorna, and Darrel spread rumors about her, too. Tom had no reason to believe that he was personally implicated in anything, but he worried about the compound effect of Darrel's rumor-mongering.

Unknown to Tom, as part of the cushy deal spun by the prosecutor and investigators with Danny, the KBI wired Darrel with a "body pack tape recorder" that allowed them to monitor and record his meeting with Tom. Darrel wanted to put on a good show for investigators, so strapped on a bulletproof vest to protect him, just in case Tom tried to shoot him. It was Danny's vest.

Later, when the taping produced no evidence, investigators claimed that they had instructed Darrel to be careful, for fear that Tom would catch on to their scheme. They also discussed using Tom's car for the meeting because, they reasoned, no one would shoot someone in their own car. Darrel had feigned fear of the preacher.

Patton, Police and KBI agents watched the meeting from strategic locations near the bowling alley parking lot. They saw Darrel waiting in his car when Tom pulled up, got out and without hesitation, got in.

(The entire transcript of that meeting follows. The author has removed superfluous words that inhibit the understanding of the conversation, preserving the factual elements presented in court at Tom's 1984 trial.)

"He's getting' in my car. How you doin' Tom?"

"All right. How are things on your end?"

"Things are a mess, ain't they?"

"Yeah. They really are."

"A friend of mine said you wanted to talk about somethin'," Darrel said, referring to Julie Palmer.

"Yeah. I just wanted to touch bases on the…you know, back in June when we talked. I know Lorna introduced us and so that's some kind of a connection. I've heard enough rumors for sure; rumors are rampant." [Darrel claimed under oath several times that this meeting occurred in May. Why didn't he correct Tom here?]

"Well of course your rumors and well, I don't know what's goin' on."

"I don't know. I was really surprised to even hear that Danny was involved in this deal. But I mean, as far as we just talked about the use of firecrackers," Tom reminded Darrel.

"Yeah. The party that you talked to doesn't know anything you know." [Here he is referring to Julie Palmer.]

"Well, I was kind of playin' an ace in the hole there. You got kids, I got kids."

"That's right."

"We don't want the kids messed up in this."

"Yeah, but she don't know anything, I've never told her anything."

"Yeah, well you handle that because I'm never going to say anything." [Tom meant that if Darrel stopped spreading rumors, he'd never say anything about Julie.]

"Good, cause after you talked to her she come around lookin' me up and she said, hey! I've heard a lot of rumors and you know. What's goin' on? Are you guys involved? And I said, hey! I don't know what the heck you're talkin' about. Then she said, well why would Tom Bird want to talk to you? I said, I don't know, maybe he just wants to talk to me, I've had a lot of people call me and talk to me."

"Well, you can handle it, just tell her you heard some rumors were comin' from you. I didn't buy it but you know, I wouldn't see that would help your brother or help anybody else."

"Well, all I'm interested in is, I don't care who did what. I'd like to know what his involvement was. He told me that he was involved and then he tried to back out of the deal." [Darrel knew the investigators were listening carefully to his every word. Here he reinforced Danny's attempt to withdraw from the murder scheme.]

"Yeah." [A portion of the tape here was inaudible.]

"Oh, he thought somebody blew the whistle on him. He wasn't gonna confess. I was right there when he went down to the Sheriff's Department. I had to go over to the apartment and turn the water on, they'd turned the water off over there. I had to go over there and turn on the water and then I showed up and here's, two or three cops. He told me well we're goin' down to the Police Department, and I said what for, and he said, well, they're gonna search my apartment. I said, all right. I'll wait here and see if you come back. I got a soccer meeting I have to go to and so I waited around there for the water guy and he got there, it was probably 9:00 o'clock and Danny never did come back. So, I went to the soccer meeting and it was over and I went home, and these guys came over about 10:00 o'clock or 11:00 o'clock. I said, where's little brother? They said, well, we have arrested him. I said, what the hell for? And he said, well, conspiracy to commit murder; and I said, well, he didn't do that. They said, well, he confessed. And I asked him later, I said, why would you have talked, I mean what possessed you to talk? And he said, well, they come in and they knew about this and they knew about that and I thought they really had me. And he said, that they knew all of that stuff, so he thought someone had ratted on 'em."

"Well, somebody had." [Tom had no information, but it was easy to see somebody turned Danny in to the police.]

"Well, he didn't know who, he thought maybe they'd talked to Lorna and Lorna had told 'em. He didn't know if they'd talked to Curry. He just got home from work, you know."

"Jumped on him."

"Yeah man, and they jumped on him and he knew that they'd been down to Burlington and had talked to 'em down there and checked out his files and stuff. I said, I can't understand why you talked to 'em. Well, then about 11:00 o'clock, I went back over to the apartment to see what was goin' on cause they never had searched it. But he was over then and they had searched it, and I asked him, don't you think we need to get an attorney? And he said, yeah, I think so. I said, why don't you keep your mouth shut now, get an attorney. By this time he had told 'em quite a bit. I had no idea that Lorna had given him the money and he had never told me that. And I had asked him several times, if he was involved in any way and he said, no, that he wasn't."

"We gotta keep each other clean here just for the sake of the kids."

"That's true."

"That's our number one concern. You're gonna probably have to testify or something, huh?"

"Well, if they knew I knew, they'd probably...yeah, hell!"

"Danny's not gonna...?"

"No, Danny's not gonna..."

"He can't help very much."

"No, Danny's not gonna say anything."

"You can't help Danny that way."

"No, he's gone, they know."

"Is he gonna try to burn Lorna with him to protect himself?" [Tom wanted to protect Lorna.]

"Well, I don't think so. He's really not sayin'. He tried to get out of the deal, and then this Curry tried to get out of the deal so I don't know."

"Well, what's Bingham got? See, I don't know any of these people, I've never met your brother."

"Yeah, Danny told me that he didn't know you. No Bingham said he didn't do it." [Both men agreed that Tom and Danny had never met.]

"Well, they didn't arrest him."

"So he said he didn't know anything about the deal."

"Of course, that may be the smartest (inaudible)..." [Did Tom speculate here that Johnny knew enough to keep his mouth shut, unlike Danny? The tape revealed nothing.]

"Yeah."

"Well, what have they got physical? They got a (inaudible)..." [Tom fished for information about any evidence investigators might have that would hurt Lorna.]

"They really don't have anything." [Darrel meant they had nothing on Johnny yet, other than Greg Curry's statements.]

"I don't think they got anything."

"They don't have anything. Did you read the reports, have you seen the reports like Lorna's seen the reports?"

"I've seen newspapers."

"Well, I've seen all the reports," Darrel asserted. [He knew a lot. Tom knew nothing, unless it was in the newspapers or Lorna told him. In either case, he might not get the truth.]

"The attorney you mean?"

"Yeah." [Danny's attorney, Mike Patton, apparently shared all of these reports with Darrel.]

"What have they got?"

"They really don't have anybody but Danny, the only one they got's Danny."

"Curry."

"And Curry."

"But they busted Lorna just to make her talk. They were gonna keep her in over Thanksgiving holiday and try to crack her." [Tom thought the sheriff's tactics were wrong and unfair.]

"Yeah, but she isn't gonna talk, is she?"

"No way. (Inaudible)"

"That's good."

"Danny's kind of in a bind right now. I don't know what's gonna come about but I think it was his girlfriend messed him up, wasn't it?"

"Well yeah, it was."

"I heard she was in a mental institution."

"I don't know anything about that."

"Well, I know everything about that."

"Yeah, I know after he got out why she did, I don't know if it was a mental institution but she did go to a hospital for about a week on this. Course he hasn't seen her but she really didn't know anything."

"Somebody knew somthin' to start all this a rollin'." [Tom believed Marty sold drugs, and this murder was drug related.]

"He thought somebody else had ratted on him. He thought Lorna. He thought that they'd broke Lorna and Lorna had talked."

"Yeah, those guys are good."

"Yeah."

"I'm steerin' clear and I just wanted to touch the bases and make sure that we just talked about possibly my youth group sellin' firecrackers for you." [Darrel had a second chance here to refute the purpose of the meeting, but said nothing to contradict Tom.]

"Yeah, but I haven't talked to 'em, I haven't said anything."

"I'm not gonna say anything cause I don't want to get your name involved, you don't want to get my name involved, we got kids to take care of. I feel sorry for Lorna's kids, and I don't know what it's gonna come out but I know for Danny and everybody else, they don't have anything physical."

"No, they really don't. I don't know how it's gonna come out. I know pretty much that Bingham didn't do it. They're pretty sure that he didn't do it, so they're lookin' for somebody else. But right now, no, I don't think they really have a clue. They're still workin' on it." [Why didn't Darrel say something like, "Tom, they think it's you?"]

"Yeah, they'll work on it, but I wonder what the deal is with this Bingham, cause who named him?"

"Well, this Curry named him, cause see, Danny didn't even know him. And like you say, you don't know Danny." [Again, Darrel reinforced the story Danny told police, that he never talked to Johnny Bingham and that Tom and Danny never knew each other.]

"There's a lot of Wolf Creek people talkin' for sure and I think that didn't help any talkin'."

"Well, there's just a lot of people that knew that Lorna and Marty weren't getting' along, and those people are all talkin'."

"Sure."

"And they're spreadin' a lot of rumors. Lorna's really done some stupid things that didn't help her any."

"When was that?" [Here Tom saw a chance to discover what was being said about Lorna.]

"Well, really pretty close to the time Marty was killed."

"Like what?"

"Well, like that insurance. Like he had a lot of insurance and she just recently took that out, and they're lookin' at that real heavy."

"Yeah, well I asked her about that because they are talkin' about that. They really didn't increase the amount of insurance, they just changed companies and got cheaper insurance, that was back in May." [Tom had no knowledge of the particulars of their insurance coverage.]

"Umhuh."

"That was right before he went to camp. You mean they'll look? They'll look at that all night."

"Yeah."

"You know, that's a lot of money, got four kids growin' up who will need it."

"That's true, that's true."

"But it's a mess, but I know you care about kids."

"She may need it before she gets out of this mess too. I'm pretty sure that they're gonna nail her, you know. It's just gonna take some time but they're gonna work on this and they've had a lot of witnesses that saw some people there."

"Saw some people where?"

"At the van."

"Oh, when the murder was...?"

"Yeah, when...when Marty was killed." [If Tom had been there, wouldn't Darrel have said something about it in this context, or wouldn't Tom have said, "I hope they can never tell who it was."]

"Yeah."

"But, there's just a lot of stories, so we really don't know."

"Yeah, well see I don't have any access to anything so I don't know, I'm just tryin' to help her out mentally and spiritually, and doin' what I can. Otherwise, I'm just stayin' clear because I can't, I can't afford." [Tom makes it plain that he is just trying to help Lorna.]

"No, really."

"The rumors are enough to wipe me out."

"There's a lot of rumors. After the meeting at the church, did she ever say anything else about this? I kinda thought maybe this thing was…"

"I thought it just had to work out. It just wasn't gonna fall in place; and when my wife died, it was God's way of sayin', you don't mess with this stuff, and I don't, I don't mess with it. Life's too valuable. You know Marty died and I ain't celebratin' but I ain't mournin' either but it's a mess, it's what I'm really mournin' about, a lot of people bein' hurt. Turned the town upside down for awhile. Danny's lawyer, what tactic they are gonna take now that he's talked or where they can go from there but ah…"

"Well, now that he's talked he's pretty well committed himself, so (blank space on tape)…."

"I know nothing about courts." [Tom would soon learn much about courts.]

"Well, I don't either and usually you really can't predict what's gonna happen but you know I'm pretty sure that they're gonna nail her. I mean there's a lot of evidence that leads up to that she had a motive to do it and her story is pretty shaky of all what happened out there, and the kids saw what happened out there and what the kids saw and what Lorna saw wasn't the same sight, so you know, I mean you just gotta face it. It really doesn't look that good."

"Umhum."

"But, I mean I'm glad I'm not in her shoes."

"Well maybe we ought to be glad that we didn't follow through," Tom answered thoughtfully. [Tom and Darrel talked in June about the two of them, along with their wives, working to get Lorna into some sort of safe house for battered women. If they had done this and then later Marty was murdered, Tom knew it would look very suspicious, given that Danny had confessed to being a part of the murder.]

"Well, that's true. I didn't want anything to do with it at the time and I'm glad I didn't have anything to do with it then and now."

"I'm not for having to do with anything. I don't want to have anything to do with anything [laughs] the rest of my life as far as me getting involved. I hope Danny does okay, but I don't know him. I hope it comes out okay for Lorna. I know they are both suffering right now even just the waitin' and stuff. [Tom's involvement had already cost him a great deal. He saw his ministry at Faith being destroyed from the rumors generated by his desire to help Lorna.]

"Yeah, really."

"She's left town."

"I thought she had."

"It's just no good stayin' in town, can't go around anywhere. But you think Danny's gonna try to burn her to get less for himself?"

"Really there's not a whole lot that he can say because she could deny that she gave him the money. I don't know where she got the money but I don't know what he could say to really help him all that much."

"Yeah, well it just kinda looks like, I mean, settin' his hearing date after her hearing date, it kinda looks like the attorney might be settin' something up, I don't know. It's pretty much in the attorney's hands now anyway."

"Yeah, it really is, but you know when she said that you wanted to talk to me, I thought maybe you might...I'd like to get him out, but I'm really not wantin' to burn anybody either in this deal, especially myself and you and..."

"There's just no use in it."

"And the uh..."

"There's no use in getting' it complicated."

"No."

"You still want to live in this town...(inaudible)..." [Darrel was an Emporia native. Tom planned to move on.]

"Oh, really."

"I think Lorna knows some things as far as you and Danny in the past, and you guys know a lot of things about her in the past and none of that wants to be threshed up either." [Lorna claimed she served as an alibi for the Carters when Darrel burned down one of his properties and filed an insurance claim. She also committed adultery with both of them.]

"That's true." [Which is true? The arson or the adultery, or both?]

"So we're okay with it...whatever our contact with the whole business. We never really followed through on anything, and so we just better be quiet, that's all. I just wanted to check the bases."

"Yeah."

"I'm sure about that. That's the way you figure?"

"That's the way I figure it. Well, I'm not gonna be able to do anything to help either one of them. I'd like to, that's why I'd like to find out, I'd really like to know who really did it. I don't care who did it but I'd just like to know who did it so we could, know what kind of a defense we could come up with or if the guys that were in the conspiracy, if they did it or they didn't do it, why then he..." [Where was Darrel going with this?]

"How come you're so sure that Bingham didn't do it?"

"I think those guys just kept that money, then this Curry left town right after he got the money, and he has already said that they weren't gonna do it." [Darrel showed he not only read the reports, he knew their content very well. He had already given a lot of thought to the case, or police had told him their plan.]

"You know, at that point you just don't know what's gonna be truthful and what's gonna be fiction and what they're gonna try to hide, because conspiracy's one thing. Doin' it is another thing. I imagine they're gonna want to keep quiet but I don't know how else to go with it, but Lorna's lawyer had already told her not to talk to anybody about any of these things so I haven't been told by her. [Lorna wasn't telling Tom much of the details. But in later years, Tom realized Lorna had many different versions of the details.] I think she probably would confide in me but she's not goin' to. She's scared, so she's not going to say anything to me about whatever's happened since all this business. I don't know whether the lawyer knows. I don't know what's been said between her and him and where they are goin' with it."

"Yeah, I don't either."

"But I do know none of it looks good. Shoot! I just, I'm just kinda tired of the rumors although everything seems to be settlin' down along that way as far as what I know. About everything gets back to me."

"Well, I really haven't heard a whole bunch of rumors, other than what we read in those reports. I mean, you hear all kinds of stuff, you know." [Darrel spread the rumors.]

"Yeah."

"But when you know the facts why you either know it's rumor or it's not rumor and so I pretty well know what the facts are, I think."

"Do you, from the reports?" [Tom would have loved to see those reports. If he had, It could have changed his entire future.]

"Umhum, I have a pretty good idea, I think, of what the facts are. I'm not puttin' a finger on anybody but some of the reports don't look good. You can put two and two together on some of those reports and they don't add up."

"What reports are you talkin' about?"

"Well..."

"... (Inaudible) from the lawyer."

"From everyone that has talked, everyone they have talked to. See, we have all the reports and the KBI has those reports. The attorneys have those reports and we've all read those reports and it don't look good. Some of the things that just don't add up. Lorna has too many different stories of what she saw and what she didn't see and Lori has too many stories."

"Well, an 8-year old girl, my gosh!"

"Well, the story that she told the person at the scene and then the story that she told a day or two later are not quite the same story, see?"

"Lori's story?"

"Yeah, and Lorna has about three stories, she changed it a little but every time she told it so I don't know just exactly what's gonna happen."

"Well they don't (long pause), they don't really have anything."

"They don't really have anything right now, no. But you know they know where Curry was and they know where Bingham was and they know where Danny was, so you know they know where Lorna was. Three of 'em were at the scene."

"Umhum."

"So they know, on that."

"Well, I guess everybody's covered."

"Yeah, that's why it don't look like that party did it. That's what I'm sayin', I don't know who…"

"Unless there was somebody else." [Tom fished for more information.]

"No, unless there was somebody else involved."

"Seems to be pretty complicated." [If Tom was involved, why didn't he ask Darrel whom he thought the police suspected? Darrel might say, "Well, you!" But Tom didn't ask because he hadn't even considered he might be a suspect.]

"It's a puzzle."

"Lorna's not going to say anything but I imagine Danny hasn't been in jail before this, has he?"

"No, nope."

"Well, they oughta go pretty light on him, we'll see what comes down I guess, won't we?"

"Yeah, before long. It's a hell of a deal, the guy to get involved in something like that when he didn't get anything out of the deal." [Darrel seemed to be playing to the investigators listening in. He states that Danny had no motive. If so, why did he do it?]

"Boy! They just caught him off guard, if he just would have kept his mouth shut."

"Yeah, everybody should, I guess. The girlfriend should have, Danny should have." [Darrel only cared that his brother got caught, not that a crime had been committed.]

"Can't do anything about that."

"That's true, so…"

"Well…"

"So if I find out anything I'll get back with you on this. If you hear anything, give me a call,"

"Okay."

"The phones aren't bugged, I know that. This was a while back, I checked, I have a friend in the phone company." [Darrel apparently knew a lot of helpful people in town. Tom knew nothing about this kind of craftiness.]

"You mean Lorna's phone? (Inaudible)"

"Yeah, to bug a phone that has to come down through security and stuff and they have to put it on the phone at the phone company, and I've checked all that out, and no one's phone is bugged, and they can only leave it on there for so many days, so no one's phone is really bugged on this deal, cause I checked that out the day after this thing all come about and I said, yeah, I have a friend down there and he's pretty much up to doin' all that stuff and he's a good enough friend that he'd tell me. He knows whose phone's bugged and whose phone's not bugged." [The investigators must have grimaced hearing Darrel confess this to Tom.]

"Well, I know these, these guys tried to nail me, I mean they tried to put it all together on me, just because rumors of our relationship with Lorna, and the fact that my wife died a few months ago. They know where I was that night. I think these guys are kinda desperate to pin it on somebody. I think they better just find out about Marty's life. I don't know what they found out about his life." [Tom referred to his belief, based on Lorna's statements to him, that Marty became a drug dealer. He thought the police should investigate the local drug scene, not his church.]

"I haven't heard anything on him."

"What he was involved in, and that's what I'm hearing, some things filtering down."

"Oh really, what was…?

"That he may be involved in something."

"He may have been involved in something, that may have been a legitimate shoot. I mean, maybe none of these guys did it, maybe somebody else on his side did it." [Darrel, who knew investigators were listening, picked up on this idea. If they started chasing drug dealers, it would take the heat off of Danny.]

"He may have been involved in gamblin', or maybe involved in drugs, maybe involved in…"

"So, who would know so we could…?"

Tom's response was inaudible.

"Who would know so a person could check that out You got any idea?"

"A whole different world than what I live in."

"I didn't know if Lorna ever said any…he had a girlfriend. I knew that. I never did know her name. Did you ever know her name?"

"The Reserves, you know."

"I never did ever hear her name."

"I know it." [Of course, his source for the name was Lorna, but he believed all she told him.]

"I'm sure Lorna said but…"

"I think she's gonna save herself, she's gonna maybe have to burn

Marty, not protect him, so that she wouldn't, and that means lettin' her attorney know a few things."

"Umhum."

"But all these people callin' the Hotline, some of 'em ought to call up and say, Hey! Why don't you check out Marty's life out a little bit, he's got some things to hide. He was pretty much hated in a whole lot of directions and I'm...that's what's filtered down to me."

"Yeah."

"There was a lot of folks didn't like him."

"Well, see, I didn't know him that well so I don't know. We've just been acquainted, some parties and stuff, through sororities, so I really didn't know him but I did know, Lorna told me one time, that he had a girlfriend that I guess he used to stay there at the house once in a while. I don't know, a different life than what I'd lead, I couldn't hardly believe it, somebody would do that, but they did."

"So I think Danny's life is gonna be drug a round a little bit and Lorna's is too. It's gonna be a mess. It looks real messy. I guess I'll just take it if they wanta drag me in the mud too." [Tom realized that no matter what he did, his life would be linked to Lorna to some extent. He believed it would take time, but eventually he could clear himself of this mess and get on with his life.]

"That's true. Do you really think that she had anything to do with it? Do you think she did it or had it done?"

"I'm pretty... I'm sure she didn't do it." [Tom believed Lorna was innocent for almost two more years.]

"Do you think she had it done?"

"I know she talked about it before. I can't tell you what I think, but I think she'd tell me, and she may one of these days." [Lorna once told Tom she had an urge to drive her van off the road into a bridge and kill herself and Marty.]

"I know she talked about it, but I really never thought she'd ever do it." [Darrel here admits that Lorna talked to him about killing Marty.]

"Yeah, I mean it was like ah...oh you know, like a kind of a test to see what would really happen, but I don't know, I don't know what it was like in their home either (inaudible)..."

"Well, I don't either cause we never went to any parties up there or anything, we always went to someone else's house."

"Well, I don't know how bad it was but I think checking on Marty's life, maybe there'd be some opening there cause he was gone a lot. He was up at Topeka, Guard duty. I know he'd kind of brag sometimes. He'd talk about some of those topless bars up there and he'd always like to talk to me about those things, see what kind of reaction I'd get, see how the preacher would act if he brags about that. He was also gettin' pretty desperate for money too. I didn't realize that until the last few months. He was really desperate for money."

"Wonder why."

"I don't know cause there was no reason to, he was makin' good salary."

"I wonder where she come up with that money that she supposedly gave 'em."

"I don't know."

"If they didn't have any money."

"I don't know. Well let's see how (inaudible)..."

"Well, hide and watch, I guess, and see what happens."

"I'm a little tense about it (inaudible) just for the rumors, but then I can see where they'd look at me. All they can do is look at me."

"Well, I think they're gonna look at everybody."

"Well that's what I figured, that's when I said I wanta touch bases with you because there's no use addin' another little niche in there. You don't wanta be involved, I don't wanta be involved, darn! I got three kids and I gotta be with them and I got a church. I can't afford to have a whole bunch of people wonderin' about me. I'm handlin' the rumors as best I can. There's nothing I can do about that. You can't do anything about rumors." [Tom once again emphasized he wanted the rumors stopped, his whole purpose for meeting Darrel.]

"Well that's true."

"But I hope it doesn't get any further than that."

"Well, it really does look bad for you too because your wife was killed." [Darrel already had linked the two together for the police. Tom had no idea how much damage Darrel had already done.]

"Yeah, I know that but..."

"And then Marty was killed and it really does look like a real coincidence. You know anybody can put two and two together on that and it don't look right."

"If they want to, but there's nothin' I can do about it."

"Yeah."

"I'm just tryin' to exist and tryin' to build back my life. I have to let 'em look at it as long as they don't try to hurt me on it. I'm sorry, I've got a job to do. I got kids to take care of, Christmas comin' up and a life to live."

"I really thought when I heard that, just read in the paper, I really thought Lorna had just pulled off the road there and shot him, cause I knew she had a gun." [How did he know she had a gun? Did she show him the eventual murder weapon? Did police ask him about this incriminating statement?]

"They checked that out though."

"Did they check out her gun or just check her out to see if she did it?"

"Well they checked her out to see if she did it, don't they have a little test on gunpowder (inaudible)?" [They tested her after she washed her hands.]

"Well, that I don't know. I guess I didn't know that. I guess that's good to know, huh? Well I just figured when I heard that he got shot, why I really thought that she did it, just the circumstances."

"Well that first article in the newspaper looked pretty bad anyway, pretty inaccurate but…"

"But then when I heard he'd been shot with a .22, why I knew she didn't have a .22." [Is he covering up his earlier comment that he knew she had a gun?]

"See I hadn't heard these things."

"Yeah, they thought it was a .22. They weren't sure but it looked like they shot him with a .22."

"Well, they'd know where the bullets went."

"Well I don't know if they got the bullets. I never saw an autopsy report on it. They just said they'd shot him with a .22 or .25 caliber handgun, or gun, they didn't say handgun, but I figure it's a handgun."

"Well, they didn't get very many details from Lorna or Lori. I imagine it was a pretty big shock anyway no matter what. How can you remember a situation like that, a little 8-year-old in question. What I heard, they talked to her a little bit at the scene and then talked to her a little bit later on about 11:00 o'clock at night."

"Uh-huh."

"What can you get out of a little 8-year-old girl at 11:00 o'clock at night when she's been through what she'd been through?"

"That's true."

"It wouldn't even be admissible."

"I don't know, all I know, we're in a lot of trouble with it."

"Humm?"

"My brother's in a lot of trouble."

"Who's in a lot of trouble?" [Tom pressed him for a clarification. He thought Darrel knew more about the way police would pursue Lorna than he revealed.]

"My brother…. I just thought maybe I could find out something."

"Oh well if I could find out anything, fine, it's probably gonna be filtered down. I don't think Lorna will ever talk to me until it's all over, and then I think maybe she'll talk to me but I don't know if it's ever gonna be all over."

"I don't know. Have you talked to her since it happened?"

"Oh yeah."

"Well I mean, well I guess you have."

"She's talked with her lawyer and he's, I think, the one that decided originally she don't talk to anybody and I think she's stickin' to that and I haven't pushed her. I really haven't pushed her at all."

"Yeah."

"So I don't know, if I find out something that will be helpful. But otherwise it's pretty much in the hands of the lawyers now and I don't know what else the investigators can come up with."

"Well I don't think anything. They may dig up something that we don't know about but ..."

"So I don't know, they had a lot of people talkin'. They have witnesses who saw the incident."

"Oh no, they don't have anybody that saw it, that actually saw it. But they had a lot of people drive by at different times with different things."

"Well, what did they see?"

"Well like they saw somebody stand' there talkin' to Lorna, and there was some reports that people had stood there, that they saw somebody stand' there talkin' to Lorna and ah..."

"Could have been Marty."

"We'll see. No it wasn't, well, like Lori said that she saw some guy standin', talkin' to her Mom after her Dad had been shot."

"So the story Lorna told me was the guy grabbed her, asked for her purse, threw her down on the ground, told her to be quiet and pulled the trigger on her, maybe just to scare her, just clicked it or somethin' and ah...ran off." [Tom believed her.]

"Uhhuh."

"Well, you know they'll put it together and maybe find out something, I don't know whatever they can do, but I've had enough troubles (inaudible) and I'm kind of at the point where...and I want Lorna to be taken care of. I don't want her to be locked up but I've got my life to live and that's why I was concerned. I just wanted to touch bases with you as far as, I heard enough about the rumors, I don't (inaudible) anything else to be involved and you're Danny's brother and when I talked to you I didn't even know..."

"Yeah."

"...your brother and so I don't want that connection to be made because that's really not even a connection, so let's just all steer clear." [Tom saw the potential connection between him, Lorna and Darrel as a problem, given that Danny had already confessed to being the bag man for the murder of Marty Anderson. He wanted to steer clear of any connection to Danny.]

"Yeah, well Danny told me he didn't know you cause I'd asked him if he'd ever talked to you and Lorna and he said, no, he didn't even know you."

"(Inaudible) if I find out something that will be helpful, but I think it's just up to lawyers now. But I figured you might be subpoenaed to talk (inaudible)."

"Yeah, course you know I'm not talkin' so they really don't have a connection with me on the deal."

"Well, I just want to make sure that stays, you don't want it to be connected to you. Let me tell you, bein' part of a rumor's no good, so you don't want any part of a rumor."

"That's true."

"Those guys...they will try to make all the connections they can. Danny told 'em Curry told 'em that they really never intended to follow through?"

"Yeah."

"They just spent the money, huh? I guess it's up to them whether they want to (inaudible) or not. But one report came out, said there was four involved."

"Well, I think they were talkin' about those three and Lorna, the four of 'em."

"Okay, well that's one party's missing, you know." [If Darrel really believed Tom was the fourth party, he could have said something at this point, but he didn't.]

"I don't know, cause I don't read too much in the paper..."

"Yeah, well reports are probably a whole lot better than the paper, but there's nobody passed me with (inaudible) of what come out now."

"No, I mean, that's as far as they went is to Bingham and..."

"That's the end of the line."

"That's the end of the line."

"As far as they know, and it's probably as far as they'll ever know."

"I don't know, you never can tell what they might dig up. I think they're gonna start back up and get off of those guys and they're probably gonna start lookin' at some other people." [Is he about to ask Tom directly if he was involved? This is a good place to do it.]

"You think so?"

"Yeah, what other channel do they have? If them guys didn't do it, they're at the end of the line. They're either going to have to look for another alternative or they may have to look at Marty's side like you said, something there."

"I suggested they dig on Marty's side."

"Yeah."

"I think he's dirty, that's just the kind of feeling I get. He was desperate and dirty, I know he was desperate and I always wondered about him because he was wantin' money."

"Uhhuh."

"He was wantin' to do a lot of things."

"Well, is that right? So ah I'll get back with you, all right, Tom."

"Yeah."

"Talk to you later."

"All right, thank you," Tom said, getting out of the car.

Darrel waited for Tom to walk away and then said, "Okay, I'm now leavin' the parking lot and Tom is also leavin' in front of me. I will meet everyone back at ALCO, same place."

Darrel failed to elicit a confession from Tom. He could have asked a question like, "Were you really serious about me hirin' someone to kill Marty? You know, that'd make you a prime suspect now."

Tom never saw the investigators watching him and Darrel, nor did he know they listened and taped the conversation. He was completely vulnerable.

Darrel could have said, "You know, if Lorna tells them you and her talked about murdering Marty, they're gonna be sure you had somethin' to do with this. You sure Lorna's gonna keep her mouth shut?"

Darrel could have found any number of ways to get Tom to confess, but he didn't.

Tom said the reason Darrel never asked these questions was simple. "The subject of hiring someone to murder Marty was never discussed. If he'd of asked the question, I would've said, 'What are you talkin' about?' and that would have blown his whole scheme. He knew the cops were listening. I didn't."

Darrel and Tom did *not* continue to update each other on the developments in the case. Their next significant meeting was in a Lyon County courtroom. This taped conversation was played for the jurors in that trial. Tom believed it would help to clear him of all charges.

Danny clarifies and expands

Feeling like they were closing in on critical evidence, Agents Winsor and Humphrey interviewed Danny Carter once again on December 19, 1983.

The interview was a bit different than those conducted earlier with Danny or others who had so far been involved in the investigation. Mike Patton, Danny's attorney, reviewed all of Winsor's questions before he would allow his client to answer.

"When did Lorna Anderson first contact you about her husband?"

"About August 22, '83."

"How long prior to this had she been talking about it?"

"She never talked to me about it before then."

"What did she say and what instructions were given by her?"

"Reference to having something done to Marty," Patton answered to clarify the question.

"She just wanted me to find somebody, she never asked me to do it," Danny answered.

"How much later did you contact Greg Curry?"

"Probably 3, 4, or 5 days later."

"Did you ask anyone else first, or anybody else other than Greg Curry?"

"Greg is the only one I ever talked to."

"What did you tell Curry?"

"I just asked him if he knew anybody that could handle something like that. He said he'd look into it."

"Is there anything in earlier statements given to Agent Winsor and sheriff's deputies that was incorrect?"

Patton interceded here and advised Carter not to answer that question.

"Did Curry ever talk to Lorna Anderson?" Winsor continued.

"Not that I know of."

"Where were you at when Lorna gave you the envelope?"

"At the Emporia State Bank Zip machine."

Agent Winsor asked if this was a prearranged meeting place and Danny agreed. Patton advised that this was on Wednesday, September 7, 1983.

"Was the payment to be $5,000 or $10,000?" Winsor asked.

"Curry told me $5,000, first he said $5,000 or $10,000 and $5,000 was agreed on."

"What information was asked for by Curry?"

"What Marty's schedule was, where he worked, what kind of vehicle he drove, what he looked like."

Winsor wondered if Greg asked for a photograph of Marty, but Danny didn't remember if he asked, but "I think I gave him some though."

"Have you ever been in contact with Johnny Bingham, or Jim Beam?"

"No."

"Did Curry get anything for passing the package on to Bingham?"

"I don't know, he never said, I wondered about it."

"Do you have any knowledge about Marty beating his wife and/or his kids?"

"I've seen her with black eyes before but I've never seen him do it, seen her with black eyes twice."

"What did you get from this (passing the package from Lorna to Greg)?"

"Nothing."

"Do you know if Marty was wanting a divorce, or was this done for the money?"

"She's mentioned something about he was going to [ask for or get a divorce]."

"Was she for the divorce or against it?"

"She really didn't say one way or the other on that."

"Did she say anything about insurance money or wanting some money?"

"No, she never really mentioned that, that was never really brought up, I didn't really think she was into it for the money."

"Do you know where the $5,000 came from?"

"No, I don't have any idea where she came up with that."

"Did you give Curry the name of Martin Anderson?"

"Yes, I gave him the money and everything, she had that all written out on a sheet."

"Was the information typed on a sheet of paper or was it a computer printout form?"

"I don't recollect that one way or the other. I think she had one of him and one of his car." (A very odd response, left unclarified.)

"Who counted the money?"

"Curry counted it out and said it was all there. He had a stack of bills there; I saw one one-hundred-dollar bill." There were several stacks of bills but Danny could not give an estimate of how many stacks or the denomination of the bills. He thought maybe he saw a $20 bill, but is sure he saw one $100 bill.

"Did you look at the contents of the envelope before you went to Curry's house?"

"No."

"Who all was present besides yourself and Greg Curry when the envelope was given to Curry and the money was counted?"

"No one else was present."

Winsor wondered how much time elapsed from the time he got the envelope from Lorna until he gave it to Greg. "Delivered it approximately 15 minutes later."

"Did you have any idea of the plans for the shooting on Highway 177?"

"No."

"Have you had any personal contact with Johnny Bingham or anyone else in reference to the shooting?"

"None."

"Do you know who pulled the trigger?"

"No."

"Did you give any instructions to Curry about the delivery of the money?"

"No."

Winsor wondered if Danny gave Greg instructions to deliver part of the money before the hit and the rest later. He denied this.

"Did you make any attempt to stop this chain of events?"

"Yes. I called Curry and told him I wanted the money back and wanted out of it. He said he would get the money back and call it off." Patton gave the date of October 20.

"Do you know whose, or what gun was used?"

"No."

"Do you know where the gun is at?"

"No."

"Did you ever give Curry any particular date and time Martin was going to be in Topeka?"

"Yeah, I did. I couldn't tell you what date they were, it was while he was going to meetings, that was information just passed on from Lorna, I knew that once in awhile he would stay at his grandmother's or his girlfriend's, I don't know that for a fact, that's what Lorna said."

Danny said that Lorna may have told him Marty's girlfriend's name but he "didn't give a s---, so it didn't stick in my head."

"Did you give a name or alias for Johnny Bingham or anyone else to use in place of your regular name?"

"He (Curry) said he'd have a guy call me and he gave me the name Letterman. Just a name Greg made up." (Along with Jim Beam.)

"Who told you the amount would be $5,000?"

"Greg Curry said it would be $5,000 or $10,000, depending on who the guy was, if he was a government official. I think he was just passing this on to me from somebody else."

"Did or does Lorna own a firearm, if so, what caliber and brand?"

"She mentioned it to me one time, I think she mentioned it was a .38."

"What denominations were the bills?"

This had been already answered, but Winsor wanted more. Danny said the money was paper-clipped together, and Greg went through the bills and peeled them off. "He stuck it in some envelopes and was writing on one of them and then took it to the back of the house."

"Did you and Lorna discuss when, where, or how, this was to be done?"

"The only thing she said is she didn't want it done in the house. Said she wanted it to look like an accident but didn't give any details. Lorna called me two or three times and told me about where he was going to be at certain times, usually on weekends."

The last weekend Lorna talked to him about Marty's location was three or four days before Danny last talked to Greg. "Curry was gone and I didn't know where to get ahold of him."

"Did you know if Curry ever had any contact with Lorna?"

"As far as I know, he didn't, what he did after he talked to me, I don't know."

"Why did you contact Curry to call it off?"

"Because it was when Marty was talking about filing for a divorce, she didn't want it called off. I wanted it called off because Greg left the area. Lorna told me there's more there than what you know about."

"Did she ever give you a deadline to have this done?"

"No. She was getting impatient about why this wasn't getting done."

"Did you know when this was going to be done?"

"Greg Curry thought it would be soon. He (Curry) said his name was Johnny, that he traveled around a lot, they were friends and the guy would stop by and see him."

Danny said that at 4:00 a.m., either October 24 or 25, Lorna called him wanting information. He told her he was trying to get her money back. "I didn't want anymore to do with it."

When Lorna talked to him earlier, she said she didn't care how much it cost. She said she had inherited some money and her father handled it for her.

Winsor asked him to speculate where the $5,000 came from. He guessed from her grandmother in Topeka, or Tom Bird. Danny said that when Lorna contacted him the first time in reference to this in August, "It seemed like it didn't take her very long to come up with the money, didn't take her over a week."

"Did you tell anybody else about doing something with Marty?"

"No."

At the end of this orchestrated interrogation, Danny learned that he had to take a polygraph test. Mike Patton agreed to it.

In all previous interviews, Danny said he knew nothing about Tom Bird. He had never met him. He did not know his name. He had only heard Lorna *claim* that her current boyfriend was a minister. During this interview, no one bothered or had permission to ask Danny why he suddenly mentioned Tom Bird as the bag man for the crime. Did Patton want to avoid such an embarrassing question?

Danny knew that Lorna had sex with many other men, perhaps even a preacher. He knew his brother Darrel, who was working hard to help him beat this rap, had sex with Lorna. None of this bothered Danny, the bagman for Lorna's husband's murder.

Many questions remained unanswered about his involvement in the murder. His attorney served him well, even if justice had to suffer.

The timely coincidence of Darrel fingering Tom Bird while Greg Curry and Danny Carter first brought up his name should have troubled investigators. Instead, they sensed a killer.

Johnny in the cross hairs

Kansas investigators sorted through new evidence about Johnny Bingham.

Greg Curry added several details to his previous statements. He insisted he had passed the money and other items to Johnny, and "I made several phone calls to him from my house in Emporia."

Police confirmed Greg had made the calls by checking with Southwestern Bell.

Greg specified that the money was to pay someone to murder Marty. Gerald Curry said, "When Gregory came home for his vacation, the very day he arrived home, about September 9th or 10th, he told me he had to go see Johnny about something." Then, on either October 21st or 22nd, Greg went to see Johnny again, "I think to ask Johnny if he could borrow $1,200 from Johnny for his move to Ohio."

During the latter trip Greg told him the hit was off. Johnny answered, "Okay, but she can't get her money back." Greg acknowledged he got some cash from Johnny, but that didn't mean the cash came from the murder money.

Danny called Greg several times in September and October wanting to know what was going on. "Lorna wants to know why Marty is still alive."

Some time around October 10, Danny called him to say that Marty would be attending a meeting in Topeka. "Give this information to your man," Danny told Greg.

Greg tried to call Johnny, but found he had no phone. He called Jimmy Bingham, Johnny's brother and got the phone number of Wilson Suitor, the farmer for whom Johnny worked. Greg called and left a message for Johnny to call him back. Phone records showed a nine-minute collect call from that number to Greg at 7:30 p.m. on October 10.

Kansas officials had a bushel basket full of evidence that implicated Johnny Bingham. They prepared to head back to Mississippi. Mississippi officials would hear none of it—or hear nothing. They were totally unresponsive.

Tracking a Bird

In early December, 1983, Tom Bird did *another* good deed for the widow Anderson. She had decided just after Marty's murder to move to Hutchinson, Kansas, where she could be close to her parents. She felt the anonymity would grant her some refuge from constant public attention.

"Tom, could you call the truck rental and reserve a truck for Lorna?" Loren Slater asked Tom by phone. "We're going to move her on the 9th. I'll pay for it. It'll save me $100 to rent it in Emporia."

Tom gladly did this favor for Loren Slater. Tom hoped that moving Lorna out of town would help her regain stability. He knew it would simplify *his* life. Agent Humphrey saw it differently. He checked with Flint Hills Towing Service manager Jana Boyer and reported:

> "Thomas Bird came into their business and reserved a truck for December 9, 1983. He came in a few days prior to December 9, but she could not provide the exact date. On the day before the truck was to be picked up, Mrs. Boyer called the Bird residence to talk about the truck and see what size they needed. The babysitter answered the phone and didn't know what size truck was needed but stated to Mrs. Boyer that Pastor Bird was moving Lorna Anderson to Hutchinson. The contract for the truck was in the name of Loren Slater and was paid for with Master Charge. Mrs. Boyer could not advise who actually picked up the truck, but it was not Tom Bird."

By now investigators believed that any kind of contact between Tom and Lorna was suspect.

Tom heard a lot of rumors about what investigators were doing. He knew they interviewed church members, and he resented it. Their sniffing around Faith only created unwanted tension. He knew Darrel Carter had read many police reports, but Darrel revealed very little the day they talked in the car. He had no idea that police listened in on that conversation. He didn't know that Darrel had also spun a condemnatory story about him.

Darrel told police that he, Tom and Lorna had met together at Faith some time in May. He stated Lorna called this meeting for the sole purpose of asking his help to find someone to murder Marty. He said it was the first time he met the young preacher.

Darrel never did pinpoint the date of the meeting, but still remembered both its purpose and content. Most astounding to police officers and satisfying to Trooper Rule, Darrel described one of the methods they discussed for killing Marty; drug him or get him drunk and run him off the road. He claimed Tom told him of just the right place on a secluded road outside of Emporia, at a bridge with a 50' drop to the riverbank.

Newspapers gave heavy coverage to Sandy Bird's death. Her car went off a bridge on a secluded road outside of Emporia, falling some 65 feet into the Cottonwood River below. Investigators, though, believed Emporian Darrel, and the fact that he could provide a "witness" to the link between

Sandy and Marty satisfied the lawmen who were eager to bring resolution to the two deaths. They discounted the fact that Darrel had just played a significant part in negotiating the plea agreement for his younger brother Danny, one of the prime suspects in Marty's murder.

Armed with Greg's and Danny's confessions, Lorna's arrest, the "love letters," a nondescript tape recording and Darrel's "witness," Agent Winsor headed back to interview Tom. He met with him at about 3 p.m. on December 20, 1983 at Faith, the day after the last interview with Danny Carter.

Tom is suspicious and upset

Winsor asked Tom whether Marty ever physically abused Lorna. Tom had no personal knowledge, but he was suspicious that something had happened between the two. "There was a time in March, 1983 that Lorna had a bruise on her cheek and she said she got it when she had almost fell and hit the side of a door."

Tom had a professional conflict. Confidentiality bound him and he refused to tell Winsor of the more private details he knew of Lorna and Marty. If he broke confidentiality in this instance, no one could ever trust him in the future, and he purposed not to cross the line. It angered Winsor.

Tom said he knew nothing about Anderson's owning a gun.

Then Winsor turned up the heat, asking Tom about where he did his banking.

"Where you going with that question?"

Winsor acted puzzled by Bird's response.

"There's been too much information put out by law enforcement in the press that has caused me problems and embarrassment," Tom said accusingly. He was becoming wary of all the attention given to him. He had begun to lose his naïve trust in police officials.

Winsor asked him about the insurance settlements from Sandy's death. This upset Tom. "That is a private matter."

Now frustrated, he glared at Winsor and stated, "You sat in that chair just weeks ago and told me that Martin Anderson had $340,000 in life insurance coverage and that Lorna was the beneficiary. That was personal information and you had no right to share that with me. That kind of information should not be put out all over."

"I shared it with you because you were her pastor," Winsor answered. "It was not put out all over."

Winsor claimed any insurance information Tom shared would remain confidential, but Tom refused to answer him.

"Did you loan any money to Lorna?"

"I don't have any idea where she came up with the $5,000. I didn't loan it to her. As far as I know, they were having financial problems."

"Do you ever wear Western clothing when you're not working?"

"That sounds accusatory. No, I don't wear Western clothing, and I'm hardly ever off duty anyway."

"You ever been to Junction City or Fort Riley with Lorna?"

"No."

"Has Lorna ever made any long distance calls from your house?"

"Maybe once when she was babysitting my kids."

"How about calls to Mississippi? Any of those made from your phone?"

"No, not as far as I know," Tom answered, trying to remain patient. "Lorna talked to me on long distance in the past, but I don't think she was at my house when she called me." There is nothing unusual about a church secretary calling the pastor when he was out of town. While he is gone, church business continues.

"Did Lorna ever make any statements to you about wanting to get rid of Marty, or get away from him in some way?"

"No."

Winsor looked Bird in the eye and asked pointedly and quietly, "Pastor, do you want to cooperate in the investigation and assist us in trying to find out who killed Martin Anderson?"

"Well of course I do."

"Then why will you not answer the question about your wife's insurance coverage? I can assure you this will be kept confidential and given only to law enforcement officials. No member of the press will get this information."

Tom relented. "Sandy was insured with AID Association for Lutherans out of Appleton, Wisconsin. She had $27,000 in life insurance and there was another check for about $7,000 from Hartford for the loss of the car. A total of about $34,000."

"You have any objection to signing a waiver of search to allow us to examine your financial records? I want to verify that no amounts of around $5,000 had been withdrawn from your account in the last several months."

Tom hesitated before answering. "I want to talk to someone first."

"You mean an attorney?"

"Yes."

"That's your right. I'll be contacting you again to ask about this." Winsor closed his note pad and stood to leave.

Tom realized he was being drawn more deeply into the murder intrigue. He had to stand strong, though, because these officers would use anything to get to Lorna, and he was not about to let that happen.

Romantic flop

Celebrations—birthdays, holidays, church observances—were always a big part of the Bird family's life and at Christmastime, 1983, the family gathered as usual. To Tom, the holiday seemed empty without Sandy. Christmas fell on a Sunday that year, so Tom left for Arkansas after the morning service. The Bird family gathered at his sister Gloria's home in Maumelle, Arkansas.

Tom and his children celebrated with the Bird family during the afternoon on the 26th and drove to the Grismers for the evening. Grismers lived in a multi-story home that sat over-looking the Arkansas River in an ritzy Little Rock neighborhood.

It started snowing agan, so the whole Bird clan stayed one more night together at Gloria's.

On Friday, Ralph and Virginia took the three children back with them to their home in Hardy. Tom was lonely and restless, despite being with family members so headed off to West Memphis, hoping to spend time with some of his former church members and other friends, and find a way to gain some freedom from his loneliness. He returned to Hardy during the evening of December 31.

Still unable to relax, Tom left Hardy on Sunday, January 1.

His folks thought he was heading right back to Emporia. Tom thought about Emporia and the joyless, empty house waiting for him; the legal stew brewing all around him and chaos in his life. He felt driven to avoid Emporia and find refuge somewhere else. He debated whether to go to Kansas City to spend time with Terry Smith, the woman he had been dating since October, or to Hutchinson, where Lorna had moved to be near her parents. Tom enjoyed Loren and Alta Slater, Lorna's parents, and all of them had suffered similar emotional distruptions during the last six months. He called Lorna and she told him to come to Hutchinson. Tom described the decision and its disappointing results:

> "The first time I had a sexual relationship with Lorna was the evening of New Year's Day, 1984. I felt the urge to leave my folks in Hardy because I was impatient having been visiting since Christmas day in Little Rock, then I went to West Memphis, then Hardy. I wanted to leave, feeling a little empty; but really not wanting to go back to Emporia.

> "I called Lorna and she said come to Hutch and have New Year's dinner with her and her parents. So the kids and I went to Hutch.

> "After dinner, her parents were leaving and I said I would be over to their place to spend the night after I put the kids to bed here at

Lorna's. He [Loren Slater] said not to worry about it, just stay there.

"In actuality, I wanted to watch the football bowl games, and some of them were on Monday that year. But it was quite a struggle to get all the children to bed. I sat on the floor and watched the late Sunday game.

"It sounds stupid and I don't remember who was playing but if it had been a good game, what happened next would probably not have happened. The game was a blow-out and at half-time, I ended up helping Lorna pull out the hide-a-bed couch and make it up for her.

"We ended up making very awkward, clumsy sex on the bed. The very thing I had worked so hard to avoid all those months, I did.

"A little while later, Aaron was coughing in the room down the hallway struggling to sleep, and I went to where he was sleeping and cuddled with him and slept into the next day."

The widow Anderson and the widower Bird experienced a very disatisfying, clumsy sexual experience. The rumor-mongers and scandalizers would have been tremendously disappointed by what really happened between the two, since Emporians believed in a raunchy image of a sex-crazed pastor willfully and often enjoying the wiles of Emporia's most promiscuous lady of lust.

"Believe me," Tom said, "It was not like in the movies," and it happened nine weeks after Marty had died. Sandy had been gone almost six months.

A pastor who commits fornication stands a chance of facing serious consequences, but a life sentence in prison is not one of them. Tom said, "I've paid for that sin many times over."

Mississippi "justice"

Kansas investigators needed help from Corinth, Mississippi officers. They found none. The Corinth officers completely ignored their requests for help after their December 2 trip. They had to request help from the district FBI office. During his January 5, 1984, phone call to Corinth, Deputy Deppish heard shocking news. He reported it:

"RO [Reporting Officer Deppish] made telephone contact…with the dispatcher of the Alcorn County (Mississippi) Sheriff's Department and asked to talk with Deputy Kenneth Marlar but was advised that Deputy Marlar no longer worked for the department.

"RO then requested to talk with Chief Deputy Terry Doles [who had participated in the interrogation of Johnny Bingham] and was told that he was not there either.

"RO then requested to talk with Jack Holt (Sheriff). Dispatcher was gone from the phone for several minutes and when he came back on the phone, he stated, 'I'm sorry sir; Jack Holt is no longer Sheriff here.' Asked who the new Sheriff was, dispatcher informed it was Bill Gant. Asked to talk with the new Sheriff, was advised that he was in conference with the Chief Deputy and could not be disturbed.

"RO advised he would call back later."

Deppish called back around 4:15 p.m., and once again made no progress. Then the dispatcher said, "David Huggins of the Mississippi Bureau of Investigation is here and wishes to talk with you."

Huggins came on the line and explained that he was familiar with the case. "Jack Holt has been removed from office. Bill Gant won the election and is the Sheriff now, but things are still a little upset."

Huggins said everyone Deppish worked with before had left the department except one man. He suggested they start working with Morris Smith, the new County Investigator, and he would help any way he could. Grossly understated, he added, "We should have been working with you before, but for some reason, the Sheriff [Holt] didn't want the MBI to be involved."

Deppish's records do not show what had gone on in the Alcorn County's Sheriff Department but it should have magnified his curiosity about Johnny. These former county officials appeared to be trying to protect him.

Deppish asked Huggins whether anyone had seen Johnny Bingham or Greg Curry recently, and was told that neither had been seen around town. In fact, Huggins thought Greg was in jail in Kansas.

Huggins told Deppish that the new staff would be very willing to help him locate Johnny, but warned him that Sheriff Gant had no previous law enforcement experience. Arresting a guy with Johnny's tough stud reputation could be complicated for the new sheriff in town.

Deppish asked about records dealing with the cash found at Johnny's house. Former Chief Deputy Doles returned the funds to Johnny in the middle of December, but even the receipt showing the funds had been seized had disappeared with Doles. Alcorn County officials arbitrarily decided the funds came from the insurance settlement.

On January 5, 1984, Geary County issued a "Material Witness Arrest Warrant" for Johnny. Deppish faxed it to Morris Smith and sent the original to him by certified mail. He told Smith the warrant called for a $35,000 bond and asked Smith to inform him as soon as they arrested Johnny. Kansas authorities waited for word, but none came. Johnny dropped out of sight.

Speed trap released

In light of what had happened on January 8, 1984, Danny Carter was either very lucky or under the careful protective watch of some very powerful people. At 9:05 p.m. on that date, Dannell W. Green of the Missouri Highway Patrol timed a "white over cream," 1976 Pontiac Grand Prix going 67 miles per hour in a 55 mph zone. He pulled it over.

Green identified the driver as Danny Carter.

"As I approached Mr. Carter's vehicle, I noticed he was holding his wallet, looking for his driver's license. After explaining to Mr. Carter my reason for stopping him, I requested he come back and have a seat in my patrol vehicle. As Mr. Carter was exiting his vehicle, I noticed a [loaded] handgun in a holster lying on the front seat in plain view on the passenger side." (Green saw the bullets in the chamber of the gun.)

Green caught Carter, an alleged conspirator in a handgun murder who was out on bail awaiting trial, with a loaded handgun sitting in plain view. The gun contained five rounds of .32-20 caliber Winchester cartridges. There was a box containing 42 more cartridges in the car.

Green told Carter to open the trunk. Here he found a .22 caliber Ruger and a .22 caliber rifle, both unloaded.

Not yet finished, Green checked the serial number on the loaded handgun and then ran an NCIC check. He learned the gun had been stolen on May 4, 1979, as reported by the Centerhill, Florida police department. Green asked for an explanation. Carter said all the guns belonged to his brother Darrel.

Missouri Trooper Larry Coulson called Darrel Carter to ask about the gun. Darrel told him "he purchased the gun from Wayne Freeman of Leroy, Kansas...for $90.00 or $100.00 in the summer of 1981." Darrel let the officer know that his brother was out on bail pending his charge for criminal conspiracy in a Geary County handgun murder.

Michael Murphy, an Assistant Clay County Prosecutor, told the officers to confiscate the loaded handgun and release Danny once they had secured a $45.00 bond for the speeding ticket. Doing this, they returned him to his car that had been left on the highway, and he presumably headed home, still a free man. No one mentioned whether he wore his bullet-proof vest that night, or explained why he carried a loaded gun in his car. Missouri officials wanted the cash for speeding, but a Kansas murder held little interest.

The next day Deputy Deppish called the Missouri Highway Patrol to talk to either Green or Coulson. They told him the story and that the guns allegedly belonged to Darrel Carter. Deppish recorded, "when a call was made to Darrel, this was apparently found to be true."

Geary County did nothing further about this strange incident, nor were charges filed against Darrel Carter for owning a stolen handgun. Geary County officials chose to protect their star witnesses rather than risk that these same witnesses might have serious ghosts in their closets—not even in their closets, but sitting on the front seat in plain view.

Mama Jane takes action

Jack Lassiter practiced law in Little Rock, Arkansas. Early in January, 1984, Jane Grismer hired Lassiter to look into the affairs of Tom Bird. Jerry and Jane had phoned Tom three times that month, pumping him for information about Sandy's death.

On January 11, 1984, Lassiter phoned Agent Winsor. "My client [Grismer] and her friends are suspicious that Sandy died of other than accidental death. I've been retained to look into the matter."

The Grismer clan had spent many hours on the phone and around dinner tables at family gatherings, wondering about Sandy's unusual death. It seemed unlikely to Grismer (and to Tom) that Sandy would have been out driving alone at 2 or 3 a.m. Jane knew Sandy had her stubborn side. She had so little contact with her, that she could not have known that it was common for Sandy to use a good drive in the country to help clear her mind. The question that bothered Jane and Tom most, though, was the time: 3 a.m.? Not likely.

Jane saw very little of Sandy once she and Tom moved to Emporia early in 1982. According to Stephanie Moore, next door neighbor to the Bird's, Jane never made the trip to Emporia until after her death except for a brief weekend during Father's Day in 1983. The Bird family trips to Arkansas were reserved for holidays. Mother and daughter occasionally talked by phone, but since converting to the Lutheran faith and marrying a Lutheran pastor, Sandy became a different person than the child Jane remembered.

Sandy remained upset with Jane for divorcing her father, Randall Stringer. This further chilled their relationship. During her developmental years, Sandy spent most her time with other family members, while Jane worked her real estate business.

The unanswered questions about Sandy's death, coupled with the natural grief of a distant mother drove Jane to find "the" answer to her untimely wreck. Hiring an attorney to find "the" answer might bring closure to Jane's loss.

Winsor, whose investigation focussed on Marty Anderson's murder, told

Lassiter what he could about the investigation, but his report did not state what he told him. Lassiter told Winsor that he would be contacting other Geary County officials and individuals involved in the case. Presumably, Lassiter also contacted Vernon Humphrey, the KBI Agent working on the suddenly revived and energized investigation of Sandy Bird's death, and others involved in that investigation.

Lorna gets tapes

As an accused felon, Lorna had a constitutional right to confront her witnesses. This right included seeing all the material that was to be used against her at trial.

Darrell Meyer, Lorna's attorney, asked for and received a body of paperwork, including investigators reports, plus transcripts of interviews with others involved in the case—Greg Curry, Danny Carter, etc.

It was on January 17, 1984 that Meyer received for the first time a copy of a most curious transcript. It was a taped, clandestine conversation between Tom Bird and Darrel Carter.

Meyer called Lorna to fill her in on the materials, yet Tom didn't learn of the tapes until after his March arrest.

As pieces of evidence appeared, word spread through town, and the pace of phone calls between Tom and Lorna increased. They spent a great deal of time together, comparing notes and updating each other. When Lorna came to Emporia, she stayed at Susan Ewert's home. Susan began to draw close to the beleaguered Emporia pastor as she tried to help both of them deal with the police. Tom and Susan saw Lorna as a victim being dragged into a hideous crime, and Tom felt himself being dragged along.

The pattern that began when Lorna moved back to Hutchinson continued, only at an accelerated pace. Tom and Lorna made an incredible number of long distance phone calls. They spent hundreds of dollars keeping in touch to keep up with developments, first in Lorna's case and following March 21, when they were both arrested the same day, in both their cases.

The legal records each collected provided insight to the other person as they both tried to fight for freedom.

Susan and Tom continued to offer sanctuary to Lorna until mid-August, 1985, when they discovered the rumors about her were true, but greatly understated.

Greg questioned again

By February 2 there still had been no arrest of Johnny Bingham. Kansas investigators decided to once again question Greg Curry with his attorney, Ralph DeZago present. Deputies Deppish and Buskey, along with Agent Winsor took part in the interview.

"Do you know a man named Harry Curry?" investigators asked. Harry was the man involved in a suspicious auto accident on September 29, 1983 with Johnny from which he received a $2,900 insurance settlement.

"He's my uncle. He travels a lot," Greg answered and, by so doing, completely contradicted the answer he had given to Deppish and Winsor just a few weeks earlier. "Oh, I didn't know then who you were talking about," he tried to cover himself.

"Do you have any gambling debts at Wolf Creek?" They had already learned he had a reputation as a big-talker and had carried a lot of cash on him during some time in September.

"Yea, I had had a $500 bet with a guy named Bev (Lnu), but I won that bet."

"What about the cash?"

"I took the $5,000 Carter gave me to Wolf Creek and used it as flash money," he admitted. "But I gave it all to Johnny. I did borrow back a $1,000 for my move about a week later, but I paid that off." (His parents had said it was a bank loan.)

"Did you ever receive anything for passing on the money? Gifts, any kind of a reward or favor?"

"No sir. None."

"Did Bingham ever tell you about his plan to kill Anderson?"

"He told me, 'tell your buddy [Danny] don't worry.' I asked him if he had enough information and he said he did."

"When did this occur?"

"Around September 17 or 18."

"In person or some other way."

"In person at Corinth."

"What else can you tell us about your October 10 phone call with Bingham?"

"Johnny said to tell Carter 'I'm already up there [in Kansas] and you [Greg] couldn't talk to me." Johnny wanted Danny to believe that everything was okay and not to worry, but Greg never told Danny what Johnny had said. He claimed he had no other contacts with Johnny nor had he ever talked to Lorna and said he didn't even recognize her photograph.

"I think Johnny just took the money and never planned to do anything. Danny accused me of doing that and then leaving Emporia."

"Do you know who pulled the trigger?"

"Yes!" Greg responded immediately.

"Who?"

"Her [Lorna] or Carter [Danny]. I think after Danny figured on getting some of the insurance money and killed Marty himself." Of course, this testimony would have been a severe blow to the prosecutor who had already settled on a plea agreement with Danny, one which would prohibit them from prosecuting him any further in Marty's death.

Not liking this response, Greg's attorney pulled him aside for a moment. Then Greg clarified his answer, saying, "It's just a guess. But I know Johnny didn't do it. His relatives say he was deer hunting and everyone knew that. He goes with someone from work."

"Who?"

"I don't remember his name."

"Has anyone talked to you about changing your story or intimidating you?"

"No, no one. But when I go out late at night, I've seen someone following me sometimes." He described a police vehicle, a Mississippi State Patrol officer.

"Why would you pick Johnny Bingham to do this?

"Years ago, when Johnny just moved to town, I heard that he was kind of a tough guy. Someone to be afraid of. And he was from Chicago." Then he added, "I never thought of anyone else to do it."

"Did Carter ever ask anyone else before you?"

"I don't know. I thought he might have been looking for someone for a time, but I have no idea."

"Who's Bingham's closest friend?"

"His brother Jimmy, I suppose."

"Did you ever discuss the conspiracy with anyone else before your arrest?"

"No."

"The reason I asked you this is because your wife seemed to know what was going on when we arrested you and how serious you were involved. Are you sure you never talked to her about it?" Deppish knew there was a hole in Greg's story.

"No, I didn't."

During a break in the interview, Greg and his attorney left the room. Upon their return, DeZago said, "Greg, tell Bill what you just told me so there will be no questions about this."

"Before I delivered the money to Johnny, Donna found the envelope containing the information and the money in the glove compartment in our car, so I guess she knew."

"But did you talk to her about the conspiracy?"

"Not really, but she knew something was wrong," Greg answered. He wanted to keep Donna out of it.

"Did you ever write any letter on yellow paper to your folks while you were in jail in Geary County? Or did you write to anyone asking them to lie for you if anyone asked?"

He sat quietly for a moment before he answered. "I did write such a letter, but to my parents. I said if anyone asked where I was at, not to tell them. They still have the letter."

"Greg, one of the questions on the polygraph test was, 'Did you ever talk to any one else besides your wife, Carter and Bingham about the conspiracy before your arrest?' The examiner told me on the phone that you failed this question. You were not telling the truth."

Greg had no comment but took another polygraph test that same day. The results were the same. He lied about this critical question. The officers believed he spoke with Johnny, but could not prove it.

On March 8, a Geary County court accepted Greg Curry's plea agreement. He pled guilty to one count of criminal solicitation to commit murder, and received a 2-5 year prison sentence. Shortly after, he received probation, serving a total of no more than 45 days.

Investigators tried once again to get the elusive truth from the young bagman at another interview on March 22. First, though the police had a Bird to cage.

Bird cage door opens the first time

March of 1984 found Tom Bird depressed, and that depression began with his loneliness and grief over Sandy. Sandy had been his closest counselor. When he had difficult decisions to make, serious conflicts to resolve, problems in his ministry or in the family, she was the one trusted person to whom he could go—but not in the spring of 1984.

He felt deeply stressed and stretched from caring for three children and a fast-growing congregation. The constant rumors and gossip circulating around Emporia and even at Faith compounded the problem.

Could he still minister at Faith? Could he even continue in the ministry anywhere?

He and Terry Smith grew close, but he had feelings for Lorna. What about a new wife? (Even Jane gave her approval of Terry months earlier.)

He saw marrying Lorna as a Pandora's Box, yet her four children were close to his in age and were friends. They had been through so much together and were close in age. She was a widow, he a widower.

He thought about just moving away and trying to put it all behind him.

He felt the Grismer's putting pressure on him to move back to Little Rock.
He could teach.

Thoughts that God had abandoned him were deeply troubling.

He thought about suicide. He saw this as irrational, of course, but he was
deeply conflicted and depressed.

As troubled as he was, Tom got no relief, just more of the same and an
avalanche of new problems.

He marked March 21, 1984, as climactic a date in his life as had been
July 17, 1983 (the day Sandy was found dead).

On that Wednesday, Tom spent a good part of the day preparing for the
Lenten Service scheduled that night. Just before 4 p.m., he headed home for
his daily whiffle-ball game with the neighborhood children. Following the
game, "As I was putting the children down for a nap at home, Lyon County
Sheriff Andrews and Agent Humphrey came to the door. Agent Humphrey
handed me a folded 11 X 14 document."

He looked at Humphrey asking, "What's this?"

"A warrant for your arrest."

"For what?" Tom stood dumbfounded.

"Solicitation to commit murder."

Tom heard the words but did not comprehend them. He read the
documents as he walked up the stairs:

"Warrant:

"The State of Kansas to any Sheriff or Peace Officer of the State
of Kansas:

"WHEREAS, it appearing upon the sworn Complaint dated
March 21, 1984, that there are reasonable grounds for believing:

"Count I:

"that during the month of May, 1983 in Lyon County, Kansas,
THOMAS E. BIRD, then and there being, did then and there
unlawfully and intentionally request another person, to wit: Darrel D.
Carter, to aid and abet in the commission of a felony, to wit: first
degree murder, contrary to the form of K.S.A. 21-3303, and against the
peace and dignity of the State of Kansas. (Class D felony)

"YOU ARE THEREFORE COMMANDED, forthwith, to arrest
the said THOMAS E. BIRD, and bring him/her before me at my office
in said County to answer said charge and then and there return this
writ.

"WITNESS, my hand and the seal of this Court in Emporia, Lyon
County, Kansas, this 21st day of March, 1984."

Lyon County District Judge Dick signed the warrant. Sheriff Andrews attested the arrest, although he failed to record the time of day. Rodney H. Symmonds, the Lyon County Attorney signed "The Complaint," which listed as witnesses Darrel D. Carter, Lorna Anderson, Michael G. Patton, Joe J. Lapping, Darrel G. Warren, Jennifer S. Palmer, J. Vernon Humphrey, Don Windsor [sic], and Daniel R. Andrews.

Tom should have immediately been suspicious of the lack of thoroughness of the investigators and the court when he noticed they spelled his name wrong on the arrest warrant. His middle name is Paul.

"I walked up the foyer stairs reading the document that said that in May, 1983 I tried to hire Darrel Carter to aid and abet the murder of Marty. This was incredible in its absurity!"

J. Vernon Humphrey, the resident KBI Agent, signed the Affidavit that contained the specific charges:

"That on December 10, 1983 affiant received information from Darrel D. Carter as follows:

"He is personally acquainted with Lorna G. Anderson who has been charged in Geary County, Kansas with the death of her husband, Martin K. Anderson. In May, 1983 Lorna Anderson contacted him and asked that he come to the Faith Lutheran Church in Emporia, Kansas and meet with her. The following day, Carter went to the Church and met with Lorna Anderson and was introduced to Tom Bird by her. During this meeting, Bird told Carter that he loved Lorna and that they had to do something with Marty. Carter knew Bird was referring to Martin Anderson, Lorna Anderson's husband. Bird told Carter he found a place with a bend in a road and a bridge outside of Emporia, which had [an] approximately fifty foot drop-off to the river and that a person could just miss the curve, especially if the person were drunk, and go off down the embankment. Bird told Carter they were going to drug Marty, take him out there, and run the car off into the river. Bird told Carter they needed his help to get Marty into the car after he was drugged. Carter did not give Bird an answer at this meeting as to whether or not he would assist Bird. Lorna Anderson was present during this conversation.

"About a week after Carter's conversation with Bird at the Church, Bird personally contacted Carter for a decision. Carter declined to assist.

"On December 1, 1983 Darrel Carter received word, through a friend, that Bird wanted to talk with Carter about this case to reaffirm their trust. Carter assumed that Bird meant 'this case' to be the death of Martin Anderson which had occurred on November 4, 1983.

"On December 12, 1983 Darrel Carter met with and engaged in conversation with Thomas E. Bird. With the permission of Carter, this conversation was overheard and recorded by the affiant and other law enforcement officers. During this conversation, Bird referred back to the aforementioned conversations between Carter and Bird and emphasized to Carter that they should both remain silent about the conversations and 'keep each other clean.'

"Therefore, affiant requests a complaint and warrant be issued charging Thomas E. Bird with one count of criminal solicitation to commit first degree murder."

"What really struck me a very hard blow, was a plot to get Marty drugged or drunk and run him off the road near a bridge and make it look like an accident," Tom said. This created an obvious connection with Sandy's death.

"I knew that Darrel was presenting this lie to save his brother," Tom reasoned. He had never met anyone so brazen and "was just blown away by such a boldness to lie." Sure, there had been a meeting, but it had been in June, and there was *never* a discussion about murdering Marty.

"What is going on here?" Bird wondered to himself. "And what's this about me wanting to get rid of Marty because I loved Lorna? This is insane."

Humphrey interrupted his thoughts. "Is anyone here with you?"

"My children," Tom answered as Andrea came down the hallway to find out what was going on.

"We have to take the kids and you."

Tom questioned what the police would do with his children as he went to wake up the boys. As he came back into the living room, he reached for his coat that lay on a dining room chair. Humphrey, reacting instinctively, quickly grabbed the coat fearing that Pastor Bird might be hiding a gun. It hit Tom full force. Humphrey really did consider him dangerous. Finding no gun, Humphrey handed him the coat.

The judge set bond at $10,000. Tom still had most of the money from Sandy's insurance settlements in the bank, so covering that amount would be no problem, but he remained mystified that any of this could even be happening.

Picking up Aaron, he scooted the other two children out the door, saying "I have to go with these men." Then he turned to Agent Humphrey. "What do I do with my kids?"

"You'll have to leave them at Social Rehabilitation Services."

Tom shooed the two older children into the back seat of the unmarked car next to Agent Humphrey, and he climbed in the front with Aaron on his lap. He begged Humphrey, "Can't we take them to the church day care? They are known there."

"That's up to the Sheriff." Sheriff Andrews nodded okay and drove to the church.

At the church, Tom herded the children into the day care center, leaving them with church friends. With Humphrey always very close behind him, Tom instructed the ladies, "I've got to go with these men so if I'm not back by closing, will you take the children to the Swint's?"

Satisfied that the childeren were in good hands, Tom, Humphrey and Sheriff Andrews walked out to the parking lot where Humphrey apolegetically said, "We've already broken procedure by taking you and the kids to church, and I didn't want to cuff you in front of the children; but now I have to cuff you," which he did in plain view of anyone watching.

"Thank you for your kindness," Tom said as he got back into the police car.

No one spoke until they got to the Sheriff's office and Tom's booking had been partially completed. Humphrey and Andrews took him to an interrogation room. Tom's mind had been running in high gear as he kept thinking, "How can we get this straightened out? What is going on here? How will the church and my ministry ever be the same again?"

Humphrey began somberly, "There are some serious things surrounding Marty Anderson's death and we need to get things straightened out."

"I agree," Tom answered. "I would like to get things straighted out."

"You need to tell us about your relationship with Lorna Anderson and what you said to Darrel Carter about the death of Martin Anderson," Humphrey demanded, pen and pad at hand.

"I think the best way for me to straighten this mess out is by talking to my lawyer."

When police had interrogated Danny Carter and Greg Curry, neither had their attorneys present. Police investigators find it easier to extract information this way. Tom wanted none of it.

Irritated and impatient at this answer, Humphrey sternly retorted, "It would serve you well to talk to us now."

"I would like to talk to my lawyer."

Humphrey led him the booking room saying, "Here is a phone. Call him."

"I don't know his number."

"You don't know his number?"

"No. I have to look it up." Tom never had a need for a criminal attorney and so, had no reason to carry a phone number either on his person or in his memory.

Tom called Emporia attorney Irv Shaw, whose office sat directly across the street from the Lyon County Courthouse. The county jail sat on the east side of the court house. Shaw, the tall, broad-shouldered, rugged and roughly handsome chain-smoker quickly arranged a hearing for Tom. The judge ordered that Tom immediately have the $10,000 bond transferred out of his bank account into the court's account. The banks had just closed making this conveniently impossible.

"They did that on purpose to keep you in. You'll be out in the morning," Shaw said.

The humiliating booking process—finger-printing, mug shot, search, personal data, surrendering personal items—tore Bird up inside. While he knew his children would be well-cared for that night, he had no idea what it was like to be in a jail cell, and even more so, not the slightest idea of what lay ahead. He believed that this phony warrant came from a devious and deceitful deal made by Darrel Carter to help his brother Danny. The truth would eventually win out, and that gave him some ill-founded solice.

The sheriif placed Tom in a single maximum cell. The fellow in the next cell had a radio on and he heard:

> "There was a major development in the Geary County murder case of Martin Anderson. Anderson was shot to death near Junction City on November 4 last year.
>
> "Two arrests were made in that case today. The Reverand Thomas P. Bird, Pastor of Faith Lutheran Church in Emporia, was arrested at his home this afternoon and charged with a single count of criminal solicitation to commit murder. He is being held in the Lyon County jail.
>
> "Darrel Carter, an Emporia business man, has alleged that Pastor Bird and Lorna Anderson, Martin's wife and at that time, church secretary at Faith Lutheran, asked Carter to find someone to murder Mr. Anderson during a meeting in the spring of 1983. Mrs. Anderson was also arrested today at her home in Hutchinson and taken to the Geary County jail. She was held on two counts of conspiracy to commit murder and one count of aiding and abetting first degree murder."

Tom felt sick to his stomach hearing the radio report. His jailmate, realizing that the story was about him, kept repeating, "They're going to nail you."

Tom burned white-hot inside, but the injustice of this claim and its results reached far beyond his present and momentary incarceration. He thought, "When I win and prove Carter to be a liar, my career here is going to be over" He thought about where he might go. He concluded, "The devil won this one."

The alarmed congregation at Faith, having gathered together for the Lenton service learned instead that their pastor was in jail. They began praying for Tom. They were confused and hurt. Some of the small fissures that had already begun in the church as the earlier rumors spread, were beginning to become stress fractures. Yet, church members stood ready to make Tom's bail the next day, a wonderful gesture, but unnecessary because Tom had the money himself.

He was released the next day and his first act was to pick up his children where he got a huge "love you and missed you daddy" hug. This little family and his faith in God were all he had left. Though devastated by the prior day's developments, Tom felt certain that very soon he could move on with his life, maybe start anew with Terry Smith—build a new home and life somewhere else.

And he did get a new home eventually, but it was not in Little Rock or Kansas City. It was in Lansing, Kansas in a state prison.

Curry changes...again and
Bingham goes away

Geary County had convicted Greg Curry and Danny Carter of solicitation to commit murder. Deputies had arrested and charged Tom Bird, now out on bail. In Hutchinson, deputies arrested Lorna who sat in the Geary County jail. There remained only one more person to apprehend: Marty Anderson's murderer, or at least the person who looked most likely.

Deputy Deppish and Agent Winsor flew off to Mississippi armed with an arrest warrant for Johnny Bingham. The earlier warrant, which had never even been served had named him as a material witness. It had been quashed on March 8. This time the charge was conspiracy to commit murder. The investigator's planned to add Bingham's scalp to those of Lorna Anderson, Danny Carter, Greg Curry and Pastor Tom Bird. The judge set Johnny's bail at $50,000.

Deppish and Winsor met with Lt. John McCullough, Morris Smith and David Huggins, the Mississippi officials who had been assigned to the case since January. The "department was in full cooperation" with them, they reported.

The officers spent some time reviewing the case and trying to learn more about Johnny. They talked of his auto "injury" from his September, 1983 accident. The Mississippi officers said, "this is not unusual here. We think that 80-90 percent of all insurance claims in our area have fraud involved." The officers named a particular insurance adjuster from Tupelo as complicit in these claims.

Lately, Johnny kept company with a girl whose former boyfriend was recently murdered in the Corinth area. They also discussed another curious incident that had occurred in September of 1981, when .22 caliber bullets were fired at the home of Alcorn County Judge Pauline Wilbanks, the judge who signed the earlier search warrants.

In the early afternoon of March 22, 1984, investigators telephoned David Coleman, Johnny Bingham's attorney, hoping for help in finding him. Coleman dodged them.

"Mr. Coleman, we want to meet with you to discuss the reasons we want to talk with Johnny," Deppish said.

"I'm not sure where to find Johnny. I haven't seen him in several weeks. He moved somewhere north of town I think."

"Well we need to talk with him. Will you help us?"

"I see no reason to talk again with Johnny. He already said he knows nothing about the homicide and he never got any money from Curry," Coleman stubbornly insisted.

"There are certain matters and other unanswered questions. It would be in Johnny's best interest if we could talk to him."

"We already know about the telephone calls to and from Kansas. These were just to discuss with Greg Curry something about a car he was having trouble getting a clear title to. Can't I just get him [Bingham] on the phone for you?"

"No, I think it would be best for all concerned if we could just sit down in person with Agent Winsor and myself to discuss the matter." Coleman agreed to meet with them later that afternoon.

They discussed various details of the case with Coleman and once again explained why they needed to talk with Johnny. "We need to know where he was on November 4."

They asked if Coleman would help them get Bingham to take a polygraph test. "I see no need for this. He's been telling you the whole truth all along and he knows nothing about the $5,000."

After more extensive conversation, Coleman finally agreed to a meeting, "If I can find him. And I must be present." He told the officers he would call if he agreed, "and we can all meet some time on Friday." (Strange that minutes earlier Coleman had no idea where Johnny was, but then agreed to a meeting the next day.)

Before looking for Johnny, though, they wisely decided to talk once again with Greg Curry. He was staying with his parents in Corinth, having already been paroled.

The questioning started with Gerald Curry, Greg's father. "Did Greg talk with you about the murder conspiracy before his arrest?"

"What? I don't understand. I mean Greg's attorney said he failed the polygraph test because …," the father protested.

Deppish interrupted. "Mr. Curry, what we want to know is your answer. Did Greg talk to you about the murder conspiracy at any time before his arrest."

"Well DeZago said Gregory failed that because of the way it was asked and the many times it was asked."

Just then, Greg came into the room.

Deppish asked Greg about a 1980 Chevy he bought in January of 1983. "I bought it from Bradley's in Corinth from Carter Bradley. I couldn't get it registered because the former owner never signed the title. So I talked to Bradley about it several times."

"By phone?"

"Phone and in person. I was trying to get the problem straightened out.".

"You ever talk with Johnny Bingham about the title problem?"

"Yes sir"

"When?"

"Out at Bradley's before I ever moved to Emporia [March, 1983]."

"You ever talk to Bingham about this by phone from Emporia?"

"Yes sir."

"Was this the call you talked about before, that you placed on October 10?"

"Yes sir."

"Did you call just to talk about the car problem?"

"Yes."

"Did you also talk about the Anderson conspiracy? About the information on Martin Anderson, and a date he would be in Topeka at a convention?"

Deppish's report does not contain an answer to this question. He continued. "Why didn't you say something before [when this phone call was discussed] that it was to discuss the vehicle title and that the Anderson information was kind of secondary?"

"I just told you what I thought you wanted to hear."

"Why did you need to talk to Bingham about the car title? How could he help you?"

"Bingham was working at Bradley when I bought the car."

The officers heard in these answers a significant change in Greg's prior testimony when he had insisted that the October call concerned arrangements for Marty's murder. Did Greg lie the first time, or had someone convinced him to change his story now that his conviction was sealed and he had been sentenced and paroled? If the October 10 call concerned a car title, the rest of the evidence against Johnny would be tainted as well. Without Greg's witness, Johnny became untouchable.

Deppish tried asking again about the conspiracy and when the two had first talked about it. Once again, father and son deflected the question by asserting that the polygraph exam was wrong. "Were you asked on the polygraph test if you discussed the conspiracy with anyone else but your wife before your arrest?" Deppish asked.

"The reason I failed the question was because of the way it was asked. I talked to a polygraph operator here in town and he said that wasn't the way I should have been asked questions. I shouldn't be asked a question over again and he also said that I couldn't pass a test because I didn't sleep the night before."

"Did you discuss the conspiracy with your wife, your mother and father, and the people who you work with?"

"My wife just saw the $1,000 in the glove compartment when we were driving to Nashville."

"You mean the $5,000?" [The dollar amount to which he had previously testified while his attorney was present.]

Incredibly, making yet another dramatic change in his story Greg insisted, "No, just a $1,000 I borrowed for vacation, from Johnny."

"She didn't see the envelope with the pictures and letter with the information on Anderson?"

"No. I didn't have it."

Mrs. Curry, the mother, and Greg's younger brother came into the room.

This time Greg asked the question. "Didn't he [Bingham] tell you that they know where he was that day?"

"What do you mean by that?"

"They can all tell you; he was out at Suitor's farm cutting beans. Eugene King and all the others; they know where he was that day."

"I saw Johnny in town one day after you were here and asked him where he was and he said he was out there at the farm cutting beans," Gerald Curry added.

Cutting beans at Suitor's is a far cry from hunting for deer at Nachez Trace, Tennessee. Bingham had said he was either at home or out hunting, not cutting beans.

The frustrated investigators asked for directions to Johnny's new place and headed on out. There they found Teresa, his wife, and their young son. "Will Johnny be home soon or is he at work?"

"No."

"Well is he at work?"

"He ain't workin'. He's just been driving back and forth to the doctor's lately."

She said she not only did not know where he was, she had no idea when he would be home. "Ma'am, would you have Johnny please call his attorney when he comes home?"

"I'll tell him, but I don't know if he'll do it," she said totally disinterested.

Johnny talks and confuses

Someone somehow did get in touch with Bingham. He joined Deppish and Winsor at David Coleman's office on March 23, at 11:30. Coleman had set a narrow time window for the interview, insisting he had to leave at noon, limiting the time they would have with Johnny.

Deppish began the interview. "Where were you on the fourth of November, 1983?"

"Working for Suitor, working with Grady Suitor hauling milo. We delivered the milo to Fuzzy's Feeds in Corinth."

"How were you paid when you worked for the Suitors?"

"Paid cash; about $150 per week." Johnny thought he hauled about four loads of milo during that period.

"When were you last deer hunting?"

"Earlier in October. I don't remember the exact dates. There are different times."

"Are you now employed?"

"Yes, tearing down a building in Henderson, Tennessee. Self employed. Selling the salvage."

"Did you make or receive any phone calls to or from Kansas during September, October, November or December of 1983?"

"Yes, Curry called about his car back in October. He asked me to call him back. I worked for Carter Bradley at the time he bought it."

"During that telephone call did you and Curry talk about anything else?"

"No sir. That was the only time I ever called that number or Kansas. Curry didn't say where he was."

"Have you ever been to Kansas? Do you know now where Kansas is?"

"No, I still don't know where Kansas is; seen it on the TV weather map, but never been there."

"About the $2,830 we found in your house. You first said it came from selling grain, then later you said it was insurance money from an accident."

"I was just confused and all that day because of everything going on; it had to be the insurance money."

"Are you still seeing a doctor because of that accident?"

"Yes."

"Would Wilson Suitor have records of your pay back during the time you were working there in November of 1983?"

"I doubt it very much."

Attorney Coleman interjected that Wilson Suitor is one of the most respected farmers in Alcorn County and is always very honest. The investigators reported that Coleman "did doubt that Suitor would keep any records because of the IRS, however." No record was made whether the investigators notified the IRS later on.

"Are you still having ear problems?"

"Yes, when I'm shooting a gun."

"Is this with just handguns?"

"It also bothers me to shoot a rifle unless I'm shooting at a deer or something like that."

"Which ear is it that you have trouble with?"

"Could be both of them, either one. This is an inner ear problem. I have an inner ear in both."

Agent Winsor recognized the contradiction in this statement. "When you talked with me in December, you said it was in your left ear. Is it your left or right?"

"I don't think I want to talk anymore. I think I've said enough." If he said more, he might implicate himself.

David Coleman realized this created a potential problem for his client and, after pondering that last response, said to Johnny, "Let's see what else they have to ask. If you don't want to, you don't have to answer, let's just see."

"Have you seen a doctor lately about the ear problem?"

"Several times, a year or so ago." [His wife Teresa said he was seeing the doctor the day before.]

"What is the doctor's name and address."

"Dr. Joseph Madara, Boonville, Mississippi."

The investigators asked for permission to get medical records from the doctor. Coleman said he would do it for them.

"Did you ever talk to anyone about going to Kansas?"

"No."

"Gentlemen, I'm sorry, we have to end this. I've got to get to another appointment," Coleman said, noting that it was 11:58 a.m.

As Deppish started to leave Coleman's office, Johnny introduced Eugene King, a man who had been sitting in the front office. "He can tell you where I was that day."

To Coleman Winsor asked, "Can we talk with Mr. King for a few moments in your office?"

"No. Sorry, I've got to go."

The five men stepped out in front of the building where the investigators tried to interview King. They made no progress due to the constant interruptions by both Coleman and Johnny. Deppish wrote, "It was apparent that Bingham had brought King along for his 'alibi.'"

Checking the alibi, but still no substance

That evening, Deppish and Winsor went to see Grady Suitor, son of Wilson Suitor who was directly involved in the management of his father's farming operation. Grady said that Johnny had worked on and off for them for about four years.

The investigators asked specifically about November 4, 1983. "We were gathering milo in early November. I couldn't account for every day. Johnny asked me about that. I looked it up. We were hauling milo to Fuzzy Feeds on the 1st, 2nd, and 3rd of November, and Johnny was taking the truck in there. You could ask Mr. Byrd at Fuzzy Feeds, he might remember, but I couldn't say for sure about Johnny on the 4th, cause they [Fuzzy Feeds] brought out a big truck that day to fill with milo."

They asked Grady Suitor about deer hunting. He knew he had not gone with Bingham the previous fall but Suitor's sister remembered that Johnny had gone one weekend "last fall sometime" with a bunch of other guys. "They had a problem with their hunting license so came back empty-handed but very tired." Ms. Suitor could not recall which weekend it was, but thought it was about "the time we were getting milo in."

Suitor had nothing else important to add, except one curious suggestion. "Johnny said to me 'I couldn't have been there. I had a summons to be in court.'" Grady explained that "Constable Smith had brought him [Johnny] a summons to be a witness for a murder trial about that time, had served him out in the field where they were working." So the officers heard yet another story.

The next day Suitor went with the officers to Fuzzy Feeds where they checked the purchase orders for Suitor's farm. They found a shipment on November 1, 2 and 3, but none for November 4.

Arthur Byrd, the manager of Fuzzy Feeds, did not know Johnny. No one else there knew him either, although Byrd thought he could have been the man directing traffic on the 4th when they brought the big truck out to Suitor's place.

Greg Curry's newest story cast doubt on some of his earlier statements about Johnny. Both of his polygraph tests indicated that he had most likely talked with someone about what really happened between him and Danny during the fall of 1983. Whether or not one of those persons was Johnny is not known.

The police had Johnny's alibi, but it was very weak. Eugene King said they were together, but if he had not been involved in nor knew anything about Marty's murder, how did Johnny know that he and King were together on just the right date? No one else could place Johnny in Corinth on November 4.

During the search of Johnny's mobile home, cash, a handgun, several .22 caliber cartridges, a blue denim jacket with silver buttons and various baseball caps with emblems on them were all seized. Junction City witnesses had described a man near the van wearing such apparel. Also seized were "Single .22 caliber shells with F & U markings," the same as those found lodged in the head of Marty Anderson, the same as those found in Danny's apartment.

Johnny first claimed the cash, $2,830, came from the sale of milo, then later said it came from an auto accident settlement. The only milo sale police found for which any kind of receipt could be produced was in April of 1983.

Did the investigators stand in the presence of Marty's murderer or was Johnny Bingham just another in a line of co-conspirators, the man who stole the hit money from the devils who wanted Marty killed? Or were these all coincidences and Johnny's only connection was a loose friendship with Greg Curry? A court never had a chance to decide because within several days of these interviews, all charges against Johnny were dropped.

❖❖❖

It would be another 17 months before Geary County officers had what they believed was the smoking gun, a first hand eyewitness to the identity of the hit man. In August of 1985, Lorna Anderson swore it was Tom Bird.

Who was Tom Bird, the man accused of a viscous cold-blooded murder? Who was Lorna Anderson, the promiscuous temptress who assisted in the murder in plain view of her own children? How did these two become twisted around the same deadly plots?

SECTION II:

"For the lips of an adulteress drip honey,
and her speech is smoother than oil;
but in the end she is bitter as gall,
as a double-edged sword.
Her feet go down to death;
her steps straight to the grave."

Proverbs 5:3-5

Bird nest built

In 1947, Concordia Theological Seminary in St. Louis, one of two American seminaries of the Lutheran Church Missouri Synod, had a student policy prohibiting seminarians from getting married. Arkansas-born Ralph Bird graduated from the seminary on June 8, 1947. The next day he married Virginia Twillmann, a St. Louis resident. They had quietly dated since 1942.

In terms of his covert marital plans, Bird was not unlike many who attended the seminaries of the conservative Lutheran denomination, but in many other ways he was unique. An avid sports fan, while still in high school he pitched for the St. John's College, Winfield, Kansas, baseball team. He won 30 games and lost 7. He threw two no-hitters and three one-hitters.

To make his message exciting for children, Bird perfected and performed magic tricks. He was very popular with children. Ralph and Virginia spent a lot of time with their own children, Mark, Tom and Gloria, and other children in the churches and communities they served.

Pastor Ralph served churches in Indiana and Texas before moving back to his native State of Arkansas. He retired from the ministry in Hardy, Arkansas.

Pastor Ralph disliked the idea of wearing a cleric's collar. He wore a business suit—less pretentious— except in the pulpit, where he wore the robes of his church. Pastor Ralph fit in with the people whom he served. He considered that his office gave him no special status. He viewed himself as equal with his parishioners, not above them.

Virginia Bird organized everything and she sang beautifully. She sewed, cooked and canned. She taught Sunday School and Vacation Bible School. She relished the traditional role of a pastor's wife, submitting herself to her husband and his ministry, willing to make significant adjustments and sacrifices, regardless of her own talents and intellect. She accepted the long hours and constant interruptions endured by Pastor Ralph. The Birds lived on a relatively meager income, as Virginia, like many pastor's wives of her generation, did not work outside the home except for helping Ralph with his church ministry. And they moved several times before retiring in Hardy, Arkansas.

Virginia gave birth to Thomas Paul Bird on June 1, 1950—the Bird's second child and son. Mark, the first born, is two years older than Tom. Gloria is the youngest.

During Tom's early life, the family lived in Bedford, Indiana. They moved to Garland, Texas during junior high school and settled in Little Rock, Arkansas. Tom graduated from Little Rock's Hall High School in 1968.

Like their father and mother, all the young Birds had a huge interest in sports. Their Little Rock home had a huge pie-shaped backyard that overlooked a small forest. Here Ralph, the Bird children and neighborhood kids played a daily whiffle-ball game.

Gloria says, "Mark made up the rules as he went along." Setting up an aluminum folding chair as the backstop, Mark measured off the distance from the pitcher's mound, next to which he put another folding chair. If the batter hit the second chair and a runner was on first, it was a double-play—unless Mark changed the rules that day. Mark insisted that no game could start unless Virginia first sang the National Anthem. And Mark had set up a special scoreboard using old number tags Pastor Ralph gave him from church. As an adult, Tom played whiffle-ball or football with his three children and neighborhood kids every day in front of his Emporia, Kansas, home.

The creativity, competitiveness, neighborliness and camaraderie expressed in these daily whiffle-ball games is characteristic of this close family. They had a good time together. They stayed attached to each other and to Ralph and Virginia.

They attended an endless string of church activities, from regular worship services, children's choir, plays and special programs to the annual summer Vacation Bible School. Joking, teasing, competing, drama, music, church, family cohesion and the Law and the Gospel formed the foundation of this talented family.

Ralph and Virginia Bird's faith had a profound effect on Tom. They took into their family homeless, unwed mothers and abused women, whom they nursed to health or to a successful delivery. The harsh realities of life evidenced in these personal tragedies exposed Tom and his siblings to the rough side of a pastor's life and, in Tom's case, watered the seed of his gift of caring.

The Birds are naturally friendly. Visitors feel immediately welcome and relaxed in their homes and presence. There is no pretense or air of superiority.

There is no record of family violence in the Bird family; nor did Tom have a reputation as a thug or bully. Nothing suggests that Tom saw violence as a way to solve personal problems. Tom obeyed his parents.

Mark Bird says he has "street smarts." The former restaurant/bar owner who never married, is the Supervisor of Officials for the Central Arkansas Officials Association in Little Rock. He also works as a referee and umpire. He hosts a Friday night sports talk show in Little Rock, where he has a reputation as a feisty, opinionated, no-holds barred expert on local high school and collegiate sports. Where Tom is laid back, Mark is aggressive, gregarious and assertive and every bit as competitive as Tom.

Gloria is a lot like her mother, strong and musically talented. She learned to be tough when her first marriage collapsed and her husband left her pregnant. Despite her tough times, Gloria's eyes sparkle when she talks about her family and her older brother Tom. Her personal travails drew her more closely to Ralph and Virginia. Eventually, she met and married Felix Cates, and now directs a day care center for a Lutheran church in Little Rock. Another Bird trait she shares, according to Ralph Bird, is that "she is not just committed to the church, but may be over-committed."

One common Bird trait is a high level of activity and total commitment to what they deem important, and a willingness to sacrifice their own comfort.

Tom learned early that he had blazing foot speed and endurance. His high school track team won state championships. He was a key member of the team. His track skills earned him a full scholarship to the University of Arkansas. He competed for four years. As a high school football end, his competitive drive and need to excel combined with his natural speed and made him a dangerous weapon.

Tom excelled as a runner because of his natural talent, but honed it through vigorous training. Daily he ran a 10-mile circuit that included a series of six long, steep hills on Reservoir Road between Rodney Perham and Cantrell Roads. Gloria said Tom topped off this run by eating a "half gallon of ice cream."

Tom's determination sometimes overruled common sense and at least once landed him in a hospital. During one Friday night high school football game, Tom took a brutal hit to the groin. It left him writhing on the ground and sick to his stomach. The hit's impact twisted his sperm duct and it became inflamed. Though in tremendous pain, he had a cross-country meet the following Saturday, and refused to sit out. Running as hard as ever, he ignored swelling and discomfort. Near the end of the race he collapsed agonizing in pain.

In 1976, a 26-year old Tom, out of the seminary and distanced from the kind of conditioning needed to run against real competition, ran against Frank Shorter, the world class Olympic marathoner. It was a hot, muggy day. Tom jogged as often as he could during seminary days, but there was no Reservoir Road-type training. Still he relished the challenge to run against Shorter.

The gun sounded and Tom took off, Shorter in his sights. He did his best to negotiate each painful step, hopeful he could finish with a respectable time. Without warning he collapsed, unconscious. A victim of severe sunstroke and dehydration, Tom's body simply shut down. Close to death for five days, with a temperature of 106 degrees, doctors packed him in ice.

Twice during his two-week hospitalization, he received kidney dialysis treatments. Then he regained consciousness, unaware of all that happened to him. He waited "while my body rebuilt itself."

Being so close to death had a profound effect on Tom's outlook. He became more focussed, studious and dedicated to his call to the ministry.

Others later suggested the near-death experience had an even more grievous effect on Tom than he realized, that something happened inside of Tom's head as a result of the heat stroke; some sort of brain atrophy, that had affected his otherwise non-violent personality. But this speculation amounted to no more than second-hand guesses by folks who seldom saw Tom.

First in a line of Stringers

Jane Stringer gave birth to Sandra Stringer on June 4, 1950. Her parents, Jane and Randall, moved Sandy and her three younger brothers from Oklahoma City to Little Rock in 1963. They lived in a middle-class home on Harmon Street, a three-bedroom rambler that blends in with the others on the block, a great place to raise a family, but not good enough for Jane.

Jane launched a successful career in real estate sales. She focussed on wealthy professionals moving in, around and out of town. She spent much of her time on the job.

Because "Mama" Jane, as she insisted the young Birds call her, worked so much, Sandy's child rearing was done by her extended family—aunts and her grandmother. Sandy cooked, sewed and cleaned house and in so doing, became an excellent seamstress. Years later, Sandy sewed two beautiful suits for Tom.

Jane is a controlling, matriarchal woman originally from Louisiana, and though Sandy inherited some of her stubborn and determined ways, she was not aggressive like Jane. Sandy had no interest in pursuing the status of high society which her intellect and personality made available.

Sandy graduated as valedictorian of her 440-member class at Hall High School. She was named one of Little Rock's Ten Outstanding Students in 1968, and was a National Merit Scholar.

A near genius in mathematics, Sandy won a full scholarship to Rice University in Houston, Texas. Jane wanted Sandy to earn a Ph.D., become a scientist and work at the National Aeronautics and Space Administration, perhaps even become an astronaut. Jane wanted Sandy to marry a wealthy professional man with status, but as a high school sophomore and junior Sandy dated very little. Jane thought Sandy needed a boyfriend.

Sandy played exceptional tennis and she rode horses. She performed with Hall High's Cheerokee [sic] Drill Team, and the Powder Puffs. Every year the Powder Puffs played football against Hall's cheerleaders. Sandy started at quarterback for the Powder Puffs.

Tom had injured his leg during his senior year of football and took time off to heal. He coached one of the girl's teams in Hall High's annual challenge football game. He drew the Powder Puff team that featured a pretty quarterback who mirrored Tom's athletic prowess—Sandra Stringer. Tom said, "She was amazingly good at imitating a quarterback."

Randy, one of Sandy's brothers, played football with Tom. He urged Tom to date Sandy. Although he had dated a couple of girls, Tom, like Sandy, was not much into dating, but between snaps of the ball and running offensive plays, they fell in love. They dated seriously by Christmastime and became high school sweethearts.

Jane Carter, Sandy's closest friend in high school and college, watched Tom and Sandy's friendship go from seed to blossom. "Sandy and I were in physics class and she had a desk by the window. The track team would walk down the street every day, and every time Tom would walk by she'd run and turn the blinds up and down [to say hello]. The teacher never could figure out what was happening."

Gloria Bird adored Sandy. "She was like the big sister I never had. We sewed together and she gave me her Cheerokee Girls pin when she went to college."

Everyone saw Sandy as bubbly, warm and affectionate. "When she came to our house the first time, Sandy went around and hugged everybody. My dad, being a German, was shocked and yet pleased by such a genuine outward expression of joy. Sandy just loved people, and people loved Sandy," Gloria said.

Sandy's three younger brothers loved her, too, but trouble loomed on the horizon. "We got the sense from Mom more than anybody that she was delighted Sandy had a steady boyfriend until it came time for her to go to college," Randy said.

While still in high school, Tom decided to follow his dad into the ministry. He had a unique perspective on what it meant to be a pastor, and it scared Jane Stringer.

> "You see, there is something about growing up in a pastor's home; especially since my dad was from Arkansas. Dad was not a staunch German, never wore a collar. I saw dad in his whole life not just his pastoral life. I mean he and mom would have arguments. He walked around in his boxer shorts at home. He hollered and yelled at baseball and football games when the Cardinals weren't doing too well.
>
> "Dad brought pregnant women into the home to protect them. If a guy down the street was struggling with a job or something, dad would

go down and have a beer with him. He umpired local ball games and played some. He dealt with families when there were suicides and things like that.

"I saw him beyond his pastoral context. I saw that he was a real person with ups and downs just like everybody else, and was able to talk at anybody's level. I learned to be like that. No one taught me that at seminary.

"I learned that the pastoral demeanor is sometimes a barrier for somebody opening up to you. It was one of the reasons I didn't go through our Lutheran school system. I felt those who did this were sheltered; certainly they had a tremendous background in theology but lacked in real life experience.

"I went to the University of Arkansas and saw real life. During Vietnam, I saw campus unrest. We had mandatory ROTC and as a freshman you had to take it, and I was not military material.

"I wanted to be a down-to-earth person who could talk to any person at any level. It's not that I was multi-personality or that I was deceitful, but I talked at the level that I would talk to a construction worker. I just do it, I don't have to think about it. I just am what I am."

Too earthy and too poor for Jane

Jane wanted more than a country preacher as her son-in-law. To Jane it meant Sandy would be throwing her life away. "I was dead set against the marriage. Sandy had a lot going for her, and I was afraid that if she married Tom she'd never realize her full potential."

Sandy left for Houston to attend Rice, and Tom went to the University of Arkansas at Fayetteville to run track. It seemed Jane's dreams for Sandy might be realized, but Tom and Sandy kept talking and visiting as often as they could. If UA had a track meet anywhere near Rice, Sandy sneaked over to see Tom. Distance made their love grow stronger. They were determined to a run a lifetime marathon together and these were two very determined young people.

Following her first year at Rice, Sandy transferred to UA to be close to Tom. She continued toward a degree in math. Tom worked toward a degree in sociology to prepare for seminary. They both became actively involved in school and church activities.

Sandy graduated in 1971, Summa Cum Laude with a Bachelor's Degree in Mathematics—in just three years. She entered the master's program and began working as a Graduate Teaching Assistant. Though Tom had another year before graduation, they decided to marry.

Tom Bird and Sandy Stringer were married on August 21, 1971. Given their popularity in Little Rock, the wedding was a huge event. Jane surrendered to their stubborn determination. "Once she married him he became a son."

Months after Tom and Sandy's wedding, Jane divorced Randall Stringer, and the relationship between mother and daughter soured. Jane dated and later married a Little Rock physician, Dr. Jerry "Papa Doc" Grismer. Sandy never moved back to Little Rock and her contact with her mother and step-father was reserved for a few family gatherings each year, and periodic phone calls.

With Sandy's strong encouragement and his native determination, Tom completed his studies and competed in track. As a senior in 1971-72 season, he captained the UA track team. The school chose him the outstanding athlete of the year in track and elected him to the hall of fame in the UA yearbook.

Sandy and Tom both graduated in the spring of 1972, he with a Bachelor of Arts degree in Sociology, and she with a Master's Degree in Mathematics.

They headed to seminary.

Tom and Sandy moved to Springfield, Illinois, where he entered Concordia Theological Seminary. Sandy taught math at Springfield College and Lincoln Land Community College. Tom concentrated on Biblical studies, but also took numerous courses in history, systematic theology and pastoral counseling, setting the tone for his future ministry.

Sandy, raised a Presbyterian, studied Lutheran theology with Tom. Friends and family report lively discussions between them about religious faith. Pastor Ralph Bird gave her Lutheran instruction. Sandy joined the Lutheran Church and, according to her brother Randy, even her politics got more conservative.

The two were a good fit—studious, intelligent, committed, focused, competitive and athletic. Sandy, with her teaching jobs, supported Tom and, unlike the days when Ralph and Virginia were forced to delay their marriage, the seminary by then had many married couples on campus.

Seminary days

Ken and Katherine Kothe lived above the "Soup," a cafeteria where seminary students at Concordia hung out. Katherine served as the seminary nurse. Ken started seminary at the age of 30, older than most of the other students.

Ken made friends with Dan Bohlken early on at seminary, and meeting him on the sidewalk one afternoon, shouted out, "Hey Dan, what's up?"

"What'd you think of [Professor] Scaer's ordination formula? Did he call it a sacrament?" Ken asked, hoping for a good theological argument.

"I'm not sure, but I thought he did," Dan answered.

Ken noticed the shorter man walking with Dan. "Who's with you?"

"Oh, this is Tom Bird."

Ken studied the thin, slightly balding man. He carried himself with his head slightly down, looking as if he would rather not say anything. "Tom, what did you think of Scaer's point?"

In his Arkansas drawl, not too loudly so as to appear pushy or arrogant, Tom said, "Well, I think the participle he used was *heretoneo* which literally means 'hands stretched on' and is often translated as 'appointed.' So there seems to be something divine connected to the laying on of the hands." Tom grinned and added, "But I'm just an ole' Arkansas boy. What do I know?"

Tom and Sharon Hackett, like Dan and Sandy Bohlken, met Tom and Sandy Bird during seminary orientation. Sharon said, "I enjoyed Tom and Sandy's friendliness and their southern accent."

Tom Hackett characterized the Bird's speech as "back woods" but said, "they were both very bright and intelligent as well as warm people."

Tom had introduced himself to Dan Bohlken during orientation. "I never knew why he picked me out of the 110 plus first year fellas, but from that initial meeting, our friendship became the best part of my seminary experience."

Dan and Ken remember Tom as a very good football player. Dan said, "At half-time of our first intramural game, we were behind, so we switched to Tom at quarterback. He was as elusive as a skitterbug and had a good arm." By the fourth year of seminary, Bird started at quarterback for the seminary's all-star team, beating the St. Louis seminary team for the first time ever. "Tom was so quick, every time he seemed to be sacked, he would run out of it and make a big gain."

Ken also remembers a pick-up game in which he played quarterback:

"Bill Parsons, Elder McCants and I, along with a few tag-along kids, were playing touch football. Bill, a bright student, was also a great athlete. I also thought Elder, a scholar at the Sem, another friend of mine, was a good athlete. He wasn't.

"I was the quarterback and I needed a wide-receiver. 'Bald' Bill was on the opposing side; Elder was on my side, and he was no wide receiver. He couldn't catch a cold in the dead of a Minnesota winter, and that meant trouble for me.

"Tom walked by, so I asked Bill if Tom could play on my team. He said, 'No problem.' I didn't know at the time that Tom had played quarterback, however, I knew he was quick, fast, competitive and didn't like to lose. That's why I wanted him on my team. I looked at Bill and told him it was all over and asked him how it felt to lose? He just smiled.

"In the huddle I said, 'Tom, go down ten yards, cut right 90 degrees and I will hit you in the chest in stride.' Tom wasn't pushy, he just accomplished things. He said, 'Got it. I'll be there. Get it there.'

"Elder hiked the ball. It came to me like a snail treading water. Parson came at me like Deacon Jones starving for a beefy quarterback. I threw the ball, it must have been a 40 yard spiral hitting Tom in the chest. He caught it and ran for the touchdown. Parson didn't touch me—as our rules required—but tackled me. I looked up and said, 'We won. You lose. Game's over. Have a nice day in the Lord.'

"Year's later, I talked to Tom about that game. He said, 'Ken, I remember you throwing a pass. I think it was about 30 yards, but I came back ten to catch it and then ran for the touchdown. And you didn't hit me in the chest, but on the top of my ankle.'"

Tom took an ankle-high pass and made a touchdown. He made sense out of an obscure Greek verb. He ran like the lightning. He played and worked through personal pain. He married a marvelous woman. He answered the call to the ministry. He comforted a hurting widow and a small child. He had many gifts and talents.

Sharon Hackett saw the Birds as a compassionate couple. "Tom and Sandy were a very friendly, caring couple. Tom had a lot of compassion for people. As I remember, he would not center the conversation on himself, but on others." Then in a statement that belied a perception shared by many that would confound them all, Sharon added, "He and Sandy were always a couple whom I felt had it all together and seeking God's will for their lives."

Dan remembers that Tom and Sandy often spent weekends house-sitting for "some of the wealthier folks of Springfield. Often they would take care of the family's children, too. Sandy was so good with kids and Tom was exceptional also—firm but gentle."

Of all the friends he made at seminary, Tom grew closest to Charles Smith. Smith and his wife Carolyn were reunited with the Birds in West Memphis following seminary. Emporia loomed on the horizon. Here Tom's gifts of caring and compassion were exploited in a deadly dance that took Sandy's life and shattered Tom's.

Pastoral calls

During his third year at Concordia, Tom and Sandy moved to

Albuquerque, New Mexico, for a year, where Tom did his vicarage. Sandy taught at the University of New Mexico and began to gain interest in computer math, a somewhat new and challenging field during the mid-1970s. Still concerned about staying in shape, Sandy rode a bicycle five miles to school while Tom jogged alongside, headed to his church. Both loved the outdoors.

In 1976, Tom graduated from Concordia with a Master's of Divinity Degree. Before Tom received his degree he completed a battery of tests and a certification interview, a process designed to ensure that the pastors Concordia graduated were stable, clear-minded, and psychologically strong. The tests helped churches looking for pastors to match their needs with the gifts, talents and accomplishments of a pastoral candidate. All seminary students took these tests.

During his four years at Concordia, Tom took the Minnesota Multiphasic Personality Inventory three times. Sandy took it once. After a thorough examination by officials in the school's counseling department, on the certification board and placement committees, the Birds passed with high marks. Tom graduated in the top ten percent of his class.

Tom and Sandy's future looked bright. They were delighted with his call to serve two mission churches in West Memphis and Forrest City, Arkansas, within 125 miles of the Birds, Grismers and Stringers.

Now 26, Tom and Sandy decided to start a family. Still, he encouraged her to continue teaching part time at Memphis State University and Eastern Arkansas Community College. The Birds had all three of their children in West Memphis: Andrea, in 1977; Paul, in 1979; Thomas Aaron (who became known as Aaron) in 1981. Tom served as Sandy's Lamaze partner during all three births.

Muriel Klingerman, a member of the West Memphis church, babysat for them. "Sandy was one of the most alive persons I've ever known. She was smart, brilliant, yet she was as down-to-earth and as humble as anyone you'd want to meet. If she was ever depressed or discouraged, she didn't show it."

Tom discovered quickly that the demands of the job were often overwhelming. Visitation, counseling, working with family problems— divorce, suicide, illness, death, juvenile delinquency, unwed teen mothers, spousal abuse—and even prison work all impinged on his time. He added the pursuit of a second master's degree in Sacred Theology at Concordia Theological Seminary, in Fort Wayne, Indiana. And he worked hard to be a devoted dad and husband.

Klingerman described Tom as very concerned about other people. "If someone had to go to the hospital, Tom was always there when they had surgery. He would be there the first thing that morning. He was the kindest person I've ever known. He always helped others," traits spotted by his professors and counselors at Concordia.

Next came an inquiry from Messiah Lutheran Church in Emporia, Kansas. Larry Kalsow, one of Tom's seminary classmates, pastored the church. Messiah enjoyed good membership growth and wanted to expand in the northwest corner of the city, following the city's growth pattern. At the invitation of Messiah's lay leadership, Tom and Sandy visited Emporia. Intrigued by the opportunity, they accepted the call to Messiah. Tom set one special requirement—that Sandy be allowed to pursue her math and teaching career.

Don Froelich, a professor at ESU, headed the search committee at Messiah, and served as a lay minister at Faith Lutheran. "Tom showed energy. He was the son of a pastor with a good reputation. He seemed very bright."

The Emporia Birds

Tom accepted the call as Mission Pastor at Messiah to work with the 65 members who started Faith. The Birds moved to Emporia in January of 1982. As she had done everywhere they had lived, Sandy landed a teaching position, this time at Emporia State University (ESU).

ESU had a great computer lab, but computer time was limited. It forced Sandy to adopt a rugged schedule around which she fit in family and faith. It forced her to go to the campus, two miles from home, at odd hours, often late at night. Sandy was designing a cutting-edge computer software program for church management, and computer time was hard to come by. Tom worked on her project with her, providing her with practical applications.

They made a great team. Sandy led the church high school youth, taught Sunday school, and participated in the church's Couples Club and Ladies Guild. Besides his duties at Faith, Tom developed a campus ministry at ESU, and taught credit courses at ESU for St. John's College in Winfield, Kansas: "History of the Life of Paul" and "Christian Ethics."

Faith knew that to grow, it needed an attractive program for the young professionals who were buying homes in the area. Many families had two working parents creating a shortage of preschool day care, so Faith started Lord's Lambs. Tom worked alongside Angie Duensing, a 20-year old recent ESU graduate, to build the program. During the fall of 1982, Lord's Lamb filled its roster with 40 children.

Tom and Sandy got involved in Emporia's active softball leagues, each playing on a team. They played co-ed volleyball together. Tom tried to continue running, but time and church duties limited him to once a week and perhaps 2-3 miles, a far cry from his college days at UA. He ran in a few charity events, but he explained, "That wasn't really running. I walked a good portion of those races. Believe me, there's no comparison with competitive racing at the collegiate level, though some of the others took it seriously."

As soon as their children were old enough, Tom resurrected the family and neighborhood whiffle-ball games, played every day at 4 p.m. in the front yard of their house on Henry Street. The house served like the stands at Royal's Stadium and the bushes along the sidewalk provided a back-stop. Pitches were thrown from the tree that grew in the middle of the front yard and first base was down near the curb. A long fly ball might make it to the street and anything hit there could be a homerun. A ball hit into the Moore's yard, though slowed by the grass, could go for extra bases. Just as when he played the game as a child, Tom reveled in leading these kids in the game of the day, though Virginia wasn't there to sing the national anthem.

Steven and Stephanie Moore lived in the house immediately to the north of the Birds. Stephanie spent a lot of time with the Birds. "Sandy was always bubbly, full of energy, she loved her children."

Gloria (Bird) Cates said the same thing. "Sandy was totally devoted to her children."

"Any time I needed something, Sandy was available," Moore added. "When we would leave on the weekends to visit my parents, she always took care of our animals [cats and dogs] and made sure the house was safe; kind of a watch guard. When we had our house fumigated for insects Sandy welcomed us into her house until the house was safe again. I always felt welcomed in their home."

Tom and Sandy gave a sense of security to the Moores. "I speak for my husband and kids too, because if they weren't here they were over at Tom and Sandy's. I always knew where they were. I didn't have to worry about them."

Though they often went in different directions, the Birds had a well-earned reputation as a close family. Moore said, "I always thought of them as a couple, not as Tom and not as Sandy. Tom liked to be with kids. When he was home, it seemed like he was always outside playing with the kids. He liked sports. He talked about sports a lot."

No one really knew what went on behind the Birds' closed doors, that is, unless the people living near them heard them fighting. "That was not the case with the Birds," Stephanie said. "I don't remember Tom getting angry around the neighborhood or with Sandy."

While widely thought of as likeable, popular, friendly, concerned and such, later on some labeled Tom as having charisma. Not according to

Moore: "I never saw anything like that with Tom. He drew me in with his sermons that he gave at church and made me feel welcome. And he had a characteristic that any pastor would have; a love for the people." Stephanie did not consider Tom necessarily a good-looking guy either. "He's balding like my husband, probably more than Steve. Not anyone that I would be interested in. But you're not looking at the physical." Moore was captivated by Tom and Sandy's consistent love of life.

Sealed lips

All pastors and priests face incredible pressures because they know private things about people. Tom had a tender heart, but controlled his outward expressions. Moore explained that, "Tom was not the type of person who would show his weaker side because he had a church to lead." His dad, Pastor Ralph Bird, was always strong. Tom had to be, too.

Tom took seriously the admonition in Luther's Confession about gossip, rumors, slander and keeping confidences. Luther's application is drawn from The Eighth Commandment, "Thou shalt not bear false witness against thy neighbor." This commandment formed the foundation of Tom's counseling ministry. If one of his church members thought for a moment that their deepest, darkest and dirtiest secrets were not safe with him, it would destroy his ministry. He went to great lengths to guard this trust.

For a pastor whose highest priorities included counseling troubled church members, who wanted to draw new members from his neighborhood, who desired a pure and solid reputation, keeping a confidence was essential. Tom committed a major portion of his ministry to keeping the Eighth Commandment.

If a wife came to him saying her husband had treated her badly, Tom wanted to counsel them both. If a church gossip passed slander on to him, he turned a cold ear. If townspeople accused one of his church women of being promiscuous or said she had something to do with murdering her husband and she denied it, he protected her.

Faith grew rapidly, more than doubling in its first nine months and doubling again nine months later.

Tom and Sandy Bird were, by all measures, a typical successful early 1980s American family. They were both highly motivated, driven professionals. They worked and played hard, but their love of softball mingled with Faith's childcare program became a volatile mix once Lorna Anderson began dropping her children at Lord's Lambs.

Lorna pitched more than a softball on Emporia's diamonds.

Mistress Lorna

In August of 1984, Betty Waystead sat with Deputy Bill Deppish to tell what she knew about Lorna Anderson. Waystead first talked to investigators on November 15, 1983, 11 days after Marty died. During that interview, she named seven Emporia-area men with whom she claimed Lorna had had a sexual relationship. Two of those men were Danny and Darrel Carter. At that time, she never heard of Tom Bird, a curious fact given her close friendship with Lorna.

Waystead, like Lorna, lived a wild adulterous lifestyle and the two often ran together. Waystead said Danny Carter slept with Lorna on a regular basis during the summer and fall of 1982—though Lorna had plenty of others as well. Betty said:

> "She and Lorna would smoke pot...Lorna was supplied by Danny Carter...Lorna had a key to Danny's house and on one occasion she and Lorna went to Danny's house when no one was home and Lorna used her key and went in and got a bag of marijuana out of the apartment."

When Deppish told Betty that investigators had located about 27 of Lorna's boyfriends by that time, Waystead asked, "Is that all?" No one could confirm the actual count of Lorna's sexual trysts and conquests, but numbers in the 50s and 60s were common. A cruel joke circulated around Emporia— if Lorna slept with as many men as people claimed, Lorna never would have slept. Bumper stickers broadcast, "Honk if you had sex with Lorna." Few honked, though, because some of the men she seduced held prominent positions in the community. Many men sweated out the possibility that their names would be publicly listed alongside hers. Emporians had a well-protected reputation of religious piety, but sexual swingers knew where to find action, and during those early 1980s, Lorna swung more than most.

Susan Ewert became another of Lorna's best friends during the first five years of the 1980s, but from church, not swingers' clubs. She and Loren Slater, Lorna's father, talked following Lorna's 1985 guilty plea. "After the plea, her dad said to me, 'Susan, what in the hell has been going on here?' He was talking about Lorna, and I said I truly don't know. I said I've heard some things, I've been told a little."

Sister Lorna

Alta Slater gave birth to Lorna Gail Slater on February 10, 1953. Lorna's brother Daryl came three years later.

Loren, a well-respected banker in Hutchinson, regularly went with his children to church. He determined to set within them a solid, Bible-based foundation. He and Alta gave them love, a strong home and material security. As a child Lorna attended the Evangelical United Brethren Church, later named United Methodist. The Slaters' strong belief in the value of faith and church meant an early bedtime on Saturday nights, even when Lorna was a teen, making sure she and her brother were well-rested for Sunday services.

With a nice home in an upper middle class neighborhood, the Slaters banned the twin "evils" of alcohol and tobacco from their home.

Lorna knew her father loved her deeply. He gave her the feminine form of his own name, as if naming a first-born son. The Slater's called Lorna by a different name after Daryl's birth; they called her "Sister." As Sister, Lorna learned to serve her younger brother's needs.

As Lorna grew older, the community knew her as "Loren Slater's daughter." A policeman refused to write her a speeding ticket because she was "Loren Slater's daughter." She got jobs because she was "Loren Slater's daughter." She had no personal identity. Her identity came from others, not from within. Her life centered on what she gave to others.

She developed an obsession to give her service, and her body, to others. She gave outside the bedroom as well, using her strong administrative gifts. These gifts won her acceptance by others. Her drive to be accepted, though, drove her to exaggerations and outright lies about her accomplishments. People saw her as an accomplished actress, but not in a theater, rather in personal relationships. She used her childish, over-awed teenager's voice to dramatize, her sultry syrupy voice to seduce, her whining and sulking voice to manipulate, and her exaggerated inflections and actions to sell her story. Scores of men succumbed to her act. Women mistrusted and despised her.

Lorna matured during the height of the sexual revolution fanned by Woodstock, Haite Ashbury, bra and draft card burning, drugs, hippies and Viet Nam war protests. Teens questioned authority. "If it feels good, do it," served as a moral guideline. Feminists wanted women to be liberated and enjoy sex just like men—and just as often.

Lorna claimed that her sexual activity began at about 16, but she had no serious regular boyfriend until her senior year. Then she fell in bed and in love with the son of a prominent Hutchinson doctor.

Upon graduation from high school, she headed to Washburn University in Topeka, while her boyfriend went to the University of Kansas. She did not do well academically. She spent too many days and nights in Lawrence with her boyfriend. Then something happened that caused her to quit school abruptly the following February and move home. The reason for her sudden retreat remained locked inside the walls of her family for years.

She eventually enrolled at Hutchinson Junior College in 1972, but never finished her education.

Lorna lied compulsively. It concealed her true nature from her parents and friends, and balanced her intense feelings of inferiority. It drove her to despair and to ecstasy—and eventually, to murder.

Married Lorna

At age 20, working part-time in a hospital, a college failure, Lorna determined to turn things around, to have a baby and build a family. She met Marty Anderson.

Maxine Anderson gave birth to Marty on December 8, 1948. She and Kenneth lived in Wellington, Kansas, where Marty grew into a big, out-going and gregarious man. His older—and only—brother Stephen became a music professor at the University of Kansas in Lawrence. Like Stephen, Marty loved bands and music, and did well in high school. He played sports, especially softball.

Marty was about five years older than Lorna and had already been once married and divorced. His first marriage lasted less than a year and according to his ex-wife ended amicably. She claimed they just were not right for each other. Some said Marty physically threatened his ex-wife, which she denied.

Marty's divorce devastated him. Though raised a Methodist, Marty found solace in the Assemblies of God, a charismatic church that gave him a chance to express himself emotionally.

Marty graduated from Southwestern College in Winfield, Kansas with a biology major. Following school, he moved to Hutchinson where he entered training as a laboratory technician. He met Lorna at the hospital in Hutchinson. He, like dozens of other men, easily fell for the 5' 6", 110-pound, chestnut-haired sensual woman. He saw her as smart enough, fun-loving, engaging and affectionate. Marty saw in Lorna a modern woman who enjoyed a drink and other, more stimulating activities. Marty proposed marriage and Lorna accepted.

The Slaters wanted Lorna to take time to get to know Marty better, but they saw him as a church-going young man with a bright future in the expanding medical field.

Four months after they met, Marty and Lorna were married in early June, 1973,.

Marty landed a job as a lab technician at the Hertzler Clinic near Hutchinson and a year later, they moved to Sterling, Kansas, where Marty worked until 1976. Here Lorna gave birth to their first daughter, Lori.

With a new baby on her hip, Lorna enjoyed the status of a stay-at-home mom. She saw her dream being fulfilled. The hospital, though, fell on hard times and closed down. Marty suddenly had no job.

Emporia Lorna

The happy marriage started to crumble when Marty took a job as Chief Technician at Newman Medical Center in Emporia. Their house in Sterling sat unsold during a time of high inflation and high home mortgage interest rates. They bought a home in Emporia, and overall living expenses were higher. Lorna abandoned her mommy-status for an unfulfilling job at Citizens National Bank. Her dream began to shatter.

She soon found a more satisfying and exciting job as an on-the-road sales representative. She worked alongside her boss, Willie Porter—actually, she spent a good amount of time underneath him. They took many sales trips together and ended their days locked in passionate liaisons. Lorna really liked Willie, and the two walked happily in plain sight, hand-in-hand while travelling together. She saw Willie as a ticket to a happier life and talked with him of marriage, but Willie chose to stay with his wife. Their adultery rekindled for a short time after Willie refused to divorce, but within several weeks, Lorna quit seeing him.

Willie's refusal to marry her triggered depression. Lorna made a feeble attempt at suicide. It landed her in a psychiatric ward in Emporia and, several months later, at another in Wichita. Lorna took a small amount of drugs, though she also admitted toying with a little gun she had in the house (in 1977). Marty found her and took her to the hospital. She detested and distrusted the care offered by her doctors and counselors and the drugs they prescribed and begged to leave the hospital.

Lorna exhibited classic symptoms of manic-depression, at one time fun loving and great to be around, and at other times, dark and angry, pushing people away. She came to blame it on Pre-Menstrual Syndrome.

Lorna left the sales position, and eventually quit having sex with Willie, but found numerous other men to fill the role.

Over the following years, Marty became more and more obsessed with the family's mounting financial problems. Lorna continued to work outside the home. Then in 1979, she gave birth to their second daughter, Julie, adding to the family's stress and financial burden.

In 1981, Lorna gave birth for the final time, to twin girls—Jennifer and Janelle. She believed Marty never wanted these two children because they added to his financial responsibilities. Marty said *she* was the one that was not happy having more children. Most who knew him saw Marty as a loving and devoted father to all four of his girls, but at the time the twins were born he could barely tolerate the financial stress. Lorna often turned to her parents for financial help. Lorna had her tubes tied to prevent further pregnancies, a decision forced on her by Marty and the doctor.

To save money, they moved to a smaller home for a time, before they bought a house on Meadowlark, in an upper-middle class neighborhood.

With four children and two adults, their finances continued to be a major irritation. They spent a lot of money on living expenses, but that was only one factor contributing to their financial dilemma. "They were always partying. Seemed like nearly every night they were out somewhere," said Reka Rosenboom, one of the Anderson's small army of babysitters.

Eventually, Marty exhibited symptoms of alcoholism and Lorna became addicted to sex.

Lorna faithfully attended Marty's many softball games. As a take-charge person, Lorna insisted on keeping score and usually sat among the men, ready to tease or be teased. The Andersons often hosted the softball team for beer after a game. At the ball-park, the men bragged that the game's MVP won Lorna for a night. The wives and girlfriends were not amused.

Danny's girl Lorna

The summer of 1982 was pivotal for the Andersons.

Lorna started a sexual liaison with her hairdresser, Danny Carter. At the same time, she seduced his very-willing brother Darrel. She met Darrel while he remodeled her home.

Danny claimed he stopped having sex with Lorna late that year. He said Lorna got too serious, talking of marriage; he wanted out. He had a stable of women and no interest in tying himself to the sexy and enigmatic woman.

Lorna belonged to Beta Sigma Phi Sorority, a haven for Emporia's swingers. There were several sorority chapters in town, and Lorna belonged to one that led to bed. "That's what the sorority was all about," remembered fellow-member Joyce Rosenboom (she belonged to a different chapter than Lorna). Lorna also belonged to a private club, The Continental, giving her many opportunities to pick up men for quick sex.

One of the men Lorna seduced at The Continental was a prominent Emporia attorney, David Guion. He knew the Andersons for a couple of years, and late in 1982 Lorna approached him for legal advice to divorce Marty. One summer evening in 1982, he sat drinking at The Continental and after several drinks, saw Lorna sitting at another table. He went over and sat down. Lorna asked him for a ride to her van she left parked downtown. On the way, Lorna performed oral sex on him. Following that night, while Marty was away, she invited him to visit her at home; he never went. He denied ever again having sex with her.

Betty Waystead said Lorna used the same ploy several times—parking downtown to get a ride from a man and then having sex with him. It was her modus operandi.

Roger Gable sold real estate in Emporia. While he showed Lorna a home, she seduced him. They had sex two or three times before Gable called it off in the fall of 1982.

Even the Anderson's insurance agent, Chris Kimble, got a visit from Lorna one night that summer.

> "Lorna came over to my apartment when I was single. She was interested in my roommate at the time who was living with me. The roommate and Lorna went back into the bedroom together and they closed the door.

> "Sometime later my roommate came back out with Lorna and she left. He later told me that they went into the bedroom and just played around, however, they did not have intercourse.

> "Lorna told my roommate that she was supposed to meet another man that night at her house, because Marty was going to be gone."

It was probably Danny Carter. He often stayed overnight when Marty went to Reserves and at other times, Lorna would rendezvous with him at his apartment. Marty found Danny one afternoon at the Anderson's sitting fully clothed on the closed toilet, watching nude Lorna bathe.

There were other sexual contacts between the insurance agent and Lorna.

> "That same summer, when I was still single, I was fixed up with a blind date. We, along with several other couples, went out to eat at Williamsburg and then drove on to Melvern Lake.

> "We all switched partners around after getting there. Lorna went off with another man that night and was gone for about 30 to 45 minutes."

The agent failed to mention that all the couples were naked.

Bob Waystead partied with the group that night.

> "In July of 1982, we all went out to eat. We had barbecued ribs at a restaurant, and since it was a nice, warm, summer night, we decided to go to Williamsburg at Lake Melvern. When we got there, we decided to go swimming and since we did not have swimming suits with us, we went skinny dipping.

> "Lorna kept trying to get everyone to pair off, that is, get everyone to switch dates or marital partners, but no one did. We did go swimming, and while in the lake, Lorna came up to me and rubbed her

breasts on me, and tried to encourage me to make a move toward her, but I did not."

On yet another occasion, the insurance agent said:

"I went to Lawrence, Kansas to get training to be the president of the Optimist Club in Emporia. I stayed at the Holiday Inn and met another couple and the Andersons.

"Martin and Lorna were arguing a lot, and Martin got drunk and was staying in another room. While he was in the room, the other man with me went in to the bathroom and was taking a shower. Lorna walked right into the bathroom there with him, and the other wife did not seem to care. In fact, while they were in the bathroom, the other wife came over and tired to hit on me, but I wasn't interested."

Betty Waystead and her husband Bob were the other couple. Betty met Lorna during that 1982 summer and they were constant companions for eight or nine months. Betty's marriage soured, "It was nice to have a good friend to have a shoulder to cry on," she said. They did more than cry together.

Bob, the man in the shower in Lawrence, had sex with Lorna at least twice while he and Betty were still married, Betty claimed.

"We were together with the Andersons partying at the Gable's, and ran out of booze. Bob and Lorna went to the Anderson's to get some more liquor. While they were there, Bob said he and Lorna had sex twice within a half hour on Lorna's kitchen table."

Later on, Bob denied it. He told Betty that to get her mad. But he spoke about a card game the Waysteads and Andersons played at Lorna's house earlier that summer, the first time they met, in June of 1982:

"The first time we went out with the Andersons, we went to the Anderson residence. We ate there, played cards, and were doing quite a bit of drinking. This was approximately in June of 1982. Lorna was my partner, and sitting opposite the table from me, and Betty was the partner of Martin Anderson in the card game.

"While sitting there at the table, I felt a foot running up and down the inside of my leg, and up into the area of my crotch, massaging me. This took me by surprise as my wife was sitting there at the table at the time. No one else seemed to notice what had gone on. I had to change positions and cross my legs to get her to stop.

"She [Lorna] kept coming on rather strong during the evening, and I had to be rude to her, but it did not do any good. I finally had to be damned rude to her before she would quit."

Betty covered "for her [Lorna] at least once a week" for several weeks, while Lorna met men for sex. Sometimes Lorna reported the sordid details of her sexual escapades. "Lorna is a very insecure person and has told me a lot of things, part of this is to cover up her insecurity."

Betty said that Lorna often called her from The Continental and told her to come over. When Betty arrived, "Lorna would have a date with her and have another man waiting for me." She personally knew many of Lorna's lovers.

One of Marty's best friends in high school visited Marty and Lorna at their home in May of 1978. The Andersons invited him to a "progressive Margarita" party and then insisted he stay overnight. The single man told the story of that evening.

> "Marty shortly went to bed and Lorna and I stayed up. Lorna made some very sexual suggestions to me and made it clear that she wanted to have sex. I refused, telling her that Marty was my good friend and, besides, he was right there in the house. Lorna insisted that we have sex right there in the house.

> "While we were talking, Lorna admitted to having an affair in 1978 with another man but it ended when Marty found out and got mad. Lorna was real unhappy with me for refusing her advances, and I often have been afraid she might use this against me when I got married."

Licentious Lorna

Donald Stein took his wife, Norma, to the Optimist Club dance at the Holiday Inn in Emporia in November of 1981. Stein led a sales division for Abbot Laboratories. He sold to Marty Anderson and Newman Medical Center.

Stein danced with Lorna that night. She asked if he knew Willie Porter. Stein did know him as they both had interviewed for the same job at Abbott. Lorna told Stein about her adultery with Willie while they both worked for C&I Products. She said, "You know, I almost left my husband for that man."

"Well, why didn't you?"

"Willie was exciting and made more money but Marty was a good husband and father to the kids, and was real reliable and steady. I don't think I want to give that up." She never told him that Porter was a married man, nor that Porter decided against marrying her.

Stein had another encounter with Lorna about two months later.

> "I had some tickets to the Royal's baseball game and invited the

Andersons to go with me and Fred Walters. Fred was a Service Engineer for Abbot. Norma, my wife, did not go along.

"When we arrived there, we sat down and Lorna sat down next to Fred. She then started rubbing her breasts against him, and told both Fred and me to come by and see her sometime, and said she wanted to have sex with us. She also volunteered that she would give both of us oral sex.

"She then invited Fred to come to Emporia that night and to spend the night with her. I saw Lorna rubbing Fred's legs, massaging them with her hands.

"Marty was only about six seats away at the time. This went on for approximately 1 hour.

"I'd guess Lorna drank, approximately four beers up to that point in time."

The men from Abbot claimed they never took her up on the offer.
Tim Barlow, a fire fighter in Lawrence, met Lorna in August of 1982.

"Betty showed up at the fire station and introduced me to Lorna...they had come to Lawrence with their husbands for a convention at the Lawrence Holidome and she and Lorna were out shopping and messing around.

"Lorna immediately came on to me in a big way. She made comments about how she wanted me, used four letter words and such. When I turned her down, she asked if I would fix her up with some of the other guys at the station."

Nothing happened then, but Lorna tried again in September. Barlow planned to run in a race in Kansas City, and Lorna wanted to meet him there. "Lorna kept talking about how great it could be, how good she thought I was." Barlow never ran the race, yet he called her a few times and on one of those occasions, Lorna mentioned American Heart Association fund raising. "I gave her the name of a friend of mine, Pete Feely, who was in the T-shirt business in Kansas City." Barlow told investigators, "All Lorna wanted to talk about was sex. I never had any sex with Lorna."

Lorna followed up on the lead, calling Pete Feely and setting an appointment over the phone. Feely described their meeting:

"We met in the park between the swimming pool and the train by Number One fire station in Lawrence. She was driving a van.

"I had talked to her on the phone once or twice prior to our meeting. I believe she called me at my shop. I arranged to meet her.

"I got in the van, we talked, left and drove to Clinton Lake by the dam, then drove down below the dam on the east side in a park. She gave me oral sex, we drove back to town, stopped by Number One fire station, and we talked to Tim Barlow for a few minutes."

Lorna drove him back to his car and the two parted. They never met again. She told him she was separated and planned on getting a divorce (a lie). "I was to meet her originally over some fund raising thing she was involved in. However, it was never mentioned at the meeting. I knew we weren't going to talk about T-shirts. Tim had indicated she was looking for some action and she had pretty well given me that impression on the phone."

Lorna turned men on. She never met a man she could not manipulate, with one notable exception—the man who became her pastor.

Church-lady Lorna

Marty belonged to many organizations, and became very active in the Emporia Optimist Club. He met Pastor Larry Kalsow of Messiah Lutheran Church there. He played basketball and, of course, softball with many of the men. The men liked Marty and he enjoyed being with them.

Most of Marty and Lorna's friends believed he knew about her adultery, but for the sake of the children, stayed with the marriage. Some friends claimed that for a time, Marty lived in the basement and tried to avoid much contact with Lorna. Lorna claimed *she* lived in the basement to avoid Marty, whom she claimed beat her several times.

Marty found additional peace, solace and money in the Army Reserves, and arranged to serve at nearby Fort Riley, up near Junction City, or in Topeka. It gave him a couple days away from Lorna and the financial pressures each month, plus an annual two-week reserve camp. Lorna took advantage of Marty's time out of town by increasing the tempo of her licentious dating. Her lovers knew whenever Marty was gone.

Most Emporia men who knew him outside of work found Marty as a fun-loving, though competitive man, especially on a softball field. David Workman, who worked for Marty at Newman, saw him as intense and difficult, their early working relationship shattered by the financial tensions of the early 1980s. Newman suffered financially. The hospital ordered Marty to cut all pay rates in his department by ten percent. He could not afford a pay cut, and it fell to him to tell his employees they would earn less for the same amount of work. Marty became more tense in the days leading up to his murder.

Several of his friends and co-workers said that Marty constantly looked for ways to make money outside of work. He inspected several home-based businesses. Lorna claimed he sold drugs, never proven by investigators nor believed by those who knew him best.

Marty told Workman as early as 1981 he considered divorcing Lorna, but felt he would lose custody of the girls. Marty did not want the girls left in her care. There were financial considerations in divorce as well; Marty could barely afford to maintain one household—two were out of the question.

Lorna told others that she wanted Marty out of her life, but not by divorce. She talked about murder. Darrel and Danny Carter both said that in the summer of 1982, Lorna talked to them about murdering Marty. She told them she needed Marty's income to live on, ruling out divorce. Marty believed strongly in life insurance, and carried a generous amount on himself—it gave her some possibilities.

They attempted marriage counseling a few times, but it failed.

The Andersons certainly did not need the complications of a church split to add tension to their marriage. During the early 1980s, they got embroiled in a messy and divisive issue at Emporia's First Presbyterian Church.

The church battle drew them closer to Jim and Susan Ewert who, like them, stood on one side of the issue. They spent a lot of time together, though there was no hint of sexual tension. With children of similar age, Susan and Lorna had much in common, and Susan, who was trained in psychology and counseling, felt needed by her deeply troubled friend.

One evening in June of 1982, Pastor Larry Kalsow introduced Lorna and Marty to Tom Bird, the new mission pastor now serving at Faith. The Andersons learned that Faith offered a preschool, and Lorna headed on over for a look. Liking what she saw, she enrolled her children and told Susan about it. Susan enrolled her children. The Bird children also attended Lord's Lambs.

By the fall of 1982, the Andersons grew comfortable with Faith. Seeking some relief from the turmoil at First Presbyterian and attracted by the ministry of Tom and Sandy Bird, the Andersons began attending and switched churches.

In December of 1982, Marty and Lorna completed Lutheran teachings taught by Pastor Tom, and joined Faith. Lorna became a regular at church; Marty less so.

That fall, Lorna landed a fund-raising job with the American Heart Association. Her organizational skills made her a good fit for the job, according to Jan Mead, her supervisor. Lorna wanted more from life though. She had her sites on the young pastor at her new church.

One Sunday, Faith advertised in its bulletin that it needed a part-time church secretary. The hours fit well with her American Heart Association job, so Lorna asked Pastor Tom about the position. He told her to apply. There were two others. Tom knew it was up to the lay ministers to hire the new secretary, and only advised them that one of the women preferred afternoon hours, leaving her free to take morning classes at ESU—he thought that would not work. Otherwise, he had no preference.

The lay ministers hired Lorna in January of 1983, starting her with 15 hours a week. Don Froelich, one of the lay ministers, said, "It was a very informal process. We all [the three lay ministers who hired Lorna] just thought that she was a nice lady. We knew nothing about her Jeykl and Hyde personality."

Froelich said there were rumors about Lorna, "but my impression was that Lorna was conjuring up the image... Because there were always rumors. So I would tell these folks to check out the facts." Just as did his pastor, Tom Bird, Froelich lived by the Eighth Commandment and The Lutheran Confessions. Rumors meant nothing without facts. And the church had a redemptive role to play in bringing reconciliation to Lorna and her troubled life and family.

Froelich remembered a little about Lorna's family troubles. "One time she came to church with a patch on her eye and I learned that Marty was roughing her up."

Now a church secretary, Lorna continued her sexual stalking. Alvin Tefft, the Laboratory Manager at Memorial Hospital in Topeka, served alongside Marty in the Reserves. He and Marty were ordered to a meeting in Kansas City in early January, 1983. A Kansas Bureau of Investigation report records how Tefft described what happened:

> "Tefft remembers that Marty Anderson and he were in the same motel room at the motel. Lorna Anderson called the motel and was talking to him when Marty walked into the room. He talked to Lorna Anderson some more and then gave the phone to Marty. Marty then said, 'she wanted to talk to you' and gave the phone back to him.
>
> "Lorna Anderson is the individual who reserved the room there for them. Lorna wanted to know if it was all right with him if she drove up to K.C. to see him that night. He said the reason she wanted to come up and see him was for sexual purposes. He told her that it was a 1-1/2 to 2 hour drive to Kansas City and he and Marty had things to do."

Tefft and Lorna talked and visited often, but none of these contacts resulted in sex. One call, though, stuck with him. During sometime in the early summer of 1983, Lorna called and asked him about whether or not a certain drug, if injected in someone's veins, would show up on an emergency room report. He wondered what prompted her to ask such a thing? Did it have anything to do with the death of Sandra Stringer Bird on July 17, 1983?

Once in a century Lorna

David Hacker, a Pulitzer prize-winning journalist contracted with Lorna in the fall of 1985, to write a book about her early years. She eventually broke the contract. Hacker told her the highest ranking person in the State of Kansas cleared his book project. And as interesting Tom's story became, Lorna's story held the most intrigue. Hacker said a woman like Lorna only comes along once in a century.

SECTION III:

"Appearances to the mind are of four kinds.
Things either are what they appear to be;
Or they neither are nor appear to be;
Or they are and do not appear to be;
Or they are not and yet appear to be.
Rightly to aim in all these cases
Is the wise man's task."

Epectitus, c. 50-120, Discourse, book 1, chapter 2

The work week at Faith

Many churches suffer a slowdown in activities following the Christmas and New Year's celebrations. Faith Lutheran, in January of 1983, got busier. Pastor Tom Bird's workload increased dramatically and regularly during his time at Faith, and January gave him no rest.

Tom tried to set aside 20 hours for preparation of his weekly sermon. He prepared for and taught two adult Bible studies, one on Sunday following the morning service, and one mid-week.

He selected hymns and when someone wanted something in the bulletin, they called Tom. He led weekly staff meeting with Angie Duensing and Lorna Anderson.

Each month he wrote an article for his church's newsletter. The church sent the newsletter to almost 800 homes that first quarter of 1983—Tom helped prepare the mailing as well.

Each day he spent time in personal devotions, and studying Greek and Hebrew.

From September to May, he taught a confirmation class. And since Faith didn't have a youth pastor, Tom and Sandy led youth activities.

Because Faith grew so rapidly, Tom almost always taught an Adult Inquiry Class, initiating new believers into the Lutheran faith.

He attended regular lay minister and church council meetings. There were committee meetings, and voters meetings where all of the church's members gathered to consider church business.

Tom counseled individuals, visited sick and shut-ins and administered private communion. He regularly did informal counseling and had simple chitchat with folks who just dropped by—for 5, 10 or 30 minutes, eating into his well-planned day. Some days he never got any of his regular work done.

He taught classes at Emporia State University, and led and planned LC-MS district events. He and Sandy taught five family life seminars around Kansas during the months leading up to her death.

He presided and preached at funerals, weddings and baptisms.

In his spare time, he attended seminars and studied to become a better pastor, husband and father. And he played daily whiffle-ball games with the neighborhood kids.

Growth required help

Church membership at Faith doubled in Tom's first nine months and within 12 months, it had doubled again. They liked what they saw in Lorna Anderson, a very good organizer, personable and friendly, though somewhat scatter-brained and hired her. Lorna took charge of everything she did, sometimes irritating those who preferred to have input into how things should be done. "I just avoided her. She wanted to run everything and I just didn't want to have anything to do with her," Joyce Rosenboom, said.

Having more hands to do more work, Tom concentrated on headier tasks, but that did not diminish his workload. He tried hard to relieve the plethora of personal crises experienced by his parishioners. Tom believed that a good pastor is available 24-hours a day, seven days a week. He opened his door to anyone who had a need, and regularly interrupted his planned activities, even those with his family.

He quickly learned that people of faith are just as prone to depression, conflict, emotional disturbance, illness, tragedy, marital and family discord, job insecurity and teenage dilemmas as are any other people. Churched people first take their woes to a pastor, not to a practitioner, being somewhat distrustful of psychologists and professional social workers. Though Tom took counseling courses as part of his seminary training, he did not see himself as a professional counselor; just the first line of first defense by making himself available this way, he could head off rumor, gossip, marital discord, financial crisis and any number of human difficulties.

The members at Faith saw Tom as likeable, a man who cared greatly about people, a man full of compassion who gave freely of himself. They saw him touch a shoulder, or give comfort with a hug or a Christian kiss on the cheek. He had "a gift of caring."

Tom, though, had a serious, dangerous hidden fault common to pastors. His devotion to the church too often took him away from his family and his wife Sandy. "I took my wife for granted and sacrificed too quickly our quality time for the sake of the needs of members of the church," Tom wrote many years later. "Calls at dinner, late night hospital visitations, or crisis counseling by phone, or lengthy emotionally draining counseling, seemed to me to take precedence over family too often."

As Tom saw it, if it was right and necessary for the ministry, "I assumed it was okay with Sandy." He took her for-granted, a common trait among men and women striving for successful careers.

Those who saw Sandy and Tom together never questioned his admiration of her.

Sandy spent a lot of time away from Tom as well, either teaching or at the ESU computer lab. They had little time for affection and conversation, because so much of their spare time centered on church or school duties. "When we did have time together as a family the focus was not on each other but because we had three preschoolers, we were devoted to their care and nurture," Tom wrote.

To everyone who knew them both, they looked like a perfect pastoral couple, at least until the spring of 1983 when Sandy showed visible signs of stress. Sandy saw Lorna as the source of her irritation.

Pastor Charles Smith, a close friend of Tom's, claimed Sandy called him three or four times beginning as early as January of 1983. She wanted advice on how to deal with the new church secretary. She saw Lorna as many women saw her; manipulative and sensual, a threat to her husband. Sandy asked Charlie why Tom dealt with Lorna as he did—Sandy trusted Tom. Charlie knew Tom better than anyone; did he have an answer? He saw Sandy as highly intelligent and he had trouble helping her understand Tom's pastoral position to a church secretary, even one so threatening as Lorna. Charlie worried about Sandy's inability to cope.

Virginia Bird saw some of the same difficulties in Sandy. Virginia had worked alongside her husband Ralph in his ministry and did not work outside the home. She loved Sandy and fully supported her lifestyle choice, but she saw that Sandy did not quite understand the role of a pastor's wife, and the sacrifice of time and intimacy it often demands.

Sandy's career placed stress on her. She taught six hours a week at Emporia State University and worked toward a second Master's Degree in Computer Math. She immersed herself in church activities, and worked hard at being a good mother and wife. Tom said, "If Sandy had a fault, it was her trying to do too much—a 'superwoman' attitude being a wife, mother with a career and a student as well."

Tom and Sandy drove themselves hard. They were both determined people, yet very human.

The stress and strain of dealing with human problems at church, along with physical fatigue, often left Tom depressed. He saw his depression as unrelated to Sandy or any perceived failure on her part. "She would take responsibility for my depression, which was not right." He knew his problems were his own, and only he could solve them. Sandy, nonetheless, felt obligated to help Tom deal with discouragement and depression and when unsuccessful, took it personally, thus compounding her frustrations.

Just as did his dad, Pastor Ralph Bird, Tom came home from a long, hard and emotionally-draining day to three small children who were full of life and energy. Most often he came home to a babysitter, not his wife. Sandy came home from a draining day at school, from a faculty meeting, or a church function, and wanted his attention and affection.

Tom summarized this:

> "It was in this atmosphere which I would call the 'stress of success,' where two people going a 100 miles an hour each, through a successful, mutually supportive career, and child-rearing that

occasional tension and depression set in.

"Sometimes our confidence was shaken. Sometimes guilt from not 'doing enough' set in. At times, depression of feeling inadequate to carry the burdens of others took hold of us.

"We lived in the classic glass house of public figures, where it is rare to be able to show true feelings. The more work we did, the more there seemed needed to be done."

In his younger years, Tom ran to relax, but given his busy schedule, running and relaxing took a back seat. In high school and at the University of Arkansas, he ran long and hard nearly every day. By 1983, he ran about once a week, a run of two to three miles. He still played softball, basketball with the Optimists and he and Sandy played co-ed volleyball, but not to the level he used to enjoy. Sometimes he ran while practicing his sermon, accomplishing two goods at the same time.

With Lorna there to help, Tom hoped he would find relief to free him up to do more of what really needed to be done. Lorna worked with enthusiasm. Marty complained that the money she made went to day care and babysitters, but he went along with it. (Months later he told the lay ministers that he was glad she worked at Faith. It made her happy, and when she was happy, his life was better.)

Lorna and Tom made a good team. Their work required them to spend a lot of time together, not unusual for any manager and his secretary. Her office sat directly across a narrow hallway from his, although their doors were offset so they could not see into each other's offices without actually getting up, walking out in the hall and down to the door.

The west wall of Tom's office at one time had been the outside wall of the building. It had a huge picture window that now opened onto a lobby. The church installed louvers on the window so he could close them for privacy.

The east wall of Lorna's office also had a window, only it had no glass in it. Rather, it allowed for materials to be handed through to someone standing on the other side in another lobby-like area of the building. A person looking into that office would have to lean over a bit, but even standing several feet away would have a clear view of anyone in the office. Lorna could never be sure of total privacy in her office. Even phone calls could easily be overheard.

Down the narrow hall on the same side as Tom's office sat the mimeograph room and storage office across from which sat the men's and women's bathrooms, both one-stoolers.

At the south end of that hallway, the door opened into the fellowship hall, where most of the church's family activities took place, or where Tom taught adult Bible studies. It has a small kitchen and the room opens both to the outside and to the Lord's Lambs preschool on its east side. It also opens into the lobby that led past Tom's office.

Faith's worship center is small, decorated simply, and comfortably seats 200 people. The building is compact, cozy and provides a very warm atmosphere. The church's members, likewise, are warm and close. Stephanie Moore remembered, "One thing that drew me to the church and helped me make my decision to join was that it was a such a family feeling; a genuine concern about everyone that was a member."

Joyce Rosenboom said, "It was a hugging church. Everyone hugged everyone. Pastor was a hugger."

Lorna, like others at Faith, hugged Pastor Tom, too. Only a few at Faith knew that her church hugs masked an enormous, unsatisfied sexual desire that always simmered below the surface of her promiscuous heart. While Tom's training and personal convictions allowed him to professionally ignore her sexual passion, he embraced her myriad personal and family problems, seeing himself as the person who could bring her to Christian teachings, helping her find order in her life.

Within weeks of Lorna's hiring, her frequent phone calls and conversations about church business became mixed with an increasing number of marital counseling sessions. These wore on Sandy. Tom ministered to hurting people and he "needed to be needed." Tom perceived that Sandy was doing so well she needed very little of his emotional support; Lorna was a different case. She had needs that grew in intensity and demanded more of his time.

During the months that followed, Sandy talked with close friends—hers and Tom's—about Lorna. She saw Lorna as a home-wrecker, determined to steal Tom's affection. She saw Lorna giving inordinate attention to the Bird children, especially Aaron, and she wanted it curtailed.

Tom only saw Lorna as a hurting person and a good secretary. He had no idea that she would eventually take everything he had: his wife, family, ministry and freedom.

Life-changing event

In things involving doctrine and church tradition, Pastor Tom Bird viewed himself as staunchly orthodox. He relied on an historical and grammatical interpretation of the Bible, and The Lutheran Confessions for guidance. He followed what he learned observing his father, Rev. Ralph Bird who, by 1983, had already logged 36 years as a Lutheran Church Missouri Synod pastor. Tom lived his life by faith, not by sight.

Tom saw cultural and political issues through a conservative prism. Sandy, following their marriage and her joining of the Lutheran church, also adopted a conservative religious and political outlook. In one significant way, though, the two deviated from the accepted norm among their LC-MS peers. Sandy worked outside the home as a college instructor, and she pursued a second Master's Degree to improve her professional standing. Tom fully supported her in this.

One issue in particular caught Tom's eye in 1983. Saturday, January 22, 1983, was the tenth anniversary of the Roe vs. Wade decision of the United States Supreme Court, legalizing abortion. Since that decision, abortion had become a political nightmare, and opened deep schisms between "liberals" and "conservatives." So powerful and pervasive a political issue had it become, it fomented a massive electoral shift in American politics. A strong national pro-life movement kept the hot issue foremost on legislator's agendas, and more militant pro-life groups regularly demonstrated at abortion clinics. Violence against abortion providers simmered and occasionally exploded in a deadly display of rage.

Amidst the tension created by the abortion debate, Tom lead a Bible study about abortion. It was Sunday, January 23, 1983. His words burned through the heart of at least one of his members that day.

Lorna came to work looking extremely glum the next day. She spoke quietly to callers and those at the church, limiting her conversations to "yes, no or okay." She spoke sadly, with a wispy, whiney voice, face downcast, teary-eyed and avoided eye contact.

"What's wrong?" Tom asked.

"Nothing," she answered sadly.

"Something *is* wrong Lorna."

"I can't talk about it."

"Why not?"

"It's your fault."

That startled Tom. "My fault. Now you have to tell me what's wrong."

"Well, it's not really your fault. It's me."

Tom looked at his full calendar and said, "Look, let's finish up what you need to do today, and then if you can, get the kids situated and come back and talk to me this afternoon. Alright?"

"Maybe."

"Maybe *if* you can get the babysitter to stay or maybe if you *feel* like it?"

"Okay."

After work, Lorna took Julie home from preschool, fixed lunch for her children and asked the babysitter to stay for a few more hours. She came back to Faith to talk with Tom.

As Lorna came into his office, Tom saw her distress in her face and body movements. Tom asked her to sit in the chair across from his desk. She hung her head, refusing to look at him. "Lorna, I want to help you, so you have to look at me," he insisted.

Lorna raised her head. The look on her face shouted for pity, tears formed in her eyes and her lips quivered. "You can't tell my parents! They can never know. Please, promise me you'll never tell my parents."

If she had known Tom better, she would have known he always kept confidant what others told him in private. "I promise. I will not tell your parents nor anybody else."

She looked up at him. "I'm a murderer." Her voice trailed off as she spoke and she buried her face in her hands, and began crying hysterically. Through her fingers she sobbed and whined, gasping for air between words.

"You said it. I'm no good. I shouldn't be working here. I killed my baby. It didn't hit me until you said it in class, in Bible study, in your sermon. You said abortion is a sin, murder. I had an abortion. You won't even want me here now. You won't understand. How can I keep on going?"

Tom never expected this and feebly tried to calm her. "Lorna, Lorna, settle down. I *did* say that about abortion and I believe it. It doesn't mean that I won't listen to you or that I won't understand or that I'll kick you out."

Tom understood the power of confession and repentance, and he prepared to express this to her.

"But I'm a murderer," she continued. "That's it. Everything was going so good here. And now, I can't go on."

Tom spoke with intimate intensity to gain control of the conversation and turn it to a positive. "Please, listen, please. Abortion *is* wrong, but look, there's a difference between saying what is okay and understanding what you did. I'm your pastor. I want to understand what happened. You see, I need to understand what happened. Please tell me about it."

"I can tell you about it. It was an awfully long time ago," she said, stuttering and on the verge of hyperventilating. She saw that Tom offered support, not condemnation.

"Please tell me about it. If what I said has touched a nerve inside you like this then it must be something that needs to get out. So take a deep breath and tell me about it," he said directly, calmly and firmly, his eyes focussed on hers.

"Okay." She regaled him with a mostly uninterrupted story of her sad experience, punctuated by sobs and gasps for air.

"I was going to Washburn and my boyfriend, his name was Tom, too. He was at Lawrence. I was so in love with him. I had to see him.

"I'd miss classes. I wouldn't study. I was out of control. Guess it was crazy. He's the reason I flunked out—partly anyway," her childish voice running the gamut of pitch from high to low, like a teenager making excuses for coming in late.

"I was really just a kid. I hadn't been away from home much. Then one day I went to the clinic and found out I was pregnant. I couldn't believe it. I mean it wasn't so bad. But my parents would die if they knew.

"I was gong to have the baby. We could have gotten married. But Tom dumped me. He would never call back, he wouldn't see me anymore. I was left all by myself.

"The people at the clinic said they would take care of me and they did.

"I dropped out of school. God has been punishing me ever since. Marty wanted a boy. He's angry at me because I had girls. He really didn't take it very well this last time when I had the twin girls.

She felt the end of her sad story approaching. Then Tom would talk, so she started tearing up, falling into her whining, syrupy voice again, the manipulative technique she used to gain sympathy. "I thought God put me working here, but now I can't keep going. You can't let a murderer be your church secretary. I just wish it never happened. Please don't hate me."

"I don't hate you." Tom stood, and moved slowly around his desk. He pushed aside a pile of files and sat on the edge of the desk facing her. He began talking compassionately. "I think your worst fears are over. You've gotten something deep inside you out. I do understand.

"You were young. You were foolish. When you do something wrong, it's natural to want to make it disappear—to cover it up. I know you were hurt and lonely when your boyfriend deserted you.

"You realize now, I think, that you didn't get the advice you should have. Even though you were broken-hearted, ashamed, scared, having an abortion was still a selfish act that involved deception of your parents and irresponsibility. Having a baby would have been difficult, I guess beyond just difficult, it would be change in your whole life. But I have faith that when God gives life, God will provide.

"But now I want you to know that in Christ's love your sins are forgiven—really forgiven. [With these words, the pastor had granted her absolution from her just-confessed sin.]

"The worst thing you could do now is live like God is punishing you. You cannot go around thinking you are no good and don't deserve any blessings.

"You shouldn't leave your job. Instead you can work at it with more joy because you know God's love so much more and you are in a position to share his love with others. Do you think you can do that?"

"I think so," she answered, but not with great confidence.

"As far as God punishing you by not letting you have boys—you need to view God as blessing you with girls. You can be a better mother if you live not like God has punished you, but blessed you to be responsible for four girls. It is only fair to the girls."

Warming slightly, but then turning sour again, she responded, "They *are* precious little girls, but I'm not a very good mother, not like Sandy or the other mothers at preschool meetings."

"You can be the best mother you can be, not by comparing yourself with others. Maybe you can learn from others, not belittling the gifts and talents that you *do* have."

"I want to try," choking out a little more positive response.

Tom knew that for Lorna to totally overcome this trauma, she eventually needed to tell her parents.

"And as far as your parents, there may come a time when you want to tell them—you don't have to but you may want to. They will be hurt, but it won't kill them. But that's up to you."

Lorna responded with one of her most effective manipulative cliches. "You don't hate me?"

"No."

"You still want me to work here?"

"More than ever," he said firmly.

"You sure are good to me. I want you to be happy with me." Lorna got up and faced Tom who was still sitting on the desk.

Tom slipped off the desk and hugged her, saying, "I am, but you better go on home now."

Lorna lingered. "You need anything else done? I want to help."

"No, no. Go on home to your kids." Tom shushed her out of his office, giving no thought to the idea that she might have had a different kind of "help" in mind.

Lorna adapted her stories to whomever listened, based on the purpose for telling the story. This day, she needed forgiveness for deep-seated guilt. Later, she told this same story to an interviewer, only she claimed her dad fully supported the decision.

So, months before the United States Supreme Court issued its Roe vs. Wade decision, Lorna aborted her first baby. She had lived with the guilt and sorrow ever since. It had a profound impact on her life.

During each pregnancy following her abortion, Lorna wanted the new baby to fill the void it left in her spirit. No new child, however, could ever fill that void, she learned. And following the birth of the twins, the doctor tied her tubes. Lorna never would birth a son. If she wanted a son, she would have to adopt him, or take him from another mother.

Church members saw Lorna as very good with children. They noticed that she spent a lot of time with Tom and Sandy's daughter and two sons. The Bird's younger son, Aaron, was actually named *Thomas* Aaron Bird. The pastor to whom Lorna now poured out her heart, and who helped her bring order to her life was also named Tom. The father of her aborted son was named Tom. Was this a mere coincidence, or was it a harbinger of something far deeper, sinister and deadly disturbing in her troubled life?

Did Lorna's extreme promiscuity and lack of sexual fulfillment flow from her abortion that proved to be such a seminal event in her life, or was it her PMS, or both? Would her confession to Pastor Bird begin the healing that seemed to elude her?

Did the abortion of a son conceived by a man named Tom create a new fantasy she began to build around this *new* Tom in her life? Lorna confessed to often living in a fantasy world, a world that seemed at times very real to her. Were her years of sorrow and a lifetime of fantasy about to be mixed together in a volatile stew that would spew death into the industrious city of Emporia?

The busy, happy Bird family had a girl and *two* boys, a strong, well-educated and popular wife, and a steady and sober husband who knew where he was going and what he needed to do to get there. Was this the kind of family Lorna always wanted ... and began to scheme to get?

The beleaguered secretary

Lorna Anderson did a good job as secretary and assistant to Tom. With her daughter Julie nestled in at Lord's Lambs every morning, and work hours from 9 a.m. to Noon, she settled nicely into the routine. She made it a point to know everything Tom did, and where he would be at all times. She liked being in control.

Lorna spent time with her children in the afternoons, unless she dated someone or fulfilled her remaining obligations to the American Heart Association, a part-time job she took prior to starting at Faith. She never told her boss Jan Mead about her new job. (Mead learned of it quite by accident later on.) She thought she could do both, as the AHA job wound down to 10 hours a week or so.

At first Mead saw Lorna's secretary job as an unwelcome nuisance. Yet, she read the work reports and they showed that Lorna did her job. To make sure Lorna stayed on target, Mead met regularly with her, meetings that often included lunch and a few drinks.

Lorna tantalized Mead, a single 24-year old woman, with tales of her sexual conquests—and she complained about Marty. Mead heard Lorna go into detail about whom she slept with and what they did. She knew only what Lorna told her. She did not know how to distinguish between Lorna's reality and her fantasy.

David Workman *did* know Lorna very well, and saw physical evidence of what was real. He worked as the Senior Technologist in charge of the evening shift at Newman Medical Center in Emporia, supervised by Marty Anderson. When the two couples first met, David and his first wife partied with the Andersons, although without sexual contact. The partying between them ended in the late 1970s. David heard the rumors about the Andersons, and knew much about what was true.

"It was fairly common knowledge that they [Marty and Lorna] had a 'hot marital situation' and I heard they were running around on each other." The rumors about Lorna's flings are rampant at Newman. He told her that nearly everyone knew about her and Danny Carter. David believed that Marty, too, played the field. He saw him at the very least a flirt.

David found a love letter of Lorna's mixed in with Marty's stuff while he moved furniture around the lab in 1978. He read the explicit letter that came from a man named "Willie," the salesman with whom Lorna later confessed she worked and slept. Because David found the letter in amongst Marty's files, he knew that Marty knew about Willie. He believed Marty knew about many of Lorna's other sex partners, too. David feared that he would put the letter back in the wrong place and Marty would know he had read it, so took it home and threw it away.

Marty's well-grounded paranoia about Lorna's sexual exploits added even more weight to his broad shoulders, according to David. "One time, approximately five or six years ago, Marty was very upset because Lorna was pregnant with Julie. He was suspicious that the child was not his."

David said Marty got angry when Lorna found herself pregnant with the twins in 1981.

He heard Marty say "a couple of times that he was having financial problems and a couple of times had to cover some checks that were at the bank." One of those may have been the bad check issued to Marty's life insurance company that caused his policy to lapse in January. It took several weeks before Lorna got him insured again.

Investigators learned that the Anderson's credit rating had suffered, and they could not secure a loan, even with their house as collateral. Marty obsessed over finding outside income.

David started working at Newman several weeks after Marty did. He originally got along well with Marty, even playing together on the same softball teams. By February of 1983, David complained that Marty got "on his case," became a taskmaster and got angry with him. He knew Marty was

piqued with him and believed it was because David knew that Marty beat
Lorna. David saw bruises on Lorna's body as early as 1978 or 1979, Lorna
told him Marty beat her.

David saw the Anderson marriage as "mutual toleration," so bad had the
relationship become. "I mean, they were civil to each other, but just barely."

A drive in the country

Angie, who managed Lord's Lambs at Faith, noticed that during March
of 1983, "Lorna was always being depressed and crying. The pastor had to
hug and counsel with her for hours and hours."

One Friday in March, Lorna became *especially* distraught. She and Tom
produced the church newsletter and prepared it for mailing—about 800
copies. They struggled each month getting the newsletter out because Faith
did not own the proper equipment.

"Lorna would type the copy at Faith, go down to the education center
downtown and cut the stencils, then run off the pages at Messiah," Tom
explained.

Then she loaded the boxes into her van and took them back to Faith to
collate and address. Tom tried to help with the boxes if his time allowed.
That Friday, Tom drove home for lunch while Lorna ran the newsletter at
Messiah. She called him about 1 p.m. saying she was finished. "I met her at
Messiah to help load the boxes into her van."

Lorna saw Tom come in the door. "You'll have to load the boxes in your
car because I'm leaving."

"What's wrong?"

"Nothing," but handed Tom four sealed envelopes. "This one is for
Marty, this one is for you to read to my children. This one for my parents and
this one is for you."

Tom noticed an empty pill bottle. He picked it up. "Did you take all
these?"

"Yes."

"How many?"

"Enough, I guess. I'm going now."

Lorna got into her van. Tom got into the passenger side. Lorna drove
around Emporia and out in to the country. Tom described her. "She was
depressed, said she was useless, no future and was going to have to have
surgery and a bunch of other stuff. She was glassy eyed and listless and
whatever the pills were they didn't kill her—but they got my attention."

Tom listened to the distressed woman as patiently as he could, trying to
reason with her. After several hours, he saw her relax. He returned home in

the early evening. Sandy confronted him when he came in. "Can't you see that she's just trying to sink her hooks deeper into you?"

"The woman was going to commit suicide. What was I supposed to do? I think you're being kind of cold to her, and not caring about her needs."

Years later, Tom thought back to the unusual counseling session. "Was it proper or professional to counsel while riding around in a van? Probably not, but being proper or professional was not my first thought. Saving her life was. Pastors are not clinical psychologists. We are, for the most part, poorly trained crisis counselors. I was a friend."

"I've counseled a drunken husband in a bar. I've counseled a depressed member in a motor boat on a lake, or a farmer out in his soybean field. I sat with a man in front of his house on the curb at midnight, and a teenager at 1 a.m. who was throwing up underneath the bleachers at the high school football field. None of that would have been considered proper or professional."

Whether proper and professional or not, Lorna told others that Tom saved her life that day.

"I was trying to help a woman who threatened to kill herself. Nothing else happened. Nothing," Tom explained. Tom saw this as a prime responsibility of a good pastor; helping a distraught member deal with depression and suicide. He discounted what others said about it as a violation of the Eighth Commandment.

Tom cared only about the truth. He knew the truth. God knew the truth. Lorna, he would discover later, had a hard time discerning truth, but she never claimed this ride included anything sexual in nature.

Battered and bruised

David Workman met and talked with Lorna many times, both at the hospital and elsewhere. He experienced her manic-depressive mannerisms. He heard her over-dramatic voice and watched her demonstrative actions. He remembered one critical conversation with her that directly related to the tragic events of 1983.

As best the date can be deduced, given that David did not recite the following information until late in 1984, and had no reason to record it the day it happened, the following event occurred on Wednesday, March 30, 1983.

Lorna worked her regular morning hours at Faith and left for home. She walked in late for the Wednesday midweek service that began at 7 p.m. that evening.

As Tom walked down the aisle following the service, he saw her sitting near the back of the church. "She was wearing large sunglasses and her face was swollen. The next day when she came to work, she had a pretty bad black eye that was pretty visible in spite of her heavy makeup."

Lorna told Tom that Marty beat her when he came home from work on Wednesday, sometime around 3 p.m. He went back to Newman following their altercation and Lorna followed him a little later. She planned to have a very public fight with him. David spotted her in the hallway and headed her off.

"She came into the hospital crying and upset with bruises on her face and I thought she'd been in an automobile accident and through the conversation it was, you know, was said that Marty just got finished beating on her." David testified during the inquisition into Marty's death. He also answered questions at the 1985 Lyon County Grand Jury investigating Sandy Bird's death.

David talked with Lorna for a time in the hall and persuaded her to head out to the parking lot. They sat in her van, talking about her present dilemma. Lorna spoke with unusual, dangerous and prophetic language to describe the methods she had considered using to solve her problem with Marty. The following is a reconstruction of that conversation based on David Workman's testimony during the inquisition and from Tom's 1990 trial.

"She told me things weren't going very well between her and Marty. I just told her she didn't have to put up with it, and there were organizations available that would protect her and keep Marty from any retaliation.

"She wanted to know if the people at Newman knew about her and Danny Carter and I said 'Yes, it's pretty much known all around the hospital.' She was a little upset at this. I guess she didn't think as many people knew as knew.

"But it was pretty common knowledge that Lorna ran around. After softball games, when the guys would have a few beers, I saw her come on to them. I saw her rub them on their rear ends or near their groins. She didn't try to hide it. This was far beyond what friends did to each other. It was very out of place. Marty saw this stuff, and sometimes he'd get mad. Other times he'd play nonchalant about it.

"I noticed that Lorna had a gun in her purse. I think it was a revolver, but I don't know much about guns. I just know that the bigger the gun the higher the caliber. It had a small bore, so I think it was a .22 caliber. She had it back in 1977 or 78, too. [In the 1990 trial, he identified the gun as the one used to murder Marty.]

"We were having the conversation about Danny Carter, and then she said 'they' were going to rough Marty up if he didn't' stop. Even though she did not say his name specifically, I took for granted that we both knew what we were talking about, that it was understood. She knew I knew she was talking about Danny. It was clear to me she meant Danny Carter or his brother, or both. It was all in the same general gist of the conversation.

"I told her again there were better alternatives, like SOS or someplace that they could hide her where he couldn't get to her.

"She told me that if he kept it up there were plans to shoot Marty or possibly getting Marty drunk or drugged running him off the road. But Marty was very much anti-drugs, so that wasn't a very good idea. No one would believe such a thing.

"Now I saw Lorna use marijuana once and maybe twice. I'm not so sure what she was using the second time. This was at softball parties.

"During this conversation the name of Tom Bird never came up. I didn't even know him until after Sandy's death, and Lorna never talked about him with me until August of 1983."

David laid out a stunning and revealing scenario from his March 30, 1983 episode with Lorna. In this scenario, he said Lorna plotted with someone, most likely Danny Carter and perhaps his brother, Darrel, to either drug Marty and run him off the road, or shoot him. Following Marty's murder, David replayed this March 1983 conversation in his mind. He should have come forward and told police what he knew, but feared for his own life.

David knew that Sandy died when her car ran off a road near a bridge; Marty died from three gun shot wounds. To David, these were "equal parts of the same scheme," as Judge Gradert said it in 1989.

David explained to investigators why he did not tell the whole story at first. "My first reason was the fact that to the best of my knowledge, Marty was Number Two and I didn't know if I wanted to be Number Three or not, to be real honest."

Lorna tells all to Mead

Jan Mead worked as a fund-raiser for the American Heart Association in 1982 and 1983. She supervised operations in 14 counties, including Lyon County. She hired Lorna in October of 1982, to serve as the residential supervisor in Emporia. Lorna reported directly to her with responsibilities for the door-to-door campaign scheduled for February, 1983.

Mead met Lorna in Emporia for the first time January 27, 1983 following a Heart Association board meeting. The two sipped a glass of wine in the bar at the Ramada Inn as Lorna started prattling on about her life in a very one-sided conversation. "She told me that she didn't love her husband anymore, that she was unhappy, but she was having an affair with her hairdresser."

During the months that followed, Lorna told Mead about "three or four other men" with whom she had sex, although Mead strangely could not recall any of their names, except Tom, Lorna's pastor.

Subsequent to this meeting, Mead spent a lot of time with Lorna both in a business and personal setting. "This was a new operation we were setting up in Emporia, and that takes a lot of work in the very beginning to make the cards and do that kind of thing and so I was in contact with her probably once a week to every 10 days."

"I don't know if you would classify it as 'friends,' but she [Lorna] opened up to me a lot."

Mead estimated that besides the regular on-site visits, she talked by phone to Lorna several times a week. Then came a period of time when she had trouble finding her. "I couldn't get ahold of her for about three or four days in a row when I needed to get ahold of her, and I kept leaving messages with the housekeeper or whoever it was that was answering the phone, and finally, she did return my call."

During this call, Mead learned that Lorna had a second job. "I learned she was working as a part-time secretary…at the church where she and her husband attended."

Mead called Lorna at the church. Caught in her deceit, Lorna immediately lied to her about the secretary's job. Lorna told her, "that the secretary who was working there was ill and Lorna was filling in while the secretary was ill and it was not going to be a permanent situation." There was no paid secretary prior to Lorna.

The AHA job took about 20 hours a week but, "she [Lorna] was getting all her work done."

Mead wanted to make sure that Lorna had her priorities in order. "I felt like her first responsibility was to the Heart Association. We were right in the middle of getting things done. I just wanted to make sure that she had enough time to do both jobs because there's a lot of critical follow-up that needs to be done in March and April, and at that time she said that she was having enough time so I didn't question her."

On November 28, 1983, Jan and a friend visited Dean Speaks, a mutual friend, when the conversation turned to Marty's murder. Mead told Speaks about all the "weird statements" Lorna made to her. She discovered that Speaks was a Park City Kansas Police Officer. He asked if she would be willing to give a voluntary statement to police. She wrote:

"On January 27, 1983 Lorna Anderson and myself went to the club at the Ramada Inn in Emporia to have a drink after the Board Meeting for the American Heart Association. This was the 1st social setting I had been with Lorna as I was her supervisor and had only met with her for business purposes. Our talk soon went from 'heart' business to men. She began telling me about a hairdresser that she slept with and how she never really loved her husband.

"I met with Lorna once every week to ten days from this date until mid-March. After we had this talk she seemed to want to tell me more about her afternoon trips to Topeka or Wichita. During February I found out that she was working part-time as a secretary at the church where she and her family attended. When I asked her if this was going to be too much work in addition to the work she was doing for me, she said no. Then she went on to explain that she and the minister, Tom, were seeing each other and it was time they could be alone, etc. [Mead believed Lorna did not need the money from the secretary's job. Lorna lied about this. The Andersons were cash poor. Lorna wanted Mead to believe she only worked at Faith so she and Tom could be together.]

"One day in March I was in Emporia on business and called Lorna about something. She wasn't home but her husband was and answered the phone. When he found out it was me he said that he thought she was in Wichita to meet with me about Heart business. I tried not to say too much. She called me the next morning to apologize. However, this began her using me to cover for her when she went places with her boyfriend(s). She would call me the morning that she was going somewhere and tell me that if Marty called that she was either on the way there or back. This happened several times."

Alvin Tefft, Marty's close friend from the Army Reserves, recalled that Marty was very upset with Lorna about April 16 or 17 in 1983. During a conversation they had on May 7, when they were together at Reserves, Marty told him about coming home and finding Lorna in the bathtub, nude of course, with Danny Carter, sitting fully clothed on the toilet. Marty walked in, saw the two, said nothing and walked out.

Mead's statement continued:

"On April 19, I gave Lorna her end-of-the-year evaluation. We met at the Holiday Inn for coffee. She was very nervous and was shaking. At first we talked about work, then I asked her if she wanted to talk about what was bothering her. She said things were getting much worse with her and Marty. She said that she and Tom were very much in love and wanted to spend their lives together. [At least three men with whom Lorna wanted a lifetime relationship had refused her: Tom, her high-school and college lover who had her abort their child; Willie Porter, her former boss; Danny Carter, who may have still availed himself of her sexual favors at that time. It was two or three days before Lorna had this discussion with Jan that Marty found Danny in the bathroom with Lorna. What Marty did or said to Lorna later is unknown, but imaginable.]

"It was at this time she said something to the effect of, 'I know this sounds awful, but sometimes I just wish that something would happen to Marty and his [Tom's] wife so Tom and I could just spend the rest of our lives together.' [Note that just several days earlier Lorna told David Workman that Danny Carter, and most likely his brother, discussed with her at least two ways of murdering Marty.]

"Our annual meeting was April 26. Lorna was there but halfway through the speaker she was called out. We were supposed to get a drink that night, but she never came back.

During these months, Lorna claimed she and Tom were in love. She told Mead she and Tom met discreetly for sex, driving to Wichita or Topeka (investigators come up empty trying to prove this). She claimed they wanted to spend their lives together. She wanted both spouses dead. As far as Jan knew, everything Lorna, the well-practiced amateur actress, told her was true.

Many months later Jan added another detail to her written statement, a detail that seemed devastating to Tom, implicating him in murder and sexual intrigue. She claimed that during one of her conversations, Lorna told her that "Tom was pretty good in bed for a minister."

Jan never talked to Tom about Lorna's claims. She took no notes and made no record of her conversations with Lorna. She never met Tom, until she testified at his trials. Everything she knew was told to her by Lorna and unverifiable.

Sitting with children, seeing too much

Given Lorna's work and play schedule, she employed a lot of babysitters. One of them, Reka Rosenboom who knew Lorna from Faith, said, "Lorna and Marty were always partying. Seemed like nearly every night they were out somewhere."

Lorna worked at Faith in the morning and for the America Heart Association some afternoons. Since the AHA work involved preparing schedules and records, she often came back to Faith to use the typewriter.

Esther Aldrete, an Hispanic woman, babysat for Lorna in 1983. She spoke broken English. Aldrete worked from 9 a.m. to Noon. Many days, though, she stayed around until 4 p.m. and sometimes until as late as 8 p.m.—a bit unpredictable given Lorna's hectic lifestyle.

She thought it strange that Lorna had so many different babysitters and asked Lori, the oldest child, "Isn't that kind of hard on you girls, having so many babysitters?"

"Yes, but that's the way mother wanted it."

A lot of different babysitters coming at various times for sundry reasons could never connect all the dots of her wanderlust. They saw only the pieces of Lorna's life during the hours they spent with her children. By virtue of her being a regular daytime sitter, Aldrete connected more dots than the others. Seeing the children, the Anderson residence and both parents close up, she observed some strikingly unusual behavior and questionable family interaction.

One morning, she believed it was in late May or early June of 1983, she worked downstairs, playing with the children. Marty left for work. "I came back upstairs a little later, unexpectedly, and found a man lying on the coffee table. Lorna was on top of him, kissing him."

She described the man as white, about 40 years old and 5' 6", chubby and bald-headed, with short hair on the side. She saw him just this one time. When she first told this to investigators on November 19, 1983, she thought the man could have been Lorna's minister. Tom stood a thin 5' 10", though he *was* balding. Esther added that at the time of this incident she had never met or seen Tom, but such were the "facts" upon which the investigators often relied.

Aldrete discovered a lot of alcoholic beverages in the Anderson home. "They had dozens of boxes of wine, beer, whisky and mixes in the basement."

Some of Marty's friends and associates witnessed him almost constantly carrying a drink. They portrayed him as an alcoholic.

Esther rather liked Marty. She said he respected her. Aldrete claimed that Marty usually cleaned the Anderson house and washed their clothes, and he did his own ironing. She said she never saw Lorna clean the house. She never witnessed a fight between them, although she knew there was serious trouble in their marriage. "Marty was mad because Lorna never stayed home."

She recalled a specific time she and Marty talked about Lorna. "One time Marty asked me if I would mind helping him clean the house. Lorna left the kids in the house alone a lot and the house was very dirty, silverware all over the floor, and trash."

As they were cleaning, Marty said, "I'm tired, I'm cleaning the house for nothing. I'm having trouble with Lorna. I don't think I can stand her anymore."

"What will you do?"

"Maybe take my kids and run away."

She noticed some time later that Lorna had a black eye, but she knew nothing about it.

That same spring, she could not specifically pinpoint the date but was sure it was a short time after seeing the man on the coffee table with Lorna, Aldrete overheard a very odd telephone conversation. She heard Lorna say, "I wish Marty was dead. I can't wait to spend all that green money I could get."

Aldrete never saw or met Tom until sometime in May of 1983, and then only on one brief occasion. Given the weight of evidence of admitted frequent visits with Lorna's confessed lovers, such as Danny Carter, it must have greatly disappointed investigators that Aldrete had no helpful information implicating Tom. She remembered once babysitting for the Bird children which, in any case was not unusual. The three little Birds spent quite a bit of time with the Anderson children, and some said Lorna had a special fascination for Aaron. Aldrete, though, opined that Tom and Lorna were dating, although, "I do not have anything to base this on."

By the time of this interview (November, 1983), gossip circulated freely about Lorna and Tom. Aldrete, who spent a generous amount of time at the Andersons, only saw Lorna with Tom that one time. She made no claims about what the two were doing during the one time she saw them together, and by then she clearly knew he was not the man on the coffee table. For all she really knew, Tom was nothing more than Lorna's supervisor, pastor, friend and counselor—all fair labels to attach to him and to which he would quickly agree.

Aldrete found herself in a frightening situation in October of 1984. It happened many weeks after Tom's 1984 trial and incarceration. Aldrete, who at that time was being questioned in relation to the Marty murder investigation, told investigators she received threatening phone calls on at least two occasions.

"She stated she had received two telephone calls, the last one about three weeks ago and the first one about a week prior to that. She stated she didn't think it was the same caller both times because the first caller had a very strong voice and the second caller had a weaker voice. Both callers were male. The callers told her that she should never open her mouth, and they either said, or she got the impression, that they would hurt her or her family if she testified against Lorna Anderson. They also told her not to call the police. The calls came during the daytime hours, prior to 3:00 PM, when she goes to work."

Someone wanted to protect Lorna or, by protecting her, protect himself. He threatened bodily harm to a potentially devastating witness. Who made those mystery calls? To this day, no one knows, but it is a certainty it was not Tom. He was in prison.

Spring Birds

The spring of 1983 saw the pace of Tom Bird's life increase again. He grew tense under the pressure.

Tom served as the first line of defense at Faith for people with problems, and he had a number of his own. The busy schedules both he and Sandy kept, sent them in opposite directions, running on emotional fumes.

Tom and Sandy together taught Family Life Seminars in their district— five in 1983. The section they taught was "Family Communications." Yet they had little time for their own personal communications.

Tom increasingly felt great doubts about his ability to handle the demanding dual chores of leading a church and a family and became quietly depressed. When Tom felt depressed, Sandy, his closest friend and constant advisor, tried to help as she always had before, but her help yielded little. She felt like a failure. Tom saw his depression driving her sense of failure, causing her great distress, but felt unable to do much to stop it.

Tom let his pastoral guard down at home where he did not have to demonstrate some superior inner strength, a perception he and other pastors try to portray in public. At home he could be irritated, sulk, pity himself— just like any man.

Tom wanted her home more, but he supported her work. Getting a Master's Degree had an end date, so he knew it would be over soon.

Sandy became more stressed. She lost weight. "She was always trying to lose weight. I don't see anything particularly significant in that," Tom said. Sandy stood 5' 2" and normally weighed 110 pounds, so her friends and family worried it was too much weight loss. They speculated that something was wrong with her.

At the same time Tom and Sandy faced these personal problems, unable to share them with anyone in Emporia, Lorna suffered her own, constant and increasingly violent problems with Marty. Unaware of how licentious Lorna was, and how her own promiscuous ways contributed to Marty's anger, Tom helped the forlorn female as often as she needed it. In February, Lorna's blood level dropped dangerously low, and she was hospitalized for several days. There was the long drive in Lorna's van, when she had taken pills and apparently had decided to end her life. There was March 30, the day she came to church wearing sunglasses and had bruises on her face.

Lorna looked for someone to lean on, someone to whom she could talk without being judged and, perhaps most importantly, someone immune to her flirtatious ways—Pastor Tom Bird. Lorna told author David Hacker that Tom was the only man she had known whom she could not manipulate.

Sandy saw Tom's open availability, especially to Lorna, as a frustration. She watched with mounting concern while Lorna stalked her husband. She never believed Tom gave in to Lorna's wiles, but she said things like, "Lorna sure is hanging on you," or "Can't you tell her not to call at suppertime?" When Lorna called during family time, Sandy complained to Tom, "Does she have to call you with every crisis in her life?"

"Sandy was jealous of my time with church work and being on call in general—rightly so in hindsight—and Lorna was just part of it. I'm sure Sandy had that woman's intuition that many had about Lorna," Tom remembered.

Sandy confided in a few others she was getting very worried. She chatted on the phone with Pastor Charles Smith, Tom's closest friend since seminary days.

She talked with Angie, the young college graduate who managed Lord's Lambs.

One time in May, while the two visited in the basement of Bird's home, Sandy told Angie that she feared Lorna was trying to steal her husband, but Tom told her there was "nothing to worry about." Angie said that Sandy was convinced that the relationship between Tom and Lorna was not sexual, but she was frustrated because she wanted "her husband [Tom] to lean more on her and not on Lorna." Sandy told the young woman that Tom had been depressed since March, and he was reluctant to discuss it with her. She wanted to help him work through his problems. Sandy saw what Lorna tried to do, and was frustrated with Tom because he failed to understand it.

According to Angie, Sandy said she feared Tom became bored with her. Maybe she acted too good. So late in May, after a pre-school picnic, Sandy bought a bottle of wine thinking alcohol would relax her. She drove to a local park and got drunk. But instead of reducing her inhibitions, she got sleepy and went home and slept.

Angie knew Marty, too. They played on the same co-ed volleyball team, attended Faith together and Julie attended Lord's Lambs. "He could be a rather gruff person," but after she got to know him, he "seemed good with the kids."

Angie talked with Marty about what he labeled his "premonition." She dated this as May of 1983, before Marty left for his two-week Reserves drill.

She saw Marty at church cleaning the carpet as if he had to get several things done before leaving. Angie heard him say that he had a premonition about death and he truly feared he would not return from camp. He told Angie that he and Lorna went to Chris Kimble's office to add a special life insurance policy—$100,000 death benefit—to cover him during the time he would be away.

Lorna mentioned Marty's premonition to Tom, and Marty personally shared it with him, too. "I thought it was weird. He just said that there were always some accidents at guard camp and his number might be up. He didn't tell me why," Tom said.

Marty's "number," turned out to be "3" (the number of bullet holes in his head) but it did not come up until his brutal ambush murder six months later.

On another occasion, Lorna told Tom a fantasy she had one day driving back from a weekend trip to Wellington. They had just visited a friend in a nursing home and she and Marty had a major argument. "Marty was very hateful toward me."

With the children asleep in the back of the van, Lorna headed back toward Emporia; Marty sat in the passenger seat. A hard spring rain pounded on the van and made visibility difficult. Lorna pictured herself speeding up and driving the van into a bridge abutment to kill them.

"But Lorna, the kids were in the car!"

"They would have been okay. They were in the back."

Lorna admitted later to fantasizing often. Tom, more used to her suicide proclamations, stored this one away in his mind. Yet, he wondered how she could ever consider such a scheme where certainly, her four little girls would either die or be injured for life.

Tom refused Marriage Encounter

Tom knew that in his ministerial practice, there were women with whom he had to be careful. He had a sense about them, but he had no such sense with Lorna.

Others believed that Tom had an unshakable blind spot as a result of his strict adherence to the Eighth Commandment and Luther's Confessions. Tom saw it as his strength. Many husbands turn a deaf ear to their wife's warnings.

Added to all this pressure, Tom wanted to strengthen his own marriage, a task made more difficult by time demands. So in an effort to both help themselves and others in their church, Tom and Sandy explored some of the marriage building programs so popular among churched people. "Marriage Encounter" and "Marriage Enrichment," two competing but similar courses, were strong. "Sandy wanted us to go to Marriage Encounter, but its roots lay in the Catholic Church and I felt uncomfortable with that. I wanted to go to Marriage Enrichment," Tom said.

Sandy told her mother about this disagreement. Later, Jane insisted in a letter to Tom that Tom and Sandy fought about this, that Tom did not want to go at all. Jane saw it as another indicator that their marriage was going badly.

From May 12-14, Tom and Sandy attended a marriage and family life seminar in Lincoln, Nebraska. While they were gone, Lorna babysat their three children. Presumably, Sandy agreed to this arrangement.

Sharon Hackett, who met the Birds during their seminary days, and her husband Pastor Tom Hackett, lunched with them during the seminar. "It didn't surprise me that they would be participating in such an event. They were always progressive thinkers wanting to learn more. They wanted to help people in their congregation in Kansas." Maybe Tom had Marty and Lorna in mind.

Sharon Hackett saw something else about the Birds. "They looked good and excited about their work."

Pastor Tom Hackett said, "They looked wonderful, happier than ever, and very excited about the work they were doing at the congregation in Emporia, Kansas where Tom was serving."

Tom remembered the seminar. "We had a great time. It was a great time for both of us." There was, however, one festering sore that followed them to Lincoln. "Lorna and I talked several times while we were gone, and Sandy was not happy about this."

More meetings

May 19, Tom drove to Topeka for the quarterly meeting of the District Family Life Committee. As usual, he drove the turnpike north out of Emporia, making sure to keep his toll receipt for income tax purposes. The receipt showed he arrived in Topeka at just after 10 a.m. He returned home the same way. The receipt showed a 7 p.m. return.

May 20, Lorna left Emporia to pick up Marty. He'd been at reserve camp since May 6. Then on May 21, Marty left for two days of weekend drill.

Tom attended a meeting of the youth board on May 21. These meetings included members from Messiah Lutheran as well, including Pastor Kalsow. The group talked about various ways to raise money for their planned summer excursions. They talked about mud wrestling. Then Kalsow showed Tom a brochure that described selling fireworks to raise money. They briefly discussed it and the meeting adjourned.

During the following week, Lorna mentioned that she knew a man,

Darrel Carter, who owned two firecracker stands—Carter's Crackers.

The following Sunday, May 29, the youth board met again and Tom mentioned the fireworks idea. He said Lorna knew a fellow—Darrel Carter—who owned a couple of firecracker stands. They agreed he should check out the details of such a sale and the meeting adjourned.

A special birthday gift

Tom turned 33 on June 1, 1983. Tom and Sandy had just finished an exhausting month. Tuesday night, May 31, Tom played softball with the church team. They just had a couple of stressful nights with their children, the kinds of nights that wake parents up for little things like runny noses or bad dreams. They felt tired. Tom had been struggling with depression at home and Sandy felt inadequate helping him work through it. She felt troubled about Lorna's constant intrusions on her husband, and wanted to do something special to remind Tom of her love for him and to reassure herself of his feelings.

The spring term at ESU had ended, so Sandy had time off of studies, but still drove to ESU to work. Her hours were more flexible.

As a special birthday present for Tom, Sandy arranged to have Angie baby-sit, giving the two a night out alone.

After the softball game, Sandy pleasantly surprised her tired, tense and sports-crazed husband. She stopped at a carry-out Chinese restaurant and picked up supper. Then she took Tom to a motel. "She said it was my birthday gift," Tom said.

Tom took a shower, they ate supper and made love. Given the difficulty they always had trying to find time alone, and the aggressive Mrs. Anderson close by his side every day, Sandy's gift of love meant much to Tom, but she had more.

"Then she said she was going back home and I had the evening to myself, undisturbed, to watch the NBA Playoffs. No kids. No phones," Tom remembered. He sat there *alone,* undisturbed. Not even Lorna could reach him.

Sandy went home. She and Angie talked late into the wee hours of the morning. Not being privy to that conversation, Tom could only guess the range of subjects the two of them covered. Angie remembered that they talked about Lorna. Sandy told her that every time she tried to talk to Tom about Lorna he would become defensive and upset with her.

Angie, the single, young recent college grad, with no children of her own, who lived a realtively carefree life, placed a lot of meaning on the events of that night. She concluded that Tom had been so distressed he wanted a night alone, away from Sandy and away from everything. She believed that somehow this night at the motel showed that Tom was dissatisfied with Sandy. "She probably could not imagine why a man would want a night to himself to watch an NBA game," Tom speculated later.

On Monday, Tom and Sandy got another birthday surprise, and it had really irritated Sandy.

The Friday before Tom's birthday, Lorna asked him if she could bake him a birthday cake. Tom said no, because Sandy would do it. Lorna persisted. "What do you really like?"

"I like pie."

"Good. It will be a birthday pie."

On Monday, his day off, Tom babysat Aaron. Andrea and Paul went to Vacation Bible School at Messiah. Lorna picked them up in the morning, along with her own kids and a few others from the neighborhood. Late that morning, Tom drove to Messiah to pick up the kids. After he dropped off the neighborhood kids, he drove to Faith, the seven children in tow. When he walked into the church fellowship hall, he saw a piece of pie and a scoop of ice cream set out for him and each child. Tom knew this spelled trouble. Just then, Sandy and Angie walked in and saw the party, and knew they had not been invited. It compounded her frustration toward Lorna. Angie saw that Lorna was very uncomfortable with her and Sandy present.

Tom thought Lorna, a terrific cook, planned to bake and give him a pie, not throw him a party that excluded his wife. But Lorna liked excluding Sandy. She wanted her permanently excluded.

Sunday, June 5, was Sandy's 33rd birthday—her last. On Thursday, when she came to church around noon, the entire crew took her out to lunch. Sandy, Tom, Lorna and Angie all walked to the Mexican restaurant across the street from the church and celebrated her birthday. The church was locked up.

While they were all gone to lunch, partying and celebrating Sandy's birthday, another Faith member, Susie Graf, stopped at the church. She saw the parked cars as she walked up to the church door. It was locked. The whole church was locked. Unable to raise anyone's attention, she sat outside waiting for someone to return and give her an explanation. Susie felt left out.

Susie spent a lot of time at church. She became quite opinionated about what happened around there, and later, had much to tell investigators.

A brief visit

Jerry and Jane Grismer made a quick trip to Emporia during Father's Day weekend. During that weekend, among other things, Jane and Sandy talked about Lorna. Jane later recalled that Sandy told her that Lorna was crazy about the Bird children, and that Lorna wanted her dead ("out of the way" would have been more characteristic of Sandy). They laughed about it, because no one took it seriously.

Sandy saw Lorna as a threat to her marriage, but she also noticed Lorna's strong attachment to Aaron. She witnessed Lorna going out of her way to pick Aaron up and carry him around, or push him in a swing. These observations added to Sandy's mounting irritation with Lorna and her frustration getting Tom to take it seriously.

An explosive fund-raising plan

During the early summer of 1983, Tom had to raise money to pay for a youth group trip to Eureka Springs, Arkansas. At a May 21 meeting, Pastor Kalsow suggested they could sell fireworks on consignment; a good idea, but without a place to sell them, Tom thought it could never work. The city would not allow their sale within city limits, and Tom saw that other than nearby farms, no location existed where a sales stand might be built. He thought about talking with the farmers.

On Monday, June 6, Lorna saw the brochure that described the Arkansas trip. She asked Tom about it again, and the two discussed the fund-raising need. They talked about Kalsow's idea of selling firecrackers on consignment.

"It's a good idea, but we have no place to sell them."

"I think I can help. Remember, I told you about this man who owns Carter's Crackers and he might help. He's got two stands in Emporia. He needs help. Maybe the kids could sell them there?"

"Who is this?"

"Darrel Carter. He's a builder in town and he owns these fireworks stands. I worked there before. Do you want to talk with him about it? I can get him on the phone."

"Well, it won't hurt asking him about it I guess."

Later that night Lorna called Tom at home — Monday was his normal day off. She said she set an appointment with Darrel for the next day, June 7, at 9 in the morning. Tom wrote "D. Carter, yth" on his day-planner that he kept at the house to remind himself of the meeting that morning.

Tom saw a man enter the church and walk past his office. A few minutes later, Lorna came and got Tom. He stepped across the hall into Lorna's office. Her L-shaped desk sat positioned so that her back angled toward the glass-less window that opened out into a lobby. Tom stood next to her desk, leaning on a file cabinet, and Darrel sat in the chair facing her desk. The office door was open.

Angie worked at Lord's Lambs, though the regular preschool had finished for the year. It was "Mother's Day Out," and women dropped their children off at the center so Angie could watch them. Kids and parents constantly came and went during these days.

Lorna introduced Tom to Darrel. As a matter of giving background about himself, Darrel mentioned that he built homes, and one of them was in the area of the church. Tom said he and Sandy just bought a house, but someday planned to build one of their own. "I'd sure like to bid on it if you do," Darrel answered.

Tom talked about the youth group's need to raise money and the idea Kalsow had suggested. "I wondered if you needed some help. Maybe this would help us both?"

Darrel talked about his volunteering as a kids' soccer coach. He said that if his team kept on winning, he would need help at the fireworks stands because the soccer season would overlap the Fourth of July sales season. "I'm behind on my construction work, too."

Darrel feared an accident might happen. If the untrained youth dropped a match and blew up the place, would his property insurance cover the incident? Darrel said he would check out the legal and insurance issues.

Tom questioned the maturity level of the teenagers. Could they be trusted to act responsibly around thousands of pounds of incendiary devices?

At the end of their discussion, Tom said it might work out. "I'll get back to you on this," he said as he left the room.

Lorna and Darrel talked a while longer in her office and then he left the church. Tom had no idea what they talked about, but while they were all together, Marty Anderson's name never came up.

Camping out

On Friday, June 10, three days after meeting with Darrel in Lorna's office, Tom took 15 teenagers on a campout at Lake Melvern. Angie Duensing and Alan Rees, the church's Youth Group Counselor, came along to chaperone.

It rained much of the night, and it was chilly. To make matters worse, some of the youth smuggled beer and vodka along. Two got drunk.

Val Kasmir, a high school junior girl, and her boyfriend, Ben Berg, who had both been drinking, got into a fight and Kasmir wandered off sometime around midnight. Tom heard about it, and became very upset, knowing that he was responsible for the safety of the youth. About to set off to find the young girl, Tom ran into Berg, the drunk boyfriend.

"I'm going to find her," Berg yelled.

"No, you go to your tent. I'll go."

"Let me go. She's my girlfriend!"

"I'm telling you to go to your tent!"

"But I'm responsible for her wandering off," Berg said, trying to push past the frustrated pastor.

Tom grabbed him by the arm and then his shirt and held him tight. He raised his voice in anger and said, "Don't tell me about being responsible. You don't know the meaning of being responsible!"

Berg pushed past Tom, but Tom blocked his path. In the struggle, they nearly bumped into Angie. Berg lost his footing and went over backward with Tom on top of him. Angie yelled at them to break it up, pulling on Tom's arm.

The incident lasted just a matter of seconds and then it was over. No punches were thrown and the two got up. Berg finally agreed to back off. Tom set out to look for the young girl alone, but without success.

Finally, around 2 a.m., Val walked back into the campsite. She never saw the altercation between Ben and the pastor. She "had wandered off to think things over."

Tom saw no humor in the incident, and took Val to the van where they talked for two hours. She knew she was in big trouble.

Tom slept very little, and the weather only made it worse, raining constantly after 3 a.m. He decided to pack up the campsite and drove the group back to Emporia early. He saw the weekend as a complete failure and he needed to decide what to tell the parents. Over the next several days, Tom took time out of his busy schedule to talk with each teen that was on the trip, hoping this would be a lesson to them.

Given their actions at Lake Malvern, Tom knew his youth were not ready to be around tons of gunpowder in a firecracker booth.

No bang for their bucks

The camping experience convinced Tom to cancel the idea of selling fireworks. "They proved they were not ready for that kind of responsibility."

He had promised Darrel during their church meeting that he would let him know whether or not the sale would move ahead. About a week after they met, Tom drove to the building site where Darrel worked to tell him to cancel the sale.

Darrel was building a home for Grover and Patricia McCullough west of the Emporia Waterworks and he was falling behind. Tom drove to the unfinished home and parked his car and walked into the house through the garage, finding Chris Carter, Darrel's younger brother, in the kitchen. Chris directed Tom to the bedroom where Darrel worked installing wood molding.

As they talked, Darrel continued his work. Tom mentioned his admiration for the house, and Darrel stopped, taking him on a tour, wanting to impress him with the work. He showed Tom the master bedroom and the living room. He felt especially proud of the big bay window and made a special effort to point it out to Tom.

During the home tour, Tom told Darrel the firecracker sale was off. Darrel agreed.

As they stood by the bay window, Darrel asked, "How's Lorna doing?"

"Fine."

"Well, you know Marty beats her."

Tom faced a dilemma common to pastors. He counseled Lorna and often talked to Marty. He had knowledge of their problems, but talking to a third party about them would violate a confidence. Tom saw Lorna's bruises, too. He confronted her about them and she acknowledged Marty abused her, but only verbally. She refused to talk about any beatings, so Tom could only speculate on what really happened. He turned his attention back to Darrel's statement.

"Well, you know Marty's gotten pretty active at church," Tom answered. "Maybe the beatings don't go on anymore. Besides, Lorna doesn't seem to want to do anything about it."

Tom found a creative alternative that would let him comfortably exit this conversation, while offering some real help to Lorna. "She's in sorority with your wife. If she becomes aware of Lorna having a problem with Marty, you contact me. I will go with you and between the two of us and your wife, maybe we can go and talk her into getting help. And if I see anything, I will call you and your wife. We can protect her and the kids, so Marty can get help. You know Marty needs help."

"Right. Well Marty better be careful, or something might happen to him," Darrel answered.

Tom said good-bye and left, assuming he would never again talk to Darrel.

After Tom left, Darrel turned to Darrell Warren and said something like, "That guy must be crazy. He's wanting a guy killed." Warren remembered it because it was such an odd statement. He did not know how to take it. "I didn't know whether to believe Carter or not."

Warren couldn't describe the man that came out to the work-site, although it stuck in his mind that Darrel said he was a preacher.

Warren remembered that Carter said something like this to him in an earlier conversation. "He said someone wanted him to kill somebody."

Carter just blurted this out to Warren, not in the midst of some related discussion, and then never brought it up again that day. Warren believed Carter said this sometime in May, weeks before Darrel met Tom.

These comments suggest that Darrel planted thoughts in the mind of the sheet-rocker, and months later, helped Warren recall and clarify his statement for the police.

Warren later told a jury that he had no reason to believe or not to believe Darrel. "It just sounded like exaggeration to me," he explained. "I mean that's a comment you just don't hear everyday. That's something that you just don't hear, you know."

Months later, Darrel insisted that he and Tom first met in May, not June.

Darrel's statements didn't make sense. Lorna agreed with Tom that the meeting at church was June 7, not during May. Darrell Warren remembered clearly that Darrel talked about someone wanting him to murder someone during May. On March 30, Lorna told David Workman that if Marty continued to beat her and mistreat her, he was going to get roughed up, and that there were plans to kill him. She said those plans included getting him drunk or drugged and running him off the road, or shooting him. She placed discussion of those plans in a conversation she had had with Danny Carter. Darrel Carter later stated that Tom Bird came to see him at a house where he was working, but claimed Tom was calling off the hit on Marty, not calling off a fireworks sale. He said this meeting occurred just days after their first meeting, which Carter claimed was in May. Warren said that Tom came out to the work site "one time last summer," not May, not "one time last spring."

In criminal investigations, little details make a big difference, especially when an allegation hinges on one person's word against another's. To a 1984 Emporia jury, though, these details slipped by. David Workman never testified at that 1984 trial about his March 30 van session with Lorna. Lorna never testified either, claiming her constitutional protection against self-incrimination. If these two had testified, the jury *would* have noticed the details and it would have changed the verdict.

Angie warns Tom

Angie Duensing directed the Lord's Lambs preschool. She was a bright, tall, attractive young woman just out of college. She was a likeable person and fit in well with the Faith "family" and she was especially good with children. (The Bird children spent a lot of time at Lambs Care, as did the Anderson girls.) By virtue of her leadership position she knew and often talked with many of the mothers.

In her capacity as a pastor's wife, Sandy spent a lot of time in church activities and at church. She often talked with Angie. Angie saw herself as Sandy's confidant.

During the spring, Angie and Sandy talked quite a bit about Lorna. Angie saw Tom as insensitive to Sandy's concerns and she heard the gossip. Angie believed Tom was vulnerable to Lorna. She complained about the extra hours Lorna put in around the church—it looked suspicious. She said that some church members called Lorna "Pastor's Puppy."

"Lorna wasn't able to give financially to the church and yes, she did give a lot of free time to the work. She felt like it was her way of contributing," Tom said.

Lorna used the church's typewriter in her work for the American Heart Association. As for the evenings, Ladies' Guild met on Mondays, Council or Board on Tuesday or Thursday, and midweek school or service on Wednesday. Faith's building was heavily used. None of these nights offered a chance for discreet romance. The snide title "Pastor's Puppy" exemplified the kind of gossip that spread like a cancer through the church and the town. At Newman Medical Center, everyone saw Lorna was a flirt and a "skirt," while at Faith, she gained a reputation as a man- and pastor-stealer.

On June 24, Angie took Tom aside to let him know what was going on and counsel him, to make a breakthrough on behalf of Sandy. She told him how concerned she was about Lorna's attachment to him. She warned him to be careful. She suggested that even though Tom was Lorna's pastor and in that role, counselor, he should quit counseling her.

Tom listened and evaluated her counsel, weighing it against his personal knowledge of both Lorna and Sandy. He knew Angie meant well, but she was young and lacking in life experience. He told her he was sure Lorna would get over her infatuation.

The young woman responded with words that really shook him up. Even *she* had been infatuated with him, though she had gotten over it. She believed Lorna was experiencing many of the same thoughts she had had.

She told Tom of a fantasy she had experienced about him. In her fantasy, Sandy and the children died in an auto accident, then she and Tom got married and had children together. Tom stood aghast at her story, and began to put distance between himself and Angie. Angie saw it differently, claiming that Tom turned cold toward her, because she had stumbled across an ugly truth—Tom and Lorna really *were* lovers. Tom said, "The woman had just told me she dreamed my wife died in a car accident and that we got married. How would you expect me to react?"

Angie saw Tom at church everyday and worked closely with him, though not as closely Lorna. Still, she spent quite a bit of time alone with Tom. Yet Angie never reported Tom flirted with her or encouraged her infatuation. Except for placing some distance between them, Tom treated Angie with the same dignity and respect he showed to all the women in church, but her fantasy left a hole in their relationship.

Nine days to Saturday

As a pastor's wife in a rapidly growing church, others had expectations of Sandy. During 1983, she never missed a worship service, taught the high school Sunday Bible class and together with Tom, conducted family life workshops in five Kansas cities. Sandy represented Faith on the Lutheran Board of Campus Ministry at least once each month. Each Thursday, she took a two-hour class at ESU's Meyer's Student Center taught by her husband.

Sandy attended multiple church meetings at Faith: Women's Circle, pre-school parents, and Couple's Club met once a month. Every other month she attended a church assembly meeting. On alternative Sunday evenings she participated in a home Bible study at Howard and Sharon Meyers' house.

She and the kids attended every one of the church's men's softball games and she played softball on the Messiah women's team.

She planned to lead the music program for the Vacation Bible School scheduled in July.

The end of her master's study project was nearing. It was a computer program for church management that she wrote at ESU's computer lab, with Tom serving as her practical advisor.

She and Tom had to work hard to find time alone and looked forward to a break in their schedule while they attended the Missouri Synod Convention, July 8-10 in St. Louis.

They drove to Hardy, Arkansas on July 7. Ralph and Virginia Bird served the church in Hardy and the near-rural atmosphere was a place of rest for the Bird family. The senior Bird's had a spacious parsonage with a huge yard that abutted Arkansas Highway 67. Tom saw the yard as a perfect place for whiffle-ball or football, and he used as much time as possible to play with the children.

When Tom and Sandy arrived in Hardy, Virginia saw Sandy's extra thin body. It startled her. "She was always dieting," Virginia wrote in her journal. "Why are you letting yourself lose so much weight?"

"Oh, Tom and I have been very busy, coming and going a lot," Sandy said. At 5' 2", Sandy had always been quite thin, and Virginia saw her weight loss as unnecessary.

The church sat just north of the house, several hundred feet beyond a small clump of pine trees. Its small platform and altar faced a sanctuary that seated 250 people. The choir and organ performed from a balcony behind the rows of pews. Under Ralph Bird's leadership, the church enjoyed numeric growth.

The three Bird children stayed with their grandparents while their mom and dad were gone. Ralph and Virginia were the kind of grandparents children wanted to see, and the older Birds enjoyed them greatly. Neither knew that in just more than a year, the three children would be living with them.

On July 8, Tom and Sandy left for St. Louis. They rode with Rev. Charles and Carolyn Smith.

During the afternoon of Saturday, July 9, Sandy and Carolyn, along with Pat Boysen, sat in a motel room, catching up on news and sharing their experiences as pastors' wives. During this conversation, Sandy became distressed and cried. She told the two women that Lorna, the church secretary, was trying to steal her husband. She feared that Lorna would destroy her family and Tom wasn't taking it seriously. She told them Tom had been depressed lately and frustrated with the increasing demands of his work. She felt unable to help him with his problems and that upset her more.

She told the women that she believed Tom's time with Lorna was purely professional. She saw him as vulnerable and felt a lack of self-confidence. It increased her paranoia and she was becoming afraid that Tom didn't love her anymore.

Carolyn and Pat, like Virginia, noticed right away that Sandy had gotten thinner. They were concerned about her. They concluded her weight loss was proof of her depression.

Sandy cried for about an hour. The two women remembered it vividly, the more so because they knew Sandy as an out-going, happy and successful person.

Later that evening, Sandy, Carolyn, and Charlie had a few drinks together in their motel room. It was unclear later whether Tom was in the room at the time (he was certain he was not there, but Charlie thought he was). They discussed their newly-acquired life insurance package with Aid Association for Lutherans. AAL policies carry a standard clause that denies the payment of benefits for someone who commits suicide in the first two years after the policy is issued. They all talked about various ways they might commit suicide to bypass this policy feature.

As the months and years following this conversation passed, angry disagreements arose over what Sandy Bird actually said to the Smiths, but the Boysen's remained clear about what Carolyn told them.

Pat Boysen rode home with Carolyn on July 10, the day after the life insurance and suicide discussion. "Carolyn, Al [her husband] and I drove back to Memphis from St. Louis together…my husband and I both feel this was the first time Carolyn mentioned Sandy's conversation about suicide. Carolyn would say 'don't you remember when Sandy said that if she would ever think about committing suicide, she knew just where she would do it?'"

According to the Boysen's, and verified by Charlie Smith, Sandy mentioned something about running her car off a road near a bridge. She claimed she knew of a place perfect for such an accident.

Before leaving St. Louis, Sandy left a personal note for Charlie in his motel room. He claimed he threw away the note after he read it, saying it had nothing to do with the question of suicide. He claimed that the note said something to the effect "that she and Tom were doing better, and everything seemed to be all right at that time." He thought Sandy "seemed to have peace of mind and was no longer particularly concerned about anything." But Charlie was not present earlier, when the two pastor's wives saw Sandy crying.

Sandy and Charlie argued angrily during that weekend. Tom said it was a "silly argument" that grew out of Sandy doing some backseat driving. "Charlie pulled the car over and said to Sandy, 'You drive, I'm leaving,' and he started walking down the road. I caught up with him and settled him down only after he said a couple of pretty bad things about Sandy."

Charlie reported that on three or four occasions Sandy called him to talk about Lorna. This puzzled Tom. "She didn't really like Charlie very much. Carolyn and she were friends, but not Charlie." Maybe Sandy counted on Charlie as Tom's best friend to reach her stubborn husband and help him understand about Lorna. Charlie made no attempt to confront Tom.

Tom and Sandy drove back to Hardy on Sunday evening, arriving after everyone had gone to bed.

They took a day off on Monday. Virginia really loved Sandy and wrote, "I shared Vacation Bible School songs with Sandy for she will be song leader also. I gave Sandy a book for craft supplies for the pre-school VBS teacher." The senior Birds felt proud of their son and his wife who were so devoted to carrying on the same ministry that served as the center of their own lives.

Ralph Bird wrote: "Sandy was very busy and stealing time whenever she could to study for her master's degree. She would go to the church study where it was quiet. But even just when she was headed over there, she would give Tom a 'good-bye' kiss. They were always saying 'I love you,' and acted like newlyweds."

Tom also stayed busy, but when the children wanted their attention, Ralph said "they'd both drop everything and take time with the kids."

They planned on returning to Emporia on Tuesday, but reserved time for a special family outing. Virginia wrote:

"Tom and Sandy and the kids decided they want to know what it's like to pick blackberries in Hardy. So Ralph takes them out to a place near Omaha Center and they have fun picking. When they return Sandy gives the youngsters a quick bath to eliminate chiggers and then they pack up (including berries) and are off for Kansas."

The Birds arrived back in Emporia late Tuesday night. Both of them had a lot of catch-up work to do.

During a brief discussion with Angie on Wednesday, Sandy told her that she found peace during her trip, and that Tom had to deal with his own problems. Sandy called Jane Grismer in Little Rock, and told her that things were good between her and Tom. She said she had gained peace and that whatever was going on with Tom was his problem. God would take care of it all.

It seemed to everyone that Sandy had a breakthrough that week. Charlie claimed she told him that she had found peace. She told Angie and Jane the same thing. Had she found true peace, or had her depression simply reached another, more deadly stage?

Playing catch up

When busy professionals go out of town for several days, upon their return home it often seems they have much more to do. This was true for Tom and Sandy. Behind on his preparation for Sunday, Tom spent extra time at church. Trying to complete her master's in computer math and being away from a computer terminal for several days, Sandy spent extra time at ESU.

These time pressures continued right into Saturday, with each of them even busier than they had been during the previous months, but they got some good news that made them both happy. Sandy was offered a promotion at ESU. They decided the announcement deserved a celebration.

Remember...
The last dance together

Very few people keep detailed records of their daily activities. If called upon days, months or years later to describe what specifically happened on a set day, they rely on recollections clouded by time and open to suggestion, interpretation, physical and mental stress, discussion with others or any number of factors. It makes an investigator's job tough. It also makes it tough for someone being investigated.

Many month later, Tom was asked to recall precisely what he did on July

16 and 17, 1983. Like many people who have experienced a traumatic loss, these details were clouded by the passage of time, and each time he told them there seemed to be a slightly different twist, a fact that pleased his defense attorney. When a person accused of a crime seems to have their story down cold when forced to recall it months later, it leaves the impression that it was too-well planned and perhaps, thought out in advance—pre-meditated.

Saturday morning July 16, Tom still had quite a bit of work ahead of him to finish preparing for four Sunday events—one more than usual. In addition to the sermon and morning adult Bible study, there was an afternoon Adult Inquiry Class for those wanting to join the church, and an evening youth meeting.

After playing with his three children for a time, at mid-morning he headed off to his study at church. Around noon he took time out to run an errand at the Wal-Mart just a few blocks north of the church. He spotted Lorna's van at the Holiday Inn across the street, so on his way back to church he went on over to deliver a message. "Lori's called the church three times this morning looking for you."

"Thanks. I'll give her a call." Lorna had been at an Optimisses' meeting that morning.

Returning to his office, he continued his work preparing for Sunday.

Around 5:00 p.m. Sandy picked up Amy Swint, one of the Bird's regular babysitters. She told the 13-year old girl she and Tom were going to spend the evening together celebrating her recent promotion. Sandy was very happy.

Around 6:00 p.m., Sandy showed up at the church with sub-sandwiches and sodas. In a rare moment alone, they had a chance to talk together without interruption while they enjoyed their sandwiches.

Sandy learned that she had received a promotion to the position of Lecturer at ESU. She had been teaching six hours a week at ESU since they moved to Emporia and it was where she would be getting her second Master's Degree, this one in computer math.

The computer model she was designing as part of her master's project was a software program for church management. Tom provided the practical application and Sandy the theoretical and soon, the workable program.

Sandy's promotion at ESU and the near completion of her Master's Degree created some unique opportunities for both of them. They had much to talk about. These events presented some exciting future opportunities.

After they finished eating they headed out to see *Return of the Jedi* at the theater across the street, just west of the church. Howard Meyer, one of Faith's lay ministers, went to the same showing of the movie, but he was far ahead of them in the exit line when they spotted him, and they failed to get his attention to say hello.

The movie let out after 9:00 p.m. Neither of them was yet ready to finish their celebration. They decided to have a couple of drinks to top off the evening, so headed home where there was a bottle of Cold Duck. Sandy went in and told Amy they would be back in an hour or so, while Tom stayed in the white Peugeot station wagon that Sandy usually drove. Sandy told Amy that the kids could stay up long enough to have another piece of pie. Then she left, returning a few moments later to retrieve a partial bottle of Seagram's whiskey, Tom's favorite.

Tom drove them back to the church where they poured the Cold Duck into red plastic cups they had retrieved from the car, the kind of cold cups one would buy at Wal-Mart. They had a drink in his office. The idea of drinking alcohol in the church made them uncomfortable so they decided to go to The Station, a nightclub at the Holiday Inn. Tom set the bottle of whiskey in a corner of the church office bookshelf. They both took the red plastic cups holding their Cold Duck with them to the car. When he was finished with his, Tom put his cup in the expandable pocket attached to the driver's side door.

Arriving at The Station sometime between 9:45 and 10:00 p.m., they ordered drinks—a slow gin fizz for Sandy and a 7 & 7 for Tom. They munched on popcorn and talked about their present situation. They both knew they were stretched too thin and that their hectic life was taking its toll on them.

They talked about future options. Sandy had also received feelers from St. Johns College in Winfield to teach math. Tom was already teaching St. John's extension courses at ESU. "Maybe we could both take teaching positions at St. John's. Move there. What do you think?" Tom asked. Teaching at St. John's would require that the school extend a call to them, but Tom felt there might be such a possibility.

Sandy's promotion at ESU was good for many reasons. The recognition received by the job offer was a payoff for Sandy's hard work and great intellect. The money was welcome. With the Master's Degree out of the way, the time pressures would be lessened. These were good problems. Good opportunities. It was a good time to celebrate.

At The Station

The solo singer who was entertaining that night began to sing a Neil Diamond tune they both loved. Making their way to the dance floor, they began a slow, intimate dance to the words of *Heartlight*, from the movie *ET*, the lyrics of which would become almost prophetic.

"Come back again.
I want you to stay next time.
Tho sometimes the world ain't kind,
When people get lost like you and me.

"I just made a friend.
A friend is someone you need.
But now that he had to go away,
I still feel the words that he might say.

"Turn on your heartlight.
Let it shine wherever you go.
Let it make a happy flow for all the world to see
Turn on your heartlight
In the middle of a young boy's dream.
Don't wake me up too soon.
Gonna take a ride across the moon—you and me.

"He's looking for a home.
'Cause everyone needs a place.
Home's the most excellent place of all
And I will be right here if you should call me."

Work. School. Church. Home. Family. These were the centers of Tom and Sandy's lives. There was no question of the mutual commitment between them despite Sandy's concerns about Lorna. This evening found them talking about priorities that had sometimes gotten off kilter, that brought added strain to their marriage, that caused depression and frustration—the same types of problems experienced by other bright, young, married professionals.

It was about 10:30 when they decided to leave The Station. Sandy wanted to go home, but Tom told her he still had to complete his sermon. The choice was to either stay up late to complete it or get up early the next morning and he preferred the late night. Sandy wasn't pleased and they had a short-lived argument in the night club parking lot, which ended with Sandy telling Tom she was going to the computer lab at ESU. He told her to go home.

At that time on a Saturday, Sandy could find uninterrupted access to the computer. She had keys to the building and the classroom, and she had gone out there before at night for the same purpose. Sometimes it was the *only* time she could get on the computer.

Tom drove them back to Faith and got out of the car. Sandy moved over to the driver's side. Sandy said, "I'll be back in an hour." It was the last time Tom would see her alive, and though she said she was going to ESU, he had no way of knowing whether she ever arrived. He recalled that she left between10:30 and 10:45. Returning an hour later meant he expected her to return at about 11:45 p.m.

Tom went into his study and picked up where he had left off with his sermon, ambivalent about the babysitter who expected them to come home by 10:30 or so. He figured that Sandy would call Amy and tell her what was going on as she usually would have done.

Tom finished writing his sermon. It was time to practice its delivery. Usually he would go into the sanctuary and practice the sermon from the pulpit. Sometimes, when he had a lot on his mind and found it difficult to concentrate, he found comfort in jogging. Occasionally he would combine jogging with practicing his sermon, and the lingering effects of the 7 & 7 made it seem even more like a good idea.

He slipped on a pair of running shorts and his tennis shoes that he kept in a sack behind the office door, and headed out into the 85-degree heat. Working up a good sweat while running and concentrating on his sermon would be an elixir. It would help him clear his mind and body from the alcohol he had just consumed. He would be confident in being well-prepared for the next morning.

Tom ran a little over two miles—maybe 2-1/2. Though he had not been doing a lot of running in the last few years, he was still in good enough shape to return to the church sometime after 11:30 p.m. While the run had caused him to break into a sweat, it had also energized him. He felt quite awake.

As he waited for Sandy, he flipped on the church's air conditioner to make sure the building was comfortable the next day. July temperatures usually reach into the mid-to high 90s.

Tom cleaned up his desk and finished his other Sunday preparations, setting his sermon on the desk so he could find it easily the next morning. It felt good to be done. It would allow him to relax a little the next day.

Sandy had a reputation for being prompt and responsible. As it grew closer to midnight, Tom started wondering about her. Given the way computers often performed and the frustrations of developing software, "she maybe has just got caught up trying to solve a problem," he thought.

After midnight he tried calling the ESU switchboard, hoping someone could check the computer lab and ask Sandy to call him. No one answered.

He was starting to get chilled from the cool air in the church and the sweaty running clothes he had on, so he slipped back into the polo shirt and slacks he had worn all day. He stuffed the shorts and shoes back into the bag behind his office door and pondered what to do next.

Impatient now to know what was keeping Sandy, he got into his Toyota, which had been left at the church, and drove up to 15th Avenue and east to ESU. He hoped he would either see her as she was driving back toward the church, or find her in the computer lab at the school.

Completing the two-mile drive to ESU, he noticed no lights were shining through any of the classroom windows. Sandy's office and the computer room were deeper inside the building, which meant he could not be sure whether she was inside. He tried the door, but it was locked. Then he drove around to the other side of the building and checked those doors, with the same result. Added to the conundrum was the fact that Sandy's car was not there either.

He drove back to the church, thinking she may have taken a different route and now was looking for him. Or maybe she came back while he was jogging and, not finding him there, either went home or looking for him.

When he returned to the church, Sandy was not there and neither was her car. He called home, hoping she would answer. He believed it was around 1 a.m. Amy answered sleepily. He could hear the TV on in the background.

Amy said Sandy had not called at all, nor had she come home. Someone else had called earlier, but failed to say anything. Instead they just hung up. There was another call, too, but not Sandy.

Tom told Amy, "I've been across town looking for Sandy but couldn't find her."

Since Amy knew nothing about her whereabouts, he started making phone calls to the ESU campus police. Scott Henderson, a dispatcher for the ESU Police Department, recorded the time of the first call as 1:11 a.m. Tom asked Henderson, "Is there some way I can call my wife?" but was told the switchboard was closed during the evening. Henderson placed him on hold and tried to raise someone in the computer lab, but to no avail.

Tom asked if someone could go over and check the computer office, explaining that he had already driven by and did not see her car. Henderson had it done. His log showed that he called Tom back around 1:30 a.m. to tell him there was no news. The ESU officer suggested he call Emporia Police.

Tom dialed 911. He was told to call the regular police number for non-emergencies. When he called the police and explained the situation, he was told they had heard no reports of anything out of the ordinary. They told him it was a busy Saturday night, and they would send an officer to talk with him as soon as someone was freed up.

He called Newman Memorial Hospital. No one there heard of anything.

Frustrated and growing more nervous, Tom finally decided to go home. He let the campus and city police know where he would be in case they learned something.

When he arrived at home, Amy saw that he was worried and anguished. Paul woke up. He took the young boy with him as he drove Amy the two blocks to her home, about 30 minutes later. Amy had heard nothing from anyone else since he had called her earlier.

Upon returning home, Tom's anxiety increased. He paced the floors and uttered prayers. He sat by the phone in the living room, waiting for a call from the police.

At 3:22 a.m., Emporia police officer Mark Summey came to the house to take a missing person's report. The two talked in the front yard. Tom told him what he knew and his concerns. The police officer wrote it off as a simple domestic dispute. "Did you have an argument?" the officer asked.

Tom said, "No we had a disagreement about how we are busy and not having enough time, but that was all."

"She's probably at a friend's house," was his response. The officer told Tom that he would have someone from the first shift in the morning come back and check, figuring that by then Sandy would either have come or called home. Summey agreed to ask Emporia police to begin watching for Sandy's car.

Tom took a shower and then spent a sleepless night in the living room, near the phone. Sometime between 6:00 and 6:30 a.m. he called Deana Koch, a colleague of Sandy's at ESU. The two had met at Faith Lutheran. "I'm sorry for calling so early, but Sandy went to work at ESU last night around 11 and didn't come home. I wondered if you had been there and you got to talking or something?"

"No, I was out of town last night."

"Oh, I forgot to give you a message from Sandy on Friday night," he apologized.

"Do you want me to go check the office?"

"No, the security people have already been there."

Next, exhausted, frustrated and now fearful, Tom called Don Froelich, a lay minister, to come by and talk. He told him what little he knew and asked Froelich to deliver his sermon, telling him where he had put it the night before. He asked, "Will you have the people pray for Sandy?"

Police come bearing grim news

Around 8:30 a.m., Emporia police Officer Scott Cronk arrived. He had no news and neither did Tom. Cronk asked him to once again explain what had happened the night before, and then he left.

Cronk returned again at 11:45 that morning following behind Kansas Trooper Charles Smith. They got out of their cars and walked up the driveway. Smith carried Sandy's purse. He told Tom about finding the Peugeot and Sandy lying dead, face down in the Cottonwood River next to the Rocky Ford Bridge.

Tom asked, "What was she doing out there? We never go out there." He stopped and asked, "Well, where is it?"

Details, body English, perceptions and the ability to accurately reconstruct events, Tom would soon learn, make all the difference in investigations and in front of juries.

A mystery at Rocky Ford Bridge

Sandy and Tom parted sometime between 10:30 and 10:45 p.m., that Saturday night. Sandy drove off toward Emporia State University saying she would return in an hour. No one saw Sandy at ESU that night, but there were good reasons why not. If indeed she ever made it to ESU, it is sure she never made it home.

Sandy may have not gone directly to ESU. She often took long drives to relax and clear her mind. She and Tom had just had a couple of drinks. She wanted him to head home right away, but he wanted to stay at church to finish preparing for Sunday. Before sitting in front of a computer terminal, she may have taken a detour, driving the eight mile route that ended with her car's plunge off the Rocky Ford Bridge, into the Cottonwood River.

Don Froelich also taught at ESU. "People out at ESU said she'd drive that route when she wanted to solve a problem."

Sandy may have driven directly to ESU, ran into a computer problem, grown frustrated and gone out for a relaxing drive before heading back to church.

If Sandy went to the computer lab, there was good reason that no one saw her enter or leave. Security records indicated no one checked her building between 9:15 and 1:15.

Sandy may have been mugged, kidnapped, taken to the bridge and murdered.

Maybe she went to ESU, finished her work and came back while Tom was out jogging. Not finding him there, she drove over to Lorna's and had a confrontation that resulted in a fatal blow. Or maybe she drove directly from the church to Lorna's to settle the issues she had with the woman, and the confrontation turned ugly. Maybe Lorna saw an opportunity to set in motion the first part of the two schemes that would take Marty's life 3-1/2 months later. Since Lorna always knew Tom's whereabouts, maybe she or someone else followed the Birds that night and saw Sandy leaving alone, setting in motion a staged auto accident to cover up a murder.

Maybe Sandy's confession of depression to her friends at the St. Louis convention a week earlier should have been taken more seriously. Her mention of suicide by driving her car off a bridge seemed trivial to Charlie. Maybe he should have warned Tom.

Was Sandy's death caused as a result of her being tired and preoccupied? Was she distracted as she drove around the unlit and poorly designed bend on the south approach to the bridge? Did she simply miss a turn and plunge to her death? Did someone brutally beat her, throw her off the bridge, and then push her car over the edge, placing her dying or dead body into the water in front of it?

Each one of these scenarios provides a plausible explanation for her death, and each one of these explanations has fatal weaknesses, except one. Investigators followed a path forged for them from scant evidence, tortured theories, gossip and rumors. They saw the Reverend Thomas P. Bird as the prime suspect. They viewed every piece of information from the perspective of his guilt.

Spooked dogs

Rocky Ford Bridge is an old, wood-planked steel structure set in a remote rural area Southeast of downtown Emporia. Mark Gibbons lived about 300 feet south of the bridge in July of 1983, and was asleep in his mobile home, an oscillating fan pointed at his body trying to make him comfortable during the hot July night. At 3:10 a.m., Gibbons heard his dogs barking at something. Day and night brought all manner of animals to the fields that lay near Gibbons' place, and the river provided a ready source of water. Gibbons left his dogs out every night.

Gibbons walked outside and quieted his dogs.

Back inside his house, Gibbons turned off the fan and lay back down. Just minutes later, he heard the dogs barking again. He shouted out the window at them to stop, but in the silence that followed, he heard something else, the "something" he believed that caused his dogs to bark. Gibbons listened and heard a very clear and easily distinguishable sound coming from the direction of the Rocky Ford Bridge, a "hissing noise," like that made as a hot engine and radiator slowly sank into the cold river.

Gibbons didn't go to the bridge to check things out, but went back to bed. What did he hear? An animal screech? Or the sound of steam when the hot radiator of Sandy's car came in contact with the river? If so, it meant that the car had plunged over the bridge sometime around 3 a.m.

Tom knew that Sandy drove out in the country late at night, but it made no sense to him for her to do so at 3:00 a.m.

At the time Gibbons heard the hissing sound, Tom sat at home by the telephone, waiting for news about Sandy. Police records show Mark Summey, an Emporia Police Officer, visited Tom at 3:22 a.m. Shortly after that, police began watching for her car.

The first autopsy

Emporia pathologist, Dr. Juan Gabriel, autopsied Sandra's body. His report stated: "[The] Autopsy revealed death to be due to thoracic and abdominal injuries; not to drowning." Sandy lay face down in the water, and Gabriel found no water in her lungs and assumed drowning was impossible.

The cause of death was a loss of blood due to a partially "transected kidney, left, lower pole, traumatic." Sandy bled to death.

Gabriel, a veteran of more than 1,000 autopsies, knew that a transected kidney was common in auto crashes. He saw Sandy's death as the tragic result of a car wreck.

The time of death was set at between midnight and 3 a.m. on July 17, 1983.

Gabriel described the body "as that of a well-developed, well-nourished white female..."

There were multiple lacerations on Sandy's right upper arm, the front of her left forearm, running at an angle on her left forehead and a deep laceration on her left check. She had lacerations on either side of her head and multiple bruises on her right shoulder, chest wall, both upper arms, left forearm, left pubic region, and the inside and outside front of both thighs and legs. Gabriel discovered several bruises on her head as well. There noted no bruises or lacerations on the back of her legs or on her back.

He moved her limbs and found her left wrist "loosely mobile from side to side," and it made a cracking sound when it was moved; it was broken. As for other broken bones, Gabriel found none in the head and neck area, but he discovered several broken ribs on her left side. There was a large amount of blood and clots in her lower left abdomen.

Her stomach contained, "Approximately 250 cc. of partially digested food." Gabriel found a partially digested tomato skin. Her blood alcohol was .01 percent, not enough to impair her driving ability. There was no evidence of drugs in her blood.

Gabriel's job was to determine the cause of death, not the method of death. The cause of death was vitally important for many reasons, not the least of which was the need of family members to know how she died. Insurance companies needed to know; so did the police.

Most of Sandy's injuries were on her left side, consistent with being thrown out the door of an automobile plunging down an embankment, especially when the riverbank below was strewn with sharp, ragged limestone rocks.

While others were content to learn of the autopsy's findings through normal means, one person was not. This fact was not available to anyone until well after Tom had been twice convicted. It came as an eyewitness report by David Workman, the man who worked for Marty at Newman Medical Center, and who had talked at length with Lorna on March 30.

Workman saw Lorna at Newman between 7:30 and 8:00 p.m. on the Tuesday or Wednesday following Sandy's death. "She told me she had a note for Dr. Ludtke," a pathologist at Newman. "I unlocked Ludtke's office and let Lorna in."

A few minutes later he came back past Ludtke's office and saw Lorna was reading something. "It was the report of Sandy Bird's autopsy."

Lorna had a need to know how Sandy died, a need strong enough to risk being spotted reading the autopsy report. The family, police and insurance companies waited for the doctor's report, but not Lorna. Why?

Months earlier she had asked Alvin Tefft, a lab technician at Newman and close friend of Marty's, about a drug that could be given to someone, but not be identified in an autopsy. Could she have been checking to make sure Tefft's advice was correct?

Looks like foul play

Some time that morning, Dennis Arb, cousin of Sheriff Dan Andrews, answered his phone. His sister told him about an accident at Rocky Ford Bridge, having picked it up on her police scanner. He hopped on his motorcycle and raced out to the bridge. What he experienced following that trip had a profound effect on him. He said, "I am about as straight a man as you can find. I got ulcers from this."

Arb joined the small crowd gathering at the site and began looking around. He saw red spots and blood on the bridge deck and on the railing, which he brought to the attention of Sheriff Andrews.

Andrews removed a sliver of wood with a sample of the blood from the bridge deck and put it into a plastic bag. He gathered similar blood samples from another bridge plank, the rail overlooking the death scene, and from a bridge cross member. Now more curious, Andrews looked more closely at the scene and saw blood on a tree below and on the rocks close to it.

Trooper John Rule also saw the blood on the tree. He noted that the tree stood directly underneath the east edge of the bridge, about 20 feet from the car.

Arb also saw a red plastic cup with the residue of some pink liquid in it near a field opening, and "peel" marks along the road. He said it looked as though a car drove away from the area very rapidly. Arb pointed these out to Andrews.

Rule found a woman's wristwatch under the bridge deck just west of the bloody tree. Looking up at the bridge, he noted there was a gap between the bridge planks through which such a watch could fall. Under the bridge he found two more red cups like the one found in the field entrance. He noticed "a trail of blood" leading from the severed car door, which lay a few feet behind the submerged car, up the bank toward the bridge. He believed the blood was fresh because it was still almost purple in color.

David Cox, an Emergency Medical Technician, who had stood by the car while it lay upside down in the water, reached in and found the ignition key. He told the police that it was turned off. If he had known anything about Peugeots, he would have realized that the ignition switch was located on the left side of the steering column, not the right as with almost every other car. When the key pointed to the rear, the ignition was on, not off. But he did *not* know this. Police believed the switch was off, adding to their belief in foul play. If Sandy died in an accident, why would she have turned off the key before going over the riverbank?

For suffering such a fall, the car's shell received remarkably little damage. The driver's door was torn off and lay 7' behind it. It had a hole in it, and the scrapings on it matched scrapes on the outside shell of the car behind the door. Its window, which investigator's believed was open at the time of the crash, was shattered.

As Larry Estes towed the car out, Dennis Arb, who stood on the bridge watching, noticed that its headlights were on, but dim. Other witnesses claimed the headlights were off. Sheriff Andrews cupped his hands over the tail- and side-marker lights, noting that they were turned on, but they, too, were dim. If the headlights were on, an accident seemed likely. If off, it could only mean the killer did not want anyone to see the foul act.

Rule discovered one wet, readable footprint about 100-150 feet east of the accident scene. It appeared to be made by a woman's shoe, but a smaller size than Sandy's.

"It was obvious right away there was foul play," Arb, the amateur detective said. Rule and Andrews agreed. But not being a trained homicide detective, Rule ordered that the car be pulled from the river.

Two tow-trucks were needed to get the car up the rough bank. Larry Estes took the car to his body shop. (It was eventually sold to a junkyard and pieces were sold to many individuals.) Pulling the car up the bank disturbed the accident scene and made collecting reliable evidence difficult.

Within 45 minutes of Trooper Smith arriving at the scene, Sandy's body and the car both had been fished from the river. All officers treated this as a single car accident.

The officers searched around the riverbank, 65 feet above the car, where it appeared it went over. They saw no brake or skid marks. Rule saw this as unusual and suspicious. It suggested that either Sandy never saw where she was going, intended to go over, or the car had been pushed over the riverbank.

The next day Andrews and Rule returned to the bridge to take more blood samples from several surfaces, including a piece of the bark, four or five feet up the tree. They saw blood at the base of the tree, but collected no sample. Rule reached down to pick up a rock on which he had spotted human tissue the prior day, but it was gone—probably an animal got it.

Two days later, at Larry Estes' Body Shop where Sandy's Peugeot had been taken, Rule, Andrews and Agent Humphrey inspected the car. They found more red plastic cups and an empty bottle of Cold Duck inside. They saw no blood inside the car, suggesting that none of Sandy's injuries occurred while she was inside. They saw that the front seat was moved back, making it unlikely that a 5' 2" person could reach the pedals, suggesting that a taller person had been in the driver's seat (it was also possible that the towing company moved the seat back to make room for the severed door that they slid in front of the seat before the car was hauled away).

The riverbanks on either side of Rocky Ford Bridge are both popular fishing sites. Fisherman use the flat rocks to clean their fish; they carry the guts back down to the river, trailing fish blood and fluid on the rocks and ground as they go. Plenty of animals live in the area surrounding the bridge. The river is a natural late-night watering hole. Many animals die colliding with bumpers of cars moving toward and across the bridge, their bodies spiraling over the edge of the bridge, bouncing off the rocks below, spraying blood, only to be carted away and devoured by one of nature's predators. Blood stains could be quite old.

Investigators knew that the quality and readability of the blood samples was essential to their case. They were not totally pleased with the results.

Sheriff Andrews believed that foul play caused Sandy's death. Andrews felt frustrated, though, because he had no real evidence. Trooper Rule said it made him feel "hinky"—some sort of reference to a macabre sensation. Andrews continued to quietly work the investigation. Agent Humphrey, though, was skeptical and didn't want to pursue a homicide investigation.

The surviving spouse commits the vast majority of murders involving a married couple, and investigators usually look there first. In this case, though, the surviving spouse was a well-respected, hard-working Lutheran pastor and the wreck still looked like an accident.

Humphrey worried how the conservative, religious townspeople would react if police went after a preacher. The officers began a half-hearted investigation, until Marty was murdered. His murder triggered a theory held by investigators that Sandy and Marty's deaths were "equal parts of the same scheme."

A caring church

Susie Graf saw Lorna Anderson that morning in church and remembered her as acting oddly. She saw her crying and leaving the sanctuary a few times. Graf knew Lorna was upset about something, but what she did not know. No one yet knew about Sandy. All they knew was that Tom said Sandy never came home the night before.

While his church family prayed and worshiped at Faith, Tom kept his vigil at home, waiting for word of Sandy. As they walked out of church, Tom opened his front door to police officers bearing the news of Sandy's death. Later that day, he had the sad chore of identifying her body and telling his family.

Many members of the church had planned to go out and help search for Sandy after the service. As word of her death became known, it spread quickly, and they began coming to the Bird' s house to pay their respects and comfort Tom.

Virginia Bird's records how she and Ralph heard the news:

"Drew and Tina are here in Hardy because our V.B.S. begins Monday and Gloria and Felix brought the two of them up. We attend Sunday School and church and come home and have a lunch together of chicken, rice and assorted vegetables and applesauce.

"I hadn't cleared the table yet when the phone rang and it was Tom. He asked if dad was home and I said, 'Yes.' Then Tom said that he was calling (his voice was a bit faint and trembly [sic]) to tell us that Sandy had been killed in an accident last night.

"I answered, 'No! No!' What happened…and about that time dad said, 'Tom, we can't believe it. What do you want us to do?'

"Tom then asked if we could be in Little Rock for the funeral and Ralph said 'Yes, Tom and I'll preach if you want me to.' By this time I was crying a little and asking more details of the accident and Tom said she was out driving to clear her head and went off a bridge approach out near her University campus. He wasn't quite sure why she was in the vicinity or if she was driving too fast or what.

"Tom said the funeral will be in Little Rock. He was going to take her home, that he had just called Jane Grismer and Tom was leaving on a plane Monday.

"Tom then asked me if I would come back to Emporia with him and I said 'Yes, of course if it will help.'

"At the hall phone the sorrow in our voices and actions had disturbed Tina and Drew, and in the hall while we were still on the phone with Tom I took Drew and Tina in my arms and tried to tell them what happened.

"We hung up and said we would be in Little Rock Monday afternoon, and would make contact with him then about arrangements.

"I took Drew and Tina into the middle bedroom where they had been sleeping and tried to explain death and accidents and God's allowing this to happen and that uncle Tom and the three cousins would need to be remembered in their prayers. And as far as I knew, the two Cate's children regularly remember Tom in prayer each night."

Don Froelich delivered Tom's sermon that morning. "Tom called early, maybe 6:30 or 7 and was panicky. He said 'Sandy should be home and I'm concerned what to do.' I went to the house and visited with him. He was totally shaken. He said, 'I just don't know what to do.' After the service, people were going to go out and look for her." But police had already found her.

Don and his wife Lois drove to Tom's to comfort their friend and pastor. They asked for details. Don remembered, "Tom said, 'I didn't even know where it was,'" referring to the location of the Rocky Ford Bridge.

Tom looked distraught, his pastoral guard lowered, and far more vulnerable than people were used to seeing him. He had one very difficult task to perform yet; telling his oldest child, Andrea, what had happened. "Tom and I went to the park to tell Andrea. I was trying to comfort Tom," Froelich said.

Later in the afternoon, Lorna came to Tom's house. The two said very little to each other, and there were a lot of people milling around, with many cars parked out front.

Stephanie Moore, Bird's next door neighbor, missed church that morning. She and Steven, her husband, returned from out of town late that afternoon and saw the cars parked in front of Tom and Sandy's house.

Stephanie was excited about that day, because for weeks she and Sandy had plotted to give a special gift to Steven. Stephanie, raised a Methodist, had decided to take instruction in Lutheran doctrine and Sandy planned to help her. It was to be their secret.

Moore said:

"I found out she had died when we came home from the weekend and called Sandy to ask her what time they needed to leave to go to church. We got back in town about 4-4:30 or 5, and classes were going to start at six or seven. I don't know what kind of stories we were going to be telling Steve, but I was going to be leaving with her, so I had to call to find out.

"We couldn't figure out why all the cars were there. And so right when we walked in the door I called immediately to talk to her. I thought they had family visiting or something. A man answered and I asked , 'Is Sandy there,' and he said 'Who is this?' And I said 'this is Stephanie next door.' He said 'just a minute, Lorna will be over there to talk to you.'"

Stephanie knew Lorna very well. They were in Sorority together and she knew her from church.

"Lorna came over here. I don't know who it was who sent her over, but I am sure it was one of the men from church. Lorna came to the door and had already been crying and was still crying and said that Sandy had died the night before. That there had been an accident and she didn't really have any information other than that. We tried to find out what had happened.

"She had been secretary at the church and I just took her as a friend being there. If my boss would have had something incredible happen, I think I would be there, too. One thing that drew me to the church and helped me make my decision to join was that it was such a family feeling, a genuine concern about everyone that was a member. So it was not unusual that Lorna was there. I didn't find it unusual that so many people were concerned. It was a family.

"We went over there. The living room and dining room were filled with people. Tom was visibly upset. Just to look at him, you could see the pain in his eyes of Sandy having died. We had no reason to suspect anything else other than the fact that a man's wife had been in a car accident. We weren't looking for anything unusual or out of the ordinary. He was a man who was desperately in despair because his wife had just died. I only saw a great deal of pain. You can read a lot about a person through their eyes and I just saw a great deal of pain, a great deal of loss."

"Did she do it?"

That same day, Carolyn Smith, wife of Rev. Charles Smith, Tom Bird's best friend, received a call informing her of the death. Charles was not at home, so she called the home of Pastor Al Boysen who was supposed to be with her husband; Charlie had already left for home.

"They found Sandy Bird dead this morning. Pat, you don't think she did it, do you?" an emotional Carolyn asked Pat. The "it" was the suicide alluded to eight days earlier in St. Louis, an off-hand comment taken as a joke. Yet was it a joke?

According to the Boysen's, Carolyn told them clearly about what Sandy had said to her and her husband. Sandy talked about where and how she would commit suicide, if she ever did. It would be at a bridge in a remote area outside of town where a car could go off an embankment. Were Sandy's words and actions linked, or prophetic, or just a strange coincidence?

Incessant phone calls

Among others Tom talked with that day were members of the Grismer family. Nancy Cotharn was Sandy's aunt, and one of the women that helped raise her. Tom talked to her twice that first day.

"I talked to Nancy twice on the phone Sunday night the 17th and again Sunday night the 24th. Both times we talked about why's, the what's and the when's, trying to understand, trying to capture those last hours and come to an understanding.

"People ask questions and I did not know answers any more than anyone else. I told Nancy that Sandy had called about having trouble with the computer earlier in the afternoon before she came with dinner, not that night."

Many months later, after rehashing the events of those last days of Sandy's life among her family members, Nancy came to believe that Tom had told her Sandy had called him from ESU at 10:30 pm Saturday, and said she was having a computer problem. But Tom stated he and Nancy had talked twice on Sunday, and one of those times was at about 10:30 pm. Over time, and clouded by numerous conversations among various family members, times, dates and stories began to run together, and that running together painted a different snapshot than what actually was discussed during those tragic days. This was further complicated by a call a week later.

"In her conversation on the 24th I was upset because I read the newspaper that the coroner had said she had died between midnight and three. I didn't understand that and wondered out loud to Nancy about the late time of death [Tom did not know about Mark Gibbons' statement at that time]. I just figured that Sandy would have died before midnight. I did not know, I only speculated."

Nancy also believed that Tom had speculated about a brake problem that may have caused Sandy's accident. Experts determined that the brakes were in good working order. She saw that as an inconsistency in his story.

"As to the car problem. Again I was speculating how Sandy could have wrecked. There was no brake problem that I knew about; but I did mention to her in my speculation that we had had a grating noise when we turned the steering wheel to the full turn and at the shop I found that I needed to add power steering fluid; so I wondered about that."

Mark Bird tried in vain for over three hours to reach his brother Tom. It was well-past 11 p.m. before he got through. "Tom kept saying he just could not understand why Sandy would be driving around that late out in the country. He was despondent and exhausted."

What Tom knew was that he was a man filled with sorrow, grief and remorse. He played out the Saturday events over and over in his mind. He knew that if he had gone home with Sandy as she wanted, she would still be alive. He tossed and turned all night, dreading the flight to Little Rock the next morning with his three little Birds and a casket carrying their mother's body.

"I remember waking up at 1:30 or so, and Sandy wasn't there." Sandy would never be there again.

Going home for good

Tom woke early on Monday, July 18, to get himself and his children ready for the trip to Little Rock. There he and Jane Grismer, would complete the arrangements for Sandy's funeral. Although her body was going home for good, Tom knew her spirit had flown home sometime Saturday night or Sunday morning.

Once the family was ready, Tom Eggeman, an ESU professor and counselor, drove the family to the Wichita airport. The children saw flying on an airplane as a big adventure, little understanding the tragic reason for the flight. Tom, the little Birds, and Sandy's body boarded the plane.

Back in Emporia later that day, Susan Ewert, Lorna's best friend, drove to the Anderson's house. She wanted to know the details of Sandy's death.

Susan recalled that strange visit.

"This is a spooky thing. Lorna called me about 11 or 11:30 the day after Sandy had been killed. She said she didn't know anything about it but she told me what she *did* know. I think I asked about the funeral and such. She was so distraught, in a state of numbness.

"I went over, but someone was there at the house, and the funny thing is, I remember that I had a red dress that was a party dress and for some reason, when Lorna came to the door, Lorna was in a party dress. And we're talking like a *new* dress. It was blue or something.

"But when I got there she didn't ask me to even sit down, which was sort of unusual. But when I left and walked off that porch, and this was the really weird thing—I denied this to myself over and over again—what I had thought to myself, in fact I don't think I thought it, but I actually said it out loud as I am walking off the porch and the door is closed. And I said, 'Lady, I hope you're not involved in this.' That forever hit home to me because there was no reason to have thought that. That statement has come back to me time and time and again. Did I have a sixth sense? I don't know. I think I buried it as I walked out the door."

Families reunited

Mark and Gloria met Tom and the children at the Little Rock airport. They took the family directly to Jane Grismer's house.

Since Jane had married Jerry Grismer, she moved from the middle-class neighborhood in which Sandy grew up, to a part of the city reserved for Little Rock's wealthy class. Her multi-story home with long porches running the length of the house, sat high on a hill overlooking the Arkansas River. The front yard and driveway were steep, providing very little play area for children. No one could play whiffle-ball in Jane's front yard.

As soon as Tom arrived, he and Jane disappeared into a back room to plan Sandy's funeral while Mark and Gloria cared for the children. The meeting dragged on.

Mark got tired of waiting and left, leaving the children with Gloria who had a difficult time entertaining them. There were no toys in the home. While Gloria searched for toys, carrying one-year old Aaron on her hip, she happened down a hallway where Jane kept a wedding picture of Tom and Sandy. Aaron saw the picture and said, "Mama."

Gloria took the children with her to K-Mart and bought a few toys.

Gloria became frustrated because she had no time to be alone with Tom and console him, because the funeral plans took so much time—Tom and

Jane had much to discuss. Jane asked Tom everything he knew about Sandy's death. He really didn't know much, and neither did Emporia investigators. Tom had never seen Rocky Ford Bridge.

Other members of Sandy's family were there also, and when Tom finally broke free from Jane, they offered condolences to Tom and the children. And they pestered Tom with questions about Sandy's sad, mysterious death.

At one point, Tom walked into the kitchen and sat on a barstool. He felt and looked physically, emotionally and spiritually exhausted. Spending time with Jane planning his wife's funeral drained him. Laura Stringer, one of Tom's sisters-in-law, saw Tom sitting in the kitchen. "Oh Tom, you look awful. You must have had a terrible night," she said.

Tom reflected on Sunday night, when he lay tossing and turning in his bed, weeping, arguing with himself, wondering why all this had happened, and very perplexed by the few details he knew about Sandy's death. It had been a terrible night, one of many he faced in days ahead. For weeks after Sandy's death, Tom could not sleep in their bedroom, choosing instead to sleep on the floor in the boy's room. But that Sunday night was one of the hardest with well-meaning friends and family calling late into the evening.

When Laura said "terrible night," she was thinking of *Saturday* night. Tom had already told the family that he had been up most of Saturday night worrying about Sandy, calling the police and such. Tom answered her wearily, "Yes. I went to sleep but woke up and Sandy was not there. I couldn't sleep and I got up and paced the whole night."

Over the months that followed, Laura interpreted Tom's remarks to mean that he was home on Saturday night trying to sleep, not tossing and turning Sunday night as Tom meant. When a jury hears these kinds of "contradictions" in a defendant's story, it affects them negatively, sending a signal that his alibi is shaky, but this exchange proved typical of the type of "evidence" stacked against Tom in the months ahead.

Ralph and Virginia come from Hardy

Monday, Ralph and Virginia Bird left Hardy to make the 3-1/2 hour journey to Little Rock. Before they left, Ralph picked up a supply of bulletin covers for the funeral. The front of the bulletin featured the Bible verse, "We too must always be ready."

When they arrived in Little Rock, they contacted Mark and asked him if he would sing at the memorial service—"The Ninety and Nine"— to which he readily agreed.

With a rough draft of the funeral program in hand, they headed to Trinity Lutheran Church where the pastor graciously allowed them to type a stencil and prepare the bulletin for printing. They headed back to Gloria's house, ready to fall into bed.

On Tuesday morning, Gloria informed them that Jane had changed the day of the funeral from Thursday to Wednesday. This meant they had to change the bulletin and rearrange logistics for those participating in the service. Jane always did what seemed most convenient to her.

As the family talked with Tom that morning, he told them that the mortician had done a great job preparing Sandy's body. "But you can still see the bruise on her cheek," he said sadly, choking back tears.

"The coroner said her death came quickly because of the bleeding, but there must have been that moment of horror." He stopped talking for several minutes, overwhelmed by grief, as he tried to compose himself. The Birds saw Tom as a hurting man, just what they expected knowing him as had Ralph and Virginia Bird.

Jane had decided that Sandy's graveside committal service on Wednesday should precede the funeral service. This unusual schedule of events troubled Tom. LC-MS churches always have their memorial services first, followed by the committal at the cemetery. But in his grief and faced with Jane's desire to be in control, Tom relented.

The group of people who Jane invited to the 10 a.m. committal service joined the funeral procession as it headed to the cemetery. On this very hot July morning, Pastors Charles Smith and Al Boysen, both of whom had been with the Birds at the LC-MS Synod Conference in St. Louis just nine days earlier, spoke and the pastor of Jane's Presbyterian church prayed. After they left, Sandy's body was lowered into her grave in the cemetery in Saline County, just outside of the city limits of Little Rock.

Tom and Sandy were popular everywhere they had been. As with their wedding ceremony, the funeral attracted a large crowd. The 11 a.m. memorial service began late. Virginia Bird wrote, "People from Emporia are there, from West Memphis (Tom's former congregation) and even some of our members from Hardy came down for the service."

Rev. Ralph Bird gave the message and Mark Bird "does a great job of singing the solo," Virginia reported. They had all planned to head down to the church basement for lunch following the service, but Jane changed that plan as well, instead insisting that everyone go to her house for lunch.

After lunch, the elder Birds and Mark left for Gloria's house, but Jane insisted that Tom remain behind. "Tom doesn't get a chance to come over. He has a hard time getting away from Jane's house. She really monopolizes a person's time," a frustrated Virginia wrote that night.

Thursday offered Tom a chance to relax and space to mourn. He spent a good part of the day at Gloria's house. "He cried most of the day," Gloria remembered. "It gave him a chance to let his guard down. It was hard to watch him suffer like that."

Later that day, Gloria answered the telephone. It was Jane. She asked Gloria what Tom was doing. Jane and the family planned to go to a birthday party for one of Tom and Sandy's former classmates at Hall High. She told Gloria they couldn't cut the cake until Tom got there. Gloria told Jane that Tom didn't want to go anywhere, but Jane insisted on talking to Tom. Jane never accepted "no" as an answer, whether it was Tom, police investigators or nosy, scandal-thirsty *Emporia Gazette* writers.

Flying home

On Friday, Tom, Virginia and the three little Birds boarded a plane back to Kansas, while Ralph drove to Hardy to preach his Sunday sermon. He planned on joining them late Sunday evening for the Monday memorial service at Faith. Before departing, Sandy's three brothers boarded the plane.

Virginia described the trip:

"We have seats on the plane close together and Andrea eventually makes her way over to my seat and sits with me when we have a snack. We have a layover in Tulsa, Oklahoma. We get off and wait in the room for our plane to be called.

"Paul has a temper tantrum in the room and is hard to control. He is showing the effects of the loss of his mom I'm sure.

"Now we board the plane for Wichita which arrives around 1 p.m. We are met at the airport by Lorna Anderson who is to drive us to Emporia two hours away."

After a quick lunch at McDonalds, the big Ford van, filled with Birds and driven by the church secretary, headed back to Emporia. After she dropped the Birds at home, Lorna left them alone.

Virginia's words describe that afternoon:

"Tom sits down in the living room exhausted. I am unpacking the clothes, etc. when I hear Tom say, 'Oh mom, the papers have it wrong.'

"When I go to see what he is reading, he holds the *Emporia Gazette* and shows me where they have printed that Tom first called police at 3 a.m. the night Sandy died. He is weeping as he says to me, 'They'll think I didn't even care, waiting 'till 3. Mom, I called from midnight on and they wouldn't come here 'till 3 a.m. saying it was Saturday night and they were short-handed and all they would do was put an all-points bulletin out about the car.'

"I try to comfort him, saying, 'Tom, people who know you are not going to believe that. So don't worry about things wrong in a newspaper. So many papers get things wrong.'"

During the years that followed that Friday afternoon experience, Virginia, who died in 1997, learned that newspapers *often* got things wrong about Tom. And those news accounts created their own inertia when read and meditated on by Jane and her family—and residents of Emporia. They created questions that Tom couldn't answer to their satisfaction other than to say, "They got it wrong!" But when your only daughter and sister and niece, who lived hundreds of miles away, died in a mysterious car crash; when her husband, grieving and exhausted, said sometimes contradictory or confusing things; when a distant family rehashed the story and memories and stories merged into mysterious, unexplainable patterns; when they naively believed newspapers *do* always get it right—a tragic drama began to be played out that destroyed the life of Tom Bird.

First weekend home

Tom answered the phone constantly that Friday afternoon. The coach of the softball team called. Friday night was a regular softball night, and he wondered if Tom wanted to play. Virginia encouraged him.

At the ballpark, Tom told the men, "I can't give 100 percent," but played the best he could. Virginia and the children watched from the stands. Some other little children came and talked with the little Birds. They asked four-year-old Paul about his mother. "She died." Virginia saw in Paul an amazing composure for a boy his age handling such a difficult question. She believed he inherited or learned some of the self-control exhibited publicly by Tom and Ralph.

The constant condolences and contacts continued on Saturday. Church members brought an endless supply of food to the family. [One of Tom's friends, another LC-MS pastor, said he is sure that the women of the church keep hot dishes frozen and ready for occasion such as this.] Virginia observed how loved her son was by the church's members. She knew they were a close-knit body, and that gave her hope for Tom's ability to cope.

That day Tom spent a good deal of time working on "Thank You" cards, and then began to try to figure out the bills. Sandy had taken care of all the family's bank and household business.

During the morning, Jane called to let Tom know they were in Emporia, at the Holiday Inn. She said she would take the children out to lunch. While picking them up, Jane informed Virginia that she and Papa Doc had bought flowers for Sunday's worship service and Monday's memorial service. Virginia saw this as a not so subtle put-down, and offered to kick in some money later to help pay for the flowers.

After supper, with the children finally in bed, Angie came to see Tom. They sat in the same basement where, just weeks earlier she and Sandy had talked about Tom and Lorna. Following that earlier conversation, the young teacher had gone to Tom to warn him about Lorna, and try to get him to understand Sandy's worry. Now that Sandy was dead, Angie once again wanted to warn Tom about Lorna. She encouraged him to stop counseling the woman, an idea Tom had been mulling over himself. Sharon Meyer, wife of one of the church lay ministers, also warned him. So had Susie Graf. Tom listened this time and made a decision to take action as soon as he could.

Tom and Angie talked late into the night. Among other things, Angie once again cautioned Tom about his vulnerability as a widowed young pastor. Virginia joined them for a while and recorded that Angie told Tom, "Sandy was very concerned about her parent's spiritual condition," and she offered to "make a point to have coffee with Grismer's and discuss religion."

It was very late before Angie left for home and the two went to bed. Virginia saw that Tom's light stayed on late into the night. "He is grieving and yet handling it pretty well," she wrote.

A hard church day

Tom and his family woke early Sunday to get ready for church. Tom struggled hard that morning, not because he wanted to avoid church or had anger toward God. It was hard because Sandy was not there to direct everything, because Larry Kalsow, not Tom, would be preaching that day, because hundreds of Tom's closest friends in the world would be there, all sorrowing with him.

When they walked into the church, Paul clung to his dad. Virginia said he was "almost hysterical" if Tom ever left his side.

Jane and Papa Doc attended the worship service, too. As Presbyterians from a big city, perhaps they felt a bit out of place in the serious, formal worship of an LC-MS service. But the people of Faith welcomed them with the same warm love they showered on their beloved pastor.

Tom chose to teach the Bible class following the Sunday service, but it was very hard to do. "Each time I would look around, I would see someone that brought back a memory of Sandy." He choked up during the teaching, and had to stop to regain his composure.

Following the service and Bible study, church members brought lunch to Bird's house, including Peggy Barnhart. She and her husband owned a house not too distant from Rocky Ford Bridge. (Sandy had been out there before, and Tom wondered if that's why she chose that route for a relaxing drive.) Once again, a steady stream of visitors stopped by to offer condolences and find ways to help the family.

Angie kept her promise to have coffee with the Grismers and talk about religious issues. Virginia reported that she was "…still arguing evolution with them when they came back to the house."

During the afternoon as things settled down, Tom, Virginia, the children and the Grismers drove to Rocky Ford Bridge in Papa Doc's van. Tom asked Robert Barnhart for directions.

As they approached the bridge, Andrea became very upset, so Jane and Virginia stayed in the van. They saw the rusty, bullet-riddled S curve sign, though barely, as it was covered with long grass and vines. They carefully negotiated the 90-degree turn to the east and then the 90-degree turn to the north. There they spotted the hulking, haunting bridge.

Papa Doc and Tom got out, looked around the site and climbed down the steep embankment onto the slippery, dangerous rocks that are plentifully strewn haphazardly on the riverbank. They talked about what could have happened to Sandy. They looked at various places her car might have gone over the riverbank. They tried to imagine how it tumbled down and came to rest. Tom showed Doc where police said her body was found.

As they drove away, Jane said to Virginia, "I understand how it could happen on that steep grade." They talked about suing Kansas for Sandy's wrongful death.

"It must have been about 2-3 miles from the bridge," Virginia wrote, when they spotted the Barnhart house. Tom pointed it out to them. Virginia described the place. "It was a typical farm house with a front porch the full length of the front of the house and had pillars holding up the porch roof."

After stopping for ice cream at Baskin & Robbins, the hot weary troupe arrived back home. Ralph Bird had already arrived. When they told him where they had been, Jane said, "Now I know what happened and can understand it since I have seen the area." Ralph wanted to see it for himself.

Jane's overbearing personality that Sunday irritated Virginia. "I was especially taken by her lack of true consideration for Tom or the children. She stayed and stayed and had only words to offer and some inappropriate looks to one grieving as Tom was. She never lifted a finger to be of any real help. Only acted the guest and even when she knew the children were waiting for Tom to say prayers with them, she monopolizes his time, but gave him very little comfort. The reason I mention this is that she was such a contrast to all the other women that had been coming in—everyone else was cooking things or lending a hand with laundry, with the children, or busy cleaning up somewhere."

Though neighbor Stephanie Moore spent less time inside Tom's house than did Virginia that weekend, she saw the same thing. "When Jane came after Sandy died, it was like she just moved in and took over and was bossy about what things should be done."

The relationship between Sandy and her mother never was close. Much of Sandy's child rearing "was by committee," as Ralph Bird later described it. Her aunts and grandmother all shared time caring for the young girl because Jane built a real estate career. The relationship really soured when Jane divorced Sandy's father Randall. "That really hurt Sandy," Tom said.

Sandy kept in touch with Jane, and the family visited Little Rock on special occasions, but Jane knew nothing about Sandy's real life as a mother and wife to a Lutheran minister. She often talked about the young Sandy, but knew little about the woman, wife and mother her daughter became. Once Sandy died, many believed that Jane tried to make up for those lost years by taking an extraordinary interest in finding out what happened to Sandy. On July 24, she saw it as an accident—pure and simple.

Tom and the family walked into Faith on Monday afternoon at 2 p.m. for a memorial service. It stood packed wall-to-wall with mourners. Pastor Larry Kalsow presided.

Later that day, the Grismers left for Little Rock. Ralph and Virginia stayed for several more days, with Ralph leaving for Hardy to serve his church. Virginia stayed behind to help her son and grandchildren.

The weary exhausted young pastor, father and widower, tried to sleep. With the public mourning over, he faced a private, deep groaning gnawing at his spirit, and continued to question: "What happened to Sandy? Why was she out there? If I had only gone home with her" Tom longed for a return to normalcy. First he had to deal with Lorna.

We're the police, and we're here to help

Trooper Rule, the accident investigator who was dispatched to the Rocky Ford Bridge Sunday morning, July 17, saw Sandy Bird's wreck as a suspicious accident. So did Sheriff Andrews. They asked for help.

Rule confronted Agent Humphrey with his suspicions. Humphrey drove to Estes' body shop and looked at Sandy's car with Andrews and Rule. What he saw made him curious enough to visit with Tom, but he wanted to keep it low key.

Humphrey called Tom on Tuesday, the day after Sandy's memorial service, and asked him to stop by his office. Tom readily agreed and drove over, and never considered bringing along an attorney. Rule joined them.

Humphrey asked Tom to tell him about Saturday night. Where had they been, what had they done? Did he have any idea why Sandy would be out in the country driving alone at that time of night? Were there marital problems? Is it possible Sandy was seeing someone, suggesting that might account for why she was out so late, and why Tom could not explain it?

Tom calmly answered Humphrey's questions. Unlike common thugs and thieves, Humphrey saw in Tom a different kind of "suspect." Tom looked almost too relaxed for the investigator, but as a pastor, he was trained to maintain a sober and strong appearance in public. Humphrey noted that Tom answered questions clearly, and made no attempt to avoid anything. Tom never said a word about calling an attorney. Tom had as many questions about the accident as the investigators, and hoped they could help him discover what happened. They had few answers.

During the interview, Rule stepped near Tom and opened a small plastic bag he had carried in with him. He emptied out a lady's wristwatch. "Do you recognize this watch?"

"Yes, it's Sandy's. Where did you find it?"

"It was under the bridge."

"How would it have gotten there?"

"That's what we want to know," Rule responded, completing his questioning for the morning. No one in that room could explain how the watch ended up under the bridge.

As they finished their talk, Humphrey assured Tom he would keep him posted on any new developments. After Tom left, Humphrey told Rule, "It's an accident."

Though Sheriff Andrews and Trooper Rule disagreed, Sandy's death continued to be treated as an auto fatality. Quietly, Andrews continued digging around for criminal "evidence," but the formal investigation ended.

Rule handed Tom Sandy's watch and, as they walked down the hall together said, "I just can't understand why'd she be out there alone so late?" It made little sense to Tom either.

Marty Anderson's murder triggered a vigorous investigation that eventually led a grand jury to decide that Sandy died by foul play, and the chief actor was her husband, Tom Bird.

Mead meets chortling Lorna

Although Lorna had worked for Faith for more than seven months, in late July, Jan Mead still wanted her to continue as an American Heart Association employee. She drove to Emporia on July 26 and met with Lorna at her house, introducing her to Kim Clark, Lorna's new supervisor. Mead had been promoted.

The three women had a brief visit. Mead saw a strange demeanor in Lorna that stuck in her mind. She explained this to Judge Clarence L. Sawyer, a District Magistrate Judge in Junction City, during the 1984 inquisition into Marty's murder.

"Is there any unusual conversation that sticks in your mind that transpired during that meeting?" Sawyer asked.

"Well, at that time it was the week after the minister's wife had been found in a car accident and had, was killed, and Lorna was in a different mood when we got there that day."

"How so?"

"Well, it's very hard to explain. Let me see if I can clarify that. We walked in and introduced Kim, the girl, to Lorna and we talked about heart business for just a few minutes and then..."

The judge interrupted her to identify Kim. "Kim is the girl who took my job."

"I see."

In her written voluntary statement given to police on November 28, 1983, Mead wrote:

> "On July 26, I was in Emporia with Kim Clark, the girl who took my job and we stopped to introduce Kim to Lorna. As soon as we got there she began telling me that Tom's wife had been killed in a car wreck the week prior to that. The details were very sketchy and she said authorities didn't know exactly what had happened. She was sort of smiling and hiding her face while she was telling this to us."

Later, Mead added more detail to her July 26, 1983 conversation. Lorna had also said, "A lot of people think she was out driving and just missed the bridge."

Kim Clark, too, remembered that conversation. Jan Mead told her about the love affair between Lorna and her minister (Lorna told Mead she and Tom were lovers, and anything Clark had to say about it would be double hearsay in a court of law). Clark had no personal knowledge of anything about Lorna except for this meeting.

About that July 26 meeting, the judge asked Clark, "Did you ever come to know a person by the name of Lorna Anderson who lived in Emporia, Kansas?"

"Yes, I did."

"Do you remember about when that happened?"

"My first and only encounter with Lorna was in July of 1983 and I don't know the day. It was July or first of August..."

"Can you relate any conversation that occurred during the meeting between yourself, Jan Mead and Lorna Anderson at Mrs. Anderson's house?"

"Well, we just primarily discussed Heart Association and then—and she was acting a little strange and Jan had asked her what the problem seemed to be, and evidently, Tom, who I did not know at that time, his wife had passed away shortly before in a strange automobile accident, and she was a little upset with that. And pertaining to this case, the only thing I know that she said was something about her and Tom had to get away and spend some time together, for the weekend....

"I thought it was a little peculiar that she would talk about...It came across as—as 'spending time with someone else' and I thought that was strange, maybe being an extra-marital affair and that she would open up like that to somebody that she didn't know.

"And—And Jan and I thought it was peculiar because she was just acting very odd—I didn't know the woman, but Jan afterwards had stated that it was odd—she was—like—covering her mouth and—like—grinning and talking about the whole situation.

"It was just strange."

Lorna continued to fill the job at AHA until after Marty's murder, but Kim Clark had no further contact with her until afterward. As part of her job, Lorna had spent considerable time organizing information about Emporia's AHA donors and storing that data on cards. After Marty died, Lorna threw them away, leaving a void in AHA's ability to raise money. But the missing cards were not the only void left by Lorna when she left town.

Resigned to a separation

July 25 was not only the day of Sandy's memorial service at Faith, it was the first day of the second week of Vacation Bible School at the church. Had she lived, Sandy would have been leading music.

VBS created a lot of human activity in and around the church, and it stretched the staff to their limit. The lay ministers relieved Tom of the greater part of his pastoral duties to give him time to recover from Sandy's death. Yet he spent considerable time at church and around Lorna.

Tom realized that week that Angie, Susie, Sharon and Sandy had all been right. He needed to stop counseling Lorna and be more careful around her—and around *other* women.

A pastor who has just lost his wife is left with a complex set of problems, especially when there are children to raise. When a pastor has established an open-door counseling ministry, the problems are greatly compounded. The

221

mere perception of sexual tension between a mourning pastor and *any* woman could cause great problems with his ministry. For this reason, it's common among pastors to remarry relatively soon after a spouse's death. Although Tom didn't actively seek a new spouse in late July, some women began entertaining thoughts about *him*.

One woman stopped to see Tom during this time and asked him for books about marriage. "My husband doesn't find me attractive anymore."

"How do you know this?"

She told Tom that her husband quit having sex with her. She wanted to know what to do. "I don't do marriage counseling without both parties present," Tom told her.

"But you have books I can read. How about these?" She moved around behind his desk and knelt down, pulling books off the shelf. She positioned herself very suggestively, and Tom grew uncomfortable. She looked up at him with passion in her eyes. Tom felt sexual tension, but excused himself from the situation. This woman became one of the gossips whose testimony hurt Tom at trial, though nothing happened between them. Did she feel scorned and embarrassed, letting that influence her testimony? She eventually divorced her husband and left the church.

Although he remained committed to Lorna as her pastor, Tom wanted to put space between them. He wanted her to resign as church secretary, and he knew she would not resign unless he asked her to. This he dreaded.

The clamor created by VBS complicated the process, but on Wednesday morning, he called her to his office. "Lorna, Angie talked to me about the rumors she and others heard about us. I'm not sure what to do about my own future. I'm worried about my ministry and my children." He looked at Lorna and said sadly, "I am sorry Lorna. I just don't need this distraction right now. I would like you to resign."

While they talked, two other people came into the office, interrupting their discussion. The phone rang and Tom answered. Helpless to do anything, stuck on the phone he watched as, "she went off and lost her temper. She stormed out of the church and got into her van."

He followed her to the parking lot, determined not to let her go away. He saw her already in the van and told her to come back into the church, but she said through her tears, "That will just make people more suspicious." He stepped in front of the van to keep her from driving away and then he climbed in the van. Tom wanted this settled, and he did not want her getting depressed and doing anything stupid. The lay ministers were scheduled to meet with him in a few days, and he wanted this issue settled.

Lorna drove out on the Kansas turnpike. Tom continued to try and explain what this meant, to put it into context. She was a good secretary. She successfully helped him and the members struggle with church growth. Other than his own personal tragedy, it had been a good time for the church. "The church cannot afford distractions, nor can I, or even the appearance of evil. The rumors are making it even harder." He paid no attention to where they had driven but thought they drove as far north as Admire, where they turned around and started back.

Lorna started to relax and pulled off the road stopping her van in front of a boarded up Howard Johnson's restaurant. "Then I'll just quit and write a letter of resignation. And Marty will write one, too, you know. He's going to be angry, because I need to have a job." Tom knew of the Anderson's financial struggles.

They talked about what Lorna's resignation letter should say and how the process would work. "You have to be professional about this. Don't write about any of your bitterness." She wanted to blast those in the church who had been her accusers. Finished with their discussion, Lorna drove them back to the church.

The next day, Pastor Kalsow called Tom. "Can you come over to Messiah and talk a while?" Tom drove right over.

"I noticed you were out with Lorna in her van yesterday. I drove by and saw you two."

"It was all about her resigning." He gave Kalsow an accounting of their meeting, though it bothered him that he involved himself with Faith's business. It bothered Tom more that Angie talked to Kalsow without either telling him she planned to do so, or doing so in his presence. What she did bordered on tale-bearing. He learned later she carried the story to Sharon and Howard Meyer, too.

"Good, but you've got to be careful. The perception of anything bad will hurt you," his friend advised. They agreed that the lay ministers needed to deal with the issue.

So concerned had Kalsow become about his friend, he called the Faith lay ministers as well. Don Froelich was out of town, but Howard Meyer and Harold Schwinn came to meet with him Friday morning. He told them about the incident and the meeting with Tom, and said Tom believed he could handle it.

This presented the lay leaders with a clear case of dealing with gossip and rumor. Appearances, misconceptions, hearsay and nonfactual assumptions plagued Tom since the day the church hired Lorna, and they were about to get worse.

Lorna's resignation torn up

Lorna wrote the resignation letter and placed a copy in each of the lay ministers' mailboxes. They found them Sunday morning. Froelich, who had been out of town, saw Lorna that morning and she told him she resigned. He told her, "No. You do not have to do that."

The lay ministers met together that evening and discussed the problem. They asked Kalsow to attend.

They met with Tom at his house on Monday morning, August 1, his day off. They discussed many issues, and Lorna's resignation was on the agenda. They concerned themselves with how best to ease Tom back into the ministry and how to share his duties. They encouraged him to take time with his children, and work to get his personal life ordered before he resumed a total ministry. They agreed, with relief on Tom's part, that he should be spared doing visitations. Also, no more counseling for a while, and especially, no more counseling with Lorna. The lay ministers wanted him to preach and teach only, and cut back his hours.

They talked of Lorna. They asked whether there was any truth at all to the rumors they had been told? "No, there is nothing romantic between us," Tom assured them. They all knew that a pastor's sexual sin meant immediate dismissal. But the leaders also knew that only one person—Angie—talked to them about the possibility of a physical relationship. Had there really been something going on, they felt others would have come forward. And these men took seriously the charge not to let gossip or rumors affect their decisions.

They told Tom of their great concern for his vulnerability to her and to other women. They discussed her resignation, but also about Marty getting angry at her and at the church. Froelich volunteered to call Marty (when they talked, Marty said he was thrilled that Lorna worked at Faith; it made her happy, and it helped him at home when she was happy).

Marty called Tom later that week and told him, "I'm not worried about you. Lorna likes working there. It's alright with me." He did not tell Tom that he had cussed Lorna out for causing yet another problem for him and for the people at Faith.

The leaders meeting ended and as far as Tom knew, in a few days Lorna would be gone from his daily schedule. He worried about completing all his duties without a secretary, but hoped they could find a way to muddle through until a new secretary could be hired.

On Tuesday, without Tom's knowledge or presence, the lay ministers met with Lorna. Whatever was discussed or whatever claims she made, or whether she practiced her best manipulative powers is unknown. What is known is that they decided to tear up her resignation and keep her on as church secretary. Tom had told them that there was nothing romantic going on between them and they were satisfied. She must have said the same. Marty wanted her to work there. That covered all the bases, except what to do about gossip.

A loan to her, no longer alone with her

Tom experienced Lorna's depressed moods many times. She needed a lot of help, and professional help, not just that of a concerned pastor. He told her it was time for her to seek out a qualified professional counselor. Since the lay ministers, with his agreement, no longer wanted him counseling her, this was a good time for her to make a move.

Lorna searched for reasons to refuse help. Her prior counseling experiences with professionals did her little good. Even if she saw someone, it could not be someone in Emporia. Marty might find out and should there be a divorce action, Marty would use it against her to win custody of the children. Besides, she could not pay for a counselor.

Tom offered to help. "I'll lend you the money and you can see someone out of town. Maybe in Wichita. You would need money for his fee and for travel costs, right?" Tom agreed to lend her $1,000. He told her to let him know when she was ready for the money.

Lorna wanted the money on September 7. Tom planned to deposit some insurance checks and paychecks that day, and he needed money to shop for a new van. Out of the $5,000 he withdrew on September 7, he loaned Lorna $1,000. He loaned his brother Mark $600 and Mark remembered additional loans totaling $500 in the following weeks. Later he helped Terry Smith pay $600 on a past due medical bill.

When Sandy died, Tom found himself embarrassed because he kept very little cash on him, perhaps $20 on a good day. Cash cards were a new item and he didn't have one, so in order to go to Little Rock for Sandy's funeral, he had to borrow cash from a friend. Of the $5,000 he withdrew on September 7, he retained a stash of cash to use for incidentals and emergencies that fall. His checkbook register showed very few checks written.

He was still looking for a car in the early part of November.

Lorna never paid back the $1,000. And she never went for counseling, at least not the kind Tom had in mind when he loaned her the money. The only counseling she did was asking Danny Carter to hire a murderer, and on September 7, she gave him $5,000 to do so.

225

Still pastoring, fathering and wondering

Tom had a difficult time adjusting to life as a single dad. Little things, like helping Andrea take care of her hair, were big things to him. Virginia stayed on for a while, and she and Ralph returned to Emporia several times to help, but it meant little in the day-to-day lives of the little Birds.

He kept up with the afternoon whiffle-ball game in the front yard. Friends helped care for the house. Others tried to provide assistance with the children, without offending Tom.

Stephanie remembered those days.

"More than anything after that time, I was concerned about the kids. They had spent so much time over here anyway they continued coming over here. I tried to help Tom as best I could because I knew he was busy.

"Andrea probably became a little bossy with her brothers. Aaron was only two, but Andrea became a little more vocal.

"One time Paul said something about his mom. I remember the emotion at the time. It was almost a non-acceptance that his mom was gone. We talked with him a bit, and the ball game distracted him and he ran off to play and the subject never came up again.

"Here's where my mothering came in. It wasn't that he wasn't taking good care of the children, I just wanted to pick up some slack that he might have been able to do if Sandy were alive. There might have been a time or two when I was watching the kids and I'd go over and do dishes and stuff. How many times do we all keep dishes in the sink?

"He was trying as hard as he could. Tom was not the type of person who would show his weaker side because he had a church to lead."

That fall, Stephanie attended the Adult Inquiry Class led by Tom, and she joined the church. This was the class she and Sandy had planned together that she would take in secret as a surprise for her husband Steve. She saw Tom as a strong teacher, confident in his knowledge and well able to present it understandably. Stephanie learned much from Tom.

Stephanie could not see Tom's heart. "Everybody told me to be strong. My father urged me to be strong for the sake of the church. But I didn't feel strong. I felt overwhelmed and weak."

He considered his options. The Grismers were pressuring him to move back near Little Rock. That would put him close to Mark and Gloria, and closer to his parents.

He had three little children to train and entertain. He relished the role of a parent, but without a mom to help, it placed enormous pressure on him. He stole as much time as possible from his daily tasks to be with them. On Tuesday, August 9, the children were hungry for a special adventure. They asked to go see the airplanes, the ones they remembered from their trip to and from Little Rock in July.

"We basically closed the church office. The kids and I went to watch the planes.

"When we came out of the terminal to the airport parking lot, there was Lorna with her kids. My kids ran and jumped in the van with them. I had no idea she would be there.

"Lorna said she was on her way to Hutchinson to stay with her parents; but they worked until 5:00 so she came here first to 'see how we were doing.'

"The kids wanted to go to the park. I saw I was outnumbered and outvoted, but I wanted to check into a motel first."

Tom shrugged his shoulders. He didn't appreciate Lorna being there, but his kids had already piled into the van. She always knew where he was, and she often showed up uninvited.

"We took the van, and left the Toyota. The first couple of places by the airport on Kellogg Road offered kids free with couples. [Tom was now a *single* parent.] That peeved me as to prejudice against single parents. So I checked into the Sheraton as 'Mr. & Mrs. Bird' and I and the kids stayed there that night.

"All of us went on to play in the park, and we stopped by a pet shop. Lorna and I were with seven children at all times! We had ice cream cones and Lorna took her kids on to Hutchinson and I spent the evening with my kids.

"So I am guilty of motel fraud for saying I was a couple, when it was me and the kids, as a protest against prejudice toward single parent families? I paid for that sin!"

He paid for that when investigators found the registration slip upon which he wrote "Mr. and Mrs. Tom Bird" of Emporia. It helped little that Lorna told Jan Mead and Kim Clark that she and Tom needed to get away alone.

One sticky detail complicated any conclusion that this Wichita trip was a "time to get away alone." August 9, 1983, was a Tuesday—not a weekend. And seven children in tow does not make for time alone.

Lorna's in love, again

David Workman loved watching softball games. He remembered one particular evening in August of 1983, weeks after Sandy's death.

He recalled this meeting in sworn testimony. Steven Opat questioned him.

"Did she [Lorna] ever talk to you about Tom Bird?"

"Just mentioned one time that she was in love with Tom."

"When was that conversation?"

"It would have been after Sandy's death, probably late July—early August of '83."

"Where did this conversation take place?"

"At Saratoma baseball—or softball complex in Emporia."

"And what was the occasion?"

"Marty was at that time—was playing church league and another friend of mine was playing on a different church league and they met in the league and I just went—took the evening off from work and went down to watch 'em play ball...."

"And she was sitting on the—the bleachers just watchin' the game and I asked her how things were going and she said, 'Well, not good.' And I said, 'Well, you're still not gonna do nothin' stupid, are ya?' And she said, 'Well, I gotta do somethin'—or 'we'—I think she said, 'We have to do somethin.' I'm not sure whether she said 'I' or 'we.'"

"Okay. Did you ask her who she was seeing or what she was doing?"

"No sir."

"Did she mention Tom Bird's name at that time?"

"I believe she as—later on in the—in the same conversation is when she told me that she was in love with him."

"And did you know who Tom was?"

"I knew of him."

"How did you know of him?"

"I'd been recruited a couple of times to play ball but never did for 'em so I knew—knew him through that and then I knew him through personal conversations with Marty."

"What did Marty have to say about Tom?"

"Well, at different times, different things. On one occasion he was upset at Tom about somethin' about a softball game that I remember—I don't remember the whole story but—and another time he was upset because Lorna was workin' for—for Reverend Bird."

"Did he say why he was upset about that?"

"I believe this was about the time when, supposedly, she was gettin' a lotta flack and, supposedly, was getting fired and had somethin' to do with money and he was upset because she was—started workin' for free and—or givin' the money back to the church and he was upset."

"Did Martin ever suggest to you that he knew Tom and Lorna were having an affair of some kind?" [Marty never said any such thing to anyone.]

"Not that I remember."

"Now, I'm gonna go back to this conversation in the ballpark. As you best recollect, what led up to the conversation about Tom Bird between you and Lorna?"

"Nothin'. She was—they were warmin' up before the game and she was sitting on the bleachers with the kids and there was nobody immediately around us so I just thought I'd stop and see how—what was goin' on. I said hi [Here he repeated what he had said earlier about their verbal exchange]....And then we chatted a little longer and then she said somethin' about bein'—bein' in love with Tom."

"Did you think that was strange?"

"No sir."

"Why?"

"Her and Marty hadn't loved each other for a long time."

"Well, you didn't think it was unusual that she should fall in love with her minister?"

"No sir."

"Had you heard rumors about her and Tom prior to this time?"

"Yes sir."

"Had you heard rumors about Tom and his wife's death?"

"Yes sir."

"When you say that you didn't think it was unusual, are you suggesting that you thought this was just the ordinary course of things insofar as Lorna was concerned?"

"I just thought that he was her latest fancy." [Unlike Jan Mead, Workman discounted most of Lorna's claims. He had witnessed her fantasies many times in the past.]

"You didn't think it was anything of a lasting nature?"

"No sir."

In actuality, Workman, like Mead, Clark, and a mounting number of Emporians, knew nothing about Tom and Lorna, except what Lorna told them. The cancerous gossip was fueled by what her closest friends *did* know about her. They *knew* she was promiscuous. Those who did not *know,* at least had heard it often enough to wonder whether the reports were true. It was easy to accept the notion that a recently widowed pastor, often in close company with her, had, like dozens of others, succumbed to her seductions.

Workman revealed a consistent characteristic of Lorna in his testimony. She lied, and she wove her lies in such a way as to accomplish her own ends. Workman didn't take seriously Lorna's proclamation about her pastor and labeled him her latest "fancy." He should have used the word "fantasy," only this time, her fantasy was a tragedy written for a real life production. And she was about to add another sinister plot twist.

Can you compute?

Sandy Bird nearly completed her master's degree in Computer Science before her death. In honor of her life, the church used proceeds from the Sandra Bird Memorials to buy the church a computer—their first computer.

Tom, Lorna and others were excited about this new piece of equipment. Concerned, too, that it be used properly and not take up even more of their time.

The computer arrived early in September and they set it up on a card table in the corner of Lorna's 9 x 12 cramped office. Tom and Lorna sat side by side on metal chairs, trying to figure out how to use the machine. Sharon Meyer joined them in the small office. Joyce Rosenboom stood outside Lorna's office in the reception area and looked in through the window. They all talked a few moments and resumed their various duties.

Sharon became disturbed about that incident, thinking Tom and Lorna were far too cozy. She saw their knees slightly touching and took it as another warning sign, rather than simply a physical necessity given the cramped nature of Lorna's office. Joyce Rosenboom, mother of two and married for the second time—an experienced woman saw nothing about which to be concerned, but Angie had talked to Sharon and Howard about her conversations with Tom. Sharon worried that this indicated the rumor might be true.

Later, Sharon went to Tom to talk to him about her concerns. Tom explained the situation and expanded on it. For a time they cried together and held hands. Sharon wanted Tom to understand the vulnerability he had and like others, once again suggested that Lorna should resign. Tom told her that Lorna was suicidal, but also that she was a great asset to him. And unlike many others, Lorna did not judge him or question him about how he dealt with his children, in fact offering advice, especially as to how to care for Andrea. Tom saw Lorna as a friend and ally, but not a lover. As Sharon left, Tom came around and hugged her.

So it became for Tom. Every time he stood, sat or walked near Lorna, others began to suspect something. It added to the tension he already felt, and undermined the unity of his church.

How to hire a killer

Sometime following Lorna's fan-in-the-stands conversation with Workman in August, she reached the boiling point. It pushed her to finally set in motion the violence against Marty that she had threatened many times before.

Darrel admitted Lorna first talked to him about finding someone to murder Marty during the summer of 1982. Workman heard her relate a murder plot to him on March 30, 1983, in the context of talking about Danny Carter. Workman said that when Lorna talked with him on March 30, she meant that she and Danny, and perhaps his brother Darrel, discussed various methods of murdering Marty,.

Lorna ruled out divorce, fearing that Marty would win custody of the children and leave her without much money. Murder done right would leave her rich.

In his June 27, 1984 court appearance before District Magistrate Judge Clarence Sawyer, Danny described the August 1983 contact made by Lorna. (When Carter testified, he was complying with the plea agreement formalized on March 8, 1984. It protected him from further prosecution in the case, as long as he told the "truth." Furthermore, his attorney had made clear to Opat that the price of Danny's cooperation included parole—no jail time. On March 8, 1984, while pleading guilty to one criminal count, Danny had indeed been paroled.)

Opat and Darrel Meyer had questioned Danny during this hearing (Meyer served as Lorna's attorney).

"Sometime in August of 1983 did you receive a phone call from Mrs. Anderson?" Opat asked.

"Yes."

"And, as you best recall, when did you get that phone call?"

"It was in the evening…It was the latter part of August. I'm not real sure. I can't remember what date."

"What was the phone call about?"

"She just called and said she wanted to see me and talk to me."

"Did you agree to meet her some place?"

"Yes. At the Village School in Emporia."

"Do you recall about what time it was you met her?"

"It was probably about 7:30 in the evening. I picked her up in my car and we went for a ride."

"What was the conversation about?"

"It was about her husband. She wanted to get rid of him."

"Tell me, as you best recall, what exactly she said to you that indicated to you she wanted to get rid of her husband."

"Well, she said that she was getting tired of getting beat up by him and abused by him and she wanted to get rid of him. She wanted to kill him."

Carter claimed the notion of murdering Marty surprised him. He suggested divorce.

"Was there any further conversation that evening about the matter of getting rid of Martin Anderson?"

"Well, she asked me if I could find somebody to do it."

"And, what did you say to her?"

"I said I'd try."

"Did that terminate the conversation?"

"Well, we just talked about it a little bit more and then I took her back and went home."

"What did the little bit more talking about it entail?"

"Well, she just wanted me to find somebody that would do it and I said I'd look around and see if I could find somebody. I didn't know anybody."

Danny said that three or four days later, while out at Wolf Creek Nuclear Power Plant, he got talked to Greg Curry about Lorna. He chose Greg because, "He just was always talking about some of the things him and his family had done and some of the people that he knew."

Greg told him he thought he knew someone who could do such a deed and he would check into it.

The two talked again a few days later. During that discussion, Greg informed Danny that he had found someone. Danny said they talked about the price, and Greg told him it would be $5,000—$10,000, depending on who the victim was—a cop or court official would cost more. (Greg disagreed on this detail, stating that Johnny Bingham and Danny Carter directly negotiated a price for the hit.) Greg said he needed more information, like an itinerary, a photograph, those types of things.

"Based on this conversation with Mr. Curry did you contact Lorna Anderson, the defendant?"

"No. She contacted me. It was probably—maybe a couple of days later."

"So, as you best recall, about what time period are we talking about here? What month? What day?"

"It'd been the latter part of August. Probably—the latter part of August, first of September."

Danny described his conversation with Lorna, telling her what Greg said, though he never mentioned Greg's name to her. He told her the cost, the details needed for the hit man. "She said she'd get it for me."

The next day Danny informed Greg that the deal was on. Danny claimed Greg told him the final price of $5,000. Danny said Greg had talked to the hit man, whom he only knew as Johnny, and that was what Johnny wanted.

"After that conversation with Mr. Curry did you again have occasion to speak with the defendant, Lorna Anderson, about what you had learned?"

"Yeah. Probably—I think it was a couple days later she called."

"And what did you tell her?"

"Well, she told me she had the money and all the information I needed."

"You told her it'd be $5,000?"

"Uh-huh."

"What was her response?"

"She said she had it."

Danny told Lorna that the next step was to wait for Greg to contact him about a date. Greg called back and suggested September 7. He planned a trip to Corinth, Mississippi the following weekend.

Danny said Lorna called him on September 6 to find out what was happening, and he informed her of the September 7 date. Danny insisted that Lorna call him because he didn't want to accidentally reach Marty. They agreed to meet the next day.

(Lorna called Tom to inform him that she wanted to accept his offer to go for counseling. She needed that $1,000 loan he offered. They agreed to meet at church after he went to the bank on September 7.)

"Did you arrange at that point in time to meet with her?" Opat continued.

"Yes."

"Tell me what arrangements were made."

"I told her to meet me at the Emporia State zip machine at Emporia. I went down and picked up the money."

"Tell me how that all occurred, Mr. Carter."

"Well, I just drove down there and I was getting some money out of the zip machine anyway. She came in with an envelope. I took the envelope. She said everything was in there that they needed."

The two met in the parking lot, but the exchange took place as he stood next to her Ford conversion van. "She just handed me the envelope. I asked her if she really wanted to go through with it? She said, 'yes.'"

As soon as the two parted, Danny drove over to Greg Curry's apartment. There he handed the envelope to the 20-year old and they exchanged small talk about the "job." Danny saw Greg count the money and separate it into two envelopes. "He just said he was going to pass half of it on before the job was done and half of it when it was done."

Danny remembered the date of the exchange because he left for South Carolina that night with Gail Wilson, his current live-in girlfriend. She wanted his help picking up her child. Wilson, after Marty's murder, turned Carter in to police and fled from Emporia in fear.

Danny told the judge that he thought the hit would take place the following weekend. It is what Greg told him. The following Monday, after returning from South Carolina, Danny again heard from Lorna. "She wanted to know why it hadn't happened." Telling her he did not know, he promised her he would contact Greg and try to find out.

Greg had gone to Corinth on vacation. He took the envelope with the $5,000 and instructions and given it all to Johnny Bingham. He believed that Johnny would do the "job" soon.

Danny asked Greg why nothing had happened, but Greg didn't know. Greg promised to get back to him and Danny so informed Lorna. Later, Greg told Danny, "He said he needed ... to have another schedule to find out where Mr. Anderson was going to be for the next weekend.... I said I'd see if I could find out."

A short time later Danny got back to Greg with Marty' schedule.

"When was the last time you had occasion to talk to Mr. Curry about this matter?" Opat asked.

"It was around the middle of October. I think it was October 20th."

"Why is it you remember that date?"

"It was the day he quit Wolf Creek."

"What conversation did you have with him on the 20th, if any?"

"I called him on the telephone that evening and asked him what was going on because he was quitting."

"Was there something that prompted you to call Mr. Curry?"

"Well, he'd—I'd given him $5,000 and he was leaving the state and I wanted to know what the deal was."

"Did he tell you what the deal was?"

"He said that he was—could get ahold of this Johnny that he'd been talking to and get my money back because I told him I didn't want any more to do with it."

"Well, why did you want to get the money back, Mr. Carter?"

"Because it wasn't my money. I just tried to find out where Curry was to get the money back. He told me he'd send it back to me but he never did."

"During that period of time did you have any conversation with the defendant, Lorna Anderson, about your efforts to get the money back?"

"She called me, I think the next day it was. She wanted to know what was going on. I told her I didn't know what was going on but I wanted out of the deal. And I was trying."

"What'd she tell you?"

"She didn't—she said, Okay, and hung up the telephone."

When Lorna's attorney Darrell Meyer asked the questions, Danny pinned down the date in August when Lorna contacted him. "It was right—

it was a day or so before my birthday…23rd of August."

In all this discussion in August that Danny had with Lorna about murdering Marty, after all the questions by Steven Opat, Lyon County Attorney Rod Symmonds, investigators from two counties, KBI Agents and Lorna's attorney, not one single time did Danny mention the name of Tom Bird. Only after making a deal with prosecutors late in 1983, following Darrel's claim that Tom had been involved in a scheme, did Danny say anything about Tom—that he thought perhaps Tom had provided the $5,000. Danny also said Lorna's grandmother in Topeka could have been her "banker." He told Opat that when Lorna had talked to him about the murder, she didn't care how much it would cost. She told him she had inherited some money and her father handled it or invested it for her.

Lorna *had* told Danny, as she had others, that she was in love with Tom and he was her "boyfriend," as Gail Wilson later testified.

Danny was Darrel's younger brother. The two were very close. In the inquiries following Marty's death, Danny made no reference to Tom ever asking Darrel to find someone to murder Marty, as Darrel alleged later that year. That should have seemed odd to investigators, because Darrel certainly made the point of telling *them* such a story, but not until Danny won a deal from Opat.

When Opat struck his plea agreement with Danny, Opat believed that Danny tried to withdraw from the murder plot. Danny claimed that about October 24 or 25, he called Greg and said to cancel the hit. He told Greg that Marty decided to get a divorce.

No doubt Lorna felt threatened by the idea of divorce, fearing she would lose the life insurance settlement she counted on as part of the murder scheme. Greg told Danny that there was nothing he could do to stop it, and Danny just shrugged his shoulders, not even worried that he could not get "his" money back. Danny referred to the $5,000 as "his" money several times. Maybe it was?

The murder plan, discussed for more than a year, had finally begun. From the day Lorna discussed the murder with Darrel Carter in 1982, and conspired with Danny Carter in August of 1983, Marty was targeted. It required the right time and place. Who planned the time and place? Lorna, of course, but she had help.

What should he do?

Tom loved the ministry and wanted to make it a lifetime career, although he also loved teaching. Following Sandy's death, he spent a great deal of time meditating and praying about what to do with his future. He could stay at Faith and provide leadership for the fast-growing congregation. If called, he could teach at St. John's in Winfield as he and Sandy discussed earlier that summer or move back to the Little Rock area, as the Grismers were pressuring him to do, and serve as pastor to a new congregation.

Despite his call to the ministry and affection for the task, he contemplated quitting the ministry altogether. As such times, he felt depressed and filled with self-doubt. Though he experienced some of these same emotions in the spring, since Sandy died his self-confidence had plummeted.

Tom tired of the gossip and rumors that followed him. He lived in a glass bowl. He felt tired of acting strong when he was weak. He had taken steps to separate himself from Lorna, first as her boss at church, and then as her counselor, but she still came to work at the church every day. He was still her pastor, and that would never change as long as he stayed at Faith.

Tom understood that he needed to plan for his marital future, too. He could not choose to ignore the void in his life left by Sandy's death—he would always miss her—but there were other considerations. For the good of his three young children, his ministry and his own personal needs, Tom needed a new spouse. There were takers at Faith, and he had been warned by both men and women in the membership to be very careful about this. At least one Faith woman (not Lorna) made a suggestion that she divorce her husband and the two of them could marry.

During the fall of 1983, Tom felt very vulnerable.

One enchanted evening

On September 30, 1983, Faith hosted a get-together for single adults. Area churches had been invited to participate—one of these was Grace Lutheran Church in Kansas City, Missouri. The Christian Education Director at Grace was a pretty young woman named Terry Smith.

Terry grew up in Flint, Michigan. She earned a Bachelor's Degree from Seward College in Nebraska, a popular Lutheran Church Missouri Synod school that emphasized training leading to lifetime ministries in the LC-MS. She did her student teaching at a school in Wichita, Kansas and became part of the school staff at Grace in 1977. Eventually she became the principal of a full-time elementary school at Grace, and for many years worked with the church's youth group. She even coached basketball.

Like Sandy Bird, Terry is intelligent, focussed, professional and a student. She continued working on a second advanced degree in administration and became heavily involved in many ministries.

Terry drove to Faith for the September single's meeting because it was part of her job. She described the event and her first meeting with the young widower, Tom Bird.

"I was called to Emporia by the district to do a workshop on friendship. I was single and avoided going to singles things. But God planned this out.

"The group was having an evening get-together at Faith. Tom was unlocking doors and introducing and showing people the facilities. And then they started some kind of a game where you had to talk to people you didn't know, where they blew a whistle and you were supposed to talk to someone else.

"I wanted to get out of there, and Tom did too. We sort of met in the middle of the room. I told him this was not my kind of thing.

"Just after Tom and I met, they blew the whistle, but we kept talking. We never moved to anyone else."

That evening after she had arrived back at home in Kansas City, Terry answered the phone. She heard the LC-MS District President asking her to drive back to Faith the next morning to help drive the seminar speakers around and pay them for their work. "I wasn't feeling well, but he begged really well."

Saturday morning, she led songs and played the piano. The guest speaker failed to show up to do his workshop—and even adults needed entertainment. While she played the piano, Tom stood in the back of the room and made faces at her, right in the middle of the song "Apples and Bananas," a favorite among pre-teens. Tom thought it was a hoot, and let her know by his actions—and it irritated her.

Going to the back of the room when she had finished leading the music, Terry gave Tom a piece of her mind. He invited her out for pizza. They had a great time together, so great that Terry decided to use one of her valuable Kansas City Chiefs football tickets as an enticement for another date. Tom declined, saying he had to preach and could not miss church. This impressed her, knowing of his great love of sports, and football in particular. Her first response was, "I couldn't understand why he couldn't get out of it." Tom put ministry first in his life.

Terry continued describing those early days.

"Later on we arranged to go out on a date, actually a few dates. This dating thing was new for him, he said. He wasn't dating anybody else.

"We saw each other quite a bit from October to November."

One of those dates included dinner and dancing, in fact more than once, when they both attended a pastor's conference in Wichita on November 10-11 that year. She did the registration and then they both left, preferring each other's company to the seminar workshops. Susie Graf and Angie Duensing from Faith both recalled seeing Tom and Terry dancing and holding hands, although Susie thought it somehow improper.

Before Tom left to meet Terry in Wichita that November day, he stopped off at Lorna's house, leaving with her a couple of greeting cards, hoping they would cheer her up. (Terry laughs out loud when talking about this, because it was these cards that investigators called "love letters" later on at trial.)

Terry described Tom, the man she met in 1983:

"I think he's very compassionate. He's not an aggressive person. He listens. He wouldn't describe himself as outgoing but I see him as outgoing and friendly. He's open to other people.

"He doesn't have an aura of power around him. People wanted to make him to be that way—especially that he would talk Lorna into something, or that I've been blinded by his charisma, but that's not it. Tom's just a guy."

She enjoyed Tom's sense of humor. As his father used magic tricks Tom used his humor to attract people to his message.

"When I went to Emporia I saw Tom preach. We took our youth group down for a lock in. I was in charge of our youth group at that time, and Tom was just a real fun-loving, caring guy. He enjoyed sports and just having fun.

"He played in a mud football game where he dressed up in a tuxedo to raise money for a charity down there in Emporia. He was fun to be around, but he was no Casanova."

Not long after meeting Tom, Terry met his children, but she never met Lorna. "Even all the times I was dating Tom I never saw her. She called one evening when we had gone out on a date, oh at least three or four or five times. She continued to call when I was there, and I said 'I don't have to answer that.'"

Terry had a sense about Lorna just like Sandy, Angie, Susie and Sharon. "Tom would put the best construction on people," she explained, but Lorna did not fool *her*. "Women see things that men don't see," even when they have never met face-to-face.

Terry continued to see Tom regularly, but there was a time when Tom told Terry to stay away. He wanted to protect her from the gossip flowing around town after Marty's murder in November. They took great care to protect her privacy, even as his suffered. When they met, she would park a block away and walk to his house or the church. He wanted to make sure there would be no potential for a blemish on her ministry at Grace.

Tom's concern about protecting Terry's privacy was well founded. Susie Graf, told Deputy Deppish about Terry and Tom, using language that suggested something immoral. "When Mrs. Graf talked to Tom Bird about his 'girlfriend,' he seemed to be trying to hide the relationship." Tom *did* try to hide the relationship from such gossip as this.

It was different when he traveled to Kansas City.

"Tom came up right before Christmas. He came up to watch a basketball game I was coaching. He told me the weekend after Marty was shot that things were really hectic. There was just a lot of busyness and he didn't know what was going on.

"I remember walking with Tom and we were walking around a track. It was in the evening and there was a shooting star and I remember asking, 'what would you wish for?' He would talk and wish that Sandy was alive. And cry."

They both thought it was not time to make a long-term commitment. "We were really good friends and just dating," Terry said.

Over the following months and years, Terry and Tom grew very close, as she did to Ralph and Virginia, and the three little Birds. They were married in August of 1988 at Lansing Correctional Facility, where he served a life sentence as a result of his 1985 conviction in Sandy Bird's death. (A complete account of their marriage can be read at http://www.cagedbird.net/excerpts.htm.) By the time they married, police investigators, Jane, some members at Faith, and especially Lorna, looked at Terry with great suspicion and a measure of jealousy. Lorna derisively labeled Terry as, "Tom's little teacher from Kansas City." Some snidely suggested that Tom married Terry to keep her from testifying at trial.

Sleazy salacious gossip oozed out of every corner of Emporia whenever it concerned Tom, a hateful, destructive gossip that enveloped the town and denied freedom to this young pastor and his future wife.

Bringing home the bread

John Waters drove a Wonder Bread truck. He lived in Council Grove. Each day between 4:00 and 6:00 p.m. he drove south on Highway 177, the time depended on how full a load he carried.

One day in October, 1983—he never could nail the date down exactly, but placed it as two to three weeks prior to November 4—while driving that stretch of road, he spotted a van and a late model full-sized car parked where

McDowell Creek Road intersects Highway 177. This is the same location Margaret Wyatt spied a car parked in the wrong direction just before Marty was murdered.

Waters saw two children and a woman sitting in the white car, and possibly two men outside by the van. "The car was facing east and the van was facing west."

In 1989, he described these vehicles to a private investigator who helped Tom prepare for his 1990 murder trial. Waters told the investigator he spotted "...a dark green van with a stripe around it along with a white car, a little bigger." Waters had no prior knowledge of what the Anderson van looked like, so it was significant to Bird's investigator that he described Lorna's van so perfectly.

Waters discussed this with police as early as February of 1984. During that interview with Agent Humphrey, Waters was less sure of what he saw. He called it "dark green." He remembered the car as a light colored "LTD type car." He was less sure of whom he saw near the vehicles. Humphrey showed him a picture of Lorna's van, but Waters could not be sure about its identification.

A year later, Agent Winsor went to see Waters. Winsor brought along photo lineup of vans and asked Waters to identify the one he had seen. Waters picked a 1980 Chevrolet van and a 1977 Dodge Tradesman. The passenger car, he told Winsor, looked elongated, like a Ford LTD or Lincoln Continental, and it was a light color and clean.

Did any friends of Lorna own a large, light colored passenger car? Did Waters see Lorna at McDowell Creek Road that day, planning the murder with her accomplice(s)? Were investigators lazy in pursuing more information about these two vehicles and their drivers? Had they already made a plea agreement with one or more of the people who stood along the road that October day? Or was Waters' witness totally unrelated to anything? Whatever the answer, Tom Bird did not drive a full-sized light-colored passenger car.

Advice meant well

As October wound down, Tom's tension wound up. Everyone had advice for him, and it often conflicted. He remained courteous and respectful, preserving the appearance of a strong leader. But it got to be too much and he finally reached a boiling point.

Faith members watched their pastor mourn his wife. They wanted to help. Most tried to ignore rumors about Lorna and him. Most, with the exception of a few gossips, strongly supported him. They saw Tom struggle to balance his family and church duties. They tried to avoid criticism and yet offer help. Some said, "He's really doing well." Others said, "He looks like he's under a lot of tension."

Stephanie was typical. "With Andrea, I didn't want to make Tom feel like he was slacking off in any way, but Andrea's hair was longer and I would bring her over to my house and we'd do the beauty shop hair conditioning, style the hair and such. He was trying as hard as he could."

Tom had no experience as a mother. Before Sandy died, he felt strong and confident, driven to the high calling God had placed on him. After her death, he lost a lot of his confidence.

That August, Faith planned to print a new pictorial church membership directory. Tom, like all the others, had an appointment with the photographer. Interrupting his busy day, he headed home and dressed his children for the picture. Tom often had trouble helping Andrea get ready and Moore was not around to comb her hair. Tom did the best he could to work out the snarls and cope with her tears. Running late, he quickly helped her slip on her dress and ushered the three children out to the car. They headed to church.

"I brought Andrea to the picture and she had on a nice dress, but it was put on backwards. I couldn't tell from the buttons." The people at church noticed. "Well, that touched my inadequacy. Not only did I really miss Sandy, but I felt stupid, too."

One morning one of the church ladies come into his office. "She told me my children were out of control. I needed to rein them in."

Later the same morning, another lady talked to him. "She told me I needed to give my children more freedom. I was too restrictive." Tom said, "I'm just trying to be the best father I can be."

He felt stupid and inadequate.

Tom saw his work literally piling up on his desk. Someone even criticized him for a messy desk. Then Lorna walked into his office and fired another small missile at his confidence. It had to do with his sermon. It was late October.

Tom stood up, walked to the side of his desk and, grabbing a stack of file folders in his arms, threw them across the room. The files and their contents spread across the floor. "There, that will clear my desk!" he said in anger.

Lorna was shocked and a bit scared. At home, Marty screamed at her and beat her. But not Tom. He was a rock. Tom kept his composure. Lorna reported this incident years later. Investigators saw it as another indicator that Tom had a pattern of violent emotional explosions.

"I'm going to Little Rock," Tom told Lorna. There was an LC-MS pastor's conference in Little Rock that week. "You take care of things here."

He called Angie and begged her to baby-sit. She reluctantly agreed. When Tom came home from Arkansas a few days later, Angie, who became Tom's chief accuser at Faith, had left the children with Lorna.

Tom let it be known at the pastor's conference that he was willing to leave Emporia. He talked with other pastors about opportunities. He spent time with his friends.

"I got together with my dad, Charlie Smith and pastors from the Memphis area and went out for a few beers and to talk."

The next day, Tom and Charlie "got up and Charlie drove me to Sandy's gravesite. I bought the headstone that day."

Tom and Charlie, joined by Les Weiser often performed comedy skits at these conferences. They called themselves "The Mighty Parson Art Players." They wrote their own scripts. Charlie said Tom's humor was dour that week. Three years later, in a statement to police, Charlie said Tom wrote jokes about having the district president killed.

"I went down there with the intent of looking for a pastorate. I know I was angry at the district president because he told me no one would want to call a widowed pastor with three kids." That cut deeply. "But look, if I had murdered my wife three months earlier and was about to murder Marty, would I be joking about murdering the district president a week before Marty was killed?"

An isolated explosion of anger, jokes about leaders, even drinking beer, were threads in a twisted tale woven together by the prosecution.

'Twas the night before...murder

There was nothing unique about November 3, 1983. Tom looked at his schedule and saw it would be a very busy day with a lot of driving.

Rising early, he got the children up and ready for the babysitter. He prepared himself to head to Topeka for a 9:00 a.m. meeting. He could confidently rely on Lorna, the church secretary, to take care of the morning details, unless she had a bad night or came in depressed. She still worked from 9 a.m. to Noon.

Tom moved fast that morning. He faced a 55 mile drive to get to his meeting at the Kansas District Office in Topeka. It helped that he could drive the Kansas Turnpike, although the speed limit was 55 mph. When he exited the turnpike in Topeka, he paid the toll and took the toll receipt from the operator, and saved it for tax purposes.

District conferences were planned at the Family Life Ministry Committee meetings in Topeka. This committee sponsored the seminars that Tom and Sandy taught earlier that year. He enjoyed this meeting, given the presence of his friend Rev. Al Burroughs, as well as Norma Jacobs, Irene Wiegert, Bob Eggold and Don Romsa. Tom actively participated in both the September and November meetings, and his presence was duly listed in the meeting minutes. The minutes also detailed his assignments for upcoming events.

Burroughs described Tom's heavy involvement with the committee. "He served as a consultant, helped set up workshops, led topics at regional seminars. He had assumed the post of co-editor of the District Family Life Newsletter. His wife [Sandy] often helped him lead these topics. We had high regard for both of them….[Faith Lutheran] was known for its advanced Family Life Program. "

The committee planned a Family Life Festival to be held in Emporia on March 31, 1984 at ESU. Burroughs said the committee had given Tom several assignments, "…such as contacting musical groups, planning the opening devotion, securing displays, enlisting the help of circuit leaders across Kansas. Tom Bird had a leadership role in these plans." At the November 3rd meeting, Tom reported that he had secured a musical group from St. John's College in Winfield.

The meeting lasted until Noon. They adjourned for lunch to McFalvind's, a Topeka restaurant. Burroughs picked up the check and kept the receipt so that the district could reimburse him. Tom next saw Burroughs at the Pastor's Professional Conference in Wichita November 10-11, only there Tom ate his meals with someone other than Burroughs—Terry Smith.

Burroughs remembered that lunch lasted until 1:00 or 1:15, but Tom left by 12:45. He rushed back to Emporia for his next duty. Upon exiting the turnpike, he once again paid the toll and collected the receipt.

He arrived at Emporia State University around 2 p.m., and prepared for his 2:30 p.m. Christian Ethics Class. He taught these classes in the Lutheran Student Center, an organization he had helped develop when he first arrived in Emporia. While these classes absorbed his precious time and contributed to his stress level, he still enjoyed them, especially because several members of his church regularly took the course. Even Sandy attended them months earlier. In his class he counted Joyce Rosenboom, Dee Waggoner and Sheri Weinmeister from Faith, each taking notes and later, thankfully for Tom, filing those notes away.

The class at ESU let out around 4:30. After cleaning up his materials, Tom drove to the Emporia Civic Center. Tom never lost his enthusiasm for sports, and it provided a necessary outlet for his tension. Thursday evening in the fall it was basketball with the Optimists Club members. Kalsow played on this team as did Mike Pruisner and Marty Anderson. Pruisner said that he and Marty "were the old men of the team."

That night, before he left for home, Tom officially joined the Optimists—finally, after a year of involvement. His application was signed by his sponsor, Marty, as the two sat together on a bench on the sidelines to complete the paperwork. Kalsow filed the application in the Club's records.

While Tom and Marty were playing basketball together, Lorna was preparing for a Beta Sigma Phi Sorority dinner. This was a big annual event, to be attended by all of the Emporia chapters. Lorna had more than the dinner on her mind. She picked up Stephanie Moore on the way to the event, but made a stop on the way, a stop that left Moore baffled.

"Lorna picked me up to go and on the way we stopped at Messiah because she had to make copies or something. I'm not sure why we stopped there. It was in the early days of Faith Lutheran Church and I don't know if we had a copier or if the copier we had wasn't working. I think she said our copier was broken, and she had to stop by Messiah to make some pictures, but I didn't see what it was.

"She was maybe a little more scatter-brained [than usual] because when we got back into the van she couldn't find her purse. She had no clue where it was. We looked all over and couldn't find it.

"The two things that stuck in my mind were that she had to make copies and I don't know what she made copies of, or maybe she could have made a phone call to someone. And number two, that she couldn't find her purse. Those two things really stuck in my mind afterwards. Lorna was scatterbrained but not to the point of losing things."

Lorna's nervousness over the purse could have been because it held a .22 caliber weapon, the one David Workman spotted in March; the one used the next day to assassinate her husband. It was a unique purse, wide but not very tall, with a clasp at the top. It provided a perfect fit for a .22 caliber Colt Woodsman, the one Marty inherited from his father.

Tom arrived at the gym around 5 p.m., and the game was played between 5:30 and 7:00 p.m. After the game, Tom drove home to his children. It had been a long day and he expected the next day to be just as busy. Friday night and Saturday he planned to attend a Church Growth Seminar at Washburn University in Topeka.

That Thursday evening he had no idea that 36 hours later, he would be driving to a hospital in Junction City. Twenty-two months later, Lorna told police that she and Tom planned a murder at the very hour that Marty passed the basketball to his fast-breaking pastor. The police believed her.

Hamburgers are great for more than food

Friday morning, November 4, 1983, Tom awoke to a gray and chilly early winter day. If he could have, Tom would have spent the day inside his study making final preparations for Sunday. Tom knew he had to complete his Sunday preparation that morning because that night and all day Saturday he planned to go with members of Faith to a church growth seminar at Washburn University in Topeka.

Angie planned to head home for a visit that night. Lorna worked in the mimeograph room down the hall.

The phone rang sometime after 10:30 a.m. and since there was no phone in the mimeo room, Tom answered. "Good morning. Faith Lutheran Church, this is Pastor Bird."

"Oh hi Tom." It was Marty. "Is Lorna there?" When Marty asked such a question of others, the veracity of the responder was always a mystery. At least he could trust Tom to not cover for Lorna.

"Sure, she's down the hall. I'll get her." Tom walked down to the mimeo room. "Lorna, it's for you. It's Marty."

He went back to his office and she went into hers. Because there was a hall and two cement block walls separating the two, he could not hear the phone conversation with Marty and anyway, had no reason to.

A few minutes later, Lorna came into Tom's office. "I can't believe it. Marty still wants to go to Fort Riley this afternoon." He wanted to buy a new camouflage coat before reporting for Reserves in the middle of November.

The Andersons had made it a habit to take a drive with the children at that time of year, and stop for a picnic. Lorna told Tom she thought that was a bad idea because of the weather, but Marty insisted. It is just as possible that Marty told her he did *not* want to go, but *she* insisted. Her murder plan depended on it. "Could I leave a little early?" she asked Tom.

"Sure. That's fine. Don't forget about the game tonight."

Angie remembered that Lorna left around 11:30 that morning, a little early. They talked about the volleyball game scheduled that night. Lorna was concerned that Angie would not be there, and there would not be enough players since so many would be at Washburn U. Little did Angie know that two players would never show up again for a volleyball game.

Following lunch, Tom decided to leave early for Topeka. He still had not found a new van, and his Thanksgiving travel was growing closer. Topeka offered more choices and better prices than Emporia.

Faith member Bart Laib showed up at Tom's house around 4:00 to ride with him to Topeka. Laib thought that was the plan, but the babysitter said Tom left earlier. Laib hitched a ride with someone else.

Tom arrived in Topeka sometime around 2 p.m. He drove his blue Toyota, and it ran poorly, another motivation to find another vehicle. That afternoon he visited three dealerships and spoke with salesmen at each, collecting their business cards. Almost a year later, Agent Winsor contacted two of the three salesmen, but they could not recall seeing Tom that day.

Tom saw a few vans he liked, but they were very pricey. Getting hungry, he headed over to the Burger King on 37th and Topeka Boulevard to get a bite to eat. As he was heading back out to his car sometime around 5:30 p.m., Sheri Weinmeister spotted him. She and Kristen Speaks, Susan Perrish, Janette Perrish and Doug Carlson (whom she eventually married) were on their way to her parents' house in Atchison. Weinmeister stated:

> "As we got out of the car and into the trunk for purses, that is when I saw Pastor Bird. He was walking away from the Burger King. We met beside Mrs. P's car and greeted each other with a hug. [No one accused Tom of having an affair with Sheri. The two had not seen each other for a while and just hugged, like he did with others in his church.]

> "There we visited about church volleyball. Pastor mentioned he was looking at vans, as his car was just too small. We talked for approximately five minutes and went our separate ways."

Sheri told the others that she had just seen Pastor Tom Bird. Then her group drove on to Atchison where later that night, her father told her he had seen Tom at Washburn. Tom had told the father how much he enjoyed Sheri. He also told her that Marty had been shot.

The following Thursday, Agent Winsor called on Sheri at ESU, and she gave him much the same statement. Later that afternoon she headed to the Lutheran Student Center at ESU for her Christian Ethics Class taught by Tom. After class Tom warned her that the KBI might be contacting her. They visited him earlier that day. She informed him they already had talked to her. "He said he just wanted to let me know." She saw nor heard no fear or alarm in Tom, other than he felt badly that she had to be involved at all. And she thought he had tears in his eyes.

After he saw Sheri and her friends at Burger King, Tom drove to White Plains Mall where he sat down on a comfortable bench. He had no idea how important that hamburger would be to his future. Sitting down, he took out the classified section of the newspaper, looking for bargains on vans.

At the same time he sat on that Topeka bench contemplating which van to purchase, Margaret Wyatt drove home and spotted a small blue-green car parked the wrong way on McDowell Creek Road South of Manhattan. And Sheryll Hoffman followed Lorna's van making its deadly drive down

Highway 177, headed toward the mailbox alongside the road exactly .9 of a mile south of McDowell Creek Road.

While Tom pondered Ford and Chevy vans, Lorna's van sat on the west shoulder of Highway 177. Several drivers saw it, including Joan Johnson. She remembered two men standing and talking near the van.

While Tom wrote notes in the margins of the want ads, Brian Huffman watched a man walk north from Lorna's van, more than 50 miles west of White Plains Mall. And Lorna flagged down Dennis and Rebecca Baylass, who then discovered the bloody dead body of Tom's fellow Optimist and basketball player, still warm and bleeding from the assassin's bullets.

Oblivious to all that was going on in Junction City, and having lost track of the time, Tom folded his paper and arrived 10 minutes late at Washburn. Within 75 minutes he learned that his church family had been hit with another tragedy—Marty Anderson had been murdered.

If Tom thought dealing with *Mrs*. Anderson was difficult, he had no idea how hard it would be to deal with the *widow* Anderson, who became to him like a millstone, dragging him deeper and deeper into the murky waters of the Kansas court system.

A recent photo of Tom taken at Lansing Correctional Facility.

A young Tom Bird

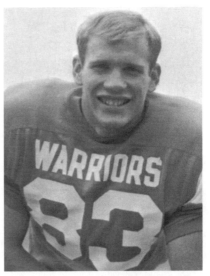

Tom Bird's senior high school football photo.

Four members of the 1968 state high school championship track team from Hall High in Little Rock, AR. Tom Bird is on the right.

Tom Bird's 1968 high school senior picture.

Sandra Stringer Bird's 1968 senior high school picture.

Sandy Bird, on the left, and the rest of the "Cheerokee Drill Team" at Hall High, in Little Rock, AR.

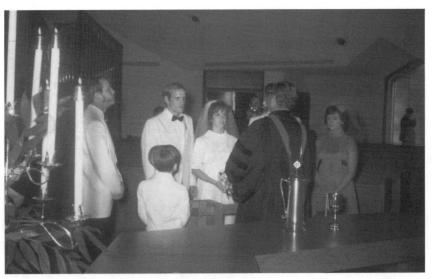

Tom and Sandy take their vows at their wedding.

Tom and Sandy Bird cut their wedding cake.

Jane Grismer, Sandy Bird, Virginia Bird ready to leave for Tom's Seminary class graduation.

Faith Lutheran Church's building.

Rev. Thomas P. Bird in the pulpit at Faith Lutheran Church.

Lorna Anderson sitting at the computer at Faith Lutheran Church in the fall of 1983.

This photo of the Bird family was taken about a year before Sandy's death and printed in the Faith Lutheran Church pictorial direction.

From left to right, Sandy Bird, Tom Bird and Carolyn Smith, one week prior to Sandy's death. Taken at the national LC-MS conference in St. Louis, MO.

Rocky Ford Bridge as seen approaching from the south end.

The decking of Rocky Ford Bridge is made of wood and is 15' 2" wide, allowing one car at a time to slowly make its way across the Cottonwood River.

The rock-strewn riverbed and the eddy in which Sandy's body was found floating face down.

257

Rev. Thomas P. Bird in his study at Faith
Lutheran Church.

Rev. Ralph and Virginia Bird visiting
Tom in prison.

Tom and Terry Bird at their wedding in
August of 1988.

Lorna and Marty Anderson with their four girls as printed in the Fall, 1983 Faith
Lutheran Church directory.

Pastor Kothe kneels down in the ditch where a gunman shot Marty Anderson to death. Mark Bird explains how Lorna said the murder had been committed.

Emporia attorney Irv Shaw represented Tom in his 1984 trial.

Susan Ewert became a close friend to both Tom Bird and Lorna Anderson.

The Lyon County Courthouse where Tom faced two criminal trials—1984, and 1985.

The Geary County Courthouse in Junction City, KS, where Tom was tried for Marty Anderson's murder in 1990.

Tom and Terry Bird meet with Dave Racer at Lansing Correctional Facility.

Jnction City attorney Mike McKone represented Tom in his 1990 trial.

Rev. Kenneth P. Kothe, seminary classmate of Tom Bird's, who began pursuing justice for Tom in 1987, and to whom this book is dedicated.

Dave Racer, Author

SECTION IV

TOM BIRD'S FIRST TRIAL

"What your determination is when you're done here will have an effect upon the defendant and his family for the rest of their lives."

Attorney Irv Shaw during his closing argument.

"Moreover I saw under the sun: in the place of judgement, wickedness was there; and in the place of righteousness, iniquity was there."

Ecclesiastes 3:16

Trial dead ahead

The scandal of a pastor being arrested hit Emporia like a Class-5 tornado; it hit Faith even harder.

When, on March 21, 1984, Tom was arrested and charged for criminal solicitation to commit the murder of Martin Anderson, he was devastated. In the past when he had encountered serious personal issues, he turned to Sandy for counsel. Through prayer, Bible study, the lay ministers and Sandy's wise words, he had been able to meet many challenges. But Sandy was gone. "I felt her loss most acutely following my arrest. I was depressed and confused. I even thought about suicide."

Angie Duensing saw Tom coming in one day late in March with scraped knuckles on his hand. She asked him what happened? He said he had put his fist through the bathroom door because, according to Duensing, "I tell you, I'm on the brink. Always living on the brink."

Tom's stress cascaded like whitewater.

The potential scandal had started slowly enough following Marty's murder. Investigators interrogated members of Faith, trying to pry loose the evidence that romantically linked Tom and Lorna. "No one wanted to talk at first," Sheriff Andrews said. Though most of the close knit church members kept quiet, the investigation began to foster discontent and division in the church. At least one person served investigators as an "inside" source. Tom found himself constantly scrutinized.

Tom knew that he could not hope to perform his official church duties while preparing for trial. The intense media scrutiny and explosive gossip around town sealed it for him. Many of the stories about his arrest for solicitation mentioned that Sandy had died in a single car accident, thus cementing the two events in the minds of readers.

He asked for a six-week leave of absence, giving the church a slight reprieve from public scrutiny. Taking time off to prepare for his trial, a trial he saw as unjust, expensive and that would strip him of his scant financial reserves. Sandy's life insurance settlement would be spent on attorney's fees.

Tom devoted full time to preparation for trial. He retained Emporia attorney Irv Shaw to represent him. Shaw's office sat directly across the street from the Lyon County Courthouse and he was well-known in the city. Shaw presented an impressive visage: tall, handsome and compelling. Tom knew he had made a great choice.

Though the media interest in his trial went national—even international as an Australian news team eventually covered the event, Tom believed strongly that justice was blind. The case would be simple. Darrel claimed they met and talked about murdering Marty. Tom said this discussion never happened. The only other witness was Lorna. Tom knew Lorna served as his ally because she knew the truth about the meeting.

During their preparations for trial, Shaw interviewed Lorna. In her statement to him, Lorna supported Tom's claim that when she, Tom and Darrel met at Faith, they talked about firecrackers, home building and soccer. She said neither murder nor Marty were discussed.

Shaw listened to the KBI tape recording of the December 12 meeting between Tom and Darrel. He heard nothing incriminating.

Tom knew the evidence showed that Darrel and Danny Carter both carried reputations of questionable character. Prosecutors listed both Danny Carter and Greg Curry on the witness list, but neither testified. As confessed felons with whom deals had been made in trade for their testimony, putting them on the stand threatened to weaken the prosecution's case.

Jan Mead's testimony could hurt him because she could provide a motive for the crime, but Tom felt certain that the judge would not let her testify, especially if Lorna claimed protection against self-incrimination. Mead's statements were completely hearsay, built entirely on statements made by Lorna that could not be proven. Furthermore, Mead's understanding of what Lorna told her was wrong. Lorna told Tom she never said anything incriminating to Mead.

Geary County Sheriffs arrested Lorna on March 21, and charged her with two counts of conspiracy to commit first-degree murder and one count of aiding and abetting first-degree murder. She had her own defense strategy. Her attorney, Darrell Meyer, advised her to plead the Fifth Amendment protection against self-incrimination in Tom's case. Tom knew this would happen and understood it. Lorna's exculpatory evidence would not be available to him. Even if she agreed to testify, it is unlikely Shaw would have put her on the stand. He saw Lorna as unstable and unpredictable, and defense attorneys do not like surprises. "Who knows what she would have said on the stand?" Shaw reasoned.

As Tom saw it, a jury of Emporians would be faced with choosing between belief in the testimony of a well-respected pastor and a shady homebuilder. He saw the trial as a frustrating distraction, but knew that within weeks he would walk free. It is the last time he trusted the Kansas justice system.

A return to normal?

The week following Easter, Tom decided to return to preaching with the blessing of the lay ministers. When he stepped into the pulpit that Sunday, he saw the front row filled with reporters. He knew his time at Faith was over.

At the end of the service, Tom stepped into the church lobby to greet his people. He saw reporters mixing among the people, and they saw him. "Pastor Bird, can we ask you a few questions?"

"No. No interviews."

"But won't you comment on this trial? How's it affecting you?"

"I said no comment. Please, I do not want to be interviewed."

A film crew from CBS in Chicago waited for him. The reporter persisted. "Let me ask you a few questions."

"My attorney has advised me not to speak to the press. I am not giving any interviews," Tom insisted.

"Okay, I don't want to ask you anything about your trial. I just want to know how this is affecting your family and your ministry," the reporter persisted.

Tom agreed to stand for an interview based on the agreement that the interview would avoid all aspects of the trial. He stepped outside and holding Paul in his arms, he did the interview. A photographer from the *Emporia Gazette* saw the interview taking place and snapped a photo from behind the camera crew. The next day, Tom saw his picture in the paper with a caption declaring that CBS had been in town covering the trial. Irv Shaw was very angry at Tom for doing this.

Try as he might to ignore it, Tom felt the growing suspicion among his friends and Sandy's family members. Many still stuck close to him, but the stress at church led him to conclude that it could no longer serve as a place of refuge for him. Even more so, his very presence in the church caused division, and he could not tolerate anything that might threaten to destroy its mission.

Gregory Miles, a member at Faith, said, "One of the worst things about this, when you run into other members in the store, you don't know which side they're on... It's one of those things where nobody can say who's right or wrong... I feel that (the congregation) would be better off if he had resigned right at first."

Miles saw the irony in Tom's arrest. "That's the sad thing about it. Guilty or innocent, his career's going to be hurt."

Even though he was convinced that he would be found not guilty, Tom had decided that once the trial was over, "I was going to have to move out of Emporia, probably back to Arkansas with my family."

On May 27, 1984, Tom spoke to the voters of his church. It would be the last message he delivered at Faith, or any other church outside prison walls. The message provides numerous insights into the way that he looked at his life, duties and expectations. Its passionate plea for Christian love shows a man desperately in need of the support of other fellow believers, but who recognized the real and, in his case, fatal harm done by gossip. As he spoke these words, he had no idea just how deadly the gossip would be.

So, tuned in to the power of rumor and innuendo and still convinced that Lorna was also a victim of sensationalism run amok, he even defended her in this last message. You can read it in its entirely at http://www.cagedbird.net/excerpts.htm. Just the opening statement is reproduced here to give an insight as to Tom's frustration.

"I feel that it is important to take this last opportunity to speak to this group even though I speak with the concern that my words may be misinterpreted. Though I feel frozen in my present situation, I must speak for the good of the church. The reasons I hesitate are because for the last two months I have experienced the following sentiments:

- If I remained silent I was judged to be unfair for not informing people.
- When I have spoken I was judged to be defensive.
- When I look depressed I was judged to be full of self-pity.
- When I smiled and looked serene I was judged to be failing to take matters seriously.
- When I acted timid I was judged to be weak.
- When I acted boldly I was judged to be manipulating.
- When I was indecisive I was judged to have lost my leadership capacity.
- When I acted decisively I was judged to be using my position to railroad matters.

"To multiply the anguish of my predicament, I only hear these judgements second or third hand, so that I cannot share directly what is in my heart and my intentions to my accusers within the congregation.

"So, as you understand my hesitation to speak, please let me have a few of your minutes to hear me out.

"As I look at my past, I see some misjudgments on my part.

- I have chosen to set aside the advice of the elders of this congregation.
- I have let myself be forced into a deceptive type of spirit for fear of being misunderstood.
- I see some bad decisions.
- I see some over zealousness.
- I see misguided talk taking place.
- I have not taken all precautions to insure that my total life be above reproach.

"No one has ever face-to-face confronted me with sin, but the above-mentioned happenings have shown beyond a shadow of a doubt that I am human.

"I live in a fish bowl." Soon he would live as a caged Bird.

May 31 was Tom's last day on the job. On June 1, Jane Grismer called Tom, the unemployed pastor, to wish him a happy birthday.

Tom gets counseling

Tom knew he needed help. He felt himself losing the ability to cope with all the pressures forced on him by Sandy's death and now the foolish trial that destroyed his ministry. He reached out to Donald Romsa, a Lutheran counselor at Lutheran Social Service in Wichita. Romsa and Bird had served together on the District Family Life Committee.

Romsa counseled Tom seven times that summer, beginning on June 8 and ending on August 27. The two-hour sessions covered a lot of ground. Tom cautioned Romsa that he could not discuss details of the criminal charges or the trial. Tom always came alone to their counseling sessions, and Romsa never saw him with Lorna. Romsa met Lorna once during a presentation he made on stress management at Redeemer Lutheran Church in Hutchinson, but never saw the two together.

Tom detailed how the possibility of being sent to jail effected his children and his hopes to build a new life once the jury vindicated him. During the August meetings, having been found guilty, the discussion turned to dealing with the real possibility of short-term incarceration, probation, schooling for him and his children, and life plans. Tom last saw Romsa on August 27, three days before his sentencing. Even facing the most dire of possibilities, Tom still took time to plan his future. Soon, though, every minute of his future would be planned by his jailers.

The trial begins

Tom Bird sat in the Lyon County Courtroom for the first time on May 31, 1984, at his preliminary hearing. The judge listened to witnesses' accusations and heard the defense and bound him over for trial. This meant that the judge saw enough evidence to convince him that a jury should weigh guilt or innocence. At his arraignment on June 4, Tom pled innocent and was released on a $10,000 bond. The judge set the trial to begin on June 25.

Unlike Danny Carter and Greg Curry, each of whom pled guilty to the same Class D felony of which Tom had been accused, prosecutors offered no deals to Tom. They saw this conviction as the first in a series of at least two and probably three convictions they planned for him. (First, solicitation to murder Marty. Second, the murder of Sandy Bird. Third, should they find the "smoking gun," Marty's murder.) The prosecution set its sights high. This series of trials provided the kind of foundational opportunities upon which legal and judicial careers could be built. So, there could be no deal for Tom (he would have refused it anyway).

Lorna's trial date had been postponed again, and would continue to be until August of 1985. Prosecutors kept her on a tight string, hoping to use her testimony to convict Tom of more than just the planning of Marty's murder. By not settling her case, prosecutors also knew they kept control over her testimony. The threat that anything she said that might weaken their case against Tom served to keep her lips sealed. The Fifth Amendment gave Lorna the shield behind which she could hide from the court.

Virginia and Ralph Bird arrived on June 3 to offer help and support to their son, and to care for the children. Virginia wrote, "No one is being a pastor to him and he needs it so badly right now! Tom needs some time to think, but he also needs guidance. Many of his congregation come by the house to visit with him and show concern."

The Birds met Terry Smith for the first time on June 4. She quickly befriended the grieving couple and helped them care for the three Bird children.

Other family members also came to the trial. Jane and Papa Doc Grismer were there, as was Randall Stringer, Sandy Bird's father, and his new wife. Sandy's aunts, June Post and Patricia Goins, as well as two of the Birds' cousins attended. The Grismers and Birds already felt the tension of separation brought about by the accusations against Tom.

Grismer family members arrived early each morning at the courthouse, eating breakfast in a second floor waiting room. The crush for seats at the sensational trial was great, and the family meant to push their way to the front. They brought cushions to sit on, softening the hard benches.

"These kind of trials bring out the worst in people. Some of these people are crazy, fighting over a seat, acting like children," reported a county employee. And why not? This trial was a soap opera script being played out in real life, and the town was caught up in its seedy plot.

"I've never been to anything like this before," gawker Lucrecia Eubanks said. "I feel like I know them all; I've heard their names so many times."

The courthouse is vintage mid-50s design, modern and government gray blah. The courtroom in which Tom was tried is moderately-sized, with its blond oak benches and sterile décor. Blond oak paneling covers its walls whose drab sameness is interrupted only by portraits of county judges. The carpeting is a nondescript gray. Nothing distinguishes this courtroom from thousands of others.

Tom sat with attorney Irv Shaw at a plain double-pedestal table on the left in front of the rail separating them from the spectators who had to share space on the court's 16 wood benches. Lyon County Prosecutor Rod Symmonds sat at the table to their right. The judge's bench sat directly ahead of Tom with the witness stand to its right. In between the witness stand and the judge sat the court reporter. The clerk and bailiff were on Tom's left. The jury box with its 18, stiff wood chairs, sat 20 feet to Tom's right, so he was at a slight angle to them. Another row of six stiff wood chairs sat directly in front of the jury box facing away from the jury. The closest juror to the witness stand sat less than 10 feet away.

Bailiff Alice Thornton entered the courtroom and saw it packed with curious spectators as she took her place to the right of the judge's bench. Never before had she seen this room jammed wall to wall. Even a television crew stood ready to broadcast a good portion of each day's activities, another first for a Kansas courtroom.

"Please rise," Thornton announced as Judge Gary Rulon climbed up behind his bench and sat down. Some in that courtroom wondered why Rulon dared sit as judge in this case. They knew he had been a close friend of Marty's, of both the Andersons for that matter. All had held their church memberships at Emporia's First Presbyterian Church. Rulon and the Andersons fought on the same side of a divisive church issue and grew quite close. The Andersons left the church and joined Faith Lutheran. Rulon belonged to the Optimists' Club with Marty. He attended Marty's funeral.

Those who knew about Rulon's friendship with Marty and how well he knew Lorna believed he should have recused himself from the case. They questioned whether he could stay neutral given how close he had been to the Andersons. Had the county known about their friendship, Rulon might have become caught trapped in the rumor mill just as had Tom Bird. Any man who knew Lorna was sure to be tainted somehow.

Years later, the governor appointed Rulon to the Kansas Court of Appeals. News accounts of his appointment described him as the "judge in the Tom Bird trials." Tom's trial brought attention, unwanted to some and desired by others, to scores of Emporians.

Pre-trial perceptions

Tom described his perception as the trial began.

"At the trial I just said let's get it over with. I saw it very simplistically. All my attorney has to do is just show Darrel Carter is just not reliable. I would get up and there and show them who I am. I didn't have a lot of tension. Irv Shaw did have his way about him relaxing you because he was laid back. I had confidence in him. I thought he's going to hit it hard and make the best of it.

"I really thought that even though many people might end up thinking I'm guilty, I'm gonna be found innocent because I believed in some basic principles. Innocent until proven guilty was the main one.

"I was intimidated by the idea that my life is in the hands of 12 people. That my life was in the hands of Irv Shaw. He was laid back, not in the sense that he wasn't going to do his job, that he didn't understand the seriousness of it. But in a confidence like way. He was confident that he was going to do everything he could and it was a crapshoot after that.

"I know I'm innocent so therefore I have a high standard of proving guilt for myself."

The Kansas press labeled Tom's 1985 trial as the news story of the year. It began with his 1984 trial.

The *Emporia Gazette,* the creation of William H. White who had been the town's biggest claim to fame before the Bird trials, provided extensive coverage as investigators plodded through their work. Townspeople saw Tom's name linked to Lorna and Marty, Danny Carter and Greg Curry regularly. Once arrested, each step of his trial merited news coverage.

"If Tom were a sewer worker, no one would show up for this trial," Pastor Larry Kalsow commented. As a pastor, the story had sensational implications.

"This is a small town where everybody knows everybody, and this is big news," stated Mike Iuen of KAKE-TV in Wichita.

Not everyone knew Tom and Lorna. Greg Jordan, the director of the Lyon County Historical Society, said they "were unknown to anyone until this all happened." The Birds were outsiders from Arkansas. They had only been in Emporia for 19 months when Sandy died. Marty and Lorna were outsiders, too, though they lived in Emporia for more than six years when Marty was murdered. Unlike the Birds, Marty and Lorna had many longer term contacts outside of church; especially Lorna. Darrel, though, had lived in Emporia all his life.

"It is sad, but it seems like most of the community have pegged him (Bird) as guilty already," lamented Alan Rees, a member at Faith, during the trial.

On June 20, Virginia wrote, "Pretrial motions are presented by attorney Shaw. We can't believe this has progressed this far. Every day there is something in the *Emporia Gazette* downtrodding [sic] Tom's reputation and undermining his character."

Shaw recognized it would be difficult to impanel a non-prejudiced jury to hear Tom's case and so entered a motion to have the trial moved to another county. Judge Rulon denied the motion.

Shaw moved to prevent Jan Mead's hearsay testimony from being heard. Judge Rulon denied the motion. The issue stemmed from the fact that Lorna would hide behind her Fifth Amendment rights against self-incrimination. Mead claimed that Lorna told her about having a long-term sexual affair with Tom during the spring of 1983. Without Lorna testifying at the trial, Shaw could not impeach this testimony.

Shaw moved to suppress any discussion of the life insurance benefits payable to Lorna upon Marty's death. Shaw showed the judge that Tom was not listed as a beneficiary, demonstrating that it was irrelevant. Judge Rulon denied the motion.

Shaw wanted the judge to bar the use of the KBI tape recording of Darrel and Tom made at their meeting on December 12, 1983. He said it violated Tom's Fifth Amendment rights against self-incrimination. Tom had no idea he was being taped and had not been advised of his rights before the tape was made. Judge Rulon denied the motion.

For the first time in the history of Kansas, television cameras were allowed at a trial. Judge Rulon denied Shaw's motion to ban live coverage.

Shaw wanted to require Julie Palmer to testify in person. Jennifer suffered a nervous breakdown once the news broke about her adultery with Darrel, and testified by deposition. Rulon denied the motion.

Jane front and center

Jane Grismer took a strong interest in Tom's predicament. Jane had hired Arkansas attorney Jack Lassiter to dig up information about the case and began feeding stories to prosecutors and the newspaper. Virginia saw Jane's direct involvement as an attack on Tom. In a section of her journal she wrote:

> "Jane Grismer comes to Emporia for the trial. She has been going against Tom's wishes and talking her head off to the District Attorney about Tom's case so we are almost afraid to talk to her. She has her facts all wrong and attorney Shaw has asked her not to speak to the press or opposition. But Jane Grismer does just whatever she wants to do without caring whether it hurts anybody or not. She is a publicity seeker in the halls outside the courtroom, talking to all the reporters. She has an obsession about Sandy and really believes she has been killed instead of an accident. We are shaking our heads."

Virginia added a marginal note to her journal a few days later.

"All during the trial Mrs. Grismer is most friendly with all the prosecution witnesses—even taking them to dinner. She and her family come at 7 a.m. with seat cushions to take up the first two rows of the visitors' rows. We have to scout around for a seat to sit in at our own son's trial.

"A lot of time we are so far back we have trouble hearing when the air conditioner goes on. There are a number of town characters who come here daily for entertainment at court trials—their amusement from other people's grief. What a predicament."

Choosing the jury

Judge Rulon looked out at the 30 Lyon County residents in the jury pool. He gave an impassioned speech about the central importance of jury service and citizenship. He warned them of the sacrifice but encouraged them to participate fully and take the responsibility seriously.

Rulon explained the process of voir dire, whereby prospective jurors are questioned thoroughly in an effort to seat an impartial jury. He told them not to be offended by the probing questions, that their personal integrity was not being questioned.

Rulon asked them, "Do any of you know anything about this case either through your own personal knowledge or by discussing the case with anyone else or by reading or hearing anything about it on any news media? If your answer is yes, please raise your hand. All right. If you would drop your hands. Was there anyone who did *not* raise their hand? All right. You might leave them up just a little bit longer if you would, please so the attorneys can make a note of that."

Then he asked if they had formed any prejudice based on these news reports. Several did, and he asked them all to step down.

Rod Symmonds, the prosecutor, took over the voir dire. "As I go through these questions I will much in the same fashion as the judge has done ask them of you as a group." He asked questions about whether any had legal business with the various attorneys or Lyon County. "Do any of you feel that words alone never hurt anybody and that the State of Kansas should never make unlawful the mere saying of certain words or phrases?" (Lyon County essentially had charged Tom with using hurtful words. The county took care not to link the solicitation charge to Marty's murder, meaning that crime consisted of talking about committing a felony—"the mere saying of certain words.")

"Have any of you heard or read anything about his particular case in the newspapers? Okay, it looks like about everyone. Was there anything about what you read or heard which you feel would affect your judgement?"

"Are there any of you that feel that the State of Kansas should never charge or file a criminal action against a minister? Do any of you because of your religious affiliation or your Christian upbringing, do you feel that it would be such that you would not be able to find a minister guilty if you were satisfied beyond a reasonable doubt that he was guilty of the offense that's alleged by the State?"

"Would the fact that there may be considerable publicity concerning this trial cause any of you difficulty in serving as a fair and impartial juror on this particular case?"

Symmonds read off the names of potential witnesses and asked whether juror prospects knew any of them and whether it would cloud their testimony. Included on the list of prosecution witnesses was David Workman, but he never did call him during the trial.

Shaw began. He asked whether anyone had any business or relationship to the County Attorney's office?

Shaw asked whether anyone had business with the Symmonds brothers (Robert and Rodney, partners in a law practice).

Shaw wanted to know whether any jurors had a social or friendship relationship with Rod Symmonds. Two in particular talked about knowing him all his life but felt it would not incline them toward his position.

A couple of jurors had dealings with Shaw's law firm, mostly with his law partner. None felt it would prejudice them in any way. (It's hard getting an impartial jury in a small town)

"Are any of you or any members of your family or friends familiar at all with the circumstances but for what I've told you here today relating to Sandy Bird's death? Any of you recall reading anything about it in the paper? Okay, we've got a bunch there (he saw many hands go up). Do any of you feel that you have any independent knowledge about how Sandy Bird died?"

Shaw asked whether anyone knew about the current case through the media and nearly everyone responded. He questioned Mr. Bailey. "And by that I mean are you talking about the newspaper, TV, radio, things of this nature?"

"Newspaper."

"Newspaper. Is there any particular story that stands out in your mind relating—that you have read in the newspapers?"

"No."

"Okay. Do you in your own mind have any opinion about the accuracy and the truth of the articles and stories that were printed in the media?"

He shook his head.

"Do you feel that they are accurate and true?"

"Some of them probably are. I don't know."

Mr. Bailey said nothing in the newspaper would keep him from making a fair judgement. Shaw reminded him that newspapers just report on the charges and not on the evidence. He asks whether Bailey can base his decision solely on the evidence. "Uh-huh."

Mr. Eldridge admitted that he had expressed opinions about Tom's guilt or innocence to others. Shaw pressed him, but he insisted he could set aside any preconceived notion or opinion and judge solely on the evidence presented at trial.

Shaw reminded the jurors that this trial had nothing to do with Marty's murder. Then he asked whether any of them knew Marty. Shaw also probed any who might personally know the witnesses, especially Darrel. Some knew him from civic involvements, school (Darrel's wife taught some of their children), the contracting business. He probed relationships with other witnesses.

"Are there any of you who feel that, for example, law enforcement officers don't lie?...Can each of you weight their testimony as well as that of all the other witnesses based upon what you see and hear on the witness stand without regard to what their status in and of itself may be?"

He asked whether any were related to a minister. Several were and from many different denominations, none of them Lutheran. Shaw asked whether any were prejudiced against Lutheran theology. "Are there any of you who feel that in a case of this nature ministers should be held to a higher standard than any other person? For example, a minister should never get into such a position and, therefore, he has to be guilty of something? Is there any of you who would feel that way as we sit here right now? Miss Kayser, you would?"

"Yes."

"Does the fact that he is a minister and the fact that he has been charged as we sit here right now make you feel that he has two strikes against him?"

"Yes."

"Do you feel then that it would be a situation of the defendant having to prove himself innocent then or overcome more evidence in this particular case in your mind than would, say, Tom Smith or John Doe on the street?"

"No, I don't think he has—there has to be more evidence, you know, to prove him innocent."

"Now, the problem and that may have been by terminology. We're not here to prove him innocent. The question is..."

"Well, okay."

"...can they prove him guilty."

"I don't, you know, feel like there's more evidence. I just think he should have stepped down maybe earlier."

Judge Rulon jumped in and reminded Kayser that she had said she believed in the presumption of innocence. She insisted that she could stick to that standard.

"This presumption of innocence which the court has talked about will not have been eroded in your mind merely because he is a minister?"

"No. I just—I guess I just feel they're like put on a higher pedestal."

Shaw reminded the jury that there would be a lot of publicity and that while they were home or in the community, the judge would prohibit them from talking about the case.

One woman who owned a beauty salon, said, "...I'm going to hear it. I mean there's not any way around that because—"

Shaw told her to tell the customers that she could not discuss it, and ask them to refrain as well. She said she guessed she could do that.

Shaw asked the jury to make sure they didn't make up their minds before hearing all the facts. "This is a criminal case and the court has alluded to the burden of proof. The burden of proof is proof beyond a reasonable doubt which differs substantially from that in the civil case. ....This burden of proof is a one-way street. The defendant is presumed innocent....Are there any of you who feel the defendant has to come forward and do something or he cannot be innocent?" No one raised their hand.

Then Shaw questioned each remaining juror independently.

Symmonds and Shaw, with Tom in tow, met in Judge Rulon's office. Each exercised their preemptory strikes and had jurors removed from the list. The final 12 were Moore, Dase, Pearson, Ensminger, Reppart, Cowden, Emley, Gardner, Gress, Markowitz, Hooern, and Sullivan. Alternates were Sayre and Wendling.

When Rulon seated the 14 chosen jurors, he gave them instructions. Rulon adjourned the trial until 9 a.m. the next day.

Present your case

Finally, on July 24, the trial began.

The attorneys made their opening statements previewing the case.

Symmonds told the jury that when Tom came into the office that day at the church, "there was then a conversation that Lorna Anderson and the defendant were wanting to have Martin Anderson killed."

They talked of two plans, one including a location southeast of town with a sharp bend in the road and a bridge. "The second plan dealt with a faked robbery at Granny's in Topeka while he [Marty] was at the Guards."

Darrel reported the "May" meeting to Mike Patton, Danny's attorney, following the December 1 meeting between Tom and Julie Palmer. Patton then contacted Vern Humphrey and arranged the meeting with Tom.

The motive for the crime was the love affair between Tom and Lorna, and she mentioned the insurance money.

Shaw said, "My purpose at this particular time like Mr. Symmonds is to give you some idea of what I anticipate the evidence is going to be, what it is you should be listening to, what it is you should be paying attention to so that when it's all said and done, it kind of fits back together."

He told them on how to evaluate a witness. "And in the course of doing so you must weigh the credibility of each particular witness. And when we use the term 'credibility' we're talking about can you believe him, do you feel this particular witness is really telling the truth, is he sitting here before you and telling you exactly what happened. And in doing so you should examine his motives for testifying, his opportunities for falsifying and the various inconsistencies that occur with respect to his testimony."

"In point of fact, their whole case, the entire case, hinges upon but one person and that one person is Mr. Darrel Carter. If Mr. Carter cannot be believed, if his testimony is false in any particular , then the State's case has its first flaw and we submit its first deficiency."

Shaw laid out the strange timing of Darrel's disclosure of the alleged solicitation, only after his brother had been charged.

Darrel had testified three times prior to this trial, and each time "his story gets better and better and better. Basically what Mr. Carter said was that he was approached completely out of the blue for a reason he knew nothing about by Lorna Anderson and asked to come to the Faith Lutheran Church. He didn't even know where it was. He went to the Faith Lutheran Church, and for the first time he met the defendant. Never met the man before in his life. I anticipate his evidence will be that at that point immediately without hesitation, with no preamble whatsoever, Tom Bird commenced to discuss how they were going to do away with Marty Anderson."

Shaw mentioned how convenient it was that one of the plots resembled how Sandy died.

Shaw described how the rumors about Tom and Lorna hurt the church and Tom's ability to minister and that is why he went to Julie. Darrel took advantage of this by concocting his bizarre tale and agreed to meet Tom with a body pack on. Shaw asked the jury to listen carefully to the tape of that conversation and especially to how Darrel attempted to get Tom to say something incriminating, but failed. Instead, the jurors would hear many references to the rumors. "Indeed an even more apt description I think is that it was two people sitting there pumping each other for information."

279

Shaw explained Tom's story to the jury, how they talked about firecrackers and Tom later met with Darrel at the building site.

He closed by reminding the jury that Darrel was the key to the case and to listen and watch him carefully. He felt confident that if they could, "you will agree that the evidence of the State is totally insufficient to find the defendant guilty beyond a reasonable doubt, that he is innocent of all charges against him. We will ask you to return a verdict in that effect."

Call the first witness: Lorna Anderson

Symmonds called Lorna, but before he did, Judge Rulon dismissed the jury and ordered that all sound and recording equipment be turned off before she testified.

Symmonds began. "If you would, would you please state your full name for the record?"

"Lorna Gail Anderson."

"Where do you currently reside at?"

"Hutchinson, Kansas."

"And how long have you resided in Hutchinson, Kansas?"

"The question calls for privileged information against self-incrimination."

Lorna refused to answer all subsequent questions. Then began a discussion between Rulon, Symmonds, Darrell Meyer (Lorna's attorney) and Shaw. Meyer explained that Lorna had been charged the day before in Geary County and, therefore, had to protect her rights against self-incrimination. Symmonds acknowledged this, but Shaw protested (the timing of her charge gave a great advantage to the state).

A debate ensued in which Shaw pushed for the right to pursue certain limited questions. Meyer and Symmonds both protested. Symmonds said, "If she is available to answer the questions set forth to her by the State of Kansas, she should do so. But I think to enable the defense as Mr. Shaw is trying to weasel this thing in and have the State be limited to two or three questions pertaining to this or that and then have the jury later wonder where in the dickens was the prosecutor's mind at the time that he failed to ask this witness questions pertaining to the issues in this case would be extremely prejudicial."

Shaw suggested that there was no reason Symmonds couldn't specify the questions he would ask as had Shaw and then the court would ask Lorna to respond.

Symmonds refused to alert Lorna to the questions he might ask and hinted that there were witnesses unknown to her that he did not want to disclose. Shaw suggested that Lorna had a right to know who those potential witnesses might be, and so did Tom.

Symmonds refused to write out specific questions for Lorna to consider, stating that the criminal law did not require him to do so.

Judge Rulon then ruled that Lorna's right to protection against self-incrimination made her unavailable as a witness.

Once Lorna stepped down, the judge asked the jury to return.

The State's star witness

The State alleged three people met at Faith and talked about killing Marty. One, Lorna, refused to testify, claiming her right to protection against self-incrimination. Tom sat as the defendant in this trial. Darrel was the third person at that meeting—the State's star witness.

Symmonds asked Darrel his name and where he lived. "How long have you lived in Lyon County."

"My lifetime."

He asked Darrel if he knew Lorna and Marty? Yes, he knew them through the sorority.

"Now, is Marty Anderson, do you know is he currently alive or is he deceased?"

"I believe he is dead."

"And do you recall what month it was that he passed away?"

"It was in November. I believe that was in December. No, I can't remember."

"Do you recall the specific day or month?"

"I think it was December the 4th. I take it back. It was November the 4th."

Symmonds asked whether Darrel ever went to Faith.

"Yes, I did."

"Where is the Faith Lutheran Church located at?"

"It's located here in Emporia at 15th and Trail Ridge Road."

"If you would, would you relate to the jury why it was that you went to the Faith Lutheran Church here in Emporia in May of 1983."

"I went to the Faith Lutheran Church on an invitation by Lorna Anderson."

"And do you recall the specific date that Lorna Anderson asked you to go to the Faith Lutheran Church?"

"I don't remember the particular date but it was sometime I believe around the middle of May, 1983."

Darrel said he went in the south side of the church, walked down a long hallway "and made a couple of turns and then went into Lorna's office which was the secretary's office." (At the preliminary hearing just weeks earlier, when asked to describe the church and how he got to her office, Darrel's description was so poor it was as if he had never been there. Between then and the trial, he brushed up on his testimony, because here he got it right.)

He and Lorna sat and talked a while, but he could not remember the subject. He really could not remember much about the office either, except that it was small. He said there were two or three chairs. "Okay, approximately five minutes after I was at the church, another guy come in to where I was seated and Lorna introduced that gentleman to me as a Reverend Tom Bird. After Tom Bird come into the office, Lorna Anderson stated to me that—after she..."

Irv Shaw rose. "Excuse me. For purposes of the record I would lodge an objection, ask that a continuing objection be made to anything that Lorna said."

"The objection you made earlier, Counsel?" Rulon asked.

"Yes, Your Honor."

"The Court's ruled on that. It will be overruled." (Thus, the judge allowed hearsay evidence allegedly given by Lorna to all others to be admitted at trial and heard by the jury.)

Lorna introduced him to Tom and then she said, "that Tom was going to help us."

"Did you ask her what she meant by that statement that he was going to help you?"

"Yes, I did. I said, 'Lorna, what's he going to help us do?' And she said, 'He's going to help us kill Martin Anderson.'"

"What if any response did you make to that statement?"

"I said, 'Lorna, I've told you before that I didn't want anything to do with that and I still don't'"

Symmonds asked Darrel to be specific.

"Okay. To the best that I can recall after Lorna Anderson told me that Tom Bird was going to help us kill Martin Anderson, I said, 'Lorna, I told you a long time ago [more than one year earlier] I wasn't going to help you do that and I didn't want any part of it.' There was some other conversation which I don't recall, and then Lorna had told me that her and Tom had outlined a couple of plans in a way that they thought they could kill him and wanted to know if I would help participate in those plans....And I said no, that I would not."

Symmonds wondered if Darrel brought up the idea of counseling or divorce.

"Yes, I did. I asked Tom, I said, 'Tom, you're the minister here at the church...Have you ever, you know, talked to Lorna about counseling and why, you know, don't you talk to her about getting a divorce?' I said, 'That would be a lot easier thing to do.' ...The Defendant told me that Lorna didn't want a divorce, that Martin Anderson had a large insurance policy and that she didn't want the divorce, that she wanted the money and the only way that they could get the money was if Martin Anderson was dead."

Symmonds asked about Lorna's feelings toward Tom. "I asked Tom Bird what his—why, you know, he didn't talk to her more about the divorce, and he told me that he—that he loved Lorna Anderson and he was doing this to help her."

The judge admonished Darrel to speak up. Each time he reached a critical point in his testimony, his voice would drop and become hard to hear.

"Was there any discussion about Martin K. Anderson's funeral?"

"Yes, there was....Well, the plan on the funeral was that Tom Bird would preside over the funeral and that way he could be close to Lorna, be by her side; and since he was the minister there, no one would really suspect the minister of having anything to do with this and he would just really be close to her. And they also—Lorna also asked me if I would want to be a pallbearer at the funeral, and I told her that there would be no way."

Symmonds asked why Tom thought Darrel would become involved in such a crime.

"I did say, 'Why do you think that I would participate in something like this, that I'm not a—you know, a cold-blooded killer and I've never done anything like this in my life.' And Tom Bird replied to me, he said, 'I haven't either.' He said, 'I'm a man of God and I'm going to kill Martin Anderson.'"

"Did one or both, referring to the Defendant and Lorna Anderson, make statements concerning the plan which they outlined to you?"

"Okay, both Lorna Anderson and Tom Bird made statements outlining the plan, the two plans that were discussed at the church that day."

"The first plan that was outlined at the church was Tom Bird told me that he had been driving around out in the country and he found a place that there was a bend in the road and a bridge. There was about a 50-foot drop off to the water and if a person was drugged or drunk and was coming down that road, they could miss that bridge and go down into the river and it would raise very little suspicion. And their plan, the plan that was outlined then, was Martin Anderson was going to be drugged at his house, loaded into the car and taken out to that place in the road; and then they were going to shove his car over that embankment. And they wanted to know if I would come out there and pick Tom Bird up after he shoved the car over the embankment. Meanwhile, Lorna Anderson was going to remain home so she wouldn't arouse suspicion and people could see that she was at the house and no one would suspect her."

When Darrel first made this statement to Humphrey on December 10, 1983, he stated the scheme was to have him help load Marty into the car. "My involvement was to go down and pick Tom Bird up at the scene after he pushed the car into the river." Darrel said he told them he wanted nothing to do with the scheme.

Symmonds asked about an "alternative plan."

"The alternative plan that was discussed at the church—and I don't recall just exactly whether it was Tom Bird or Lorna Anderson that initiated this plan, but they both had information on the plan and that was Martin Anderson was in a reserve unit in Topeka and he stayed sometimes overnight with an aunt or a grandmother. And I don't know if it was his relative or hers, but he stayed there several nights when he would go to the reserve meeting. The plan was Tom Bird was going to go to the house on one of the nights that Martin Anderson was going to be staying there, go into the house, rough it up and make it look like a robbery; and then when Martin Anderson come home, he was going to shoot him and then he was just going to leave and it would just look like a robbery had occurred at the house and that Martin Anderson walked in on the robbery."

"What if any emotional reaction did you have to the plans?"

"Well, I had never really talked to anybody about killing anyone before and I didn't realize when I went up to the church that that was what was going to be discussed up there, and the longer I sat there and two people are talking about killing a friend of mine, I started to get pretty nervous about this deal because I knew they had talked to me about it and if I didn't give them a decision on whether I was going to help or I wasn't going to help, you know, I may not be leaving the church either. And so I really never gave them my decision right there at the church. I told them I would have to think about it because I was really concerned about just getting out of the church myself."

Darrel said he could not be sure whether Tom and Lorna were serious about these plans or just talking. Just before this, though, he had testified that he feared for his own life.

Symmonds asked him about fireworks. "When I left the church, Tom Bird told me, he said that, 'Anyone has seen you here or wants to know why you were here, just tell them that I was talking to you about my youth group selling fireworks'"

Darrel said he left the church but that Tom came to see him again, "...two to three days after our meeting at the church."

"Tom Bird came out to the house where I was working, he asked me if I had made a decision yet on whether I wanted to help participate in the plot to kill Martin Anderson or not." Other men worked at the house that day, his brother Chris and Darrell Warren, a subcontractor. He could not remember whether Warren was at the site, but knew Chris had gone home.

Darrel said Tom caught him by surprise and so, "I told him I really hadn't had time to think about it and if he would drop back by in a couple days that I would give him my decision then."

To establish the May date, Symmonds asked how Darrel paid Warren for his services. He paid by check, and furthermore, he claimed he previously paid Jim Russell, a sheet rocker to hang the material so Warren could finish it. Darrel produced two checks, one for Russell and one for Warren. (The fact that Darrel paid Warren in May didn't preclude him paying him again in June, July or any other time.)

Symmonds tried to nail down the specific date that Darrell Warren worked at the house. Carter could not identify it any better than stating "around the 23rd or the 24th that Tom Bird come out to the house and talked to me...I'm unclear whether Darrell Warren was out there at the house or not."

No matter how hard Symmonds tried, Carter could not specify what date he and Warren worked together when Tom came to the house.

Darrel's testimony started getting confusing and Shaw objected to it as speculation. "Everything he's said so far is 'it seems like, I think, I can't recall.' I think the witnesses can testify about what happened and what he remembers, but everything else is just guesswork at this point and I would object to it."

Symmonds said it was reasonable for a witness to speculate on some details 14 months following the occurrence of an event. Rulon agreed with Symmonds and overruled Shaw once again. (Later, when Tom had trouble remembering specific dates, Symmonds said it proved he was guilty.)

Darrel claimed that when Tom came to the house a second time, he still didn't give him an answer, and told him to come back a third time. He said that on that appointed date and time, he made sure he wasn't there. Instead, he called Tom on the phone "...and told him who I was and that I didn't want anything to do with the murder of Martin Anderson."

Symmonds asked whether he had any further contact with Tom. He said it was in December when he called Tom to set up a meeting. He called him because Tom had gone to see Julie Palmer.

Symmonds asked whether Darrel and Julie ever met for sex. "Yes, we did."

Darrel said that following Julie's visit, he went to see the attorney, Mike Patton and Patton called Agent Humphrey. Darrel called Faith to set up a meeting with Tom, placing the call from Patton's office. Tom answered and

Darrel told him he wanted to meet to talk about Marty's murder. (Actually, Darrel never even used Marty's name in the call.) He said that Tom set up the time and place.

"Do you recall if that conversation was recorded?" Symmonds asked.

"Yes, the conversation was recorded."

Darrel said they agreed to meet at the Emporia Bowl at 5 p.m., but was unsure of the date. He drove his brown pick-up truck and said Tom sat waiting in his car when he arrived. He said the KBI met him behind the Alco store and wired him with a body pack prior to the meeting. That way they could both listen to the dialogue and record it.

Symmonds knew Darrel made a mistake here and asked him whether he had visited Mike Patton's office earlier that day? "Yes. After the meeting at Mike Patton's office and before they placed the body pack on, I did go home. I had a bullet-proof vest that I did wear as just a precautionary measure."

"Mr. Carter, what was your motivation in agreeing to wear this body pack and trying to record a conversation between yourself and the defendant?"

"I think the main motivation in this was my brother Daniel Carter had been arrested in connection with the murder of Martin Anderson, and I was working in cooperation with the KBI in trying to gain any information that we could to help them solve this case."

Symmonds wondered if Darrel had contacted anyone in law enforcement between May, 1983 and Marty's murder. He hadn't. "I think the main reason is I just wasn't wanting to get involved in this deal and I was just trying to stay clear. I really never felt that maybe anything would ever—would ever come of this. It's not just every day that someone sits around talking about killing somebody, and quite a time period had passed I guess and I really kept thinking nothing was going to happen."

Darrel told a neighbor about the incident, a man named Joe Lapping, but no one else. What about Mike Patton?

"I had talked to Michael Patton after the death of Martin Anderson about this, and I told him on November the 18th." (Strange how easily Darrel recalled some dates that were crucial to his story, but conveniently forgot others that might impeach his testimony.)

"Did you at any time ever have sexual relations with Lorna Anderson?"

"Yes, I did."

"Did you recall approximately when it was that you had sexual relations with her?"

Shaw objected and the attorneys once again approached the bench. They had a lengthy conversation about the relevance of Darrel's adultery with Lorna to the charge against Tom. Symmonds argued that it was important to establish why Lorna would dare ask Darrel to do such a thing. Shaw got impatient and said, "If he wants to profess to be a man about town and lady killer and slept with everybody in town while he's been married 19 years, that's his problem; but it certainly doesn't have anything to do with this case."

To resolve this dispute, Symmonds agreed to withdraw the question about when they had sex and the Judge ordered a recess. He planned to have the taped phone call played when the jury returned.

Play the tape, please

Upon return from recess, Symmonds showed Darrel several pictures of Faith Lutheran Church. He identified them as the building, doorway and halls that he had entered.

Symmonds produced the tape of the phone conversation that set up the meeting between Darrel and Tom.

The tape rolled.

"Faith Lutheran Church."

"Yes, is a Pastor Bird there?"

"Yes, this is Pastor Bird."

"Hey, this is Darrel Carter."

"Yes."

"Hey, I wonder if we could set up some time when I could talk to you."

"Okay. What—what have you got in mind as far as getting together?"

"I just need some information on what my brother's involvement in this deal is if you know. I would rather not say too much on the phone."

"Sure, well, I—I can't give you much information but let's—where are you working now?"

"Ah, we're working all over town. Not really any one spot. If you've got a place maybe we could meet or just maybe meet in the parking lot or something somewhere."

"Okay. I'll meet you over at—"

"It's going to have to probably maybe have to be a little later on today."

"Okay. Well, you name the time."

"4:30, 5:00 or sometime after there," Darrel said, setting the time.

"Okay, let's say 5:00," Tom agreed. "I'll just meet you at the, oh—just like the bowling alley up there off Graham."

"Okay, that would be fine."

"All right." The call ended.

Argue in private

Symmonds turned to the judge and said, "I would advise the court at this time that my line of questioning will be changing." This had to do with prior agreements concerning admissibility of evidence. Rulon decided to dismiss the jury until 9 a.m. the next morning.   Several times during the trial, Rulon dismissed the jury so that he could meet privately with the lawyers. Here they discussed disagreements over testimony, evidence, procedures and legal issues. Each time, Rulon noted for the record that Symmonds, Shaw and usually Bird participated in the meeting (in a few instances, Tom waived his right to be present, leaving the negotiations in Shaw's hands).

On this day, Darrel Carter remained in the courtroom as well.

Symmonds asked Darrel about a time 2 or 2-1/2 years prior when Lorna flagged him down and asked him "at that time if I knew of anyone that would kill Martin Anderson?" Three or four months later, she flagged him down again and "asked me if I had found anyone to kill Martin Anderson."

Darrel insisted that at the time, he and Lorna were just good friends. He claimed to also be a friend of Marty's, but there had not yet been sex between them.

Shaw began his cross-examination. He asked Carter for a specific date when Lorna asked him these things. He again said it was 2 to 2-1/2 years earlier.

"Do you remember what day of the week it was?"

"No, I do not."

"Do you even recall what month it was?"

"To the best of my knowledge it was sometime during the summer months but no."

Shaw pursued another line of questioning, trying to identify where Darrel was the night Lorna flagged him down. He said he had left the apartment building on 8th Avenue, saw her, and went over to her van. Leaning in, she asked him to help her find someone to murder Marty.

Shaw pressed him on how well he knew Lorna. He said they met five or six times at sorority events prior to this street meeting. "And based upon this, just out of the clear blue you're trying to tell the court today that she said, 'I want you to help me kill Martin Anderson?'"

"That is correct."

"What were her precise words?"

"She asked me if I knew of anyone that would kill Martin Anderson."

Shaw pressed him on why Lorna wanted Marty killed, and he claimed he didn't know.

"So can we assume then that you weren't really that upset about the fact that you had been approached by her or this statement had been made?"

"No, I wasn't upset that she approached me."

Rulon dismissed Darrel.

Before Rulon heard the tape, he asked whether there were any objections. Shaw stated that the tape was a violation of Tom's Fifth Amendment rights since he didn't know he was being taped. He said it was a form of self-incrimination, and though he knew he would lose the argument, he wanted his objection recorded.

Symmonds argued that Darrel wasn't an employee or agent of the state while wearing the body pack, and that at the time, investigators were in a fact-gathering mode anyway. No one had been accused of anything. Given these facts, he felt there had been no need to inform Tom of his rights.

Rulon overruled the motion to suppress the tape.

Shaw objected to playing the tape because of how the state proposed the jurors should listen to it. They wanted to rig special earphones for all the jurors, the judge, attorneys, Tom and the court reporter, and also broadcast it via a larger speaker to those in the courtroom. Shaw imagined what it would look like. He pictured the tape recorder with special amplifiers and microphone cords running across the room and said it would make a visual impression on the jurors. He believed the jurors would place undo weight on the tape's contents given all this attention it received. He argued aggressively against the use of earphones. He said the jury should hear it just like anyone else.

Symmonds wanted the jury to wear earphones so they could clearly hear all the words.

Rulon decided to use the earphones. Symmonds was pleased.

Shaw said, "I would like to have it in the record that these earphones which we're talking about are plastic head pieces which go over with pretty yellow earmuffs on them and they are connected—at least the one I see comes off of two wires with some kind of a switch going to some kind of a junction box which has no more than three or four outlets which leads to this magic machine we have up here.

"I would further suggest that again we're changing what would appear to be a public trial into a public spectacle by taking the microphone now and set it back here so everyone can hear to the tape. Who cares? They're here. They can hear what comes over the tape. They're not entitled to have it broadcast to them in any way, shape or form.

"Finally, I would object to all of this being done as a violation of the defendant's right to a fair trial; and if the court insists on doing it that way, I would request the court to make it very evident and very plain to the jury that this method of presenting this evidence is being done solely for their convenience because of the noise level contained within the courtroom and is not to be considered in any way as adding any additional weight, credit or any other factor to this particular item of evidence because I submit to the court that by this particular procedure we are isolating this out of the entire set of circumstances.

"I can see myself, my client sitting here with earphones in the middle of the evening news tomorrow night saying, 'Isn't this wonderful? We've got earphones because this is such a crucial piece of evidence.' It's not better than any evidence that the defendant might present.

"I'm, well, literally beside myself with the whole situation." He learned about the method of presentation during a casual conversation with Symmonds in his office the previous Saturday. "I was just dumbfounded and remain so to this day."

Before the jury returned the next morning, Rulon met with the attorneys once again to talk again about the rules for listening to the tape. He said he would order that no photographs be taken, lest some newspaper run a demeaning picture of Tom wearing little yellow earphones. He ordered that the equipment would be removed immediately following the playing of the tape, and the jury would be removed from the courtroom while this was being done. Rulon asked Shaw if he had prepared an instruction to the jury.

Shaw restated his objection to using the earphones, saying, "If I were to ask to have my testimony, my witnesses' testimony played over earphones so that the jurors not be disturbed that certainly wouldn't happen....I think it's a denial of my client's right to a fair and public trial. It is causing undue emphasis on one particular item of evidence. It is infringing upon the jury's right, if you will, to either listen or not listen to a specific item of evidence."

"I certainly don't see anything prejudicial about it," Symmonds answered.

Symmonds asked permission to let an FBI agent test play a music tape so that the jurors could adjust their earphone volume. Shaw called this "silly" and Rulon said there would be no music in his courtroom, but the agent could instruct the jurors how to use the equipment. (Shaw really saw a dilemma here. Not only would the specialized equipment make the evidence seem more important than it was, but an FBI agent, standing in plain view of the jury, would advise and assist them in the hearing of the tape.)

Darrel took the stand again, once everyone was in the courtroom and the jury seated. He described motioning Tom to get into his truck, and acknowledged certain phrases he used to begin the taping session. Symmonds wanted to establish whose voices were on the tape. Then Symmonds introduced the tape as evidence.

The tape was played. Once the tape finished, the jury left the room while the playback equipment was removed.

While the jury was out, Judge Rulon ruled on the question of whether statements Lorna made to Darrel years earlier could be admitted during this trial. He ruled against it, stating they were not relevant to the case against Tom. Shaw won one.

Dissecting the tape

Darrel took the stand again and Symmonds asked, "Mr. Carter, what if any training have you received in homicide investigation?"

"None."

"On how many occasions have you been asked to assist the KBI with a homicide investigation?"

"One."

Shaw leapt to his feet. "Your honor, I'm going to object to that question. I'm going to object to the term 'homicide.' I don't think there's anything in this particular case to indicate there was a homicide involved as a result of any of the charges here."

Symmonds defended his question by stating he could find many nouns to use to "describe the killing of another human being." He offered to use a different phrase.

"On how many occasions have you assisted the KBI on investigations in which a person has been killed?"

"Just one."

"And which case was that?"

"That was a case involving Martin Anderson's death."

Shaw stood again, and this time asked to approach the bench. He reminded the judge that Tom was not being tried for murder in this case and there should be no mention of homicide or Martin Anderson's death. The instant case was solicitation, not murder.

Symmonds said he used the term anticipating that the defense would try to imply that Darrel never asked certain questions because he knew Tom was innocent. By asking these questions about Darrel's experience in homicide investigations, Symmonds hoped to mitigate this deficiency. Rulon told Symmonds to stop this line of questioning.

Shaw began his cross examination.

"Mr. Carter, if you would please, first of all I believe you are married and have been for 19 years. Is that your testimony?"

"That's correct."

"And have three children."

"That's right."

"Perhaps I'm a little bit confused but it is correct, is it not, sir, that you testified at the preliminary hearing in this particular case on May the 31st, 1984? Is that right?"

"I believe that is right."

"You do recall testifying at least in this particular matter on one other occasion?"

"Yes."

"At that time, sir, you were asked if you knew Lorna Anderson. Do you recall that question?"

"Yes."

"At that time you said that you only knew her through the sorority which your wife was a member of. Do you recall that answer?"

"Yes, I believe that's correct."

"And you also further indicated in response on questions that you only saw her on social occasions when husbands would be invited. Do you recall that?"

"I don't recall making that exact statement, no."

Shaw read from the transcript. Carter said, "About the only time that I ever saw Lorna was at some of the socials." "Do you recall that testimony?"

"That's correct."

"And then further I believe on cross examination you were asked about how many social occasions were there, and I believe you indicated that there could not have been more than five or six. Would that sound about right?"

"Yes, that sounds correct."

"And do you recall, sir, that at the time of your testimony on cross examination in the preliminary hearing you were asked if you had ever formed any kind of a relationship with Lorna Anderson and you responded 'No.' Do you recall that?"

"That's correct."

"You were asked, 'Did you ever see her other than at these social-type functions?'; and you responded, 'Yes, I've seen her on the street and talked to her.' You were asked, 'Have you ever met with her on other than social-type functions? And by that I mean for a protracted period of time, anywhere from 30 minutes to an hour to two hours?' Do you recall those questions?"

"Yes, I do."

"And do you recall what your response was to that last question?"

"No, I do not recall my response."

Shaw read it back. "Not that I can recall right off." "Do you recall that answer now?"

"I believe that's correct."

"Yet if I understood you correctly yesterday, you indicated that you had

had sexual relations with Lorna Anderson. Is that right?"

"That's correct."

"And how many times has that occurred?"

"One—"

"How often?"

"One time."

"I see. You also were asked at the preliminary about this Julie Palmer who we've had substantial conversation about. Do you recall that testimony?"

"Yes, I do."

"Do you recall being asked who Julie Palmer was?"

"Yes, I do."

"And at that time you said she was a friend of yours. Is that correct?"

"That's correct."

"Do you recall being asked if you were involved with her in any other way?"

"I don't remember the exact question."

"Do you recall these questions and answers: 'Who is Julie Palmer?' 'A neighbor of Birds.' 'What is she to you?' 'A friend of mine.' 'How close a friend?' 'A good friend.' 'Indeed, sir, are you involved with her in any other way?' 'No.' Do you recall those questions and answers?"

"Yes, I do."

"Do you recall further, sir, that I even went further and asked you if you had ever been involved with her romantically or otherwise? Do you recall those questions and answers?"

"That's correct."

"And what did you respond, sir?"

"I responded, 'No.'"

"And do you recall me saying—asking the question, 'No?'; and you saying, 'No.'; and I reminded you at that time that you were under oath? Do you remember that?"

"Yes, I remember that."

"Then I believe we had a lunch break, did we not?"

"That's correct."

"During the intervening lunch break, did you not have occasion to discuss with your attorney, Mr. Michael Patton who I believe is in the courtroom with you today, and with Mr. Symmonds the fact that it was absolutely necessary for you to tell the truth?"

"That's correct."

"And then you came back and on redirect examination you were asked, 'For clarification I would ask have you ever had sexual relations with Julie

Palmer?'; and you said, 'Yes, I did.'"

"That's correct."

"And then again on re-cross examination I asked, 'Are you then saying that your original answer is incorrect?'; to which you responded, "yes.' Do you recall that?"

"Yes."

"Mr. Carter, how often have you had sexual relations with Julie Palmer?"

"I really never kept track."

"It was more than once then; is that correct?"

"That's correct."

"Would you agree with her testimony that this is a sexual affair which has been going on for a period in excess of two years?"

"That's correct."

"I guess then my question is that—what is it we are to believe today, what you testified to in May or what you're testifying to here today or what you've testified to or made statements about in the past?"

"What I'm testifying here today is to the best of my knowledge correct."

"Surely, sir, when you testified on May 31st, 1984, you did not forget if you had had sexual relations with Lorna, did you?"

Symmonds objected to this question stating that Shaw had not laid a foundation for the question and was only about trying to prove inconsistencies in Darrel's answers. Further, Symmonds claimed there had been no inconsistency in Darrel's May 31 testimony, because he clarified it after lunch. Rulon sustained the objection.

"What does the term 'involved' mean to you, Mr. Carter?" Shaw continued.

"I really don't have a definition for that. 'Involved' could mean a lot of things I guess."

"Was this relationship then, the sexual relations with Lorna, the sexual relations too numerous to mention with Jennifer, they did not constitute any type of an involvement?"

"Not to me they did not."

"But did they constitute in your opinion any kind of romantic attachment?"

"No, they did not."

"Mr. Carter, when you indicated at the time of the preliminary that your answer to the first question involving Julie Palmer—asked you if that question was incorrect and you said yes, it was. Is that right?"

"That's right."

"Are you adverse to lying to a jury under oath?"

"No, I am not."

"Thank you. In fact, you have in the past bragged about being a liar, have you not?"

"I don't recall that."

"In fact, you have in the past said, 'Take me to court and see what kind of liar I am,' haven't you?"

"I don't believe I said that."

"Do you know Mr. and Mrs. McCullough?"

"Yes, I do."

"Mr. Carter, I'm a little bit more confused now about the house situation, the second meeting that you had with Tom Bird wherein you said you met him at the house. And is it your testimony today that Mr. Bird came back to the house a second time?"

"I'm not going to say definitely that he did come back a second time, but I know that he did come one time and possibly the second time. I just—I'm unclear on that. That's been quite a while ago."

"It certainly has. May, 1983, has been even longer ago, has it not?"

"That's correct."

"And your memory about May, 1983, seems to be crystal clear insofar as what went on at that particular meeting at the church. Is that right?"

"I would say that my memory is not crystal clear but I do remember some of the important facts."

"Some of the important facts. Who made up those important facts?"

"The two people that I met with at the church apparently made those up."

"When did they become important facts to you?"

"After the death of Martin Anderson."

"Do you recall, sir, that you were asked at the preliminary hearing how many conversations you had had with Mr. Bird and you indicated that there were only three? Do you recall that?"

"I can't remember how many I said that I had had with him."

"You indicated that you had talked to him at the church on one occasion which is the first time you had ever even seen the defendant, period. You testified that you had talked to him at the house on one occasion, and you testified you had talked to him on the phone on one occasion and then you had the tape recorded conversation. Do you recall that testimony?"

"To the best of my knowledge, yes, I recall that testimony."

"In fact, sir, you were asked that because of your reactions from this particular meeting, because of your reactions at the house if you were so scared of Mr. Bird, wasn't it true that his face was indelibly printed upon your mind to which you responded, 'Yes.' Do you recall that?"

"Yes, I do."

"Would you agree, sir, that if you had seen Mr. Bird then if you were so scared at any time from and after the date of the meeting at the church, you would have remembered that occasion?"

"I think that would be a situation if I saw Mr. Bird just a one-on-one situation when there wasn't anyone else around. I think if there were other people around it really wouldn't bother me."

"In fact I asked you I think at the time of the preliminary hearing if you remembered him being at the fireworks stand in 1983 to which you responded, 'No.' Do you recall those questions and answers?"

"Yes, I remember you asking me that and, no, I don't remember him being at the fireworks stand. There are a lot of customers there."

"And now you say that he has come to the house on several different occasions or at least two occasions. Is that right?"

"I said that he come to the house definitely on one occasion and possibly two."

"Which is it?"

"It's definitely one occasion and possibly two."

"I see. Does that leave us to believe then that your testimony at the time of the preliminary hearing was incorrect?"

"I later recalled that maybe he did come to the house a second time."

"That's where my problem is. When do you recall this, Mr. Carter?"

"After I go home and think about this for a little while. I try to put the pieces together."

"So it is that—on December 10th, 1983, the first time you talked with the KBI agents, you told them about what went on at the church. Is that correct?"

"To the best of my knowledge at that time."

"And at that time you gave them the version about the fact that you had been contacted, asked to go to the church. You went to the church; you were told after being introduced to Tom Bird, 'This is the man who is going to help us get rid of Marty'; and then they outlined the plan about the situation with respect to going down the road, running the car off the road and your assistance at that time in putting Marty Anderson in the car. Is that correct?"

"I don't know if that's correct or not. I didn't write those statements down. The KBI wrote those down. That could be a mistake on their part."

"I see. Was Mr. Vern Humphreys the KBI agent that was there?"

"Yes, he was."

"Was he taking notes as you sat there and as you talked to him?"

"I believe he was."

"All right. Then on December 10th, 1983, you also gave them the version about the plan wherein someone was going to go to the house in

Topeka, rob the house and kill Martin Anderson and make it look like a robbery. Is that correct?"

"Yes, that's correct."

"And this was the sum and substance of your statement on December 10th, 1983, was it not?"

"That was the best that I could recall when I gave that statement at that time."

"December 10th was within, what, six to seven months of when this particular incident had allegedly occurred? Is that correct?"

"That's correct."

"Do you recall giving a statement to Mr. Winsor or to Mr. Opat relative to the particular incident back in June of 1983 or May of 1983?" [On April 20, 1984]

"I remember talking to Mr. Opat."

"At that time, sir, isn't it true that for the very first time some almost ten months later you brought up the fact that the defendant at the time said, 'I am a man of God. I'm going to kill Martin Anderson?'"

"Yes, I made that statement."

"And that was the first time you raised that, isn't it?"

"Yes, it is."

"You also for the very first time in April, some 11 months later, brought up the fact that they said he was a preacher and nobody would ever suspect him of having killed Martin Anderson. Is that not correct?"

"That's correct."

"You did also in April of 1984 bring up the fact that they asked you to be a pallbearer at Martin Anderson's funeral for which the defendant was going to preside. Is that not correct?"

"That is correct."

"Those are the first times you ever raised any of those particular statements to the KBI or anybody else apparently."

"That's apparently the first time they ever wrote those down." (He blamed his own inconsistencies on bad police reports, not a creative memory.)

"In May at the time of the preliminary hearing for the very first time you brought up the fact of insurance as the motive for this particular solicitation."

"I really don't recall bringing that up."

"Do you recall these questions and answers: 'And then but for the money that was the only motive apparently that was ever told to you. The insurance money was the only motive ever told to you why they wanted to get rid of Marty?' 'That's true.' Do you recall that?"

"I don't recall that but if it's there, I must have said that."

"Then for the first time in May of 1984 you saw fit—you were asked about the question of fireworks or the sale of fireworks, and at that time for the first time you brought up, Mr. Carter, that at the end of the meeting Mr. Bird had said something about, 'If anybody asks you what we talked about, we talked about fireworks.' Is that correct?"

"That's correct."

"This was first brought up then in May, some 12 months, one year, later."

"That's correct."

"Are you asking the jury to infer then, sir, that your memory improves as time goes on?"

"Yes, I think as I remember back to the first meeting in May I do remember more and more each time I think about it."

"I see. With respect to these various statements at various times, you've identified various times, you've been involved in court, Mr. Carter, I believe the first such occasion for your conference with the KBI was December the 10th, 1983. That conference took place at Mr. Michael Patton's office here in Emporia. Is that correct?"

"I'm not sure of the date but I had a meeting with the KBI at Mike Patton's office."

"Mike Patton was acting as, in part, your attorney at that time, wasn't he?"

"That's correct."

"When this tape recorded conversation occurred, Mr. Patton was involved in all of the arrangements going to that; that is, the telephone call was made from his office; the conversation, he was there to observe when it went on at the taping out at Emporia Bowl. Is that not correct?"

"That is correct."

Shaw quizzed Darrel on Mike Patton's involvement in helping him prepare to testify, and to put together his various stories. Patton attended every meeting and trial where Darrel's sworn statements were given or when he talked to police officers.

"What are you afraid of?"

"I'm not afraid of anything, Mr. Shaw."

"Mr. Carter, make sure we're clear on this. I believe your brother is, as we've already established, Danny Carter. Is that right?"

"That's correct."

"Danny Carter was arrested, if I'm not mistaken, on November the 17th, 1983, for conspiracy to commit murder. Is that correct?"

"That's correct."

"You went with Danny Carter the first time he went to Junction City. Is that not correct?"

"No, that's not correct."

"Did you go with him when he went to Junction City and had his first appearance?"

"Yes, I did."

"At that time when you were there, sir, did you not receive some statements from KBI showing who all they had interviewed?"

"Yes, I received those reports."

"And I believe there were some 60 or 70 reports which were delivered to you, Mr. Patton and Danny, your younger brother. Is that right?"

"I didn't—I didn't count them. I don't know how many reports there were."

"Would you agree there were quite a few?"

"There were quite a few, yes."

"Danny Carter lives or works for you now, does he not?"

"Yes, he does."

"At the time of his arrest he was employed at Wolf Creek, was he not?"

"That's correct."

"He was either suspended or fired from that job at the time of his arrest?"

"He was suspended from the job."

"Since that time you have continued to give him a job?"

"That's correct."

"Danny Carter in fact lives in an apartment house that is owned by you, does he not?"

"That's correct."

"You were quite concerned about your brother Danny Carter, were you not?"

"Yes, I was."

"And indeed it was after you had gone through these reports and around this point of time that you and your attorney decided you would work with the KBI for Danny's benefit. Is that not correct?"

"I'm not sure that was the time that we decided that. We decided we would work with the KBI from the start."

"Indeed I think eventually it was your cooperation with the KBI which had a substantial influence in getting the ultimate punishment which was meted out to Danny Carter. Is that not correct?"

"The KBI's never mentioned that to me."

"Do you recall, sir, and I think we talked about this at the time of the preliminary hearing, the statement by your attorney at the time of Daniel Carter's sentencing wherein the reference was made to his brother has done a substantial amount to help the KBI in Emporia? Do you recall those statements being made?"

"Yes, I do."

"So would you agree, sir, that it was your cooperation with the KBI that got Danny Carter his ultimate sentence?"

"I'm sure that it had something to do with his sentence."

"Now, if I'm to understand correctly, you were first approached sometime in May or June of 1983 relative to soliciting the murder of Martin Anderson. Is that right?"

"It was the month of May, 1983."

"And during the intervening period you did nothing to contact law enforcement officers or anyone else relative to this particular contact."

"That's correct."

"Yet if I recall, you said on direct that you were somewhat concerned about these people talking about killing a 'friend' of mine."

"That's correct."

"But not concerned enough to go to any authorities. Is that right?"

"That's right." (Did he go to Marty? Apparently not, but Shaw did not ask the question.)

"Yet you would have us all believe that you are a law abiding citizen. Is that correct?"

"That's correct."

"And indeed, sir, it wasn't until some six or seven months later that you came forward with this particular information, was it?"

"That's correct."

"And it was from this particular information that these charges eventually developed. Is that not correct?"

"I guess that's right."

"In that regard, sir, if I understand correctly it is your testimony that two people, one who was totally unknown to you, approached you to kill somebody. Is that correct?"

"That's correct."

"And they came to you completely out of the blue. Is that correct?"

"That's correct."

"At the time you made this first report you were aware of various rumors that had been reported or contained within the reports relating to Lorna and Tom, were you not?"

"Yes, I knew the rumors."

"And I believe you were also familiar or at least you've previously testified about the manner and method of—in which Sandy Bird, who was Tom's wife, was killed. Is that not correct?"

"I think that is correct."

"And indeed that particular accident was substantially similar to the first, quote-unquote, reported plan which you gave to the KBI. Is that right?"

"That is correct."

Shaw referred to a specific question at the preliminary hearing relating to the possibility that he made up his story about Tom. He had asked, "So after having reviewed that, it would not be inconceivable or even difficult to concoct a version that would be somewhat credible because of the accident involving Mrs. Bird, would it?"

"No, it would not be."

"And your answer at that time was, 'That's true' as well. Is that correct?"

"That's correct."

"Mr. Carter, I believe your primary occupation is construction work. Is that right?"

"That is correct."

"Going back to May and June of 1983, at that particular time did you have—how many projects did you have going on?"

"I don't have any idea. Several I'm sure."

"All right. At that particular time, sir, you were working at the house at 2521 West View. Is that correct?"

"That is correct."

"And at that particular time, sir, you were working for Mr. McCullough. Is that correct?"

"That's correct."

"And were you at that time behind in your work?"

"Not that I recall." (McCullough certainly didn't agree.)

"At that particular—now, is it your testimony that on a given day—do you recall what day of the week it was when Lorna Anderson came to the house and contact you the first time?"

"Not the exact day, no."

"Was it a work day?"

"Yes, it was."

"What time of the day was it?"

"It was in the morning hours. I'm not certain on just what morning hour it was."

"It could have been any one of the days then from Monday through Friday. Is that correct?"

"That's correct."

"Would you agree, sir, that at this house at 2521 West View you had a lot of people coming and going?"

"Yes, there were."

"Then at that particular time did Lorna give you any particular reason why she wanted you to come to the church?"

"No, she did not. She just stopped by the house and wanted me to come up by the church. She wanted to talk to me."

"So then with your busy schedule, you just dropped what you were doing, your several projects which you had going on at that time, and went to this church for a reason you knew nothing about. Is that right?"

"Well, I'm not going to say that I just dropped everything and went running right down there. I had several people working for me and I did go over to work that day that I went to the church and got everyone lined out on the projects and then went up there to see—I thought maybe she might want a project. I didn't know what she might want me to do."

"Now, so in point of fact you knew of no reason why you were being called to the church."

"That is correct."

"All right. Now, do you recall, sir, when you arrived which was approximately 9:00, is that right, in the morning?"

"Around 9 to 9:30 I believe."

"Do you recall, sir, was there any activity, any other people contained in that long hall?"

"No, I did not see anyone in the long hall."

"So you went into this office. Would you describe, sir, what that office looked like."

"No, I really can't. I just remember going into the office, and there was a desk and two or three chairs, and that's the best I can describe the office."

"I believe at the time of the preliminary you also indicated that there might well have been a big window on one of the walls. Is that correct?"

"It seems to me like maybe there was a window."

"Or an open space or something?"

"Or an open space on one of the walls, but I'm not sure on that."

"If there had been an open space, was it—I mean it had to have been opened if you noticed either a window or an open space. Is that a fair statement?"

"I believe if it was there, it was a solid glass window." (It is an open window with no glass, and it opens onto a reception area.)

"When you walked in, sir, was the door open?"

"To the office?"

"Yes."

"Yes, I believe it was."

"You don't recall anybody specifically closing that particular office door then. Is that right?"

"No, I do not."

"Were you seated?"

"I believe I was seated across the desk from Lorna."

"Then do you recall at all what conversation, if any, you had with Lorna at this particular time?"

"I don't recall just the conversation right at the few moments that I was in there."

"When you say a few moments, are you talking about minutes or are you talking about seconds or what?"

"I'm talking about the first three or four minutes."

"Did you have any conversation with her at all at that time?"

"Yes, I'm sure that I did."

"Were you aware at that particular time about any wife abuse or any abuse she had taken?"

"Not that I can recall."

"How did—is it possible you were?"

"That first that I recall knowing that Martin Anderson possibly beat Lorna Anderson was at the church that day."

"You had never heard that before?"

"Not that I recall." (In closed court, Darrel had stated that Lorna asked him to help murder Marty in 1982. She claimed Marty beat her. Yet, he feigned ignorance, knowing that Rulon refused to allow this fact to be introduced at trial.)

"After this two or three minutes is it my understanding that Mr. Bird then walked in?"

"Yes, that's correct."

"And how were you introduced to Pastor Bird?"

"Lorna introduced me to Pastor Bird."

"What did she say, the best of your recollection?"

"The best of my recollection she introduced him as Tom Bird."

"And was it at that point then that this conversation commenced about 'Tom is the one who's gong to help us kill Marty Anderson'?"

"That's correct."

"That was the next thing out of her mouth at that point?"

"I'm not sure that was exactly the next thing out of her mouth but it was the very first of the conversation that I can recall."

"And indeed, sir, at that point you made some comment about, 'Lorna, I'm not interested in this.' You refused it at that point. Is that correct?"

"That's correct."

"Then with that in mind, they proceeded to give you some sort of a tale, if I recall it correctly, whereby they were going to go put—drug or get Martin Anderson drunk, put him in a vehicle, take him out and run him off a bridge.

Is that correct?"

"That is correct."

"And again you said, 'I'm not interested in that.' Is that right?"

"That's correct."

"And in fact, sir, if I'm not mistaken I think on at least three different occasions you refused to be a participant in any of this particular matter at all. Is that right?"

"That's right."

"And yet with those three different refusals it is your testimony they proceeded to tell you about a plan to kill Martin Anderson in Topeka without any of your participation?"

"That's correct."

"And you were known to be a law abiding citizen?"

"That's correct."

"And it was at this point then, sir, am I to understand that you said, 'Hey, I'll let you know. I'll get back with you,' and then you departed?"

"That is right."

"And there was no other conversation with Tom Bird?"

"Not that I can recall other than right after—right when I was leaving he told me—Tom Bird told me, 'If anyone wants to know why you were here or saw us here, just tell them it was because my youth group was interested in selling fireworks."

"Was there ever any conversation to the best of your recollection about your—his youth group working with you or selling firecrackers and asking your advice?"

"No, there was not."

"Was there ever any conversation at that time about your building and being possibly behind on the house you were working on?"

"I don't recall that conversation."

"Well, you don't recall it. I would like for you, if you can at all, to be more specific. Was there or wasn't there?"

He said no, not that he could recall.

What about soccer?

Shaw asked whether there was talk of soccer during the church meeting. He said no. Shaw pursued information about when and if Darrel took his kids to an invitational soccer meet and he did. "It was on July 3rd and 4th."

Shaw went back to Darrel's December 10, 1983, interview by Humphrey. He told the agent that day that he had related his story to two other individuals, Joe Lapping, a neighbor, and Darrell Warren, an employee.

Shaw read from Humphrey's statement. "He stated he talked to Joe Lapping and Darrell Warren of Lyndon. He talked to them soon after his conversation at the church with Bird and Lorna Anderson."

Darrel said this was an accurate report. Shaw reminded Darrel that in the preliminary hearing, he narrowed the date down to May 18, 19 or 20 as when he talked with these men. He insisted Tom came out to see him on a workday and that no one else was around—no witnesses. Darrel agreed that he talked with Warren within 2-3 days of Tom's visit to the house.

Shaw asked about the second time that Tom allegedly came to see him at the house, as Darrel had reported it on December 10. Darrel could not recall anything specific about that meeting or even whether it occurred.

Shaw returned to the taped conversation about setting up a meeting between the two men. Darrel had insisted in several interviews that Tom initiated the meeting, decided on its location and set the time. Shaw reminded him that when they listened to the tape the prior day, they heard him say, "I wanted to get together with you some time and see what you knew about this deal my brother's in."

Shaw asked if the whole point of the meeting was presented to Tom as a chance for Darrel to learn more about Danny's trouble. "I think, yeah, that would be correct."

Shaw established that Darrel suggested a time—"late in the day"—and the place—"somewhere like maybe a parking lot or something."

"Between 10:10 a.m. and 5:00 p.m. you had an opportunity to discuss this matter further with the KBI agents, your attorney and whatever. Is that not correct?"

"That is correct."

"And they gave you some guidelines as to what you were to be looking for. Is that not correct?"

"They gave me a few, yes."

"And of course, your whole purpose in going into this meeting was to try to get any type of incriminating evidence from the defendant that you possibly could. Is that not correct?"

"That is correct."

Shaw turned to the tape itself. "I think at the time of the preliminary we even agreed that at that particular point in time in that 45-minute tape there were no less than ten different statement by Mr. Bird about 'the rumors that are going around are about to get me under; there are rumors going on all over; I've heard that some of these rumors were coming from you.' Is that correct?"

"Yes, he did state that."

Shaw stated that twice on the tape Tom talked about fireworks and that

Darrel never commented nor disputed those remarks. "I'm not—I'm sure he asked me about the fireworks. I don't know how many times," Darrel answered.

"In point of fact, Mr. Carter, despite your purpose, admitted purpose to be there to get incriminating statements, despite your admitted purpose to support your story which you had developed or concocted or whatever about what happened at the church, in the whole 45-minute tape you never indeed asked him one direct question if he did do the plan or follow up on the plan, did you?"

"No, I did not."

"In the whole 45-minute tape you never once made reference to the fact that Mr. Bird had solicited you, did you?"

"No, I did not."

"In the whole 45-minute tape you never made any reference to the fact that Mr. Bird might have had something to do with Marty's death, did you?"

"No, I did not."

"In the whole 45-minute tape you never made reference once to the fact that Pastor Bird and Lorna were supposedly in love, did you?"

"No, I did not."

"You never once mentioned the plan about the bridge."

"No, I did not."

"You never once mentioned the plan or the statement that Lorna was going to offer you any kind of money or insurance proceeds to engage in this particular plan."

"No, I did not."

"You never once mentioned the meeting at the house."

"No, I did not."

"In fact, sir, if I recall during the course of this you seem to be somewhat surprised about the insurance issue, and I believe if I recall you told Mr. Bird that having read the reports you had ascertained that she did have a lot of insurance, that she had just recently taken this insurance out. Is that right?"

"That's correct. I knew that."

Shaw asked if helping Danny gave Darrel the motive to do this taping. "I had a motive to get him off, yes."

Shaw returned to the various KBI reports Darrel had read before he met with Tom. "Isn't it true in one of those the officers said there were a lot of rumors to which Pastor Bird had replied, 'Yeah, I know there are and I don't know what to do about it'?"

"I don't recall just that statement, no."

"But at any rate, you were aware of some complaints or some talk relative to Tom and Lorna. Is that correct?"

"Yes."

"Therefore, you had an opportunity to create this story, did you not?"

"I really didn't create this story. This story actually happened."

"Answer my question. Did you have the opportunity?"

"I had the opportunity to concoct this story, yes."

"And on each occasion your story has expanded and become more and more embellished, has it not?"

"The story has expanded as I remember details."

"And become different?"

"Yes, they have."

"And I believe you've already indicated that it was not difficult—not hard for you to concoct this credible story."

"That's right. Anyone that had the reports I think could have done that."

"And you have stated already under oath that you are not adverse to lying under oath."

"On that statement, I misunderstood that statement and I meant that I would not lie to this jury."

"Would you lie under oath?"

"No, I will not."

Symmonds again

Symmonds stepped back up and asked whether Darrel had ever been convicted of a crime. He had not. Did Darrel have any concerns about the plots to murder Marty? "Well, after I had told Tom Bird that I didn't want anything to do with it, I just kind of dropped this matter and I really never thought any more about it."

After Sandy's death, he became concerned. Symmonds tried to pursue a line of questioning that would have suggested Tom murdered Sandy and therefore, Darrel became afraid for his life. Shaw objected and a bench meeting was held. Rulon told Symmonds to steer clear of any discussion that would suggest Tom might be involved in any other crime.

Symmonds asked whether Darrel had testified truthfully as to all of the facts of his meeting with Tom and Lorna. "Yes, I have."

"Where did you get the bulletproof vest that you put on in December of 1983?"

"My brother—it belonged to my brother I guess."

"Why did you go get the bulletproof vest?"

"Wearing the bulletproof vest was my idea. I felt like two people had already been killed and I didn't want to be the third person."

Darrel said he answered truthfully when he spoke with investigators, and he acknowledged that Tom might have stopped by one of the fireworks stands in June or July.

"Are you on good relations with Grover McCullough at the current time?"

"No, I am not."

"Have you had disagreements with him in the past?"

"Yes, I have."

Shaw began re-cross examination.

He reminded Darrel that during preliminary hearings, he said he became fearful during the meeting at the church, so much so that he would not give Tom and Lorna an answer. He said he feared Tom when he came to the house, and again, refused to give an answer and so called Tom on the phone with his "No."

"And yet today you're telling us, 'Well, I wasn't really that fearful of it until we'll say July 17th when his wife passed away.' Isn't that right?"

"That is correct."

Shaw had caught Darrel in a lie.

"On direct examination you indicated that Marty Anderson was 'a friend,' did you not?"

"That's correct."

"And you did nothing to tell anybody including Marty Anderson or anybody else that you had been solicited, quote-unquote, to commit his murder, did you?"

"That's correct."

He reminded the jury, via questions directed at Darrel, that in fact, he had lied under oath at the preliminary hearing when asked about sexual relations with Lorna. Darrel insisted that he had never been asked whether he had sexual relations with her, only whether he had been involved with her. To him, that question did not touch on sex.

Symmonds returned. "With respect to indelibly. If you would have seen the defendant in, pick a month, August of 1983, would you have remembered his face from your meeting?"

"Yes, I would have."

"When you see his face today here in the courtroom, can you recall that it was the same person that you saw in May of 1983 at the Faith Lutheran Church?"

"Yes, it was."

Both sides rested and the court took a break.

(Late in 1985, Joan Baker interviewed Lorna for a *Kansas Magazine* article. Baker asked Lorna, "Did he [Darrel] lie or was this just an exaggeration?"

Lorna answered adamantly, "It's not exaggerations. It's not playing games. He lied intentionally," Lorna insisted, "The bridge was never discussed but he had to say that to add to [the] creditability of the story."

Baker wanted this clarified. "The bridge is something you're convinced he just made up?"

"He did that. We read about that in the paper. He did it to make his story work.")

Workman didn't do any work here

David Workman worked for Marty Anderson at Newman Medical Center. Investigators talked with him several times about Marty and Lorna and he gave them quite a bit of information, though it was spread over several months.

Symmonds listed him as a prosecution witness but never called him to testify. Had Shaw known Workman's testimony, he would certainly have put him on the witness stand, but Workman never made it to trial until 1990.

Had Workman testified, the jury would have learned that there was a lot of evidence that Marty beat Lorna and had for many years. They would have known that Danny and Darrel knew about these beatings for months before Tom ever met Lorna. They would have heard Workman describe the gun he spotted in Lorna's purse, even though it had not yet been determined to have been the murder weapon (it was found more than a year after this trial). The jury would have heard Workman describe Lorna's comments about how Danny and Darrel were going to rough Marty up, maybe even kill him if he didn't quit hurting her.

Workman's powerful testimony would have shot a cannonball through Darrel's testimony. But no one heard it.

Symmonds builds his case

Symmonds moved ahead to try and corroborate it. He called Darrell Warren to the stand.

Warren said he had worked for Darrel for 8-10 years as a sheet rocker and trucker. He remembered working on two houses for Darrel in 1983, one of them being the house near the water works. He recognized the check by which Darrel paid him near the end of May, 1983, stating he got paid the day he finished the job.

"Do you recall any statements in particular that Darrel Carter made to you during this period of time that you were working on that house west of the water works?"

"Yes. He said someone wanted him to kill somebody."

"Did you consider this statement which he made to you to be a little bit out of the ordinary?"

"Yes, I did."

Symmonds turned him over to Shaw.

"I believe you have indicated at least to me earlier that when you were out at this house out west of the water works there were always a lot of people coming and going. Is that right?"

"Yeah, there are people coming and going in a new home."

"I believe you gave a statement to Mr. Humphrey in January of 1984. Is that correct?"

"Yes."

"And at that time you said you didn't know whether to believe Carter or not, didn't you?"

"Yes, sir."

"And I believe you've previously indicated that as far as you know it sounded like he was exaggerating, right?"

"Yes."

On redirect, Symmonds wanted to clarify the statement about exaggeration. Warren said, "I mean that's a comment that you just don't hear every day. That's something that you just don't hear, you know."

Symmonds called Joe Lapping to the stand.

Lapping lived two houses north of Darrel. Lapping worked on his Corvette one night he recalled as sometime in the summer—perhaps the end of June or first of July—when Darrel came over. In the midst of that conversation, Darrel told him that someone wanted to hire him to kill someone. Lapping thought it was crazy and said, "Well, you're surely not going to get involved in that mess, are you?"

"And what did he say if anything?"

"And he said, no, he sure wasn't; and that was about the end of the conversation about that topic."

Shaw's cross-examination attempted to establish the date firmly in the mind of the jurors. Lapping remembered clearly that it was summertime, and he felt late June.

(No one bothered to ask Lapping whether Darrel referred to a man or woman trying to solicit him. Neither Warren nor Lapping mentioned anything about a minister or pastor during their testimony, though Warren suggested this during one of the KBI interviews. Once faced with the pressure of perjury, his story changed.)

Attorney Mike Patton took the stand.

Patton had known Darrel for many years and served on the soccer board with him. He represented him and eventually Danny Carter also retained him. "If you would, would you relate to the jury the circumstances which surrounded that," Symmonds asked.

"I received a phone call the early morning hours of November the 18th and I went to the Lyon County jail. There I met Darrel Carter, Ron Carter who's Darrel's brother, and Danny Carter was in jail. And I went back and talked to Danny Carter for a—the time span was about two hours."

"After you visited with Danny Carter, did you visit with anyone else?"

"I talked with Darrel and Ron Carter both."

After Ron left them, Patton and Darrel talked alone. "Darrel walked up to me, and I had already talked to Danny so I knew some of the things that were going on. Darrel walked up to me and said, 'There's a lot more involved here. This concerns the death of Sandy Bird; and the Reverend Bird is involved in this.' And he started going through these things, and I started shaking my head and I said, 'It's like 4:00 in the morning.' And I said, 'Why don't you come in and see me later on today.'"

They met later that day for about 1-1/2 hours. "Do you recall whether or not Darrel Carter at that time mentioned a meeting with the defendant and Lorna Anderson in May of 1983."

"Yes, he did."

"If you would, would you relate to the jury what if anything he said concerning that meeting that you recall."

"He told me that they had—he had had a meeting at the church; that Lorna Anderson was there, that Reverend Bird was there; that they had asked him to participate in the murder of Martin Anderson."

"Did he at that time outline any plans to you pertaining to the killing of Martin Anderson?"

"He told me that there was a plan about drugging him and going over a bridge and drowning in water or the water underneath the bridge. It was outside of town and that he thought—he thought that they were serious but then he didn't—wondered if they were or they weren't later on because nothing happened. And then when Sandra Bird died in that location as outlined to him, that's when he became very nervous and upset about this and very concerned and very worried. And he also talked about going to Topeka. There was a relative in Topeka; that they were going to push the furniture around, rearrange the house and then kill Martin Anderson when he walked in the door."

(While Patton testified, Shaw did a slow burn. Shaw had quizzed Patton on the phone about the crime. Never before had Patton mentioned this alleged November 18 statement of Darrel's. Even if this did happen as Patton now testified, it did not negate the fact that Danny knew eventually he would be arrested after Marty's murder. Thirteen days elapsed between the murder and his arrest, giving Danny and Darrel plenty of time to concoct a story.)

Patton he didn't receive any police reports until December 7. "I know that Darrel Carter read those reports in my vehicle. He rode up with me and Dan Carter was in the car, and we read the reports and went over the reports on December the 7th."

Symmonds asked if there were any other statements Darrel made that first day. "I do remember the one statement about that Bird had said that he was a man of God and that he was going to help kill Martin Anderson. That statement was made at the beginning....I really wasn't writing down all the information that Darrel Carter was telling me about how he was involved in all this." (This made no sense to Shaw. Patton served as Darrel's attorney in a number of matters. Protocol required him to record the subject of meetings with his client. By not doing so, Patton could be accused of fabricating a story after the fact.)

Patton said that he received a phone call from Darrel on December 1, about a contact made with him from Tom. Julie Palmer said Tom wanted a meeting. Patton called Agent Humphrey, who had been his friend for many years and the two met at Patton's house that evening.

"I was interested in what could we get for Dan Carter in this. I was representing Dan Carter, and I was trying to see what kind of a deal we could get for Dan Carter. And I explained to Mr. Humphrey that if we were able to help clear up the murder of Martin Anderson and what happened to Sandra Bird through our efforts, would that be of value to the KBI and the law enforcement officers; and he obviously said, 'Yes.' He also told me that he wasn't in a position to deal on behalf of any prosecutor but he certainly would make a recommendation. And I related to him that Darrel had been contacted by the Reverend Bird, and I related to him the contact at the church and that information."

Another meeting was held with Darrel and Humphrey on December 10, but the case belonged to Don Winsor from Geary County. Patton wanted to be sure that he worked with someone he knew and trusted. They discussed the church meeting details before bringing Winsor in on it.

Patton recalled that Darrel made a call to Tom from his law office on December 12 to set up the taped meeting. Darrel, Humphrey, Sheriff Andrews, Don Winsor and he were all present. Patton recorded the conversation. Darrel put on the body pack, but his shirt made a scratching sound. They sent him home to change shirts—there he put on the bulletproof vest—and they met him behind the Alco building to put the body pack back on.

Patton drove around with Humphrey, waiting for the meeting. Police vehicles were wired with receivers and Humphrey used a tape recorder held next to the speaker to record the meeting. They parked behind J.C. Hines and Sons, about half a block away.

Symmonds asked about the deal Patton cut with Opat. Patton explained it as a "Santobello agreement," named after a Supreme Court case. Patton said it meant that the judge could accept the plea agreement as offered by the defense and place Danny on probation, or reject it, thereby nullifying the agreement. Since the judge had accepted the agreement, Danny did no jail time.

Symmonds asked him to describe the procedures agreed upon for Darrel to do the taping.

Patton said Humphrey wanted Darrel to try and get any information he could about Sandy or Marty, but not to push too hard, "To see how it goes." They could go back and do it again sometime if they needed more.

Symmonds asked if something had happened to preclude another taped meeting. "Yes, I received a call from Darrell Meyer." [Lorna's attorney.] Meyer had learned about the taped meeting somehow. "I first off said, 'What meeting?'; and he said—because I was surprised he knew about. My understanding was, we weren't going to pass out this information."

Symmonds asked about Darrel's demeanor. Did he have any fear, especially the day he left for the taping. "Well, he was afraid like I was to go out there and do that. I mean there was a lot of concern on everybody's part."

Shaw began. He asked about time sheets that reflected work Patton did for Danny Carter. He asked how Patton charged? By 6-minute increments. Most of Shaw's questions were answered with a note of sarcasm, as if Patton wanted to embarrass him.

Shaw asked about just exactly whom Patton represented, Darrel or Danny? He noted that Patton worked many hours on behalf of Danny during that time. "Was Darrel your client?"

"Well, I didn't hope he was going to be."

"Well, is he now?"

"Well, he's a client in a civil case with a Mr. McCullough but I'm not—he's not my client in this case."

Shaw asked about the preliminary hearing. (Patton sat in the courtroom, feet propped up on a bench, for much of the testimony during the preliminary hearing. It struck many as unusual and unwarranted. They believed his purpose for sitting there was to ascertain how Darrel should answer questions, and that it interfered with Tom's right to a fair trial.)

"And you did in fact sit in the courtroom while Mr. Darrel Carter was testifying, did you not?"

"Yes."

Shaw established that Patton was present on numerous occasions when Darrel testified, including in the present case. "And you were present on December 10th, 1983, when Darrel Carter made his first statement to the KBI agent. Is that not correct?"

"That's correct."

"And there on the 12th when we went through all of this Mickey Mouse with the tape; is that not correct?"

"I'm not sure it's Mickey Mouse, but I was there."

"All right. So you have then, can we assume, established a relationship with Darrel Carter whereby you are representing him in the course of these proceedings?"

"Well, I would have to think about that, Mr. Shaw."

"How long do you need?"

Symmonds jumped to his feet at this, and Rulon reminded Shaw and Patton to watch their behavior.

Shaw reminded Patton that acting as Darrel's attorney, he had "certain fidelity, certain duties, certain supportive reactions" for his client. Patton agreed. Shaw asked him about any notes he took of his meetings with Darrel during the time period of November 18 through December 10, 1983. There were none.

Shaw pressed him to be more specific about why his time sheets and notes didn't reflect anything dealing with these statements by Darrel. Patton remained adamant that he had, in fact, had such a conversation that morning in the parking lot.

Shaw changed directions. He said that Danny made very incriminating statements to the police on November 17, and was in serious trouble. "And was it and isn't it true, sir, that you and Darrel and everybody else was doing the level best you could to try and get the best possible deal for Danny Carter?"

Patton agreed.

Shaw moved to Danny's sentencing. Patton had told the judge that Danny "...and his other members of his family have cooperated with the KBI, his brother did certain things with the KBI to try to solve a case, this murder case of Mr. Anderson and another case in Emporia."

Patton insisted that though it was his job to win the best deal for Danny, he cooperated in all the rest to help the police solve a puzzle.

"I see. And that's the reason why we; i.e. you and Darrel Carter, waited from November 18, 1983, when this information was disclosed to you until 12-10-1983 when it was first literally revealed to the KBI or 12-11-1983 when you first talked with Vern Humphrey, depending on which date this came down. That's the reason we waited was because we were concerned about solving this whole problem."

"No, that's not true, Mr. Shaw. I can explain if you'll let me."

Shaw left that explanation to Symmonds on redirect. He then began to show that Patton, without any notes of his conversations with Darrel, could not possibly specifically recall what he had been told.

Shaw went to the May 31, 1984, preliminary hearing. He reminded Patton that he had attended that hearing. "Is it true, sir, as Mr., Carter testified that during the lunch recess you and Mr. Symmonds did see fit to tell him that he was going to have to tell the truth?"

"We've always said that."

"And what were you speaking with reference to at that particular time?"

"The whole case in general. The most specific ones were that—were his relationships with other women."

Shaw went back to the December 10, 1983, meeting with Humphrey.

"And did he make a full and complete disclosure at the time to the best of your knowledge and information?"

"He—at that time a lot of things were talked about. Whether—he didn't talk—a lot of things have come up subsequent to that."

Patton stepped down.

Winsor's turn

KBI Agent Don Winsor took the stand.

Symmonds asked about Winsor's December 20, 1983, interview with Tom when he had asked him whether Lorna ever talked to him about murdering Marty. Tom said no she had not.

Symmonds asked about Winsor's meeting with Darrel on December 12, the first time the two had met and talked at any length. Winsor strapped on the body pack that day and told Darrel how to use the equipment. "We mostly asked him to not be too obvious." He and Sheriff Andrews took a position about a block away, near Gibson's Discount, where they could watch the entry to the bowling alley.

Winsor said he made a tape of the conversation in the bowling alley parking lot and Symmonds showed him the enhanced version of that tape, then entered it into evidence.

Winsor first met Tom on November 5, 1983, at the hospital in Junction City, but first formally interviewed him on November 10. Tom had been relaxed and fully cooperative during this interview, even when he mentioned the rumors about him and Lorna. Tom told Winsor that pastors were subject to these kinds of rumors and he hoped they had been put to rest.

When Winsor interviewed Tom on December 20, he asked about

315

whether Lorna ever said anything about wanting Marty dead. Tom said "No." Winsor said that though the second interview followed the taping, he asked no questions related to that taping nor the alleged criminal solicitation.

Shaw turned to a report Winsor wrote about the taped conversation. "During the conversation Darrel Carter stated that he had observed copies of the investigative reports and that a good investigation had been conducted. Carter was inquiring as to whether Lorna Anderson was going to be burned. The conversation was centered around the investigation and involved the participants already arrested." Shaw asked whether this statement was correct and if it reflected Winsor's thoughts about the taped interview. Winsor said it was only a summary, but acknowledged that it was correct.

On redirect, Symmonds asked whether Winsor's summary "was supposed to be a definitive statement of the conversation between the defendant and Darrel Carter?"

"No. The transcript itself is 19 pages long, and this is just a very—very brief statement made by me."

This ended the third day of the trial. Court recessed until 9:00 a.m. the next morning.

A new day

Chris Kimble came next. He served as the Anderson's life insurance agent and wrote a new policy on Marty's life for $300,000 during June of 1982. Marty named Lorna as beneficiary. The policy lapsed in January, 1983. In April, the insurance company notified the Anderson's of the lapse and Lorna immediately contacted Kimble. Kimble told her that to reinstate the policy, they would need to pay all the back premium. They opted to apply for new insurance coverage instead.

Lorna met with Kimble and he took an application on Marty's life for a new policy. It carried $60,000 in whole life coverage, $150,000 in term and a $60,000 rider in case of accidental death. The total face value, in the case of an accidental death, was $270,000. Lorna took the application home for Marty's signature. Marty brought it to Optimists and signed the papers in Kimble's presence.

Marty carried an additional $35,000 in group insurance from Newman Medical Center and had another $30,000 through the Reserves.

On May 6, Lorna showed up at Kimble's office. He saw Marty sitting in the van outside. Kimble took an application for another $100,000 coverage, but it became a temporary policy to cover the period during which Marty would be at Reserves. Had Marty died prior to June 6, the total pay out would have been $435,000, if it had been an accident. A murder, though, might have negated the accidental death policy.

Symmonds asked Kimble if he knew Tom. Yes, from Optimists.

"Did you ever have occasion to see the defendant and Lorna Anderson together?"

"Yes sir."

"Where?"

"On two occasions in Mrs. Anderson's van."

"And who was driving the van on those occasions when you saw the defendant and Lorna Anderson?"

"Thomas Bird."

"And what if anything did you note about them when you saw them in Lorna Anderson's van?"

"I would say they were a couple of happy people."

"And do you recall approximately when it was that you saw them, Lorna Anderson and the defendant, riding around in the Lorna Anderson's van?"

"I would have to say the spring of '83"...inside the city limits." (Lorna had tried seducing Kimble at least once, according to his statement to police. She did come to his apartment one night and went to bed with his roommate. Knowing her as he did, he assumed that any man, even a preacher, had to be alone with Lorna for only one reason—sex.)

Shaw took over and showed that Kimble's income depended on selling new life insurance policies. He also reviewed that prior to June, 1982, the Anderson's already owned a $300,000 term policy, as well as the Reserve and Group Life polices, for a total of $365,000 coverage. When Kimble took the new application, he added no new coverage, even though computer models showed the Anderson's needed more coverage. Kimble agreed.

Following the lapse of the policy, the Anderson's carried just the $65,000 from Reserves and the hospital. With the new policy, minus the accidental death benefit, they actually purchased less coverage than before, but given the whole life portion of the policy, Kimble had made a greater commission.

Shaw forced Kimble to clarify the $100,000 additional insurance bought on May 6. Marty wrote a $30 check for the premium and Kimble accepted the payment, but never processed it. When Marty safely returned from Reserves, Kimble tore up the check, in effect, giving Marty two week's free coverage.

Shaw turned to Kimble's knowledge of Tom. He knew him vaguely from Optimists and he knew that Marty sponsored Tom's membership. He asked Kimble about spotting Tom and Lorna, and Kimble admitted he was going in the opposite direction of Lorna's van.

Symmonds asked Kimble to clarify what constituted accidental death.

Kimble said some shootings could be accidental, even homicides, but the insurance company made that determination, not him. He said Lorna handled the entire transaction for the additional $100,000 and that he understood Marty headed to camp right after signing the forms. He never got out of the van. Lorna helped Kimble complete the application and took it to the van, Marty signed it, and she brought it back in with the $30 check.

Kimble stepped down.

Next was Michael Robinson, a Sergeant in the Army Reserve. He testified that Marty attended reserve camp from May 7 through May 20, 1983. Upon his return, Marty attended weekend drills at Topeka, on May 21 and 22. Marty also attended drills in Topeka in June, July and August. Symmonds established this because one of the methods Darrel said had been discussed was to shoot Marty during a reserve weekend in Topeka.

Robinson stepped down.

A jealous young lady took the stand

Angie Duensing came next.

She described how with Tom's help, she started Lord's Lambs preschool and described her duties. She said Lorna worked from 9-Noon, but during March, that had changed dramatically. "I noticed that she started coming earlier, spending time in the afternoons. She would be there in the evenings sometimes if Pastor had a counseling session. I remember occasions where she would be there in the evening. I remember on occasions on Saturdays when I could come in she would be there also working on Saturday's."

She said Tom and Lorna often sat in the fellowship hall, having brought their children to the preschool, and ate breakfast together.

During March, 1983, Angie saw Lorna crying at her desk as a result of depression. As for Tom, "He spent time—I don't know, large amounts of time, comforting her, counseling her, talking to her, being there for her."

Symmonds asked whether Angie observed a difference during March in the way Tom and Lorna interacted compared to January and February. "The difference in the amount of time Lorna spent at the church which meant that it differed in the amount of time that she spent with the defendant." (Angie addressed Tom as the defendant, choosing not to use his name. This hinted at a level of disgust or disappointment with him. Later, witnesses showed how she held responsibility for carrying her gossip to several people at Faith, and at least one outside the church. Did she feed Jane Grismer's anger as well?)

Symmonds asked Angie to describe any specific situations in which she saw Tom and Lorna interacting. "I can think of two specific instances. I don't have dates for them. One time Lorna was sitting at her desk crying. She was holding a Kleenex up to her face. She was crying, and the defendant was standing near her desk. He leaned down on her desk. He put his arm on her back stroking her back, comforting her.

"And another time she was standing at the opening behind her desk...crying, and Pastor took her in his arms."

Angie either saw them in Lorna's office where Tom sat across the desk from her, or in his office, where sometimes they sat in the two chairs facing Tom's desk and sometimes Lorna came around behind him, leaning over to observe what he typed or wrote.

Shaw objected strongly to this line of questioning. He said it was impossible for him to defend against general statements and Angie simply described impressions she gained during a long period of time, not specific instances. Rulon overruled him.

Symmonds asked Angie how often she spotted them close together. She said maybe six times. "Well, like when they were sitting side by side, their knees would often be touching or shoulders touching. It seemed out of the ordinary." She said she estimated seeing them sit this way once a week. (Once a week times 10 or 11 months does not equal six times. Angie seemed very prone to exaggeration.)

Angie said Tom told her about Lorna's unhappy marriage. She became concerned when Lorna started leaning on him because "in my view marital counseling is to improve the marriage, not to have the person unhappy lean on someone else."

"Well, did the defendant counsel Lorna Anderson?"

"That's what I was told by him and by Lorna."

"Did you ever observe the defendant and Lorna Anderson acting in some way which you thought was somewhat out of the ordinary for a minister and a secretary?"

"Yes, I did."

"Describe what you observed."

"I saw a sparkle in their eyes when they talked to each other. I felt electricity in the air. I saw a physical attraction. I saw devotion on the part of Lorna."

"Devotion to what?"

"As in whatever he asked her to do, she did. She praised him a lot, what a wonderful minister he was, what a caring person he was, et cetera...I can give a specific time frame. In May of 1983 at a parent conference I spent with Lorna when Marty was at guard camp. She spent several minutes of that parent conference discussing Pastor Bird."

Symmonds asked her what Lorna told her about Tom, and Shaw

objected. He said such testimony would be hearsay, and given that Lorna was not available for testimony, there would be no way he could discover the truth of any of these statements. Rulon overruled him.

"Did Lorna Anderson ever describe to you her feelings about Reverend Bird or the defendant, however you wish to refer to him?"

"Yes. She said she thought he was a wonderful minister, a caring person, that she appreciated the help he gave her as far as emotional support when she was struggling."

"Did the defendant after May of 1983 ever describe to you his feelings towards Lorna Anderson?"

"Yes. He said, 'I care so much'; and he also—he expressed that he felt sorry for her."

"Did you ever discuss with the defendant your concern over his relationship with Lorna Anderson?"

"Yes, I did."

"And when was that?"

"As near as I can pinpoint it, June 24th, 1983."

"And what if anything was said between the defendant and yourself at the that time?"

"I expressed my concerns over what I saw as dependency and infatuation on the part of Lorna, and I told him that I realized her marriage was bad but that I thought he was coming between her and Marty instead of helping the marriage. And I told him that if he needed a counselor if she needed him, it should be a professional form of counseling where they would meet once a week like a normal counseling situation is."

She saw Tom and Lorna on several occasions together in either of their offices, talking with each other. True, she spent most of her time in the back of the building tending to the children, but occasionally came to the office area. She could not be specific how many times she saw them together. She suggested it was on a regular, on-going basis. (Of course, they did work together five days a week.)

On July 15, 1983. She saw them in Tom's office. "The phone rang. He was sitting at his desk. The phone was over here; Lorna was over here. I was sitting in a chair in front of his desk. And the phone rang, and she reached across Pastor Bird to answer it in what I considered a suggestive manner."

"Can you think of any other specific instances?"

"Not that I would have a date for."

Symmonds asked Angie whether she ever observed Tom counseling or speaking with other women. She had occasionally, but not to the same extent and she did not recall him ever touching the others.

"And what was the difference between what you're trying to describe to the jury and what you saw the defendant do with other women?"

"There was more physical touching; there was more time spent." (Other women were not church secretaries.)

Symmonds asked whether she ever told Tom that Lorna needed to quit her job, but she could not specifically recall that she had done this. She did, however, talk to several others following Sandy's death. "Reverend Larry Kalsow, his wife Becky, Howard and Sharon Meyer. Howard is an elder of the church."

Symmonds showed Angie some sort of document and asked her whether she recognized the handwriting. She said it was Tom's.

Shaw objected. Angie had no professional qualifications as a handwriting expert, he said. But something else irked him even more. "Again this is one of the many new exhibits which we asked about as much as two months ago and were assured there were no more. We're now finding more and more exhibits. I would have to object to this in its entirety and perhaps even ask for some form of an out-of-court hearing on it."

Symmonds agreed to limit his questions to her opinion of whose handwriting she saw and showed her another document. Lorna's? Yes. Shaw once again objected. Rulon overruled.

Symmonds showed her two more documents and asked if she saw Tom's handwriting. Yes. Shaw objected. Rulon overruled.

Symmonds asked whether Angie ever talked to Tom about Marty. Yes, on June 24. She believed Tom was agitated at him. He told her Marty beat Lorna and treated her with disrespect. She had seen Tom and Marty together also, and they were cordial to each other, shaking hands after Sunday services and the like.

Shaw asked her how it was she could see Tom and Lorna, and she said as she walked down the hall she would glance into either of their offices.

Shaw asked her how she came to lead Lord's Lamb preschool. She met Tom at the Lutheran Student Center he founded at ESU, and they began a discussion. She graduated from ESU in 1982, and they decided she should put the preschool together, committing to the task in May or June of 1982.

"Was Pastor Bird excited about this or encouraging towards doing this? Was he anxious to get done?"

"Yes, he wanted a preschool."

"And did he ever tell you why?"

"Because he thought it was a good time to introduce the Word of God to children when they were young."

Shaw asked how much involvement Tom had in getting the preschool up and running. He had given her quite a bit of assistance with filing papers with the Lutheran church district and moving the process along. He helped her with an advertising program and saw that 800 letters were mailed out. Tom attended the large group parent meeting and went with her on a couple of occasions to visit with prospective enrollees. She said it was part of his evangelism program. The program eventually grew to 40 children, starting with 25.

Shaw asked her when during the day she took a break and walked down to get a snack.

Lord's Lambs' schedule paralleled the public school year. In the summer, Angie offered a "Mother's Day Out program," which was a drop-in babysitting service. The program operated on Tuesdays and Thursday s.

"Did you notice or was it unusual for people to come and go through the church? And by that I mean the whole facility. I'm not just talking about the church itself."

"Well, like the treasurer would come by sometimes to pick things up or the financial secretary. The treasurer and financial secretary would come by once or twice a week I guess, and people who needed to talk to Pastor or wanted to put something in the bulletin or put something in the news letter or—"

"Really we had a fair amount of traffic in and out of there. Is that correct?"

"I think so."

"Would you agree that this is relatively an open, public area then right in here?"

"Lorna's office more than Pastor's."

Angie said that the church member's mailboxes were close by the opening to Lorna's office and that many times, members and church officials would come by and check their boxes.

Shaw asked about Lorna's emotional nature. "She's kind of hard to describe," Angie claimed.

"With respect to Tom Bird, would you describe him as an outgoing type of person?"

"Yes, in addition to other things."

"Would you describe him as a caring person."

"He appears that way."

"How about a loving type of person?"

"He appears that way."

Shaw asked whether she had ever seen Tom touch or hug other parishioners, "or touch their arm or things of this nature, hold their hand, whatever?"

"I've seen him touch arms before, never hug like he did with Lorna."

"Has he ever hugged you?"

"Yes, a few times."

"Was there anything about that that made you feel uncomfortable as if it was…"

"Yes."

"—something more than just a supportive-type situation?"

"I felt uncomfortable with a lot of physical contact from a married man, yes."

Shaw asked about the times Angie saw Tom and Lorna hugging. She said one time they stood in the door and she noticed them as she walked by. The other time, they were in an office and she walked by. Shaw asked whether her presence caused them to make any movement or motion indicating she surprised them. She said no, but described their reaction as a "sheepish" look.

"Angie, it's true, is it not, that there was a time when you yourself had feelings for Pastor Bird?"

"Yes, there is—there was."

"And I believe you have even told people that because of your attraction to Tom, this may very well have been one of the reason why you were resentful of Lorna."

"That's taken out of context I believe."

"Did you ever tell Tom or anyone else for that matter that on occasion you had been attracted to the point that you had wished that something would happen to Sandy so that you and Tom could be together?"

"That's out of context also. What I said was I was struggling with my feelings which were really more hero worship than anything else. It was the first young pastor I had ever had and I knew my feelings were wrong and I was having difficulty with them, so the thought crossed my mind that if he was single it wouldn't be quite so bad."

"I see. Did you discuss that when you and he had your meeting on June 24th, 1983?"

"Yes, I did because I thought it would help him—I thought if I went in there and just told him what I thought he would say, 'You're a single woman who knows nothing about this'; but I thought if I could share with him that I went through the same struggle that Lorna was going through that maybe he would take my word."

"Did he ask you about that? Had he ever done anything to encourage this type of activity?"

"In his mind probably no."

"Had he in your mind?"

"The physical contact."

"Had encouraged you?"

"Well, it encouraged me to go from hero worship to infatuation."

"And Lorna had indicated to you at one other time that she felt him to be a wonderful person, a wonderful minister and that he had given her a lot of help. Is that correct?"

"Yes, and she would use other statements, too, like she wold say, 'Marty has no respect for women but Tom has a lot of respect for women,' the comparison."

"You apparently felt that, too, did you not?"

"That he had respect for women? Not really. I wouldn't say that's his strong point."

Shaw asked her about her afternoon schedule. The school adjourned at noon and she often came back to the church in the afternoons. She stated that several times she came down the hall to Lorna's office and or the conference room to get supplies and equipment she needed to do her job, and on occasion, once or twice a week, she would go into Tom's office to talk. She saw others come to the pastor's office as well.

Shaw asked her about evenings. She said she came to the church very infrequently in the evenings, perhaps once a month. She left town between July 15 and August 15, so obviously could not have seen Tom and Lorna during those times. In fact, she could not have spotted them together at the church in the evenings very often since she, herself, wasn't there.

Symmonds asked about June 7 and June 9. "Did the defendant indicate to you what was significant about either June 7th or June 9th?"

"Yes. He said it was a date that he had met with Darrel Carter."

"And did he indicate how he knew that?"

"He said he had found the name in his appointment book."

Symmonds asked how many people might come into the church on a busy day. Perhaps a dozen, but there were times when no one came in— sometimes for hours. (The fact remained, though, that visits were unpredictable. At any moment, someone could have walked into either Tom or Lorna's office and they would have had no advance warning. The floors were carpeted and if someone approached from the east, neither Tom nor Lorna could have seen them coming. This presented a very poor accommodation for moments of intimacy.)

He asked her to go into more detail about June 24th when she talked to him about Lorna.

"He said, 'Well, I know she likes me'; and when I talked to him about coming between her and Marty, he said—he agreed that he probably was coming between she and Marty. And then he also related to me the details of a beating that had taken place....And I said that I thought she needed to lean on him less; and he said, 'I don't think she could make it if she couldn't lean on me,' or words to that effect."

He returned to the question of flirting. What did she mean by flirting?

"Well, for example, when they would talk, well, like—well, I've already talked about his office or it seemed like they couldn't even keep the desk between them. They had to be side by side touching or like if he would be in the office talking to her, he would be leaning up against the wall, you know, like…"

Shaw objected. He said her answer was "…conclusionary. Geez, I object to this line of questioning unless we have some specifics…. We have nothing that we can really contest on this." Rulon overruled him.

"With respect to these afternoon and evenings that you discussed on cross examination, do you recall anything in particular about the afternoon of June 1st of 1983?"

"Yes. That's the pastor's birthday and… I had stopped by the preschool to prepare for Mother's Day Out which was beginning the next day."

"I stopped by to prepare for Mother's Day out and I happened to go in the fellowship hall. And Lorna was there with her children, and I asked her what she was doing, and she said, 'Well, I called Tom and he's going to bring the kids over and we're going to have a little birthday party.' And then Sandy walked in on it, too; so Sandy and I joined them in their birthday party. And during the party Lorna was kind of embarrassed that we had walked in on it, and she said…"

Shaw objected. This time Rulon told Angie she could not state what Lorna might or might not have said. Symmonds rested.

Shaw asked her to confirm that she, Lorna and Tom took Sandy out for lunch on Sandy's birthday. They had. He reaffirmed that she had much the same feelings for Tom that she ascribed to Lorna. She did. He rested.

Symmonds called Jan Mead. Shaw jumped to his feet. "Anything this woman has to say is pure, rank hearsay. I thought we had already gone through this and over this and around it, I thought we had determined that Jan Mead was not going to be used as a witness."

"Was not to be used as a witness?" Symmonds countered.

Rulon said, "I don't think we said that she was not to be used as a witness. I thought that I instructed counsel that this may be a witness that we would have to have—"

Shaw cut the judge off mid-sentence. "Then we'd better have it, Your Honor."

"Isn't there some other witness that you can call at this time other than—"

Symmonds said he could call other witnesses, but Mead had flown in from Cincinnati that morning just to testify. Rulon told Symmonds they previously had agreed she would testify on Friday, and he apologized for getting the day wrong. Rulon ordered him to leave her testimony until he conducted a hearing on it without the jury present.

Lori gets it "wrong"

Symmonds called Lori Anderson, Lorna's oldest child.

Earlier that day, Susan Ewert and Lorna talked about picking Lori up at a camp somewhere near Junction City where she had been all week. Susan offered to make the drive for or with Lorna, but Lorna demanded to go alone. It gave her an hour with her daughter outside the hearing of anyone else.

Symmonds asked her general questions about her age (nine years old), where she lived now and before, where she went to school and church.

"Do you remember what the name of your minister was when you went to the Faith Lutheran Church?"

"Yes."

"And can you tell me what your minister's name was?"

"Tom Bird."

"And did Tom Bird, did he come to your house once in a while?"

"After the ball games he came over to our house to drink beer with my dad." (This must have shocked the Baptists. Did they note that he did this with Marty?)

"And do you remember when you visited with Don Winsor who was with the KBI?"

"Yes."

"And do you remember that he asked you certain questions?"

"Uh-huh."

"And do you remember if he asked you if you ever saw your mom and Tom Bird kissing?"

"Yes."

"Do you remember what you told him?"

"Yes. I said they were hugging."

Symmonds asked whether this happened more than once, but she didn't remember. She said this happened after Bible class at her house. (KBI agents interviewed Lori more than once. Each time her story had varied somewhat.)

"Lori, did you ever see your mother and Pastor Bird kissing?" Shaw asked her.

"No."

Shaw asked her just one question: to name several of her babysitters, and then he rested.

Symmonds had no redirect, but asked that Lori stay in town until he finished questioning his next two witnesses, Stephen Anderson and Don Winsor. Rulon ordered it and Stephen Anderson was called to the stand.

Symmonds asked about the interview Winsor conducted of Lori on November 22, 1983. Had the agent asked about Lorna kissing Tom? Yes he remembered it, "quite clearly."

"Agent Winsor asked Lori if she had ever observed her mother, Lorna, and Pastor Bird kissing. She said, 'Yes, on two occasions.' I remember one was after Bible study and the other one I don't know that it was identified in any other way."

Symmonds asked whether Winsor specified a part of the body on which Tom kissed Lorna. With great drama he answered, "I will never forget it."

"If you would, please relate that to the jury."

"She said they were kissing on the mouth."

Symmonds rested.

Shaw asked who initiated the interview and Anderson said it was Winsor. Shaw wondered who used the word "kissing" first? It was Winsor. Did he also talk about hugging? Anderson did not remember. Shaw rested and there was no redirect.

Symmonds called Agent Winsor.

"Do you recall whether or not you at some point during the course of that interview asked Lori Anderson if she had ever observed an individual by the name of Pastor Bird and her mother kissing?"

"Yes, I did."

"And do you recall what her response was to that question?"

"Yes, I do."

"What was her response?"

"She observed them kissing twice."

"Did she indicate to you the location at which she had observed them kissing?"

"Yes. It was at the Anderson residence, and she said that one time she thought that she herself was in the kitchen area and one time in the bathroom area, and both times her father was gone from the house and one time..."

Winsor said Lori answered that her father was not home either time she saw Tom and Lorna kiss, and that they kissed on the mouth.

Symmonds referred to Winsor's November 10, 1983, interview with Tom. Tom said he had an emotional relationship with Lorna, but not a physical relationship.

Shaw took over.

Winsor said someone in the Geary County Sheriff's office told him Lori was at Anderson's house and that the interview lasted 45 minutes. "It was a long interview for someone that was 8 years old. Would you agree?" Shaw asked.

"No, it wasn't that long I wouldn't think."

"For an 8 year old?"

"It wasn't continual, you know, conversation. A couple times Steven had to get up and leave the room so we stopped talking until he came back. It was not continuous."

"Did you just sit there and not say anything, just stare at each other?"

"No. I visited with her." He said he was just being friendly with a little girl.

Winsor said he went through many details about the night of Marty's death and the questions about kissing came at the end of the interview. Shaw asked him whether he normally wrote out his questions before meeting with a person, and he said no, and he had not done so for this interview. (Earlier he had testified differently, that he often wrote out the questions first.)

Shaw wondered if he could have asked Lori, "Did you ever see your mother and Pastor Bird hugging and kissing?"

Winsor said no, but Shaw pressed him. By that time, Winsor had done 25 to 30 interviews and without notes specifying his questions, there was no way he could be sure exactly what he asked Lori more than nine months earlier. Winsor said he partially agreed with that statement. Shaw finished and Winsor stepped down.

Symmonds called Pastor Larry Kalsow.

Kalsow answered questions about his background and how he knew Tom. "And do you recall whether or not you had occasion to see the defendant during the last week of July of 1983?" Symmonds asked.

"Yes, on July 27th."

"And how is it that you're able to recall the fact that you saw the defendant during that particular week?"

"I remember it because of the situation."

"Was the defendant's wife's memorial service that preceding Monday?"

"Yes."

"And did you have occasion that week to contact the defendant?"

"Yes."

"And why did you contact the defendant?"

"I wanted to discuss some concerns I had with him about his relationship with Lorna."

"And what prompted you to contact the defendant."

"I had a visit from a member of his congregation."

"And what was the name of that person?"

"Angie Duensing."

"And do you recall approximately when that conversation was in relationship to the 27th day of July of 1983?"

"The conversation with Angie or Tom?"

"With Angie."

"It would have been after Sandy's death, the weekend after Sandy's death."

Kalsow waited to talk to Tom because he had gone on vacation. But he spotted Tom and Lorna in her van out on the turnpike on Wednesday, July 27.

Kalsow called Tom the next day and they met that afternoon at Messiah. Kalsow told Tom about Angie's discussion with him and he wanted an explanation. He said he saw the van the day before and asked Tom if he and Lorna were together. Tom said yes, but did not tell him why they were there.

"Did you at that time ask him what his feelings were towards Lorna Anderson?"

"I asked him to describe to me the relationship between him and Lorna."

"What if anything did he say?"

"He described that he was counseling with her, that she had the problems with the marriage and he was working with her." He used the words that he cared for Lorna. "I expressed the concern that I didn't think that he was in a position to counsel with her given his circumstances of having just lost his wife....That the counseling situation, for example, of the two of them being together on the turnpike, were not the kind of counseling situations that I felt would be helpful for a client....I suggested to him that I didn't—that he not counsel with Lorna anymore....I also suggested that it might be better if she was not secretary at the church."

Tom said he would talk with the lay ministers about it—whether Lorna worked or not was their decision, not his.

Kalsow said Lorna came into his office the next morning, and she cried and was very upset.

Kalsow said he talked with Harold Schwinn and Howard Meyer. "I shared with them my concerns that Angie had presented to me, and I shared with them the substance of the visits that I had with Tom and with Lorna and also what I had seen on the turnpike." He told them that Tom should quit counseling Lorna and that she should leave her job.

"That Sunday evening I was called and asked to attend a meeting with Howard Meyer and Don Froelich and Harold Schwinn, and at that point they told me or asked me more questions and told me what their decision was at that point...To retain Lorna as secretary and ask her to keep strict watch on her hours which meant that she should stay there 20 hours and not work so much overtime."

Shaw established that Kalsow and Bird had known each other a long time and that Tom basically started the work at Faith. He acknowledged that the core group of 65 members grew to 150 by October, 1982, and that he was impressed with Tom's work.

Shaw bored in on the July 27 incident and Kalsow's general impressions of Tom. He agreed Tom was a caring, touching kind of person, and that Tom never used the word "love" when referring to Lorna. Shaw suggested that Kalsow counseled Tom based on the substance of what Angie had said, not personal knowledge, and Tom's grieving. Kalsow agreed.

Shaw asked him about the role of lay ministers, and he explained they were responsible for the overall operation of the church, and the pastors "physical well being, his family life." Kalsow presented his concerns to the lay ministers on his own volition.

Shaw asked Kalsow to describe the duties of a pastor to the jury. He asked him about counseling and Kalsow agreed it could take as much as 30 percent of a pastor's time. The seminary offered optional counseling courses to their students and counseling is an attempt to help people find a way to find answers.

"Do you feel that or is there some danger that frequently a counselor becomes that fulfillment when these people are looking for something?"

"That's a risk."

"And that also when that happens, you end up with having a congregation which may in fact become divided or create dissension among a congregation. Is that a fair statement?"

"As a result of becoming involved with your client?"

"Yes, becoming the fulfillment of what their need is."

"That's a potential problem."

"As the pastor of Messiah and Tom being the pastor of Faith, did the two churches have combined activities?"

Yes, especially youth groups. Shaw asked about a youth board meeting on May 21, 1983. Did they discuss fireworks at that meeting? Kalsow could not recall it, but he knew he gave Tom a brochure about fireworks. "I passed it along to him and suggested that this might be something that his youth groups could use to raise the money they needed for their trip."

"And this was in the May 21st meeting. Is that correct?"

"Uh-huh."

Tom reported back to him sometime later that they could not sell fireworks inside the city limit. He also said that he knew Tom personally and believed he lived his life in accordance with the Bible.

Symmonds began his redirect. He asked Kalsow that, since he knew Tom so well, could he imagine him saying about Marty's death, "I ain't celebrating but I ain't mourning either." (This statement came from the

December 12 taped conversation.)

"That does not seem to fit his character."

He asked him about the statement, "We got to keep each other clean here just for the sake of the kids." Kalsow said that did not sound like the Tom he knew.

"Reverend Kalsow, would you describe the defendant to be somewhat vindictive?"

"Somewhat."

He asked Kalsow whether Tom could be persuasive when talking in front of group. Kalsow said yes.

Symmonds wondered if Tom called Kalsow after his meeting with Darrel. "No."

"Did the defendant contact you after his arrest and ask you if you recalled this discussion concerning the fireworks?"

"Yes."

On re-cross examination, Shaw asked whether Kalsow had any knowledge of Tom's state of mind when he made the tape-recorded conversation with Darrel. "No, just from what I've learned attending the trial."

Shaw addressed the issue of Tom being "vindictive." He asked Kalsow if there had been a falling out between Messiah and Faith, and if that fallout was related to Kalsow's recent divorce from his wife. "Yes." Kalsow said it involved his ex-wife, "To some degree."

Kalsow agreed that he and Tom had disagreements about how a church should be run and the extent to which a church should be involved in counseling. Messiah was more conservative than Faith in this.

Kalsow stepped down and Symmonds called Gladys Simmons, Lorna's grandmother from Topeka. Simmons said that Marty usually stayed at her house when he came to Topeka for reserve duty.

Irv Shaw asked her if she was retired. "Yes." She never gave Marty a key to the house, so she would always be home when he was there. (Darrel said Tom would hide in the house and murder Marty when he came home. If this scheme had been true, he would have had to murder Granny as well as Marty.)

Symmonds called Sharon Meyer. She was the wife of Howard Meyer, a lay minister at Faith.

She first met Lorna in January of 1983, at the time Lorna began working at the church.

Symmonds asked whether she ever saw Tom and Lorna together? Yes, at church and at Fellowship Club. The Club met once a month; Tom and Lorna attended, but so did Marty and Sandy.

Symmonds asked about seeing them working together and Sharon recalled a time in late August or September of 1983. "Well, I had come into the secretary's office to talk with Pastor Bird about something, and we had just gotten the church computer shortly before that time, and he and Lorna were working with the computer and they were sitting in metal chairs in front of the computer and they were very close together. Their knees were touching, and it just took me back a little bit to see them that way because I had been concerned about their relationship."

Sharon thought Lorna had become too dependent on Tom. "Because of things that I had observed about Lorna that she seemed to make Pastor Bird her friend to the exclusion of the other people in the congregation. She did not open up to other people like she did to Pastor Bird. She seemed to light up when he was around and really go to him with whatever problem she had."

After the "knees touching" incident, Sharon found Angie in the preschool and told her "that I realized that the lay ministers told Lorna that she could keep her job but I was still concerned about the relationship that was developing between Lorna and Pastor."

Sharon went to Tom and talked at length with him about her concerns. He said others had told him the same. Tom told her that Lorna was suicidal and that the job gave her fulfillment, but Sharon thought she should resign. They talked about other options, "And he told me that if I really felt that way that maybe—that he would ask her to leave."

Later that same day she told her husband about the conversation and the next day, during a clean up session at church, they both talked with Tom. Howard made a statement about Lorna starting over fresh, and Sharon believed Tom thought that meant that Lorna should stay.

Symmonds asked whether Sharon talked with Tom about the turnpike incident. She had. "He said it was a dumb move, and he said that he should have known people would talk about it if they saw him out there with her. He said that he was out there talking with her about her resignation."

During their September discussion, Tom told her about Marty's abuse of Lorna.

She said that Lorna would just basically do whatever Tom asked her to do around the office. "She would just do it and that basically she was good for his ego I think."

"Did he indicate to you whether or not that she gave him strength?"

"Yes, he did....I just remember those words, 'She gives me strength.'"

Tom said Lorna never judged him nor complained about how he handled his children.

Shaw asked her whether she spent a good deal of time at the church. Yes.

She said she only saw Tom and Lorna on the one occasion at the computer and that Joyce Rosenboom was also in the church that day.

Shaw showed Sharon a picture of Lorna's office with the computer in view. She recognized it and agreed that the computer was new, and that Tom and Lorna were both trying to learn how to use it.

She said that Angie had talked to her previously about Tom and Lorna.

Shaw reminded Sharon that they had previously talked about the case. "At that time I believe you described Tom as a warm, sensitive, loving person. Would you agree with that description?"

"Yes."

"Would you consider him to be a person who would do anything for anybody to try and help them out?"

"Pretty much."

"I believe you've also described him on occasion as a huggy, touchy person. Is that—outgoing, touchy type individual. Is that a correct statement?"

"Yes."

"Indeed I believe you have told me earlier that during the course of this first meeting that lasted approximately an hour and a half, you and Tom in the course of your discussion actually ended up holding hands for a while. Is that correct?"

"Yes. He became very emotional....As well as I did."

"When it was over I believe the two of you even hugged each other. Is that a fair statement?"

"Yes."

"Did you feel anything unusual or untoward about this hugging and holding of hands while you were sitting there talking?"

"I didn't feel anything unusual about holding hands. I felt a little uncomfortable with the hug."

She said she felt Christian love toward him, and that meant caring about him.

"When he talked about the criticism, the fact that Lorna did not criticize him, did not judge him, was he referring to the best of your knowledge to things such as the way he raised his children, the way he dressed his children, how he was taking care of his children at that time?"

"I think he stated that."

"This was in fact a very difficult time all the way around for Pastor Bird, was it not?"

"Yes. We talked about how he was living in a fish bowl and everyone was watching him."

On redirect, Symmonds asked whether Sharon attended Marty's funeral and whether Tom presided. She said "Yes" (but Tom had not presided, though he did give a message—Pastor Kalsow presided).

Symmonds started to ask questions about Sandy Bird. Had Sharon noticed she lost a lot of weight and such? Shaw strongly objected. He believed Symmonds crossed into an area not only far outside his examination of Sharon, but that he was trying to introduce a suggestion to the jury about Sandy's mysterious death. "I'm going to move to have that last question and answer stricken. It's inflammatory, it's prejudicial, it's improper conduct counsel because he knew darn good and well he couldn't get anywhere with it. The only reason he asked it is to inflame the jury. I'm going to ask for a mistrial and—"

Rulon cut him off and told Symmonds to drop it. He told Shaw he would not have it stricken from the record because it would bring weight to the statement.

Symmonds said he had no further questions. Neither did Shaw.

Symmonds called Howard Meyer to the stand.

Meyer served as a lay minister at Faith and one of his duties was to deal with payroll issues. He said the lay ministers hired Lorna in January of 1983 for 15 hours a week and paid her $60 a week.

"Did Lorna Anderson submit to you a resignation in July of 1983? When I say 'you' I refer to the lay ministers."

"She had not personally. She had typed up a copy of a letter of resignation and put into each one of the slots for the lay ministers at the church, and that's where I found mine."

"Do you know what precipitated the offer of a resignation?"

"I know personally several things that happened beforehand. I don't know exactly what led to that letter, but Ill relate a couple things. On July 29th Reverend Kalsow gave me a call...about 9:30, 9:45 in the morning and asked if I could come over to Messiah to meet with him; and I had no idea what he wanted to talk about but I did. And Harold Schwinn also came a few minutes after I got there, so we had a brief meeting on July 29th. I think it was, a Friday."

Symmonds asked when the lay ministers were able to meet with Tom and Lorna and talk about the letter? It was the 31st. The three lay ministers met that night and then on Monday morning, August 1, they met with Tom. Howard said the reason Lorna stated for resigning was "some people in the congregation questioning her relationship with Pastor."

Symmonds asked whether the meeting with Kalsow had precipitated the resignation, and Howard could not be sure, though it "certainly entered into it." He believed there were other contributing factors.

"Mr. Meyer, ultimately the resignation was not accepted by the board, was it?" Irv Shaw asked.

"No, it was not."

"And as a matter of fact, in your conversation with Pastor Bird he had never indicated to you in any way that, 'If you get rid of Lorna, you lose me, too,' had he?"

"No, sir."

Howard Meyer stepped down the court recessed.

Love letters debated

The attorneys remained in court to debate more motions. Shaw knew that the state intended to use two letters the police had seized during their search of Lorna's home. They labeled them "love letters." Shaw objected to their use, but Rulon disagreed.

Jan Mead entered the courtroom to give Symmonds and Shaw a chance to go over her testimony. Shaw strongly contended her testimony was total hearsay and had no place in the trial. Both men grilled her with Shaw concentrating on how her statement changed over time.

Rulon decided to allow her to testify. Shaw again protested. Rulon spoke about a legal doctrine called a "declaration against interest." This doctrine states that a person generally will not tell another person something that would debase their standing in the community. Rulon believed that the things Mead testified to about Lorna had to be true, because they were so sordid they could not be lies. No one, he argued, would lie about such things that would have the tendency to bring them ridicule and dishonor. (Had Rulon been able to rule on this motion with the benefit of seeing the future, given the scores of lies Lorna told to investigators, in court and to journalists, he might have realized that she was totally capable of fabricating anything that brought her temporary relief or enjoyment. Even one of his court employee's spouse had at least one sexual encounter with Lorna, showing she had no regard for her reputation in the community.)

Rulon said the way Mead handled the questions during this private hearing convinced him to let her testify. He limited her and Symmonds, though, to questions only pertaining to what Lorna allegedly told her.

Shaw didn't give up. "...We're losing sight of what in the world this case is all about. We're here because the defendant is accused of soliciting somebody. We're not here because he's accused of having Lorna Anderson having fallen in love with him, assuming she did and even if she did.

"These statements are not attributable to the defendant in any way; and to go in there and have her make these grandiose statements which we've never heard before is so far prejudicial and so far outside anything else that has ever been testified to that even if they did have any merit, which I suggest they do not, it just does not seem they can be admissible at all. It is clearly unqualifiedly, blatantly hearsay from someone who isn't here."

Rulon restated his decision that Mead would be allowed to testify.

The jury came back into the courtroom and Symmonds called Alan Rees. Rees said he was a long time member of Faith and that he sat as a "youth board director," with responsibilities to "dictate and supervise all activities of the youth." Rees described a few of the fund raising projects he had helped with at the church, one which was selling sun catchers. "That was something Pastor Bird had arranged."

Symmonds asked about a May, 1983, youth board meeting and Rees recalled being there. "Do you recall if at that board meeting there was any discussion concerning the sale of fireworks?"

"To the best of my recollection we didn't discuss it. We did discuss some fund-raising projects I believe though for the trip to Eureka Springs, but what they were I don't know, but we ended up not doing any fund-raising projects."

"Did you at any time have occasion to hear the defendant mention anything pertaining to the youth group selling fireworks?"

"Not that I recall. Not until after his arrest." Rees said Tom talked to him a couple weeks after his arrest. Tom asked if he remembered the discussion and he did not, but he might have come late to the meeting, he said. Tom asked him to look in his notes, but Rees just two weeks earlier had thrown all his notes away.

Shaw asked whether Rees gave a statement to Agent Humphrey just a few weeks earlier. He had. He told Humphrey that Tom had asked him about the fireworks discussion. Shaw asked, "and that time did he ask you to fabricate a story about fireworks?"

"No, sir, he didn't."

"In fact, didn't he tell you to tell the truth?"

"Yes, he did."

Rees would only know about fund-raising that had been approved, had commenced or was about to be commenced. He agreed there was a trip planned for August to Eureka Springs and that they needed to raise funds to make the trip.

"Do you recall, sir, in June a campout that occurred at Lake Melvern with the youth group?"

"Yes, sir, I do."

"And I believe that caused or you had some problems with some of the youth out there, did you not?"

"Yeah, I think we had a few."

Deppish steps up

Deputy Sheriff Bill Deppish took the stand. Symmonds asked him if he executed a search warrant on Lorna's house on November 22, 1983. Yes, he had. Did he make any field notes? No, he did not.

"Did you have occasion to search the master bedroom of that home during the course of the search of the residence?"

"Yes, I did."

"And did you have occasion to search a chest of drawers which was located in the master bedroom of the Anderson residence?"

"Yes, I did."

"What if anything did you discover in that chest of drawers which was taken as evidence at that time?"

"I discovered two letters or two notes and perhaps a letter, described as a letter, in dresser drawer in the master bedroom."

"And where in the dresser drawer did you discover these two notes and the letter?"

"It was in a drawer containing ladies undergarments, and it was—all the letters were towards the bottom of the drawer, under the under-garments."

Deppish said he read the letters after finding them, and Symmonds showed him three exhibits; an unfinished letter and the two cards that became referred to as love letters. Deppish identified them for the record.

Once he found the letters, he called the other officers into the bedroom and they read and photographed them. The officers decided they were relevant to the search warrant so turned them over to the custodian.

Symmonds called Tommy Thompson, an officer at the Lyon County State Bank. Thompson testified that he knew both Marty and Lorna, served as their personal banker and knew Marty from Optimists.

Symmonds asked Thompson questions pertaining to a loan application Lorna made in May of 1983. He offered the Anderson's bank statements for that period as exhibits. Shaw objected to the relevancy of Lorna's banking problems to the instant case. Rulon overruled him again.

Symmonds asked about the type of checking account the Anderson's had and determined it carried a $10,000 life insurance rider, payable upon accidental death.

Shaw clarified that the $10,000 insurance rider had been in place since 1981.

Thompson stepped down.

The attorneys approached the bench and discussed the reading of Julie Palmer's deposition. Rulon ruled it admissible and allowed that it could be read. Symmonds said his secretary would read it. Donna Hughs read the deposition into the record in front of the jury. (The author presented this testimony in Section I of the book.)

The deposition simply reported that Tom came to Julie's house and asked for a meeting with Darrel. Julie said Tom was very nervous and she had trouble understanding just why he wanted her to do this. She said she went to see Darrel later that day and gave him the message. She asked Darrel what it was about, and he told her not to worry. Darrel told her that he and Tom had talked about fireworks. She admitted to having a two-year sexual relationship with Darrel.

Agent Humphrey took the stand.

Humphrey described his assistance in the execution of the search warrant at Lorna's. Also, he had picked up the letters from the KBI and kept them until he delivered them to Symmonds earlier that day.

Symmonds had Humphrey look at the various pictures of Faith Lutheran's building and he acknowledged they were accurate. Humphrey also identified writing samples of Tom that he picked up at Faith on July 19. Lois Froelich, the church secretary, gave them to him.

Symmonds began to ask Humphrey what Lois told him that day, but Shaw objected, saying it was hearsay. Symmonds answered that Lois had been subpoenaed, but Shaw said she wasn't on the witness list. Symmonds gulped and said he meant to add her and asked that she be added. The judge said he'd take in under advisement but ordered Symmonds to refrain from asking about statements Lois may have made.

Symmonds began to ask Humphrey about the December 1, 1983, meeting he had with Mike Patton and once again, Shaw objected. He said this testimony had already been given. Rulon warned Symmonds not to repeat earlier testimony, but Symmonds claimed Humphrey had the right to confirm the earlier testimony. Rulon told him to proceed, but very carefully.

Humphrey stated that Patton told him about the December 1 meeting between Tom and Julie and then later, Julie's meeting with Darrel. He said he attended a meeting on December 7 where investigation documents were turned over to Darrel and Danny. He attended a December 10 meeting to hear Darrel's story and then, on December 12, he provided a tape recorder for the call to Tom. He confirmed his presence during the taped meeting in the bowling alley parking lot and he verified it was Tom's voice on the tape.

Irv Shaw showed Humphrey another photograph taken at Faith. It showed the opening in Lorna's office taken from a large hallway that sat outside the wall of her office. Humphrey acknowledged that it was accurate. Shaw admitted it into evidence. (This showed the open window that greatly restricted any privacy.)

Shaw asked Humphrey about his field notes. Did he consider them to be an accurate reflection of his interviews? Yes. And the typed records, were they accurate? Yes.

He asked about the various meetings Humphrey had with Darrel and on all occasions, except a few, Mike Patton had been present. The exceptions were when Humphrey drove to a work site to collect bits and pieces of information.

"You report relating to the events on December 10th, 1983, related the story about the involvement with the car accident. If I'm not mistaken, sir, at that time you were told, were you not, that Mr. Carter's involvement was to help get Marty into the car."

"Yes, that's what he told me."

He reminded Humphrey that the December 10 meeting was in the context of finding some sort of deal for Danny, to which he agreed. "Apparently, sir, from looking at your notes and from looking at the other matters contained therein, at the very first meeting with Darrel nothing was mentioned relative to pallbearers, was there?"

"No."

"The very first meeting there was nothing said relative to Pastor Bird saying, 'I am a man of God. I am going to kill Martin Anderson,' was there?"

"No, there wasn't."

On redirect, Humphrey said he never asked Darrel questions that would have resulted in the answers about which Shaw had just asked. He also stated that it was common for people to add detail to their statements over time as they recalled more things.

Humphrey stepped down.

Symmonds called Sue Graf.

Sue started attending Faith in March of 1983, and she enrolled her children in Lord's Lambs. Symmonds asked whether Sue attended Faith regularly. Yes. Did she go to the church often? Yes, nearly every day. Did she see Tom and Lorna together? Yes.

"Did you based on your observation of the two of them form any opinions as to whether or not they had feelings for one another?"

"Not right away, not immediately."

"And based on your observations of them over that period of time, did you formulate any opinion as to whether Lorna Anderson had any feelings for the defendant?"

"After a few weeks it seemed like she was attracted to him somehow."

"What caused you to feel that way?"

"Just the look in her eye and her manner I imagine."

Shaw began his cross-examination. He asked her about the hallway outside Lorna's office and about looking in through the window. Sue said it was a busy place and others also would walk through there. "The mornings were always busier."

Sue stepped down and Symmonds called Esther Aldrete who had served as one of Lorna's babysitters during 1983. Lorna fired her because she called in sick one day; had a bad cold.

Symmonds asked if Aldrete knew Tom? She pointed him out. "How did you become acquainted with the defendant?"

"Lorna and him, they took their kids for me to baby-sit. Lorna, she never ask me to baby-sit his kids. They never call me up to say, you know, 'You want to baby-sit my kids' or something like this. They just drop the kids off."

She remembered three occasions when the Bird children came over, and she thought it started four months after she started working. "The first time I saw him was about April, the middle of April. The second time was June, and the third time was July."

"When the defendant came to the Anderson home in April, can you describe what happened after he arrived?"

"They dropped the kids and they left. They say they were going to go out to eat lunch or go back to work."

"And do you recall did they leave together?"

"Yes."

"In one car?"

"Yeah."

"And in June of 1983, can you describe was it a similar procedure?"

"They came over to the house; and Lorna, she brought one of her little girls, no Lori, the next one; and she ask if he want to stay for lunch. And he said, 'No. We better go out and eat in a restaurant or something.' That's when Lorna, you know, she got real close to him and make—"

Shaw objected. He said Esther was getting into hearsay. Rulon overruled him.

"I was ready to go home and that's when she told me that, you know, she was going out with him to eat lunch."

"And without indicating what she said, because we can't get into that, what if anything did you observe in June?"

"That's when, you know. They were getting ready to go eat lunch and she—you know, she got real close to him. She hardly saying anything. You know, the only thing she say was, 'Let's go'; but she got real close to him and she give one of those sexy eyes or whatever you call like."

The audience reacted to her statement and the judge cautioned them to keep quiet.

"What did—what if anything else did you observe?"

"Well, you know, she got real close and she make those sexy eyes or whatever you make when you like somebody like, you know, 'Well, let's go, honey,' like that. She say that, 'Let's go, honey'; and she looked at him real, you know, like real loud something like this (indicating). And they left and get in the car real close they left. I didn't see nothing else."

Aldrete said it was 7:00 or 8:00 p.m. before she returned.

Symmonds asked her about a specific event when she overheard Lorna on the telephone. "It was about April the 23rd I heard she was speaking in the telephone, but I don't know who it was, but I overheard when she say, 'I cannot wait for Marty to die. I wanted to spend—I wanted to count his green money or green stuff.' She say, 'I can't—cannot wait for Marty to die. I can't wait to count the green stuff.'"

Shaw questioned her about various versions of the dates she had given for her employment with Lorna and what she did afterward. She admitted she was fired in June. (Obviously, she hadn't seen Tom and Lorna at the house in July as she had testified.)

When Agent Winsor interviewed her, she had said she never met Tom until much later. Shaw asked about the discrepancy and she said the agent misunderstood her. He asked why she never mentioned the three times that she now claimed Tom's children stayed with her. She said they never asked. She agreed that it was just her opinion that Tom and Lorna were dating.

Shaw clarified the date when she overheard the phone conversation and she insisted it was April 23; payday. She said Lorna was very serious on the phone.

Other than these three occasions she now testified to, she never had been near Tom.

Symmonds recalled Tommy Thompson. Thompson explained that the Anderson's had 20 overdrafts in May of 1983. They ended June with a balance of over $900. Shaw objected once again that Lorna's financial problems had no relevance to this trial, as she was not the defendant. (Years later, as Tom reflected on the trial, he came to believe that in a sense, Lorna served as a co-defendant in abstentia. Much of the trial dwelt on her problems and her attitudes toward Tom and others, especially allegations of an affair and looking for a financial motive. Tom felt like the jury needed to punish her for her misdeeds, but he sat on trial, not her.)

Lorie Roelfs took the stand despite Shaw's objection. She had not previously been listed as a witness and Shaw said this was prejudicial to Tom. Symmonds said Roelfs was there just to prove chain of custody of earlier evidence and Rulon agreed to let her testify to the same.

Charles Kaufman was next. He testified about the handwriting and concluded that Tom wrote the two cards. (Tom much earlier acknowledged that he wrote the cards. This had not been challenged evidence. Yet by questioning Kaufman in this manner, Symmonds added more drama to the matter, even setting up an enlargement of the handwriting on the cards for identification purposes. At one point, Kaufman focussed on the way Tom wrote the "L" in the word "Love," thereby drawing attention to the word. In terms of establishing fact, Kaufman's testimony was unnecessary.)

Hearsay personified

Next up was Jan Mead. Though it did not come out in this trial, Mead was but 24 years old and single when she employed the sexually experienced Lorna Anderson. Those who have spent time studying and getting to know Lorna realize she is a rare type, almost unique both in her story spinning and range of sexual experiences (investigators eventually set the number of documented sex partners at about 60). The Kansas Department of Corrections labels her a "master manipulator." Lorna impressed the younger more impressionable woman with her stories of sexual dalliances.

Before she was allowed to testify, Rulon called the attorneys to the bench. He reminded Symmonds to steer clear of any questions about what Marty might have said.

He asked Shaw if he still wanted to object to the testimony. He did. "We would object to any statements that were made to this witness by Lorna Anderson or any testimony about them at all as they occurred well prior to any allegation of a crime or criminal solicitation and further all being outside of any exception to the hearsay rule, finally being too prejudicial and inflammatory as to outweigh any probative merit they may have. So our objection is threefold."

Rulon restated his earlier decision to allow the testimony.

Symmonds asked Mead to identify herself and her job, how she met Lorna and such.

Mead said the two met weekly at Lorna's house and sometime in February she learned Lorna worked at Faith. She placed it as before February 11, in a person-to-person meeting at Lorna's house. No one else was present. Lorna told her, "Tom and I are seeing each other, and this is one chance that we have to be alone and I enjoy working there." She said Tom was her minister.

"Did she indicate to you whether or not that she was from time to time going outside the city limits of Emporia with this individual?"

"Yes. In March she began using her Heart Association job as an excuse for afternoon trips to Wichita or Topeka. She would call me and say, 'I've told my husband I'm going to meet with you in Wichita; and if he calls, would you tell him that I'm on my way to or from to meet with you.'"

"Who did she say that she went with?"

"Tom."

Symmonds asked what Lorna told her they did when they went to the hotel or motel. "It was something like, 'He's pretty good in bed for a minister.'"

Symmonds moved to the April 19, 1983, meeting between Mead and Lorna. They met at the Holiday Inn and no one else was present. "What if anything did Lorna Anderson say to you on that date?"

"She was very upset when she got there so before we started with the evaluation I thought maybe if we talked a little bit and had a cup of coffee it would calm her down. So I asked her, I said, 'Do you want to talk about it?'; and she told me that things with her and Marty were much worse and that things with her and Tom were more involved....She made the comment and she was very nervous that 'I know this sounds really awful but sometimes I just wish something would happen to Marty and his wife so Tom and I could spend the rest of our lives together.'" (Lorna told Tom out of court that spring that what she really said to Mead was more like, "I wish something would happen so that Marty and I could have the same kind of lives together as Tom and his wife.")

Symmonds asked whether there were other dates of which she was aware when Lorna said she and Tom left town together. She recalled one time during March. "She told me about some trip that her and Tom had taken just recently within the last few days; and she said, 'It was so nice to be in'—I can't remember the name of the town—'so we could walk down the street and hold hands.'"

Mead said Lorna also told her that her daughter saw her and Tom kissing and feared she might tell Marty.

Irv Shaw asked Mead whether she met with Lorna regularly from October until April. Yes, every week to ten days.

Shaw showed that Mead kept written records of when she met with various employees—like Lorna—but she took no notes of what was discussed. He asked her about the voluntary statement she gave to police in November of 1983. She explained how she decided to write it out at the urging of a friend, a police officer. She gave the statement to police but heard nothing until Steven Opat called her from Geary County.

Shaw tried to place the conversations Mead had with Lorna in context. He asked if they were "girl talk" where each one gave a little? Yes.

He asked about the first man Lorna mentioned to her, the hairdresser. "Yes."

"Then your testimony here today is that within two weeks she suddenly was telling you about another man she was sleeping with. Is that correct?"

"In those first two weeks she didn't say she was sleeping with him."

Shaw placed the first mention of Tom into the discussion about Mead's concern over Lorna having a second job. That's when Lorna mentioned she and Tom were "seeing each other."

Mead had never met or talked with Tom to check out any of Lorna's stories.

"Did you in your conversations with Lorna ever consider her to be somewhat of an emotional type of person?"

"High strung is how I would explain it."

"Somewhat flighty?"

"Correct."

He reminded her that in one of her statements she referred to Lorna's "boyfriends" but Mead insisted she knew only the one name—Tom. She acknowledged that the comment about him being good in bed for a minister was not in her original statement to police.

Mead said she and Lorna met 12 times during 1983, and on five of those occasions Lorna told her about her affairs, four of those referring to Tom. She admitted that she did not know specifically who Tom was, and she never heard his last name.

Mead stepped down and the court recessed until Monday. Jurors had an entire weekend to mull over this sensational testimony. Given the reports in The Gazette about Jan Mead, were the jurors able to resist talking about the trial that weekend?

Meanwhile, at Ewert's

At Susan Ewert's house that day, Mead's testimony drew a completely different response than that of the jury's. During a break in the testimony, Darrell Meyer phoned Ewert's and asked to speak to Lorna. Lorna stayed there because Judge Rulon ordered her to stay in town until the trial ended, and Susan provided her with physical and emotional shelter. Susan handed Lorna the phone and Lorna listened as Meyer told her about Mead's testimony.

When she hung up the phone, Lorna went upstairs to the bedroom she used while in town, and knelt down next to the bed. Susan followed her upstairs after a few minutes and found her sobbing, her hands buried in her face. Susan tried to comfort her and asked her what caused this outburst? She told Susan that when Mead talked about Tom being good in bed for a minister, she never told her that. She told her about Willie Porter, her former boss with whom she had a long term affair. They used to walk around hand-in-hand and people commented on how happy they looked. No, Mead had it wrong. Lorna knew her testimony had hurt Tom badly.

The jury never knew about this outburst, not until Susan testified during the 1990 trial.

Defense ready

With Mead as his last witness, Symmonds rested his case.

Shaw called his first defense witness, Rev. Larry Kalsow.

"Reverend Kalsow, one question which was asked of you on redirect examination with respect to your opinions concerning the defendant was whether you felt him to be somewhat vindictive. You and I have since that time had an opportunity to discuss that question a little bit further. What precisely did you mean when you said you felt him to be somewhat vindictive?"

"I hesitated when I answered the question. What came to my mind was sports and Tom's competitive nature especially like a softball game. He and I were on the same teams in seminary, football and softball; and he was very competitive. And if we were to get beat or he was to make an out, the next time up he would try that much harder."

"All right. Did you mean to infer by that statement in any way that he was the type of person that if he was slighted by someone he would aim to get even with that particular person?"

"That's not what I was referring to."

Shaw also asked for a clarification about Tom's abilities as a speaker. Kalsow referred to Tom as a preacher and said his abilities were comparable to Kalsow's; he did not mean to imply that Tom was better than others.

Kalsow stepped down.

Tom takes the stand

All eyes in the courtroom were fixed on Tom as he walked toward the witness stand. He felt confident that he could set the record straight about all the gossip, innuendo and outright lies he had heard the previous week.

"Do you solemnly swear to tell the truth, the whole truth and nothing but the truth, so help you God?"

"Yes." Tom saw the truth as his best defense. Pastor's are known for telling the truth. Shaw had told him not to testify, which was his right, but Tom insisted. In his mind, telling the truth was all that mattered.

Taking the witness stand, Tom looked out at the crowd of people jammed into the courtroom. He saw his mother and father on one side, expectantly awaiting his vindication.

On the other side he saw Jane Grismer and her family. He knew Jane had been talking to the press, prosecutors and prosecution witnesses. He didn't understand Jane any more that day than he had during all the years he and Sandy were together.

He looked at the gawkers, scandal-hungry Emporians who lined up daily in front of the courtroom to win a choice seat, like they were going to a Royals' baseball game and wanted to sit behind home plate.

He noticed a number of members from Faith, and that gave him confidence.

He looked to his left at the jury; six men and six women who held his life in their hands. They were good people, he thought, who wanted to do the right thing.

He looked at Rod Symmonds, the prosecutor, and wondered how Judge Rulon could tolerate his antics and volatile behavior.

He felt the presence of the court reporter and the judge sitting to his right.

He saw the media who had come from around the country to watch and report on this trial. This he did not understand. What made his trial such a circus? It was all just a misunderstanding, he believed. They would be very disappointed at the end.

Lastly, he saw the investigators from two counties who compiled the shaky evidence against him.

Shaw asked Tom several personal questions, including where he lived, where he was born and about his family. He asked about Tom's call to the ministry.

Tom explained that Sandy died in a car accident on July 16, 1983, and that he had three children.

Shaw asked about the process of being called to Messiah.

"I received a call from the calling committee at Messiah. This is a committee of people who would be evaluating candidates and deciding who they wanted to come to this position. It was made up of—basically two people were behind this, Gilbert Dieckhoff who was the head elder and Mike Pruisner who was the president of the congregation and, of course, Larry Kalsow."

Shaw wanted an explanation of how the LC-MS congregations function organizationally. "Well, the way the organization functions and what we believe is the correct way to do this is we have a voting assembly which is an assembly of adults, and all members qualified to vote on major decisions. Then there are a number of boards that report and do specific work. One of those boards would be the board of elders, our lay ministers. They are in charge of the spiritual care of members of the congregation, the spiritual and physical care of the pastor; and they oversee the worship and teachings of the church."

Shaw established that each congregation also elects a president, but that person is not the pastor. "Who specifically or is there any specific person that a pastor in a Lutheran church would answer to?"

"No specific person but he would answer to the board of lay ministry or elders."

"How big is your office? Do you recall?"

"I think it's about 12 by 12."

"Did you have any windows in your office?"

"There were windows—the structure to the west had been added on later. The section to the west would be a—that would be kind of a welcome area, yes. So originally there were windows there. There still are windows there but there are drapes over there."

"Were they ever opened, the windows?"

"No."

"How big was the secretary's office?"

"It's about 9 by 12."

"And were there windows in that particular office?"

"Yes."

"Where at?"

"On the west side...it's an open reception area type of thing. It's not really a glass window, it's an open reception area....The purpose of the office being right there is to be a reception area, and so entering through the long hallway someone who would want to talk with me or talk with the secretary and do business there—there's also a set of mailboxes there, too, for communication purposes—would come to that area and then speak with the secretary if they wanted to make an appointment with me or wanted to know if I was in. There's kind of a large open area just to the right of that open window where you could wait for an appointment or whatever."

Tom said that the door to the secretary's office normally was left open. He described the layout of the furniture in each room.

Tom described his duties. "You also indicated counseling. What all were your duties with respect to counseling? What type of counseling are we talking about?"

"There are a variety of types of counseling. There's supportive counseling; there's crisis counseling; there's comfort counseling if someone's going into a surgery or hospital. I counsel on a one-to-one basis; I counsel on family basis; counsel in preparation for a couple being married."

Shaw asked how much time Tom spent on each of these. During his normal 65-hour week, and given how the dynamics of a growing church force regular change on a pastor's schedule, he estimated that he spent

"...about ten hours of administration training, ten hours sermon and preparation, ten hours of the, oh, what we call the outreach, and then probably 15 hours teaching, and it got to be maybe 20 hours counseling." Counseling consumed about 30 percent of Tom's time.

Shaw asked about the circumstances under which counseling took place. "It wouldn't be limited to appointment-type counseling. Pastoral counseling is different than professional counseling in the sense a professional counselor would be appointments. He sees a person and then they leave.

"Pastoral counseling means you work with people in the settings of their own and in the atmosphere of the church, that you counsel with them on an informal basis quite often because you see them worshiping, you see them at Bible classes, you visit them in their homes, you know their family, you get to know their spiritual needs and so counseling can be on an informal basis quite often.

"As a matter of fact, I think some of the best comforting and support comes with just talking to a person standing in the parking lot after a meeting before you go home at night."

Shaw asked about counselor training in seminary. Yes, he took a number of courses. "Generally, what is your method and approach then in going through counseling?"

"When someone comes to see me...with a need or a problem, I try to find out what the presenting problem is, seek to listen—that's the most important thing is listening—and then usually you find an underlying problem that's maybe more real and is more long term in its needs. The underlying problem then can be dealt with again after listening.

"And the our purpose in pastoral counseling would be to give Biblical guidance and direction and support to shore this person up and let them know they're loved of God and help them that way."

Shaw asked about Angie. "She just graduated with an early childhood education degree from Emporia State University, sent out a number of applications and didn't really receive any job because of I guess the number of teachers available. And I had talked with her and, you know, she was concerned about what to do. And I talked with her, and I already had a goal because I have three young children, a goal of having a preschool, a Christian preschool here in town at our church. And she was very much committed to that idea, too.

"So we began to work toward that and presented that as an idea to our church...We had to work together to make grant applications; we had to again put together a policy booklet for licensing; and we had to make plans by way of surveys and by way of advertising and by way of reaching out to parents of young preschoolers to encourage them to commit themselves to this."

The church opened Lord's Lambs in September, 1982. Tom spent a lot of time working with Angie both on launching this preschool and at the ESU student center.

"Do you know Lorna Anderson?"

"Yes."

"Where and how did you meet Lorna Anderson?"

"I met her for the first time at a softball game. That's the first time I met Marty Anderson, at a softball game and just by way of saying hello. And she said she read the newsletter and was interested in the preschool. The first time I really ever talked with her was in '82 in the—September, '82, when her child started coming to preschool." Andersons started attending services in November.

Shaw asked about Lorna's hiring as church secretary. "The first year of our operation we didn't have in the budget enough money to hire a secretary so we were relying on volunteer work to do the secretarial work. The church grew quite quickly in '82 and there was a strong need causing a backlog of record keeping and paperwork. There came a need to hire a secretary, and the voting assembly put in the budget to hire a secretary to being in January.

"When I was visiting Marty and Lorna, I was—it was an outreach visitation. They had visited our church and I was wanting to see if they were interested in taking instruction in the church and joining our church, became a part of it. And at the time I was talking to Marty and Lorna, and I mentioned the idea that we were hiring a secretary. She said she had worked as a church secretary before. I think it was in Sterling, Kansas, was the town...And she worked at St. Mary's hospital and such, and she was interested in a part-time job like that, especially if it would be during the times when her little girl would be in preschool there."

"Was she subsequently hired then? Is that correct?"

"Yes. The board of lay ministers who would be in charge of making that decision—the board of lay ministers hired Lorna to being work at our church."

Shaw asked about how the Andersons came to join the church. Tom explained that all members go a six-week course and that this particular class was held at the Andersons' home. "...there were a number of other people who participated in those classes and eventually joined the church."

Shaw asked about Tom's relationship with Marty. Tom said they became friends, played several sports together and belonged to the Optimists (Marty sponsored Tom). They remained friends up to Marty's death in November.

Shaw returned to Tom's relationship with Lorna. "Going to April, May, June of 1983, what if anything was your relationship with Lorna at that time?"

"May and June of 1983? My relationship with Lorna was one of—well, it was a number of things. The pastor and member; it was boss-secretary; it was one of family and friends together and I consider her a friend of mine. And I think we also—it was a relationship of counselor-counselee, and it was a relationship—we had a good working relationship, very comfortable in the work; and I think after that time she understood the goals and ideas and we worked together very well."

Shaw bored in on the counseling. Tom said most of it was privileged information, but could describe her situation in general. Lorna suffered from depression and low self-esteem. He started counseling her in March, 1983.

Angie testified to seeing Tom with Lorna when the lady was crying. Tom remembered the incidents but not that Angie was there. Shaw asked what sparked Lorna's bouts of depression?

"Well, number one, there were some health problems that she had and caused her some depression, and then also sometimes when she was low, a little bit of criticism or maybe something going wrong would set her off such as, you know, the children maybe doing something or—"

"What would you do when Lorna would have these problems, this crying or this depression or the reaction to some form of criticism?"

"Well, she would start to spiral down."

Tom remembered that the problems first surfaced in March. Sometimes the depression reached the point of totally giving up.

"There's been testimony that in March at least on two occasions Angie Duensing felt that she had observed you I believe either rubbing Lorna's back or holding her to the extent—I'm not sure what, but is that possible?"

"Oh, yes."

"Why?"

"Well, to tell someone that God loves them and that people care about them and that I care about her and that she is okay and nobody's, you know, rejecting her because of a mistake, nobody's rejecting her because maybe she's failed with the kids a couple times, to say that and stand across the room when she's crying and hurting would be not a full communication of that. So, sure, like many people I would comfort her that way, give her affirmation."

"Was this unique to Lorna, this method of comforting…"

"No."

"—and affirmation?"

"No. It's just the way I am."

"Is it something that you use in counseling or even in your day-to-day relationships with people?"

"I have a pretty open relationship. I express myself that way, yes."

Tom met Darrel, June 7

Shaw asked about Darrel. Tom met him through Lorna on June 7, 1983, when he came to church that morning. No, he had never met him previously.

"You indicated this occurred on June 7, 1983. Is that correct?"

"Yes, I did."

"How are you so sure of that particular day?"

"Well, I knew it was June and then it's also in my calendar book."

Shaw had the calendar book marked for identification.

"Let's back up a little bit of time if we can, Mr. Bird. First of all, prior to this meeting on whatever date it may have been, had you ever met Mr. Carter before?"

"No."

"And is there any question in your mind but what this particular meeting that we're talking about occurred in the church?"

"Yes."

"And where did this particular meeting take place that you're talking about?"

"In the secretary's office."

Shaw asked whether Tom heard Darrel's testimony alleging the meeting took place most likely on May 18, 19 or 20.

"Well, first of all, were you here on the 19th?"

"No, the 19th I was in Topeka...I'm a member of the Family Life Committee of the Kansas District of the Lutheran Church, Missouri Synod...a committee made up of pastors and laymen who work in various churches to encourage family programs throughout the year."

Tom produced a receipt from May 19 showing he entered the Kansas turnpike at Emporia and exited at 10:05 a.m., about an hour drive (55 mile per hour speed limits were in place in 1983). He produced a second receipt showing he arrived back in Emporia at 1906—7:06 p.m. Certainly, Tom could not have met Darrel on May 19.

"How about the 20th?"

"The 20th? Lorna Anderson was taking the day off that day. She wasn't present....Marty Anderson was returning from his two-week leave—I mean not his—his two weeks of guard duty up in Washington, and she took her children and she went up there to greet him on the airplane."

"How about the 18th of May? Do you think you were there on that day or that meeting could have been held that day?"

"I don't think so."

"And do you have any specific reason why you don't think so?"

"Well, I haven't accounted for every bit of my time in 1983. In my knowledge, I mean I know that Mrs. Anderson called me on a Monday and told me that she had set up an appointment with Darrel Carter, and I know we met the next day and it was Tuesday. It was a Tuesday we met."

Shaw asked Tom to explain the purpose of the meeting. "The youth were planning a trip to Eureka Springs, Arkansas, in August; and I work with the youth along with Alan Rees and some of the other youth board members. And we were making plans not only for the trip but we were also working toward fund raisers to help the youth in that trip because it would be a fairly expensive trip per child."

"And so what happened?"

"Going all the way to, well, on the calendar there May 21st we had a youth board meeting which is a combination of the youth board at Messiah and a combination of the youth board at Faith. And that that time—I can't remember. It wasn't—it was like right before the meeting or after the meeting, Reverend Kalsow brought me a brochure among a lot of the mailings that we get for fund raisers. And that brochure was a brochure concerning well—well, buying firecrackers on consignment, fireworks, and selling them; and Larry said maybe this would be a good idea to check out to see if we could sell fireworks with the youth, maybe set up a stand there at Faith's parking lot."

"What happened next?"

"It was discussed a very short time at that point among some of the people, and then the next week I thought it over some more and I recognized that we couldn't—couldn't sell fireworks in the city limits as far as I knew, and setting up a booth would be not feasible there at the church parking lot.

"I looked through my membership list to see if there was anybody on a road outside of town that might be on a good road that had a lot of traffic where we could maybe set up a booth if they would agree to it, and there really wasn't anybody in my membership who would be in a good spot.

"And I bounced this idea back and forth with Lorna. This would have been—I don't know what day it would have been. It would have to have been sometime between the 21st and 24th we discussed it. And she said, 'Well, Darrel Carter has had a fireworks stand here in Emporia for a long time, and maybe he would agree to some of the youth working for him.'

"And I thought, well, maybe that would be pretty good because that way we won't have to order the material and go through that hassle, we wouldn't have to build a booth, we wouldn't have to do a lot of things. It would just be a matter of going and working and it would cut down on a lot of the organizing. And so I said, 'Well, maybe we will present that idea.' And on—"

"Now, did you have another meeting with the youth board or anyone involved with the youth group?"

"We didn't meet with the youth board anymore, but on the 29th we had what's called the Lutheran Youth Fellowship meeting which would be the youth, the actual youth; and that was a planning meeting.

"On the 29th of May we were planning a campout which was to be the 10th and 11th of June, and we were also planning the Eureka Springs trip which was going to be in August. During that meeting we assigned work to do of various youth to prepare for this campout and prepare for our trip to Eureka Springs Passion Play. And we discussed the plans for both, tried to figure out how much the cost would be for both and then presented a few ideas about how to raise money to help pay for those."

"Did one of these plans or ideas concern the use or the selling of fireworks?"

"Yeah. We went through a list of possibilities for fund raisers, bake sale, garage sale, a car wash, a kind of a youth slave day, selling firecrackers, and then tried to see what kind of response the youth would make to those ideas."

Shaw referred to Tom's calendar. "The charge which was filed against you has alleged a meeting but it didn't really give a specific date. Is that right?"

"I think it said on or about—"

"May?"

"The month of May."

Shaw asked whether the purpose of Tom giving him the date book was to show that the meeting occurred on June 7. Yes. He asked Tom whether or not he had mentioned June during the tape recorded meeting with Darrel, and didn't Darrel respond, "Yeah." Yes, that is true.

Shaw had Tom identify the notations for May 21 and May 29. Then he asked what it was Tom wrote in on June 7? "'9:00, D. Carter,' and then it says, "Yth,' stands for youth."

Tom said Lorna called him Monday night to set up the meeting—it was his day off.

Darrel goes to church

Shaw asked Tom to describe the meeting at the church. "Darrel Carter had come in and I had never met him. I was in my office, and I saw him walk by my office and go into the office of Lorna Anderson which is the secretary's office. And I had to finish up some paperwork of some kind so I was there a couple minutes doing some paperwork in my office, and then I went in there and joined them in the secretary's office." It was "about 9:15."

"Lorna Anderson was seated behind the secretary's desk in that small circle (office chair) there (he pointed at the floor plan displayed for the jurors to see)....I, well—Lorna introduced us and I shook hands with Darrel Carter, and then I just backed up and I leaned against that file cabinet that's right there by that A (again, he pointed at the floor plan)"

Tom leaned on the file cabinet during the entire discussion. The office window and door remained open the entire time.

"Tell us what happened then after you were introduced to Mr. Carter."

"Lorna introduced us and she said that, 'This is Darrel Carter. He is a homebuilder here in town' and done some work at her house; and then I proceeded to say, 'Well, we just moved here and—a couple years ago and we were thinking about building a house but we couldn't afford it at the time but we may build a house one of these days. We came and rented for a while and then we bought a house. We might want to build one of these days.' And Darrel responded by saying he would be sure to give a bid on it if that time ever came.

"Then I proceeded to talk to him about the idea that Lorna and I had talked about, the—we wanted to see if he was open to the idea of maybe the youth group selling firecrackers for him working in his booth. I understood that he had two booths here in town, and maybe sometime before the 4th of July holidays he would like some youth to be scheduled in working. I told him that we were taking this Eureka Springs trip and the youth group were trying to raise money and we wanted to work out that as a possibility.

"Darrel Carter—he responded by saying that he was behind in the house that he was building over in West Ridge and was wanting to get it finished by the end of June, and he was going to have to work pretty hard and stay pretty busy to get it finished by the end of June.

"He also said that he had a soccer tournament or game coming up I think in Wichita or at least against a Wichita team—I don't remember which there—and that was coming up at the end of June and so that would take him away for a while when he would be selling the firecrackers.

"And then—well we got off on a tangent talking about soccer for a while. He talked about how he worked at—you know, with the soccer league and worked helping build those soccer fields out there, and I talked about my boys growing up and maybe playing soccer. I thought it was a good sport; he thought it was a good sport. We shared the idea that it doesn't cost a lot of money for equipment, you know, and there's not as many injuries as like football and so I thought it was a real growing sport and I would like my boys to participate in it someday. I had a four-year-old and two-year-old coming up.

"And Lorna shared that she had some girls growing up and girls can play soccer, too. It's not like football, you know, that eliminates girls.

"So we got back on track I guess talking about the fireworks possibilities again, and we discussed maybe some of the problems that would be involved we needed to decide before we made that kind of decision like organizing my youth and would those youth be responsible if they're there and Darrel expressed some concern about whether, you know, some accident would happen or something with fireworks, something be set off, somebody burned or hurt. And that was a real concern." (Tom developed his own concern as he testified at length. He feared he was putting the jury to sleep.)

He asked him about the various concerns over firecrackers. "There was just a lot of questions to be answered before any decisions would be made. He wanted to check his schedule, just see exactly when they would be needed if they were going to be needed; so some questions were still to be asked."

One question dealt with how the kids would be paid. There were legal and insurance issues to settle. They came to the close of their meeting. "Darrel still wanted to think about it and I still had to work on answering some questions, and so it was pretty much still left up in the air and we decided we would get back with each other about it."

"Were there any set plans as to who was to get back with who or how that was to take place?"

"No set plans. I told him I would contact him." Darrel told him the approximate location of the house on West Ridge and told Tom just to look for a brown truck. Tom left the room and saw Darrel leave the church moments later.

"Now, during this conversation, Mr. Bird, did you ever ask Darrel Carter to help you or assist you in any way in getting rid of Martin Anderson?"

"No."

"Did Lorna in your presence ever make statements at this meeting about getting rid of Martin Anderson?"

"No."

"Did you ever tell Darrel Carter that you were going to do it or go to Topeka and kill Martin Anderson?"

"No."

"Did Lorna in your presence?"

"No."

"Did you at that time ever tell Darrel Carter that you loved Lorna Anderson?"

"No."

"Did you ever say to him, 'I am a man of God. I am going to kill Martin Anderson?'"

"I never said anything like that."

"Did you say that you would preside at the funeral and Darrel Carter could be a pallbearer?"

"No."

"Were you familiar with Andersons' insurance status?"

"No."

House inspection

Shaw asked Tom to describe the next contact he had with Darrel. "It was the next week and I can't recall the exact day, and it was not an appointment type of thing so I didn't write it down. As close as I can understand trying to picture it in my mind, it was—it would have been either the 13th, 14th or 15th of June, one of those three days."

"Where did you see him?"

"At his house that he was building."

"What was your purpose in going to the house where Darrel Carter was working?"

"Well, to wrap up the previous conversation about what we were going to do with the fireworks proposal."

"Okay. What was your feeling or your thoughts relative to the fireworks proposal when you went out there?"

"My thoughts were that I pretty much wanted to scrap the idea as far as, you know, my concern with it was…I had recognized over the weekend that it would probably be too much work to get them organized and I didn't really want to do that organizational work.

"We had had a campout in between those meetings. We had a campout with the youth that I and a number of youth, Alan Rees, the youth director, went to Lake Melvern on the 10th and 11th of June. And we had a problem with the youth.

"There were about 16 youth there, and three or four of them had stashed away some alcohol and had been drinking, and so I was very disappointed and troubled by that. And so I wanted to—I had decided I was going to spend my time working with youth as far as topics and growth and things like that rather than—rather than fund raisers, spending time with fund raisers; and so it was just a matter of deciding what I was going to do with my time. And by then I thought, it would just be too much to organize from my point of view."

"What happened when you arrived at the house?"

"I just walked in the room—I walked in through the garage and stepped up into a kitchen and saw a young man there, and I asked him where Darrel Carter was, and he said, 'He's around in the back part of the house.' And just as I started to step that way, Darrel Carter walked in."

Tom noticed that the house remained uncompleted, but the walls were up and sheet-rocked. He remembered some of the trim had been installed and, in fact, Darrel was working on the trim in the bedroom when he arrived.

"I just said, 'Well, what have you thought, you know, concerning this possibility, this proposal?' And he was saying he really didn't think it would work out because it would cut into the profits too much and he was just going to try to find a way to get everything done himself. And I think he had just some concerns about turning things over to some young people, and I told him that I shared the same concern and that I didn't think it would work out either." They both agreed to scrap the idea.

Then Tom, who admired the house, said to Darrel, "It looks like it's a pretty nice house."

Darrel proudly took him on a tour, ending up in front of the big picture window in front. "He asked me how Lorna and Marty were getting along?"

"And what did you say?"

"I said that I knew that they had some troubles in the past. It seemed like things were getting a little bit better now and I had some concern...I meant I had been counseling and talking with both of them."

"What did he say?"

"Darrel said he knew that they had had some marital problems and that they were pretty serious in the summer of '82. He said that Lorna had been beaten up pretty bad and he had seen her and it was kind of upsetting.

"I told him in March that I had noticed that Lorna had come to church a couple times with black eyes and I had asked her about that and she had made up some excuse about some accident holding the kids and being thrown off balance, and that I suspected that Marty had beaten her at that time."

"What did he say?"

"He said that, he knew it for sure and Marty's a pretty tough fellow sometimes and that—well, he was just kind of mouthing off, he said somebody, does something like that to his wife ought to be shot."

"Did you take that serious?"

"No. I mean that was just a figure of speech."

"Did you come to any conclusion as a result of this conversation the two of you were having?"

"Yes. I told him, something ought to be done when it's like this. I said, 'I know they speak harsh words sometimes, Lorna and Marty; but, if Marty loses his temper, he could really hurt her bad.' And so I said, 'Something ought to be done.'"

"Did you come to any conclusion as to what should be done?"

"Yes. I told Darrel that maybe we ought to confront Lorna and have her to go to a wife-abuse agency and let them tell her what to do about this and also to deal with Marty by not turning him in to the police, but to find out what to do with Marty to give her support along that line.

"And Darrel agreed that something ought to be done but, he had seen her beaten a whole year ago and so—and I had seen her beaten back early in the spring, I had seen the black eye. And so nothing had happened recently; and together we concluded, there's no use doing anything now.

"I said, 'Well, if you ever see her with black eyes and, you know, suspicion of anything happening, would you call me?' And if I ever see her with black eyes and am suspicious of her being beaten that I would call him and we would both together encourage this.

"And he thought that would be a good idea. We would try something along that line to encourage her to go to a wife-abuse agency."

July and later

He next saw Darrel on July 4 at the firecracker stand on 24th Avenue.

"I got out of the car and I started walking toward the booth, and I saw Darrel Carter inside the booth and he was talking with Kermit Grother who's a member of my congregation. He was leaning on the booth.

"And I stepped up to them and said hello and 'How are you doing' to both of them. And they greeted me and I just joined their conversation with them.

"They were talking about soccer, and I asked Darrel Carter how their soccer team did because he told me they had this big tournament. And he said they got beat pretty bad by this Wichita team, and he said they kind of had the teams stacked against them I guess."

They talked for about 10 minutes. Tom asked how the business was going? Darrel told him that a big rain had washed out a huge part of their inventory. Tom bought some fireworks and asked Darrel for a discount, but got none.

Shaw made sure the jury understood Tom's claim. He had met Darrel three times in his life, and the first time was June 7.

Shaw shifted gears, asking Tom about his vacation in July. Tom described the trip to Hardy and St. Louis where he and Sandy stayed with Charlie and Carolyn Smith.

"Mr. Bird, you have testified earlier that your wife Sandy was killed in a car wreck on July the 17th, 1983. Is that correct?"

"Yes."

"Was she alone at that time?"

"Yes."

"Was the death and her—was the accident and her death publicized in the local newspaper to your knowledge?"

"Yes, it was."

"Prior to her death had you ever been to that location where the accident occurred?"

"No."

"Was the manner of her death similar to the first plot which Darrel Carter described when he testified earlier?"

"Yes, it was."

"How did this death of Sandy affect you?"

"I was pretty much devastated."

"After her burial when did you return back to Emporia?"

"Friday the 22nd of July."

Shaw turned to Angie's testimony. He remembered meeting with her on June 24. "Angie came into my office one day and said she wanted to talk to me, and she seemed serious, and so we sat down together and I asked her what was her concerns. She shared that she thought that Lorna was getting too dependent upon me and too close to me in her counseling and that she didn't know if this was healthy or not.

"I said that I had counseled with Lorna a lot and that I thought Lorna was growing as a person. She had self-esteem problems, that I wanted to continue to help her. I recognized her dependence upon me for counseling and for her self-esteem just because I was her boss and she was doing the job of secretary and she felt good about her work and I helped make her feel good about her work."

Shaw asked whether these were formal counseling sessions or casual? "Well, in March and April there was a set time we were meeting. And then other times I would see just in her work whether she was down or not, and I would say, 'What's the matter? How are you doing?' And then she would share with me and I would talk with her there. So at that point it was an informal type of thing. I could tell when she was down."

Tom told Angie that he hoped Lorna would, "hold her self-esteem and self-worth independent of anybody else. That would be the goal."

"Did you on June 24th, 1983—was this what she was conveying to you? Did she eventually tell you that at some point in time she had had strong feelings for you?"

"Yes."

"What was your reaction to that?"

"Well, my first reaction was, 'What did I do to make you feel that way?' I asked her, 'Did I ever make a pass at you or anything like that?'; and she said, 'Oh, no, you didn't do that. It's just because we've talked. We talked about everything. We've shared so much when we work together and we share the same kind of ideals and we share the same kind of work and goals.' It was our talking together and our closeness and openness as far as the talk."

During the summer of 1983, Tom and Angie's daily contact had lessened. Unlike the previous summer when they spent a great amount of time laying the groundwork for the preschool, now they each had more than enough to keep them separately busy.

Shaw clarified that no one had talked to Tom prior to June 24, complaining about Lorna. Then he asked about the July 23rd talk Tom had with Angie at his house. "Mostly we just talked about Sandy, but she expressed a concern that I'm vulnerable now; I'm in a different situation and that she was concerned maybe that dependency would really go overboard at this time."

Subsequent to that talk, Tom met with Lorna. "I wasn't working at the church [again yet] but I went back to the church because a number of memorial cards and letters were coming in and I wanted to collect those to write thank you's. And I saw Lorna there, and I asked her to step into my office for a minute, that there were some concerns to deal with. And I told her that there was a feeling that there was some vulnerability here, the problem of dependency and that it had been expressed and we needed to deal with it."

"What were you saying?"

"I was basically saying that if people are bothered or are going to be bothered, there's a potential for that, then the church shouldn't be hurt and so we need to respond to it and do something. Lorna became upset. She started crying. This is one of the things that bothers her is criticism. And so she just stared crying."

Tom tried to talk to her but the phone rang, and people were coming and going because it was Vacation Bible School week. She left while he was on the phone. He finished his call and followed her out to the parking lot.

"I knew I needed to deal with the situation. That's why I started talking to her, and I knew she was upset and I didn't know what she was going to do. She was leaving in a pretty upset state and I didn't want to let her go out at that point."

Tom found her in the van already pulling out. He stepped in front of the van and she stopped. She sat crying. "I got in on the passenger's side, and I said, 'We've got to talk it out. We've got to settle down.'" Tom felt upset as well and didn't want to have to deal with the problem at all. "She said she couldn't go back in there if people are thinking things. She didn't want to be seen in my office crying and like that, 'People are going to say things no matter what we do'; so she wanted to just forget it and go; and I said, 'No.'"

She started driving and they ended up at the turnpike rest area, but he could not recall anything about how they got there. He spent the time talking to her, not noticing where she drove. "We had talked. We had settled each other down; and I said, 'There's just some things to do and the proper thing to do would be to respond through the lay ministers.' They were the ones who hired her, and I thought it would be best if she would submit her resignation to them and put the choice in their hands.

"Lorna expressed that she would write a letter of resignation, but the way she expressed it I thought that resignation would be pretty bitter and I wanted to again continue to settle her down. I didn't think it would be right to write a bitter, angry type of resignation. And so we talked about maybe what would be written."

Shaw asked how long this trip took. Maybe 45 minutes to an hour fifteen minutes. When did it occur? Late afternoon, perhaps 4:30 to 6:30.

"Was there anything to these rumors insofar as you were concerned? And by that I mean were you having any feelings or relationships developing with Lorna?"

"No." Tom said they worked together and "understood each other very well." He saw her as a friend. They shared thoughts and ideas about their children. "I got where I counted on her a lot for the work she did and the help she gave, and there was an emotional dependency on her part to always talk to me about her feelings toward things." And no, Tom harbored no feelings about a long term relationship with Lorna.

Shaw asked about Larry Kalsow's call the next day. Kalsow told him about Angie's call and wanted to talk. "I talked to him about our relationship and he expressed the concern and said, well, you know, maybe after talking with Angie and he thinks that maybe Lorna should resign."

"What did you say?"

"I said that I was a little upset because I didn't think it was his position to make that decision, and so I told him I would handle it through the board of lay ministers. He agreed with that."

Shaw asked him what he meant when he told Kalsow he cared for Lorna. "I cared about her as a person, as a friend, as someone that I had a good, close working relationship with that I didn't just want to cut off because I didn't want to hurt; and so I mean I really cared for her with a genuine Christian love."

"You've used the term 'Christian love.' What does that mean to you, Pastor?"

"I believe in open relationships. I mean open emotions and feelings and sharing. And Christian love means when someone hurts, you hurt with them; when someone mourns, you mourn with them; when someone is happy, you're happy with them and that you accept people where they're at; who they are. You don't judge them; you don't put conditions upon them."

Tom related coming to church on Sunday and finding Lorna's resignation letter on his desk. Don Froelich stopped in his office and said he got one, too, and "We'll just all have to talk about this."

The lay ministers came to his house the next day. "They shared with me that the—any kind of rumors were not inside the church and they had heard nothing from any members except for Angie and that they were concerned about my vulnerability and they were concerned about what people would think, and I agreed with that concern that I didn't want the church to be hurt or any members to be having any doubts or problems with anything like that. And I put it in their hands. I said, 'You decide.'"

They planned to accept Lorna's resignation but wanted to talk some more. "Ultimately they didn't accept the resignation....Don Froelich told me that they had talked about it some more and that he had talked with Martin Anderson. Martin Anderson had called him and was very angry at this situation. He said he didn't believe any of this and he felt that any kind of action like accepting a resignation would be bad and wrong and he wanted Lorna to stay working at the church."

The leaders met with Lorna and "gave her a vote of confidence to continue to work." But they reduced the pressures on Tom. They wanted him to preach and teach, then slowly go back to other duties. They told him not to do any counseling for a while. "I agreed with that. I was very low and hurting pretty bad and I wasn't really ready to continue any kind of emotionally draining type of work."

Shaw asked whether Tom ever threatened to quit if the leaders accepted Lorna's resignation. "No."

Lunch time

After a much-needed lunch recess, Tom once again took the stand. Shaw asked him about the day when he and Lorna worked together on the computer. The church had purchased the computer—a Zenith 100—with funds from a memorial to Sandy Bird.

"We just had unboxed the computer and plugged in the monitor on the computer and the printer, and Lorna and I had begun to work on the word processor. We had just opened up the notebook that deals with word processing. And we began to work on that."

"Do you recall Sharon Meyer coming in at that time?"

"Yes."

"What were you doing?"

"We were excited about having the computer there but I was also a little bit nervous about how it was going to be used. We had just begun working on it. Joyce Rosenboom came to the reception window and was talking to us, and she was asking about the computer, and I was looking. I was on the left side of the desk looking at the notebook. Lorna was next to me at the keyboard."

Shaw asked whether Tom talked with Sharon about that day at a later meeting. Yes. He asked for specifics about that conversation. "I could tell Sharon was depressed and she wanted to talk to me, and I was down that day, too. And we both began talking, and she expressed that she and Angie had talked about my relationship with Lorna and whether Lorna was again too dependent upon me. And then she expressed the idea that maybe it would be better if Lorna would resign."

Tom told Sharon he thought the lay ministers had settled the matter. He told her he had quit counseling Lorna, that they just worked together. He said he "didn't really want to deal with it. I was upset. I had just gotten back going to work full time and I was struggling with that. I didn't have a lot of emotional energy still. I was still hurting and I was till spread real thin trying to take care of the three children and take care of the work. And so I was kind of let down that this cropped up again."

Tom told Sharon he would not fire Lorna. If she felt strongly she should go back to the lay ministers and tell them.

"Did you have any conversations with her at that point about whether Lorna was judgmental or critical or anything of that nature?"

"As a matter of fact, Lorna was very helpful with me. I was struggling with the idea of getting three kids up, changing diapers, taking one to the babysitter's, one to kindergarten and one to preschool on these days; and that wore me out.

"And I was trying to do a lot and I was struggling with it. A lot of people were really helping me. The people of the church were tremendous to me at this time.

"And Lorna was a support, too. And I relied on her and I would ask her, 'How do you brush a little girl's hair when you get them ready in the morning?'; and a lot of questions along that line. She was helpful because she had little children, too.

"There were times when I was very sensitive to people's criticism, and other people would criticize me sometimes about, 'Well, you're too lenient with the children'; and then somebody would come the next week and say I'm too harsh with the children; and I was very sensitive to that.

"So I shared with Sharon that Lorna was not critical of me, that she was helpful without being judgmental or critical in the way I took care of my children."

"Did you at that time talk at all about the turnpike incident?"

"Yes. She asked me about that. I guess her husband told her about that and that bothered her. And I said, 'Well, that was probably a dumb thing to do but it was just what happened.'"

Shaw asked whether they both became emotional, held hands and cried. Yes. Tom thought that the conversation had ended and the issue resolved.

Chris Kimble had referenced twice seeing Tom driving with Lorna in her van. Shaw asked what Kimble witnessed? "'Cause we were a new church we didn't have very much equipment for doing the clerical work. We put out a newsletter each month and we sent it out to 800 residents, and this was about a ten, twelve page newsletter.

"We don't have a mimeograph machine or an electronic stencil cutter or a coping machine at our church. Messiah had a copying machine and we had an arrangement to use theirs.

"I had a routine each month and a deadline to meet because we had a number of people who would come in to collate these newsletters. So to make a long story short, the only time that I can remember where I would be driving the van would be when I took her to the School Board of Education building, where they had an electronic stencil cutter; and there she would take the copy material and the pictures that we would copy and she would copy those.

"Each electronic stencil would take about ten minutes to do so I would drop her off; I would put up a couple boxes to box these things up in and then I would go to Messiah and use their copy machine to get the rest of the newsletter ready.

"Then I would go pick her up, come back to Messiah and then she would run them off on a mimeograph." They did this every month.

Back to Lorna again

Shaw asked about the Lord's Lamb school year. It ran the same as the public schools. Then they started Mother's Day Out? Yes. "That was basically just a childcare, drop-in childcare type of program."

Mother's Day Out meant a regular stream of people coming and going on Tuesdays and Thursdays. Yes, it was busier at church, like in May, during the school year.

Shaw asked Tom about his relationship with Marty during the fall of 1983. "We were good friends."

And Lorna? "We were also very good friends."

Shaw asked about a trip Tom took to Little Rock during October. Why did you do that?

"I would say I just generally hit rock bottom in my grief at that point. Work had gotten to me and the daily care of the children had gotten to me, and I just one day when I was really feeling down, I was feeling lonely, upset and tired, just one of those get up early in the morning and fix breakfast and dress the kids and you run one over to the babysitter and another to the kindergarten and another dropped off at preschool; and I walked into the office and it was 9:00 in the morning and I was already tired. And I was already feeling like I didn't have any energy for the rest of the day, and so I made arrangements for the kids to be taken care of and I just left for Little Rock."

Tom saw Charlie Smith in Little Rock and stayed about two days.

During April, June and July, did the children ever stay at Lorna's house? Yes. "Sandy's babysitter had lupus, and every once in a while she would have a spell."

"Who was that?"

"Brenda Schwinn."

Tom kind of remembered Esther Aldrete, but insisted he never left the children there until 7:00 or 8:00 in the evening. Perhaps they stayed until noon or 5:00 p.m. a couple of times.

Jan Mead's scandalous testimony addressed

"We've also had some testimony from a Miss Jan Mead indicating that Lorna had told her that the two of you had had sexual relations and left town on occasion. Did you back in February, March or April or May ever have sexual relations with Lorna Anderson?"

"No."

"Did you ever go to Topeka or Wichita with Lorna Anderson?"

"Not just by ourselves."

"Did you go in a group for some type of church group activities?"

"Yes."

"How many times?"

"One time."

"Did you other than the time on the turnpike ever leave town with Lorna Anderson?"

"Yes."

"When was that?"

"That was back in March."

"And what was that occasion then?"

"That was the very first time Lorna presented to me a real deep depression. It was right after we had done one of those newsletters, and I could tell she was depressed. And she made the statement that when she gets through with this newsletter, then she's just going to be through all together, meaning she was going to take her life." Tom got into Lorna's van and they drove around for "a couple of hours" talking. They left the city limits during part of that drive, but other than the turnpike incident of July 24, it was the only time they left town alone together.

Shaw asked about Marty's murder. Where were you? In Topeka. He saw Lorna at the hospital the next day. And the funeral was on the following Tuesday, November 8, at Faith. "Pastor Kalsow led the service and I preached the sermon."

"Would it be normal for you to preside at or preach the sermon at a funeral of one of your parishioners?"

"Yes."

Shaw asked about Agent Winsor's interview on November 9. "Did he remind you or say anything to you about rumors that were going around?"

"Yes. He said there had been some rumors and he would like more information about." Tom told the investigator he had heard about rumors, too, and "I hope they will be laid to rest pretty soon."

Following Winsor's interview, Tom left for a two-day conference in Wichita (but still he did not mention meeting Terry Smith there, though the two dated several times at the conference). "It was a very difficult week as far as getting a lot of my work done at the church and I was going to this meeting and I had a lot of arrangements to make. I was also very concerned about Lorna and how she was doing at this point being a couple of days after the funeral."

"Why?"

"She had expressed a lot of grief in her situation, and that day that her parents were leaving and a lot of other people were leaving and I knew she was heading for a deep depression of emptiness because everybody was going their own way which it happens in a funeral—after a funeral is that everybody is gathered together and there's a lot of support there all at once: and then after the funeral, people were going back to their homes; and then all the sudden a sudden emptiness. And that was part of it for me, too. I was leaving town for a while and everybody else was soon to be going their way, that's hard on a person who is in the state or situation she was in."

"Could you identify with what you anticipated she would be going through?"

"Yes. I think a lot of people recognize I could identify with that."

"Why?"

"Well, I lost my wife and I knew the kind of depressions that hit...You have a feeling of emptiness; you feel sapped; you feel like all the sudden there's a million decisions to make and there's nobody to talk to get support on those decisions. You feel like you're hurting. Wherever you go in the house you're reminded constantly of the person who's gone."

"Like how?"

"You see pictures or you see letters or you see things that constantly remind you that someone else lived here, too, and was part of your life. The kids mention their mom and you have to talk to them about it even though you don't want to. So I know how difficult that is. It's a long, hard day and then put the children to bed at night and then just empty."

"Is it scary?"

"I guess it's scary. You're afraid of the future. You wonder about hope for the future; you wonder about making it. There's a lot of questions still left, yes."

"Do you have concerns about other people, your relationships with other people?"

"Well, you're called as a minister not just to preach and teach but you're called to care about people; a commitment to people, giving to people."

Shaw referred to November 10 and the two cards Tom gave Lorna that day. Had he given her anything else? Yes, "a booklet on what to do at the sudden death of a loved one."

Shaw showed him the cards. Tom identified the handwriting as his. He found the cards "in a cellophane envelope in a package that had been sitting on my dresser for a number of months, and these are some things that my wife had ordered from some kind of gift company..." Even now, there still were several cards in the packet.

"Now, why did you prepare these documents?"

"Well, I felt kind of bad about—as Lorna had expressed the feeling she was being kind of deserted by everybody. I thought, 'Well, I'll give her a couple cards here, write out a couple notes, keep her going. I'll come back after this conference and talk with her, help her though some troubled times." He expected to return Friday night, but his church duties would keep him busy until Saturday night, the first chance he would have to talk with her.

"Did you search out specific cards for specific printed messages?"

"No, I just pulled them out."

"How did these get to Lorna?"

"On my way out of town I dropped them by."

"Did you make any explanation to her when you did this or anything?"

"Yes. I didn't have much time because I was running late, and I had this note and I had one written Thursday. And I said, 'Lorna, you're going to get depressed. You're going to have some down times. The day is going to seem long. When you get down, read these. You know, read this one on Thursday anytime you get down." He told her to do the same with the other card on Friday.

Shaw asked Tom to read the handwriting on one of the cards out loud.

"I love you and I'm confident of the future and that makes the present okay. Take care of the kids. Love you always, Tom."

"What did the term 'I love you' mean?"

"It meant that I was committed to care for her as long as she needed that care and I was committed to stick and stand beside her through the grief or whatever was going to go on in her life, in her troubles, and that I wouldn't give up on that commitment."

"What is the statement 'I am confident of the future' intended to mean?"

"The future is a big question in a situation like this. I remember after my wife died I didn't know what the future was going to bring; I didn't know if I should move on to another job, if I could handle the kids, if I could handle all the decisions I was making. A feeling of inadequacy makes you wonder about the future, but I knew I was making it step by step.

"When you're in the thick of a loss, you wonder whether you're going to make it. The tendency is to just kind of give up and let yourself slide. So I told her I was confident of the future. That means even though there were troubles right then, she was going to make it through that."

Tom read the next card. "You are so very special. I hope time goes fast until Saturday evening. It should with all the work and the children. I love you so very much and that's forever. Tom."

"What did the term 'I love you so very much' refer to?"

"It referred to the amount of commitment I had toward her and the caring I had toward her."

"What did the term, 'Your are so very special' mean?"

"When I would talk to her about her self-esteem, I believe she was a very special person and had a tremendous amount of potential." Tom used similar words to encourage others. "Everybody's special."

Shaw asked whether this meant, "an ongoing commitment to, for example, share your lives together?"

"No. Stand beside her."

"What was your feeling, what was your relationship, with Lorna at this particular time?"

"I felt a very strong bond with her because of her experience of the loss. People that shared with me, 'Pastor, you're going to be able to minister to people. You're going to be able to help people. You're going to be able to be closer to people because of what you've been through yourself in the future'; and that was true. When people died in my congregation and I did their funeral, I felt closer to the families and a particular bond with Lorna because

I had been working with her for a year."

"Was this bond anything in the nature of a physical attraction to her?"

"No. I enjoyed her being around."

"Was this bond anything in the nature of a sexual relationship with her?"

"No."

Meeting Darrel again

Shaw moved to the December 12 meeting between Tom and Darrel.

Shaw asked how the meeting came about.

Susan told him about all the rumors and that she traced them to Darrel Carter. "It was rumors concerning my relationship with Lorna and rumors concerning an involvement in the death of Martin Anderson."

"Did this upset you?"

"Yes, it did….Rumors tear a person up personally, and that's what it was doing to me, because there's no way to fight rumors. You can't confront them and work through those.

"Then also I was concerned about the church. I know that many people in the church had been questioned concerning matters, and it hurts the church 'cause it plants doubts in people's minds, it causes them to freeze up and just wonder."

"What did you do after you were advised of this information from Susan Ewert?"

He remembered that Lorna claimed that Darrel had an ongoing affair with Julie Palmer, and he had also heard that elsewhere around town. "And I thought, okay, everybody is vulnerable to rumors and it really wasn't fair to spread rumors; and if Darrel Carter was spreading them, he needs to be confronted with that."

Tom felt that by going to Julie and telling her that he wanted to talk to Darrel, he would send the message that everybody is subject to rumors, and Darrel would stop. Shaw asked him to describe the meeting with Julie.

"I was all ready to go to visit her and to tell this to her to get this message to Darrel Carter, but right when she answered the door, then I realized, 'Well, this is a person here. I shouldn't be doing something like that.' I was a friend of Julie Palmer's and I didn't really want to her to be hurt. So I kind of stammered around a little bit, and then I just went ahead and said, 'Go ahead—please give a message to Darrel Carter that I want to see him."

"Did you make the statement during the course of that conversation that you didn't want to use any phones?"

"Yes."

"Why?"

"I wanted to talk to Darrel face to face."

Tom said Darrel called him on December 12. It surprised him because he did not expect a call. Since he did not hear from Darrel right after seeing Julie, he thought perhaps Darrel had gotten the message and there was no need for a confrontation.

"Do you recall how it was that the meeting at the bowling alley was set up?"

"When Darrel called me, he said that he wanted to meet with me; and I said, 'Okay'; he said he wanted to talk about this deal that his brother was involved in."

"How was it to the best of your recollection that the meeting was established at the bowling alley?"

"He told me he was working all over the place so I couldn't come there. He suggested a parking lot of some kind, and then he said he couldn't meet during the morning or he couldn't meet at that time, he would have to wait until later on in the day. He suggested 4:30 or 5:00; and I said, 'Okay, 5:00.' And then I thought for a while and said, 'The bowling alley on Graham Street.'"

"What was your purpose in going to this meeting, Mr. Bird?"

"I wanted to talk about how rumors were hurting me, and I just surmised whether he was involved in those rumors."

To the tapes

Shaw asked whether it was true that several times on the tape Tom talked about rumors? Yes.

"There were occasions when you made reference to the fact that, 'I have kids, you have kids.' What were those references to?"

"That was another concern of mine, that kids can be pretty blunt to each other sometimes in school and some older kid could say something to my son or daughter and hurt them; and I didn't want that to happen."

Shaw mentioned that twice Tom referenced selling of firecrackers. Yes. Why did you mention this?

"That was a reminder, 'This is how we met. This was our point of contact. This is how Lorna introduced us.'"

Darrel never denied meeting to talk about firecrackers. Shaw repeated various quotes from the tape and asked Tom to explain them. "Okay, I was kind of playing an ace in the hole there. You know, you got kids, I got kids," he had said.

"We were discussing Julie Palmer, contacting her; and the ace in the hole there meant that I was saying, 'Darrel, you're vulnerable to rumors, too, because the rumors were that you were having a relationship with her so you're vulnerable to that, too. You have kids. Your children could be hurt if things like that spread. My children could be hurt if things like that spread.' And I wanted him to recognize that. I had kind of hoped that would make a strong point."

"We've got to keep each other clean here just for the sake of the kids. Now, that's our number one concern," Shaw quoted Tom from the tape.

"I think that these rumors just muddy people's lives and reputations, and I felt that's what was happening to me, that these rumors were muddying my life. And I was hurt by it, and I felt my kids were going to be hurt by it."

"During the course of this conversation Mr. Carter had indicated that he had seen all of the reports. Do you recall that?"

"Yes."

"Had you at that time seen any of the reports?"

"No."

Shaw read another quote. "Well, I'm steering clear. I just wanted to touch bases and make sure that we just—all we talked about was possibly my youth group selling firecrackers for you."

"One of my concerns was that somebody would make a connection by way of these rumors saying that, 'Well, Lorna introduced Darrel Carter to Pastor Bird'; and Darrel Carter's brother had been arrested at this time and Lorna had been arrested at this time and people would ask 'What is the connection there?' Who knows who and who's part of what. And I wanted him to understand that I was steering clear of any kind of connection with the fact that his brother was arrested."

Next statement. "I'm not going to say anything 'cause I don't want to get your name involved; you don't want to get my name involved. We got kids to take care of."

"I was concerned that the investigators in asking questions would talk to members of the church. They had already talked to some members of the church, and that they would ask about me and my relationship with Lorna, and I didn't want my name involved in that kind of asking."

"Had you in the past when you had discussed with the KBI or when they had investigated you had any qualms about things that they had told you?"

"I didn't like that they gave me some information I felt I didn't need to know....I felt sometimes that when they talk with people I think it was a method that they use in their investigation was to give out a little bit of information, and I'm sure that they were seeking to make someone comfortable enough to give back information for them.

"That's what I felt when they talked to me, that they told me some things and hoped that I would give them information, and so I felt that when they would question other people, they would bring out some things about me in order to flush information out."

Next statement from the tape. "Well, see, of course, I don't have any access to anything so I don't know. I'm just trying to help her out mentally and in that spiritually and doing—doing what I can. I ain't otherwise—I'm just steering clear. I can't afford or I can't I can't afford—" Carter responded, "Not really." Tom finished. "The rumors are enough to wipe me out."

"What did you mean when you said again, 'I'm just steering clear?'"

"I didn't want to get involved in all the investigation. I'm not a private investigator and I'm not involved in the case that Lorna was arrested and this Dan Carter was arrested. I'm just trying to help her out spiritually and mentally."

"Mr. Carter then asked you, 'After the meeting at the church did she ever say anything else about this? I kind of thought maybe this thing was—' to which you responded, 'I thought it just had to work out. It just wasn't going to work. It wasn't going to fall in place. And when my wife died, it was God's way of saying, "You don't mess with this stuff" and I don't. I don't mess with it. Life's too—life's too valuable. I don't care who it is'; and so on. What were you talking about in response to his question?"

"Darrel had said that Lorna had talked about Marty beating her, and then at the house Darrel and I talked about Marty beating her. We talked about Marty and her relationship and possibly doing something about it together to help her any way we could. And that's the way we left it at the meeting, that we were going to help in this relationship that we were talking about between Marty and her.

"That's the way we left the meeting in June. But then when my wife died and I became completely and totally drained and the lay ministers came and said, 'Cut out counseling. Don't counsel with Lorna, don't do any counseling at all until you get yourself back on your feet, until you're emotionally strong,' I felt that I didn't get involved in such a way as to take on their burdens anymore.

"I was still in mourning; I was still hurting. It seemed like things kept happening in the next few months that kept bringing me down to a low point emotionally, and I was at a low point emotionally then and I had Christmas coming up and I just—I didn't want to take on the burden of people's lives anymore. I was steering clear of that."

The next statement Shaw read had been used several times in previous examination of witnesses. "Life's too valuable. I don't care who it is and I'm not—you know, Marty died and I ain't celebrating but I ain't mourning either. It's a mess is what I'm really mourning about, a lot of people being hurt."

"I said life is valuable and I believe it is valuable. It had been 40 days since Marty had died. Marty was a friend, but in that time over those 40 days I had heard so many things and I was so confused by what was going on, and I was really struggling with what was going on and what had been heard, and I had heard some things along the line that I felt there was a possibility that Marty was responsible for his own life being taken in that he might have been involved in something illegal or something that got him into trouble. And I expressed that later on in the tape. And so I was questioning whether I was really concerned with Marty.

"He was dead, and a lot of other people were being hurt now. A lot of lives were in disruption, and I didn't know how that would turn out but I was very confused by that. So I was mourning the fact that there were just so many people being hurt in this whole episode."

"When you use the term, 'I ain't celebrating,' what were you referring to there?"

"Well, I'm not celebrating that Marty died."

"Mr. Carter made some statement to you, 'But I don't think I am. I'm glad I'm not in her shoes but—' to which you responded, 'Well, maybe we ought to be glad that we didn't follow through.' What did that mean?"

Tom said it had to be answered in the context of the discussion. "Right up above there Darrel Carter said that, 'I mean everything. There's a lot of evidence that leads up to—that she had a motive to do it.' One of the motives that I had read in the newspaper that had been presented was that she had been badly beaten by Marty, and Darrel and I had talked at the house about helping Lorna by bringing her to a wife-abuse agency and possibly turning Marty in so that he could get help. We were going to see about doing it and we decided not to do that. And I'm glad we didn't follow through on that."

"Why?"

"I thought it would be the right thing to do if Marty would ever beat her again, but now two reasons, I guess. It's a tendency to use everything against someone when they're arrested, and I felt that they would even use that, that she had been beaten, use that against her as far as a motive. If there was an actual record that she had been in a wife-abuse agency, they would probably use that against her.

"And another reason was that if Darrel and I were the ones that took her to the wife-abuse agency, then there would be a record of that and that would be more reasons for rumors because it's Darrel's brother that had been arrested, and Lorna had been arrested. So I was concerned about involvement there, so I'm kind of glad we didn't follow through on that point."

"What did you mean by 'There's no use getting it complicated?'"

"I felt that would make it complicated if the pastor of the secretary who was arrested had turned in with Darrel Carter, the brother of the other man who was arrested, had turned in Lorna to a wife-abuse agency for care because of being beaten. That would make things complicated, and from my point of view that didn't have anything to do with the case at all."

Next Shaw read, "So we're by whatever, we're—you know, our contact with the whole business, we never really followed through, never did follow through on anything and we just better be quiet. That's all. I just wanted to check the bases."

"I just didn't want to use the fact that Lorna was beaten and the knowledge of Lorna being beaten to be used against her after her arrest. And so our contact with the whole business was just a discussion about it and it was a discussion that we didn't follow through on as far as taking any kind of action."

"You made reference in response to a question from Mr. Carter. He said, 'Do you think she had it done,' to which you responded, 'I know she talked about it before. I don't—I can't tell you what I think, you know; but I think she would tell me and maybe—she may one of these days.' What did you mean when you said, 'I know she talked about it before?'"

"I didn't have any direct knowledge of her talking about anything like that, but she had been arrested and since her arrest there had been news articles and talk, and from what I gathered at that point a Gail Wilson and Dan Carter and Greg Curry had said she talked about it before. That's what I was talking about.

"And I wasn't going to challenge Darrel Carter at that point, you know, call his brother a liar or anything; and I just was speculating. And what I was considering was that I didn't know what I thought but I think she would tell me if she was involved in this in any way but she hadn't told me anything."

Shaw asked about the statement that Lorna claimed she knew things about the Carters and they knew things about her. What was that all about? Tom talked about Danny's drug dealing and the charge that Darrel purposely burned down a house. Darrel's response to this was, "That's true," agreeing with Tom.

"Now, at that time were you attempting to get information from Mr. Carter relative to what all was going on regarding Lorna's case?" Shaw asked.

"I was very confused by everything that was going on and I wanted to just talk to him about rumors; but when he said he had read all the reports, I was interested and I was kind of wanting to know what he was saying. I think everybody was interested at that time."

Shaw referred to the December 20 interview by Agent Winsor. During that interview, Winsor wondered whether Lorna ever made any statements to him about getting rid of Marty. Tom said she hadn't. "I had no direct knowledge of Lorna ever talking about it."

What about his questions about her being attacked or abused? "...You apparently responded you had no direct or personal knowledge of any physical abuse of Lorna Anderson."

"Yes."

"Was that a correct statement?"

"I think I said I was suspicious of her being beaten."

"Did you have any direct knowledge?"

"No. No, she never would talk to me about that."

Shaw wanted Tom to summarize the relationship between him and Lorna during the spring of 1983.

"I think we had a friendship and a good working relationship and a counseling relationship."

"How about in June, July and August of 1983?"

"I think we had a close relationship. We shared a lot of things together, we had an understanding of each other."

"How about September, October and November of 1983?"

"I think we had a good friendship, and she helped me out a lot and I depended on her a lot as far as child-care advice and work, so I depended on her some, too."

"In November of 1983 did you have any love, feelings toward Lorna Anderson?"

"Not a romantic type of love. I had great caring for her."

"Had you ever at that point ever had sexual relations with Lorna Anderson?"

"No."

"Finally, Mr. Bird, did you solicit Darrel Carter to murder Martin Anderson?"

"No, I did not."

"Did you participate in any such event?"

"No, I did not."

"No further questions," Shaw told the judge.

Tom felt a great relief from finally telling his story. He felt confident he could endure the grilling Symmonds was about to unleash because, after all, the whole purpose in testifying was to tell the truth. He had just done so.

It was mid-afternoon and Judge Rulon called a recess.

Bird on a hot seat

Rod Symmonds took his place in front of the witness stand. He had prepared his questions and was determined to break down Tom's story. Symmonds employed an effective but curious questioning technique, often repeating verbatim the words Tom spoke on the tape recording or in previous testimony. But as he repeated those words, he did so in such a way as to suggest they had some sinister or negative meaning, even though the words might vindicate Tom. Or, he placed different emphasis on Tom's words or changed the punctuation to change the meaning of a sentence altogether. Most often, he left Tom with a yes or no answer, and it sometimes had the effect of changing Tom's previous testimony altogether.

"I believe you indicated, did you not, that you observed Lorna Anderson with two black eyes in March of 1983? Is that correct?"

"Yeah, that she was bruised."

"I believe you indicated on direct examination that you observed blackened eyes, did you not?"

"Twice, uh-huh."

Agent Winsor asked him whether he had any direct knowledge of physical abuse of Lorna by Marty. Tom told Winsor he had only been suspicious because "Lorna Anderson told you she received a bruise on the side of her face by hitting a door? Isn't that correct?"

"Yes."

"You never mentioned at that time anything about black eyes, did you?"

"She had a bruise right here (indicating), yes."

"You did not mention specifically anything about black eyes at that time, did you?"

"No. I don't recall."

Symmonds reminded him that he told Winsor that Lorna never made "any statements to you about wanting to be rid of or away from her husband, did you not?"

"Yes."

"And I believe you indicated 'no' to Don Winsor, didn't you?"

"Right, yes, sir."

"And on the taped interview of December 12th of 1983 between yourself and Darrel Carter, you stated, 'I know she talked about it before,' did you not?"

"Yes."

"And today you're saying that she did not say that. Is that correct?"

"She didn't say anything to me concerning that."

"So at the time that you indicated that you knew she talked about it before and spoke with certainty that you knew it, you were not speaking correctly. Is that right?"

"I don't—what you just said to me, no, I don't think that is right, sir."

"Well, when you said that you knew that she talked about it before, was that a correct statement?"

"I had no direct knowledge of her speaking to me before. I knew she had talked about it before from other people."

"So then that statement on the tape would not be correct because you did not actually know it. It was just something you said on that date. Is that correct?"

"Yes."

Symmonds asked to introduce his version of the typed transcript of the conversation into evidence. Shaw objected because the version Symmonds had contained some small variations from the version Tom and Shaw used. Rulon took it under advisement.

"I believe you indicated on direct examination that you ran outside the church, saw Lorna Anderson pulling away from the church in her van and that you hopped in fearing that she might leave without having an opportunity to visit with her. Is that correct?"

"I don't think I ran out the church but, yeah, I went on out the church and stepped in front as she pulled out."

"And then at that point in time you don't recall exactly how but at some—in some manner you made your way to a service area on the turnpike. Is that correct?"

"Yes."

"You don't recall Lorna Anderson getting on the turnpike then. Would that be correct?"

"I try to picture it but I just wasn't paying any attention to where we were going."

Symmonds asked about Tom's talk with Sharon Meyer a few days after the computer arrived.

"And you told her that you wanted to talk to Lorna about her resignation at the church but you did not want to do it at the church so you drove to a rest area on the turnpike and sat in a van and helped her work on her resignation. Is that correct?"

"As much as I can recall, yes."

"Well, that would seem to indicate, would it not, that it was a situation where you didn't want to visit at the church? Wouldn't that be correct?"

"Well, Lorna didn't want to visit at the church so we just went on from there."

"And you said later you knew that was a dumb move and you should have known that people would talk about it. Is that correct?"

"Yes. Yeah, it was probably a dumb move, yes."

Symmonds pursues the tapes

"When you first met with Darrel Carter," referring to the taped meeting, "he said that things were a mess, didn't he?"

"Yes, I think so."

"And you agreed that things were a mess, didn't you?"

"Yes."

"And he said that 'A friend of mine said you wanted to talk about something,' didn't he?"

"Yes."

"And I believe you indicated that, yes, you did want to visit; you just wanted to touch bases, didn't you?"

"Yes."

"And as I understood this meeting at the church from your testimony here today, you agreed that Lorna Anderson set up this meeting between yourself and Darrel Carter, didn't you?"

"Which meeting are you talking about now, the one at the church?"

"This is the one in May."

"In May? No, it was in June, and Lorna Anderson did set it up, yes."

Symmonds asked whether Tom knew how Lorna contacted Darrel. No. She contacted you at home? Yes. You did meet with Darrel at Faith, right? Yes. Then you went to see him at a house on West View? Yes.

"When you visited with Darrel Carter [in December] I believe you indicated that you just wanted to touch bases with him and you stated that you had heard rumors and that rumors were rampant, didn't you?"

"Yes."

"You didn't indicate at that time that you had heard any rumors were coming from Darrel Carter, did you?"

"I think just a few seconds later."

"Now. This reference that you make to later, is this the statement made by yourself to Darrel Carter's statement that—I believe he had indicated that he had visited with Julie Palmer just prior to that, hadn't he?"

"I think so."

"And he indicated that she had stated that—something to the effect, 'Are you guys involved? What the heck are you talking about?' with referring to the meeting with yourself. Is that correct?"

"Yes, sir."

"And it was in response to that line of questioning that you made the following statement: "Well, you can handle it. Just tell her—tell her you heard some rumors out. Say, I've heard some rumors were coming from you. I didn't buy it but, you know, I wouldn't see why you would—that would help your brother or help anyone else.' You made that statement, didn't you?" (Symmonds had heard the tape more than once. Yet here, in the hearing of the jury, he distorted the meaning of the words by placing punctuation and emphasis differently than they had been spoken.)

"I think that's an improper way that you read it. If I could share with you where the quotes end."

Symmonds referred Tom to the written transcript and repeated the phrase, once again asking if that is not what Tom had said. Again Tom insisted Symmonds read it wrong. "Could I read it as I remember I said it?"

"If I might, what portion of that are you contending that I'm not reading properly?"

"You say, 'Well, you can handle it. Just tell her I heard some rumors out. Say I heard some rumors were coming from you. I didn't buy it.' The different meaning, I told her—I said, 'Tell her you just heard some rumors out."

"That's correct."

"And that's all I wanted to tell her; and then I said, 'Hey, I heard some rumors were coming from you. I didn't buy it, you know. I wouldn't see why you would—that you would help your brother or help anyone else.' That's the way I heard it. I don't know if that's clear or not."

"I think it's clear, Mr. Bird."

He asked about Tom going to see Julie Palmer. Did he say some people say and do things they wish they hadn't? Yes. You knew she was a sensitive person?

"I don't think so. I mean I assume she has some sensitivities, yes."

She was your friend? Yes. You knew it would upset her and Darrel?

"I wasn't going to confront her directly so I don't think it would upset her, but I thought it would make Darrel think, yes."

"And you thought it would keep him quiet, didn't you?"

"About the rumors, yes."

"You didn't think he would say anything to anyone about this incident, did you?"

"About the rumors, yes."

"And then I believe, Mr. Bird, that you made a statement, 'But I mean as far as we—we just talked about the use of firecrackers.' Isn't that correct?"

"Yes."

"And I believe right after that that Darrel Carter said, 'Yeah, the—the party that you talked to doesn't know anything. I mean, you know.' Isn't that correct?"

"Yes."

"And this was right after you had been talking about the fact that you had contacted a friend of his. Isn't that correct?"

"Yes."

"And then you indicated that you had contacted her because you were playing an ace in the hole. Isn't that correct?"

"Yes."

Symmonds referred to comments about a soccer meet and that several times he said, "you had kids and he had kids." Yes.

"And you were aware of the fact, were you not, that Darrel Carter was having an affair with Julie Palmer?"

"Yes, right. I wasn't sure. I don't know for sure."

"And you knew that Mr. Carter had a wife, didn't you?"

"Yes."

"And you knew that he had had sexual relations with Lorna Anderson, didn't you?"

"No, I didn't know that."

"But with respect to Julie Palmer you knew that Mr. Carter like any married man would fear exposure of this affair, didn't you?"

"I'm sure."

"In fact, you were counting on that, weren't you?"

"I was hoping he would recognize that, yes."

Symmonds read one of Tom's quotes from the tape. "But they—they busted Lorna just to make her talk. They were going to keep her in over Thanksgiving holiday and try to crack her." He asked if Tom said that? Yes.

"And you contacted an attorney at the time there was a warrant issued for her arrest on her behalf, didn't you?"

"I talked to Irv sometime. I don't know when it was.... I called Darrell Meyer."

"And I believe Darrel Carter stated to you, 'Yeah, but she isn't going to talk, is she?' Isn't that correct?"

"Yes."

"And you said, 'No way,' didn't you?"

"Yes. And then there's an inaudible, yes."

Symmonds referred to comments about Danny Carter maybe burning Lorna. "And you were concerned about that, weren't you?"

"Yes. It seemed like that's what was happening."

"Thank you. And then I believe there was a discussion and Darrel Carter stated to you that he didn't think his brother was going to talk, didn't he?"

"I think so."

"And there was a discussion about the fact that the police didn't have anything physical, wasn't there?"

"Yes."

"And I believe you indicated that somebody knew something to start all this rolling, didn't you?"

"Yes."

"And you indicated that the police officers were dumb but they were good, didn't you?"

"Yes."

"And then I believe you made the statement which you referred to and discussed on direct examination about how you were steering clear and you just wanted to touch bases and make sure that the two of you just possibly talked about your group selling firecrackers. Isn't that correct?"

"Yes."

"And didn't Darrel Carter at that time respond by saying, 'Yeah, but I haven't talked to them. I haven't said anything, you know.' Didn't he say that?"

"Yes."

"Both times when you referred to the firecrackers, he responded once by saying that Julie Palmer or the person you had talked to didn't know anything, and the next time he responded by saying that he hadn't talked to anyone. Isn't that correct?"

"The first time he did what?"

"I believe the first time you had referred to the—you referred to it as the use of firecrackers, and I believe he said, 'Yeah, the party you talked to doesn't know anything.'"

"He was concerned about her."

"And then the next time you mentioned the sale of firecrackers he said that he hadn't talked to anyone. Isn't that correct?"

"He said that after that, yeah."

"And at the time you had met with Darrel Carter at the church, you had told him if anyone asked about our meeting to just say that it pertained to the sale of fireworks by the youth group, didn't you?"

"No."

Symmonds read another quote of Darrel's. "After the meeting at the church, did she ever say anything else about this? I kind of thought maybe this thing was..." "And then you responded. I've correctly read that, haven't I?"

"Yes."

"And he referred to the meeting at the church, didn't he?"

"Yes."

"Not at the house, did he?"

"No."

"And you didn't discuss the SOS and the wife beating at the church, did you?" (SOS provides shelter and legal services for battered women.)

"No. He and Lorna did. Well, he and Lorna discussed her and Marty at the church."

"You learned that fact at the preliminary hearing, didn't you?" Symmonds thought he scored. The only place Tom could have learned that Darrel claimed he and Lorna talked about SOS or getting her protection would have been at the preliminary hearing. He believed he caught Tom refreshing his story instead of relating the truth.

"No. Darrel told me — are you asking me where I heard — "

"And then Darrel had told you at the house that he had learned that Lorna was beaten at the church? Is that correct?"

"No, he knew Lorna was beat a year ago. He told me that he asked how Lorna and she were doing — Lorna and Marty were doing at the church. That was — I wasn't there — "

"Thank you."

" — yet."

Symmonds read Tom's statement. "I thought it just had to work out. It just wasn't going to — it just wasn't going to fall in place. And when my wife died, it was God's way of saying 'you don't mess with this stuff.'" "Didn't you make that statement?"

"Yeah."

Tom and Marty questions

Symmonds asked about Tom's claim to be good friends with Marty. He asked whether he played volleyball, basketball and other sports with him. Yes, and softball. "And he was a good friend of yours right up to the date of his death. Isn't that what you said?"

"Yes."

"And you presided at his funeral, didn't you?"

"I preached at his funeral, yes."

"And yet you could turn around just a few short days later and say, 'You know, Marty died and I'm — I'm — I ain't celebrating but I ain't mourning either; but it's a mess. It's what I'm really mourning about, a lot of people being hurt.' You said that, didn't you?" Symmonds feigned incredulity.

"Yes."

"And at that time you weren't even mourning the loss of this Christian brother, were you?"

"I was confused about a lot of things I'd heard about, yes."

Symmonds asked whether Tom read anything in the paper to change his mind about Marty? No. Did you hear something on TV then? No. (Had he asked whether Lorna told him about Marty's alleged selling of drugs and such, Tom could have clarified this.)

Symmonds read another of Tom's quotes. "When my wife died, it was God's way of saying 'you don't mess with this stuff'"; and that's referring once again to the SOS and the beating of Lorna Anderson. Isn't that correct?"

"I don't think it had to do with SOS. Take on the burden of people's marriages."

Symmonds said Tom claimed he and Darrel talked about Lorna's marital problems and Marty's beating her at the house. Yes. "And you weren't one bit concerned about her privilege as a patient of yours that you were counseling. Isn't that correct?"

"Oh, I didn't go into detail with Darrel Carter."

Symmonds reminded Tom that he said something should be done because Marty might lose his temper. Yes. And something about getting her into SOS. Yes. And Darrel thought it would be good to contact SOS. Yes. "And in fact because he thought it was such as good idea was the reason he said on page 8, 'Well, that's true. Like I said, I didn't want anything to do with it at the time and I'm glad I didn't have anything to do with it then and now and.' He made that statement, didn't he?"

"Yes."

"But now you're saying that in fact he did want to have something to do with the SOS?"

"Well, we decided not to. If Lorna was ever beat again, we would."

Symmonds then quoted Darrel again. "But I'm really not wanting to burn anybody either on this deal, especially myself and you." Tom responded by saying, 'There's just no use in it."

"And I believe that's when you indicated that Lorna knew some things about he and Danny and the past and that he didn't want that drug up or threshed up or whatever the word was. Isn't that correct?"

"Yes."

He again quoted Tom. "So let's—we're by with it, whatever. We're—you know, our contact with the whole business. We never really followed through. Never did follow through on anything, and so we had better or so we just better be quiet. That's all. I just wanted to check the bases." Yes, that's what Tom had said.

"And I believe you indicated in that December 12th meeting that all of the rumors seemed to be settling down as far as you knew, didn't you?"

"I was hoping so, yes."

Symmonds reminded Tom that earlier he told the jury that he had been very upset when he went to Julie's house. He had said he wanted to confront Darrel face to face. He had said "no phones." Yes, all this was true. "And when you visited with him on December 12th you had had a chance to regain your composure and you were no longer really upset, were you?"

"Right."

"And at that point you did what any of us would do, you just told him on the phone what your concerns were. Is that correct?"

"I don't think I did."

"In fact you agreed to go and meet him in a parking lot at Emporia Bowl, didn't you?"

"Yes."

"You didn't have to worry about anybody recording the conversation at that location on a telephone, did you?"

"Didn't have to worry about it? I don't know. I didn't worry about it, no."

Back to the transcript, Symmonds lead Tom through a series of quotes, some already covered by earlier testimony, but put in a different way. They had already discussed the quote, "I know she talked about it before." Symmonds referred to a few lines that preceded that. Darrel said, "Do you really think that she—that she had anything to do with it? Do you think she did it or had it done." Tom answered, "I'm pretty sure or I'm sure she didn't do it."

Darrel asked again, "Do you think she had it done?" Tom answered, "I know she talked about it before...I don't—I can't tell you what I think, you know, but I think she would tell me and she may one of these days." Symmonds continued reading Darrel's response. "I know she talked about it, you know, but I really never thought she would ever do it."

"And you responded, 'Yeah. I mean it was like, oh, you know, like kind of a test to see what would really happen.' You said that, didn't you?" Symmonds asked.

"Yes."

"Now, is that test that you were referring to, Mr. Bird, is that something that you didn't know as well? You were just presuming? I believe you indicated—"

"I don't understand."

"—you didn't have any direct knowledge referring to the first part of that, 'I know she talked about it before.' You said you really didn't have any direct knowledge on that. Isn't that correct?"

"Correct."

"And are you telling the jury that your last response, 'Yeah. I mean it was like, oh, you know, like kind of a test to see what would really happen,' is that something you didn't have direct knowledge on, that you were just speculating on as well?"

"Yes."

"And I believe on page 15 you said, 'Well, that's what I figured. That's when I said I want to touch bases with you because there's no use adding another—another little niche in there so, you know, you don't want to be involved.' You said that, didn't you?"

"Yes."

"And you didn't feel you had to worry about Lori Anderson ever appearing and giving testimony against you, did you?"

"I wasn't talking about me at this point."

"You were concerned about Darrel Carter being subpoenaed to testify, weren't you, in the hearing in Geary County?"

"I think I expressed that."

"I believe in fact you said, 'I figured you might be subpoenaed to talk,' didn't you?"

"Yes."

"And I believe Darrel Carter responded by saying, 'Yeah, they don't like—well, of course, you know I'm not talking so they really don't have a connection with me on this deal,' didn't he?" (Darrel was protecting himself from prosecution.)

"Yes."

"I believe you indicated at that point, 'Well, I just want to make sure that stays,' didn't you?"

"Yes."

"And at one point in here, Mr. Bird, is it not correct that Darrel Carter very explicitly said, 'If they knew I knew,' then he would be subpoenaed, didn't he? Do you recall that?"

"Something like that. I don't know what the context was at or anything."

"Thank you. You didn't tell the police about your meeting with Darrel Carter at the Faith Lutheran Church, did you?" (Why would he? It had nothing to do with a crime, and so he certainly didn't want to bring it up.)

"No."

On to the letters

Symmonds reminded Tom that he said he had planned to be away for a few days in November—Symmonds referred to it as a "little outing," and Tom corrected him: "It was a conference."

"You were going to be away from Lorna, weren't you?"

"Being out of town, yes. Yeah, I would be away from Lorna."

"And I believe you indicated that you really didn't pay a bit of attention to the cards that you were going to send to her. Isn't that what you said?"

"Right. As far as what I wrote?"

"As far as the card that you picked."

"Right."

"Never even checked to see if you were sending her a card that said, 'Congratulations on the birth of your new baby' or something. Is that correct?"

"No, I didn't check that. I don' think that would have been in that packet."

"So you didn't bother to check to see that this thing coincidentally reads, 'Miss you, miss you, miss you. Everything I do echoes with the laughter and the voice of you,' and continuing on. It just coincidentally happened that this 'Miss you' appeared on the same card at the time you were leaving town. Is that what you are saying?" he asked sarcastically.

"Well, yeah. I just picked them out, yes."

"Thank you. And I believe you indicated that you wrote both of those to give her inspiration during your absence. Isn't that correct?"

"Lift her up."

"In March of 1983 didn't you indicate to Angie Duensing that you were burned out on being a minister?"

"I don't remember that."

"Do you recall going to St. John's College to visit with them about being a professor at that institution? Do you recall that?"

"I went to St. John's College for a different purpose."

Symmonds asked about the March, 1983, drive in the van. Did Lorna make suicidal statements? Yes. You were gone two hours? Yes. Driving around the county. Yes, in the north part of the county.

"And I believe that you indicated, did you not, that Angie Duensing was the only one that expressed concern to you about your relationship with Lorna Anderson. Is that correct?"

"No."

Who else then? Sharon Meyer, Larry Kalsow, Howard Meyer, his in-laws in July. And after Angie talked to you, the July van incident happened? Yes. "Do you remember what you told Reverend Kalsow that you talked about when you and Lorna Anderson were in the van out at the rest area?"

"Not specifically. I don't recall anything specifically that I told him."

"Do you recall anything you told him?"

"I recall that I told him that I was going to take care of it. I told him I cared about Lorna."

"You never mentioned the discussion about the resignation talk that you had with Lorna Anderson to Reverend Kalsow, did you?"

"I don't think so."

"In fact, you told him that you were out there just generally visiting with Lorna Anderson and talking about Sandy's death, didn't you?"

"I don't remember that."

"You never told Reverend Kalsow or Sharon Meyers anything concerning this incident where you hopped in the van and sped out of town onto the turnpike, did you?"

Shaw objected to this question. He said it was ambiguous and impossible to answer, but Rulon overruled him. "The witness can answer that if he can."

"Okay. I don't recall what I told them specifically about anything. I told them that I did do it, I was out there and—"

"You told Reverend Kalsow about that after he called and confronted you about the fact that he had seen you out there at that service area."

"Yes."

"Didn't you? And I believe you indicated that you were gone no more than an hour and a half I believe was your estimate. Is that correct?"

"Yes, sir."

"Where did you get on the turnpike at?"

"I don't specifically know. I assume at the entrance here in Emporia."

"You don't recall then whether you just drove out to the service area and she pulled in there or anything about that. Is that correct?"

"I assume we went to Admire and turned around." (This is the only place between Emporia and Topeka, other than the rest stop, where one can turn around and head south without leaving the turnpike altogether.)

He asked when it was Tom quit counseling Lorna. The end of July. He clarified what that meant. "I didn't counsel her concerning her marriage or, things like that. I still talked to her and worked with her, and such as that. I had no formal counseling with her."

"So any contact which you made with her was—after that time was either business or personal in nature. Is that correct?"

"Well, practical matters. She helped me out with the kids, such as that."

Symmonds returned to December. Tom said he wanted to do everything he could to stop the rumors.   "So then you didn't do anything which would cause rumors? You wouldn't have done that, would you?" he asked sarcastically.

"I guess I would try not to. I wouldn't want to."

"Well," Symmonds began, thinking he just hit a homerun, "you made arrangements with the Hydro Truck Line, wasn't it, to assist Lorna Anderson in moving from Emporia?"

"Yes."

"You went out there personally and made those arrangements, didn't you?"

"Yes."

"And I believe you indicted that you went on a trip at the end of November, is that correct, or when was that little jaunt that you—"

"Conference in Wichita? That was the 10th and 11th, I think."

Symmonds meant the Thanksgiving trip to Fort Worth. He asked if it was true that Tom drove by way Hutchinson on the way back from that trip? Yes. Did you see Lorna? Yes. Did you help her with her moving in December? Yes.

"How frequently did you continue to call Lorna Anderson?"

"I kept in constant contact with her."

"What do you mean by constant contact?"

Shaw objected. He wanted Symmonds to specify a time frame. Symmonds obliged by asking Tom about December of 1983, then January, February, March, April, May and June of 1984. Yes to each of those months. Tom and Lorna talked daily during that time and, yes, sometimes more than once a day.

"You weren't counseling her at that time, were you?"

"Oh, yes."

"Oh, you resumed your counseling?"

"After the death of Marty Anderson, sure."

Did you visit her in Hutchinson during this time? Yes.

Confusing a few more details before resting

Symmonds proceeded to ask a variety of questions, trying to clarify or confuse a few points. Did Tom know Darrell Warren or Joe Lapping? No. Did he get along with Lori Anderson? Yes. Once again, other than Sharon Meyer, who had he talked with about Lorna? Kalsow, Angie, the Grismers. All of those discussion preceded his talk with Sharon.

"And you told Julie Palmer that you wanted to reaffirm the trust with Darrel Carter, didn't you?"

"I don't know if I used that exact word or not. I don't recall that. Probably affirm a trust, conform a trust. I don't know, something like that probably."

"And this was a trust of not going to the SOS office at the time of your meeting in June of 1983. Wouldn't that be correct?"

"A trust not to talk about each other in terms of rumors."

"And you and Lorna Anderson used to go to Topeka, didn't you?"

"No."

"The two of you used to go to Wichita, didn't you?"

"No."

"You had never met Jan Mead before she testified here in court, had you?"

"No, I didn't."

Symmonds asked him when he asked Angie if he ever made a pass at her, was it because he forgot when he had done it? "I was wondering if she had interpreted something as a pass."

Symmonds sat down.

Redirect and re-cross examination

Shaw asked Tom about two discussions he had had with Angie. One was on June 24. And the van incident was July 27? Yes. "So this would have been at least a month in between there between the first presentation of concern and your ultimate confrontation with Lorna. Is that right?"

"Yes."

"You were also asked about some time in December making arrangements for Lorna to move to Hutchinson. Why did you make those arrangements, Mr. Bird?"

"Her father called from Hutchinson, and how as the one that was really moving her and he was going to bring up a carload of men that he had hired down there to load the truck up and take back. He called me up and said, 'Would you put a deposit down' and then he'll take care of it when he gets up. He'll take it from there." All Tom did was put down a deposit. Loren Slater did the rest. Tom tore up the deposit receipt.

Shaw turned back to the tape. He mentioned the numerous references to the rumors. "I've heard—I know Lorna introduced us and that's some kind of a connection, and I've heard enough—you know, enough rumors for sure that rumors are rampant." Yes, he said that.

He referenced the remark about rumors coming from Darrel and Wolf Creek people. Darrel responded to that, saying, "you know, and they're spreading a lot of rumors."

Tom said, "The rumors are enough to wipe me out." He said he was tired of the rumors. He said he was tense because of all the rumors. He said he couldn't afford to have people wondering about him, and he was handling the rumors the best he could.

"Now, you indicated that you had gone to St. John's College. When and why did you go down there, sir?"

"I went down to St. John's College in June. I was meeting with Professor Helmer down there who is in New Testament studies, and I was setting up a series of courses that I would be teaching at the Lutheran Student Center here in Emporia, credit courses….and at the same time I was also interested in the possibility of later on having a position of teaching down there."

Shaw asked whether or not Tom's contact with Lorna increased after March or April, 1984. Yes. Why? "It was after my arrest....We were in such a predicament that we needed to talk with each other and share each other's bad experience." (Sheriffs arrested Lorna the same day Tom had been arrested.) "We felt kind of like lepers. Lepers who are outcast, who all the sudden didn't have the support we used to have and kind of needed to gather together to shore each other up."

Shaw rested and Symmonds had no further questions. An exhausted Tom Bird stepped down and returned to his seat at the defendant's table. He had no idea how well he had done. He just knew he had told the truth, and had to trust the jurors to believe him.

Defense continues

Shaw called Jody Bryant to the stand. She served on the joint youth board that planned combined youth activities for Faith and Messiah. "Did you have occasion to attend a joint meeting between Messiah and Faith Lutheran Church on May 21st, 1983?"

"Yes, I remember that meeting." She sat between Larry Kalsow and Alan Rees. Tom chaired the meeting.

Shaw asked what they discussed at the meeting. She said youth outings and the trip to Eureka Springs. She also recalled talking about fund raising. "I do remember two of them that were discussed very clearly."

"Okay. What were they?"

"One was a mud football type thing...And then I remember the fireworks discussion because, you know, the legality of it." Since it had been her first time at a youth board meeting, she remembered it well.

"Did Pastor Bird take any interest in this or do anything with respect to it as far as you knew?"

"Oh, Pastor Bird was very interested in all aspects of it, you know; very much so."

Symmonds took over. He asked her to clarify the question of legality, and she could not specific, but felt it had to do with whether they could be sold inside city limits. He tried to clarify the date of the meeting. Was it the 21st or 29th? She felt pretty sure it was the 21st.

Symmonds wondered whether there was more emphasis placed on the mud football game than fireworks. No, they got about equal time. He finished with her.

Shaw called Kermit Grother to the stand. Grother said he saw and talked to Tom at Darrel's fireworks stand on July 4, 1983. "Tom Bird showed up and Darrel Carter exchanged hellos. He said, 'Hello, Pastor Tom'; and they started talking about soccer and I entered into that discussion.'...I believe that Tom Bird asked him if he had been to Wichita and how things went with the soccer game up there, and I think Darrel Carter said they got beat, and then they went on talking more about soccer."

"While you were there, did you notice any problems or any ill feelings between either Mr. Carter or Mr. Bird?"

"No. I assumed that they were the best of friends the way that they greeted each other and with visiting."

"What happened after that?"

"My kids were at the one end of the fireworks stand with Darrel Carter. He was showing them some fireworks. And Pastor Bird was at the other end, and he mentioned to me that—he said, 'The church is thinking about selling fireworks'; and then half a minute later he says, 'That is if we can get Darrel to help us or if Darrel will help us' or something like that...And that was all that was said."

Symmonds had no cross-examination, and that caught Shaw off guard. "I was hardly anticipating such a succinct and effective cross-examination. I do not have any witnesses present at the present time I don't think," Shaw told the judge.

They agreed to adjourn to 8:30 Tuesday morning, hoping the trial could go to jury before the day was through.

The last day of the trial

Tuesday morning, Jeff Shipley took the stand. He belonged to Faith and served on the "board of young people's work from September of '82 through approximately May of '83." Shipley also attended the May 21, 1983, youth board meeting.

"Do you recall, sir, any particular topics that were discussed at the May 21st meeting?"

"The youth was planning several camping activities for the summer, and a couple things that were discussed were possible fund raisers for the campouts."

"Did any of them include the possible sale of fireworks?"

"Yes, it did....Well, we were trying to come up with several ideas as to what we could use to raise money for the youth. One was possibly a car wash, possibly a slave auction, and then the fireworks was one that I've always felt was a good fund raiser."

"What was done with the particular idea relating to the fireworks?"

"We decided we would bring it up for a vote at the Sunday meeting, and at that point was when Pastor Bird said he wold talk with Darrel Carter as far as letting the youth sell fireworks."

"When was your Sunday meeting?"

"It was the 29th of May." (Tom said it was at this meeting that the name of Darrel Carter first surfaced, though he had not met him yet. Lorna told him briefly about Carter's Crackers during the prior week.)

"Did the subject of fireworks come up at that particular meeting?"

"Yes, it did."

"And what if anything was discussed at that time to the best of your recollection?"

"I remember the youth thought it seemed like a pretty good idea and we left it in the hands of Pastor Bird to talk with Darrel Carter about us working for Carter's Crackers at a couple of his stands for the Fourth of July season."

Shipley said he never saw anything in Tom's actions or character causing him to question his integrity.

Symmonds began his cross-examination. He asked Shipley whether Tom ever mentioned the meeting with Darrel after the May 29, meeting. No. He asked whether Shipley knew whether or not Tom ever met with Darrel. No.

Shipley quit the youth board following that meeting and, therefore, never attended subsequent meetings. (Given that he left the youth board, he had no reason to learn of the board's decisions thereafter.)

Shaw called Grover McCullough to the stand. McCullough bought the house Darrel had built, the one where Tom visited. McCullough had executed a contract with Darrel in late February or early March of 1983. Once the building began, he made nearly daily trips to the building site, checking on progress.

"During those periods of time did you have occasion to talk with Darrel Carter and get to know him?"

"Quite a bit, yes."

"Drawing your attention to this particular home, when was it promised to you, if you can recall, that the house would be completed?"

"He told us we could have it the first of June...We took possession of it June the 25th...We moved in maybe June the 27th."

"On June the 25th, was the work in your opinion completed?"

"No, there wasn't even windows in the basement."

Shaw began to ask whether McCullough had formed an opinion of Darrel's character, but Symmonds objected. He objected to Shaw asking about a specific situation versus a general opinion of a person's standing in the community. Shaw said he would try to phrase the question more broadly.

"Mr. McCullough, do you have an opinion about Mr. Carter's truthfulness and veracity within the community?"

"Yeah, I sure do."

"And what is your opinion?"

"Well, the man lied to us so many times that—"

"Objection, Your Honor. It's not being responsive to the question," Symmonds complained.

"Sustained," Rulon answered.

"And I would ask that that be stricken, the last response." Rulon dismissed it and told the jury to disregard the statement.

"Without regard to any specifics, Mr. McCullough, can you tell us what your opinion is of Mr. Carter's character trait for truthfulness and honestly?"

"Well, I think he's the biggest liar in ten counties."

Symmonds began. McCullough had a legal disagreement with Darrel concerning the house. Shaw served as his attorney. Darrel had filed a mechanic's lien on the house because McCullough refused to pay him.

Shaw began his redirect and asked why McCullough refused to pay the bill?

"Well, on June the 25th it was his last day of work there. He stuck a final bill on the kitchen cabinets when he left there that day, and that was for 2700 and some dollars. About three weeks later he come back demanding his money, and I told him that I wasn't going to pay him until he finished the house. He asked me what he needed to do, and I told him he could start with putting a window in the basement that he had done—he put a single strength window in there instead of a casement window. And he just laughed; and he says, 'If I have to take you to court.'"

Symmonds objected, but Shaw said, "He opened the door." Symmonds said the questioning went far beyond the latitude allowed. Rulon agreed.

Grover McCullough stepped down and his wife, Patricia took the stand.

She said the McCullough's had pressed Darrel to get the house done. He promised them it would take about 60 days, barring bad weather. "His problems were that he only spent about two days a week on the job."

"In the course of your contact with Mr. Carter, did you have occasion to form an opinion as to his truthfulness and honesty?"

"Darrel Carter is without a doubt the worst liar I've ever encountered in my entire life. He enjoys it; he has fun with it; he brags about it—"

"Objection, Your Honor," Symmonds yelled.

"And in my opinion, he's sick. He needs professional help."

"Just a minute, please," Rulon interrupted.

"Your Honor, object, and I would ask that response be stricken. She's not been responsive to the question," Symmonds protested.

Rulon sustained the objection.

"Without regard to specific feelings and specific instances that you've had with Mr. Carter, okay, do you have an opinion about Darrel Carter's truthfulness and honesty?"

"He's a habitual liar. He's sick and he needs professional help."

Seeing the same thing differently

Joyce Rosenboom took the stand. Shaw asked whether she remembered when the church bought its computer. Yes. Was she there the first day it was used? Yes, so were Sharon Meyer, Pastor Bird and Lorna Anderson. Rosenboom saw Sharon standing in Lorna's office next to Tom. She noticed how Sharon studied Lorna.

"At that time did you observe anything unusual about Tom and Lorna as they were working on the machine?"

"No, nothing unusual."

"Did you observe any touching or unusual closeness between them at that time?"

"Not a thing."

She said she left the room but Sharon stayed behind.

"Was there anything about that particular incident that caused you any problems?"

"I was a little concerned about Sharon. She acted like maybe she needed to visit with Pastor or maybe she just finished visiting with him and needed some more reassurance. I knew that at that time she was going through some problems at home with an addition of some more children to her household. I felt maybe that was why she was not receptive and excited about getting the computer."

"In the time that you have known Pastor Bird, have you known him to be the type of person who would touch others?"

"Definitely, yes."

"Is this his usual character trait?"

"Yes, it certainly is."

She considered herself a friend of Tom's and knew him well. Shaw asked whether she considered him a truthful person. "I definitely do. I think he's very truthful. I think he's very honest."

"Are you familiar at all with his feelings concerning the Bible?"

"Yes. I think I am. I've been in Bible class with him and ethics class which I took under him....I feel that he has a great concern for life, that his opinion is based on the Bible, that the Lord gives life and the Lord takes away life."

Shaw next called Harold Schwinn, one of the lay ministers. He worked at ESU in the data processing and education measurement center. He served as a lay minister from the beginning of the church. He knew Marty Anderson, he said, from coaching softball during the summer of 1983.

Shaw asked him to describe Marty. "Marty was the type of person that was very sure about what he was doing on that field. He certainly had a definite ability and he knew what that ability was. He was the kind of guy that always went in hard at second base. He—you know, he would stretch the run. He was really into the activity of it and the competitiveness of it."

"Did you have occasion to observe him and Tom Bird together?"

"Definitely."

"And how did they seem to get along?"

"Very fine."

Shaw asked about Lorna's resignation and Schwinn parroted much of the information Howard Meyer shared earlier, about meeting with Larry Kalsow, getting the resignation letter and such. He confirmed that her resignation was not accepted. He started to say that he talked with Marty about it and what Marty said, but Symmonds objected, Anything Marty may have said would be hearsay, and Rulon wanted no hearsay (except Jan Mead's, that is).

Schwinn confirmed that Tom never threatened to quit and that the lay ministers' greatest concern was what they could do to help him.

Symmonds pressed Schwinn on the issue of counseling Lorna. Did the lay ministers suggest that Tom stop counseling her? Yes, but Schwinn tried to say they felt it should be done over a period of time, not all at once; Symmonds cut him off. Schwinn had no idea whether or not Tom stopped the counseling.

Schwinn confirmed that Lorna's work hours were limited to 20 a week. Symmonds asked whether Tom denied having a sexual relationship with her. Yes, he had. Symmonds tried to suggest that, based on Tom's denial, the lay ministers tore up her resignation. Schwinn said, "Not totally." Symmonds did not try to clarify that answer.

Shaw asked Schwinn more questions about the lay minister's meeting with Tom. Wasn't it true that they talked about a number of ministry issues? Yes. And wasn't it true that the issue of counseling applied to all of his counseling, not just Lorna? Yes. "So he could resume his duties as a preacher and a teacher and an administrator?"

"Yes, to work back into it slowly."

Shaw asked about church growth and weren't they considering hiring a full time secretary? Yes, but Schwinn felt they could not afford it. They asked Lorna to keep track of her hours to evaluate whether or not there was a greater need for secretarial help.

Shaw called Don Froelich to the stand. He served as the chief lay minister. (These three lay ministers were well educated and professional men, not the mindless dolts portrayed in *Murder Ordained*.)

"If you find a deviation in the acts of the minister, what would you do in that particular instance?"

"It's our duty then to investigate and to be assured that some error is being committed or whatever, and then we would call for his termination of duties."

Froelich described Lorna's resignation. He came to church Sunday morning. "I was sitting in the office, and she said, 'I will submit my resignation,' and she didn't mention too much about it. I said, 'No, I don't know anything about it so as far as I'm concerned that's not valid.'" Froelich felt it would be wrong for Lorna to resign just based on rumors.

The lay ministers "determined that this was not sufficient to warrant her resignation." (Like Tom, the lay minister's took the Eighth Commandment and the Lutheran Confession seriously.)

Froelich said they traced the rumors about Tom and Lorna to a few members in the church, but did not reveal who they were.

(The fact that the men took no action to fire Lorna further indicates that they had no firsthand knowledge of her promiscuity nor had anyone brought them proof. It showed another side of Lorna in that she apparently took great care not to mess with the men at Faith, a clever move on her part. If she treated Faith like The Continental, to recruit lovers, the lay ministers would have fired her month's earlier.)

Shaw asked him his opinion of Tom. "I believe he's a truthful person. I believe he's a quality individual. He's a dedicated minister of the Word of the Lord, and I trust him totally."

Symmonds asked Froelich if it were true that Tom denied being sexually involved with Lorna. Yes. And if he had not, he would have been fired. Yes. "So, in other words, his job was dependent upon his answer, was it not?"

"I didn't sense that."

Had Tom ever told him he had started once again counseling Lorna, in November or December? No. He asked about Froelich's reaction when he saw the large phone bills created by Tom calling Lorna regularly in Hutchinson following Marty's death. Yes, that surprised him, and yes, Tom made a lot of calls on a monthly basis.

Shaw made a point that even after Lorna moved to Hutchinson, she still belonged to Faith. Yes, and needed "support and encouragement from friends?" Yes.

Symmonds jumped up and again badgered Froelich about the phone calls. Do you really believe Tom was fulfilling his pastoral duties calling Lorna over a 6-1/2 month period following Marty's death? "I trust the man." Symmonds asked whether Tom did that for others who moved away or had a death in the family. Froelich could not answer.

Next up was Stephanie Moore.   Moore said she helped Tom quite a bit with the children after Sandy's death. Asked about his honesty and truthfulness, she responded, "I've never had any reason to doubt what he told me or talked about."

Shaw finished and Symmonds had no cross-examination.

Shaw called John Rath to the stand. Rath served as the pastor at Faith Lutheran Church in Topeka. He installed Tom after his call to Messiah and at Faith in Emporia.

Rath served as the circuit counselor for the Lutheran Church-Missouri Synod and spent time with Tom each month. There the circuit pastors shared information about their circuits, studied scripture together and prayed for their work. They planned circuit functions at these meetings. In his capacity as circuit counselor, he often advised pastors who inquired of him how to handle various situations and concerns in their churches and ministries.

"Have you been able to observe Tom with respect to his feelings about people and touching? By that I mean having application of the Bible to people."

"Yes, I have. First of all, Tom is very knowledgeable man as far as his understanding of scripture, but he was also very careful as we would discuss the Bible to seek ways and means of applying the truth of the Bible to the lives of people so that it became really an alive thing and instrument for him. It was not just some dry words but a way in which he could find ways of being of assistance and of help to people."

"How would you describe Tom Bird?"

"I know it's an overused word in this trial but I would certainly describe my relationship with Tom and my observations of Tom as a very caring and people-connected person, one who generally was concerned and very caring for the people of his congregation."

"With respect to the Lutheran theology, can you tell us briefly what does the Lutheran theology or the Lutheran church feel with respect to life itself?"

"That life is a creation of God, that the Fifth Commandment, 'Thou shalt not kill' is applicable at all times; and on the positive, we should do everything we can to be of help and assistance to better the life of our fellow man rather than to tear it down or to destroy it."

Symmonds began. He asked whether Rath could see into Tom's heart? "No, sir."

"Is that correct?"

"Not even yours, sir," Rath answered.

Symmonds asked whether it would be normal for a Lutheran to mourn the loss of the life of the spouse of a friend? "Certainly."

"And can you imagine this individual whom you have so recently described referring to an individual that he had played softball, volleyball, basketball, and other sports, can you imagine him just really a few short days after his death, after he presided at that funeral, saying, 'I ain't celebrating but I ain't mourning either'? Does that sound like the man you've just described?"

"I would have to know in what connection as you mention, what his feelings and his understanding of those words were."

"Does that sound like the—a statement though that you would expect from this man you just described to the jury?"

"No, it would not."

Shaw called Mike Pruisner to the stand. Pruisner worked for John North Ford in Emporia and attended Messiah Lutheran where he served as president of the congregation. In his duties at Messiah, he helped hire Tom in 1982. "I did work with Pastor Bird. I counseled with him a few times for myself. We were in the Optimists together. We played basketball together. I feel I know him as a pastor, a friend....I firmly believe that Pastor Bird is a man of God. I believe he teaches the Word of God and he lives it with God's help to the best of his ability."

Shaw asked whether Pruisner knew Darrel. No, but he knew people who did know him. Shaw asked about Darrel's reputation as Pruisner knew it through these friends and acquaintances of his.

"I would ask again then being familiar with his reputation for honesty and truthfulness, what is his reputation in the community for honesty and truthfulness?"

"It's not good."

Symmonds began. He asked whether everyone who ever bought a car at John North Ford said good things about their experience? No, some didn't. Symmonds implied that a specific instance may have made someone unhappy, though overall, others thought highly of the dealership.

Pastor Al and friend Susan take the stand

Shaw called Pastor Al Burroughs to the stand. Burroughs knew Tom from his service with the LC-MS's Family Life Committee. Burroughs chaired it and Tom served as an active member. The committee "addresses itself to broken homes, families, strengthening the family spiritually, having better Christian homes, how to discipline children, and compassionate understanding of persons and family life."

Shaw asked whether Tom attended the committee meeting on May 19, 1983? Yes. He asked him about Tom's belief in the Bible, his character and truthfulness. Burroughs strongly endorsed Tom.

Symmonds had no questions.

Shaw called Susan Ewert to the stand. He asked about a meeting Ewert had with Tom on November 29, 1983. "We had formed a relationship after Marty's death. I had known Tom for some time; but after Marty's death we had formed a—we became friends. After Marty's death we had become friends and we had discussed Marty's death at length prior to that time following the death. When I went in that day, I—I had several things I wanted to talk to him about, but one of the things that was most troubling was a rumor that I had heard a couple days before."

"You had heard a rumor relative to Darrel Carter I believe was your testimony. Is that right?"

"Yes."

"Where had you heard this?"

"Mary Kretsinger, Dr. Kretsinger's wife, told me that she had heard the rumor."

"And did she give you any indication where she had heard it from?"

"Not at that time. I did not ask."

"Did she specifically say that this particular rumor had stemmed from Darrel Carter?"

"Yes."

Symmonds objected to this as hearsay, but Rulon overruled him.

"And basically what was the nature of that particular rumor?"

"Mary said it was reported to her that Darrel was saying downtown that Dan Carter's relationship, his brother's relationship, with Lorna Anderson had been over for a month and that Lorna's involvement in Marty's death was due to her involvement with the minister of the church. I also went on to tell him that Darrel had, according to the rumor, had stated the investigation into Sandy Bird's death was going to be reopened."

"All right. You related all that to Pastor Bird?"

"Yes."

"What was his reaction, if any? Do you recall? Was he upset about it?"

"He was upset about it. He was concerned about it."

Shaw asked whether she had seen any changes in the relationship between Tom and Lorna since November 4. "Very definitely...There has been a strengthening of the bond between the two." (This testimony resulted from a discussion with Irv Shaw and Tom. They felt it wise to open the door slightly to the growth of the relationship between the two following Marty's death. Susan, though, had also urged Tom to let Terry Smith testify. He had dated Terry since early October of 1983, and Susan believed that fact would offset any of the allegations about Tom and Lorna. Tom insisted on protecting Terry. He feared she might receive some sort of a negative mark against her that would hurt her standing in the LC-MS, and he did not want that to happen.)

Symmonds began questioning Susan by reinforcing this idea that the bond between Tom and Lorna had grown stronger. He asked her about the bond prior to November 4, did she have any personal knowledge of that?

"I was aware of the fact that Lorna was working with Tom in the fall in the beginning of the spring of 1983. I was aware of the working relationship. I was aware of the fact that they did join—both Marty and Lorna joined Faith Lutheran Church, and she spoke very highly—"

Symmonds cut her off and simply reinforced the strong bond presently existing.

That ended the defense's case.

Rebuttal witnesses called

Symmonds called rebuttal witnesses, starting with Sharon Meyer. He asked whether it was true that Tom told her Angie Duensing, Larry Kalsow and Tom's in-laws expressed concern about Lorna to him. And was there anyone else Tom said expressed the same? "Yes, he did. He told me Sandy Bird expressed a concern."

Shaw objected to this because all through the trial they had avoided bringing Sandy into the testimony. Rulon said that Tom raised it himself during his testimony. The answer stood.

Shaw had Sharon clarify that the topic of her discussion with Tom was Lorna's dependency on him, nothing else? "That was my understanding."

Symmonds asked again, "Did the defendant say that Sandra Bird was concerned about Lorna's dependency upon him or about his relationship with or about the relationship between the two?"

"My understanding was that he said that Sandy was concerned about Lorna's relationship toward him."

Sharon Meyer stepped down.

Symmonds called Darrel back to the stand. Symmonds asked about the soccer tournament in Wichita. Did Darrel go to such an event? Yes. Did he remember seeing Kermit Grover at the fireworks stand? Yes.

Did you meet with Tom at Faith during May, 1983? Shaw objected. This was not a proper question for a rebuttal witness, it was simply repeating earlier testimony. Rulon overruled him thereby allowing the jury to hear Darrel's testimony one more time. To prove it was a May meeting, Darrel said he knew it to be so because Darrell Warren worked with him at that time. Darrel stepped down.

With this the state and the defense rested their cases. They argued about admissibility of certain exhibits of evidence and then Rulon told the jury they were dismissed until 1:30 that afternoon when closing arguments would be made and the case submitted to them.

Symmonds closes first and last

Kansas rules of procedure allow the prosecutor to go first during closing arguments. He chooses whether to split his argument into two sections, allowing him to present half of his argument following the defense attorney. Symmonds chose to go first and last.

[Author's note to readers: The entire transcript of the closing arguments of Rod Symmonds and Irv Shaw are posted on the website, http://www.cagedbird.net/excerpts.htm.]

He reminded the jury that Darrel had a wife and children, and that he lived his entire life in Emporia. Darrel had no criminal record and employed "a number of persons."

Symmonds justified Darrel's delay in reporting the solicitation as a means of protecting himself from public embarrassment over his affair with Lorna. Besides, "had he gone out at that time, who would have believed him?" He suggested that pieces of the puzzle fell into place over time.

Everyone agreed the church meeting had happened. The reality that the story evolved over time proved its truthfulness, Symmonds claimed.

Symmonds repeated the statements Darrel said had been made by Tom and Lorna. Love, insurance, presiding at the funeral, Darrel as a pallbearer. "Those are cold statements."

He repeated the two plots of how to kill Marty. Darrel told them he'd think about it. "Get back to me later," or words to that effect.

He told them Tom came to the house on West View but Darrel brushed him off. Then Darrel called and told him, "Hey, I'm not participating." He claimed this happened weeks later. Since Marty still walked around alive, "I suppose Darrel Carter, like any one of us, would have thought, well, it's one of those things that was mentioned but nothing's ever going to happen." But Sandy's death caused him to think and to worry.

Though he waited until Danny's arrest to tell anyone about the May meeting, Darrel told Darrell Warren that "he had been approached by a man to kill someone else." The cancelled check proved the time period.

He reminded the jury that Darrel told Mike Patton this story during the morning of November 18. Patton testified to this. Patton said he remembered Darrel making "the statement about the defendant being a man of God and going to kill Martin Anderson; could not remember what other statements."

Tom "told Julie Palmer he wanted, one, to reaffirm a trust. What else did he say? When she asked him or made the statement something to the effect, 'Why don't you give him a call'; and he said, 'No, no phones.' Now, you've heard the defendant's explanation for that. But if you were excited and if you were upset about this rumor which you heard Susan Ewert mention, wouldn't you want to immediately talk to that person? You could pick up the phone; and you would say, 'What the heck are you doing' if you were upset about it." Tom had told Julie that sometimes people said things they wish they hadn't. Symmonds implied that meant a discussion about murder, not rumors about a sexual affair.

He rehearsed the chain of events between Patton and KBI Agent Humphrey, that the first meeting occurred before a deal had been cut for Danny. Then he referenced testimony that Darrel showed nervousness before meeting with Tom in the parking lot and wore a bulletproof vest. Though Darrel had no experience "like a trained investigator that had participated in a hundred undercover operations," he still produced a useful audiotape record of that meeting. "You've heard the preposterous explanation as to certain statements on that tape by the defendant, absolutely incredible explanations as to what they were really talking about."

He recalled KBI Agent Don Winsor's testimony about interviewing Tom. Tom said he saw Lorna with a bruise on the side of her face. She told him she ran into a door. And Tom said he never heard Lorna say anything "about wanting to be rid of or be away from her husband."

He talked about the life insurance, with a potential payoff of $445,000. He reminded them of the May 6 policy application adding $100,000 coverage on Marty's life. "And if you start looking at the time period there, it becomes very obvious that they—had this killing occurred within that period of time, had it occurred soon after the meeting at the church, well, there wold have been another hundred thousand on the life of Martin Anderson."

Angie "talked about the flirting which occurred between the defendant and Lorna Anderson, the electricity in the air, the sparkle in their eyes and things of that nature."   "Lori Anderson, she testified as to the kissing." Steven Anderson and Don Winsor said Lori used the word "kissing," and that it had been on the mouth.

Larry Kalsow testified about the van; "it was headed south."

"And you heard the testimony of Jan Mead pertaining to the relationship, pertaining to the fact that the defendant, the minister, he was pretty good in bed."

Esther Aldrete, the babysitter, testified about Lorna telling someone on the phone about counting the green stuff.

Neither Aldrete nor Mead had a motive to make up a story.

Symmonds first 20 minutes expired. He sat down, listening carefully to Shaw's closing arguments, fine-tuning his final statement.

Shaw gives his closing argument

Shaw reminded them of the pledge they took during voir dire, to rely only on evidence and to hold the state to proving their case beyond a reasonable doubt. "I am confident that you will do so and I appreciate it."

"At the outset I would like to try to isolate and get down to exactly what it is we're talking about. The defendant, Tom Bird, is tried in this courtroom at this time with the crime of criminal solicitation, and that crime and that crime alone is all that is alleged. He is not charged with being a victim or responsible for rumors. He is not charged with being involved in insurance. He is not charged in the death of Martin Anderson...the sole and only question before you here today, is whether the defendant is in fact guilty of the crime of criminal solicitation."

Shaw reminded the jury to evaluate the credibility of testimony and the motives behind it. "I would suggest to you, it is necessary for you to believe, as the state has presented the evidence at the present time, that in May of 1983 Darrel Carter went to the Faith Lutheran Church and met for the very first time the defendant, Tom Bird. That the defendant immediately upon being introduced without an preliminary introductions proceeded to request Darrel Carter, a person he had never met or knew anything about, to assist him the perpetration of the criminal act of murder in the first degree. That despite not one, but three refusals by Darrel Carter that the defendant proceeded on to go forward and outline" three murder plans in an open office. Shaw called the state's allegation "bizarreness."

The state tried to bolster it's claim by introducing a discussion about insurance and trying to prove a sordid love affair existed between Tom and Lorna. "I suggest to you again the defendant is not charged and neither of those are before you for consideration. Those are not crimes."

Shaw addressed Jan Mead's testimony. "We don't know even if those things were said. We do know that the defendant has denied it." He dissected Mead's testimony, showing that Lorna's claims went from an affair with a hairdresser in January to a minister in March, and the claim Lorna met Tom at motels in Wichita and Topeka. "Where are the motel receipts? Where are the people from the motels to identify this?" Even with the KBI and the FBI, no proof could be found to support Mead's hearsay evidence.

Shaw discussed the testimony of Angie and Sharon Meyer. Both testified to Lorna's infatuation with Tom or her dependence on him. Neither accused

Tom of reciprocating. Lorna worked for Tom and she was his friend. He relied on her and became concerned about her. "But that in and of itself does not make the boss-employee or the co-employees bed partners, lovers or paramours." If Tom's concerns for Lorna became a motive for solicitation, then every human being that gets angry on behalf of a friend would be guilty of "carrying a motive to solicit murder; and that's not so."

He pointed to Tom's grief and mourning that crescendoed until he went to Little Rock in October, unable to bear any more stress.

"Let's look at these letters. These letters, if you will recall, were written after Lorna Anderson's husband had passed away. The defendant could identify with the grief...with the low point she would have." Given that he would be out of town those two critical nights, "he selected these cards at random and wrote on there words that he considered to be words of encouragement, of love, the Christian love that 'I am not going to abandon you. I'm not going to go off and lead my own life. Don't give up hope.' Of the future but not of the future together but of the future so that she would not give up hope." Shaw said that in retrospect, these words might have been a bad choice, "but it does not establish a love affair."

Shaw turned to Darrel's veracity. What about Darrell Warren? What about Joe Lapping? What about Mike Patton? Their testimony relies solely on whatever Darrel told them.

Warren and Lapping both said Darrel talked about somebody wanting him to kill somebody. The state tried to establish that as happening prior to May 30. Neither man took it seriously. "Indeed Lapping just kind of passed it off and Warren considered it an exaggeration...But that is not to say someone didn't approach Darrel Carter. Indeed they may very have approached him. Anyone who has a bulletproof vest at home is running in, pardon the expression from the tape, a different crowd than I'm familiar with."

Darrel's best guess of the meeting date was May 18-20. Tom drove to Topeka on the 19th. Lorna drove to pick up Marty on the 20th. That left the 18th, and Darrel stated he told Warren about the meeting at the house a few days after Tom came out to see him. That meant he spoke to Warren at the earliest on the 21st—it could be no other day. But several testified that Tom met with the youth board on the 21st and they briefly discussed fireworks that day. "More importantly, if what Mr. Carter is saying is true, then you have the unbelievable situation of Thomas Bird having given Reverend Kalsow a brochure somehow surreptitiously so he would never know about it for Reverend Kalsow to give back to him in front of witnesses so we could have the onset, the first mention, of firecrackers relating to this particular incident."

Kermit Grother saw Tom and Darrel at the fireworks stand. He said they looked like old buddies.

Even Rod Symmonds stipulated that Darrel's "only motive in reporting this, was to help his brother, Danny. Shaw demonstrated how even starting on November 17, the date of Danny's arrest, Darrel's story began to evolve and expand.

Once Lyon County filed charges against Tom, Darrel had no choice but to testify. "And if he doesn't, his brother's approved plea and the probation could be revoked; and it is with that that he proceeds to embellish, to expand, to create a new and different story."

Darrel took possession of police reports, including statements made by Angie, Sharon Meyer and even Tom. From those reports, Darrel fashioned his evolving story.

Shaw said, "These things, if they did in fact happen, are so bizarre and so outrageous that any person in their right mind would have told them the very first time they talked to the authorities. But did he? No. It's not until May the 31st, 1984, when he testifies that for the first time he explains or attempts to explain away the firecracker situation." Not until Darrel listened to the tape a few times before his May 31 testimony, and heard Tom mention firecrackers, did he add that twist to his story.

Darrel testified that, given all of the public knowledge of Sandy's death, it was not hard to concoct a story.

Darrel first said he only knew Lorna socially. Then he confessed to having sex with her. He called Julie Palmer a friend. Then he admitted to a two year sexual relationship with her, but only after a lunch break and consulting with Mike Patton and Rod Symmonds.

What about the taped meeting in the bowling alley? Darrel, even after being trained by the police, could not elicit one single incriminating statement from Tom.

The jury heard Darrel refer to getting and reading all the police reports. Not once did Tom ask whether those reports included anything about him— not once. Shaw quoted Agent Winsor's conclusion about the tape. "This is nothing more than two individuals talking about the investigation to date and the parties already charged."

Shaw reminded the jurors that Tom testified voluntarily, and that his testimony was corroborated by witnesses. Shipley, Bryant and Kalsow all recalled the May 21 meeting. Shipley recalled the brief discussion of Carter's Crackers on May 29.

Tom pointed out the June 7 date he had written on his calendar. "If the defendant was in fact guilty, he would never, never include on his calendar the name of Darrel Carter, and yet it is here for everyone to see."

Tom acknowledged a meeting at the house in mid-June. They talked about whether Marty beat Lorna and what to do about it.

Susan Ewert testified that she told Tom about Darrel spreading rumors, the same rumors mentioned several times on the tape.

"His testimony here, unlike Darrel Carter's, does not stand alone. Mr. Bird's testimony, sufficient in and of itself, stands with independent observations and reports, support."

Tom might have made unwise decisions in dealing with rumors, but it was the responsibility of the board of lay ministers to "insure the integrity, the theological devotion, if you will, of the ministry and the church; and had they had one shred of evidence in July or August of 1983 of any type of fooling around...they would have terminated him. There would have been no fact-finding. It would have been automatic, complete and final. But they would not act on rumors."

Shaw reminded the jury that they had to have evidence that Tom solicited Darrel. No such evidence existed, "and a verdict of not guilty should be returned."

Symmonds finishes

Judge Rulon allowed the jury to stand and stretch. Then he asked Symmonds to begin.

Yes, Tom did testify. He asked the jury to believe that those cards he gave to Lorna were just to get her through her time of grief while he went to Wichita. "And you heard him say that, gosh, he didn't really look at them, didn't really pay any attention; and yet these letters start off with the 'Miss you, miss you, miss you' that I referred to earlier. These are love letters," Symmonds insisted.

Symmonds claimed that not even Lorna believed these cards were just to lift her spirits. Otherwise, why did she hide them away in a drawer under her "lingerie"? "That shows you that she thought these things were love letters."

"Now, you can sit here and talk all day long about Christian love and brotherly love; and when you start ending up—when you start saying, 'I love you and am confident of the future and love you always' on an envelope that looks like this and to presume that a minister, somebody with two master's degrees wouldn't even have been considerate enough to look to see what was on the outside to know whether he was sending a get well card or a sympathy card is absolutely incredible. Nobody would do that."

Symmonds admitted that the state did not have to prove Tom had a love affair with Lorna. But, the state showed this provided a motive for the solicitation of someone to murder Marty. "And if it isn't love and it isn't money, and those we all know are some of the oldest motives that ever existed since Biblical times."

He mentioned credibility. "You believe Darrel Carter and the defendant is guilty. You believe Thomas Bird and he is innocent."

Symmonds next totally twisted Susan Ewert's testimony. (This misuse of her statement so rankled her that she brought a complaint against Symmonds to the Kansas State Attorney General.) "And Susan Ewert, what did she say about this when she was testifying? She said they were closer today than ever."

Referring to Susan telling Tom about hearing rumors, Symmonds minimized the impact by saying, "But interestingly enough, the defendant would have you believe that he heard this, just that little bit, that he and Lorna Anderson were having a relationship, he heard that rumor and he was so excited that he immediately walked over there, confronted Julie Palmer...and the whole purpose being it's going to shut the mouth of Darrel Carter."

Symmonds said that Tom should have told Lorna to quit spreading rumors. She's the one who talked to Jan Mead and Esther Aldrete. Now, Susan says that Tom and Lorna are closer than ever. "What didn't he take offense at the fact that Lorna Anderson was running around spreading these rumors? Because he knew they were true. Just that simple." (Actually, Tom never knew she had been doing this, nor did the lay ministers.)

He addressed the lack of motel receipts. He derided the idea that police could have found motel receipts to prove Tom and Lorna visited motels. (They had tried and failed, but he did not mention this.)

What about the bulletproof vest? "And by golly, if I had just confessed to my involvement in a murder charge that was underway over there, I think I would get me a bulletproof vest over there, too, if somebody had already been killed and I had been the type that made a confession to it."

He addressed the issue of the date of the offense. The state charged that this crime took place on or about the month of May. "The state isn't contending this thing took place on the 18th or 19th. We are saying that this occurred in the month of May." He believed it made more sense that it happened the following week so that the youth had already discussed fireworks.

Addressing the evolution of Darrel's testimony, Symmonds said that when Humphrey talked with Darrel on December 10, it was not a formal interview. But Darrel did tell Patton about Tom saying he was a man of God who would kill Marty. And he insisted that the reason the story evolved was because over time, people would ask him if there was anything else he remembered. That is only normal.

He said Darrel didn't plan the church meeting, Tom did. Then he brought in witnesses to say, "Gee, he's a minister and we all know ministers read the Bible." "Ladies and gentlemen, we've all been raised; we've all been taught to respect people who are ministers, who are priests, who are men of the cloth. We all do. Those persons who are entitled to our respect should receive it. And those persons who would abuse their position have no right to expect that to save their neck when they're sitting here on trial."

He spoke to the idea of reasonable doubt. "The state doesn't have to prove this beyond all doubt...We just have to prove it beyond a reasonable doubt."

"Ladies and gentlemen, with respect to this matter, you can sit here and tell me a hundred times that those statements aren't incriminating, and I heard those explanations and I still just quake to think that anybody would actually believe somebody would swallow it." (Symmonds here suggested that any juror who voted to acquit, then, would be stupid.)

He quoted Tom saying that after his wife died it was God's way of saying, "You don't mess with this stuff." "And that shows, ladies and gentlemen, that at that point in time he may have learned—you know, he may have learned that he shouldn't have been talking about it and soliciting murder."

"The statement that—and then the most damning, 'We're by with it, whatever we're—you know, our contact with the whole business. We never followed through, never did follow through on anything.' To suggest that this refers back to some SOS meeting where they both agreed that, well, they weren't going to report it to SOS, Darrel Carter said he didn't even mention that." Darrel said they never talked about the SOS.

Symmonds insisted that Tom had many inconsistencies in his story.

"And I think the evidence leads you to one conclusion, the very thing that I asked you at the time that we started this case, and that was would you be able if the evidence established beyond a reasonable doubt that the defendant was guilty, would you be able to convict that man. And I submit, ladies and gentlemen, the state has met that burden and I ask you to find the defendant guilty as charged. Thank you."

The jury returns a verdict

Judge Rulon sent the jury out in the afternoon on August 1. Virginia wrote about it:

> "When all testimony is heard and the jury is in session we are forced to reside in this feeling of limbo. We are sure Tom is innocent yet we feel the jury will be biased. The whole city seems to be biased.

408

We do a lot of praying about this as we await the verdict.

"The jury goes in session at around 10 o'clock in the morning and I go home with the children to wait. Tom and attorney Shaw stay at Shaw's office until he closes. Tom and his friends seek refuge in a nearby restaurant to be close at hand.

"At 10 p.m. the jury is sent home for the night and we spend a very sleepless, disturbed night, not to be compared with any other. [The jury was not sequestered. The judge trusted them not to discuss the case with anyone, nor watch or read news about the case.]

"Early next morning Ralph and Tom go again to Shaw's office to wait. At around 10:30 a.m. a call comes to us at the house that they have reached a verdict. We quickly take the kids to a babysitter and race downtown..."

At about 10:45 a.m., Tom entered the courtroom and sat down. He watched the nervous jurors return to their seats and the judge to his bench. They jury had deliberated a total of eight hours, indicating a level of difficulty in reaching a verdict. "Has the jury reached a verdict?" Rulon asked.

"Yes we have your honor."

Alice Thornton took the piece of paper with the jury's decision to Judge Rulon. He unfolded and read it, and handed it back to Thornton. "Mr. Bird, will you please rise? The bailiff will read the verdict."

"We, the jury, find Thomas P. Bird guilty as charged," Thornton raised her eyes and looked briefly at Tom.

Tom stood looking down when the verdict was read. He spent years developing an outer appearance of strength under pressure. He kept his professional composure.

Terry Smith watched Tom react and thoughts flew through her mind like a whirlwind. "It was unbelief. I was in shock. I remember Tom didn't react because he was so on guard, they were always watching and he didn't react, and they called him stoic. He couldn't win either way. A dull hollowness went through me. What do we tell the kids?"

Virginia wrote, "We got there just in time for the jury to come in and give a verdict of GUILTY. We are numb and just can't believe this is happening to our family."

Jane Grismer declined comment, saying, "To us, it's a family thing and we've got three grandchildren (Bird's)." Jane had retained Little Rock attorney Jack Lassiter to look into Sandy Bird's death. Tom's conviction, and what she learned while quizzing prosecutors and their witnesses, added to her belief that there was more to Sandy's death than had previously been known.

She intensified her efforts to win "justice."

Lyon County Attorney Rod Symmonds said he was surprised the jury took so long to reach its verdict, but otherwise was pleased. He recognized a potential appeal point when he said, "I don't think the media's attention in this case harmed it in any way. I wasn't bothered by the cameras and I don't think the jury was either."

"I think it is the wrong decision, but we will go on and carry out our mission," said Don Froelich.

"I think it would be worth his while to appeal," said Alan Rees. "They should move the trial somewhere where the jury hasn't already made up its mind. Everybody in this town had decided Tom was guilty."

Shaw said he would consider appealing. "It's too early to tell. We will have to sit back and look at it for a while."

Rulon set Tom's sentencing at 9 a.m. Aug. 30.

The jury told Rulon they had voted as a group not to comment to news reporters and others concerning their deliberations. Their lips remained sealed and no one but these six men and six women know why they believed Darrel and not Tom.

If the jury had heard Susan Ewert's testimony that Lorna never told Jan Mead she wanted Marty and Sandy out of the way; if they had heard her say the man Lorna referred to was Willie Potter, not Tom; if they had known how Lorna cried and wailed when she heard Mead's testimony, would the jury have voted guilty?

If the jury had heard Lorna say that the meeting was in June, not May; that Marty's name was never discussed at the meeting; that they discussed fireworks, soccer and homebuilding, would the jury have voted guilty?

If the jury had heard David Workman describe his March 30 meeting with Lorna after Marty had beaten her, where she told him Marty had better be careful or he would be roughed up or shot; if they had heard Workman place this in the context of a discussion of Danny Carter; if Workman had told the jury he saw a gun in Lorna's purse that day, fully seven weeks before Darrel said he met Tom, would the jury have voted guilty?

Darrel could never specify the date of the alleged May meeting. He thought it was maybe in the middle of the month. Both Tom and Lorna could prove neither was available on the only days this meeting could have occurred.

If Judge Rulon had refused to allow Jan Mead's hearsay testimony, would the jury have voted guilty?

These and other questions remain unanswered until 1990.

The jury voted guilty because they believed Tom, a minister, had sex with Lorna. A pastor who had sex with his church secretary could have been guilty of just about anything.

Rod Symmonds mocked Tom as a minister trying to hide his hideous crimes behind the collar of a pastor. At the time, Jim and Tammy Baker's demise filled the airwaves. Jimmy Swaggert's sexual affair made the tabloids.

Once Symmonds got Tom convicted, part "A" of the state's three-part strategy was complete. They could move ahead with part B, finding a way to convict Tom of murdering Sandy, even though they had no evidence.

Tom left the court and went home with his parents and children. Many well-wishers stopped by to express their continuing support, and that offered him some slight comfort, but it did not erase the injustice of the verdict.

Jane Grismer stopped, too. Jane reminded Tom that her son Joe Stringer was to be married on August 9. She demanded, with threat of suing for grandmothers' rights, that the three Bird children be allowed to attend the wedding.

Later that day, Tom went to the door and picked up the *Emporia Gazette*. He dreaded the stories that chronicled his conviction but it was the editorial page that caused him the most grief. Tom read the editorial that called Darrel Carter a hero. "A hero! A hero! He is a liar, not a hero!"

Tom ran downstairs and threw himself on a bed. Ralph and Virginia saw their son looking pathetic and destroyed. They heard him wail and sob, "Dad, I'm not a bad boy. I am innocent!" They knew it, but Emporia had believed Darrel, one of their own.

On August 3, Virginia, Ralph and the three Bird children left for Hardy, Arkansas. Tom had time to spend planning the next phase of his life which he believed would be several years of probation.

Preparation for life after guilty verdict

Lorna saw Tom's conviction as a danger signal. The court had moved her trial date back several times, waiting until they had Tom convicted. She hired Jack Focht, a well-known defense lawyer, to fight for her freedom, but it would still be more than a year before her charges were settled. Lyon County needed to keep her on a tight string until they were done with Tom.

Irv Shaw met with the family and with Tom. They decided to appeal the decision and felt certain Tom would be released on appeal bond until his hearing, as much as 120 days after sentencing. Given the 4-year probation Danny Carter received for admitting guilt to a Class D Felony, the same charge as Tom's, Shaw saw much the same ahead for Tom. A Geary County judge placed Greg Curry on parole just 45 days into his sentence for the same charge.

To insure that the court looked favorably on him, Tom began to put together a plan for him and his family. Though he knew pastoring another church remained out of the question until this wrongful conviction could be overturned, he believed that going to and teaching school would serve two purposes: satisfy the court that he would be gainfully and productively employed, and prepare himself for a better future.

He enrolled his three children at Bethany Lutheran School in Wichita and himself at Wichita State University. He settled on pointing toward another master's degree, this time as a Specialist in Education. He began negotiations with the Board of Missions of the Kansas District to teach at the Lutheran Student Center at Wichita State or with Lutheran Social Services. The District President, Rev. George Bruening, worked with Tom to develop a writing project chronicling the history of the Lutheran Church in Kansas.

Tom continued seeing Don Romsa to deal with his personal frustrations and gain an objective opinion on how to proceed, now that he had lost in court.

Though his confidence in the court system was shaken by the guilty verdict, Tom saw some relief coming once the sentencing phase was completed. In Wichita, Tom saw hope that he could begin rebuilding his life.

Mark marks Marty's murder spot

Tom's older brother Mark is aggressive and outgoing, a take-charge and driven person who transparently displays his convictions. Mark's friend Fred Geller drove him from Little Rock to Emporia after the guilty verdict. Tom asked Mark to help him sort through all that had happened and help him do some of the investigative work he had left undone.

Soon after arriving, Fred drove Mark, Tom and Lorna out to the site of Marty's murder along Highway 177. Mark watched and listened to Lorna carefully that day, and soon became convinced that Tom had been totally conned by her. He describes their trip to the murder scene:

"I'm in the front seat, passenger side, Fred's on the driver's side. We've already picked up Tom and he's sitting in the middle of the back. Lorna gets in and leans over absolutely as positively close as she can get to Tom. I mean this is the clinging female; immediately I saw that.

"Keep in mind that I talked to Sue Ewert about how dependent she was. She said Lorna is not the type who can be single. Lorna needs a man around. That whole drive there, her hands were constantly clinging to Tom.

"While we drove, I was describing what I read, they were

describing what they knew and then I said 'when we get out there what I want to do is park the car like you parked the van and walk through the whole thing step-by-step. This we did."

Lorna led Mark and Tom around the site, pointed to where the hit man first appeared, explained how he fired at Marty. She took them down into the ditch where Marty had laid, and to the telephone pole where the hit man had pulled her down on the ground and fired the empty gun at her.

Mark continued:

"At the time, there were some things that really bothered me. When I read the material there was nothing in the material about Lorna having mud on her. That was one of the things we talked about, that there should have been mud on her knees. Then in the autopsy report they said there were only three shots fired. Lorna's story was that the man was by the van and shot down toward the field. [Mark recognized that it would take a professional marksman to hit a target from 40-50 feet away with a .22 caliber pistol, and put them in the kind of close cluster found in Marty's head.] I told Lorna this was a guy I wanted to line up for a shooting team."

When Tom and Mark returned home that day, they talked late into the night about things that made no sense. The shooting itself, seemed improbable. Dr. Eckert said Marty died from three bullets in the rear of his head. Eckert noted there was mud on Marty's knees, as though he had been kneeling down, and the shots were from above and behind him.

Tom left the room and returned with a box of materials. "Look at this stuff and see what you think," he told Mark.

"There were two things that struck me. In Sandy's death, none of the officers' reports suggested anything but an accident. Nobody said anything that talked about anything foul or out of place or unusual or suspicious. That was the first thing I noticed.

"The second thing I noticed was the fact that the bullets that they found when they searched Danny Carter's place were the same name brand as those that killed Marty. Now this was an important factor because of the history of guns in our family. This silly story that Darrel came up with that Tom planned to go to Marty's grandmother's house and when he walked in he would shoot them. I mean that's just outrageous. It's foolish. No one in our family owned, used or shot guns.

"After reading the autopsy report, I showed it to Tom that there is no way that Martin could turn his back and this guy shot him from the van. And I remember this distinctly, Tom said, 'What you think is that Lorna is lying?' And I said, 'Tom the picture I saw of Lorna today is not the picture I saw on the phone.' Over the phone she comes off as very timid, very sweet, very withdrawn. But as soon as we got there she was very clinging."

Mark saw Lorna as a dangerous seductress.

The second day he read the material about Danny Carter and the transcript of the taping done in Darrel's car. "At that time, I was convinced that this was all awry; something just didn't make sense. Why didn't Darrel Carter confront Tom with the questions? Tom did not say a word about the transcript, he just said 'you read it. Tell me what you think he said, because I'm just looking for the answers. When you're involved, sometimes you don't see that stuff.' So we went through all that."

Mark asked Lorna for permission to talk with Lori, now nine years old. The Bird children loved Uncle Mark, and Lori took to him immediately. The two of them sat on a curb together and talked about the night of Marty's murder. "The girls did not recognize the voice, which really made me think twice. I thought, well they know Tom's voice and they know Danny Carter's voice, why did they not recognize the voice? The only thing I can come up with, was that they confused this conversation with the conversation between the man and wife who first arrived who gave the CPR. He was consoling Lorna and the girls. They certainly remembered the flash."

Mark sensed Lori told the story as she remembered it, and left open the possibility that Lorna may have coached her.

"My final night with Tom, he bused me around everywhere. He showed me the place where the money was exchanged, the house where Carter lived. He took me out to the bridge. We went to Hutchinson for a meal with Lorna's family. I took along the legal pad with about seven questions written down. I asked Lorna to answer them. She did, pretty much as she answered them earlier in the day, except that there were two things that bothered me.

"One was could she tell by the voice who was the man with the mask, and she said she couldn't. I thought that in that situation she would have remembered the voice. Been able to put a name on him. The rest of her description is a pretty good description, even the morning Tom went and talked to her in the hospital. Here it is a month later, in the sanctuary of her home, where she's feeling safe and she could not answer."

As Mark and Tom prepared to leave, Loren Slater came up to Mark, shook his hand and said, "Thank you for all that you can do because we need to get this mess taken care of."

"I hope we can."

Then, still holding Mark's hand, Loren pointed at him and said, "You know and I know she knows who did it."

"That may or may not be true, but maybe she will tell us when the time comes."

Loren's comment shook Mark, and he decided on a strategy. He believed Lorna withheld the identify of the killer because she feared for her own safety or that of her children. He took Lorna aside and said, "Put it down in writing the person who did this, and send it to me. I promised I would put it somewhere safe. She did not do this."

Tom heard this conversation. Lorna cried and whined, stating she felt threatened and was in "all kinds of trouble."

"Lorna, the only protection you have is for them to know that you have sent this to someone, so that if it does happen, you are protected. She never sent anything."

Mark quickly became convinced that Lorna was at the center of Tom's trouble.

"I felt that this was all an inner circle game. If you read the police reports carefully, a lot of the paths lead to her. Loren was pretty certain that everybody knew everybody and they were all still around the area. This was Lorna's dad. I assume he was hoping Lorna would break down and tell somebody what really happened."

Lorna did confess, but not for another year. Her eventual confession made all her other lies pale in comparison, but her present problem centered on how to avoid her own conviction. Her legal strategies centered on her own needs, and Tom became nothing more to her than a way to collect information to help her beat her own rap.

Task force formed

With Tom convicted of solicitation, investigators began to focus on finding the evidence to convict him of Sandy Bird's murder and, eventually, Marty's—equal parts of the same deadly scheme.

They formed a task forced chaired by Steven Opat, Geary County Attorney that met for the first time on August 16, 1984. Members of the task forced included:

Deputy Bill Deppish, Geary County Sheriff's Office;
Deputy Al Buskey, Geary County Sheriff's Office;
David Klamm, Junction City Police Department;

Tom Lesher, Junction City Police Department;
Agent Don Winsor, Kansas Bureau of Investigation for Geary County;
Agent Vern Humphrey, Kansas Bureau of Investigation for Lyon
    County;
Lt. Billy Persinger, Kansas Highway Patrol;
Trooper John Rule, Kansas Highway Patrol;
Sheriff Dan Andrews, Lyon County;
Deputy Gary Eichorn, Lyon County Sheriff's Office.

Opat saw the task force as a vehicle to coordinate the two investigations, one of Marty's murder and the other of Sandy's mysterious death. Clearly, the members of the task force now believed Sandy had been murdered.

At this first meeting, Opat reported that Stephen Anderson, Marty's brother, recalled that an old handgun previously owned by his father had been passed on to Marty. Stephen looked at pictures of various types of guns and identified a few as similar to the old gun. He marked the Colt Woodsman as one of his choices, and Deppish noted that it matched the type of gun that could have been used in Marty's murder.

Opat reported on a copy of a letter Stephen Anderson recently received from Lorna. Its contents seemed strange to Stephen but it was the handwriting sample that Opat needed. He ordered the handwriting be compared with an incomplete letter Lorna wrote to Tom, found next to the greeting cards in her lingerie drawer. Opat saw this incomplete and never sent letter as more proof of an affair between Lorna and Tom, though once again it was but an indicator of the world as seen through Lorna's eyes. Her perception had been bought by the first jury.

Opat advised the task force that Sandy Bird's body would be exhumed as soon as the district judge could sign the proper paperwork. He mentioned that Tom owned the burial plot so before they could move ahead, he would have to be notified. It is unclear whether Opat considered Tom to be Sandy's closest living relative, or if he appealed to Jane Grismer. For certain, he never got Tom's approval. Opat explained that Dr. William Eckert had agreed to perform a second autopsy.

Opat did not record in writing whether he mentioned that Eckert previously talked about the case with Deppish, nor does it state what Eckert confessed to a reporter in a 1985 interview. "I gave a private report to Opat that was not public knowledge after talking to Deppish," Eckert told Joan Baker in a November, 1985, interview. She wrote a 1986 article about the deaths for *KS Magazine*.

In his "secret memo," Eckert wrote to Opat on July 24, during Tom's first trial, and pushed for the second autopsy. "I have had a conference with

Mr. Bill Deppish of the Geary County Sheriff's Department on July 22, 1984 at my home in Wichita in which we discussed the various aspects of the death of Sandra Bird. He suggested that I write to you with my thoughts and opinion as the value of the disinterrment of the body of Ms. Bird." Eckert stated the reasons of this disinterrment in vague terms, emphasizing the early treatment of the death as an accident and the inexperience of the first pathologist in criminal matters. Eckert made his living doing this type of work and he had a penchant for high profile cases.

"Was there a pattern of injuries?" Baker asked, wondering why they chose to consider a second autopsy on Sandy's body.

"See, *we decided before the autopsy,* the question was should we do an autopsy, and I pretty well felt that, in the first place, there's such a question that you gotta check it out. You gotta have someone experienced to check it out. *So we had a fairly good concept ahead of time.* It may not be a good approach, but at least you had a degree of suspicion." [Emphasis added.] A degree of suspicion is appropriate, but predetermining what one will find during the autopsy invalidates the results.

The task force also heard that Lt. Billy Persinger, a Kansas Highway Patrolman with limited experience in accident reconstruction, had agreed to examine the Bird case. Trooper Rule assisted him. Opat reported that, "Sandra always used seat belts." This information came from the Grismer family, none of whom lived in or near Emporia. How did they know whether or not Sandy "always" wore a seat belt? The Grismers also told Opat and various investigators that Tom had told them "different stories" about what happened to Sandy. Those "different stories" seemed, to Grismer, that Tom lied and if he lied to them, he must be guilty of something. The "different stories," though, were nothing more than explanations given by a weary sorrowful widower who had scant facts during the hours and days immediately following Sandy's death.

The task force continued to drive the investigation to prove Tom murdered Sandy. They showed no inclination to look at various alternatives to her death. Their minds were made up.

Emporians wanted someone to answer for the unusual death of Sandy Bird. Public pressure began building against Sheriff Andrews to "do something." Andrews believed he was doing everything he could, but he did it quietly, behind the scenes. He resented "those people up in Junction City who think they know everything." Cliff Hacker, Andrews' opponent in the fall election, used the perception of inaction by Andrews as a campaign issue, and Andrews lost the election. The Tom Bird case, as it evolved, became a vehicle for the political and career hopes of prosecutors, investigators, sheriffs and at least one judge.

Sentencing

Tom stood once again before Judge Gary Rulon on August 30, 1984. He believed the next several months would be tough but eventually, following a successful appeal of the guilty verdict, his name would be cleared.

Tom explained the plan he had devised to teach and serve in the Wichita area while attending Wichita State University. He told Rulon about enrolling his children in a Lutheran School. He presented evidence that he would be gainfully employed. He felt certain the judge would order probation.

Let Virginia Bird relate the judge's decision. "Tom is sentenced to 2-1/2 to 7 years. We are shocked and surprised. Even for a first offense this is severe. Also he was denied bail and denied the right to go take care of his last minute details. He is ushered off to jail immediately."

Judge Rulon saw no need to give Tom anything except immediate incarceration. "The court cannot overlook the extent of the harm that can be caused in a community by such solicitations."

No public record exists that Judge Rulon had knowledge of the work of the two-county murder task force that had already decided Tom murdered Sandy, but his unusually tough sentence and denial of appeal bond sent a strong signal: The Kansas legal system wanted Tom Bird in a cage and didn't want to chance that he might fly away if given any freedom.

With this sentence, Tom faced a minimum of 17 months in prison before his first parole hearing. Rod Symmonds strongly argued for a longer sentence, suggesting he wanted more time to develop his prosecution of Tom for Sandy Bird's murder. The judge's decision placed pressure on the task force to get their case assembled quickly.

Irv Shaw implored the judge to place Tom on probation to give his children "the emotional, financial and guiding support" they needed from their only living parent. Now jailed, Tom could do nothing for his children. Jane, though, had her own plans and wasted no time taking action against him. Within two hours of his sentencing, Jane filed suit to win temporary custody of the children.

On August 31, Tom met with his parents at the Lyon County Jail. He asked them to assume temporary custody of the children. Tom expected his jail-time not to exceed 120 days, and he felt the kids would be best off in the home of his Lutheran parents despite Jane's protestations. Tom knew little of Jane's involvement in the developing case against him, but he knew the spiritual and family needs of his children would best be met by Ralph and Virginia.

While the Birds met at the jail, Tom's aunt and uncle came from Hardy to begin packing Tom's possessions at the Henry Street house and move them to Arkansas. The Bird's had rented a short-term storage unit to keep them safe until Tom could leave jail.

Tom's children wanted to see their dad every day, but the visitation room at the Lyon County jail was small, and it allowed no direct contact. Ralph and Virginia brought the children downtown where they played together across the street from the jail. By pulling himself up on a bar in his basement cell and holding himself there, Tom looked out the window to watch his children play. After a time, his muscles would spasm and he would let himself down to relax, then pull himself again.

Aaron's birthday was on September 4. Virginia described the event:

> "We plan a party of the family and Terry Smith... Terry and I shop for a gift from Tom for Aaron and we find a cute shuffle-toy. I go by the store and get six coconut cupcakes that we can put candles in. We have hats. Napkins and birthday plates. Aaron is happy and we take a lot of pictures. Our hearts are aching for Tom who cannot be with us.

> "We saw Tom in jail today and he saved a cookie from his lunch and gave it to Aaron for his birthday. We are almost in tears.

> "This afternoon we all go to the hearing where we are awarded temporary custody of the three children."

Jane attended the custody hearing, too. She sat dumbfounded at the judge's decision to give custody to the Birds, and she demanded to be heard. The judge refused to pay attention to her. Following the hearing, Jane left the courthouse by the same door as Tom. As they went through the door, she said to him, "Now I know how you felt when the judge wouldn't listen to you." Those were the last words Jane ever spoke directly to Tom. Jane left for Little Rock, but she purposed to push Kansas authorities to solve Sandy's "murder" case.

Strange friends at Lansing

The state moved Tom to Kansas State Penitentiary (later named Lansing Correctional Facility) and placed him in a large barracks-type transition cell with 107 other recently incarcerated men. After several days, they moved him to Topeka for psychological evaluation, standard operating procedure for all convicted Kansas felons.

In the transition cell each man had a cot, but not much else. They had nothing to do but read, watch TV or sleep 23 of the 24 hours of the day. One hour was for exercise.

Prisoners are a strangely jealous lot, and when one of them gets a lot of attention, they want part of the action. Tom got a lot of media attention.

On September 12, 1984, the *Emporia Gazette* carried an article titled "Emporian's Body Has Not Been Exhumed." Newspapers seldom publish stories about events that have *not* happened, but the Gazette felt this one merited mention. Roberta Birk wrote:

> "Contrary to rumors that are circulating in Lyon County, the body of Sandra Bird has not been exhumed. Dr. Fahmy Malak, Arkansas Medical Examiner, said this week that he has not received a request to remove Mrs. Bird's body from the Pine Crest Cemetery in Little Rock [sic], Ark. Dr. Malak said that an exhumation cannot be done in Arkansas without this approval and that approval has not been requested by Lyon County authorities."

The Gazette article about exhumation described Sandy's death and the alleged link between it and Tom's recent conviction. "According to testimony given during the trial, Mr. Bird and his secretary, Lorna Anderson, plotted to kill Mrs. Anderson's husband, Martin, by drugging him and pushing him and his car off a bridge across the Cottonwood River southeast of Emporia."

Having strongly implied that Tom may be culpable in Sandy's death, Birk wrote, "Recently, rumors have circulated contending that Mrs. Bird's body has been exhumed and that a second autopsy has been performed." Birk wrote there was no truth to the rumor; the exhumation had not yet been done. She failed to report on how the rumor was started, but the idea of an exhumation came from the task force effort to find the "truth" about Sandy. Clearly, someone had leaked the information.

The balance of her article fluffs Dr. Eckert's resume as a world-renowned forensic pathologist, even describing his medical training and 30 years of experience. Birk quoted Eckert, "'We run a center at the university here (Wichita State) which is a definitive center internationally for the field,' he said. A center in Sao Paulo, Brazil, named for Dr. Eckert, is 'modeled after the center we have at Wichita State University.'"

When Birk finally stopped writing, she had constructed a 21-paragraph story, only seven of which spoke to the question of rumors. The remaining 14 paragraphs established Eckert as the first authority among world-class forensic pathologists. The reader knew that Lyon County had sought help from the best. The reader did not know that Eckert had already made up his mind about what he would find once the second autopsy had been done. Such a comment would have certainly demeaned his world-class status.

On September 13, Nancy Horst wrote a story titled, "Death of Sandra Bird Being Investigated." This 23-paragraph story quoted Rod Symmonds,

Lyon County Attorney. "There is a very active investigation of the death."

Symmonds mentioned the cooperation of the Lyon County Sheriff's Department and the Kansas Bureau of Investigation. "His remarks were the first public admission that law-enforcement agencies considered Mrs. Bird's death suspicious."

Coming a day after Birk's story about the potential for a second autopsy, Horst's story stirred great passion in Emporia. She provided details of Sandy's death and the findings of the first autopsy report. She misrepresented Dr. Gabriel's qualifications, stating it "was the first he had ever performed." When added to the previous day's story about the acclaimed Dr. Eckert, Gabriel looked pathetic and weak. The public saw the need for a stepped-up investigation.

Horst reported that the investigation never *had* been closed, but investigators became more aggressive once Marty Anderson had been murdered. Sheriff Andrews "worked the case as a traffic accident....He said there was some question about the death then, but there were no facts to indicate it was anything other than an accident."

Andrews directed a low-key investigation for about two weeks following Sandy's death. With Marty's murder, though, the pace quickened. "After the death of Martin Anderson many people who had information made the information known to persons in law enforcement," Symmonds claimed. Horst closed the article asking for persons with any information to contact the Sheriff's Department.

Horst was on a roll, and her next Bird story appeared on September 14. This 30-paragraph story delved into the details of Sandy's death. It carried the title, "Circumstances of Death Raise Suspicions."

"Many people in Lyon County have not been comfortable in calling the death of Sandra Bird an accident," opened the Horst article. "Suspicion about the circumstances of Mrs. Bird's death began to circulate [sic] Lyon County almost immediately after her body was found in the Cottonwood River...Mrs. Bird's family was puzzled by the unusual circumstances and in December initiated a private investigation in her death."

Horst's reference to "Mrs. Bird's family" meant Jane. Jane spent a great deal of time during Tom's solicitation trial learning as much as she could from local sources. She entertained some of the prosecution witnesses and talked frequently with the prosecution team. Jane saw Sandy as a murder victim, and Tom as the murderer. She hired Little Rock attorney Jack Lassiter to help her prove her suspicions. Jane became a prime source of information for the Gazette writers and regularly pumped them for information.

Horst quoted some of the men who came early to the death scene. The article left no doubt that, as Dennis Arb stated it, "there was foul play."

Birk followed up the September 14, article with another on September 15—four days in a row. This article meant to set straight Dr. Gabriel's record as a pathologist. "Dr. Gabriel actually had participated in more than 1,000 autopsies before he came to Emporia...The autopsy done on Mrs. Bird was Dr. Gabriel's first in Emporia." Still, those who earlier read that Sandy's body was the first Gabriel autopsied were left with an impression that the first autopsy was a failure.

Birk used the balance of the article to explain the difference between a clinical pathologist and a forensic pathologist. She emphasized that the Emporia lab lacked the proper equipment and Gabriel the proper training to determine the instrumentality of death—the object that severed Sandy's kidney.

Meanwhile, back at the cell

Tom sat with the other men in the cell listening to all this news and non-news about the investigation into Sandy's death. He heard the rumors of an exhumation and saw the articles that came close to naming him a murderer. He heard the radio and TV reports as well. He had nothing else to do. The other men in the cell heard the same, including Randy Rahal and Charles Henderson. Tom had minimal contact with them during this time, but everyone in the cell knew he was the subject of the numerous media stories.

The convicts' ears picked up when the news of a reward hit the airwaves. On Tuesday, September 18, Birk wrote a story titled, "Reward of $2,500 Offered To Solve Sandra Bird Case." Birk wrote, "The reward...will be given in one of two situations: to the person or persons who offer proof that Mrs. Bird died accidentally, or to the person or person whose information leads to the arrest and conviction of her killer or killers." The *Emporia Gazette* offered the first $2,500 of the reward money.

Birk updated this article several times over the next few months as the reward grew to $5,000. To Randy Rahal and Charles Henderson, the thought of winning a $5,000 reward for turning state's "evidence" against Tom became very enticing. Each acted on this impulse in the spring of 1985, contacting the KBI to tell them about Tom's "confession."

The KBI talked to both men, and to others who spent time near Tom. Investigators regularly question inmates about other inmates, hoping to find a snitch that will seal their case.

Rahal provided the KBI with an extensive version of Tom's "confession," alleging that the mere thought that Dr. Eckert would perform a second autopsy caused Tom to panic. (Rahal agreed to testify against Tom and found himself paroled with a new suit and $200 cash in his pocket. He never testified, though. Instead, he jumped parole and fled from Kansas.)

Agent Humphrey interviewed Charles Henderson while he was on parole during the spring of 1985. During the interview, Charles mentioned the potential reward and Humphrey implied he had it coming for his assistance. Charles also asked for help with his parole and Humphrey said he would look into it. Henderson gave Humphrey his version of Tom's "confession." He became a star witness for the prosecution in Tom's next trial.

KBI agents talked with other convicts as well. They sought out one in particular, a man named Harold MacMillen who had become a close friend of Tom's in prison. Looking for dirt on Tom, an agent asked prison authorities to call MacMillen out to chat. They called others named MacMillen before they found the right one. Harold, the one whom Tom befriended, submitted an affidavit about the interrogation.

"In the Spring of 1985 while incarcerated at Kansas State Penitentiary I was called to the front office where I met an agent for the Kansas Bureau of Investigation. (The agent's name I cannot remember).

"The KBI agent told me that they had information that an inmate named MacMillen had become friends with Tomas Bird while he was incarcerated at KSP.

"The agent questioned whether I knew Tom Bird, was friends with him, and knew that Tom Bird had been charged with murder. All of which I answered affirmatively. [Note: A Lyon County Grand Jury indicted Tom for murder in February of 1985. Humphrey interrogated MacMillen as the prosecution prepared its case for trial.]

"The agent then asked if I knew any information which would help them in the upcoming trial of Tom Bird. To which I replied that I believed Tom Bird was innocent and I had no information.

"The KBI agent said that they had evidence against Mr. Bird. I responded by asking, 'Why were they talking with me?' For the second time I said I had no information for them.

"At that point the KBI agent opened a file on the desk which he said was my file. As he opened it he said, 'I see here that you are doing a pretty long sentence. Maybe we can help you out if you cooperate with us.' He was implying that they would make a deal with my prison time in trade for testimony.

"For the third time I told him I had no information and I requested that the interview cease.

"I know that after word got out about the KBI coming to KSP, that inmate Charles Henderson then contacted and talked to the KBI.

"I know that Charles Henderson from the Orientation Annex of KSP in the Fall of 1984. He continually read newspapers, watched TV news and talked about the highly publicized case of Tom Bird."

Did Humphrey and other KBI agents offer rewards for testimony? MacMillen certified it, Rahal got money and freedom. Henderson denied that Humphrey offered anything, but changed his tune by 1989 when he hired an attorney to sue the state of Kansas because he never received the reward.

Numerous people interviewed by Humphrey claimed he used questionable tactics. Keith and Dee Waggoner, members at Faith, threw him out of their house because they became so upset. Stephanie Moore described him as aggressive and obnoxious. Mark Bird said he often began his interviews saying something to the effect, "We know Tom Bird is guilty, but we wanted to check out some facts." Were these simply effective investigative techniques, or outside the limits of justice and fairness?

Nancy Horst wrote again on September 18, chronicling the arrest of Lorna Anderson by Lyon County officials. Geary County had previously charged Lorna with two counts of conspiracy to commit murder and one count of aiding and abetting murder. Lorna's Geary County trial was scheduled for October 1. Lyon County's charge for one count of solicitation to commit murder was the same charge that convicted Tom.

Symmonds pushed for the Lyon County charges, but was vague about the timing of the arrest. "I felt the timing was important for a number of reasons which I am not in a position to comment on." Looking ahead, Symmonds saw how valuable Lorna could be once the next case against Tom was filed.

Again, Horst used this article to restate the allegations about Lorna and Tom.

Bird Analyzed

In Kansas, first-time offenders are sent to the Reception and Diagnostic Center in Topeka. Tom arrived there expecting up to a five-week stay. His next stop depended on the results of tests and interviews conducted at the center.

As part of the evaluation process, Ralph and Virginia received a five-page questionnaire about Tom "concerning his past life and childhood, to illnesses and toilet training...They have a psychiatrist, psychologist and a social worker who will analyze everything about Tom and report back to Lyon County their findings and recommendations," Virginia wrote.

The state used these evaluations to determine how to deal with new prisoners and, in some cases, which ones should be released. The process required several tests and personal interviews by experienced professionals. Tom did what he could to make the best of a bad situation by cooperating with the people assigned to his case.

Tom also planned on cooperating with Lyon County authorities in their attempt to exhume Sandy's body, but he wanted the second autopsy done in Arkansas. He didn't trust the Kansans to be objective. Symmonds did an end-run around Tom to get Sandy's body back to Kansas.

Sandy's body exhumed

Symmonds expected Sandy's body to be exhumed in mid-September, but Kansas officials fouled up the paperwork. They assumed that Sandy had been buried in Pulaski County, because most of Little Rock falls within its borders. But Sandy had been buried in Saline County, in an area known as Alexandria. Pulaski County officials refused to do anything to help Symmonds.

Symmonds filed corrected paperwork and a Saline County judge signed the order on September 20. Dr. Malak approved the exhumation order on September 24, and Symmonds set the date as September 27. He delayed it until October 1 suggesting a vague fear of some kind of interference with the process. He probably meant Mark Bird.

Mark Bird heard about the exhumation on the morning of October 1. As quickly as he could he drove to Pine Crest Cemetery only to find the grave open and the body gone. "May I see the paperwork?" he asked cemetery officials.

No one bothered to get Tom's release for the autopsy. "When I told them that Tom was the next of kin and showed them that his signature never appeared on the document, they panicked and immediately called their attorneys. It seemed odd to me that in all this, Kansas officials could break Arkansas rules to get what they wanted, but they never gave Tom a break."

Tom let Kansas officials know through his attorney that he would have approved an exhumation as long as a qualified Arkansas pathologist did the autopsy. He strongly disagreed with the idea of bringing the body back to Kansas and had he known that Dr. Eckert had decided before the autopsy what he planned to find, he would have fought harder. Once the body was in Kansas, there was nothing he could do but await the results, and pray.

Birk wrote the story about the exhumation for the October 2 *Emporia Gazette*. She wrote the "autopsy was done by an internationally known forensic pathologist, Dr. William G. Eckert of Wichita."

Once again, Birk recounted the details of Sandy's death, Marty's murder, Lorna's pending trials and Tom's conviction. She reminded readers of the secret witness fund with the reward awaiting anyone with information about Sandy's death. By now, nearly every Emporian knew the allegation of an affair between Tom and Lorna's and presumed it played a role in the death of both of their spouses—a rare quadrangle murder case.

Diagnostic results

On October 3, 1984, the Reception and Diagnostic Center issued its "Report of Clinical Evaluation" of Tom Bird.

These reports recount much personal information as background, such as family history, education and such. Many convicted felons come from broken or violence-filled homes, are of lessor intelligence or lacking in education. Many never married or had rocky marriages. Financial problems are common. In Tom's case, his background indicated a strength of character from a superb upbringing and an exemplary life. The report pictured Tom as a cut above the average convict.

The report stated:

"Mr. Bird ... is cooperative with the examinational process. He is mildly to moderately depressed and anxious. This emotional state is considered commensurate with his current predicament. He functions in the bright-normal to superior range of intelligence...

"Mr. Bird is a man of high achievement and success oriented and who has tended to measure his own self-worth in terms of the attention, admiration and recognition of others...

"He said that he had thought about suicide after his arrest and had considered several ways of taking his life. At the present time, he is relatively certain that this is not an alternative for him as he would not want to leave such a legacy for his children...Mr. Bird reports that he had the continued support of a number of people. He is grateful that he has not been abandoned."

The report described Tom as normal, not suffering from any psychiatric condition or disorder, except for mild depression. It saw him as functioning within the normal perimeters of acceptable behavior, and it reported no use of alcohol or drugs.

When Tom and his family read the report's recommendation, they were ecstatic! Underlined, in bold italicized print, the report concluded:

"There are no prior felony offenses in this man's life. In our

clinical opinion, extended incarceration would serve little purpose for this man or for society."

The report closed with a statement that Tom had been transferred to the Kansas State Penitentiary to await the Lyon County Court's decision on sentencing. Tom saw maximum security at the old prison as a frightening and tough place to be, but felt confident he would be released shortly, given the good report of the diagnostic center.

When TV stories broke about Tom's diagnostic center report, they totally contradicted what the Bird's had just read. Mark called the stations. "I asked, 'how could you guys get this wrong? Let me read the last paragraph.' It said that Tom Bird was not a threat to society, that incarceration would serve no purpose. And I read that to him, and he said, 'Well Mr. Bird, I don't know what to tell you. We got an AP report out of Emporia, and that's what it said.' And I asked him where he got it, and he said, 'We got it from the *Emporia Gazette*.' So those goofy little girls [Birk and Horst] who were covering that crime that whole time botched that up."

Dr. Gabriel, too, knew these two writers often botched the details when they wrote that Sandy's autopsy was his first. That suggestion of possible incompetence, like this false report on his sentencing recommendation, reinforced Tom's negative public image.

Tom still protects Lorna

While Tom sat at Lansing prison, Lorna awaited trial at her home in Hutchinson. Originally scheduled for October 1 in Geary County, the trial was postponed to November 5, December 10, and then to January 14.

In January, Lorna's new attorney Jack Focht moved to have the Geary County charges against her dropped. He stated the court had a jurisdictional problem since the alleged crimes of conspiracy, and aiding and abetting had occurred in Lyon County. Judge Melvin Gradert agreed and dropped the charges. She still faced one count of solicitation in Lyon County.

(Both Greg Curry and Danny Carter entered into plea agreements in Geary County. Their crimes, like Lorna's, had also been committed in Lyon County. Their attorneys decided the best deal could be obtained outside of Lyon County and so decided against raising the jurisdictional question.)

During this time, Tom and Lorna used each other to gather and compare information. This resulted in near daily phone calls. Tom offered Lorna continued emotional support from behind prison walls and suggested how to move ahead in her trials. Given his recent negative experience, he urged her to be careful and take nothing for-granted. The two of them ran up enormous phone bills for Lorna, another "proof" offered by the prosecution that they were co-conspirators in crime. Tom continued to believe that Lorna was, like him, a victim. They needed and relied on each other, and on their mutual friend, Susan Ewert. (Tom called Susan several times as well, but no one alleged they had an affair just because of the phone calls. He called Terry Smith and his folks as well.)

Mark pursued as many leads as he could, concentrating on the whereabouts of Danny, learning what he could about Darrel, Johnny Bingham, Greg Curry and the others. He warned Tom about Lorna, believing she would betray him, but to little avail.

Early in November, the KBI moved Tom to Junction City for a week. They interrogated him about his knowledge of Marty's murder. On the advice of Irv Shaw, he refused to testify.

Shaw also advised the Bird family about Jane's efforts to win custody of the children. Jane's attorney asked that the custody hearing be moved to February 4, and the Bird's agreed. They saw this as a way to grow the bond between them and the children, and believed that Tom would be released from prison on parole far in advance of February.

The *Emporia Gazette* continued to carry regular stories about progress in the investigation into Sandy's death. Several stories recounted the mounting dollars given to the reward fund, listing the individuals who gave money. These included Jane Grismer and other members of her family.

Horst wrote a piece about Trooper Rule, who claimed "that the case was never worked as a traffic accident...I never believed it was a traffic accident, but I didn't have proof enough that it was [anything else]. I couldn't convince anybody really." (Each time these stories appeared, Horst and Birk reinforced the links between Tom, Lorna and the deaths of both spouses.)

Two more court losses

On November 27, 1984, Horst penned an article titled, "Grand Jurors will Probe Bird Case."

"Lyon county Attorney Rodney Symmonds said today he is pleased with the decision of the district judges to summon a grand jury to investigate the death of Sandra Bird." Judge Rulon and Associate Judge William Dick "filed an order with the court Monday afternoon granting the request."

For the second time in Lyon County's history, a grand jury would be convened. The county avoided grand juries preferring a simpler method of charging persons with crimes, rather than seeking indictments.

The grand jury offered Symmonds a chance to win community support to take on this emotionally-charged case. Yet, neither Symmonds nor other court officials knew how to conduct a grand jury.

Horst described the process of forming a grand jury and the various options open to it. "The only people present during a grand jury investigation are the jurors, witnesses who are testifying, and a court reporter. The prosecuting attorney may be present at the jury's request. He may also make a request to present information to the jury. The jury also may employ a special prosecutor and a special investigator. Witnesses also are allowed to have an attorney present."

Grand juries are freewheeling bodies, and once convened can follow many threads leading them off on tangents. The flow of information between the jurors and the witnesses is less formal and few rules apply. Indictments occur when at least 12 of the 15 jurors agree to indict.

The Gazette missed the news that Agent Winsor drove to Hardy, Arkansas during this time. Winsor convinced a judge to grant him a search warrant to look through Tom's possessions, now partly in storage at Ralph's home and in a locked storage unit. Virginia watched as Winsor searched the parsonage. He took pictures of the clothes Tom wore while in the Lyon County jail, and looked for Tom's tennis shoes and a log book he supposedly used to keep a record of his running.

Finding nothing, Winsor returned the next day with a warrant to search the locked storage unit. Virginia and Aaron rode with Winsor in a squad car to the storage unit, and watched as he poked through Tom's possessions. He found a box of shoes, but took nothing. The pattern on the shoes didn't match those at Marty's murder site.

About that parole, Your Honor

Two days after approving the formation of a grand jury, Judge Rulon looked down from his courtroom bench at Irv Shaw who represented the absent Tom Bird. Tom had planned on attending, but Rulon said no.

Rulon reviewed the report from the diagnostic center and heard Shaw request releasing Tom on a bond while his appeal was pending. Shaw presented Rulon with Tom's probation plans, and asked for a sentence modification—probation. Following Tom's August 1 conviction, Shaw had told the Bird family to expect probation. With the diagnostic center's report, his prediction seemed likely.

Rulon rejected the diagnostic center's advice and denied Shaw's motions. Tom stayed at Lansing. Rulon saw the real potential that the Lyon County Grand Jury would soon indict Tom in one of the two "equal parts in a scheme."

Tom and Ralph Bird decided to hire Robert Hecht, a well-respected

Topeka attorney, to represent him. Tom wanted Hecht to oversee his appeal, made simpler by his proximity to the court in Topeka. He also asked Hecht to consider a wrongful death suit against Kansas on behalf of the three Bird children. Tom believed the dangerous approach to Rocky Ford Bridge played a central role in Sandy's death, and he felt the state should pay for it. Jane saw it the same way during the summer of 1983, but by this time, she saw only the blood of Sandy on Tom's hands.

SECTION V:

TRIAL #2

"Acquitting the guilty and condemning the innocent—
the LORD detests them both."

Proverbs 17:15

Prepping for Grand Jury

Just before convening a grand jury, Rod Symmonds moved to drop Lyon County's charge against Lorna Anderson. The county previously had charged her with one count of solicitation to commit murder, the same offense for which Tom now sat in prison. Symmonds saw it was to his advantage to present the evidence about Lorna to the grand jury.

Wednesday, January 2, 1985, Symmonds led the selection of the grand jury. He announced that "the grand jury had asked him to be present during the sessions and give legal advice." The jury could have conducted their investigation without him, but they felt inadequate. They believed Symmonds would provide unbiased assistance.

The grand jury planned to begin its work on January 8, the following Tuesday.

During this time, Geary County continued the inquisition into Marty Anderson's murder. An inquisition is similar to a grand jury, but the witnesses appear before a judge. The prosecution has wide leeway into lines of questioning, and hearsay evidence is permitted. The defense is restricted to challenging witnesses only about constitutional issues.

Deputy Deppish picked Tom up at Lansing prison on Friday, January 4, and headed back toward Junction City. Tom asked Deppish why he was being moved, but he just grunted that he had a court order to do so. Once Deppish booked Tom into the jail, he handed him a subpoena to appear as a witness at the inquisition. "Why wasn't I given this at Lansing so I could call my attorney?" Tom asked.

"I'm just doing what I've been told."

Tom asked permission to call an attorney, but was refused.

With Judge Melvin Gradert presiding, Opat put Tom on the stand and presented him with a sworn statement to sign stating that Tom agreed not to disclose any information about the inquisition. Tom felt like he was being ambushed and refused to sign the statement, demanding his right to have an attorney present.

Opat had no choice but to agree to Tom's request forcing the court to hold Tom over the weekend until he could find an attorney. On Monday, Tom appeared once again for the inquisition, his attorney at hand, and taking the witness stand, refused to testify, claiming his constitutional right to protection from self-incrimination. A frustrated Opat ordered Tom's guards to take him back to Lansing.

Press covers details, again and again

Reporters are locked out of inquisitions and grand juries. Witnesses are ordered to keep silent about their testimony and the proceedings. Still, newspapers needed to write stories.

Roberta Birk's *Emporia Gazette* story about the first day of the grand jury closed with this paragraph. "Interest in the incident was rekindled when testimony during the Bird trial indicated that the circumstances of Mrs. Bird's death were similar to those described in one of the plots to kill Mr. Anderson."

Birk referred to Darrel Carter's claim that one of Tom's schemes to murder Marty included getting him drugged or drunk and running him off the road near a bridge. Darrel said Tom described a bridge with a 50-foot drop. Investigators jumped on this story because it sounded so much like the way Sandy Bird died. It should have. Darrel made it up, according to Lorna.

Mark Bird testifies and tests

Mark Bird drove to Emporia on Sunday, February 10. His turn in front of the grand jury was to be the next day and he would be one of the last to testify. Leaving early in the morning, Mark encountered rain, then freezing ice and finally, as he entered Kansas, snow—8" before it stopped. This made him late for his scheduled time with Tom at the Lyon County jail.

Mark walked into the jail and signed in. He entered the visitation area and saw Tom sitting in a closet-sized room on the other side of a door that had a head-sized window in it. It reminded him of someone ordering a ticket at a movie theater.

The deputy on duty talked with Mark about time limits—one hour, maximum. "I just drove in from Little Rock on icy roads and through a blizzard to get here. That's why I'm late." Mark explained.

"You drove through all that?"

"Sure did."

"Well, you take as long as you want. You can stay until I go off duty." Mark stayed more than two hours.

Tom needed to know how the grand jury was being led because it would give him an insight into the prosecution's strategy. They devised a plan.

On Monday morning, Mark walked into the grand jury room along with his attorney. He informed the jury that he had a statement he wished to read before starting. He asked the jury to dismiss Symmonds, as they had a right to do, so they could question him directly. He carefully watched Symmonds and the grand jury react to his request. It shook all of them. Symmonds never anticipated this. After a few clumsy questions, the grand jury foreman asked Symmonds to dismiss Mark for a few minutes while they talked about their options.

When Mark came back into the room, Symmonds explained that the grand jury had every right to dismiss him if they wished, but they wanted his advice. Symmonds then proceeded to ask all the questions. When he finished, grand jury members passed a few handwritten questions to him and he relayed those to Mark. This confirmed what Tom and Mark had feared. Symmonds controlled and directed the grand jury. Any indictments, or a decision not to indict, would accrue directly to his influence.

Mark wanted to make sure the grand jury dealt with all the alternative explanations that could have affected Sandy's death. He pointed the finger at Danny and Darrel Carter: their mutual intimate involvement with Lorna; the burning down of Darrel's building; the .22 caliber shells found in Danny's apartment that perfectly matched those at Marty's death site. He believed the grand jury should explore all the tangential aspects of the case before settling the question of indictments.

Instead of reading the statement, Mark gave Symmonds the list of issues, asking him to present them to the grand jury. These issues required calling certain other witnesses and extending the grand jury's time schedule. The list was ignored.

Grand jury testimony is secret. No one, including the Bird family, knew the outcome until Symmonds released the jurors. Still, it took weeks before Tom's attorney had a chance to read the testimony of grand jury witnesses to analyze the state's case.

Lorna gets a temporary pass

On January 14, 1985, Scott Faust of the Wichita *Eagle-Bulletin* wrote about Lorna's upcoming trial in Junction City. He asked the question that intrigued most of the state of Kansas: was Lorna an innocent victim of a vicious murder or "a woman of fierce passion and greed whose love affair with her minister and her desire to receive a $400,000 life insurance settlement led her to arrange her husband's death?"

Scott's conclusions assumed Tom's guilt as an adulterer, and reinforced the possibility that Lorna was an innocent victim of circumstances. Prophetically, Scott wrote, "But regardless of what happens in the Geary County courtroom, there will be little left unknown of the once private lives of Lorna Anderson and the man prosecutors say she loved, Lutheran minister Thomas Bird. At least outwardly, they [had been] small-town people living pleasant quiet lives."

Scott's article described the details of Marty's murder and rehearsed the charges leading to Tom's conviction. Scott stirred the emotions of his readers, writing, "Sandra Bird died in an auto accident a few months before Martin Anderson was killed...But suspicions raised by Martin Anderson's death...prompted authorities to exhume her body and do a second autopsy. The results of that autopsy have been kept secret, but authorities have been investigating her death."

Scott's mention of the mysterious second autopsy built public expectation and kept the story alive. Symmonds counted on this as he built momentum toward the eventual trial.

Scott described perfectly the sense that many had about these unfolding events. "The witness list filed by Geary County Attorney Opat reads like the cast from murder-mystery theater. That's exactly what will be sketched in the prosecution case in Junction City—a plot of love, money and violence." But Opat was denied his command performance.

Opat made it clear that he could re-file charges against Lorna because she had not stood trial. "Jeopardy has not [been] attached," he stated. "Basically the court is saying that venue for the conspiracy is in Lyon County and that we need more evidence about the identity of the killer before we go any further."

Lorna reacted to the judge's decision with a broad smile and generous hug of Attorney Focht. "I think that he ruled exactly consistently in accordance with the law," Focht said. "She's free...presumed to be innocent...and in my judgement, that's the way she's going to stay."

Focht, like others in her life, knew little about the real Lorna. Had he known the truth, he would have avoided bragging about maintaining her innocence. He would have avoided a display of affection as well. Such actions with Lorna destroyed the lives of many men.

Back in Hutchinson, Mark Enoch interviewed Lorna about her most recent travails in Geary County. Lorna told Enoch, "I was just extremely happy and very thankful because our prayers had been answered. I know I'm innocent. The Lord's gotten me through it. I've leaned on him and I've had wonderful support from family and friends."

Enoch reported that Lorna had enrolled in school at Hutchinson Community College, majoring in family development. He mentioned how busy she was caring for her four children as a single parent. "It's been difficult to adjust to doing it alone. He [Marty] was my husband and I love him. I go over and over it, even hoping I can come up with something to find whoever it was."

Loren Slater, like Tom Bird and Susan Ewert, believed Lorna. "I believe in my daughter's innocence all the way. There's no describing the agony we've gone through. It's one of those things that happens to the other guy. We're not the kind of people who do these things."

Investigators felt that Lorna knew the identity of the killer but she refused to cooperate. Eight months later they would coax a confession from her that sealed their theory about Tom.

Ironically, at the same time the judge dismissed charges against Lorna, the Kansas County and District Attorneys' Association named Opat "Outstanding Prosecutor in 1984." The newspaper stated, "Mr. Opat has been involved locally with the recent investigations into the 1983 murders of Emporians Martin Anderson and Sandra Bird." Their deaths accrued to Opat's success.

Back in Emporia, Rod Symmonds informed the media that "he could not comment on how he plans to proceed in that [Lorna's] case. All I can say is that the grand jury can look into any public offenses that have been committed in this county."

For a few brief weeks, Lorna thought she might escape all punishment, but her hopes for $270,000 in life insurance benefits suddenly were put in jeopardy. Lawyers for the New England Mutual Life Insurance Company filed a petition to have a guardian ad litem appointed on behalf of the Anderson children. The company set in motion a plan to refund the Anderson's insurance premiums and deny paying her anything from the insurance policy because they saw Lorna as a willing participant in Marty's murder.

The insurance issue began to pale for Lorna when compared to the events of February 21.

The Lyon County Grand Jury wanted to issue four indictments. Symmonds convinced them not to indict Danny and Darrel Carter for conspiracy/solicitation. Symmonds supported the other two indictments.

The grand jury indicted Lorna for one count of criminal solicitation to commit first-degree murder and one count of conspiracy to commit first-degree murder. Both indictments stemmed from Marty's murder. The Reno County sheriff arrested her and that day brought her to Emporia where she appeared in court the next day. Judge Dick entered a plea of not guilty for her and set her trial for May 6.

Once the grand jury was formally dismissed that Thursday and Lorna had been arrested, Symmonds told the media that he could not "confirm or deny whether any other indictments have been issued." He refused to explain what the grand jury decided about Sandy Bird's death. (In their report, the *Gazette* once again mentioned the second autopsy; "...the results have not been made public.")

Like the newspapers and a growing number of Emporians, Tom wanted to know about the second autopsy, too. Since Symmonds refused to release it to him, Mark looked to Arkansas officials for a copy of the autopsy. Arkansas law required that the results be filed in that state. But Kansas had yet to file the autopsy in Arkansas.

No party to be had

On Friday, February 23, in Hardy, Arkansas, Ralph and Virginia Bird packed the three little Birds in their car and drove to Lansing for a weekend visit with Tom. Little Paul looked forward to celebrating his birthday with his daddy, though it meant going back into prison. Once there, guards turned them away, telling the frustrated family that they had moved Tom to "A & T." They could tell them nothing else. Tom wrote:

"I'll start with Thursday, February 21, 1985. I had come back to my cell from work. Two members of the shake down squad came to my cell, cuffed me up and escorted me across the compound to A & T. It is the Adjustment and Treatment building, what we call 'the Hole.' This building houses those who are put in isolation for bad behavior.

"The building had three wings stacked two high with cells. On the east wing, north side, bottom run is a dozen cells that are called the 'double slam door' cells, because there is a solid metal door you must enter and then an additional cell door. This area is reserved for extreme isolation. This is where they took me Thursday evening. I had no idea why.

"A few hours after being put in the isolation cell, I was served Department of Correction papers that said I was being held in Administrative Segregation due to a pending investigation. They can hold a person for 72 hours for this reason without any further explanation.

"I only saw three human beings from Thursday evening until Monday morning. They denied me contact with anyone besides one orderly who came by and mopped outside my cell and two officers who brought me my meals. [They refused to allow him to call an attorney.]

"An inmate who was crazy a few cells up from me had stopped up his toilet and flooded all the cells east of him, so for two days my cell was in one inch of water. I had one towel, one blanket, a bar of soap and one set of clothes.

"I continually wrote what were called 'Form 9s' with the pencil and paper they provided me, but I received no answers, until Sunday when an officer who brought me lunch said there would be no visit.

This hit me very hard because it was Paul's birthday and mom and dad had gone to a great deal of trouble to bring the children up here from Arkansas and I had not even been allowed to contact them to keep them from coming.

"It was Monday morning when I was cuffed and taken to the Unit Team office and told that instructions to hold me in segregation came from the 'front' office and that was all I needed to know.

"Later on that Monday, I was escorted to Admissions and Discharge and placed into the custody of Lyon County deputies who served me my indictment by the grand jury for Sandy's death. I was taken to Emporia.

(Lyon County Undersheriff Merton DeBoer served Tom with the arrest warrant in the squad car while they were sitting in the parking lot at Lansing Correctional Facility, about 3 p.m. that day. Because no official from Leavenworth County or an agent of the KBI aided DeBoer in this arrest, the arrest was technically illegal. Lyon County had no arrest jurisdiction in Leavenworth County. If Tom had understood this, he could have moved to have the charges dropped and forced Lyon County to abide by the letter of the Kansas state laws, as they forced him to do during his appeals.)

"I also noticed that a guard handed a deputy my address book before we left. I never saw that address book again. Later I learned that most of the people in the address book were contacted and asked how and why they knew me.

"A couple of years later a guard told me that it was the Kansas Bureau of Investigation that had called the institution and ordered me to be put in isolation. You see, the grand jury indicted me on Thursday and they did not want me to hear about it or contact anyone until they picked me up on Monday."

Ralph Bird drove back to Lansing prison on Monday and wanted an answer about Tom. Prison officials refused to tell him anything, save one guard who quietly mentioned he had been taken to Emporia. The Bird's gathered the children and drove back to Hardy where they learned the grand jury had indicted their father and son for murdering Sandy.

Since grand jury hearings are sealed, no one knew at that time that Symmonds tried to get the grand jury to also indict Tom for conspiracy to commit murder. The grand jury did not buy Symmonds' request. They indicted him for the single count of first-degree murder.

Nancy Horst wrote the lead story about Tom's indictment and arrest. It provided another opportunity to remind people of the details of the allegations and of his first conviction. And she wrote about the second autopsy. "In October, Mrs. Bird's body was exhumed and a second autopsy was performed by a forensic pathologist in Wichita. The results of that autopsy have not been make public."

Why such mystery about the autopsy? What did the world-renowned Dr. Eckert find that seemed so compelling that it led to a first-degree murder indictment? The public wanted to know. Tom wanted to know, but Symmonds refused to send him a copy until just before the trial began.

Looking to a second trial

Tom endured more than 72 hours of isolation at Lansing before deputies moved him to the Lyon County jail. After a restless night, he stood before Judge Gary Rulon on Tuesday. Robert Hecht, his Topeka attorney, chose not to enter a plea at the hearing, so Judge Rulon entered a not-guilty plea for him and scheduled an April 18 hearing for pretrial motions.

Following his 15-minute arraignment, deputies escorted Tom out of the courtroom and returned him to Lansing prison.

Hecht filed a motion to compel the county to produce transcripts of the grand jury testimony and Rulon ordered it to be done. Thus began a long, grueling process for Tom, his attorney and family members to prepare for the unthinkable; defending him against charges that he murdered Sandy.

The grand jury indictment, though, lacked any clarity. Its ambiguous wording left Tom without a defense.

"COUNT I: that on or about the 16th day of July, 1983 in Lyon County, Kansas, one THOMAS P. BIRD, then and there being, did then and there unlawfully, willfully, maliciously, deliberately, and with premeditation, kill a certain human being, to-wit: Sandra S. Bird, contrary to the form of K.S.A. 21-3401, and against the peace and dignity of the State of Kansas. (Class A Felony)."

Hecht and Bird read and re-read the indictment. How did Tom supposedly murder Sandy? What was the instrument of her death? Did he beat her with a stick, tree branch, tire iron, wine bottle, rock or his fists? Did he violently throw her against a railing, wall, down the steps, over the bridge or off a cliff? Did he kick her in the back causing kidney damage? Did he drug her first or get her drunk? Tom's ability to defend himself against the murder charges depended on knowing exactly how the state alleged he killed Sandy.

Had the grand jury said he killed her with a baseball bat, he could have asked where he got it, how he held it, why the type of bruises found on her didn't fit the pattern made by a baseball bat? He could have asked the prosecution to prove that her blood or skin tissue was found on a baseball bat, or even that he had a bat at his disposal. If a bat, did the state find his fingerprints on it? But the grand jury had failed to specify the means of death. They failed to do this because they didn't know the answer; neither did Symmonds, Agent Humphrey, Trooper Rule, or any other person associated with the prosecution.

Kansas statutes require a detailed description in an indictment of how a crime was committed. "The...indictment shall be a plain and concise written statement of the essential facts constituting the crime charged. (K.S.A. 22-3401)"

U.S. Supreme Court Justice Oliver Wendell Holmes wrote in State vs. Carpenter, that the Federal Rules of Criminal Procedure requires that an indictment contain a "plain, concise and definite written statement of the essential facts constituting the offense charged."

The U.S. Supreme Court wrote in 1962, "the rationale for these rules is clear: they guard against the possibility, however, slight, that a defendant could...be convicted on the basis of facts not found by, and perhaps not even presented, to the grand jury which indicted him." (Russell v. United State). Russell reinforced the absolute necessity of providing accused criminals with the specifics about the crimes they allegedly committed. Russell said it is insufficient to simply accuse someone of a crime without specifying the alleged method of committing the crime.

Without such protections, guaranteed by the U.S. Constitution, prosecutors would be free to use their office for any manner of indictments, with a wide range of motivations: personal vendettas, political agendas, hiding the real criminal from justice. This is a basic and extremely profound constitutional protection and is jealously guarded, except in Tom's case in Lyon County.

Judge Rulon denied Attorney Hecht's attempt to dismiss the case based on the defective indictment, so Hecht asked the court to direct Symmonds to produce a "Bill of Particulars." It failed to provide any help to Tom's defense.

"COMES NOW the plaintiff, by and through its attorney, Rodney H. Symmonds, Lyon County Attorney, and relative to the defendant's criminal agency on Count I of the Indictment hereby alleges and states as follows:

"1. That the defendant did feloniously touch and apply force to the person of Sandra S. Bird which caused her to sustain and suffer blunt injuries to her person, including but not limited to her kidney, which caused her death."

The Bill of Particulars was not particular. About the only method of murder it excluded was poisoning. It included information not specified by the grand jury—"feloniously touch and apply force." Symmonds served as an agent of the grand jury, not as the charging authority and therefore, he had no freedom to add to their indictment. Because the grand jury had no clue as to the method of "murder" it could not be specific, and no possible means could be applied to resolve this problem. Judge Rulon chose to ignore all this and let the Indictment and Bill of Particulars, as severely deficient as they were, to stand.

Trying to strategize how to defend himself when he knew only that he had been accused of murder, Tom saw his only hope in proving that Sandy had died by accident. This placed him in the untenable position of proving his innocence, rather than having the state prove his guilt. He had to prove an alternative explanation for Sandy's death.

Hecht, along with Mark and Ralph Bird, all set out to read the grand jury transcripts to try and find the answer to the question, how did Tom murder Sandy (Tom never saw the grand jury transcripts until the jury selection process had begun. Jane Grismer had told the grand jury she thought Tom should be hung up in the front yard by his thumbs. Though that statement never made it to trial, it left a lasting impression on both the jury and Tom.)

They concentrated on Trooper John Rule, accident reconstructionist Billy Persinger and Dr. William Eckert's testimony, believing those to be the most potentially destructive to their defense. Because their time to prepare for trial was limited, they only concentrated on the testimony of those witnesses on the list provided by Symmonds.

One witness Symmonds left off his list was David Workman. Symmonds had Workman's testimony about Lorna's claims on Tom. Lorna told him the previous August that she was in love with Tom. Workman's hearsay testimony matched in many ways that of Jan Mead. She testified in the first trial that Lorna wanted Sandy and Marty out of the way so she and Tom could spend their lives together. Since Judge Rulon allowed her hearsay testimony in the first trial, why would Symmonds not want to reinforce it in the second trial?

Symmonds knew that putting Workman on the stand would allow discovery and cross-examination that hurt his case. Workman certainly would have testified to the March 30, 1983, meeting where Lorna talked about having Marty killed in the context of Danny and Darrel Carter. Had Workman testified to this in the first trial, it is unlikely Tom would have been convicted. The Bird defense team concerned itself with the grand jury testimony of the called witnesses and so, never bothered to read Workman's testimony, or call him as a witness.

Hecht commissioned Captial Research Services to conduct a market survey to assess whether or not the extensive pre-trial publicity would preclude picking an impartial jury. CRS reported "that virtually everyone in Emporia had heard about the case. Only 2.6 percent of those interviewed said they had not heard or read that Thomas Bird had been charged with murdering his wife. Two-thirds of Emporians admitted "they had heard a lot." Less than 10% said, "they had not heard very much."

Referring to Marty's murder, CRS asked if "they had heard that Bird had been implicated in another murder, 80% replied affirmatively.... This is a relatively high percentage given the amount of time that has elapsed since the case was tried."

CRS also tested whether pretrial publicity has "predisposed them [potential jurors] in one direction or another.... When asked if they thought he was guilty or innocent of the charge that he had murdered his wife, almost half (47%) said they thought he is guilty... only 2.8% of the people in Emporia think that he is innocent."

Though not as scientific as asking a person directly what they believe, CRS asked "how they thought their friends and neighbors felt about this case... A majority indicated that they felt the same way that they did. In other words, most Emporia residents think that Bird is guilty as charged and think that the rest of the community concurs with them."

More than two-thirds of Emporians believed that Tom and Lorna were lovers, and nearly 40 percent believed Lorna had something to do with Sandy's death.

CRS concluded, "We have found that virtually everyone in Emporia has heard that Thomas Bird has been charged with the murder of his wife... Finding a jury that has not been exposed to extensive pretrial publicity of one type or another will be virtually impossible."

Hecht moved for a change of venue. Rulon denied it. Rulon argued that Tom had participated in pretrial publicity, citing his interview with a Chicago news team. The *Emporia Gazette* ran a photo of that interview, reporting that a CBS crew talked with Tom outside his church. The subject of that "interview" never made it into print. Tom had told the crew how he and his family were coping and said nothing about the case.

Pre-Trial Motions

Attorney Hecht had made several pre-trial motions.

He wanted to suppress all information and testimony from the first trial. Hecht said the murder indictment presented a different charge and Tom should not be subjected to the testimony that convicted him the first time. Allowing in this testimony presented an issue of double jeopardy by, in essence, retrying Tom for solicitation. Symmonds argued that it was relevant and spoke to motive. Rulon denied the motion.

Hecht moved to dismiss the indictment altogether because Rod Symmonds led the grand jury to their conclusion, rather than letting them conduct their own inquiry. Rulon denied the motion.

Hecht moved to question jurors independently, called individual voir dire. This protected Tom from each juror hearing questions repeated over and over, giving more weight to various questions than they deserved. Rulon denied the motion, but did allow for some individual voir dire after the questions were first directed to the group.

Hecht moved to require the prosecution to release all information relevant to the second autopsy. He argued that the autopsy itself should be suppressed given that Kansas officials violated both Kansas and Arkansas law in obtaining the writ of exhumation. Rulon denied the motion.

Hecht said the indictment failed to establish the cause of death and therefore, the case should be dismissed. Rulon denied the motion and let the defective indictment stand.

Hecht wanted the jury sequestered, given the great amount of publicity and exposure the case garnered. Rulon denied the motion.

Rulon conducted a preliminary hearing on May 31, 1985. Then on June 3, Rulon said he wanted time to read the entire grand jury transcript before the trial began.

Tom returned to Lansing to await the start of his trial, but even during this time, there were new developments. Terry Smith called Ralph and Virginia about Harold McMillan. Virginia wrote on June 17, 1985, "Terry Smith told us McMillan's wife told her 'Mac' was questioned a fourth time and threatened by KBI about his upcoming sentencing in order to get him to talk about Tom. There is nothing he can say." Perhaps the KBI knew that Charles Henderson's testimony would be weak and Randy Rahal, their other snitch, had left the state.

Tom could do very little but wait for his next visit to Emporia to meet his new jury.

Getting the trial started

On June 26, 1985, Tom Bird sat at the defendant's table in the Lyon County Courthouse. Robert Hecht, his defense attorney, sat to his right. Rod Symmonds once again readied himself to prosecute Tom. Judge Gary Rulon sat as the judge.

Hecht had a strong reputation as one of the best defense attorneys in Kansas. Many people told Tom he was fortunate to get him assigned to the case. A smooth, well-educated and articulate man, Susan Ewert said he had "Hollywood looks," handsome and winsome. By the time of this trial, he had practiced law in Topeka for 25 years, and had previously served as a prosecutor.

He had one major flaw: he was not a hometown boy. Symmonds knew this, and trial observers said Symmonds familiarity and down-home style appealed more to the jury than did Hecht's professionalism. As an "outsider," Hecht didn't know the local personalities either, rendering it more difficult to pick neutral jurors.

Jury selection

Alice Thorton, the bailiff, brought in the 49 persons called for the jury panel, from which the attorneys and the judge would select 12 jurors and three alternates. If Capital Research had done their work accurately, one to two people in this pool were totally neutral.

The voir dire process patterned that of the first trial. When Rulon asked whether anyone was familiar with the case or information about the case, virtually everyone raised their hand. Several stated they had previously made a decision in the case, and they stepped out of the room. Some said they knew quite a bit, formed an opinion, but felt they could be unbiased. Others said they knew quite a bit, but had no opinion.

Dale Barger, who eventually became the presiding juror, gave typical answers. He knew quite a bit about the case, but mostly from his wife, a nurse on leave of absence from Newman Medical Center. She read about the case in the Gazette. A shipping clerk at Dolly Madison Kitchens in Emporia, Barger felt he could be neutral and no, he would not listen to his wife nor discuss the case with her.

Symmonds voir dire went quite quickly, but Hecht bored in on specifics. He searched the potential jurors for bias. "Is there any among you who believes that a crime was committed by somebody in this case?" The state first had to prove a murder had been committed, then prove Tom did the crime. "No one has raised a hand so you are all telling me to the best of your knowledge none of you believes that a crime was committed. Is that what you are saying?"

"Will you restate that, please?" Mr. Beemer asked.

"My question is is there any among you who believes that a crime was committed by somebody? Mr. Hannigan?"

"Somebody did it, didn't they?"

"Do you have a belief that somebody committed a crime?"

"I do, yes."

"As opposed you mean to an accident?" Mrs. Holmes asked.

"Do you believe somebody committed a crime?"

"The question is whether or not it's an accident or intended, and we don't know," Holmes answered.

"My question is, do you believe that a crime was committed in this case by somebody? I think I saw a hand in the back some place. So other than Mr. Hannigan, you all are telling me that to the best of your knowledge, you have no reason at this point in time to believe that a crime was committed by anybody. Is that a fair statement on my part? Mr. Morris?"

"I'm kind of like Mr. Hannigan. I thought somebody committed something."

"You think at this point in time you have the impression that somebody committed something? By that I take it you mean that somebody committed some kind of crime."

"Must have," Morris answered.

"Must have," Hecht responded thoughtfully. "Anyone else of that same impression? Mr. Hogan"

"Yes. I think there's been a crime committed or we wouldn't be here."

Hecht asked whether there were others of the same opinion. Mrs. Woodworth, Mrs. Lang, Mrs. Morgan all said yes, they felt that way. Mr. Dreyer said, "I would say so myself. I don't think we would be here if there wasn't a crime committed."

Hecht explained the purpose of a grand jury and its function.

A grand jury hears only the prosecution's case. The defense is not even present. The grand jury asks a wide range of questions not subject to rebuttal or cross-examination. Grand juries can determine their own procedures or allow the prosecutor to lead them. In Lyon County, the grand jury let Rod Symmonds lead them, and he had led them to an indictment. Hecht wanted the jurors to clearly understand this to expunge any pre-conceived idea of guilt just because an indictment had been issued against Tom.

"I just need a clarification as to what you're askng now. On what basis is the case decided to fit into the grand jury category where there is no— possibly no evidence presented by the witness?" Miss Rice asked.

"A grand jury is nothing more or nothing less than an investigative tool," Hecht responded.

Rulon interrupted Hecht. "I would advise the jury that the manner in which this case has reached this point in the proceedings is no concern. Whether this case was commenced by grand jury or information as the attorneys have asked, that is of no concern at this point and it shouldn't bother any of you."

All parties expected a long trial, perhaps two weeks or more. Hecht asked questions about health and employment. Some had doctor appointments. Others feared losing their jobs or an opportunity for a new job. Could they stay neutral or would they hold this against Tom?

Hecht pursued many angles. Had they discussed the case with others? Had they formed or expressed an opinion? Could they remain neutral? Could they look at grotesque and horrific autopsy photos? Had they previously served on a jury that reached a verdict? If the state proved a crime had been committed, but failed to prove that Tom did it, could they find him innocent?

He asked questions about their family, education, occupation, faith and church attendance. Had they ever been accused of a crime? Had they ever been in a court or legal dispute? Did they drive a car? Had they ever been in a car accident? Did any of them have knowledge of auto mechanics? Did they drive an American or foreign car? How about an automatic or standard transmission? Did they know anyone who had been injured or died in a car accident? Had any of them been out to Rocky Ford Bridge?

Had any been involved in police or prosecutorial work and, if so, would that bias them toward the state? How about newsgathering and dissemination?

"Would you be bothered by the fact that there had been an awful lot of time and an awful lot of money spent to prove that there wasn't even a crime committed by anybody?"

"Absolutely not," Miss Rice claimed.

Could you remain neutral when you listened to state's witnesses? Do you understand that the state has the burden of proving guilt beyond a reasonable doubt? So that if the state's witnesses and defense witnesses disagreed on what constituted the facts, "would you resolve that difference or that dispute in favor of the defendant?"

Hecht found that Bruce Webb worked at the Emporia State University bookstore. He questioned him in depth. His wife, too, worked at ESU as an instructor in the Computer Science department (Sandy studied for her second master's degree in that department).

Hecht asked to conduct individual voir dire on 17 people. These were brought one at a time into a separate courtroom where counsel could ask questions outside the hearing of other jurors. Kimberly Marsh had indicated the prior day that she had heard opinions about the case. Rulon asked her what she had heard.

"Well, I've just heard that he is the one that killed his wife and that he's the one that pushed the car into the river, that bridge, by that bridge; and that's basically all that I've heard really."

"Was the source of this information other than a newspaper or television news report or a radio news report?" Hecht asked.

"Yes.

"It was a comment?"

"Just from people, yeah."

"Can you tell me whether the people were members of your family, friends, fellow employees or a combination of all of those."

"A combination."

Hecht asked how often she heard these comments and from whom? It was gossip passed around her circle of friends, she said.

"The information that was given to you or the opinions that were expressed to you did it cause you to form an opinion of your own?"

"No, it didn't. I just listened to what they said."

Mr. Beemer came next. Earlier, he had answered that a crime must have been committed, otherwise there was no reason for them all to be there. Hecht took him through a series of questions to try and understand what he meant. He had trouble answering, but claimed he could keep an open mind.

"If you didn't have any choice but to have to vote right now, what would your vote be?" Hecht asked, referring to whether or not Sandy died by accident or murder.

"Well, that's a little difficult question to answer because some of the accounts I've read in the paper made it look very clearly like there had been, and on the other hand it seems to me like it's yet to be proven that there has been [a murder]," Beemer answered. Later he answered, "Well, from what I've heard and read, I'll have to frankly admit that I lean toward that there probably was a crime..."

Beemer insisted that he could keep an open mind and that the evidence would have to convince him one way or the other. (He became one of the 12 jurors.)

Rick Harris came next. He worked with Dennis Arb and Arb told him and others what he saw at Rocky Ford Bridge the day of Sandy's death. Still, he felt could be neutral. He rented land from Sharon and Howard Meyer, but claimed they never discussed the case. He heard several of his employees discussing the case with Arb just prior to being called to serve on the jury and told them to get back to work. He described what he overheard, and one question dealt with blood on the bridge. He often fished off the bridge and implied that he understood why blood might be present.

Hecht asked whether Arb expressed any opinions to him. Yes. Could you stay neutral? Yes, he said he didn't let others make up his mind for him and as far as he was concerned, it had been all hearsay anyway. (He became one of the 12 jurors.)

They all returned to the main courtroom to continue the group voir dire.

Did anyone know the various witnesses to be called by either side? Had anyone ever testified in a court case? Had anyone given a statement to police? What kind of magazines or periodicals did they read? Had anyone worked in a medical facility? Did you ever witness a medical procedure?

Did anyone know Martin Anderson? Sandy Bird? Tom Bird?

What do you do with your leisure time? Do you fish? Do you fish off a bridge?

Do you go to church regularly? If so, which one? Does the fact that Mr. Bird had been a pastor make a difference to anyone?

Does anyone have an opinion about this case based on the first trial? Or based on the Martin Anderson murder?

Mrs. Langley heard and read about Tom's case and discussed it with, "My mother, my father, my brothers and sisters, friends, acquaintances." Perhaps other people as well. She named several acquaintances with whom she had discussed the case.

"Will you tell me what you remember about those discussions."

"We was just discussing what had come out in the newspapers and they would give opinions."

Hecht asked what were the opinions she heard? "They thought he was guilty."

"And that was an opinion expressed by your parents?"

"Yes."

"Your brothers and sisters?"

"Yes."

"Your friends or acquaintances that you have identified?"

"Yes."

"Did you express any opinions?"

"Yes, I did."

"Okay, what opinions did you express?"

"I expressed that from what I had read in the newspaper, I thought he was guilty."

She said her opinion was based mostly on what had come out about the second autopsy. Hecht asked her what she remembered about that story? "That she had been beaten to death."

Hecht asked whether she had her earlier opinion in the back of her mind when she arrived the first day of jury duty. "It was in the back of my mind but I'm a fair-minded person. I make up—you know, I use facts and make my own decisions."

Langley left the room. Later on, Rulon allowed for her removal from the jury. He also removed a Mrs. Boles who, during questioning, indicated she was a close friend of Sandy and Tom and felt a bias toward them. Releasing these two preserved a balance.

Hecht questioned Mrs. Freymouth. Her husband knew Marty and Lorna, Larry Kalsow and other members of the Optimists. She heard them talking about the case. Hecht asked her to explain.

"Well, I guess that they just felt that they were of the opinion or had heard of a relationship between Mr. Bird and Lorna Anderson. Therefore, when the death of Sandra Bird and the death of Marty Anderson and these happened, they just formed their own opinions maybe or had heard hearsay."

The court asked whether any jurors had ever been to Rocky Ford Bridge. Most had not, but a few knew it well. Mrs. Pike lived southwest of the bridge and used it occasionally. Symmonds asked whether she would "formulate and make any conclusions regarding the incident [Sandy's death, based on her own experience with the bridge]?"

"No, because it's a bad bridge and I don't like it anyway. I mean, you know, it's just—it's just curvy and it's a bad bridge, bad road to travel when you get right down to it...just that I don't like the bridge itself....when you're coming—you come in on a curve and then you go down and then you go out on a curve, and it's pretty blind from both sides and it's just a one-way bridge."

It took until nearly 4 p.m. on the third day to finish voir dire. The final jury included Mr. Beemer, Mrs. Castor, Mrs. Price, Mr. Harris, Mr. Webb, Mr. Gehring, Mr. Kessinger, Mrs. McCloud, Mr. Barger, Mr. Rohling, Dr. Barden and Mr. Davis. The alternates were Mr. Dreyer, Mr. Harmony and Mr. Kneer.

During the first trial, the Bird family often had trouble finding seating. This time, Rulon ordered that four seats be reserved for the Birds directly behind Tom next to the rail. He reserved a row of seats for Jane Grismer and her family members. Rulon wanted to avoid forcing family members to come early to get the choice seats.

The judge read a series of detailed instructions to the chosen jurors and told them to report to the courthouse by 9:00 a.m. Monday morning. The jurors spent the weekend mulling over and thinking through the four days it took to winnow the panel down, and the days ahead. Did they stay away from newspapers, radio and television? Did they keep from discussing the case with friends, relatives and acquaintances? They all promised to do so.

Tom returned to his cell. Before his first trial he had felt confident. Not this time.

First day of the trial

On July 1, 1985, Tom sat at the defendant's table in the Lyon County facing a jury. He saw this trial differently from his first.

"I didn't have any confidence. Especially when the judge was taking all this stuff from the previous trial, refused change of venue again, I had to prove my innocence.

"In the first trial, a juror said I testified and that hurt me more than anything. I wanted to tell my story and my attorney said no you don't. We wanted to keep the tape out of that trial. We weren't attacking anything. I wanted Shaw to attack Darrel. No we can't do that. When Irv got through, I kind of shrugged my shoulder and said, is that it?

It was more serious the second time, therefore the stakes were higher. You see, mine were the only trials. People were psyched up for Dan Carter's trial. Didn't happen. They were psyched up for Curry's trial. Didn't happen. They were psyched up for Lorna's trial. Didn't happen. Then here came my trial and it's happening. It's like here's some food, take it away. Here's some more food, take it away. They gobble it up. Then they got the trial they wanted.

"Lorna's kept getting postponed, filed and re-filed. I've been in jail.

"Support in the town at the second trial was pretty isolated. Supportive people were not very verbal about it anymore."

Before the trial began, Susan Ewert delivered a strange and surprising piece of news to Tom. Lorna had married Randall Eldridge, a singer in a Southern Gospel group from Hutchinson. She met him in church. Tom and Susan stood confused and shocked, having been so close to and protective of Lorna, neither could imagine why she would marry without informing either of them. But as surprising as had been this marriage it paled in comparison to the surprises Lorna had in store for Tom that would affect him for the rest of his life.

A few loose ends

About opening statements, Rulon said, "I would hope that you would be reasonable about the time." Symmonds felt they would take the better part of the morning.

Lorna sent a letter by way of her attorney stating she planned to claim protection against self-incrimination if called to testify. Rather than bring her to court to receive that news, the parties accepted her refusal to testify. Once again, anything she told another would be hearsay.

Symmonds laid out the state's case in his opening remarks. He shocked Tom and his attorney by finally revealing the state's theory of how Tom killed Sandy: he threw her off the bridge, Symmonds said.

When Hecht finished his opening statement around 10:30 a.m., Rulon ordered a short recess. Counsel met with the judge to consider new issues that had arisen. Hecht moved to dismiss the trial altogether, stating, "Counsel in opening statement said for the first time that the state's theory in this case was that Sandra Bird met her death by being thrown off of the bridge. The accusation made against Mr. Bird in the Bill of Particulars states that he did unlawfully and feloniously touch Sandy S. Bird and as a result thereof she suffered a blunt injury. There's no reference in the Bill of Particulars that she was thrown off of any bridge but rather that it was felonious touching."

Symmonds answered, "The state would contend that concerning throwing or dropping or tossing somebody off a bridge would be encompassed within the term touching or applying force to the person of another which resulted in injuries, and the blunt injuries which we described are still—I think I haven't really disputed what caused the death, and certainly the exact—well, I guess the state would just contend that it certainly is encompassed within what was described with the Bill of Particulars and certainly doesn't surprise the defense in light of the testimony presented at the grand jury."

"We've been trying for six months to find out whether the state claimed that she was beaten to death, run over by an automobile or in what manner she met her death; and today's the first time anybody has said the state's theory was that she was thrown off a bridge." This lack of clarity in the indictment is precisely why Hecht moved for dismissal of the case altogether. "You can't properly defend if you can't determine what is the state's theory as to the exact cause of death."

Symmonds argued that the defense had reviewed all the grand jury testimony and it should have been clear to them what applying force and feloniously touching could include. Furthermore, the state clearly excluded certain actions like a gunshot wound.

Rulon denied Hecht's motion.

Hecht moved that the state be limited in the balance of the trial to the argument that Tom threw Sandy off the bridge, "and that there be no testimony concerning then any allegation that she met her death in any manner or sustained her injuries in any other manner...The state didn't charge, this gentleman has not been indicted with, an assault and battery or aggravated battery or any other form of battery. He has only been charged with murdering his wife, and the state now says in its opening statement that he murdered his wife by throwing her off the bridge." The Bill of Particulars said nothing about this. The defense had repeatedly begged for a clear statement about how Tom allegedly killed Sandy. Not until the opening statement did the state express its theory, and Hecht believed it should then be limited to only that theory.

Rulon also denied this motion.

Witnesses begin their testimony

Symmonds called Brian Fletcher to the stand. Fletcher arrived at Rocky Ford Bridge the morning of July 17, 1983 and spotted Sandy and the car in the river beneath the bridge. "After you looked over the bridge the second time and saw the car and the body, what did you do?"

"I got back in my Blazer and drove up to the trailer house up at the top of the hill and called for the person there to call the sheriff."

Fletcher said that after this he "just got out and kind of milled around until somebody showed up." He described in detail what he actually saw — the car, the body, the location of each. He stayed on the bridge. He said the second highway patrolman who arrived was the first to go down to the car.

Symmonds showed Fletcher a photograph of the accident scene and asked him to verify that it represented what he saw that day. This photograph was one of dozens introduced during the trial and became part of the "170 or more pieces of evidence" Symmonds presented to the jury. More than 100 of those "pieces of evidence" were photographs.

Did you notice if the lights were on? No. Did you hear any discussion about whether or not the ignition was on? Yes, but I don't know what they actually decided. Did you see blood on the bridge? No, I only looked for a second.

Symmonds asked about the roadway south of the bridge. Did you see any skid marks or disturbance of the rocks "which might indicate that someone had lost control of a vehicle?" No.

Fletcher described the roads as gravel and the bridge deck as wood. He said Sandy's body lay partially submerged and it "seemed dirty...The person was real light skinned and, you know, you could see the dirt that had like drifted up on her and just kind of sat there. It looked real dirty."

Symmonds asked for a more specific description of the bridge. Wood planks ran lengthways that one drives on, and then east to west, under the long planks."

Hecht began his cross-examination. How often do you drive that route. Often, I have friends out there. I hunt around there. And fish, too. He couldn't quite identify the time he arrived, but thought it could have been within an hour of 9:00 a.m. (Why would Fletcher think to record the time of his arrival? He had no experience in criminal matters. Most non-criminals seldom note the time of every action or event in their lives—just an estimate of the time within an hour or so, even when it's traumatic such as finding a dead body.)

Hecht asked specific questions about where he and his girlfriend parked, where he walked on the bridge and how far he got before looking over. He looked over to check the condition of the water for canoeing. The first thing he saw was the body and he estimated it could have been 50 yards from the bridge. (Fletcher, a common citizen who had no investigative training, missed this dimension by a wide margin. Hecht used this to demonstrate that normal people, even with the adrenaline rush of finding a dead body in a river, make mistakes. Mistakes are human.)

You saw a body and believed it was dead? Yes. What was the first thing you did? Told my girlfriend to stay in the car and then looked over the bridge again, spotting the car. He had leaned over the railing a little further and had moved up the bridge somewhat.

Hecht asked about the river's current. On the west side of the bridge, it's deeper and faster than the east side. (Sandy's body lay on the east side.) The current runs west to east. Hecht used Fletcher to explain how the current acted at about the point where the car and Sandy's body had been found. In a sense, the river's curve and the bank deflected it back out away from the riverbank. "And it leaves, does it not, kind of a quiet water pool there in the vicinity where the motor vehicle was and the deceased person was?"

"Yes."

"There is no current, so to speak, at that location, is there?"

"It would be very slow."

He quizzed him about the arrival of the officers, who came first, what did they do? He tried to determine the intervals between the arrival of each officer and from the time he first saw the body. "I don't have any estimate on the time. It didn't seem really like it took the highway patrol that long to get there."

Fletcher described in detail the position of the car and the body. The wheels were up in the air and the car faced away from the bridge. "The body was in the water." The car sat partly in the water, and part on the riverbank.

The discussion you heard about lights and the ignition switch, who did that? The rescue people and the highway patrol. They all stood fairly close to each other, but not huddled together. He couldn't say whether any conclusion had been reached about the lights and the ignition.

About the substance on the bridge, did you walk in or around it or stand on it? No, just glanced down, but it never caught his attention. How about the gravel road? No, never saw a disturbance or skid marks. The gravel seemed to be pretty plain and flat.

About the body, Hecht asked, "And it didn't look to you like a dirty body had gotten into the water but that a body had gotten dirty in the water."

"Well, I don't know what it looked like before it was in the water, but I would say most of what I noticed was from the water."

"Drifting up, washing onto it?"

"Yes."

Fletcher stepped down.

Symmonds called Mark Gibbons to the stand.

Gibbons lived in a mobile home "approximately two to three hundred feet almost directly south of the bridge, just a little west of the actual bridge."

Symmonds asked Gibbons to specifically locate his home on a diagram he posted on a display board. Hecht objected because the diagram had not been entered as an exhibit and it was not drawn to scale. Symmonds explained, "Your Honor, I would state for the court that the diagram is not drawn to scale. It was prepared by Trooper John Rule who we do anticipate calling tomorrow as a witness."

Rulon told Symmonds to establish a foundation for the diagram by asking Gibbons to identify various entries on it. As Gibbons began, Hecht objected once more. "It's not to scale and design, and curvature of this road is an issue in this lawsuit, and we don't think the witness should be put in the position of attempting to decide whether or not a nonscale diagram correctly depicts the curvature of the road."

Rulon asked Symmonds the purpose of using the nonscale diagram. He said only to help Gibbons describe where he lived in relation to the bridge. Rulon allowed him to continue, saying, "As to whether or not that diagram properly relates the road situation, I don't want you to get into that with this witness."

Gibbons pointed to the location of his mobile home and sat back down in the witness stand.

Symmonds asked several questions about Saturday evening and early Sunday morning, July 16 and 17. When did you go to bed? 10:00 or 11:00 p.m. Did you use a fan to cool yourself? Yes. What happened after you went to bed? "I was awakened in the middle of the night by my dog or one of them I heard barking and just carrying on."

"What did you do when you heard your dog barking?"

"I got up, and I went out on the front porch of the house and called the dog more or less up to me and scolded him for waking me up."

"After you scolded the dog, what did you do?"

"I returned to bed, and at that time being in the middle of the night it had cooled off enough that the fan was actually cold, so I turned the fan off and just returned to bed." He looked at the clock. It said 3:10 a.m.

"After I went to bed and was laying there just trying to go back to sleep, the dog again started barking and growling standing at the end of the driveway. This time I didn't get up and go to the door. I just sat up in the window and yelled at the dog to be quiet which finally it settled down and I went back to bed."

"Did you hear anything further on that particular evening?"

"Yes. While laying there trying to go back to sleep, I started hearing some noises outside."

"Is it uncommon for you to hear noises outside?"

"Not uncommon, no. That's out of town; and with the wildlife, the deer and coyotes and all the different animals running around, you hear noises most all the time."

"Can you describe the noise that you heard?"

"The first reaction I had to the noise was just the cats hissing at each other or the dog and the cats fighting or it was a hissing noise kind of; I don't know, raspy kind of like noise." He did nothing except try to figure out what the noise had been. It didn't resemble any of the normal noises he had heard from time to time. Gibbons fell back asleep.

Good morning, Mr. Gibbons

On Sunday morning, Gibbons heard a knock at his door. He opened it to a man who said "that there had been an accident at the bridge with a car in the river and there was a body." He called the sheriff and then went to the bridge. The man, Fletcher, told him there was no need of an ambulance. The person in the river lay dead.

Gibbons had walked down the gravel road toward the bridge and Symmonds asked him to describe what he saw. He saw nothing. At the bridge he saw Fletcher and his girlfriend. "What did you do?" Symmonds asked.

"We at first tried to find out how the car could have gotten down there. There was no damage to the bridge itself....We tried to determine what path the car took to get to the river, naturally our first guess was it went through the railing of the bridge which with the type structure the bridge is, it just couldn't have without breaking the railing through."

He walked to the north end of the bridge and saw nothing that indicated the car had gone over at that point. He walked back south and on the river bank, saw that some bushes looked damaged, bark had been torn away and branches torn off. He described the concrete abutment near the south end of the bridge and placed the bushes east of there. Then he walked up the road in the direction it appeared the car had traveled, but saw no skid marks or disturbed gravel. Then he, Fletcher and his girlfriend waited for the highway patrol.

Gibbons said that the only damage to the car that he could see from up above was a door lying on the riverbank.

Symmonds returned to the question of the noise that he had heard earlier that morning. Did he ever begin to think it had not been an animal. Yes, "after we had discovered the body."

Hecht began his cross-examination. He established that Gibbons had lived in rural areas for many years.

Gibbons said he drove across the bridge perhaps 10 times a week to and from work. He also used it to get to town at various other times, day or night. How many times in a month, total? Perhaps 50.

He knew it to be a popular spot for sportsmen, hunters, fishers and canoeists. "Yes, there was always people down there."

He thought Fletcher knocked on his door at 10:00 a.m. He called the sheriff's department.

It took 10 to 15 minutes from the time of the call for the first trooper to arrive. The second came, he thought, within five minutes of the first.

Had he mostly been on the bridge while waiting? Yes, mostly on the south end of the bridge.

He noticed that part of the car sat on the bank so that someone could walk up to the driver's side without getting their feet wet. He thought the door lay 30 feet from the car to the right.

No, he saw no damage to the bridge itself, but noticed scrape marks on the concrete abutment. And he noticed the damage to the vegetation to the east of the abutment.

No, he saw no tire marks at all, except some that had been in the mud for what appeared to be a long time. Other than the damage to the vegetation he saw no evidence of the car having passed that way. Is it a fair statement that the car went in on the south side of the bridge? Yes.

Hecht asked about the dogs barking. One dog would often bark if someone turned around in his driveway or if there was something going on down at the bridge. Sometimes people turned around in his driveway at night.

"Your dogs are also excited in the morning hours or in the nighttime by the presence of wildlife?"

"Not usually. This dog that I had, the person I bought the house from, it was his dog; and the dog had always been out there and it was more or less accustomed to the natural happenings of the area."

The dogs barked like that only one time—that early Sunday morning of Sandy's death. They barked loud enough to awaken him over the hum of a whirling fan, and they did it twice.

It had to have been after 3:10 a.m.

Hecht asked, "If a highway patrol officer or deputy sheriff was at Mr. Bird's house at 3:00 in the morning on July 17, 1983, having a conversation with him in the front yard, would you agree with me he could not have been at the bridge when you heard the noise?"

"Yes."

Symmonds began his re-direct.

Gibbons said his dogs had awakened him a couple of times during the two years he lived out there. Yes, there were more than two times that people had been at the bridge during the middle of the night. No, the dogs didn't always keep barking when someone went out there.

Were there ever times the dogs barked if a coyote came into the yard? Yes. The dogs protected their territory.

Gibbons described the location of the scrape on the concrete abutment as being on the right side as he faced it, toward the river. He thought it looked like it had been recently scraped. Symmonds showed him a photo of the abutment. Do you see the scrape mark? No, but I see the area where it had been, "a point to where there was a discoloration."

Hecht had more. He asked Gibbons to circle the area on the picture of the concrete abutment where he noticed scrape marks. Gibbons stepped down.

After the afternoon recess, Symmonds called Trooper Charles Smith. Smith held the rank of Sergeant with the Kansas Highway Patrol—a 15-year veteran.

Smith received the call to head to Rocky Ford Bridge at 10:40 a.m., according to his log. He spotted Trooper Rule on the highway and advised him of the call. Smith arrived at the bridge first with Rule about a minute behind him. (Fletcher and Gibbons both felt several minutes passed before Rule arrived.)

He got out of his car, noticing three people on the bridge, and looked over the edge down to the river. He spotted the car and went back to radio for help. He requested the sheriff's office to send out a coroner and to locate Sheriff Dan Andrews. He checked to see whether a rescue unit and ambulance had been dispatched and then moved his car out of the way. About then, Rule arrived.

Smith took out his camera and shot a roll of film before he left. He explained the method the troopers used to mark their film and then identified one for the jury to help them understand the system.

Smith identified other photographs and certified that they represented what he saw that morning.

Within minutes of his arrival, Trooper Rule and "several of the firemen were down at the scene." He noted that the driver's door lay several feet from the car, the exterior side facing down.

He described the terrain as "very rocky at that point."

He described the car as lying so that the front end "would be down to the front a little bit." (It tilted down and to the right.)

Symmonds asked him to describe the damage he saw on the car and to identify several photos and certify that they depicted exactly what he saw that day. He identified them all, noting one in particular that showed the pocket on the inside of the door "that you can place road maps and stuff like that."

"On the rocks near the car door we also noted some substance that appeared to be in my opinion blood...It was red in texture, and my experience as a police officer I've seen blood many times, and it appeared to be blood."

Smith said the body lay "partially submerged, mostly submerged in the water face down with the feet lying toward the vehicle."

Symmonds asked whether Smith noticed a blood-like substance anywhere else.

"There was a couple different locations. In the areas of the rock we also noted some that appeared to be blood on the leaves; and on the bridge, on the east side of the bridge. He failed to photograph the substance on the bridge.

Smith mentioned that he took photos of the blood on the leaves of the tree that stood directly beneath the edge of the bridge. He remembered seeing blood, or at least what appeared to be blood on the rocks near the tree.

Symmonds asked about the headlights. Were they on? Smith didn't remember.

Did you look inside the car? Yes. What did you see? A purse "and numerous other items and what appeared to be a bundle or a large amount of computer printout sheets."

Fireman David Cox had retrieved the purse and handed it to him. He pulled out the driver's license and saw it belonged to Sandra Stringer Bird. The photo and measurements on the license matched the body in the water. She wore a "summer dress or an evening dress possibly."

Smith left the scene and drove to the sheriff's office. He met Officer Scott Cronk there. He checked the license plate registration and noted it belonged to the Birds. He and Cronk drove to the Bird's house. Cronk followed behind in his own car; he had taken a missing person's report from Tom earlier that morning.

Upon arriving at the house, Tom opened the door. "As I recall, he said, 'Do you have any information about my wife?' I said, 'Yes, sir, I do; and the news is not good.'"

"After you made this statement, what happened?"

"Mr. Bird invited us into the living room of their home at that time, and Officer Cronk and I went into the living room with him and we were seated on the couch in the residence. Mr. Bird sat across from us in a chair.

"After telling him that the news was not good, he said, 'Well, what can you tell me?' And as I recall I believe my statement to him was that there had been apparently an accident and I would—I can't remember the exact words but I probably said to Mr. Bird that his wife had been fatally injured. I do not use the word 'dead' or 'killed' in making notifications and I believe I stated it that way. And he asked me, 'What else can you tell me about it?'; and I said that the accident happened at a location southeast of Emporia on the Cottonwood River known as the Rocky Ford Bridge."

"What did the defendant say?"

"Well, he was shaken by it for a few moments there and I gave him a few moments to regain his composure, and I don't recall just exactly what was said then. Several more comments were made and I asked him if he had—if they had some children; and he said, 'Yes, but they're not here at this time. I had a friend come and get them.'"

Smith did not recall whether or not Tom cried. After Smith told him this, he remembered Tom said, "Well, what's she doing out there? We don't know anything about that part of town."

Was there further conversation with the defendant?

"Yes, sir. Some more of the conversation was I asked Mr. Bird if he could relate to me where they had been earlier in the evening. He mentioned to me they had been to a movie and been to a club and had a couple of drinks. And as I recall they went back to the church and Sandy let him out there and she was to go to the college to her office to get some work or do some work at the college. I'm not sure which way the statement was made to me at this time. I asked him if there had been an argument or anything and he said, no, there had not been but he said once in a while when she has things to think out she'll go out for a drive."

Symmonds asked how many times that Smith had delivered such sad news. Numerous times. "Is there any way to predict how a person will act?"

"No, sir, there sure isn't."

Symmonds yielded to Hecht.

Hecht asked Smith to clarify his testimony about the damage to the car. Smith misspoke in his earlier testimony stating there had been damage to the right side of the car. "It would be the left side, all of the damage, sir," he corrected himself.

Hecht asked him whether or not he knew he would be testifying in this trial? Yes. And he took time to prepare his testimony? Yes. You made an honest mistake. We all make mistakes.

"Did you make any diagrams?"

"No, I did not."

"Did you make any notes wherein you reflected the measurements from various points of references as to where the photographs that you took portrayed a substance that you believed to be blood?"

"No, I did not make any diagram of any kind." Neither did he take measurements or take notes of any kind. This meant that he could not tell anyone exactly where the blood had been that he noticed. He could only offer an opinion after looking at the photos, and then only the photos that included the door.

As for the blood on the leaves, Smith felt sure he looked down at the tree from the third span of the bridge right above the tree, but he had to rely on his recollection to offer an opinion. And the same held true for the substance on the bridge that he thought might be blood—no measurements, just his recollection where the spot sat.

He asked about the debris Smith saw in the car. Yes, it pretty much seemed like what you would expect in a car belonging to a family with three small children.

Hecht went to the issue of notifying someone of a death. Smith said not every one sheds tears. "It's not uncommon, no."

Smith testified that Tom had been shaken by the news. It fell within the normal reactions he had previously observed.

Hecht asked about the conversation with Tom as Smith recalled it. It was not exactly what had been said, but the sum and substance of the discussion. Did Tom tell you they had been to a movie? "He probably did."

Hecht rehearsed the rest of the story as Smith recalled it. It fit Tom's consistent statements.

How long were you at the accident scene? Maybe 30-45 minutes. Did they move Sandy's body while you were there? Yes, to identify it. They took it out of the water.

Hecht asked if Smith had seen the car door at a later time and noticed any damage. "There was a hole in the left door on the outside skin." Since then, he saw the photos and noticed the bottom of the door had been rolled under.

Hecht asked him about the rough rocks. Did they pretty much cover all the area down on the beach and around where the car had been found? "As I recall, pretty much so, sir, especially the bottom half of the terrain there."

Smith said he arrived at the scene at 10:52 a.m. and believed he got to Tom's around 11:45 a.m. and left around noon. He couldn't be exactly sure of those times.

On redirect, Symmonds asked Smith to explain what he meant that Tom had been shaken and then regained his composure. "When I told him his wife had been fatally injured, he took a deep breath and just kind of sat back for a little bit, and I didn't say anything for a few seconds or a moment or so."

Smith said he went back to the bridge several hours after notifying Tom and saw the spot on the bridge that looked like blood.

Hecht asked whether Smith noticed the leaves on the trees when he went back that day? No, he noticed them that morning when Trooper Rule pointed them out. Where they still there? He didn't know. Smith thought it was 6:00 p.m. by the time he got back to the bridge.

More accident scene testimony

Symmonds called Michael Younkin to the stand. Younkin worked for the Emporia Fire Department. He arrived at the Rocky Ford Bridge at 10:54 a.m. in a rescue truck driven by David Cox, another fireman.

Cox had parked the rescue vehicle south of the bridge. "We went down the riverbank to the edge of the river to see what we were going to need at the scene, see if the person was alive or dead, make sure that the person was indeed dead."

One of Younkin's duties is to make sure the area is safe for others who might work near the scene. He assigned the task of checking the ignition of the car to Cox. Then they removed the body.

"The body had some—had a small laceration on the left side of the head and it was partly covered with river debris....Small particles of moss, small particles of dirt coming out of the river." He said the body was "very stiff."

He described the eddy in which the body had been found as "a place where the water does not flow very fast."

He ordered a body bag to be brought down and then they removed the body to the "Roberts-Blue Funeral Home." (Actually, they moved it to Newman Hospital, but even trained EMT personnel make honest mistakes.)

Younkin stepped down and Rulon announced the court would be in recess until the next morning.

The next morning, Symmonds called Earl Eugene Bryant to the stand. Bryant served as an Emporia fireman and did emergency rescue work.

Bryant arrived at the bridge around 11:00 a.m. Sunday morning. Terry Kramer drove the ambulance. They parked on the bridge and went down to the body. He saw David Cox climb in the car and bring out a purse. He never touched the car himself.

Symmonds asked him to describe the body. "It was discolored from murky water, of course, river water. There was a laceration on the left cheek area approximately one inch in length, fairly deep, half inch deep. That's basically all I observed. The body was clothed." He said it was rigid, too.

He said the water was about 12 inches deep where the body lay.

Bryant said that he saw no tire marks on the road. "There was a scrape mark on the end of the abutment."

Hecht asked, "Do you know whether or not a body that is left in cool water such as river water will become rigid faster or slower than a body that is left in either the July weather outdoors or in the ordinary room temperature?"

"No, I don't.

Hecht asked Bryant about skid marks. "Do you mean you did not discover any skid marks?"

"Yes, that's exactly what I mean."

"And by skid marks you would mean I assume black rubber left on the surface of the roadway from the severe application of brakes."

"Or the gravel being disturbed."

Bryant agreed that he saw nothing to indicate that the car did not pass next to the abutment and go over the bank. Bryant stepped down.

Symmonds called David Earl Cox, the man who drove the rescue truck. Cox said that before they went down to the car they retrieved the stretcher and body bag. (His partner testified the day before that they had brought the body bag and stretcher down after first inspecting the body. These were two professional men who had been at the same place at the same time, but had different stories. The testimony had been an honest mistake, but it grew out of the fact that no one treated the incident as anything but an auto accident. Therefore, careful notes had not been made of each activity.)

"When you got down to the river's edge, what if anything did you do?"

"The first thing I did was to enter the car to check for any fire hazard or safety hazard at the scene."

"What do you do as far as checking for any fire or safety hazard?"

"In normal circumstances·we check the ignition [sic] of the car to make sure if it's in park or in a safe position where it won't travel in any direction, and we disconnect the battery. In this case the only option open to us was checking the ignition to make sure it was off." They didn't do anything with the battery because it was submerged in water, and since the car lay upside down, whether it was in gear didn't matter.

"Did you in fact check the ignition on the car?"

"Yes."

"What if anything did you note?"

"It was in the off position."

"How do you know that?"

"It would not go in any direction and it was labeled as such."

"Was there anything else that caused you to feel that the car was in the off position?"

"When I entered the car I had to crawl down through a small bit of water, and to help myself in I grabbed the steering wheel and it felt locked like if the ignition had been turned off."

Cox failed to notice whether the lights were on, saying he looked at the dashboard and saw nothing out of place. Inside the car, Cox saw Sandy's purse, some bottles, children's clothing and paper and other debris.

"What kind of bottles?"

"They appeared to be like a wine bottle, a dark green in color."

He helped three other men carry Sandy's body to the rescue vehicle. He drove to Newman Hospital where a law enforcement officer took charge of the body. Then he left.

Hecht asked Cox about whom he saw down by the car when he arrived. No one. Yes, Trooper Smith was still there. After removing his equipment from the van, he climbed down to the car, making him the first person at the wreck. He had no idea whether anyone had been down there before him.

Hecht asked whether Cox went in through a door or a window? Cox said a door. "I went through an opening. I really don't remember whether it was a door or not." But his recollection was that he went through a door on the driver's side. (The door lay detached several feet away from the car up on the beach.)

Hecht mentioned that Cox had laid on the roof of the car inside looking up at the "gadgetry." Yes, that would be correct. Hecht went to great lengths to identify exactly the position Cox's body sat in the car. Once he got Cox to explain his position relative to the steering wheel, he asked, "Then what did you do, sir?"

"I checked the ignition."

"How did you do that?"

"By visual and manual means."

"Tell me please what you did manually."

"I checked to make sure that there was a key in the ignition, tired to turn it, couldn't get it to go either way, looked at it and it was in the off position."

"Tried to turn it?"

"Yes, sir."

"Would go neither way?"

"Yes, sir."

"And then you looked."

"I looked and turned approximately at the same time."

"When you looked, what did you see?"

"I saw a key in the ignition."

"Now, where was the ignition in regards to the automobile?"

"Well, it was on the steering column."

"Where?"

"Towards the inside of the car, towards the middle."

Hecht forced as clear a definition from Cox as he could get. Cox remembered the ignition switch as being on the passenger side of the steering column. Cox said he looked at the ignition switch and it said "off," and that the key was centered on the word "off."

Hecht asked him if he knew what the other side of the key pointed to, and he said, "I have no idea."

Hecht asked for specifics about the steering wheel. Cox meant that he grabbed it and it didn't turn, not that it couldn't turn. It just didn't when he grabbed it. He could not be sure if it had been in a locked position.

Hecht asked about the contents of the car, especially whether there had been quite a bit of computer paper. Cox remembered the paper, but not the volume of paper.

Hecht clarified the comment about the lights. Cox hadn't noticed whether the switch was on or off.

Terrence L. Kramer came next. He rode with Earl Bryant in the ambulance to the bridge. He testified to helping remove the body. He added one detail. Sandy's body lay in shallow water, but the riverbed itself was rock-strewn.

Hecht once again asked for many details. His technique seemed to probe small issues to be certain whether or not testimony corroborated that of others, or perhaps, to set up questions to ask future witnesses and show inconsistencies in their testimony.

Hecht asked Kramer if he remembered seeing Trooper Smith down by the car? Kramer could not recall one way or the other, but he didn't think so. Hecht referred to testimony Kramer gave to the grand jury. He had testified that Charles Smith stood near the body down by the car and told the rescue crew that she was deceased. "Do you recall that question and that answer?"

"Yes." And he said he answered truthfully the first time.

Kramer stepped down and Symmonds called Dennis Arb.

Arb described how his sister called him after hearing about the accident on her police scanner. He thought he went to the bridge around 9:00 a.m., but admitted that couldn't be since the police call came close to 10:30.

He rode his motorcycle to the bridge, approaching from the south. He parked on the north side of the bridge and walked back to the middle and looked over the edge. Then he talked with two of his relatives who were also there, "and we just started talking about it."

Arb said the body wasn't there when he arrived, nor were there ambulances. He didn't recall a tow truck either. He remembered the car being upside down. He thought he saw some debris in the back of the car and noticed the door had been torn off.

Symmonds tried to find a way to get Arb to describe finding blood on the bridge, but Arb kept answering incorrectly, raising objections from Hecht. Finally, Symmonds took him step by step through a description of the bridge. He described how the planks ran across and east and west. Then Symmonds asked, "And when you looked at the plank that was running on the bridge floor, describe what if anything you observed to the jury."

"I'm afraid to say anything."

"You needn't worry about that. We just need to have you relate to the jury what it was that you saw when you looked at the plank."

"Well, I myself didn't see anything. Another person seen it."

Hecht objected. Rulon sustained the objection.

Then Symmonds asked, when he *did* look at the bridge plank, what had he seen?

"Well, there was blood on the bridge plank."

Symmonds asked him what it was that caused him to think it was blood? Arb said he had no doubt that he saw blood. Why did you draw that conclusion? "Well, right on the edge of the bridge there was a pool of blood, and it was—there was also blood on the hand railing and there was two cross members that go across beside the bridge that ties the bridge together. There was drops of blood on that and there was also drops of blood on the tree directly below and also on the rocks right directly below where it was on the railing."

Arb said that he began looking at other areas on the bridge and found another set of blood spots, about eight by eight inches across. He said the blood on the railing was uniform in position with the blood on the bridge deck, and the pool of blood was bigger than the spot he found closer to the end of the bridge.

Symmonds asked Arb if he had looked through the planks where he noticed the blood spots. Yes. Describe what you saw. "Well, there was a tree directly below that there was blood droppings. You could see them on the tree and on the leaf and on the wreck—on the rocks directly below, and there was one smear on the tree." He thought the smear on the tree was about six to eight feet off the ground and maybe four inches long.

Arb said he saw blood spots on both the railing and on a cross member that sits directly below the railing on the side of the bridge.

Symmonds showed Arb several photos and had him identify the blood spots. He asked whether he stepped in one of the spots. Yes, he had, but the blood had dried so it did not stick to his shoes. He said it wasn't red, more of a brown color.

Arb said, "Dan Andrews, the sheriff, took a sample of every blood stain he could see." (No one asked Arb about Andrews being his cousin.) Arb described how cousin Dan meticulously collected blood samples and put them into plastic bags.

Arb wandered to a road on the south side of the bridge that enters a field. "And there we found a red plastic cup." He said the cup reminded him of the kind he saw at keg parties, red on the outside and white on the inside.

Symmonds asked him what else he saw at that road. "Right where the cup was there was peel out marks in the gravel that went up the hill, came out right where the plastic cup was and went up the hill south."

Symmonds asked him about head and taillights, but Arb could not give a definitive answer.

Hecht began his cross-examination.

He used Arb to describe the area on the south side of the bridge, and then asked him about the red plastic cup. "Did you notice anything unusual about the red plastic cup?"

"I remember it as being smashed."

"And by smashed you mean essentially flat?"

"Yeah."

Hecht quizzed him about arriving at 9:00 a.m. Arb felt sure that was accurate, but having heard other testimony, he knew he was wrong. By so quizzing Arb, Hecht cast doubt on the accuracy of all his testimony.

"And when you arrived there at what you thought to be 9:00 in the morning, the automobile was sitting on its wheels, was it not?"

"No, it was on its top."

"Have you ever testified before, sir, that it was on its wheels?"

"Yes, I did." Arb gave that testimony to the grand jury in January. He said his memory had improved since January. Then he had testified that the headlights had been on and that, in fact, as the tow truck pulled the car up the bank, he saw the headlights on.

"They had another man down there at the car. After they turned it over, they loaded—they put something in the car which was the door, and then it was just kind of an inch your way up the embankment. There was big rocks to go over." The rear end went up first, giving Arb a clear look at the headlights. The tow truck sat on the bank above the car and a man attached a cable to the car. The tow cable pulled the car over onto its wheels.

Arb said he could not remember if the taillights had been on, but now seemed sure about the headlights. Yes, they were on. He felt sure he saw someone reach into the car once it was up on the road and turn off the headlights.

Symmonds showed him a picture of the car in the river as taken from the bridge. Yes, he could only see the taillights and no, he could not remember if they were on or off. Then Arb added that much of what he said about the lights had not been his observation but what he heard others say.

Hecht again read from the grand jury transcript. Arb stated clearly that he could see the headlights as they pulled the car up the bank. He remembered others talking about how unusual it was that the headlights remained on given how long the car had laid in the water. Arb said his grand jury testimony was true and claimed nothing happened since then to change it.

Pulling out more testimony

Larry Estes came next. He owned Larry Estes Body and Wrecker and operated the truck that pulled the car out of the water and up on the bank. He towed the car to his garage.

Estes believed he arrived between 10:45 and 11:00 a.m. No, the rescue truck was not there, but he remembered the ambulance. He parked on the southwest side of the bridge and "run a cable down to the car or to a tree to the side of the car, pulled it over and picked up the stuff around the car."

Symmonds asked Estes to indicate various positions and directions on the diagram Rule had prepared. Hecht once again objected. A distorted diagram prejudiced the jury against Tom. Symmonds said all the diagram did was to help Estes clarify his testimony. Since Rule had prepared the diagram, Symmonds felt that made it adequate enough for this purpose and since he planned to call Rule to testify, the diagram could be dealt with later. Rulon disagreed and sustained the objection.

Symmonds asked Estes to step down and called John Rule.

Rule explained his training, background and specialty. "As a part of your training do you receive instruction on how to make diagrams?"

"Yes, sir."

"Do you recall, Officer Rule, did you prior to this date have occasion to make several diagrams pertaining to the location around the Rocky Ford Bridge?"

"Yes, sir."

"Were those drawings drawn to scale?"

"No, sir."

Symmonds turned to the diagrams. Rule then identified several facets of the diagram to establish that it represented the site at the time of the incident. Though he believed the diagrams to be accurate, he added, "There are no abutments here. I put these on just to merely show where the end of the bridge was at."

"And does that diagram fairly and accurately depict, recognizing that it's not drawn to scale, the general relationship between the bridge and various roads and drives that are out at that particular location?"

"Yes, sir."

"Was it drawn with the idea of depicting the actual curvature of the road?"

"No, sir. The diagram was drawn from my notes and measurements that I have made of the area. It's not to scale." He prepared the diagram to help him with his testimony.

Symmonds asked him to point to the location of the car. Hecht stood again. "The officer's already testified that it's not to scale in any sense of the word, and now to be testifying as to the placement of things by the use of this diagram will give a distorted view of the facts. Surely the county or the state can prepare a diagram to scale. The highway patrol does it all the time. You have a county engineer here."

Rulon overruled him. He said the jury understood it was not drawn to scale and it would just be used to "show a general location of where objects are located."

Hecht took over. Was the diagram drawn to scale? No, repeated several times. "Would you agree with me, sir, the diagram is not accurate in any sense of the word other than that it shows a line which is sort of an S curve with a line on both sides?"

"The accuracy of this diagram was made to give you an overview of the area. I didn't count fence posts; and to be to scale, I would have had to measure the trees and the shrubs, and that's why the diagram is not to scale."

"To be more accurate, if it was to scale it would show the nature and extent of each curve, wouldn't it?"

"Yes, sir."

Symmonds asked whether Rule had in mind to use the diagram to distort the facts. "No, sir, I did not."

"Do you feel that that diagram fairly and accurately generally depicts the relationship of various objects which exist out at that scene?"

"Yes."

"To which we would object, Your Honor," Hecht asserted. "He's already testified it's inaccurate in every measurement."

Rulon sustained the objection to the degree that the diagram represented any semblance of accuracy. He instructed the jury that it "cannot consider this document as accurate in any type of measurements. The only purpose that it can be considered by the jury at this time is to show a general location of objects…"

Larry Estes returned to the stand. Symmonds returned to questions based on the diagram. Estes described in detail the process of removing the car from the river.

Bob Bell helped pull the car out. Estes needed a second wrecker to help protect the car as it was pulled up the bank. A cable from Bell's truck accomplished this task.

Estes said he checked to see what gear the car was in, but didn't recall what it was. No, he didn't check the ignition. He did check the lights, though. "They were on and very, very dim."

"Which lights are you referring to that you would have observed?"

"The light I observed being on was a side marker light on the car, clearance light you might say…I thought I turned the lights off."

On July 27, Estes said he towed the car to Olathe, Kansas and left it with Dave Dehaemers at I-35 Auto Parts. As far as he knew, prior to delivering it there, no parts had been removed from the car. He waited to move the car because Rule and Andrews had placed a hold on it. They released it on July 20.

(If investigators had seriously believed some mystery existed about the wreck, they would have impounded the car for future evidence—but they didn't. This allowed the car to be moved several times, creating doubt about whether damage occurred during the wreck or at a later date. By the end of 1984, parts had been sold off the car, further complicating both the prosecution and the defense.)

Estes remembered Tom coming out and removing personal items and that the insurance company asked to have it towed to Olathe.

"Was the car to the best of your knowledge and belief in the same condition on the day that it left as the day that you towed it into the…"

"Yes, sir, it was."

Estes told Hecht that he did not throw the car door into the vehicle. He left it there until the police finished their investigation.

Hecht asked very specific questions about how Estes managed to flip the car over and pull it out. How many cables did he use? Where were they attached? In which direction did the car face? (Because Hecht had to prove to the jury that Sandy died by accident, identifying when damage occurred to the car was critical. Since Rule had failed to impound the car as evidence, every scratch, dent and broken window became suspect.)

Hecht wondered whether anyone got into the car and checked to see what gear the car had been in. Estes could not specifically recall, but said it was a habit to do this. They wanted the car in neutral.

Hecht asked him whether he checked the headlights after noticing the clearing light had been on. "I tried to see if the headlights were on but the clearance light was so dim that I don't know whether it had enough juice to run the headlights." He said he looked at the headlights but "didn't notice them on." Yes, he did in fact turn off the lights.

Estes repeated that to his knowledge, no other damaged had been done to the car once he received it.

Time for a break

Rulon called the lunch recess. Before he left the court, Symmonds asked to approach the bench. He informed the judge that he next planned to call Jim Crahan, an accident investigator, to the stand. Crahan had prepared a report for both attorneys but neither of them had reviewed it. Crahan gave it to them sometime around noon. Hecht never saw it until Symmonds put a copy in his hand while they stood in front of the bench.

After lunch, Hecht continued his cross-examination of Estes. He asked whether Estes found a liquor bottle in the car? No. But he acknowledged there could have been one. He just didn't find it.

Hecht showed him six photos of the car's interior, and Estes identified them all. One of the photos showed the driver's door sitting inside the car. One of Estes' workers put it there, he said. (This action probably required moving the seat back.)

Estes stepped down.

Bob Bell took the stand. On July 17, 1983, he worked for Larry Estes and operated the second tow truck at the bridge. Symmonds asked Bell about the car door.

"Well, when the car was uprighted we put the car door back in the front seat."

No, he didn't turn off any lights. And no, he didn't remember whether the car had been in gear.

Hecht again asked very specific questions about how Bell went about his work helping pull the car out. He knew nothing about whether the car had been in neutral or not, but said they normally checked it. Same with turning off the lights. He thought the car got hung up on its suspension as they pulled it up.

Bell stepped down.

Symmonds called Joseph Richardson to the stand, the president of Rich Industries in Kansas City. His company recycled imported cars, and he purchased Sandy's car from I-35 Auto Parts. He received the car on January 23, 1984.

Richardson placed the car in their salvage line "and we almost immediately started selling parts off of it." (All this was normal activity for a car that had been involved in an auto *accident,* even one with a hint of mystery.)

One of his employees started the car a week or so after receiving it and it ran fine. As far as he saw, everything was on the car except for the door.

Trooper Rule came to view the car in September, 1984, after it arrived at Rich Industries.

Hecht showed Richardson three photos of the car's interior and began asking him questions about it. Richardson said the lever protruding from the left side of the steering wheel column was a switch used to turn the lights on and off, also to turn on and off the high beams.

"Where is the ignition switch on the automobile?"

"It's just below the turn signal-light switch."

"And which side of the steering wheel column is the ignition switch?"

"It's on the left side."

"And is that consistent with where ignition switches are on American automobiles?"

"No, sir." American cars have their ignition switches on the right side of the steering column. In fact, the same is true of nearly all other cars no matter where they're made.

"And if somebody said that they reached in and turned it off on the right side of the steering wheel column, they would not be speaking of this automobile, would they?"

"That's true." And no one could look at the dashboard and tell whether or not the lights were on either.

(Both the prosecution and the defense saw this testimony about the switch and the lights as crucial. If the ignition and lights had been off, it added to the possibility someone pushed the car over the riverbank. If on, it made an accident more probable. Hecht seemed to have won this argument, and in so doing, showed how unreliable memories could be, especially when distorted by someone's unproven theory of how Sandy's death occurred.)

The insurance adjuster is called

Symmonds called Jim Crahan, the Hartford Insurance adjuster to the stand, but Hecht objected. He moved to suppress the testimony since he had just received Crahan's report during the noon recess. Hecht said that though the purpose and content of Crahan's testimony had been known from the grand jury, yet the report hadn't been handed over until just a few minutes earlier.

Great confusion and suspicion surrounded Crahan's reports and testimony. He wrote his first report on August 16, 1983. His supervisor edited that report, removing much of Crahan's professional speculation as to what had actually occurred, and his first impression seemed more favorable to the accident scenario. Then in September of 1984, he wrote a third version of the report. Finally, following the grand jury, he wrote a fourth version, the one handed to Symmonds and Hecht at the trial. This version, however, contained an additional three pages and appeared to be based on an interview Crahan had with Trooper Rule several days after the grand jury had been dismissed. Hecht felt the report had been influenced by Rule's version of events and no longer constituted an expert opinion.

Rulon ordered that Crahan be allowed to testify and that Hecht could read the reports overnight and recall him the next day, if he chose.

Crahan worked as an insurance adjuster for Nixon and Company in Kansas City, Missouri. He first came to Emporia on July 28, 1983, to see Rocky Ford Bridge for himself. At the bridge, armed with the highway patrol report of the accident, he surveyed the scene.

"I went back for a distance of about I would say four-tenths of a mile and then drove north to the bridge, and I observed that there was an S curve and that there was a curve sign."

Crahan brought with him many photographs he had taken that day. Symmonds walked him through each photograph. The first showed the warning sign with the S curve on it, about two-tenths of a mile south of the bridge. It stood about three feet high off to the right-hand side of the road.

Crahan took photos at approximately 50-foot intervals as he approached the bridge. Symmonds asked him what he saw in each photo. "Photograph seven was taken at a point 150 feet south of the bridge, and in this photograph you can just begin to see the bridge come into view." At 100 feet, Crahan saw that the bridge "goes over something, probably a river."

Crahan took one photo about 10 feet short of the bridge. He identified the concrete and wood abutments to the right of the bridge. He also took pictures from the north side of the bridge facing south, and pictures of the place where Sandy's car had been. He noted the rough terrain on the rock-strewn beach, as well as some glass that might have been from the car.

Crahan said he drove to Estes' body shop to view the car on July 29. He took several pictures of the car and verified each one for the record.

[Both the prosecution and the defense extracted highly detailed testimony from several experts about the car. The author had chosen not to belabor the reader with this detail except to give a general sense of the damage to the car.]

Crahan described the damage he saw. "Starting from the front and going back, the left front fender is heavily damaged, the driver's door has a gouge and is no longer attached to the vehicle. The windshield is smashed. The top of the car in the vicinity of the driver's compartment is pushed down I would say five or six inches. The back door on the driver's side has a crease in it. It's pushed in several inches starting at the front of the door and the door appears to be shoved back a little bit, and there's a crease in the quarter panel right above the left rear tire." The wheel had been crushed somewhat and caused the flat. All other tires remained inflated.

Rulon called for a recess. Once the jury left the room, he informed counsel that the media had asked to take pictures of some of the evidence that had been entered. He wanted to allow this, but would not let them see what had yet to be admitted. Hecht argued meekly that it was improper to let the media see close up what the jury observed from a distance until the jury had a chance to more closely review it. Rulon felt confident "that this is a conscientious jury" and none of the them would read the papers anyway. He decided to allow it.

Crahan returned to the witness stand. He said he saw many miscellaneous items in the car—coloring books, crayons and the like that would indicate young children often rode in the car. He had tested the brakes and they functioned normally. He checked the master cylinder and it had ample brake fluid. He checked the transmission while the operator had the car suspended in the air and saw no damage. The drive train remained intact.

Crahan noted that to check the steering he had to get a key. A Peugeot's steering wheel remains locked without the key in the ignition. Once he put the key in the ignition, he could turn it to the on position then move the wheel left to right.

He tested the suspension by simple observance and the shocks by pushing on the bumper. Again, they seemed operational.

He noted that the door glass had fallen down inside the driver's door. (This indicated that the window had been down when the door tore off.)

Hecht began by showing him pictures taken at a later time and asked whether they appeared to be the same as those Crahan took. He answered carefully, mentioning the rust and maybe, more damage. Hecht wanted specific confirmation of various types of damage done to the car, but Crahan made it difficult by mentioning he could not testify to the accuracy of the newer photos, though they appeared to be similar.

Hecht asked whether the damage to the outside of the door was sufficient enough to show that the door tore off during the accident. "I think it's hard to refute that since it's off. Yes."

Hecht asked about some specific damage to the rear of the car. Crahan claimed he could offer no opinion based on the photos. Hecht reminded him that he had made such a statement in his written report, and then Crahan agreed—yes, the impact could have caused the damage to which Hecht referred.

Hecht asked whether Crahan felt sure he saw the vehicle at Estes' place on July 29. Yes. But Estes said he towed it to Olathe on the 27th. One of you is wrong. Yes.

Crahan next said he could not be sure he actually got into the car, since there had been glass on the seat. No, he didn't actually drive it.

"Are you telling the jury that the steering wheel was locked and the key was in the ignition when the steering wheel was locked?"

"I believe on this particular car, yes."

"Are you sure of that?"

"I'm not positive, no."

"Do you know whether or not the steering wheel can be locked if the key is in the ignition?"

"I think that it can...I don't recall testing it, no."

"Do you know whether or not the key was in the ignition when the steering wheel was in a locked position?"

"No, I don't know that."

Symmonds asked about the copy of the report Crahan had submitted that day. "The report that you're reading from is a copy that's edited from my original report." He said he first provided the report when he reported to court that day. He used a different version when he testified at the grand jury.

Symmonds bored in on the door. Did Crahan believe the door ripped off from contact with something? Yes. Did you see wood chips? I can't testify to that. He thought the door had to have been open when it hit whatever tore it off. He said he was not qualified as an accident reconstructionist.

Hecht turned to a discussion about the door. Crahan just said he thought the door had to have been open, so Hecht asked him how much force it would take to tear off a door. He didn't know and didn't want to speculate.

Crahan stepped down and Symmonds called Robert Nevitt. Nevitt lived south of Rocky Ford Bridge and traveled across it regularly. He drove south across the bridge between 1:00 and 2:00 a.m. on July 17, 1983. He didn't see any lights shining down in the river.

Hecht established that Nevitt drove across the bridge 15 or more times a week. It served as the best route to get to downtown Emporia. He had been to a private club on July 16, and had been drinking. He could not remember how many drinks he might have consumed, but it was more than one or two. He felt he had control of his faculties, otherwise he would not be driving that night.

Nevitt said he drove about five miles an hour across the bridge. He mentioned the curve that lies just before the bridge from the north and thought maybe someone could make it at 30 miles an hour, but not him—20 was acceptable. From the south, he never drove faster than 15 miles an hour. Nevitt added that 10 miles an hour became necessary as one approached the bridge in case "you got a car coming off that bridge and there's not much room there."

Hecht asked about Sandy's car. "If that vehicle would have been there [down on the riverbank] between the hours of 1:00 and 2:00 a.m. on July the 17th with its lights on, would you have seen it?"

"If it had shined across the water, that would be the only way you could see it." But if the car wreck happened at 3:10 or later, you wouldn't have seen the lights? Right.

Rulon ordered the afternoon recess.

After resting, the next day begins

The next morning, Hecht called James Crahan back to the stand to cross-examine him. He drilled him about all his various reports, insinuating that Crahan rigged his reports to favor the prosecution.

Symmonds probed Crahan about his motives for testifying. The man said he felt he needed to do his civic duty and gained nothing from being there.

Symmonds asked whether anyone told Crahan how to testify at this trial. No. Or arrive at a specific conclusion? No. Were you paid the same no matter what you found? Yes.

Crahan stepped down, but Hecht wanted him to stay around until he finished with John Rule. Since Crahan had confessed to having interviewed Rule while preparing his last version of the report, Hecht thought he might want to put him back on the stand.

Symmonds called Dan Andrews, the former Lyon County Sheriff, to the stand. Andrews said he responded to a call on July 17, 1983, and headed out to Rocky Ford Bridge. He arrived "somewhere between ten and eleven." (Jurors must have found themselves confused by the variety of times folks said they got to the bridge. Trooper Smith recorded his arrival at 10:52 and he was the first law enforcement officer on the scene. Now comes the sheriff and he gives a range of on hour. Would the jury later accept Tom's story if it contained so many vague references to time?)

By the time Andrews had arrived, Sandy's body had been removed. He saw the ambulance and rescue truck leaving as he arrived. He found Smith and Rule and asked what they knew "and a little bit later somebody mentioned that they saw some things that they thought might be blood. I went over and looked at them myself and decided that I ought to collect some samples."

Andrews helped Rule measure the distances related to the spots that appeared to be blood. "One was the—the bridge decking run east and west. There are some runners that run north and south on the bridge deck which the tires roll on. One of those samples was on the runner that runs north and south. One was right next to the edge of the cement or, I'm sorry, the steel edge on the bottom of the deck. One was on the top of the steel railing, and another one was what I call a girder on the outside of the bridge about a foot outside."

He described one spot as a set of "reddish-colored spots, kind of rust-colored," in a pattern about a foot square. Andrews scraped up a small sample of the blood and wood and put it in an evidence bag.

At this point Symmonds requested a recess. He told the judge he had quite a bit of evidence to bring in and wanted to do so in an orderly fashion. Rulon ordered the recess.

The method Symmonds used to convey and store much of the evidence seemed very odd to many observers. Investigators had put various items of evidence into paper bags, some similar to what one would get at a liquor store when buying a bottle of booze. Each bag carried dates and initials of those who handled it.

Each day Symmonds assembled an assortment of these bags along with other evidence on the table in front of the judge. As he presented an item of evidence, it would be removed from the bag and then both the bag and the contents were marked as exhibits. In this manner, it appeared by sheer count that the prosecution had amassed far more evidence than it actually had. Added to the dozens of photos, each one considered a separate exhibit, Symmonds bragged to having presented more than 170 pieces of evidence in the Bird trial (not one piece of that evidence consisted of a witness who could place Tom at Rocky Ford Bridge).

Andrews returned to the stand following the recess. Symmonds had him describe exactly how he collected each substance sample and the exact location of each. Andrews described how he handled and secured each sample after he left the scene. He said that three of the spots, on the bridge deck, railing and the support girder, lined up with each other. The other spot sat south of the others.

Symmonds asked him to identify a paper sack with the number 23 (for the exhibit number) on it. "I have a number five on the sack. I have my initials, D.R.A., have a date of 7-18 of 83, a time of 12:20, and I have a notation 'rock with reddish stain.'"

"If you would, would you remove Exhibit No. 24 from the sack which had been marked as Exhibit No. 23. I believe that would be one of the small envelopes." And so it went with other items Andrews had collected.

Symmonds asked if Andrews did any investigation at the site besides collecting samples. Yes, he talked with the coroner, Dr. Butcher. He told the doctor an autopsy needed to be completed. Kansas law required it in unattended deaths.

Before Andrews finished his work that day, he had an officer retrieve Sandy's clothes and take her fingerprints.

At the bridge, Andrews watched the tow truck remove the car. Once on the bank, he went over and got down by the left rear side marker and cupped his hands to see if the light was on. It was. So was the taillight. "Very dim."

Symmonds asked about the cup found near the road south of the bridge. Andrews saw some sort of color—orange or pinkish—in it, but remembered it as not being crushed. (His cousin, Dennis Arb, felt strongly that it had been crushed.) Andrews saw Rule holding the cup and the two had a short discussion about it, then Rule dropped it back on the ground. It wasn't until the next day that Andrews picked it up again. By then it had been exposed to 24 more hours of the elements, at least two more sets of fingerprints, and mysteriously was no longer crushed. When Andrews later had it tested it for latent fingerprints, it had no value.

Andrews identified a rock as the one Rule handed him at the bridge.

Symmonds walked Andrews through several photos the sheriff took of the Peugeot on July 19. He took pictures of both the interior and exterior of the car, a fortunate development given that within months the car would be diced and sliced with parts sold to unknown individuals. Symmonds added 20 more photos to his stock of evidence. During this identification process, Andrews identified one photo showing the driver's door sitting on the passenger side of the front seat.

Andrews pointed at a red plastic cup in a photo of the car, identical to the one found on the road south of the bridge, the kind Dennis Arb suggested as common at keg parties. (Cups, broken bottle and cans commonly lay strewn near the bridge, near the road and down on the riverbank. This might explain why no officer paid much attention to the cups the first day, and why they had very little evidentiary value.)

Yes, Andrews photographed the seat belt. He saw "a number of papers sitting on the seat, an Andre Cold Duck wine bottle, a Sprite can and a piece of wire or something along with glass fragments."

Symmonds picked up one of the paper bags from the table and handed it to Andrews. Andrews took the cold duck bottle from the paper sack and announced it was the same one he found in the car. He could not recall how much wine had been in the bottle that day, but he called it a "small amount," certainly less than half. No latent fingerprints had been found on the wine bottle, nor the apple juice bottle he had also collected.

Andrews opened yet another sack and identified several unused red plastic cups as those he collected that day. They had been inside the car.

Thinking they might find blood, the officers "took a sun visor off of the driver's side and retained it was well as took a sample of the carpet on the driver's side of the vehicle, took a section of it out and kept it as well as removed the door panel off of the driver's door to see the position of the door glass." Symmonds then showed him items taken from other paper sacks and Andrews identified them as the visor and carpet.

Rule handed Andrews another red plastic cup he had found on July 19, two days after Sandy's death. Rule also handed him some human hair along with the cup. Andrews saw that the cup matched the cups found in the car and the one down the road, so he kept it as possible evidence. Symmonds showed him another sack and in it was an identical cup. Andrews identified it as the second one Rule gave him that day. Both had been tested for fingerprints, but Andrews said Agent Humphrey knew the results—he did not.

Andrews identified other rocks, each in their own paper sack.

Andrews had released the blood samples to the KBI on July 18, 1983, along with other items needing crime lab work. He stored the balance of the items in the sheriff's evidence room. Andrews released items collected after July 18 to Agent Humphrey on October 22, 1984.

Symmonds asked about the bridge. Did you look over the edge? Yes. What did you see. Trees. Anything on the trees? "Blood or what appeared to be blood. It was a reddish stain." (But no one collected a single leaf to determine whether or not the substance was, in fact, blood.)

Andrews later climbed down the embankment and inspected the tree. "There was just a [blood] smear on the side of a tree that I would estimate it somewhere between five and six inches in length and went around the west side of the tree." He saw similar substances on nearby rocks.

After the lunch recess, Andrews returned to the stand. He identified more bags that had light bulbs and headlamps taken from the Peugeot, plus several other items Rule gave him on July 17 and 18. These he had stored in the evidence room at the Lyon County jail, except while various labs ran tests on them.

"Did you have occasion on the 18th to once again observe the stains which you had noted on the preceding day?"

"Yes, sir....They were not near as visible as they were the day before on the 17th."

Hecht began his cross-examination. He asked whether any of the filaments of the bulbs were broken. No, just distorted. Andrews did not test the bulbs himself, but he did test the wine and apple juice bottles, and the cups, checking for fingerprints.

Andrews found fingerprints, but felt none of them were good enough to make any comparison for identification purposes. Hecht explained, through his questions of Andrews, that fingerprints were not always reliable, especially on uneven surfaces like cups and bottles. "So your inability to discover latent fingerprints on those objects of a sufficient quality to be used for comparison purposes is not unusual at all in your experience as a law officer?"

"No, sir." (Hecht anticipated that Symmonds might claim Tom wiped the car and debris of fingerprints to cover up his crime.)

Hecht asked about the time of day Andrews had arrived at the scene. He couldn't be specific. He asked how many people and vehicles were there when Andrews arrived. He guessed, but could not specifically recall how many. He knew the body had been taken away and that the coroner came after he arrived.

Hecht asked about the cup found south of the bridge. Yes, the one in the bag appeared to be the same one. No, it wasn't crushed. Yes, it now had a crack in it that wasn't there at first. Yes, the cup had been tested for content and fingerprints. Nothing definitive could be found.

Andrews helped take measurements at the bridge on July 17 dealing with the discolored, reddish spots on the bridge. He measured only from the end of the bridge to the spots, not from the east or west edge. He also assisted in measuring the height of the bridge from the ground and other measurements indicating how far the car lay from various points on the bridge.

Hecht quizzed Andrews about the car lights. He saw the side markers and taillights had been on, but very dimly. They were running off the battery, correct? Yes. And had been for some time? Yes. Do you think someone turned them on after they discovered the car? "That, sir, I don't know. There's been some discrepancy amongst people that have been interviewed and so forth, so I don't know."

"A lot of discrepancy among the people who have been interviewed?

"Yes, sir."

"Everybody sees it differently, don't they?"

"Yes, sir."

He returned to questions about the red cup found south of the bridge. Did Mr. Arb see it? "He may have." (Arb told the author that he found the cup first and pointed it out to the sheriff.)

Andrews, as sheriff had viewed, inspected and collected evidence from numerous car accidents. Hecht handed him a stack of photos of the driver's door and asked him questions about the door, then the doorpost, chrome strips and other parts of the car. He asked Andrews his opinion about how these various dents, scrapes, breaks and tears had been made. Did this all make it appear the car moved forward and struck "the bridge or some portion of it to cause that damage?" Yes.

"Would you agree with me, sir, that it would take some considerable amount of force to do that damage to the door and rip the door off of the automobile?"

"I rather doubt that that particular damage there would have ripped the door off without any further damage to the entire framing of the door."

"But the combination of the damage to the door and doorpost and left rear door and that area would have required considerable force necessary to do that damage and rip that door off of the car?"

"Force or weight, yes."

"Or both?"

"Yes."

If the door had been open, wouldn't the contact have slammed it shut? "Depending on where it was hit and other factors involved."

During Hecht's cross-examination, Andrews pointed out two evidence bags that contained empty envelopes. Symmonds needed to clarify this. When he sent them to the KBI lab they contained samples scraped off the bridge cross member and railing. "It was a very small amount in both envelopes because there just wasn't that much that I could get scraped off of the metal."

Andrews stepped down and the judge released him from his subpoena.

As the chief county law enforcement officer, the court felt no need for Andrews to play a role more significant than that of custodian of items of evidence. The new sheriff, Cliff Hacker, had beaten Andrews in a 1984 election, insisting that Andrews didn't do enough to bring Sandy's case to a conclusion. Andrews' testimony here indicated he had quite a bit of involvement at the beginning, but perhaps proceeded more carefully than had Trooper Rule and much too methodically for *Emporia Gazette* writers.

Identifying Peugeot's uniqueness

David Dehaemers operated I-35 Auto Parts in Olathe, Kansas. He bought Sandy's Peugeot from The Hartford. Larry Estes brought it to him on a flatbed truck on August 27, 1983. I-35 paid the insurance company on January 21, 1984. Thereafter, Dehaemers sold the car to Rich Industries. Estes said he delivered the car to Dehaemers on July 27. The Hartford Insurance Company thought it still sat in Estes' garage as late as October 25. (Three businesses with three different records of the same event again showed how easy errors could be made in critical testimony.)

Dehaemers said as far as he knew, the car came in and left in the same condition. No one sold anything off of it.

Hecht asked Dehaemers to specifically describe how a car is put onto and taken off a flatbed truck. He wanted to clarify whether the transportation of the car had caused any specific damage. Hecht needed to show that damage to the undercarriage of the car occurred at the river, not during transportation.

Dehaemers stepped down.

Symmonds called Dr. Robert Ford from West Memphis, Arkansas, to the stand. Ford cared for Sandy Bird when she and Tom lived in West Memphis. He delivered two of her children. Yes, he took a blood sample. Yes he kept a record. No, blood type does not change over time. Therefore the jury could be sure that Sandy's blood type was A-positive. No other record existed in Emporia to prove this, and Symmonds needed to prove that blood found on Sandy's dress matched her blood type.

Hecht asked about Sandy's medical history. Ford had delivered her first baby and his records said he used the Lamaze technique. Someone acted as her coach, but his records and memory failed him as to whom that had been. (Tom coached Sandy at the birth of all three of their children.)

In 1980, Sandy had a miscarriage. Ford delivered the second child in 1981. He could not be sure whether Tom attended Sandy in this delivery, but he knew he had been at at least one of them.

"During the course of your care or treatment of Sandra Bird, did you become acquainted with her husband?"

"Yes, sir, I did." But he knew him outside his medical practice. "He was a minister in our town and was active in various civic functions, and I knew him socially as well as being the husband of one of my patients...I thought they were a very nice family, a nice young family."

Symmonds asked whether Ford knew anything about Tom and Sandy during the spring of 1983. No. And over time, marriages have good and bad time? Yes.

Ford left the stand and Rulon ordered the afternoon recess.

Horse-loving attorney called next

Symmonds called Linda Glaze, an Emporia attorney who also served as the Emporia municipal prosecutor, to the stand. She owned horses that she pastured south and east of Rocky Ford Bridge. To get to the pasture, she usually drove south across the bridge, as often as twice each day. On July 17, about 3:30 a.m., Glaze drove out to load the horses up and bring them to Hartford, Kansas, for an early morning ride.

"Do you recall as you were going across the Rocky Ford Bridge on that particular date about 3:30 a.m., did you form any mental impressions?"

"Yes, a very distinct one....The impression was that particular night was very, very dark; and as I was getting ready to go across the bridge or driving out there, I was driving somewhat slower than I normally do because I was ahead of myself and I did not want to get there before my friends had gotten up, so I was driving slower.

"And as I came from the intersection and approached the bridge, I just have a very distinct mental impression as I got on the bridge of thinking how dark it was and how that it was somewhat of an eerie place to be at 3:30 in the morning.

"It is an unusual bridge and kind of a, to some degree, mysterious place."

She remembered specifically looking to the east as she drove across the bridge. She glanced down the river. Did you see lights? "I didn't see anything. It was absolutely pitch black."

She felt that 10 to 15 miles an hour was a safe speed to cross the bridge while driving south.

Hecht asked if she saw anything when she looked to the left, right, along the banks, on the road? No, nothing.

"Could you see the river itself?"

"Only down the road, and I could not actually see the water because it was dark." By "road" she meant to express distance, not the physical road.

Glaze said she drove 10 miles an hour across the bridge, a speed "unusually" slower than normal.

Driving north toward the bridge as you come down the grade, do you feel 10-15 miles an hour is a safe speed? Yes.

And that night, it was pitch dark? Yes. Darker than usual? Yes, I had a clear impression of that. Why? Because I could not see my horses when I got to the pasture, and two of them are white. Did you see the moon? It was moonless. The stars? No. "Is that because they weren't visible or because you never looked to see?"

"No, I recall looking but it was just darker than usual." (But it had been a clear night. For one whom the prosecution planned to claim had been so observant she should have seen headlights, Hecht implied she also should have noticed the stars. She didn't.)

Symmonds called Douglas Peck, a highway patrolman.

Peck attended the autopsy of Sandy's body at the request of Rule. He saw Undersheriff Charles Schreck and two others there that day. One he knew as the pathologist, but he wasn't sure whether the other might have been an assistant or another doctor. He and Schreck both took photos of the autopsy.

Symmonds began handing Peck 12 photos and asked him to identify

Sandy's injuries. Peck authenticated them all and gave a general description of the injuries they portrayed. Then Peck stood down.

Symmonds called Charles Schreck, who had been the Lyon County Undersheriff. Schreck transported some of the exhibits to and from law enforcement officers. Symmonds handed him exhibit number 43, a paper bag, and from within he removed exhibit 44, three packages of rocks—exhibits 46, 47, 44—and an empty envelope marked 45.

Schreck identified other items taken from other paper bags as those things he delivered to the KBI in Topeka on July 18. Later, he brought them all back from Topeka and returned them to the property room in Lyon County. He described how each sack and bag had been sealed, the precautions taken to protect the items inside.

Symmonds turned to the subject of the autopsy and handed him a series of photos. Yes, they accurately represent the condition of Sandy's body.

Hecht asked who took the photos? He did, except for three. (Earlier, Peck had said he took these photos. Once again, two professionals testified differently about the same items and the same event.)

Rulon ordered a recess until the following Monday. He gave the jury Friday off, since one juror had previously scheduled a family outing.

Friday morning, with the jury on holiday, Rulon met with the attorneys and Tom to discuss handling of various exhibits and possible contested testimony as well as the expected time it might take to complete the trial. Rulon led a debate over admitting testimony about Marty's murder. He told the attorneys they could raise any issue that had been addressed during the solicitation trial, but nothing else about Marty.

More chain of custody

Without the prosecution carefully establishing how evidence had been collected, processed, stored and transported, the defense could claim it had been tampered with. Symmonds worked hard to establish chain of custody, as it's called, for each item he planned to use as evidence against Tom.

Kenton Thomas came next. Thomas worked for the funeral home that removed Sandy's body from Newman Medical Center following the autopsy. Once at the funeral home, Thomas embalmed the body. Symmonds asked detailed questions about the embalming process.

Thomas drew one blood sample for blood alcohol testing prior to the embalming, and one during the process. A deputy had called and requested a second sample. (Embalming fluid ruined the value of the two blood samples, as the jury heard later. Trooper Rule had failed to protect this vital source of potential evidence by waiting too long to get the samples.)

Thomas did no damage to the body except for two small incisions needed for embalming.

He focussed on the wrists. They showed a liner pattern of bruising. No, we did not cause that, Thomas said.

Hecht had no questions of Thomas and Symmonds called Mack Long. On July 17, Long served as a deputy sheriff in Lyon County. He transported Sandy's clothing from the funeral home to the sheriff's evidence room. Since the clothes were still wet, he carried them in plastic bags to the sheriff's office. There he hung them on a line beneath which he placed a white linen sheet. In this way, he collected any residue that fell off them either while hanging or drying.

Long identified various items Symmonds presented to him as those he transported on July 17. He signed them over to Deputy Schreck on July 19 and had no further custody of them.

Hecht did an interesting thing to Long. Though he had no questions about chain of custody, he still asked about a specific answer Long had given earlier. "You were in error, were you not, Mr. Long, when you testified that you obtained the dress on July the 19th, 1983? You in fact obtained it on July the 17th, 1983?"

"I corrected myself."

"Yes, you did....And you had at the time you testified that it was the 19th in your hand the documents known as a property receipt?" Yes.

Hecht had accomplished his goal. Even a sworn officer holding a receipt could err in his testimony.

Long first testified that he had obtained two blood samples from the funeral home. Later he said one. Then he said maybe Rule picked up the second. No, he never said he took two. Well, maybe he did, but he could not be sure since he had no receipt.

"If you said that, that was an honest mistake, was it not?" Hecht asked.

"Yes, sir."

"And that's because your memory isn't perfect, is it?"

"No, sir."

"Do you know anybody whose memory is perfect?"

"No, sir."

Symmonds called Deputy Gary Eichorn. During 1983, Eichorn served as an Emporia police officer. On July 18, he interviewed "the babysitter" and stopped at The Station, a nightclub located in the Holiday Inn. He went to the nightclub searching for anyone who might have seen Tom and Sandy there eating supper that night. (No one claimed they ate supper there—just drinks and dancing after 9:30 p.m.)

Eichorn measured the distance from Faith Lutheran to Rocky Ford

Bridge using his squad car odometer—eight miles.

Eichorn received some of the evidence back from Agent Humphrey on January 15, 1985 and placed it in the property room. He completed the chain of custody as it pertained to getting the exhibits into court. As with other witnesses, Symmonds walked Eichorn through a long line of exhibits establishing chain of custody. Suddenly, Symmonds couldn't find one specific exhibit he needed at that moment. He had gotten confused by all the paper bags and begged the court to recess while he checked them. Rulon complied and called the mid-morning recess.

Hecht discovered that Eichorn never took possession of the blood drawn at the funeral home. He also pointed out a date error in Eichorn's testimony.

Symmonds called KBI Agent J. Vernon Humphrey to the stand. Humphrey explained that though he had visited the bridge, he did not collect any evidence there.

He, along with Rule and Andrews, viewed Sandy's car at Estes' place on July 19. The three men inspected the mechanical systems of the car and found no failures. They inspected the interior looking for anything that might have evidentiary value.

Humphrey testified to his involvement in chain of custody of various exhibits. When Symmonds got to the cups, Humphrey mentioned that one of them had been smashed, and it was not that way when he first saw it. (Could this be the one Arb saw? Did the officers mix them up?) Humphrey had no idea how it got damaged.

Humphrey acknowledged receiving a vial of blood on October 2, 1984, from Dr. Eckert. Eckert drew the blood during the second autopsy. Humphrey delivered it to the KBI lab for a drug screen and to determine its type.

During Humphrey's long, detailed and somewhat boring chain of custody testimony, Symmonds asked him whether or not fingerprints had been found on one of the red cups. He said no, nothing distinguishable. Hecht challenged this on cross-examination.

"You testified to the grand jury, did you not?"

"Yes."

"Commencing on page 20 of your testimony before the grand jury, Mr. Humphrey, you testified, did you not, concerning a fingerprint examination of the red cups?"

"Probably did."

"And do you recall on page 22 making this statement, 'There were some good fingerprints on some of these items but they did not match with Tom Bird, Lorna Anderson or Daniel Carter. We don't know if they matched with Sandra Bird'?"

"That would sound right, yes."

Rule steps up the first time

Kansas Highway Patrolman John Rule eventually became a celebrity because of the prosecution of Tom Bird. (Keith Carradine played Rule in a 1987 CBS mini-series, *Murder Ordained.)*

He arrived at the Rocky Ford Bridge at 10:52 a.m. He saw Trooper Smith there when he arrived.

His testimony about the location of the car and body paralleled earlier testimony. He added, "The front part of the car was entirely surrounded by water. The rear of the car was partially surrounded by water. It was at the river's edge."

He noted spotting a white shoe just south of the car. It was Sandy's.

He and Smith began measuring various distances "which is a common practice at an accident scene." The door lay seven feet from the car.

Symmonds asked him to describe several photos. "This photograph shows the lack of damage to the passenger's side of the car. It also shows that there was leaves and branches picked up by the car as it traveled down over the embankment."

Rule explained the procedures an accident specialist is supposed to follow. "We document evidence of accidents mainly for the victims of accidents and decide at the scene if there's been a violation of the law. Mainly we just document, photograph and take evidence."

Symmonds asked him to describe the scene. "There were blood stains on rocks in the vicinity of the door.... The bloodstains at this location appeared to be droplets. There was two to three rather large droplets just to the west edge of this driver's door, and, of course, from that area I was able to track the blood stains back up the hill towards the bridge."

Rule said some of the bloodstains were of sufficient volume to run down the edge of the rocks, that others were just drops. "The blood was dried. It still had a lot of color left in it. It was almost a purple, kind of a cross between blood red and purple. It was fairly obvious that it hadn't been there for a great length of time."

As for the car's interior, "There wasn't any scratches or tears in it indicating that it had slid on the upholstered side of the car. It was basically undamaged."

Symmonds asked him to refer to the diagram, the one he drew without regard to scale, marked as exhibit 118. Rulon refused to allow it to be entered as evidence at that time.

Hecht had several questions about the diagram because it presented the jury with a false impression of the scene of the wreck. He asked if one inch equals about five feet is that accurate? No, I'm not a mechanical engineer.

Are you aware that every Kansas county provides scale drawings of every road? Yes. Did you look at their drawings? Yes. But you didn't use them in preparing yours? No.

Rule said the county's drawing he saw didn't show the river and embankment. This surprised Hecht. Didn't you know the county had topography maps? "No, sir, I only saw the one drawing at the county attorney's office."

Rule claimed his drawing was very close to the actual layout of the terrain. But even being off a bit could greatly affect the conclusions the jurors might make based on the diagram. Finished establishing that Rule's diagram was woefully inadequate, Hecht said, "Judge, we would object to the use of this diagram for any purpose. It's not to scale in any sense of the word and, frankly, I don't understand if they're going to use diagrams why they don't use them to scale. They're right here in the courthouse."

Hecht said that the relationship between locations was critical to the case. Symmonds planned to have Rule use the diagram to locate items and talk about their relationship to each other. The diagram presented a distorted view to the jury.

Rulon told the jury that Rule could use the diagram, but they were to ignore anything that spoke to exact locations.

The car lay 65 feet down the embankment from the bridge. The bridge measured just over 15 feet wide and 215 feet long. The south roadway where it met the bridge measured 19 feet wide. At its widest point, the parking area just south of the bridge was 22 feet wide.

He pointed to the 12-foot long concrete abutments that sat on either side of the south end of the bridge. Just above and parallel to the abutment on the east side of the bridge sat a wood plank attached to three horizontal posts. The wood plank hung out over the concrete abutment about 18".

Rule estimated that the rear end of the car nearest the bridge sat 10-12 feet from the bridge.

The only place he found auto glass was in the area immediately around the severed door.

He gave a detailed description of the damage he observed on the car while it remained in the water. He said the undercarriage "appeared to be in good shape." The only major structural damage to the undercarriage sat just ahead of the engine compartment underneath the front bumper.

Rule said the only lights he saw on were the side markers and rear lights.

He next described in detail the various significant distances south of the river; about 300 feet to where the first curve was and 300 more feet west to the second. He called them 90-degree curves. "The roadway is fairly coarse gravel. When the roadway is dry, it doesn't have very good traction. The rocks have a tendency to act like marbles and you don't get real good traction on it when it's dry."

Did you see anything indicating someone lost control of a car? "There was no evidence to indicate at all. If you think of losing control of an automobile, you think of heavy braking and sliding; and of course on a surface of this type it has a tendency to push the gravel out of the way and it will leave you a pretty good track on the roadway. There just wasn't any of that kind of evidence at all. I walked up the road for a considerable distance and I could find no signs of damage to the ditches on the fence rows or any indication that anybody had slid off the road."

Neither did he find any evidence of braking "being done by the car that supposedly went over the embankment.... The only evidence I had of an accident at that end was the bridge abutment."

Rule said he found the grass pressed down east of the bridge near some shrubs but the ground remained undisturbed there, suggesting the wheel passed over freely. This area sat "right at the edge of the embankment."

Rule described the grade of the road as 10 percent leading from south of the bridge to the embankment. Though the grade lessened just before the embankment, it would have little effect on a car that had been coming down the road.

He identified the abutment in a photo. "Plainly on this exhibit it shows some white area on the end of that abutment that in my opinion was paint transferred from the station wagon as it went by."

Rule indicated the distance between the abutment and the natural barriers on the east of the abutment to be 11 feet. Nothing sat there to impede a car travelling past that spot.

Symmonds showed him a picture of the wooden plank that sat above the concrete abutment. Rule said he personally took that picture. He pointed to some glass and a bottle cap that sat on the plank. Symmonds told him to circle the bottle cap and glass on the photo.

Rule described the spots he saw on the bridge deck. "It appeared to be possible blood to me. It had a reddish color to it. It was laying on the bridge planks that tire tracks set on, and there was some of it in the dirt adjacent to the planks. It's the area that was about 30 feet from the south end of the bridge."

Rule testified about other spots that he saw that day. "There was a stain on the planking that was 35 feet from the south edge of the bridge. These were on the east-west planks," near the east edge of the bridge. He pointed out the stains on the steel cross bar just east of the stains on the plank. "This substance was dark in color. It's hard to describe. It's kind of a cross between black and purple. It was obviously dry. And on the steel it showed up as much darker than it did on the wood."

He noted that the blood on the planks, rail and cross bar all measured between 32 and 35 feet from the south end of the bridge, as though lined up.

Symmonds asked whether or not Rule saw blood below the bridge. "I was down below, and I had followed a blood trail from the door up to a tree that was directly underneath the east edge of the bridge. I found a lady's wristwatch when I went up the hill, also."

Rule mentioned a tree that stood 20 feet from the rear end of the car, back toward the bridge. "I took a blood sample that was approximately two foot south of that tree. That was as far south as I could find blood under the bridge....The base of this tree would have been directly under the east edge of this bridge.... Standing at the guardrail of the bridge and looking straight down, you would have been directly over the top of this tree."

The tree stood 12 to 16 feet tall, but bent sharply to the east. Rule estimated its diameter at four to five inches at the base. The base of the tree sat 21-1/2 feet below the bridge deck.

Rule collected a sample of the tree bark and three rocks from the beach area, which, he believed, had blood on them. "There was blood droplets all over the leaves and area around this tree here that I took the wood bark out of. There was several leaves there that had blood droplets on that. There was also blood droplets from this tree down to the edge of this door here. I observed a blood droplet on a rock here and another rock here that had what I believe a tissue sample of some kind."

Rule went back to the site on July 18. He picked up another rock that looked as though it had a bloodstain on it. Some rocks he left undisturbed, saying they were too big and heavy to provide good samples.

He described finding two red plastic cups directly under the bridge on July 17, but he left them there. Investigators found them when they went back on July 18 and put them in evidence bags. Rule remembered them as being between 12 and 20 feet west of the wristwatch, and closer to the river.

Rule described the lady's wristwatch. Later Tom identified it as Sandy's. The crystal had cracked and the chain that held it closed had broken. "I don't believe the watch was running." He suggested that the watch lay directly underneath the bridge planks, and that a crack of nearly one inch existed between the planks. Rule believed the watch fell out on the bridge and fell through the crack to the riverbank below.

He identified a large number of photos taken of the car at Estes' body shop and others at the bridge site. He described one as "the area that I picked up the tissue that I talked about earlier. In my opinion it was a piece of scalp." The shoe lay nearby. After saying this, Rule seemed to correct himself. He apparently thought he had retrieved the body tissue but picked up the wrong rock.

"Have you had occasion in the past to push an automobile off the roadway if it was blocking the travel of other persons on the highway?"

"Yes."

"And have you had occasion to hand push a car off of the roadway?"

"Yes, sir."

Do you think a car could be hand pushed over the embankment? "I believe that it could."

Symmonds asked him about his trip to Rich Industries on September 6, 1984, to take photos of the Peugeot and collect more evidence. By then, Rich Industries had sold several pieces of the car. Rule took all the lights and the gearshift.

After Rule described each light bulb and proved chain of custody, Rulon called the afternoon recess and dismissed the jury until the next morning.

Rule continues

"What if anything did you do with that wristwatch after you took it into your possession?" Symmonds asked Trooper Rule as the trial entered its sixth day.

He intended to give it to Trooper Smith, but kept it until meeting with Tom on July 26. On that date, Rule and Agent Humphrey briefly interviewed Tom. "I had the watch in a sack. I asked him about some jewelry that his wife might have been wearing the night of the accident. He stated that he didn't remember her wearing any jewelry, and I laid the watch out on the table in front of him and he indicated that it was his wife's watch… I could see no reason at that point to retain the watch so it was released to Mr. Bird." (This action seems consistent for one who believed an auto accident had occurred. Had Rule so strongly believed it to be a murder, he would have held the watch as evidence.)

He identified several exhibits as the various rocks he picked up at the bridge site. He circled their location on his diagram.

Symmonds asked what might constitute a comfortable rate of speed while driving the S curves south of the bridge. "Twenty miles an hour is comfortable."

Did you notice any damage to the wood railing that runs above the concrete abutment? No, and no paint or splintering either. And he saw no scrape marks on the top of the abutment, or any tire marks or any evidence that a car had driven over the embankment. Did you see wood splinters imbedded in any of the damage to the car? No.

"And in investigating an accident, what do you do?"

"We photograph and measure the scene and try to reconstruct what happened during the accident and check and see if we have reason to believe that a violation of the law caused the accident and document the information and send it in to the Department of Vehicles in Topeka." (Certainly, had Rule seriously believed there had been foul play at the bridge, he would have reported the same to the DOV. Did he?)

Using his non-scaled diagram, Rule described in general terms the path of the car as he saw it. The car struck the abutment and proceeded down the embankment. He provided a fairly specific description of how he believed the car ended up in the water as it did.

Hecht showed Rule a number of photos taken by James Crahan that showed the approach to the bridge from the south. On one, Rule pointed out the gravel area east of the road, the area he called the "parking." Rule's non-scale diagram failed to include that area. As well, Rule drew the 19-foot wide road as the same width as the 15-foot wide bridge.

Hecht spent several questions to get Rule to admit that yes, he had a lot of training as a driver, yes, he was probably a better driver than most people and yes, the highway patrol car had a special suspension system. "And under those circumstances operating that motor vehicle with all of the training that you have, 20 miles an hour was a comfortable speed for you."

"Yes, sir."

Hecht showed that Rule could not possibly testify that the light bulbs he removed on September 6, 1984, were identical to those in the car on July 17, 1983. The car had been moved to three different locations by then. He had previously testified that the bulbs were in the same condition as the day of the accident. Rule said he had to remove the lens cover to retrieve the bulbs, thereby suggesting they must be the same. (Had this been considered a crime from the beginning the lights would have been in a crime lab within a few days.)

Hecht presented photos of the concrete abutment and the wood plank that sat above it. Rule identified two marks on the concrete and admitted to a chip and a split in the wood plank.

Hecht used other photos to show the car in relation to various trees and shrubs. He planned to use all this information to assist his reconstructionist as he proved an accident had occurred.

Hecht next showed Rule a series of photos taken on September 6, 1984. They showed scrape marks on the bottom of the chassis, beneath the driver's door. Rule said those scrape marks hadn't been there on July 17, but had no personal knowledge of how they occurred.

Rule admitted, though, that no close-up photos existed of the car's undercarriage taken on July 17. Nether had he personally closely inspected the undercarriage while the car still lay in the water.

Both attorneys saw the debate about which photos fairly depicted damage to the car as crucial, and terribly confusing. If the prosecution won the debate, the jury would view some pictures more favorably than others, and they would see in the pictures what the prosecution wanted them to see.

Hecht wanted the jury to see the pictures from Tom's perspective, and it meant that he wanted them to disregard other pictures.

Rulon admitted various photographs as exhibits but had to give the attorneys special instructions as to how they could use the photos. He had to tell the jury how they were to view the photos. Given that there were more than 100 photos admitted into evidence, this debate left the jury filled with heightened confusion. Had Trooper Rule treated the wreck as a suspicious accident from day one, much of this confusion would have been eliminated.

Rule said he only looked inside the car on July 17 to get the odometer readings and serial numbers. At Estes' body shop, he removed several items from the car, including the visor and a piece of carpeting. "We were trying to find blood or hair or some kind of indication that the driver of the car had been thrown up against something in the car, left some blood or some hair on the interior of the car."

"As long as the key is in the ignition, the steering wheel is operational?"

"If I can clarify that a little bit."

"Is that the case?"

"Yes. If the key is in the on position and shut off, the steering wheel will not lock until the key is removed."

Hecht used Rule to show how the car most likely traveled as it went over the embankment. Rule said it headed north but, in his opinion, turned somewhat to the west when it hit the concrete abutment.

Hecht pointed to a substance on a rock near where the car door had laid. You thought that was blood or tissue? Yes. Was it tested. No. Did you take a sample? No. "Could a sample have been removed?

"If I would have got it when I first observed it, yes, sir." When Rule returned on the 18th, it had disappeared. He agreed there were other samples he marked on his diagram but failed to collect. Some he picked up on the 18th.

As for the lights, did you see the taillights on? No. But if Sheriff Andrews said he saw them on, you wouldn't argue with that? No. Did you see the headlights on? No. But if Dennis Arb said he saw the headlights on, you wouldn't argue with that? "I didn't see them. I couldn't argue with him if he did."

No, no one collected a paint sample from the abutment.

As for two blood samples you took to the KBI lab, can you prove by your records who provided those samples? No. Can you prove who received them at the KBI lab? No, just who signed the report once the tests had been completed.

Hecht showed that Rule testified in error earlier when he stated a sample of the tissue had been collected for testing. "And that was an honest mistake in testimony on your part when you testified?"

"Yes, sir."

Who walked there? I don't know.

Rule described finding a right footprint along the shore of the river 100-150 feet east of the bridge. "It was in wet ground right next to the water's edge." He saw nothing growing in the footprint. He saw a tread pattern and he believed it to represent a woman's shoe—it did not match Sandy's. It pointed toward the bridge. Rule saw no other discernable footprints.

Hecht moved to the lack of warning signs at the site. "Would you agree with me that they [photos] show no traffic control devices, warning signs, narrow bridge ahead signs or reflectorization as you approach the bridge from the south headed north other than on the bridge itself being a weight limit sign?"

"Yes, sir, that's accurate." The only warning sign Rule saw showed an S curve lay ahead, and that sat south of Gibbons' house, on the east side of the road. That S curve sign stood about three feet tall and weeds and long grass surrounded it.

"You would agree with me that on July the 17th, 1983, at this particular bridge as you approach it from the south headed north there was no sign that said to the effect, 'bridge ahead.'"

"No, sir, there wasn't."

"No sign that said to the effect that there is a one-lane bridge ahead?"

"No, sir."

Neither could Rule point to reflectorized warning signs near the curves in the road. There hadn't been any.

Hecht asked what the time was as shown on Sandy's wristwatch? Rule had never looked. No one wrote down the time. (Why would they? They thought it to be an accident and treated it as such.)

After the lunch recess, Symmonds began his redirect of Rule. The watch, did you wind it? Yes, and it started running. Had it wound down, do you know? No. Was it self-winding? I don't know.

Did you notice anything at the first S curve to suggest Sandy's car had gone out of control? "There was no evidence to indicate the car was ever out of control until it crossed the embankment."

He described the spots on the bridge deck and the metal portions of the bridge as darker on July 18, harder to see.

He said the only time troopers collect transfer paint—paint found on a surface that appears to have come from another vehicle—was in a hit-and-run situation.

Back to steering wheel locks, Rule described his procedure when he checked it on September 6. "You turn the key to the on position, release the steering wheel and then you shut the key back off to the off position, the wheel would remain unlocked until the key was removed from the ignition switch. You put the key back into the switch and it would remain locked until you turn the key on. The only time you shut the switch off the wheel is locked is where you pull the key out."

(The author repeats that getting the facts right about the key and steering wheel lock is crucial to prove that Sandy died in an accident. Had the grand jury properly indicted Tom by specifically naming the method he allegedly used to commit murder, this discussion would have been moot. It, instead, created great confusion and conflict between so-called expert witnesses.)

On re-cross examination, Hecht asked Rule how many accidents he had investigated where the door tore off a car in motion. "I can't think of any, sir." So you have never investigated an accident where the door tore off and no hair or blood could be found inside the car. "I don't think I that I've ever worked an accident that would meet all those criteria."

Rule stepped down.

Autopsy number one

Dr. Juan Gabriel took the stand. Gabriel spoke with a thick accent and several times he had to clarify or repeat his testimony. The attorneys often had to repeat their questions as well. This effected the jury by creating slightly more confusion about what he found when he autopsied Sandy's body on July 18, 1983.

Dr. "Mike" Miguelino had assisted him.

As Symmonds got into the most horrific aspects of Gabriel's testimony, it grew quite gruesome. Observers reported that Jane Grismer made a dramatic exit from the courtroom that, no doubt, caught the jury's eye.

Gabriel identified various autopsy photos and described each. He gave a detailed description of the injuries he spotted. (The author provided the detail of Gabriel's autopsy in an earlier chapter.)

Gabriel said he first checked for fractures. He saw none except for the wrist.

Symmonds quizzed him about the lungs. Did you find any foreign matter there? No. Why is that important? To see if there was any evidence of drowning. He had been told she was found face down in the water and found no evidence of drowning.

"What if anything did you note, doctor, concerning the kidneys?"

"The right kidney was essentially within normal limits or I didn't see any abnormality there; however, in the left kidney the lower pole of the kidney was almost completely transected [torn in two] with ragged margins, and it was covered with blood clots on all sides of the injury."

What caused her death? "My impression to this case would be she died of loss of blood or hemorrhage due to internal injuries caused by blunt trauma." The transected kidney and resultant bleeding caused her death. The loss of blood and loss of kidney function is deadly, within 30 minutes to an hour. These injuries could cause shock and render a person unconscious.

What did you find in the stomach? The only identifiable item "was tomato skin."

Hecht began his cross-examination. (Nothing in Gabriel's report had suggested foul play, nor did it rule it out.)

In your opinion, could any of the injuries you saw to the head cause death? Probably not, but I could not totally rule it out. Did any of the injuries you saw above the shoulder, in your opinion, cause her to lose consciousness? No.

Hecht had Gabriel mark on a chart the location of various injuries he found on the body. He marked lacerations with an L, bruises with a B, fractures with an F and indicated the location of the damaged kidney. Once finished, Hecht asked him if he agreed, "all the major injuries were on the left side of the deceased?"

"Yeah, that was my observation, on the left side." The only fractures were five ribs on the front left side and the left wrist.

Hecht asked how long it might have taken for Sandy to become unconscious and bleed to death. Again Gabriel said 30 minutes to an hour. "Do you have an opinion based upon the examination that you conducted as to her time of death?"

"My basis on the time of death would be within three hours from the last meal." Rigidity and lividity are both affected by temperature and the environment in which the body is found, so were useless in determining time of death.

(Years later, Tom discovered an article about determining time of death based on stomach contents. The article said that it is a poor and inaccurate method, given all the variables affecting digestion, such as fatigue, other foods consumed, stress and the like. Dr. William Eckert had authored the article, but Hecht knew nothing about it during this trial. Since the coroner originally had indicated the time of death as between midnight and 3:00 a.m., changing it to sometime around 10:00 p.m., three hours after Sandy's last meal, made a critical difference to Tom's defense.)

Hecht asked Gabriel to define blunt trauma. "It's a blunt force."

"Is that just the application of external force to the body?"

"Yeah, it's when a body is struck or compressed by a hard object."

"That is the kind of injury that persons receive in motor vehicle accidents?"

"Yeah, you can see that in a motor vehicle accident."

Gabriel stepped down.

Dr. Quincy, you're wanted in the courtroom

Since September 12, 1984, all of Emporia had waited with great expectation for this moment. Dr. William Eckert, the man on whom the TV character Dr. Quincy was based, took the stand. He had performed the mysterious second autopsy on Sandy's body after Kansas' authorities had it exhumed—illegally—and brought to Eckert's Wichita office.

The media trumpeted the second autopsy so effectively that at least one prospective juror said plainly that it showed that Tom beat Sandy to death.

As a forensic pathologist, Eckert served a different purpose than someone like Gabriel. Gabriel looked for the cause of death, but not the instrumentality of death. Eckert reasoned from his research, observation and experience, how somebody died—the cause and manner of death. Where Gabriel observed that Sandy died from a partially transected left kidney, Eckert would say what specifically caused the kidney to become transected. From his observation, investigators then could form their theory of how the alleged murderer committed the act.

No one doubted Eckert's credentials. He stood at the top of the profession, but there were others just as competent, and who had been in the field longer than he had.

With great drama, Eckert took his oath and climbed into the witness stand. Symmonds anticipated a knockout punch.

It took Symmonds and Eckert several minutes to establish his long list of credentials and to separate him from a mere hospital pathologist. He had performed more than 10,000 autopsies.

"What if any information were you able to obtain as a result of the examination relative to the exhumation of Sandra Bird?" Even Tom hung on the edge of his seat, awaiting this answer. Tom saw nothing particularly startling in the second autopsy report (which Hecht finally received just before the trial began) and he had wondered himself exactly how Sandy died.

"Well, there were several points that were evident that represented a pattern that had not been demonstrated on the first autopsy. One was a fracture of the shoulder blade or the scapula on her left side." Eckert classified this as a vital injury, done while Sandy still lived.

Eckert said he could confirm nearly all the injuries Gabriel found during his autopsy. He described in detail the condition of the body. The jury needed to hear that there actually was enough left of the body to draw a conclusion.

Have you visited Rocky Ford Bridge? Yes. Have you reviewed photos of the bridge, the site of the car wreck and such? Yes.

Did you note any injury that was life threatening? He saw a laceration on the head that might have rendered Sandy unconscious, and could have been life-threatening under the right conditions.

Eckert described the areas near the brain and face that showed a collection of blood beneath the skin. He said these injuries were caused by blunt trauma.

"What other injuries with respect to the body did you find to be of significance in formulating any opinion relative to this particular case?"

"Well, the injuries that are on the wrists and the arm of the individual. It had a pattern of compression which is the type that is seen if a heavy object but a nonsharp object makes impact to the skin." He pointed at injuries above her left wrist and in the area of her right elbow.

Eckert said the injuries on the arms had been caused by blunt trauma. Symmonds asked him to be more specific. Eckert called them defensive injuries. What do you mean by defensive injuries?

Eckert stood near a diagram while providing this testimony. To this question, he dramatically raised his arms and hands, crossing them in front of his face and head while he said, "Well, when someone is confronted with a weapon or in some way trying to protect themselves against an attack of any type, they will make an effort to defend themselves, and the defense could be an outstretched arm or if there's impact to a specific area the hands might just try to cover that area or in fact the legs. The head, it could be the hands holding off or trying to ward off any type of impact; and in the process fingers may be injured, the arms may be injured as well as the target of the attack which would be the head."

Eckert described the injuries on the arms and above the wrist. He said they were rectangular, "slightly rounded edges or ends," and they happened before death.

"In what manner can such an injury be received?"

"By a heavy object, a branch of a tree, baseball bat, a pool cue. Mostly of a noncutting nature, a tire iron, something of that nature where there's a linear component. In other words, it's long and it has the weight to produce an effect, and the effect is that the skin is compressed against bone by the weight of this object and that produces the line or the outline of the instrument." (Eckert could not explain how the bruises, which followed the curve around the arm bone, got there. No solid, stiff item would have caused such damage.)

Eckert described what he believed to be scrapes and "circular injuries which meant focused pressure" on Sandy's legs. He implied that someone had held her tightly by the legs.

Eckert saw no punctures in Sandy's body. Since no puncture wound appeared on Sandy's back, the kidney had been subjected to some sort of "severe impact and force so as to produce this fracturing of the kidney."

What types of things could have created such force? It would be "an object of a size and significance, say a large stone or a piece of timber, or the body itself moving and impacting a surface that is protruding, either a stone or a stump of something of that nature." Even a person falling just right from a height as little as five feet could incur such an injury. Certainly someone falling 20 feet could as well.

Symmonds asked Eckert to describe the types of injuries common in auto crashes where the body is ejected. These kind produce some of the worst types of injuries to the "major body areas." Did you see these types of injuries on Sandy's body? "I didn't see any injuries on this body that I would relate to an ejection type of process or for that matter involved in an accident at mild speed or low speed."

Did the broken shoulder blade and damaged kidney occur at the same time? Yes, the blood collected around the wounds show that, and how they line up. Eckert believed this blunt force came from behind Sandy. Since the broken ribs were on the front, how were they fractured? "I think that the ribs themselves on the outer side might have been a result of impact or forces that were directed to the left side of her body. The ribs that are closer to the midline could have been part of another process, part of another trauma situation involving the whole, total picture."

Eckert believed that given the loss of blood Sandy sustained she could have died within 10-15 minutes of the injury to her kidney. He thought the bleeding from her broken shoulder and cut face affected this short amount of time.

He saw enough blood collected on the brain to suggest a concussion and, therefore, believed Sandy had been knocked unconscious.

Building to a crescendo, Symmonds asked his most dramatic question. "Doctor, do you feel that in your opinion based upon your observations of the photographs and your examination that the injuries to the person of Sandra Bird would be consistent with being dropped from the Rocky Ford Bridge and landing on a rocky surface 21 feet six inches below the bridge floor?"

Hecht jumped to his feet. "I would object, Your Honor. It's a hypothetical question not predicated upon any fact in evidence."

"Your Honor, at this time I believe that there has been evidence to support that question."

"If the court please, if we're going to argue this, I prefer it be outside the presence of the jury," Hecht answered angrily. Rulon agreed and had the jury removed.

After hearing out both attorneys, Rulon instructed Symmonds, "At this point in the proceedings there is no evidence that I've heard that someone fell anywhere. Now, what the court is ruling is that you can ask the doctor based upon his autopsy and based upon his inspection of evidence that's already in the record how these injuries could have occurred, but there's been no one testify anything about someone falling off of a bridge."

The jury came back into the room and Symmonds finally asked the question everyone had waited ten months to hear. "Doctor, do you have an opinion based upon the autopsy photos and your inspection of the evidence in this case how the injuries to Sandra Bird's scapula, kidney and ribs could have been received?"

"Yes."

"What is your opinion?"

The tension in the courtroom peaked as each person listened breathlessly. Mark Bird expected to hear "tire iron" or "wine bottle." Others had their own opinion. Tom actually hoped for a definitive answer.

"By blunt trauma to the back which resulted in all three of the areas of injury being—having occurred."

The air went out of the room. Eckert had answered the same as had Dr. Gabriel. Ten months of speculation found nothing but a broken scapula and blunt force—everyone knew that and felt disappointed.

Hecht questions Eckert

Eckert acknowledged that during the second autopsy, he found everything Gabriel had found, plus "a fracture to the shoulder blade, scapula." Nothing else.

"The type of injury that a person's head would sustain being ejected from an automobile at a speed of 15 to 20 miles an hour and striking a stone would depend, would it not, on the manner in which the head struck the stone? By that I mean whether it was a glancing blow, a head-on blow, and whether or not the stone was rigid or moved and also the weight of the body and the speed at which it was traveling."

"Yes." By so winning agreement, Hecht set up his later argument that in fact, even Eckert testified that an ejection from the car comfortably explained Sandy's injuries.

Hecht mentioned that Sandy had lost 2200 CCs of blood, perhaps more. "Would a loss of consciousness have occurred previously to [death]?"

"Yes."

"And would a person have entered into a state of shock also prior to death?"

"As soon as the blood loss was perhaps a third or up to a half of the body blood, yes."

"As you well know, I'm not a doctor and I don't pretend to be. Is there a difference between shock and unconsciousness?"

"Well, yes, there's no relationship...A shock can produce unconsciousness but unconsciousness can go on at the same time shock can go on."

"You can be unconscious without being in shock?"

"Yes."

"And you can be in shock but that will ultimately produce unconsciousness?"

"Yes."

"The injuries that you saw in the photographs and during the performance of your postmortem were sufficient in your opinion to have produced unconsciousness?"

"To the head, yes, sir." Furthermore, Eckert believed in a case such as this one, unconsciousness could have occurred within seconds.

Hecht stepped down and Symmonds had no further questions. The great Dr. Eckert wished the court a good day and left. Rulon dismissed the jury until the next morning.

Tom and his attorney had mixed feelings about Eckert's testimony. The great doctor failed to state the instrumentality of death. This continued to leave the defense vulnerable with no way to defend. They suspected, of course, from Symmonds' opening statement that somehow he would assert Tom beat Sandy and threw her off the bridge. He had tried to get Eckert to say as much.

Yet, overall, Eckert's testimony added little to the prosecution's case. Sandy died from internal bleeding. Eckert said blunt trauma caused the bleeding. Proving Sandy's death an auto accident still seemed the best defense. Accident reconstructionists would next battle over pictures, measurements, laws of nature and some very strange reasoning that passed for science.

Reconstructing a tragedy

Opat listed Lt. William Persinger as one of the members of the bi-county murder task force on August 16, 1984. At least since that day, Persinger participated to some extent in formulating the state's case against Tom. No official record states that he began with an assumption that foul play had occurred, as in the case of Dr. Eckert and the second autopsy, but his answers at trial and the strange and deficient methods he used to conduct his investigation suggested John Rule did more of the reconstructing than had Persinger.

Symmonds saw Persinger's testimony as critical to his case against Tom. Since no one could place Tom at the scene of the wreck, nor did any other evidence exist that he murdered Sandy, it fell on Persinger to prove she could not have died in a simple, one-car auto accident, at least not without help.

Persinger had served 27 years with the Kansas Highway Patrol, a great portion of which was running the training school and handling the food, linen service and repair contracts. He received many formal classroom hours in reporting on accidents and, to a very limited degree, doing actual accident reconstruction. He also received two week's training as an accident reconstructionist at Minnesota's vaunted school for the same, and at Northwestern University's acclaimed school for reconstructionists. Michael Loffgren, who ran the Minnesota school, designed a good portion of Northwestern's curriculum.

Passing an exam means only that someone completed a course. It does not prove expertise, and for the greatest amount of his active service time, Persinger acted in a management capacity or as an instructor. By Tom's trial, he claimed to have performed perhaps 50 accident reconstructions.

Persinger lacked any training in physics or engineering so it wasn't surprising that he made no calculations to determine the effects of rate of speed, coefficient of friction, inertia or any other calculation to arrive at his opinion. He never even determined the weight of the car.

Responding to Symmonds question about the job of a reconstructionist, Persinger said, "You rely on the laws of nature, the physical forces, the momentum of a vehicle, the speed of the vehicle, the damage and location of damage to the vehicle, the type of damage that the vehicle has to it that's been put there by objects that it has struck."

He visited Rocky Ford Bridge 14 months after the car wreck and took no measurements. He climbed up and down the embankment and strolled on the shore, comparing what he saw with the photos taken by various law enforcement officers.

Symmonds asked him the length of the concrete abutment. Persinger said 18 feet then admitted he never measured it. Trooper Rule had, and it was 12 feet long. He attempted to provide a measurement from the miss-measured abutment to the car, but the car had been removed 14 months earlier.

He never visited Rich Industries to view the car. Instead, he relied on photos taken at the time of the wreck and by investigators on September 6. Hecht objected strenuously to using the newer photos since, at the time they had been taken, several parts of the car had been removed and sold. The car no longer appeared as it had on the day of the wreck.

Persinger's testimony at trial contradicted his testimony at the grand jury and, in fact, contradicted itself during trial questioning.

So concerned were investigators at the poor job Persinger might do on the stand, that the morning of his testimony, he and Trooper Rule drove to the bridge and conducted an experiment. They hand-pushed his 4,380-pound pickup truck down the road toward the embankment to prove that Tom, acting on his own, could have done the same thing. Using a completely different vehicle under conditions that may not have represented those present on July 16 and 17, 1983, made this test useless. Rulon ordered that it be stricken from the record and told the jury to disregard it.

Persinger ostensibly conducted the push test to show a Peugeot could have been traveling 15 miles an hour when it reached the embankment. Earlier, though, he testified the car traveled five miles an hour when it went over and, in fact, based his opinion on how the car came to rest on the lower rate of speed.

He wrote much of his opinion in a report dated October 19, 1984. In his report, he speculated that the car traveled north down the embankment next to the bridge abutment, continued traveling north, made almost a half turn to the east, and traveled at least 80 feet. But at trial, he changed his mind. He said the car struck the abutment and was sent in a northwesterly direction, then was pointed back to the north by "riprap" (loose rocks and debris) and underbrush. As it traveled north, the car did a slow rollover.

Much of his testimony focused on the driver's door that had been ripped off the car and thrown onto the beach. He believed the car hit the back part of the concrete abutment and that collision caused the car to turn. He believed the door had been open when it hit the abutment and had struck a rock. He circled a rock on one photograph, insisting that was the one the door hit, but under cross examination, admitted he "probably didn't recognize" the rock, nor had he viewed damage to or paint on the rock.

Hecht challenged him about the door latch. He identified photos that clearly showed the latch had been damaged and he had, in fact, testified that way in the grand jury. Here he said by latch be meant to include part of the doorpost.

Persinger testified about the light bulbs and headlights as well. He said the taillights and side marker lights had been on because they sagged and were not broken. He said the headlights were off because they only showed sag from age, not from use and had they been on, they would have shown sag. Hecht challenged him bulb by bulb, reading from the Northwestern reconstructionists' manual, showing that his conclusions were, at best, dubious.

Over and over Hecht objected to Persinger's testimony for lack of foundation, lack of science, lack of measurements. Hecht wanted his testimony struck from the record.

Writing in Tom's appeal months later, attorney Ben Wood wrote, "Billy Persinger's testimony was critical to the state's case: He was used to establish that what the state had originally thought was an accident, before it prosecuted Thomas Bird, was a staged wreck. Billy Persinger told his story. Where his story came from no reader of the record will ever know. Men or women pulled from the street might have told the same story. Certainly, they could have made the same calculations he made in this case. A conviction of first degree murder cannot stand on such 'evidence.'"

When Persinger mercifully finished, the jury had been totally bored with technical discussion and, worse, the constant interruptions as Hecht objected, Symmonds argued and Rulon overruled—at least most of the time.

Blood and drugs

Symmonds called Richard Pierce to the stand. Pierce analyzed blood sample for the Kansas Department of Health and Environment in Topeka. He analyzed the blood sample Rule sent him on July 19, 1983. "What were the results of your examination of this sample?"

"The blood alcohol content on sample on Sandra Bird was 0.01 percent by weight ethyl alcohol." This fell far below the legal limit of 0.10 used to determined whether somebody was legally drunk. Sandy had been sober at the time of her death.

Rakesh Mohan stepped up the witness stand. He, too, worked at the Kansas Department of Health and Environment. He performed toxicological tests on Sandy's urine and gastric fluids on July 20, 1983. He found no trace of drugs or other toxic substances in Sandy's body.

Then Symmonds called Dr. Timothy Rohrig to the stand. He performed forensic toxicological tests for the KBI, looking for drugs and poisons. On October 10, 1984, he performed tests on fluids drawn during the second autopsy. "I did not detect any drugs present in the blood sample."

Hecht probed Rohrig a bit about the types of drugs and poisons he might have found in Sandy's body. "I tested for many of the common drugs that are seen in bodies that I've experienced, the antihistamines, the tricyclic and depressants, the barbiturates, the alkaloid drugs."

"Drugs that could be obtained in a community like Emporia?"

"That's correct, sir." He found none of this in the fluids Agent Humphrey gave him drawn from Sandy's body.

Since the next witness's testimony dealt with blood evidence from the accident scene, and the afternoon was getting late, Rulon dismissed the jurors, but with a special instruction. All of them were to report back to the courthouse at 9:15 p.m. Rulon decided to have them all visit Rocky Ford Bridge the night of July 10, 1985, almost two years after Sandy's death.

When they assembled that evening, Rulon explained that cars driven by court employees would carry them in groups of three to the site. He told them they would drive north, around the curves and across the bridge. They were to view whatever they could see as they drove and no one was to talk about it. The new reflective signs had been covered with bags (Hecht wanted them removed to make the site as much like it was the night of the car wreck as possible) but other than that, it was assumed everything appeared much as it did two years earlier.

Without getting out and inspecting the site at night, the defense lost its ability to show how impossible it would have been in utter darkness for one person to perform the crime the state alleged. The hour of the drive-by was earlier than the state alleged the murder occurred. Still, it seemed of value that the jurors could actually see this mysterious, infamous bridge that took the life of a young mother and wife.

Critical blood tests next

Eileen Burnau took the stand. A 12-year veteran criminalist, her primary duties included, "Various and physical and chemical examinations on different pieces of evidence that are submitted" and then testifying on the same.

She analyzed blood samples and other items associated with Sandy's death. These items included "dirt and tree bark and clothing and rocks to determine if any blood was present; and if so, the nature and further identification of that blood."

Burnau tested each sample first to determine if it was blood, then whether it was human blood and last, to try and type it. Burnau found one of the spots on the bridge deck as unidentifiable, a second as human blood, but not able to be typed. As for the blood Andrews scraped from the metal ledge of the bridge, "I could not make a determination as to whether the stain was of human origin."

Andrews found blood directly below the metal railing. Burnau identified it as human blood, but, "I was not able to arrive at a type."

Burnau found no blood on one of the rocks but did on others, some human some unidentifiable. The human blood she identified, even within a few feet of the car, could not be typed. One rock had human blood on it, but the officers collected such a small sample, it could not be further tested.

Burnau identified an envelope that had contained pieces of bark the tree that stood directly below the bridge. Burnau identified human blood, type A.

She explained that the ability to determine blood type deteriorates over time. Exposed to the environment as had been the tree, rocks and bridge, after about three months it becomes difficult to type the blood. This suggested, though, that the blood on the bridge, if it had been blood at all, could have been old.

Burnau tested Sandy's clothes and identified type A blood on her dress.

The blood on her dress matched the blood on the tree, but no other blood could be matched to hers. DNA tests had not yet come into practice, so no one knows for sure whether the tree blood was, in fact, Sandy's. Hecht had a theory how Sandy's blood got on the tree, so it made no difference to the defense at the time.

Hecht pressed Burnau on whether her tests could provide a false positive or negative. Could she, for instance, determine from testing that a particular sample was human blood but the test provided a false reading. Burnau insisted that though it could happen, she operated with such strict control that it virtually eliminated any false readings.

During re-direct questioning, Burnau said that some samples are rendered useless in as short as a week, using the enzyme test, and others might be testable if gathered up to three months. An antigen test could be used on older samples, as she had done on the dress.

Burnau tested the red cups and found no blood. She also tested the sun visor and carpeting from the car. Again, she found no blood. Prosecutors theorized that Tom murdered Sandy outside the car and so the absence of blood in the car seemed to favor their theory. (But Trooper Rule treated the wreck as a single-car accident from the beginning.)

Burnau closed her testimony describing the blood taken at the funeral home. Kenton Thomas had already begun embalming Sandy before officers retrieved the samples. Burnau found the two samples useless.

(Burnau identified type A blood on Sandy's dress and on the tree. Dr. Ford stated Sandy's blood type as A. Trooper Rule insisted he followed a trail of blood on the rocks leading from the car to the tree and that he spotted blood directly above the tree on the bridge railing, cross member and deck. Burnau showed some of that blood, though not typable, had been human; others seemed to be animal. The conclusion? Science could not determine this case, as long as the defense had an explanation for the blood on the tree.)

Before dispensing with this testimony, Symmonds offered all the rocks, wood splinters, chips and other items Burnau tested to be entered as items of evidence. Hecht objected to all those not identified as human blood type A. The others, Hecht said, were irrelevant since they proved nothing. Rulon allowed them all to be entered. The jury sat confronted by what appeared to be overwhelming evidence that Sandy's blood dripped off the bridge and on the rocks, even though Burnau couldn't assert much of it had even been human.

Before they broke for lunch, Rulon dealt with a personal problem encountered by Mr. Harris, one of the jurors. He had developed a dental problem that needed attention. Dr. Barden, a dentist who also was a juror, agreed to meet him later that evening and take care of the problem. Did Harris do more than spit and moan during his dental visit?

Peugeot specialist called next

After lunch, Donald White, a Peugeot mechanic, took the stand. Symmonds went directly to the ignition question. "Do you know what position the key is in on a 1978 Peugeot station wagon if the ignition is off?"

"In the off position the key would be in an 11:00 position."

Where is the ignition located? "Sitting in the driver's seat, it is located on the left side of the steering column....The steering wheel is locked when the key is out of the car."

"Can a person turn the key into the off position irrespective of what gear the automobile is in?"

"Yes. The gearshift and the ignition lock are not coupled at all." The gearshift can be moved through all the gears even if the key is out of the ignition switch.

"What causes the steering wheel to lock into a certain position?"

"If the car was running, you come to a stop, turn the ignition off, the only way the steering wheel could lock would be if you pulled the key out of the ignition lock. Then it would lock."

"Would the steering wheel remain locked if the key were then once again inserted into the ignition switch?"

"Yes. To unlock the steering wheel you have to insert the key and then turn the key to unlock it. It remains locked until you turn the key on."

(What did all this mean? If a murder occurred, the steering wheel needed to be locked so the car could be pushed straight ahead. Otherwise the car could turn to the right or the left. If the engine had been turned off, the wheel locked into place, then the key reinserted but left in the off position, the wheel would remain locked. The car could then be shifted into neutral since the steering lock and gearshift were not linked.)

White said the car weighed 3200 pounds without any fuel or oil in it. The only fuses tied to lights were the side markers. The main headlights and parking lights had no fuses. They drew their power directly from the battery. Turning off the ignition would not affect the headlights or parking lights in any way.

Hecht began by showing White the same photo Symmonds showed him earlier. He asked, "There has been testimony that that photograph was taken on July the 19th, 1983. Can you tell me by looking at that photograph what position the key was in on July the 17th, 1983?"

"Since this photograph was not taken on July 17th I can in no way tell from this photograph what the position of the key was then."

White said the July 19 photo showed the gearshift in neutral. Hecht wondered whether an individual could push the car by hand if it is in drive? Yes, he said he could do that himself. "How fast could you push it by hand by yourself?"

"Slow roll, very slow roll."

"If you quit applying force to it, would it come to a stop rather rapidly?"

"Yes, it would."

Before White left the stand, Hecht was able to extract from him the observation that to tow the Peugeot, one normally raises the rear end. Before doing so, they make sure the steering wheel is locked and gearshift in neutral. (Larry Estes, Bob Bell and David Cox gave confusing and conflicting testimony about these issues so that no conclusions could be drawn. Estes, who had been in the towing business for a long time, indicated that certain actions were performed habitually, like turning off lights, the ignition and checking the gearshift. Since no one could testify with credibility as to the exact position of all these items and, in fact, testified falsely about much of it, Hecht implied that the tow truck driver had locked the wheel and put the car into neutral—not a murderer.)

Sandy's "confidant" steps up again

Symmonds called Angie Duensing to the stand. The state had to prove motive, method and opportunity. Angie helped convince an earlier jury that Tom and Lorna had an affair and this affair provided motive.

By this time, Angie had moved to California and once again, ran a day care center.

Symmonds led her to a discussion she had had with Sandy in late May, 1983. Hecht objected because "it's hearsay, denies confrontation and cross-examination with no establishment of reliability."

Rulon dismissed the jury so the attorneys could present their arguments about Angie's testimony.

Hecht said Angie could not testify about her conversations with Sandy because Sandy could not be cross-examined. (During the first trial, Rulon forbid any conversations in which Marty had participated for this very reason. Marty is dead. Marty cannot be questioned. Hecht asserted the same argument.)

Symmonds argued that in a case of murder based on marital discord, such testimony is admissible to establish motive and intent. But the case he cited had involved letters written by the wife before her murder. Hecht said it didn't apply in this case.

Rulon had prepared for this fight. He cited a recent case from Shawnee County in which the judge admitted hearsay testimony. The person testifying had the alleged conversation fairly recently, and the deceased had no motive to lie. The conversation took place before any alleged crime.

Hecht asked how often Angie had visited Sandy in her home. Maybe 10 times. Was Tom present? Most of the time. How often did you see her when he wasn't there? Two or three times. When? She had trouble being specific.

About this late May meeting, was Tom there? No, he had gone to St. John's College in Winfield and, she thought, to Wichita State. Why? Inquiring about teaching there. For himself? No, for both he and Sandy. "So it was a joint venture, so to speak, that they both were looking at the possibility that they would both work at the Winfield College, whatever its name is, as professors or instructors of some sort?"

"Yes."

That night, did you have anything to drink? I'm not sure, maybe wine or maybe just Pepsi. She stayed until 2:30 or 3:00 a.m. Later, Angie talked about another similar discussion she had with Sandy, on Tom's birthday, perhaps a week later.

Symmonds asked whether Sandy showed any concern about her marriage? Yes, she was sad and concerned. "Because her voice broke and there were tears in her eyes and she told me she was worried."

Symmonds asked what was the subject matter that caused Sandy to be concerned. "Well, mainly she was talking about how Pastor had been depressed for so long...and then she went on to describe why she felt he was depressed."

Angie answered several questions dealing with this late May discussion, then the birthday night, at church the day of Tom's birthday and a phone call. Finally she said it was hard to be specific about dates and times because the conversations sort of ran together and they had been similar.

Symmonds asked, "During this period of time that she made these statements, did she continue to make statements regarding her love for the defendant?"

"Yes."

"Did she ever speak poorly of the defendant?"

"No."

Sandy asked her to talk to Tom because he wouldn't listen to her. The implication of all this discussion was that Sandy had a problem with Lorna, though her name never surfaced during this questioning.

Hecht resumed questioning her. Is it true you had been infatuated with Tom? Yes, for maybe three months in the summer of 1982.

"And are you telling the court that a 33-year old woman who had been married for a number of years and had three children and one masters degree and was completing a second masters degree whose husband had at least two college degrees and was a practicing pastor is going to ask a 21-year old college girl to talk to her husband about serious marital problems?"

"That's what happened."

Hecht asked whether she had any training as a marriage counselor? No, nor training in psychology or sociology. She had never been married nor lived with a man.

Hecht returned to Angie's statement that Sandy loved Tom and never spoke ill of him, nor would she allow anyone else to do so. Did she ever accuse him of being an alcoholic, beating her, hitting her, choking her, inflicting any kind of physical abuse on her or her children? No.

Did Sandy ever tell her that Tom threatened to kill her, physically or verbally? No. Did he ever threaten to divorce her or move out of the house? No.

Rulon decided to let Symmonds continue questioning Angie with the jury present as he had begun before Hecht's objection. He limited the inquiry to May through July, 1983. (The addition of July seems curious since the entire voir dire of Angie dealt only with May and June. Rulon perhaps remembered some of Angie's testimony it the first trial dealing with July 23.)

Symmonds asked Angie to describe the content of her discussion with Sandy during late May, 1983. "She said he [Tom] had been very depressed since March and that it was unusual for him to be depressed for that long of a time and it was especially unusual because when she would try to talk to him about it, he wouldn't discuss it with her. He wouldn't discuss the things that were causing him to be depressed."

Angie mentioned her discussion with Sandy the Tuesday night before Tom's birthday. She testified to this during the first trial, saying Tom needed time to be alone. Again she made no mention of the romantic time Sandy spent with Tom prior to coming home that evening.

Angie claimed that one time when Sandy tried to talk to Tom about his depression, he responded by telling her, "Sandy, quit pushing me." He stomped out of the basement.

She told about the time Sandy bought a bottle of wine, went to the park and got drunk.

Angie recalled a phone conversation "the weekend of her birthday which was in June also." Sandy's brother and sister had been in town and Tom acted cold toward her. "She didn't go into any detail but she said, 'Angie, will you please tell me every nice thing that Tom has ever said about me because I'm afraid that he doesn't love me anymore.'"

She recalled one more conversation, the day after Tom's birthday. They stood in the fellowship hall at church and Sandy said "that the weekend before she had been so upset that she couldn't keep food down and that she was losing a lot of weight and that she was having a lot of trouble sleeping." Sandy said it was, "The tension between her and her husband."

Sandy laid the blame for her tension on Lorna. Sandy asked her to talk to Tom about Lorna. Why her? Because she had once been infatuated with Tom and maybe could identify for him what Lorna might be feeling.

About their time at the Family Life Seminar in Lincoln during May, Angie said Sandy became very upset because Lorna called Tom, and Tom called Lorna, while they had been away.

About the March incident, when Tom drove around in Lorna's van, Angie said Sandy described that to her as well. Sandy told her Tom was gone from 1:00 to 7:00 p.m. and that he told her Lorna was suicidal; that's why he went with her. Sandy warned him that Lorna was trying to sink her "hooks deeper into you" and Tom got "angry at her for saying that and said she was cold and not caring about Lorna."

They had one more conversation, the Wednesday before Sandy's death. "I asked her how she was doing and how their vacation had been, and she said they had a real enjoyable time and that her and her husband had been able to talk and that it was really good and she was very positive. She was in a very positive frame of mind that night. She said, 'I've just realized that it's not my problem, it's his problem'; and we discussed the fact that Lorna had handed in her resignation at the end of June, that she was going to quit her job. And I said, 'Well, it's sure going to help now that Lorna's not going to be working here'; and she said, 'She is still going to be working here.' And she seemed saddened by that fact but yet she was still positive, in a positive frame of mind."

Hecht goes next

Hecht demonstrated to the jury that Angie had no qualifications as a marriage counselor and, though she finished several college courses on educating young children, she had none of her own. "Would you agree with me, ma'am, that to work full time and go to school and attempt to raise three children together with a husband who had a full time occupation that required more than 40 hours of work is the kind of lifestyle that can place a lot of stress on people?"

"Yes."

Someone so busy could become depressed? Yes. Have you ever been depressed? Yes. Do you get teary-eyed when you get depressed and does your voice crack when you talk? Yes.

Hecht repeated for the jury his line of questioning about any abuse Tom may have laid on Sandy. Angie knew of none. "Did she tell you at any time that she believed that Thomas Bird was sexually involved with another woman?"

"No."

Angie admitted that Sandy never told her about going to the motel with Tom the night of May 31. (Perhaps a married woman doesn't share *everything* with a single young lady.)

Hecht probed Lorna's obvious signs of depression and threats of suicide. Did Angie understand that a pastor's job included counseling a parishioner who might commit suicide? Yes.

"In any of these conversations that you had with Sandra Bird did she ever talk badly about her husband?"

"She would express frustration but never speak badly." Yes, it's pretty normal for a woman to express frustration about her husband.

As for returning from vacation, did you talk to Sandy about that? Yes, she said they had a good time and a long talk. Things were better, more relaxed and satisfied.

"It's true, is it not, that a pastor who participates in some kind of counseling relationship with a parishioner is under an ethical obligation not to disclose the contents of their conversations?"

"I'm not aware of it but I suppose there is." (She had been trained in the Lutheran faith and certainly must have been aware of their teachings on gossip and keeping confidences.)

"You wouldn't have much confidence in a counselor if you expected that they gossiped about what you told them would you?"

"Right."

Symmonds asked Angie whether Sandy generally came home on time.

"Yes. I don't remember ever waiting up for her." (Angie babysat occasionally. She had no knowledge that Sandy generally came home on time; only Tom and the children knew that for certain.)

Returning to the line of questioning from the first trial, Symmonds asked if Angie saw Tom counsel Lorna? Yes, informally, and she leaned on him a lot. If she cried, he would "sometimes hold her in his arms and comfort her or put his arm around her to comfort her."

Hecht referred to police reports of interviews with Angie. Then she stated her disappointment that Tom "did not turn to [her] or lean on [her] and counsel with [her] following the death of his wife."

She did not remember saying that, yet the police reports stated it clearly. She denied it now.

Angie stepped down. Her testimony alleged several conversations with Sandy. Rulon allowed these, even though they were hearsay, because the allegation against Tom was that he murdered her. Jan Mead came next. With Mead, the rules to allow hearsay had to change because Lorna still lived— just refused to testify.

Mead's next

Jan Mead took the stand. She repeated her credentials for the jury's sake and her employment relationship to Lorna. Symmonds then asked her a question about what Lorna told her and Hecht objected, just as he had done with Angie.

Rulon cleared the court and the two sides argued but with the same result. This time, Rulon stepped more lightly than in the first trial giving a long, rambling monologue about being careful to protect rights and the legislature's intent to provide some latitude on hearsay evidence. He again decided that a declaration against interest—no one would say what Lorna had said and hold themselves up to ridicule, so her statements must be true— drove him to conclude that Mead could once again give her hearsay testimony.

Mead's testimony parroted the first trial. She repeated the accusation that Lorna and Tom took trips out of town together and that "he was pretty good in bed for a minister." She repeated Lorna's statement that she wished something would happen to Marty and Sandy so she and Tom could spend their lives together.

Hecht added a few wrinkles to the cross examination. Mead testified that Lorna shook and cried during their April 19, 1983, meeting. Hecht asked whether she held a coffee cup while she was shaking? Mead said it was water, but then said she didn't remember.

Did Lorna ever say that Tom was in love with her? No. Did Lorna ever say Tom planned to leave his wife? No. Did she say Tom planned to bring harm to his wife? No. That didn't love his wife? No. Did Lorna ever say that Tom wanted to "spend the rest of his life with her?" No.

"Did you ever meet Thomas Bird?"

"No, sir." (Nor had she talked to him, a curious thing for a boss who feigned concern that Lorna had a second job.)

"Were you aware at any time from and after October, 1982, to the present time of Lorna Anderson's reputation in this community for fidelity and chastity?"

"No, sir."

"Were you aware from October, 1982, to the present time as to what her reputation was for honesty?"

"No, sir."

Did Mead know Lorna's shoe size? No. Is her shoe size larger or smaller than yours? She had no idea.

Mead finished. Symmonds planned to call Darrel Carter as the next morning's first witness. After such a long day, Rulon allowed the jury to go home to ponder the sensationalized hearsay testimony just given by Jan Mead.

Darrel Carter is next

Symmonds probed Darrel's long connection to the community as a builder and family man, a life-long Emporian. He walked him through the testimony about the "May" meeting at Faith, especially about the plot to push Marty off the road near a bridge.

Darrel repeated that Tom said he loved Lorna and planned to help her, that he was a man of God and planned to murder Marty. He repeated allegations about Tom presiding at the funeral and him being a pallbearer. He walked him through the meeting at the house and his telling of the story to Mike Patton in November, 1983. He spared the jury from listening to the December 12 taped conversation.

Hecht's objective was to impeach Darrel's testimony. He showed that Darrel's entire motivation in telling his story was to keep Danny out of jail, and he succeeded in doing so. He demonstrated that Darrel was an adulterer and that he owned a stolen handgun, the one Missouri police found in Danny's car. Darrel agreed Lorna asked him to help murder Marty at least a year, and perhaps as much as two years, before he met Tom. Darrel constantly confused dates while testifying, as he had during the first trial.

"Do you have a reputation in Emporia, Kansas, for being available to be solicited to help murder other people?"

"Not that I'm aware of."

"Did you have a reputation in Emporia, Kansas, for being available for the commission of serious crime?"

"Not that I'm aware of."

"Do people that are total strangers to you normally ask you to help commit a crime?"

"No, they do not."

"And you're telling the jury that a man you had never met before and never seen before and never talked with before and had no knowledge of you asked you to help him commit a murder."

"That is correct."

Hecht probed Darrel's adultery. Yes, he had sex with Lorna. Yes, he had sex with Julie. "Aside from Julie Palmer and Lorna Anderson, how many other affairs have you had during the course of this marriage?"

Symmonds jumped to his feet. "Objection, Your Honor, totally irrelevant and I ask the jury to be admonished to disregard that question."

"Well now, counsel, I thought you argued to the court that having an affair holds a person up to ridicule and embarrassment and degradation in this community. Do you not now think so?" He referred to Symmonds' earlier arguments that Lorna had to be telling Mead the truth about Tom because no one would admit to such behavior unless it was true.

Rulon overruled the objection and Darrel said he had no other adulterous relationships.

Before Darrel stepped down, Symmonds clarified that it was Tom who got Julie involved as a go-between him and Darrel. (In his mind, perhaps this equaled going to bed with her every Tuesday for two years.)

Symmonds called Lori Anderson, now 10 years old, to the stand. Grandpa Loren sat at the prosecutor's table to help her relax, and Rulon ordered all the cameras to be turned off.

After identifying where she had lived, gone to school and church, Lori pointed out Tom, indicating him as her former pastor.

"Did Tom Bird ever come to the house where you lived?"

"I can't think of a time right now."

"Did you ever observe your mother and Tom Bird together?"

"Yes."

"Did you ever see them together at the home where you lived at?"

"I don't know."

"Did you ever observe Tom Bird and your mother touch one another?"

"Yes."

"And do you remember where you were at the time that you saw that?"

"The church."

"And what did you see at the church, Lori?"

"They were—they just got a computer or something like that and they were trying to figure out how it worked."

"And did you see them touch one another?"

"Yes."

"Can you tell me what you saw?"

"I'm sorry, I can't. I don't know. I can't think right now."

"Do you recall whether or not you ever saw your mother and Tom Bird kissing?"

"Yes."

"And do you recall where you were at that time?"

"At the church."

She said she never saw them kiss at the house and the kiss was on the cheek or the mouth. No, she didn't remember what she told Agent Winsor.

Hecht asked simply whether she had told the truth. Yes.

Lori stepped down and Stephen Anderson took the stand.

He repeated his testimony from the first trial. Lori told Winsor that Tom kissed Lorna on the mouth in the living room of the Anderson's Emporia home.

That ended the week's testimony. Rulon dismissed the jurors, telling them to keep away from news reports and not to discuss the case with anyone.

July 15, trial resumes

Following the weekend recess, Symmonds called Amy Swint to the stand. Sandy hired Amy as a regular babysitter beginning in March, 1983. Swint, 14 years old at the time of Sandy's death, babysat the night of July 17.

Normally, Sandy picked Amy up and Tom brought her home on the weekdays she babysat. "She would usually have books in her front seat and she would have to move them for me, and she would wear a seatbelt."

"Do you recall were there times that she did not wear her seat belt?"

"Just a few times."

When she picked you up on July 16, was she wearing a seat belt? "Yes, I think she did."

When they arrived at the Birds, Tom wasn't there. Sandy told her she had made pie and the kids could have a piece before they went to bed. She said the couple planned to celebrate Sandy's promotion by going to "A movie and supper."

"Did she indicate to you what time that she anticipated that they would

517

be home?"

"No." (Interesting. Others indicated Sandy always returned on time and phoned when she found herself running late. Amy would testify this way in a few moments, but on this night, Sandy gave her no return time. Perhaps Sandy wasn't always as precise as people remembered her to be.)

Sandy appeared happy when she left for the church, driving her Peugeot.

She returned at 9:30, coming in the house alone. Amy saw her retrieve a bottle of wine and say hello to the kids. She told them they could have another piece of pie and went out the door. (At this point, Sandy said nothing about a return time.) Then Sandy came back in, retrieved a second bottle and left, saying she expected to be home at about 10:30. Amy said Sandy usually called her if she thought she would run more than 10 minutes late.

Amy saw Tom's blue car in the driveway and someone sitting in the passenger's seat, though she could not tell whom it was. She said Sandy drove. Sandy didn't tell her where they planned to go after leaving the house and she appeared very happy when she left.

After Sandy left, the phone rang twice. One was from someone out of state and the other, nobody responded when she said hello.

Amy remembered that Tom called her "between 1:30 and two" the following morning. "He said that he had been looking for Sandy and he had been looking all over town for her and he was worried about her." Tom came home a few minutes after the phone call.

"Do you recall how he was dressed?"

"He was wearing a suit and he had a jacket over his arm."

"When you say he was wearing a suit, what do you mean?"

"A shirt, tie, slacks and dress shoes and jacket." (Tom disputes this to this day. He says that Amy babysat for the Birds perhaps 75 times by that night, and on as many as 70 of those occasions, he came home in a suit and tie. But, he said, he came home that morning wearing a brown tweed sport-shirt and slacks. What he wore became a major issue for the jury during their deliberations.)

No, Tom didn't appear to have recently showered or bathed. He seemed worried and had trouble controlling his voice, Amy said. Then Tom took her home, she thought between 2:15 and 2:30.

Hecht walked Amy through a series of questions to restate the events leading up to 9:30, including that Sandy had changed into a sundress sometime after leaving the house the first time.

He asked what Amy did after she put the children to bed. She said she watched TV, but no, she did not fall asleep nor doze off.

She believed it took Tom a half-hour to get home after he called her around 1:30. Hecht asked several specific questions about Tom's appearance, especially whether there was any indication that he had recently bathed or showered. No.

"Did you think his mannerisms, his voice, his words, his attitude and his appearance was consistent with what you would expect to see or hear from Thomas Bird or any other man whose wife couldn't be found at that time of the night?"

"Yes."

"And when he got home, would you tell the jury please, ma'am, as best you can everything that he said and everything that you said. I know that's hard but do your best."

"He asked if she was home yet and I said no. And he said that he wasn't able to find her anywhere, and he told me that he would take me home." Tom took Paul with him and Amy noticed that he held Paul closely, as he usually did.

Hecht closed by referring to Amy's grand jury testimony. At that time she stated that Sandy did not have her seat belt on when she picked her up on July 16, and when she made the statement, it was accurate to the best of her recollection. Yes, memories fade over time, she agreed.

Carol Swint, Amy's mother, took the stand. The Swint family attended and held their church membership at Faith Lutheran. She remembered that Amy arrived home just after 2:00, and she had been upset. Hecht had no questions for Carol and she stepped down.

Deputy Deppish takes the stand

Symmonds called Deppish to the stand. Since Marty's murder, Deppish won election as the Geary County Sheriff. He described finding the two cards in Lorna's dresser, underneath her lingerie.

Hecht asked about Deppish searching Danny's apartment and his participation in Danny's arrest. Deppish said Darrel came to the apartment before the deputies left for the sheriff's office. This contradicted Darrel's earlier testimony where he stated the police had not been there when he arrived. Yes, he knew Darrel stayed at the apartment after the deputy's left.

Returning about an hour later, among other things, Deppish found .22 caliber ammunition. Deppish would not admit that the shells he found at Danny's were the same as the casings found near Marty's body, except to say they were the same brand. He had failed to bring his notes to court that day and testified from memory.

Hecht and Symmonds played a cat and mouse game with Deppish over the shells. Though Deppish admitted they were the same brand and caliber, he could not testify that they were drawn from the same production lot. The

FBI never performed a test on Danny's shells.

Next up was Scott Henderson, a former security officer at ESU. Henderson said he received a call at 1:11 a.m. "The individual identified himself as Reverend Bird, and he stated that his wife, Sandra, who was a graduate assistant at Emporia State in the mathematics department had gone to her office on the upper level of the science hall to retrieve some materials and books for a computer class." Henderson said that in one of the calls, Tom said she had gone out there around 10:00 p.m.

Tom had asked him to transfer his call to Sandy in the math lab, but that could not be done. The switchboard closed on the weekends, so after placing Tom on hold, Henderson dialed up the lab, but no one answered. Henderson offered to have someone check the area and Tom agreed.

"During the first part of the phone call when I was taking more information that I could relay to the officer, he described the type of vehicle that she was driving and he stated that she often parks on the west side of the building which is the faculty parking lot. I stated that this would help me to notify the officers. And he stated that he had been to the area and drove by that same parking lot and there was no vehicle."

Tom told Henderson that Sandy "was to return to the church to meet him."

Henderson sent Tim Sadowski, an ESU guard, to check out the building. He called Tom back to give him the news around 1:30, and he felt sure he called him at the church. Henderson advised Tom to call the police and Tom indicated he had already done so.

"Several times during the course of our conversations he repeated over and over that he was worried that his wife's never been gone that long without calling and telling, that this is not like her to be this long; and several times he stated that 'I don't know where she would be. She has three children at home'"

Tom called Henderson back around 2:30 and asked if someone could check again. Henderson sent Sadowski back to the building. Henderson said he called Tom back at the church right around the same time to tell him Sadowski found nothing. (Swints testified that Tom took Amy home sometime between 2 and 2:30 a.m., and that he had Paul with him. Furthermore, Amy testified that Tom felt uneasy leaving the children alone at home. Though Henderson testified otherwise, he had called Tom at home at 2:30.)

Henderson reported on one more phone conversation with Tom between 3:20 and 3:30. "And he says, 'I would like to thank you very much for all the help that you've done in attempting to locate my wife.' He just thanked me several times that I had put so much time and effort into helping him. He stated at that time that when things were upsetting his wife that she would go driving in the country and that recently in the past few days she had been upset about something and he just thought that she could possibly be out driving."

Henderson believed that Tom's voice changed on the last call, from worried and upset to more one of "relief."

Tom told him that they had been to a club and had a couple of drinks. He worried that something related to the alcohol might have happened.

Hecht began his cross-examination. Henderson said it was common for ESU to receive calls such as Tom's. As a matter of practice, the only call Henderson logged was the first. No official record existed of subsequent calls.

Henderson gave a report to police on the evening of July 17. Hecht had him read from that report, made less than 24 hours after Sandy's disappearance. He told the police that Tom said, "My office phone number is 342-3590 and my home phone number is 343-1480." Henderson earlier testified to looking up the church phone number in the yellow pages, and felt certain he called Tom back there at 1:30, because he had no other number for him.

Referencing a rough transcript Henderson made of that second call, Hecht showed him that Tom mentioned having called both the sheriff and police department. Yes, that's true. But earlier, Henderson said Tom didn't tell him about the sheriff until a later call.

Tim Sadowski testified about checking the building at 1:13 a.m., looking for Sandy. He saw no one, nor did he see any lights on.

Guy Kidd served as the supervisor of security at ESU. He showed that on July 16, a student guard, Jim Azar, walked through the math building sometime between 8:57 and 9:16. No one made any other check that night, except Sadowski's at 1:13 a.m. Kidd found no record that anyone requested to enter the building that night, though a person with a key could enter without telling anyone.

Howard Meyer is next

Lay minister Howard Meyer took the stand. He covered all the ground about when and how the church called Tom, when and why they hired Lorna and organizational questions about Faith. All this parroted the first trial.

Meyer reviewed the discussion of the August 1, 1983, meeting at Tom's house. Yes, Tom told them about counseling Lorna and they discussed the turnpike and gravel road incidents.

Symmonds asked whether Faith had rest rooms. Yes. Do they have soap in them? Yes. Showers? No.

Meyer said he played a number of different sports with Tom including running a 10K race in April. Meyer finished in 42 minutes, but it took Tom longer. He estimated Tom ran an 8-1/2 minute per mile pace (far off his times when he had been in shape back at the University of Arkansas).

Meyer said he had a long talk with Tom on July 17, but prior to learning of Sandy's death. No, Tom never said anything about eating the night before. Yes, he did mention the movie because they saw Howard in the line ahead of them. Tom told him they went to the club at the Holiday Inn, but he called it the Continental (located at the Ramada Inn—even lay ministers make mistakes).

"My memory serves me that Sandy dropped him off at church for him to work on his sermon notes or other office work, and then she went on to the university to work on a computer program." Tom told him that sometime between 11:30 and 12 he drove to ESU to see if Sandy's car might be there. He remembered vaguely some reference to Tom jogging that night.

Hecht reviewed the start and stop times of the movie. Yes, Tom could have gotten home at 9:30.

About the 10K-race time, Tom felt very disappointed in his time. Yes, it could even have been slower than an 8-1/2 minute per mile pace.

"Have you ever tried to run six miles or more on gravel?"

"Yes."

"Is it harder or easier than to run on asphalt?"

"Depends on whether the road's been freshly graded or not. There's a lot of different factors. I prefer at times a gravel road over asphalt." Rougher and looser gravel, though, slows down running time.

Yes, the lay ministers asked Lorna to reconsider her resignation. Yes, she stayed on. Yes, we expect pastors to counsel.

Symmonds knew that Tom said he had jogged about two miles the night of July 16, so he asked Meyer if someone would perspire running two miles. Yes.

"Were the lay ministers concerned about the fact that there might be counseling going on out in the country in automobiles?"

"Yes."

That's where Symmonds left it. He called police officer Mark Summey to the stand.

Summey answered a missing person's call and drove to Tom's house at 3:22 a.m., July 17. Summey asked Tom when and where he last saw his wife. Summey remembered him saying it was at the house and that she had left about 11:15 p.m.

Sandy probably had gone to ESU and that sometimes she went for long drives. Summey left saying he would notify other officers to watch for Sandy's car.

Hecht asked whether the officer knew earlier calls had been placed to the police. No, at the time no one had told him that. When did you prepare your report of the 3:22 a.m. meeting? At 5:00 a.m. on July 19, 48 hours after the conversation.

Hecht asked Summey how Tom appeared to him. He said he seemed organized and had all the information needed. He said since Tom told him Sandy often took drives, "I assumed that if she was usually gone at times that maybe this is why he didn't appear real upset." Yes, Tom told him she usually had not been gone that late.

Next up was police officer Scott Cronk. Cronk visited with Tom at 8:30 Sunday morning, following up on the missing person's report.

Cronk said Tom provided him with information for his report. He last saw Sandy between 11 and 11:30 the night before. She dropped him off at the church "to pick up his car." Tom told him they had gone to a movie and then to The Station. Sandy went to ESU to work because "It was easier for her to work on her programs at night."

Had Tom and Sandy argued? "He advised me that he had had a disagreement with his wife over the amount of time that she was spending working with the computers." But this argument was no big deal, certainly not enough to keep her from coming home that night. No, Tom said nothing to him about being out jogging or about having a drink at the church.

Cronk stopped back at Tom's around 11:15 a.m. because Tom had placed so many calls during the night, looking for Sandy. Tom said he didn't think Sandy planned to spend much time at ESU that night.

"I again asked him about the argument and if possible his wife was more upset than he had thought."

"And what did he say?"

"Mr. Bird stated, and I quote, 'Oh, no. She's not suicidal. She wouldn't commit suicide,' end of quote."

Cronk went back with Trooper Smith at 11:50 a.m. to deliver the sad news of Sandy's death. "What if any response do you recall the defendant making?"

"After being or advised that she had been involved in a car wreck and at the Rocky Ford Bridge, Mr. Bird stated something to the effect of, 'What was she doing out there? We never go out there.' And then he stopped and said, 'Well, where is it?' like he caught himself or something to that effect."

Hecht objected and Rulon sustained the objection.

Tom asked Cronk where the car had been towed. "He stated he just wanted to make sure that the vehicle wasn't out in the open where people could gawk at it."

Hecht asked whether this had been Cronk's first death notification. Yes, it had been.

Hecht reviewed all the statements Cronk had given about Tom and the various times. Yes, each time Cronk questioned Tom he had given pretty much the same answer, except the last time when he added, "That his wife wasn't going to work very long.... And the other was that his wife was supposed to come back and meet him at the church so that they could go home together so that one could stay with the children while the other one took the baby-sitter home."

More chemistry

After Cronk stepped down, Symmonds called Stanley Heffley, a chemist with the KBI lab in Topeka. Heffley tested the wine bottle; "a large container containing a clear liquid, and then there was a cup containing purple residue in the bottom."

He identified Cold Duck in the wine bottle and water in the other. Neither contained any evidence of drugs. He couldn't extract anything from the cup to make any test at all.

Hecht asked a series of questions. You examined the wine bottle and found Cold Duck? Yes. You examined the other bottle and found water? Yes. You examined the cup and found nothing? Yes. "That's the first thing in this case that is as it appears to be. Thank you, sir."

Symmonds called Deana Koch to the stand. Koch, like Sandy, served as a graduate assistant at ESU and was a member at Faith. She shared an office with Sandy and saw her nearly every day.

Koch described how many computers and what types were available. Yes, sometimes it was hard to get on the computer. Sometimes she worked in the evenings, just like Sandy. "She went a lot more than I did and she worked more often with another graduate assistant later at night. They would talk about sometimes the next day about how late they worked. She didn't like to work too much past midnight because she said she got kind of creepy that late."

Koch described Sandy as very organized, though she had a messy desk, and extremely popular on campus. Students wanted to take her classes because she had been so helpful, even beyond their work assignments, on a personal level. Sandy loved Coke and often took Coke breaks when she became frustrated with her work, but always returned within 15-20 minutes.

Koch described the process of developing software on an IBM mainframe computer, the one Sandy used. She said complicated programs could take days and days, and Sandy had to work an hour or so at time, given how full her daily schedule usually was.

Koch rode in Sandy's car maybe six times, and Sandy always wore her seat belt (at least on those occasions).

Koch got a phone call from Tom sometime between 6 and 6:30 a.m. on the morning of July 17. "The first thing he did was apologize for calling so early and then he said that Sandy had gone up to work in the computer room the night before about 11 and that she hadn't returned home, and he wondered if maybe I had been up there also and we had been talking all night long and maybe I knew where she had gone after that or had seen her." Koch had been out of town the night before.

Koch had called Sandy at home on Friday evening, but she was in the shower. Tom forgot to give Sandy the message. He apologized for forgetting. "I got the feeling that he was really sorry for calling so early and he was really worried, and he just two or three times in a row, he said, 'I'm sorry you didn't get to talk to her. I'm sorry I didn't give her the message. I'm sorry you never got to talk to her again.'"

Koch went up to the math department later than morning and searched the area. She found the usual mess on Sandy's desk, but nothing in the wastebaskets or elsewhere showing that Sandy had been there. A few days later, she found the floppy disk Sandy stored her program on, but it indicated no date of any entry. Sandy had bypassed that option, presumably to save disk space.

Sandy never told her she took drives in the country to relax.

When Faith bought their computer later that year, Koch assisted in transferring data from Sandy's program to the new computer. She observed Tom and Lorna working together and heard them call each other, "honey" and "sweetie," "which I didn't think was very appropriate."

Hecht began questioning Koch about how close she had been with Sandy during the summer of 1983. Koch took a class from 10-Noon, and usually left her books on Sandy's desk; Koch worked in a different building the rest of the day. She had socialized with Sandy, but mostly together with others from Faith. They had never socialized alone together.

"Mr. Bird called you between 6 and 6:30 in the morning?"

"That's correct."

"And he sounded worried?"

"Yes, he did."

"Sounded concerned?"

"Sounded tired, yes."

"And worried about his wife?"

"That was the impression I got."

Koch said when she saw Sandy's messy desk the morning of July 17, she couldn't tell from it whether or not Sandy had been there.

Symmonds asked about computer availability, especially the limited number of IBM PCs in the computer lab. Koch said they were well used up until the lab closed at 11:00 p.m. each night.

Sharon Meyer, again

Symmonds called Sharon Meyer to the stand. Meyer's testimony parroted that of the first trial, mostly focussing on the "knees touching" incident in front of the computer and the conversation she had had with Tom. She mentioned riding with Sandy three or four times and yes; Sandy always wore a seat belt.

Hecht had Sharon describe the layout of Lorna's office and how tightly the computer sat on a card table in the corner. She saw Tom basically studying the manual and Lorna doing the keyboarding. The office was crowded and they had to sit close together—there was no choice.

Sharon agreed that Tom often showed affection by touching, hugging or holding hands. But she believed Lorna misunderstood his gestures and saw them as love for her. That's what she wanted to caution him about.

Symmonds called Larry Kalsow. He parroted the same testimony about the van incident. Kalsow said he could not recall Tom discussing Lorna's resignation or doing any counseling out there. "I raised some concerns with him about his ability to counsel with Lorna in light of his wife's death. I felt that he wasn't in a best position to deal with her and her emotions because of him and his emotions due to his wife's death...He indicated that he had too much on his mind at the time to deal with that. He basically was wanting to know my opinion about the situation and then indicated that he would handle it."

"What was your opinion?"

"I felt that the secretary position held by Lorna was putting her and Tom under too much pressure as far as each other was concerned and that it would probably be best if Lorna would leave her position at the church." Tom told him he couldn't handle that pressure and would let the lay ministers deal with it.

Kalsow reported the meeting on July 29 with Lorna, then with Harold Schwinn and Howard Meyer. He said he never saw Tom at any other time or place alone with Lorna.

Hecht asked Kalsow if, as a pastor, he counseled with people who were having problems? Yes. Do you consider it wrong for a pastor to touch or show affection in a physical manner? No, but he did not do this.

Kalsow visited Tom's house the afternoon of July 17. He saw him again several times over the next week or so, and every time he saw him, Tom showed the kind of demeanor he expected from someone mourning such a loss.

"Would you agree with me, sir, that the life of a minister places unusual stresses and strains up on both a minister and his family?"

"Yes."

"That it is a job or a career that requires substantially more than 40 hours a week?"

"That's correct."

"And do you agree with me that the work that you do sometimes places you under stress and strain that your experience teaches you is not consistent with the usual stresses and strains of an office worker."

"Yes."

"And would you also agree with me that it places ever more stress and stain or unusual stress and strains upon the spouse of a minister?"

"That's for sure."

Kalsow agreed that going to school and raising children while pastoring, or being a pastor's wife, can bring on depression from time to time.

Symmonds asked Kalsow whether he felt counseling on a road or a turnpike in a van was appropriate. No. Church is an appropriate place to counsel someone. Tom told him he disagreed, and that it was appropriate to counsel Lorna as he had done.

Lorna told Kalsow there were "times" when she and Tom talked privately, but failed to disclose the number of times or the locations.

Hecht stepped up again. This examination became a bit of a ping-pong game, with each attorney trying to better the other. Kalsow agreed that the dictates of his church meant that counselors had to keep conversations private.

Kalsow agreed that just because a pastor gets divorced, in the LC-MS it does not necessarily mean they lose their job.

Symmonds stepped back up and tossed a cynical bomb at Hecht and Tom. "Are there many people in the Faith Lutheran Church and in the Lutheran church who do not look favorably upon a preacher divorcing his wife and marrying his secretary?"

Hecht objected loudly. Rulon sustained him. Kalsow stepped down.

First of the Grismer clan testifies

Symmonds called Laura Stringer to the stand. She married Randy Stringer, Sandy's brother. They lived in Arlington, Virginia and gathered with the family for Sandy's funeral in July, 1983.

During the day of July 18, Laura talked with Tom in the kitchen of Mama Jane's home. She saw Tom standing by the counter, went to him and they hugged. "What if anything did Tom Bird tell you concerning Sandy's death?"

"I asked him what happened and he said that—he woke up at about 1:00 in the morning, Sunday morning, and discovered that Sandy was not there; and at that time he called the police."

"Did he say anything else at that time?"

"Yes, he did. Let's see, I knew that she didn't—they didn't discover her until the next day, and I made the statement that 'that must have been awful for you that night'; and he said, 'Yes, it was the longest night of my life.'"

Hecht asked her what time of the day she had that conversation with Tom? Perhaps late afternoon or early evening, the day after Sandy's death. Do you have children? No. Does Tom? Yes, three.

"And you know as a matter of fact, do you not, that a police officer was in Thomas Bird's driveway speaking with him concerning the whereabouts of Sandra Bird at 3:22 A.M. on July the 17th, 1983."

"Yes, I believe he testified to that." And he saw a police officer at 8:30 a.m.? Yes. And talked to Deana Koch sometime around 6 a.m. Yes. And late in the morning of July 17, he learned his wife had been found dead? Yes. And he made arrangements to bring Sandy's body and his children to Arkansas? Yes. Given all this, doesn't it seem that he had very little sleep from Saturday night until you saw him Monday? Yes.

Hecht finished with Laura and Symmonds called Nancy Cotharn to the stand.

Nancy was Mama Jane's sister, Sandy's aunt. Sandy often stayed a month to six weeks with her during the summer, and rode her horses. Sandy visited her home every year from age 10 until the summer of her death. Of course, once married, the visits had been shorter.

Jerry Grismer called and told her about Sandy's death. Then, sometime around 12:30 p.m. she thought, she called Tom. They talked briefly but she called again, around 10:30 that evening.

"And if you would, would you relate to the jury what it was that he told you concerning the events of July the 16th of 1983 when you visited with him on the telephone on the 17th."

"He told me that it had been a very normal Saturday night, that Sandy got a baby-sitter and they went out to dinner and he went to the church and she went out the school, and she called him and said that she was having a problem with the computer and she was running a little late and he said, 'That's all right,' that he was doing his work.

528

"And then he said that after a while he called the school and he didn't get an answer and so he thought maybe he misunderstood what she had said to him, so he went on home. And I asked Tom what he did then, and he said that he called security at school.

"And I asked him what time this was and he said, 'Who knows about time when you're busy. It was probably about 11:00.'

"And I asked him if he had ever been out to the site of the accident, and he said no, that he had never been there and to his knowledge, Sandy never had.

"And then I asked him what time he thought she died, and Tom was very adamant in his response in that he said that that's what made him so angry, that the coroner said about 3 a.m. and that that was ridiculous, that by 11:00 he had already called the police and the sheriff was sitting outside his house.

"And I said, 'Tom, what time do you think she died?' And he said, 'Between 11 and 12, about 11:30 probably.' And I said, I don't understand. It doesn't make sense for her to be out on a gravel road at night. Why?'

"And he said that he figured that she had driven out the highway and just to let the wind blow and think over her computer problem and that she had realized how late it was and she decided to cut through that way to get back to town, and then Tom told me that he had learned that day that two of his church members lived on that road and maybe they had told Sandy that she could cut through that way.

"And I said, 'Tom, it doesn't make sense for her to be on a dirt road at night with the wind blowing or no seat belt.' And I asked him if she was in her car or his, and he told me that she was in her car."

Nancy said she asked him about the car and he said Sandy had it in the garage with brake problems. He hoped nothing happened to it before he could get back and check on it.

Hecht began. Nancy hadn't seen Sandy since just after Christmas, 1982. Her responses to Hecht were confusing, as if she had trouble understanding his questions. She admitted that by the time she talked to Tom, he had been through a terrible night and day. She agreed that to both of them, the idea of Sandy dying at 3 a.m. made no sense, that 11-11:30 seemed more likely.

Nancy stepped down. Symmonds planned to call Agent Humphrey next, and it was already 4:45. Rulon recessed the court to the next day.

A true con job

Instead of Humphrey, Symmonds called Charles Henderson to the stand.

Henderson met Tom in the transitional cell at Lansing Correctional Facility. He had begun serving an involuntary manslaughter charge that got reduced to car theft. Henderson had a long rap sheet extending back to 1975 and included charges of strong armed and aggravated robbery, first and second-degree murder, theft and auto theft. He had been in and out of prison four times by then.

"Do you recall what if anything you were told by Tom Bird concerning his wife's death?"

"He said that he had conspired with Lorna Anderson to have his wife killed."

"Did he use the word that he had conspired with her to have his wife killed or how did he phrase that?"

"Well, to the best of my knowledge it was just conspired. He said that him and Lorna and two or three other people had met somewhere and talked it over, and I guess that's what he meant by conspired. I don't know."

Henderson said Tom worried about Dr. Eckert, but he had no idea why.

"Do you recall was there any discussion concerning insurance?"

"Yes, he said at one time he had collected 300,000 or was going to collect 300,000, and he said something like Lorna Anderson was going to get 400,000."

"Did Tom Bird ever discuss with you anything concerning a relationship with Lorna Anderson?"

"He said him and her had an affair going for I think it was two or three years, something like that."

Henderson said he first talked with KBI agents during April of 1985, and he had been on parole—still was. "Have you been promised anything in exchange for giving this testimony here today?"

"No, sir."

Hecht asked how many times Henderson had been to prison? Twice. How many times have you been arrested? Symmonds objected. He said arrest questions were out of bounds when trying to impeach a witness. Hecht said he believed getting arrested for a felony "brings discredit." Rulon agreed with Symmonds and disallowed that question.

He had Henderson repeat his previous testimony and then asked, "Do you have any understanding why J. Vernon Humphrey's report of his interview with you on April the 1st, 1985, says that you said 'Bird never told Henderson that he had killed his wife?'"

Henderson said he had used the word "conspired." Why hadn't Humphrey written that in his report? "I don't have no idea. I never wrote the report."

Hecht asked how it could be that Tom had an affair with Lorna dating back three years when he lived in Arkansas at that time? "I don't have no idea, sir."

Symmonds tried to clarify Henderson's disjointed statement. "Is it your testimony today that he told you that he killed his wife?"

"Yes, sir, had her killed."

J. Vernon Humphrey

On July 26, 1983, Agent Humphrey met Tom Bird for the first time. Tom voluntarily visited with the agent at the Lyon County Sheriff's office and as far as Tom knew, they met to reason together what could have happened to Sandy to cause her death.

Humphrey told the jury that Tom related the events of that evening to him. Sandy worked at ESU earlier in the day, she came to church and brought along hamburgers, they went to see "Return of the Jedi," then they drove to their house and picked up the wine and bourbon at about 9:30. Sandy changed from her shorts and top into a sun dress and dress shoes at the church. Tom had been working at the church most of the day.

At the church, Tom mixed a bourbon and 7, while Sandy drank wine from one of the red plastic cups, the same ones found at the scene of the wreck. They left the church and went to The Station, taking the wine bottle along and the two cups from which they had been drinking. There was "very little left in the bottom of the bottle." At The Station, Sandy drank two sloe gin fizzes and he had two more bourbon and 7's.

Leaving The Station around 10:45, "They went back to the church," and he went inside. Sandy left for ESU for, Tom, thought perhaps 45 minutes. Tom said they had had a disagreement about how many hours she worked at ESU, but it wasn't really an argument. Though Humphrey could not recall whether Tom told him why he went back to the church, he remembered something about a sermon.

Tom said he stayed at the church until around midnight. He left the church twice that night. He jogged from about 11:15 to 11:45. Tom provided Humphrey with the route he jogged and it measured about 2.6 miles.

Humphrey had no idea what time Tom returned from jogging, but sometime after that, Tom drove to ESU looking for Sandy. Checking the buildings, he noticed Sandy's car was not in the parking lot. He drove back to the church and, "I believe that's when he called the baby-sitter to see if the baby-sitter had heard from Sandy."

Tom described making phone calls to the police department, sheriff's office, ESU security and Newman Hospital's emergency room. He said he went home and took the baby-sitter home.

Sometimes Sandy went for drives to clear her mind, but the latest she had ever stayed out before was 12:30 a.m.

Symmonds changed directions and asked questions about the Peugeot. Humphrey inspected it on July 19 at Estes' body shop. The seat belts both worked perfectly. "What if anything did you observe relative to the position of the driver's seat in the Peugeot station wagon?"

"Once we moved the seat back to see how much father back it would go and it would move back very little. Then we slid it forward to see how far forward it would go and it went, well, a considerable distance, probably two to three inches."

The officers asked Linda Schreck to sit in the seat. She stood between 5' 4" and 5' 5". "Her arms had to be completely outstretched to reach the steering wheel."

Symmonds showed Humphrey the telephone records of phone calls between Tom and Lorna from December 11, 1983 to September 19, 1984. They were in excess of 100.

Humphrey said that sometime soon after Tom's first conviction, Jane and Jerry Grismer took him to a location out near Rocky Ford Bridge. They pointed out a "rural farm house" to him, but here Hecht objected. Rulon would not let Humphrey continued as Symmonds planned to call the two Grismers as his next witnesses.

Before his next question, Symmonds asked for a bench discussion. He told Rulon that Humphrey conducted a push test similar to the one Billy Persinger attempted to describe in earlier testimony. Humphrey used two different cars, similar in weight and size to a Peugeot wagon. Symmonds wanted him to testify about the ability for a person to push one of these cars down toward the embankment.

Hecht objected. "You can't offer testimony of a test where the circumstances are not similar. It's not the same type of car, not the same weight of car. The surface conditions are not the same. There wasn't any similarity according to counsel's statement."

Rulon sustained the objection but Symmonds refused to let it go. "I would at some time like to make a proffer of that evidence I think so that we could have that as a matter of record, the speeds at which the car was pushed and things of that matter."

"It cannot be a matter of record unless it's a matter of evidence," Hecht said, and the judge refused to let it become a matter of evidence.

Symmonds claimed he could, indeed, make a proffer of evidence for the record, and Rulon told him to do so, but to him at the bench, not to the jury. "Well, I think perhaps it would be best to have him explain all the details so that would be fully a part of the record as far as the tests and things of that nature," Symmonds argued, refusing to give up.

"Can't you advise the Court [judge] what the testimony would be?"

Rulon asked.

"Well, I think generally, Your Honor, but not specifically and I think it would be just as well to make it a matter—to just offer testimony relative to that proffer."

Rulon took it under advisement. (Rulon later ruled against allowing this oddly construed "evidence" to be heard by the jury.)

Hecht began his cross-examination. He directed his questions to Humphrey's report of his April 1, 1985, interview of convict Henderson. "In your report of interview does Mr. Henderson tell you that Mr. Bird told him that he had killed his wife?"

"No, it doesn't say that."

"It says in fact that 'Bird never told Henderson that he killed his wife.'"

"That's correct."

"On the last page of the report does it state that Mr. Henderson felt that the information he had was of no real benefit to anyone?"

"That's what he told me at that time, yes."

Hecht led Humphrey through a series of questions dealing with his July 26 interview of Tom. In every instance leading up to 9:30, every detail checked perfectly with testimony of others. Hecht continued exploring the details Tom gave him up until midnight. Once again, everything checked out, even to the reading of the sermon by Don Froelich the next morning. Tom had left the sermon on his desk when he finished Saturday night.

Humphrey verified completely Tom's recollection of the various phone calls he made after midnight. Newman Medical Center had no record of a call, but they kept no records either.

Hecht turned to questions about the car. Humphrey acknowledged that it had been pulled up out of the river, 65 feet up an embankment, causing the car to be bumped on rocks and such. He agreed that two days had passed since the wreck and the day he inspected it, meaning he could not vouch for the position of the driver's seat.

Hecht pointed to Henderson's rap sheet, asking Humphrey how many convictions it showed—four. (Henderson testified earlier that he had had two previous convictions.)

Symmonds referred to an earlier interview Humphrey had with Henderson, on March 5. Following that interview, Humphrey wrote, "Bird never told Henderson that he killed his wife. He did say that he and Lorna Anderson had talked about killing his wife."

"Did you promise Mr. Henderson anything in exchange for his testimony?"

"No, sir."

Symmonds asked whether it was "the customary fashion at the church to always have a prepared sermon for Sunday morning?" Humphrey had no idea. (Why should he? Symmonds could have asked Kalsow, and the answer would have been, yes, in the LC-MS, this is common.)

Lastly, Humphrey said no one could verify the Bird's presence at The Station that night.

Hecht asked Humphrey to clarify whether or not the Bird's had gone to The Station. "No, we don't know whether he was or not."

Hecht asked about life insurance coverage on Sandy. Had there been $300,000? No. "$100,000? No. "How much insurance was there?"

"Well, there was—as he explained it to me, there was two polices. One for 25,000 thousand and one was for 2500."

Symmonds reminded Humphrey that Tom received an insurance payment from the auto insurance company. Hecht clarified that. The auto insurance did not pay a death benefit.

Humphrey stepped down. Rulon noticed it was close to 10:00 a.m. and called the morning recess. This gave the gawkers and media a few more minutes to work themselves up a little more in anticipation of the next two witnesses—Jane and Jerry Grismer, the aggrieved parents, though Jerry was just the stepfather. Much like the anticipated testimony of Dr. Eckert, the crowd expected a dramatic climax to the prosecution's case.

Dr. Jerome Grismer took the stand. He practiced medicine in Little Rock and married Mama Jane several years earlier, following their divorces.

Grismer said he and Jane visited Emporia on Father's Day weekend, June 17-19, 1983, and they talked with Sandy about "marital difficulties" that day. "Sandy said that for the first time she and her husband were unable to communicate, that she was excluded from doing the usual things she had done for years of marriage to Tom as a wife of a minister, that Tom had told her not to come to church because she would be spying on him and not call the church to check up on him. She felt that the problem was because of Tom's secretary....She had approached Tom about the problem but Tom was not responsive to her."

"Did you have occasion after that particular date to visit with Sandy either on the telephone or in person?"

"When we returned to Little Rock, we had two telephone conversations with Sandy, one the latter part of June and the other the Wednesday before she died in July."

No, neither of them talked to Tom about Sandy's concerns.

Jerry said he and Sandy had a sort of father and daughter talk later in June, discussing the "stresses that married couples go through." Jerry suggested counseling but he thought she said Tom would never agree to it.

"What if anything did she say to you on the telephone when you visited with her on the Wednesday before she died?"

"Sandy was kind of in an upbeat mood. She felt good she said, that she had her life straightened out with God, and Tom's problem was Tom's problem and not hers and it was up to him to straighten out his life."

Symmonds asked about July 17. "Tom telephoned us at approximately 11:00 a.m. in the morning. We had just returned from church." (Police told Tom of Sandy's death no earlier than 11:45. Who got the time wrong, here?)

Jerry recalled the conversation as short, and that Tom told them "Sandy had been out on a road and had run off the road by a bridge and had been killed, and I think that's about as much as we discussed at that point."

Sometime in January, 1984, Jerry talked with Tom by phone three times. "The conversations with Tom, the first two conversations were how was he, was there anything unusual going on in Emporia or the Emporia area, and he said, 'No.' The third conversation which was on the 12th of January I asked Tom what was going on relative to Marty Anderson and Lorna; and he said, 'What do you mean?' And I said I had heard that Marty Anderson had been murdered and that Lorna Anderson was indicted. And he said, 'Well, where did you hear that?' and I said, 'We heard it from some relatives.' I asked him at that point, I said, 'What is your relationship with Lorna;' and he said, 'If you mean have I slept with her, no. I am counseling her. She is a friend. She will listen to me. She listens to me when other people are always after me or against me.' I asked him if he thought Lorna had anything to do with Sandy's death and he said, 'No.'"

Jerry then asked Tom for a step-by-step sequence of events the night of Sandy's death. "He said that Sandy had arranged to have a baby-sitter for the afternoon and the evening of the 16th, the Saturday; that she went over and worked on the computer during the afternoon and then came by the church and brought him wine and some hamburgers. They ate at church. Then they went to a movie. Following the movie they came back to the church and—no, I'm sorry, following the movie they went to a club, they went to the Holiday. After that they—Sandy brought him back to church and dropped him off about 10:00 p.m."

Tom said they had a drink.

"He said that she was going over to the computer center to do some work on the computer and he was going to work on his sermon. He said he worked on his sermon for about a half hour and then couldn't concentrate on it so decided to go for a jog and went for a jog and returned about 11:30.

"He said Sandy was not at the church and he had not heard from her and he became concerned, and about midnight he called the baby-sitter. Sandy's wasn't there. He called the math department, got no answer. He then went over to the university and did not find Sandy's car. He returned to the church and then he said between—I asked him what time and he said about midnight or right around midnight, and then he made a series of calls to the police, the hospitals and the sheriff's office.

"He went home somewhere around 1:00 and took the baby-sitter home he said and then called the Emporia police again from home."

Jerry recalled driving Tom to the Rocky Ford Bridge on July 24. He said Jane and two of the children were in the back of the van. Tom gave them directions, saying he had been out there with his dad earlier and feared he could not find it. On the way out, Jerry said Tom pointed out a house on the east side of the road, saying it belonged to a church member. Jerry pointed that house out to Agent Humphrey just after Tom's first conviction.

Hecht questioned Jerry about his role in parenting Sandy. Since he married Jane in 1979, long after Sandy left home, he admitted to playing no significant role in Sandy's life. Yes, they did talk the weekend of Father's Day, and yes, they talked about Sandy's marriage. Jerry admitted that he had stress in his marriage and, in fact, he had gone through divorce. Being married to a professional man was hard.

As for the morning of July 17, Jerry said church let out at about 10:00. He remembered getting Tom's call just after they got home from church, thinking it to be 11:00. No, he had not written it down—had no reason to do so. Yes, it could have been later.

How did Tom sound on the phone? He had trouble understanding him, but here, he refused to say Tom had been emotional. Hecht read from the grand jury transcript where Jerry said, "Tom was kind of—he kind of broke down on the phone."

Jerry remembered seeing both Ralph and Virginia on Sunday, the 24th, but said Virginia took care of the youngest child that day. Jerry insisted Tom told him that he had visited Rocky Ford Bridge with Ralph earlier that week, despite the fact that Ralph didn't come to town until the 24th.

Before calling Jane Grismer, Symmonds recalled Agent Humphrey to the stand. Did the Grismer's point out a house near Rocky Ford Bridge to you? Yes. Who owned that house? Harry Fowler, Junior.

Symmonds called Harry Fowler to the stand. Yes, he lived out near the bridge in a white house. No, neither he nor any of his children belonged to Faith Lutheran Church and never had.

When Humphrey returned to the stand, Hecht made a point that his trip with Grismer's to see the house occurred almost 14 months after the car wreck.

Jane Stringer Grismer, next up

Finally, Symmonds called Jane to the witness stand. How often did you see Sandy and her family?

"Well, always at Christmas they were home; and once that my children had married, I really have not been that much of a visiting mother but at least once a year I would go and visit them, and they would always be home almost every summer, most of the children."

Prior to June, 1983, Sandy never had any marital problems of which Jane had been aware. She gave her version of the Father's Day conversation with Sandy.

"Tom had a secretary that—whose name was Lorna Anderson, and Sandy felt that their communication had been cut off, that where they used to talk together, she was, you know, used to doing things with him for the years in Springfield and one year in Fayetteville and like critiquing his sermons and discussing things with him, that she did not get to do this anymore.

"We're a very touching family and she wasn't touching Tom. She said that. I asked her about it and she said she was afraid of rejection.

"And in the course of our conversation she told us that the things that she was concerned about was—one thing was that if she came by the church, she was accused of being nosey and if she called him, she was checking up on him. And I believe that she used two or three adjectives to describe how she was feeling.

"But I also want to tell you that she was not running Tom down.

"This had come about because of a great weight loss that I noticed in her when we got there, and I brought that out. It wasn't something that she just suddenly started complaining about Tom."

Symmonds asked her when Sandy told her these problems had begun? Jane said in March, and then began giving a long answer, unrelated to the question. Hecht objected twice, but Jane kept on going until the judge stopped her and told her to just answer the question.

Jane said that she noticed a change in Sandy during March. Prior to that, "Sandy was a fun child. She was bright. She loved her family, her children, her husband. She loved my husband, her father, his wife, all of her brothers. She loved friends. You know. Along this line. I can't say enough nice things, but I wish I were as good as I thought she was. She was a good person."

Jane related her memories of the July 12 phone conversation with Sandy. "She told me that they had returned from a trip to St. Louis. It was kind of a fun trip. Tom's parents had kept the babies. And we talked for quite a while. As I remember on my telephone bill it was like 41 minutes.

"Jerry and I were both talking to her. And she talked a little bit about

537

visiting I believe a minister friend of his and his wife had been in St. Louis....The minister's name was Charlie Smith and his wife.

"And I asked her how she and Tom were doing; and she said that she—Sandy believed in God. She was a true believer. And she said that her life was right with God and that she had—she's made the decision that it was up to Tom to get his life right with God."

Jane testified to finding a record of calls made from her house on the Tuesday following Sandy's death. They were to his house in Emporia, one to Lorna's house and the other to Hutchinson. She also received a call from Lorna that day. (At that time, Lorna still served as church secretary. As well, Tom needed to coordinate plans for the following Sunday service and Monday memorial service for Sandy. This could only be done after all other funeral arrangements had been finalized.)

Symmonds asked Jane to describe the Thanksgiving visit Tom made to her house following Sandy's death. "It was on Friday and Tom had become very upset and decided to leave, and I asked him to go into the bedroom with me and talk. And he said he wasn't going to, that my sister and I had exactly one hour to visit with the children and he was leaving.

"And he went out to get some things, and he came back. He was going up to pack. And so I said, 'Tom, I want you to come in this bedroom and talk to me because you owe it to me'; and we went into the bedroom and I basically talked to him about trying to keep our lines of communication open, that I had lost a daughter and that though I had never wanted Sandy to marry him, once she did, he was mine, he was my son and I did not want to lose him and I did not want to lose the grandchildren. That's all we had left of her was Tom and the children."

Jane said they talked in that bedroom for quite a long time and Tom agreed to stay.

"Did he make any statement concerning Sandy that you recall?"

"Well, one I recall very well, that if Sandy were not so much like Nancy and I that she would be alive today."

Symmonds asked Jane about talking with Tom in April of 1984 during a visit to Emporia. (Tom had been arrested on March 21.) What did Tom tell you about the food they ate that night?

Jane began to say she came to Emporia because she had heard so many different stories about Sandy's death. Hecht objected, but she kept on. Once again the judge settled her down. Then followed a confused story about wine bottles, hamburgers and potato chips.

Returning to the trip to the bridge in July, Jane said Tom talked about suing the county that day.

Jane said she gave the watch to Sandy that had been found on the riverbank.

Hecht began his cross-examination. It dealt with the location of the S curve warning sign and any other warning signs near the bridge on July 24, 1983. Jane remembered the S curve sign, but vaguely and had no idea of the others. She said she sat in the back seat of the van with the babies and remembered little else. Yes, she agreed that there should have been ample warning signs at the bridge.

Jane stepped down. Though she tried to dramatize some of her answers, once again the crowded courtroom had been denied their climax. Most of the stories told by Jane and Jerry corroborated those told by Tom, save for minor details that changed as time passed. The critical difference dealt with identifying a house near the bridge. Who got that detail wrong? The court would find out soon enough.

Time for a rest

Rulon released the jury at about 11:40 for a long lunch break. He wanted them back at 3:00 p.m. Hecht would soon begin presenting the defense's case and needed time to line up his witnesses.

Before the attorneys could go to lunch, several items needed to be addressed outside the hearing of the jury.

Agent Humphrey took the stand and Symmonds dealt with the push test Humphrey conducted the prior Sunday with help from Emporia police officer Dennis Delmont. They tested pushing a Plymouth Volare and a Chevrolet Malibu. No Peugeot wagons could be found. They did this to determine whether someone, acting alone, could get the car up to a speed of 15-20 miles an hour. Persinger tried this with his 4300-pound pick-up truck and Rulon had refused to allow the test to be entered into evidence.

Humphrey sat in the driver's seat with the door open while Delmont pushed the car. One car achieved 22 mile an hour; the other, 15.

Rulon ruled against allowing this testimony to be heard. Humphrey had no credentials to give such expert testimony. The cars were different and the road conditions had changed.

One more item of business needed attention. To formally conclude the presentation of the state's case, Symmonds needed to enter various exhibits into evidence. Hecht objected to the admission of exhibit 23, a plain brown paper sack. Symmonds asked that it be admitted because it had held four other items.

Symmonds attempted to enter John Rule's non-scaled drawing as evidence along with three other similar diagrams. Hecht had objected to Rule's drawing from the beginning because it distorted the road's curve and the relative position of items at the bridge site. When they first argued this, Symmonds said he only wanted to use it to help explain testimony, not as an item of evidence. Now he argued that the jury had already been admonished so they knew it had not been drawn to scale. Rulon allowed them to be admitted, but he planned to give a limiting instruction to the jury so they would remember it was a non-scale drawing.

Hecht next moved to dismiss the case. He contended the state did not prove a crime had been committed and certainly did not show that Tom murdered Sandy. Citing several cases to make his point, Hecht then deferred to Symmonds, who naturally, chose other cases from which to quote. When those two finished their legal dance, Judge Rulon gave a lengthy argument defending his decision to let the case move ahead.

The time had arrived for Tom to prove his innocence to a jury of his peers. He had no choice, since the state still had not told him what he did that caused Sandy's death.

Defense calls...

Robert Hecht took control, ready to prove Tom's innocence. He called Dr. Thomas Butcher to the stand. A general surgeon who practiced in Emporia, Butcher had served as Lyon County Coroner since 1978.

Butcher signed Sandy's death certificate. He reviewed Dr. Gabriel's autopsy report as a normal course of business and approved his findings. Butcher read from the death certificate what he had written about the cause of death. "Death due to severe hemorrhage from extensive abdominal and thoracic injuries." He listed "accident" as the instrumentality.

Hecht asked about coroner's inquests. They are called on occasion to help determine a cause of death and require a hearing in front of a jury. No one requested such a hearing in this case.

Symmonds established that Butcher had no standing as a forensic pathologist.

John Carlson, a math professor at ESU, came next. He knew Sandy as a graduate assistant at the school where he served as interim chairman of the math department. He promoted her to a position as a part-time instructor sometime during June, 1983.

He supervised the independent study Sandy conducted. Sandy spent many days working on the project.

He knew Sandy had a key to the math building, as he did. He commonly went to the building late at night and on weekends, and seldom informed the campus police about it. He knew Sandy often worked late at night because it provided the best chance to use the computers for long periods of time without interruption.

Carlson described visiting the Henry Street house on July 17, 1983. "When I first arrived, he [Tom] was visiting on the telephone and I stood there at the back of the living room. And there were a number of people in the living room and the kitchen area there together. After he was off the phone, he came over and talked to me and he expressed to me that he felt that Sandy had perhaps got lost, got confused, had got on the road she wasn't familiar with; and the other thing I remember talking about was that she had been very, very excited about the opportunity to teach for us and she was very, very excited about working with the computers. And then he said something to the effect, 'And I ruined it.'"

Hecht hadn't expected the last comment, but it caught Symmonds ears. "Pardon me? I couldn't—excuse me, I couldn't hear your answer."

He repeated the statement. (Tom meant by this that had he gone home with Sandy the previous night, she would still be living. Instead, he insisted on going to church to finish his sermon, which caused her to decide to go back to ESU.)

Carlson noted that Tom showed all the signs of grief he had observed in others under the same circumstances.

Symmonds asked if Carlson had seen Sandy anytime during Saturday, July 16, at ESU? No, and he had been there almost all day. Hecht clarified that Sandy's office sat one floor above Carlson's and it was possible for her to be there and he would not know it. But, Symmonds said, if Sandy used one of the personal computers, they sat on the same floor as Carlson's office. Hecht asked what time he left that day—about 5:30, so he could not possibly know if Sandy had been there later that evening.

Hecht called John Gerits, an associate math professor at ESU. He knew Sandy both from his membership at Messiah and as a graduate assistant at school. He, too, admitted that he failed to notify campus security when entering the building after hours. He never saw Sandy after hours, but he seldom worked after hours. He stepped down.

Hecht called Lou Lowrey to the stand. A Civil Engineer, Lowrey served as the Lyon County engineer and had been since 1984. "As county engineer it's my duty to administrate the road and bridge department, to see that the roads and bridges are maintained and to construct or design and oversee the construction of new projects." These duties included assuring roads and bridges had the proper warning signs installed.

Hecht showed Lowrey two manuals that served as the standard in Kansas for the location and installation of warning and other road signs. Hecht referred to a section on low volume gravel roads and then asked whether Lowrey brought along work records relating to installation of safety signs near Rocky Ford Bridge.

Symmonds saw where this was heading and objected. Rulon sent the jury out so Symmonds could question Lowrey.

Symmonds told the judge that he objected because it seemed apparent the defense planned to show the county made improvements to the road and bridge following Sandy's death. He claimed that to be irrelevant.

Hecht said this testimony served several purposes: to show the dangerous condition of the road; to show what should have been there and "which if present would have given adequate warning to a driver." He said these warning devices were required by law to be there and he wanted to show that the county engineer took steps to correct the deficiency. Hecht said that this testimony would demonstrate that someone unfamiliar with the road bereft of the warning devices "could easily be deceived by the topography and the geography of the roadway" and end up in the river.

Rulon allowed testimony about the road conditions at the time of the wreck, but took under advisement any testimony about remedial actions taken by the county.

Lowrey said that in his opinion, warning signs should have been placed on the gravel road south of the bridge and on the S curves, including reflectorized signs indicating the curve, and slow bridge signs as well. There should have been a sign 50-100 feet south of the bridge showing that the road narrowed from two lanes to one at the bridge.

Hecht deferred to Symmonds.

Symmonds referred to the two sign manuals. Both of them said that the ultimate decision about locating signs fell on the experience and judgement of the engineer. These two manuals contained no legal requirements. Lowrey agreed and then stepped down.

Hecht called Peggy Barnhart to the stand. The Barnhart family attended Faith Lutheran and had known Tom and Sandy since the spring of 1983. They lived in a 1-1/2 story white house out southeast of town that featured a large porch.

Symmonds asked specifically where she lived relative to Rocky Ford Bridge. "You would go another half mile east and turn and go south, and it would be about another two and a half miles south."

He asked whether Tom had ever visited the Barnhart's home? Yes, in May of 1983. (Again, Symmonds thought he discovered a helpful fact. Testimony now showed Tom had been someone near the bridge prior to Sandy's death and, in fact, during May, the month Darrel Carter alleged to have met with Tom.)

Hecht called Virginia Bird to the stand. She testified to having traveled back to Emporia with Tom the Friday after Sandy's funeral, and that Ralph arrived late on Sunday.

"Mrs. Bird, on the Sunday following the funeral and this day prior to the memorial service, did you go to the Rocky Ford Bridge?"

"On that Sunday afternoon I most certainly did."

"And who did you go with?"

"I was in Dr. Grismer's van with Mrs. Grismer and the three children and Tom." Ralph and Tom had not gone out there; Ralph hadn't even come to Emporia yet.

"Were there any houses pointed out?"

"Not on the way out."

"Was there any houses pointed out on the way back?"

"Yes."

"Would you please describe the house that was pointed out."

She gave a detailed description. "Tom pointed out that his member lived in that home and that he was speculating I guess as to whether maybe Sandy had come out on that road knowing that one house."

"Who lived at that house?"

"Mr. and Mrs. Barnhart," the lady who had just testified.

Symmonds' cross-examination only reestablished the facts. Jane and Jerry Grismer got it wrong, as they did with many other "facts." Mama Jane was observed after this court session apologizing to Rod Symmonds for the false testimony. The observer saw him just smile and he said nothing. (It is hard to know just how much damage Jane did to Tom with her recurring errors and omissions.)

The court recessed for the day.

Lose two more, Tom

Before testimony resumed the next morning, Rulon had to deal with three motions.

Hecht wanted to introduce Henderson's rap sheet as evidence. It showed he lied to the court, had four convictions and several arrests. Rulon refused to admit it, saying it contained too much extraneous information and went beyond the issue of impeaching Henderson for previous crimes of dishonesty.

Rulon refused to admit Dr. Butcher's file containing all his records on Sandy's death. "The best evidence regarding Dr. Butcher would be his testimony."

Then Rulon agreed to allow some limited questioning about the placing of warning signs that occurred after July 17, as long as Hecht didn't imply that newly installed signs would have prevented Sandy's death. The jury could decide that issue on its own.

Hecht called Gary Dirks, a forensic scientist "with the Johnson County Crime Lab" to the stand. Dirks previously held a similar job with the KBI where he had worked with forensic serology and trace evidence examination.

"Will you tell me please what forensic serology and trace evidence is."

"Forensic serology is examination of biological materials such as blood, hair, body tissue, things along this order while trace evidence examinations take—it's an umbrella that covers several disciplines including head lamps."

Dirks estimated he had tested thousands of samples for the KBI. He testified that heat and moisture affect the deterioration of blood samples. A hot, wet environment accelerates the deterioration.

Dirks estimated that during his career, he had examined thousands of headlamps. Hecht showed him a treatise that dealt with how to tell whether headlights had been on or off during an accident. Persinger claimed he used the same treatise in his work. Hecht planned to show that the treatise completely contradicted Persinger's testimony.

Hecht carefully described the condition of each of the four headlights from Sandy's car. In all four cases, Dirks said no scientific determination could be made from the lights whether or not they had been on or off at the time of the wreck.

Symmonds determined that Dirks never examined the bulbs from Sandy's car.

Symmonds tried to show that when two headlights located next to each other show different damage to filaments, it is possible to conclude that one had been on and the other one off. Dirks agreed, but Hecht objected because what Symmonds described didn't relate to the damage done to Sandy's car. Rulon overruled Hecht.

Symmonds asked whether it is customary when reconstructing an accident to personally inspect all the bulbs? Yes, of course. By so quizzing Dirks, he suggested to the jury that they should disregard this testimony. (But his own expert, Billy Persinger, never even bothered to inspect Sandy's car, though it had been available to him. Was Symmonds impeaching his own expert's testimony? Did the jury perceive it that way?)

If a side marker light showed damage, does that mean anything when determining the condition of the headlights, Hecht asked Dirks? No, they are unrelated.

More law enforcement officers

Hecht called Lyon County Sheriff Cliff Hacker to the stand. Hacker brought along the log of telephone calls received by the sheriff's office on

July 16 and 17, 1983. The log showed that Tom called the sheriff's office at 1:20 a.m. Hacker marked the log with an "X" next to the call from Tom. The log showed no other communication with Tom.

Hecht had Hacker identify the call from Mark Gibbons; it came at 10:39 a.m.

Hecht called Emporia Chief of Police Larry Blomenkamp to the stand. Blomenkamp brought tape recordings of phone calls made by Tom to the police on July 16 and 17, 1983.

Police received the first call on the 911 line. Blomenkamp's voice was heard telling Tom to call back on the regular number. Tom called back and the police recorded that conversation as well.

Hecht wanted the jury to listen to the calls. Before he could do so, Rulon asked the jury to leave so the sound system could be tested. Unlike Tom's first trial where each juror received a set of earphones, Rulon had the tape played over the court's loudspeaker system.

Hecht called Raymond Olson to the stand. He served as "chief of rural and urban development with the Kansas Department of Transportation"—an engineer by profession. Olson administered federal highway funds for Kansas, but previously served as an engineer in the secondary roads department. County roads fell within his purview.

Hecht showed Olson the safety manual he had earlier used when questioning Lou Lowrey. Olson said the federal government required states to adopt such a manual and Kansas had used this one and its predecessor for many years. The manual had been adopted by statute and was binding "upon the states, cities and counties as such." It allowed an engineer to use his best judgement when making decisions about where to install signs.

Hecht recalled Lowrey to the stand. Lowrey referred to work orders that showed warning signs had been installed after July 17, 1983, out at the site of the Rocky Ford Bridge. The work orders did not specify whether those signs were place north or south of the bridge.

Because of the severe restrictions Rulon laid on Hecht, no matter how hard he tried, he couldn't prove the county installed chevrons south of the bridge following Sandy's wreck. Showing that the county installed them just after her death would indicate they believed the road to be dangerous, and meant to fix it quickly. The fact remained that sometime following Sandy's death, whether days or months, Lyon County did install several chevrons on the S-curve.

Ministerial testimony

Rev. Al Burroughs took the oath and sat down. His testimony parroted that of the first trial, indicating the great work Tom and Sandy did for the family life seminars. The Birds participated in several seminars, including one the evening of June 23, 1983. "Their particular topic that night was premarital and marriage." (Note that it was June 24 when Angie said she talked to Tom of Sandy's worries about Lorna.)

Burroughs' records did not reflect whether Sandy attended every conference with Tom, but he recalled a few specifically. On February 19, 1983, they team-taught a section on divorce and separation. (During this same time period, Lorna told Jan Mead she and Tom were in love and she worked at Faith to be close to him.)

He recalled the seminar on April 17, 1983. Once again they taught on divorce and separation. (Two days later, Lorna told Jan Mead she wished something would happen to Marty and Sandy so she and Tom could spend the rest of their lives together. She said they were in love.)

"I remember them again as pleasant people, and I remember my wife met them there at that workshop since we live in Topeka. And when we came home, she told me about Sandra and Tom and what the positive reaction she had toward them."

Burroughs and his wife attended the Family Life Seminar in Lincoln, Nebraska, during May of 1983. Tom and Sandy had been there along with Dr. Ken and Becky Eggemen, members of Faith. "Did you notice anything positive about their relationship?"

"Well, the way they looked at each other, the way they talked in a group of Ken and Becky Eggeman and myself. There was every indication that the relationship was positive." (This seminar occurred during the time Darrel Carter alleged that Tom asked him to help murder Marty, and said he loved Lorna enough to kill her husband.)

Hecht called Agent Winsor to the stand as a defense witness. Winsor handled the Marty Anderson murder investigation and belonged to the bi-county murder task force. He seemed an odd choice as a defense witness.

Hecht asked Winsor about his report of his interview with Angie. Winsor read from his interview. "She stated that after Sandy Bird's death that she herself was very upset because Tom Bird depended more upon Lorna Anderson."

"Than on Angie Duensing?"

"Yes, that's right."

Symmonds had Winsor look at the report. Hecht had added the words, "Than on Angie Duensing," and the report didn't say that, did it? No.

"The preceding line shows that Angie was concerned because she knew that Sandy Bird had been hurt and expressed concern about the relationship between Tom Bird and Lorna Anderson, doesn't it?"

"Yes, sir, that's right."

"And Angie Duensing didn't want to see Tom and Lorna continue to get closer, did she?"

"That's correct."

Hecht asked, "And Angie Duensing was upset because she thought they were getting close, wasn't she?"

"Yes, sir."

Hecht called Stephanie Moore. Hecht asked whether she saw any change in Tom and Sandy's relationship during the time she knew them. No, she saw no change at all.

Hecht asked her to describe what she saw in Tom's behavior the afternoon of July 17, 1983. "He was definitely upset with what had happened to Sandy. I don't know how to describe it any more. To me, when there's a death in the family, you're upset. There's just not much more. I didn't notice anything unusual at the time other than his wife had died and he was definitely upset about that fact." His actions and demeanor during the following months indicated a grieving man who struggled caring for his young children.

Symmonds asked Stephanie if there was any way to predict how someone would act after a spouse had been killed. No, there is not. She saw Tom upset the day of Sandy's death; that's where Symmonds left it.

Rev. Smith, please

Rev. Charles Smith came next.

Charlie and Carolyn, his wife, met Tom and Sandy in Hardy on July 7, 1983, and then drove to St. Louis together for the LC-MS convention. They stayed together in the same room.

Hecht asked Charlie to describe what he observed of the Birds during the stay at the convention. "Their relationship seemed to be strained but it did not seem to be—I mean I made no value judgement on their relationship at the time. I made judgements about Sandy's emotional state; but as far as their interaction, I don't think I really connected the two."

"What if any judgements did you make of Sandra's emotional state?"

"Sandy had been losing weight. She was very thin. She seemed somewhat agitated, and the two of us sort of got into conflict...During that weekend she didn't discuss directly with me what the source of her agitation was."

Charlie saw Tom that weekend, too, of course, and noticed nothing unusual about his attitudes or expressions toward Sandy.

Symmonds asked whether Sandy ever called Charlie to express concerns about Lorna. "Yes, she did…three or four [times] to be exact."

Charlie tried to counsel Sandy.

Charlie stepped down.

(At no time did anyone address the issue of suicide during this testimony. The prior September, Agent Humphrey traveled to Florida to interview Charlie and Carolyn about the possibility Sandy committed suicide. Charlie related that Sandy had mentioned it to them while they were in St. Louis. He told Humphrey he absolutely did not think Tom could kill Sandy, but the suicide could have been possible. Two years after the jury convicted Tom of Sandy's murder, Charlie changed his story, claiming the suicide issue was a joke, the result of some silly story telling.)

Don Froelich took the stand. Once again the described his duties as the chief lay minister, and detailed his knowledge of Tom and Sandy Bird. Hecht asked whether he saw any decline in Sandy's activities at the church during the spring and summer of 1983. "I wasn't aware of a particular change."

"If there had been any dramatic change or reduction in her activities, is that something that you would have expected to have been aware of?"

"It seems likely I would have been aware of it, yes."

On the morning of July 17, Froelich delivered Tom's sermon. "I obtained it from the pastor's office on his desk." It was an original new Tom Bird sermon.

Symmonds asked him whether it was common to type the sermon to distribute it to hearing-impaired members? Yes. And normally, wouldn't the secretary type it on Fridays? "I think that's the typical arrangement." (Symmonds meant to leave the impression that Tom lied about working on his sermon on Saturday. He failed to mention, of course, that Tom had been out of town earlier that week, so it was not a "normal" situation.)

Hecht called Jeanne Turner to the stand. Turner served as the Clerk of District Court for Lyon County, assuming that job in June of 1981. He asked her to specify certain reports she had brought to court at his request. "The first page is the report of death that was filed in my office on August the 2nd of 1983. The next report is a toxicology analysis which was filed May the 7th. There's a blood alcohol examination result also attached to that. And the last report is the report of autopsy that was filed in my office on August the 5th of 1983."

Hecht asked whether all those reports were required by law to be filed with the clerk's office. "The autopsy is," Turner responded.

Symmonds asked one question. Were those reports she referred to available to the public? "That's correct. They are not confidential records."

Hecht asked, "Was there ever a report field in your office of the second autopsy?"

"No."

"Are you familiar with the provisions of K.S.A. 19-1034 that requires all autopsies to be filed in your office?"

"Yes."

Reconstructing an accident

William Kennedy, a consulting engineer, came next. "My degree is in mechanical engineering and I specialize in forensic engineering....My activity is to analyze vehicle accidents and product accidents and give a technical description to attorneys and help them to understand the situation."

Kennedy had testified in 50 different Kansas counties and in numerous counties in surrounding states. He began this line of work in 1974.

"On the 2nd of May I traveled to Kansas City and inspected the Peugeot station wagon. I took measurements, observed the damage and photographed it.

"On May 21st I inspected the accident scene, took measurements and photographs. I returned to the office and prepared scale diagrams and studied the numerous photographs and the investigating officer's report and analyzed the accident."

Kennedy said that if at all possible, the reconstructionist should inspect the damaged vehicle and take careful measurements at the scene of the accident, which he had done (Persinger had not done this). "If there are no measurements taken, specific analysis cannot be performed, a numerical analysis."

Scale drawings are "used to determine positions and paths of the vehicle, collision points; and it helps to establish the motion of the vehicle." (Persinger drew no scale drawings.)

Hecht showed him every photograph of the accident scene. Some had been taken on the day of the wreck and others later. He showed him all of the photos of the Peugeot. Kennedy had studied them all, plus those he took himself.

Hecht took great pains to show the jury that a properly scaled diagram could actually be produced of the bridge scene, drawing a sharp contrast to Rule's amateurish attempt to do so.

"I prepared the diagram to scale. I reviewed the investigating officer's [Rule] reports that notes the vehicle final positions. I reviewed the photographs and ... noted the final position. I considered the damage pattern to the vehicle, and I considered the physical characteristics of the accident scene." Kennedy did his homework.

"And what if anything did you do when you considered those things?"

"I analyzed the motion of the vehicle which was required to do the damage that was evidenced on the vehicle and proceed from the collision to its final position. I also made a speed calculation based on its travel and path."

Hecht began to ask Kennedy his opinion based on all he had studied when Symmonds objected. He claimed Kennedy planned to testify based on evidence that had not yet been admitted, and his conclusions relied on road conditions nearly two years after the wreck. This argument mirrored Hecht's objection to testimony given by Persinger who had done his site "inspection" 14 months after the wreck; that reality didn't bother Symmonds when it favored the prosecution.

As with Persinger, Hecht spent several questions on damage to the driver's door. Kennedy showed that the damage to the door, starting about six inches behind its front most edge, were parallel to the trim, and the metal had wadded up at the end of the tear. Furthermore, the tear lined up with damage on the side of the car behind the door.

Hecht showed Kennedy a photo on which Persinger had circled a rock. He asked whether the damage to the door was consistent with the kind caused by striking a rock. No, it isn't. Why? "The wadding up of the sheet metal indicates motion of the door with respect to the object that is struck. A motion and the contact starts just behind the front edge of the door, and the motion is parallel to the mold strip and indicates striking a fixed object.... Falling on the rock would produce more of a penetrating damage from the initial start."

The wadding could only have occurred if the door had been moving forward.

Kennedy said the damage to the door hinges and the lower corner of the door indicated the door had been torn free of the car while it had been in motion. Otherwise the lower corner of the door would have acted as a pivot and had greater damage.

He believed that some fixed object caused the damage to the left front door and that the same object damaged the rear door. All the markings and bent metal were horizontal and ran below the auto trim in nearly a straight line, though the damage to the rear door occurred slightly lower than the front. This signaled that the car's front end had begun to drop as the rear door hit the object.

"Do you have an opinion, sir, as to what caused that damage to wad up the material on the driver's door and to pull the front door post to the rear ripping the hinges off?"

"The damage considering the total damage pattern of the automobile is consistent with both the damage pattern and the vertical height having impacted the east end of the wood beam that is immediately adjacent to the concrete abutment at the southeast corner of the bridge."

Kennedy showed that the concrete abutment fell below the road level, but "The left side of the automobile would be immediately adjacent to the east end of the wood beam."

He pointed out a large rock sticking up out of the embankment just beyond the concrete abutment. Then he indicated on the bottom of the car, several areas of the pinch weld that holds the undercarriage to the frame of the car had been bent at a 90-degree angle. These bends followed a line down the left side of the car.

"This damage is consistent with having occurred when the left front wheel of the automobile dropped over the top edge of the concrete abutment and the left side of the car fell with the side rail contacting the top of the concrete abutment and the left front door impacting the wood beam."

Much of this testimony proved time-consuming and tedious. Though the record does not specifically show it, Rulon must have noticed that many jurors had lost concentration. He called for a brief recess to let the jury stand and stretch.

Kennedy indicated that the damage to the left rear wheel and deflation of its tire occurred when it hit the concrete abutment. This damage occurred immediately following the damage to the pinch weld.

He showed that at the time the left side of the car hit the wood beam, the other side hit the vegetation on the right side. He gave a very detailed description of how the car passed over the abutment, indicating the line of travel and how each portion of the car touched the ground, rock outcroppings or the abutment. His opinion included carefully describing the mechanical motion of the suspension as it compressed and expanded. As the car passed over the abutment, Kennedy offered this analysis:

"The left front wheel would fall over the abutment and the side rail on the left side scraped along the abutment. Dropping the left front wheel causes a rolling pitching of the automobile which allows the wood beam to contact the left front door. The car is proceeding generally to the north.

"The door is hung up or restricted by the wood beam, and the door is torn from its hinge attachment to the doorjamb at the car. The car continues generally north and the rear of the door is pushed forward. The door rotates about the contact point with the wood beam and the front end falls and then recontacts the wood beam making the scrape mark along the bottom edge of the door.

"The door separates from the vehicle and the wood beam contacts the front edge of the left rear door. The front edge of the Peugeot station wagon is falling, and the left rear wheel is striking the concrete abutment, indenting the wheel and blowing the tire as it rides up over the abutment raising the car with respect to the wood beam, leaving the angled scrape marks on the left rear door."

"The car has begun to roll and pitch with its left front corner dropping causing the vehicle to separate from the beam and the abutment."

[The author understands that most readers struggle with such detailed descriptions. He imagines the jury trying to comprehend it all, and sees them nodding off, forgetting most of it. He sees them, however, left with an impression: Kennedy knew his stuff and did his homework; Persinger's testimony was a joke. Symmonds, though, cut through it all by focussing on a minor issue. Keep reading.]

"The damage to the automobile indicates a rolling of the automobile one-half of a revolution. The pitching movement and the yawing movement initiated by this contact with the wood beam and the concrete abutment, the front end of the vehicle north of the beam is dropping and the car is rolling to its left with the left front corner of the automobile striking the ground and rolling onto its top."

"And would it come to that location then as its final resting place?"

"Yes." [Whew!]

Kennedy showed that the car could not have moved in a northwesterly direction as Persinger indicated. He pointed out tree limbs that grew on the right side of the vehicle's path that were broken off.

His detailed analysis led him to conclude that the car had been going between 15 and 19 miles an hour when it made its first impact. He provided a physics lesson to the jury, detailing rates of speed, resistance, gravitational forces and affects of collision to show how he arrived at his conclusion. When finished, Hecht said, "Now, tell me what this means."

He proceeded to give a point by point analysis of the movement of the car, its drop, which wheels touched the ground and when, and showed the point of time and place when the car lost contact with the embankment.

Kennedy gave a long dissertation on why the damage to the left rear wheel could not possibly have occurred the way Persinger described it. Persinger's theory would have required the car to be moving broadside first, and no other damage correlated to such a motion. Kennedy   said   he measured the distance from the bridge south to the point where he could first see it. Depending on where on the road the car traveled—center, right, or slightly left—the first full view of the bridge came at 100-120 feet. At 15 miles an hour, four seconds would elapse from that point until the car arrives at the bridge. At 17 miles an hour, it would take the car about 3.7 seconds to reach the bridge abutment. Normal braking reaction time is estimated at .75 seconds, Kennedy said.

If Persinger's theory about direction had been correct, the car would have had to have driven out of the ditch on the right side of the road, or from as far right as the fence line.

Kennedy said that he saw no damage to the concrete abutment indicating that it caused the damage Persinger had described. In fact, the discoloration in the abutment came from its casting at the time it had been constructed. The chipping mentioned earlier was smaller than a fingernail. There had been no paint transfer identified in any photographs.

Kennedy inspected the wood beam and found splinters consistent with his theory that the door had hit it. He noted that the discoloration of the wood also was consistent with the effects of moisture on splintered wood over time.

The court reporter's paper ran out. Hecht, sensing a need to extend mercy to the jury, suggested taking the afternoon recess. Rulon agreed.

Throw the body from the car

Hecht asked if it was consistent that a body could be thrown from the car. "The car as it rolls has a pitching movement and some rotational acceleration to the body, and as the vehicle rolls to its left, the door opening, it would be down and the driver could separate from the vehicle."

Trooper Rule had said a person would be thrown around in a car like a rock in a box. Kennedy said that could be true, but "If the box had a hole in the top the rock could fall out."

Hecht asked whether a driver needed to make an adjustment to their direction as they approached the bridge from the south. The curve of the road as it met the bridge lined up imperfectly—a failure of either the design engineers or the construction crew—and a driver needed to begin steering back to the right while negotiating the leftward curve. Kennedy said that at 17 miles an hour, this directional change needed to begin at 100 feet south of the bridge. The scene as he saw it indicated Sandy didn't make that adjustment.

Kennedy noted that the road construction included the parking area immediately southeast of the bridge. He saw no distinction between that area and the road surface, thereby making the parking area appear to be part of the road. It led directly to the embankment.

So ended Mr. Kennedy's afternoon testimony. A mentally exhausted jury recessed until the next morning, brains abuzz with pitching, yawing, coefficients of friction and throwing of bodies.

Symmonds gets Kennedy

Hecht saw William Kennedy's excellent detailed scientific testimony as critical to proving Tom's innocence. But unlike Dr. Eckert's dramatic flair, arms raised to fend off a brutal beating, Kennedy's testimony proved long and dull, yet far more convincing than the doctor's for those who cared enough to listen. Using physical evidence of auto damage that had been painstakingly studied, applying laws of physics and mathematics with a dose of common sense, Kennedy's precise details lacked the sensationalism of human damage. Jurors gave more weight to Eckert than Kennedy.

The morning belonged to Rod Symmonds. He asked whether Kennedy had reviewed Persinger's report. Yes, but he didn't use it for his analysis. Did you review Persinger's grand jury testimony prior to testifying here? Yes.

The day Kennedy did his inspection at the bridge he drove a standard 1981 Pontiac Grand Prix. On one of his drives toward the bridge, he negotiated the curve at 20 miles an hour without slipping or sliding, but crossed the bridge at 5 miles an hour.

Symmonds established that it was normal for a reconstructionist to be called in sometimes years after an accident and that Kennedy often testified when asked by an attorney or insurance company. This suggested that he had a bias.

Kennedy insisted that on a dirt road it would not be unusual for such an accident to occur and not leave any kind of skid marks. Perhaps a furrow, but skid marks are made on pavement. Wouldn't someone see a disruption of the gravel? Could be, but "it may not be noticed."

Symmonds asked numerous questions to establish that a car could be hand-pushed down the road south of the bridge and cause the damage as Kennedy saw it. Though he found the pitch of the road to drop 24-1/2 feet from 300 feet south of the bridge, Kennedy deftly avoided answering directly; each time throwing in a factor that would negatively affect Symmonds' theory. What gear was the car in? Were the tires fully inflated? How heavy was the car?

Symmonds turned to a discussion about the wood beam and the chips Kennedy had described. It appeared to be about three inches long, though the photos made it hard to be sure. Symmonds asked whether or not Kennedy based his theory of the car impacting the wood beam on the missing three-inch chip? No, nor on the crack.

Symmonds spent a number of questions trying to clarify how Kennedy saw the car going over the abutment, causing the bend in the pinch weld. Once established, he handed Kennedy a photo taken by Trooper Rule on July 17, 1983. "Tell me what it is that's sitting on that concrete abutment, Mr.

Kennedy."

"It appears to be the broken neck of a bottle."

Kennedy admitted that none of the photos showed damage or scrape marks on the top of the abutment. So, you agree there is nothing on the abutment indicating the damage you claim it caused to the car?

"The grease and oil generally is not collected on the side rail and is more generally along the drive line of the automobile. I would not expect to see grease or oil deposited on the concrete abutment. There may or may not be rubber marks exhibited. There may be some faint scratch marks. The pinch weld is not a structurally sound element of the car compared to say a frame member or the suspension component, and it can more easily be deformed. The concrete is a much stronger, harder element than that pinch weld. There may be some slight scrape marks but not gouging or severe scratching."

Symmonds spent numerous questions trying to show that Kennedy's theory of damage to the driver's door didn't line up with the damage to the rear door, relying on what he called buckling of the rear door and vertical scrape marks. Kennedy provided no answer to the slight buckling, but his theory fit the vertical marks.

Symmonds asked in what direction would the door fly if the wood plank had torn it off. Generally in a northerly direction. Once separated from the car, the door flew in much the same direction as the car, except as influenced by other objects.

Kennedy said the door tumbled and rolled down the hill and Symmonds jumped on that, suggested that if true, it would indicate other damage. Kennedy said the motion would be very complex, "with yawing, pitching and rolling of the door." He then explained the difference to the jury [the author spares the details].

Symmonds asked about the bottle cap and broken bottle. If it had been sitting on the abutment prior to the car going over the bank, the car would have knocked it off, right? Yes, if it had been sitting there. It could have been put there between the accident and the taking of the photo. Does any evidence exist that it had been placed there after the accident? No.

Symmonds handed Kennedy photos of the door and car lying in their final resting place. Do you see any glass there? No, the pictures don't show it. But if someone testified they saw glass, could there have been glass? Yes. Do you see glass anywhere along the path the door would have taken if it had been ripped off by the beam? No, but "lack of evidence does not indicate that it didn't follow that path. It just means there is no glass along that path."

Symmonds tried to disprove Kennedy's theory about how the left rear wheel and tire had been damaged. Wouldn't the front right tire first hit the depression in the road? Yes, and it would cause a jolt. Then wouldn't it have been damaged? Not necessarily. Then how can you say the left rear wheel would have been damaged when it was now going slower? Because it carried the weight of the vehicle at that point.

Symmonds questioned more about the door. Isn't it true that as it pitched, rolled and yawed its way down the embankment that it would have received damage on the inside of the door? Not necessarily.

"How did the car get from the top of the embankment to the river bed, Mr. Kennedy?"

"After the car went north of the concrete abutment, there is no support for the front end and the front end drops and initiates a pitching and develops an angular rotation. The left front corner of the vehicle dropped, and the vehicle dropped with its left nose down, left front corner of the car hit the ground producing the damage in the photographs and rolled onto its top." This dropping occurred after the door hit the wood beam and the right front wheel went over the abutment.

Symmonds spent several questions defining where certain rock ledges sat and how far from the bridge the car came to rest. He suggested the door went in a northwesterly direction, but Kennedy said no, it was just west of north. To an engineer—or an experienced accident reconstructionist— northwest meant an approximate 45 degree angle from direct north.

Kennedy said he thought the car slid on its left front fender for up to 10 feet before turning over on to its top. It slid less than five feet on its top before it came to rest. Symmonds tried hard to disprove this theory, but Kennedy persisted.

Symmonds asked Kennedy to describe what had happened to Sandy, given his theory that she had been thrown from the car. "Because of her speed and the acceleration that she undergoes from being thrown by the car because of the rolling action of the car, she would act similar to a projectile and travel over the embankment until she contacted the embankment and rolled and tumbled to her final position." Though he had not calculated how far Sandy would have been thrown toward the river, he estimated perhaps 20 to 30 feet.

Kennedy described how rotational forces acted on Sandy's body and without knowing specifically where her body separated from the car, he could not be perfectly sure in which direction she ultimately flew. It could have been near the tree, but he thought not. Rather, he believed she more closely followed the line of the car.

Symmonds tried to trip him up using the debris in the car as a red herring. If Sandy had been separated from the car as Kennedy indicated, wouldn't all the debris in the car have fallen all along a path down the hill? No, it depended on where it was inside the car.   "Mr. Kennedy, one last question. Would articles from inside of that car be found underneath the bridge as a result of this rolling action that you've described?"

"Not in my opinion as a result of this rolling action."

Hecht suggested that a light breeze could have caused the cups to act differently than heavier items. Kennedy readily agreed.

Hecht asked, "Does an automobile engine become hot as it is driven or running?"

"It operates at a higher than atmosphere temperature. Cars operate in the 175 to 195 degree temperature range normally." Kennedy described several parts of a car that get very hot during operation.

"If a hot engine and hood and component parts of a motor vehicle are thrust suddenly into cool running water of a river, will they hiss?"

"The hissing would be noise that would indicate steam was generated. If the parts were hot enough to generate steam, there could be hissing detected."

Hecht continued to reinforce earlier testimony and answer each specific doubt Symmonds had raised. One of those dealt with the speed of 20 miles an hour Kennedy said he drove around the S curve. Hecht asked when he began slowing down? At about 150 feet south of the bridge, at the time he began to see its eastern edge. He slowed to 5 miles an hour to properly align his tires with the planks on the bridge, and he did this in broad daylight, not in the pure dark of a moonless night.

Symmonds showed Kennedy a number of photos of the bottom of the car and asked him to point out the damage to the pinch weld. Kennedy insisted the photos did not show whether or not there had been damage. In fact, some were taken as far as 35 feet away. Hecht asked him if he could have seen a fingernail from 35 feet away, implying that would be the size of the pinch weld. He said no, of course not. Symmonds asked if he didn't see the lines along the edge of the frame as shown in the photo and Kennedy said yes, he saw the lines, but they didn't answer the question about the pinch welds nor the damage to the undercarriage of the car.

Finally Kennedy stepped down. Rulon dismissed the jury for lunch and those 15 stiff bodies rose, stretched, tried to clear their minds and left the courtroom.

So what is one to conclude?

Kennedy provided a very careful, scientific and well-documented case to prove Sandy died in an auto accident. Any juror who stuck closely to his testimony had to have been convinced it was a plausible explanation, far more plausible than the sad and simple testimony of Billy Persinger. Yet, did Kennedy prove Sandy died in an accident?

Four questions remained unanswered. How did she actually get into the river in front of the car? How did type A blood get on the tree under the bridge? How did Sandy's watch end up under the bridge? Did the blood on the bridge above the tree have anything to do with Sandy's death, or did it come from a fisherman who cut himself, or a wild animal hit by a car?

Before we call the Dr.,
what time did you say the death occurred?

Before the jury re-entered the courtroom, Rulon needed to decide whether or not to admit Dr. Butcher's file as evidence. The critical matter involved in this decision dealt with the issue of time of death.

Butcher's report showed that Sandy had died between Midnight and 3:00 a.m. Dr. Gabriel later suggested she most likely died about three hours after her last meal—interpreted as around 10:00 p.m.. He based this on finding a partially digested tomato skin in her stomach.

Time of death became critical because Tom had no evidence to prove his whereabouts between 9:30 p.m. and sometime after midnight. If Sandy died at 10:00 p.m. or so, it looked bad for him. If she died at 3:00 a.m., it was likely that Mark Gibbons heard her car sinking in the river at that time.

Symmonds talked with Butcher about his method of recording of time of death. Though he could not say who provided him with the information upon which that decision had been made, it was deduced from talking with others, not from an examination of the body. That made the entry hearsay. Rulon had been very selective about which hearsay he allowed into Tom's trials and this one he refused. Butcher's reports could be entered, but the reference to time of death had to be expunged.

James Bridgens, M.D.

Dr. Bridgens took the stand to provide his expert opinion of how Sandy died. Like Eckert, he had performed thousands of autopsies as a forensic pathologist and had practiced medicine since 1947. His credentials rivaled those of Eckert's, save that no one had ever created a TV series based on his life.

Perhaps because of his age and comfort while testifying, Bridgens had a tendency to get very wordy in his answers and this caused him to breach a subject that turned against Tom—dry drowning.

To prepare to testify, Bridgens had studied all the autopsy reports and photos taken during both autopsies. He had also traveled to Rocky Ford Bridge.

Based on everything he had seen and studied, Hecht asked him if "the injuries that are there depicted [in autopsy photos] are consistent with the decedent having been ejected from that motor vehicle as it crossed the embankment or concrete abutment on the south side of the Rocky Ford Bridge on the Cottonwood River and as it proceeded to its point of final rest."

Just as they had with Eckert, courtroom spectators and the jurors ear's perked up. Maybe finally someone could tell them how Sandy died.

"Sandra Bird died as the result of massive blunt injuries which caused massive hemorrhage; in other words, the cause of death is blunt injuries. The mechanism of death is massive hemorrhage." For a moment, the crowd sat disappointed again. He continued. "She fell out of the vehicle as it rolled over in its descent down that steep, rough, rugged embankment, struck that rugged terrain, bounced around on those rocks, trees, shrubs and ended up in the river on a—between the vehicle and the bridge."

But her body came to rest on the other side of the car. They needed more information.

"The flow of the current would have moved her body downstream which would have been to the east; and because of the obstruction slightly upstream which produces an eddy pool just beyond where the vehicle terminated its path, the body was deposited there literally to the front of the vehicle in the stream."

He said Sandy's injuries were consistent with those expected by someone thrown from a car onto such a terrain.

Hecht asked about defensive wounds. Bridgens saw none on Sandy. He said defensive wounds happen on the inside of the arms because people point their hands away from the body while covering themselves. He could not accept the explanation that Sandy's wrist could be broken and her outer arms bruised from defensive maneuvers.

What about the broken scapula Dr. Eckert found? Gabriel had missed that. Bridgens said that such an injury is quite uncommon and easily missed during an autopsy. Eckert found it because he was looking very closely for anything different from Gabriel's finding. Almost all the injuries had been to Sandy's left side. Bridgens saw that as consistent with being thrown from the car in the manner he described.

Do you think Sandy could have been thrown or pushed off the bridge? No. "In most instances in individuals that fall from a height frequently because of the weight of their trunk they will tend to injure the upper portion of their body more frequently than, say, the lower portion or one side. It's a little difficult for a body to fall and not end up with head and shoulder-type injuries; and, of course, along with that, frequently if they're really in a vertical position they'll have fractured backs and all that sort of thing; but by and large, the bulk of the injuries are in the upper portion of the torso rather than along a whole side."

If Sandy had been dropped feet first, her ankles would have shown injury. He found none. If she had been thrown over horizontally, there still would have been head injuries. Besides, he asked, how did she get all those bruises?

What about someone beating her? "It would be an exceedingly uncommon circumstance that it would cause these type of injuries…. Most assaults are aimed at the head, not the trunk; and the bulk of the injuries literally are on the trunk, the shoulder, the chest, the kidney. She had some bruising of the head; but in numerous cases of battery or assault where the individual has been beaten with a ball bat or a beer bottle or whatever, there's largely little of anything except injuries to the head and defense wounds."

He said had Sandy been beaten she would have had several lacerations and there would have been evidence of hemorrhaging. He saw none and neither had the others.

Hecht said there were four ways that a person could die: natural causes, suicide, homicide and accidentally. Obviously, Sandy had not died from natural causes. How about suicide?

"Suicide in that you are referring to autocide?" Bridgens began to offer.

Symmonds objected loudly. "I'm going to object as far as the—this witness testifying as to the ultimate question." Rulon sustained him. He forbade Hecht from pursuing this question. That had to be left for the jury to decide.

But Bridgens answer came back to haunt Tom in a 1987 appeal. Tom asserted at that time that Sandy might have committed suicide. He called it new evidence. Symmonds, writing for the state, disagreed and quoted Bridgens' answer in part to explain that Tom could have or should have raised suicide during this trial. In his 1987 decision, Rulon agreed with Symmonds and denied a new trial.

Symmonds steps up

"Dr. Bridgens, you haven't received any training in accident reconstruction, have you?"

"Only related to pathology, forensic pathology in—no, this is part of the field. One must be…"

"Thank you."

"…acquainted with accidents and mechanism of accidents, what happens to bodies in accidents, yes…I wouldn't hold myself out as an expert in accident reconstruction."

Symmonds suggested he had testified as a layman regarding Sandy being thrown from the car. "No, I'm offering it as an expert in forensic pathology. We're talking about the body, not the accident and how this came to pass."

Symmonds challenged his credentials again, suggesting that they were more equal to Dr. Gabriel's than Eckert's. He responded, "No, no, no way."

Symmonds reviewed Bridgens' theory that Sandy had been thrown from the car and tumbled down the bank. He asked him what kinds of injuries a person sustained from being thrown from a car, but Bridgens forced him to give very specific parameters. "All right, let's roll the vehicle over. All right, then we're going to present to the terrain essentially their left side because that's going to be the side that falls out of the vehicle first."

Then how did she get the broken scapula and transected kidney, both of which require a force from behind? From falling on the rocks and such, he said.

Bridgens believed she became unconscious after going into shock but that she remained breathing until the internal bleeding caused her death.

Does hitting a stone cause a laceration or a bruise? "It depends on the size of the surface that's presented to the head. If the surface is relatively large, you'll get an area of bruising....If the surface is relatively confined, you'll get a laceration and associated bruising. If the extent of the injury is such, you may cause some hemorrhage into the brain or onto the surface of the brain itself or into the brain case."

Symmonds pointed to a small laceration on Sandy's head beneath which there had been some internal hemorrhaging. Yes, Bridgens saw it and identified it. Well, didn't a blow to the head cause that laceration and bleeding? No, an injury caused it.

Symmonds asked whether or not Sandy suffered a skull fracture? No, there were none. Aren't skull fractures common in ejection-type injuries? It depends on the terrain. Symmonds kept pressing him on this and he finally agreed it would not be uncommon to find such an injury on a person who had been thrown from a car.

If Sandy had been killed as you suggest, doctor, wouldn't you find bruises all over her body? Well yes, of course, and that's what I saw on her. But doctor, the first autopsy said she had no bruises on the back of her legs nor her back. Bridgens pointed out the bruises he could see on the back of Sandy's legs as shown in the pictures. But he had seen no photos of the back of Sandy's body.

"So on the back you would accept Dr. Gabriel's finding in the evidence in this case that there were no such bruises on her back?"

"I would be curious about it. Just like scapulas, they don't often look at the back."

Symmonds asked about the linear bruises on Sandy's forearms, on the thumb side. "What type of injuries are those consistent with, doctor?"

"Some type of blunt injury to the wrist, to the forearm. I can't tell you what, but striking a small limb on a tree, some such thing as that, something that will produce a linear mark." He admitted they were unusual marks, so unusual he couldn't figure out what caused them, "and so one night I even tried tying my wife up to reproduce them and I couldn't do it."

Rulon had to quiet the court down.

Bridgens insisted that in every frontal assault case he had studied, the palms of the hands pointed outward in an effort to fend off the attack. Even if she had been attacked from the back, the palms would have been outward, and it made no difference if she had been kneeling.

The linear marks on her forearms wrapped around the bone on the thumb side. A stiff stick or club could not have made those marks, Bridgens argued. A pliable thing, like a tree branch could have, but no one would have hit her with a tree branch thin enough to make those marks. Such a branch would have been ineffective.

Symmonds asked about drowning. Gabriel found no water in her lungs, so he concluded the cause of death could not have been drowning, don't you agree? "Not necessarily. There are two types of drowning. There's wet drowning and dry drowning, and some people—we're talking about people that have drowned in swimming pools and the death has occurred there and there's no question about it, and in the autopsy they don't have water in their lungs. This is known as a dry drowning...I can't explain it but it happens."

(At least one juror hung onto this answer. Having had EMT training, Bruce Webb believed the idea of dry drowning was preposterous. He said he knew better. This answer caused him to doubt the balance of Bridgens' testimony. While it was unfortunate for Tom that the doctor got into this, several years later Tom uncovered a learned treatise on dry drowning. They do happen. The doctor had been right.)

Bridgens said that he could not discount the possibility that Sandy died from dry drowning. Symmonds attacked him on this. Earlier Bridgens had testified conclusively that Sandy died from blunt trauma that caused her to bleed to death. Furthermore, he said her tumbling down the rocks had caused the blunt trauma. Now he claimed it could have been dry drowning.

Symmonds asked whether or not a body hitting a tree as it fell would change the direction of the fall? Yes, if it were big and strong enough. And if someone fell, say 20 feet and hit the tree on their side, that would produce enough force to cause severe injury and even fracture their ribs? It could.

Bridgens agreed that digestion stops at the time of death.

Symmonds pressed Bridgens on other inconsistencies with his theory.

Why didn't Sandy have lacerations on her knees and elbows if she tumbled to her death? Because it depended on how she tumbled and what she hit. But wouldn't her dress have been torn? Maybe, maybe not.

Hecht tries to counter

Bridgens gave an honest, scientific answer about how dry drowning could occur. Hecht carefully walked him through this, but it drew attention to the issue. Hecht nor Bridgens ever meant to suggest that Sandy died by drowning, but once the words came out, Symmonds jumped on them. It sullied Bridgens' testimony.

Hecht called Louise Hinrichs. She had served as the church organist at Messiah and knew Sandy quite well. She knew Tom, too, and had from the time they came to Emporia.

Louise sat in the Hornet's Nest, a coffee shop at ESU, one day in the later part of June, 1983. Sandy sat a few tables away. Seeing Louise, Sandy came over and sat down. They talked about their projects and about being "working mothers and all the adjustments you have to make, all the stresses and strains that go with that and so on."

"What if anything did she tell you in that regard?"

"Well, she said that she was maybe having an adjustment problem getting it all put together. She was working very hard. And I told her I could appreciate that because I had obtained a masters degree when my daughter was about there years old; and I said, 'It takes a lot of cooperation, a lot of work'; but I told her not to be too hard on herself."

"And what if anything did she say in response?"

"She did say that she wasn't feeling well and she couldn't eat very well and maybe she was being too hard on herself. And I told her maybe she should go to a doctor. She said maybe that would be a good idea."

"And what if anything else did you say and what if anything else did she say?"

"I said that a working mother always has to put away a little time for herself; and I said, 'Do you have anything you do to relax'…She replied that she went for drives."

Louise told her to be careful when she drove. Sandy answered that she always knew where she was going.

Sandy told her about the upcoming trip to St. Louis and the chance to relax and be with Tom. She looked forward to the trip.

Symmonds had no questions and Louise stepped down.

Hecht planned to rest his defense, but wanted time overnight to review everything. Symmonds didn't plan to call any rebuttal witnesses, but also wanted time to review his notes. Rulon recessed the court until the following morning.

Cleaning up loose ends

Before court resumed the next morning, Hecht, Symmonds and Tom met with the judge to go over the admission of evidence. Hecht went first. Symmonds objected to the admission of the various manuals dealing with warning signs and lights because much of the material was irrelevant to this case. Hecht agreed to photocopy the relevant parts.

Symmonds objected to admission of the pamphlet dealing with headlamps, but Rulon admitted it.

Symmonds had no exhibits to admit, but wanted to withdraw two. One was the empty apple juice bottle found in Sandy's car. The other was an empty brown paper bag. The evidence it had been admitted without it, "so it would appear to be a waste of everybody's time to send to the jury an empty brown paper sack." Hecht and the judge agreed.

Symmonds tried again to allow Agent Humphrey to testify about his push test. This time Symmonds argued from case law and said the purpose of allowing this testimony was simply to demonstrate that it could be done; one person could push a car down that road fast enough to shove it over the embankment. Symmonds said he had no plans to offer an opinion based on the test, but he felt the jury would benefit from knowing about it.

Hecht showed that Symmonds arguments failed miserably. First, the cases he cited were civil, not criminal cases. Secondly, in one of the cases the judge refused to allow the test. Thirdly, in those cases the court required that a trained expert perform the tests. Lastly, the only purpose for allowing such a test would be to render an opinion based on its results.

Furthermore, Hecht showed that during the trial there had been no testimony that the car had, in fact, been pushed "either by hand or by another automobile." (Symmonds would later, during his closing arguments, claim that Trooper Rule had testified as such.)

Rulon said he would not allow this testimony from Agent Humphrey.

Rulon ordered the jury to be brought into the courtroom and be seated. Hecht rested his case. Symmonds said he had no rebuttal witnesses.

Rulon told the jury that he and the attorneys had to finish up some business that afternoon to prepare to give them the case on Monday. He told them to go home, keep their mouths and ears shut about the case, and, of course, be sure not to expose themselves to any news about the trial. Tom knew this would be hard for them and had strongly hoped Rulon would have sequestered the jury, but he didn't.

After the jury left, Rulon and the attorneys reviewed all the instructions the judge would read to the jury before sending them out to deliberate. Hecht had a concern about an instruction dealing with the state's requirement to prove the crime beyond reasonable doubt. Rulon took it under advisement. Hecht had very little control over choosing the instructions, though he had written language of his own. Rulon rejected his language and chose instead to use a more standard language generally accepted by the courts. Finally, the parties agreed on the instructions.

Then Hecht moved either for a mistrial or at least to strike all of Charles Henderson's testimony. Henderson had testified that Tom had his wife killed. He had offered no testimony that Tom killed his wife. Henderson testified to a crime of either conspiracy to commit murder or solicitation, but not murder.

Symmonds argued against either option—mistrial or striking Henderson's testimony. He said that the defense did not make any contemporaneous objection to the testimony during the trial.

Hecht argued that the contemporaneous objection rule applied to objections made before trial, not during trial. Either declare a mistrial or throw Henderson's testimony out, Hecht said.

Rulon took it under advisement.

Hecht again moved to dismiss the charges because the state had not proven a homicide had been committed to the exclusion of all other possibilities. Rulon denied the motion.

Rulon reviewed the portion of the highway road sign manuals that Hecht wanted admitted into evidence. He said they were too complicated and would confuse the jury. He would not admit them.

All that remained, Rulon said, was deciding on the Henderson issue. He'd give them an answer on Monday morning. "So we'll see you all on Monday."

Before closing arguments, let's deal with the snitch

Rulon met with Hecht, Symmonds and Tom in chambers early Monday morning July 22, 1983. One more major issue needed to be settled. Should Jude Rulon declare a mistrial or should he expunge Charles Henderson's testimony?

Rulon had spent a good part of the weekend reviewing applicable cases. He had laid out a 15-point argument that Henderson's testimony could stand on its own merits. He said that Hecht had heard Henderson's testimony as he gave it and failed to object at that time. He also failed to object before the trial, and he had been given adequate time to review all the investigative reports. Hecht should have made his objection before trial began. But given the nature of the testimony, Rulon decided to add one more instruction to those that he would present to the jury in a few minutes.

"That proposed instruction reads as follows: 'A person who either before or during its commission intentionally aids, abets, advises, hires, counsels or procures another to commit a crime with the intent to promote or assist in its commission is criminally responsible for the crime committed regardless of the extent of the defendant's participation if any in the actual commission of the crime."

Hecht became incensed. First, it constituted Rulon interjecting himself "into the trial of the case in the roll of advocate rather than as trial judge because this is not an instruction that has been requested by either of the parties and it's after the instructions have been settled upon Friday of last week."

Henderson never testified that Tom aided, abetted, advised, hired, counseled or procured anyone to commit a crime. The jury didn't indict Tom for aiding, abetting, advising, hiring, counseling or procuring someone to commit a crime. Hecht read the indictment to the judge. He read the Bill of Particulars to the judge. Neither of them said anything about aiding, abetting, advising, hiring, counseling or procuring someone to commit a crime. It seemed outrageous to Hecht that Rulon would now come with such a suggestion.

Because the indictment failed so miserably to tell Tom what he had done to murder Sandy, the defense already had one arm tied behind its back. Then, in opening statements, Symmonds said that Tom threw Sandy off the bridge, the first time the defense had heard the state's theory. The indictment said nothing about being thrown off a bridge. With this new prejudicial instruction, Rulon now wanted to tie up Tom's other arm.

Symmonds argued that Darrel Carter testified that Tom did conspire with Lorna to hire someone to murder Marty, so Henderson's testimony should stand. Furthermore, Henderson claimed Tom told him he had had his wife killed. Besides, since Hecht failed to object at the time, he cannot do so now.

Hecht showed Rulon he erred saying the objection had to occur before trial, and he cited a number of cases. In a long and emotional argument, Hecht showed that the objection had to be made prior to closing arguments, and he had complied. He restated how the state had utterly failed to properly present its indictment and now attempted to try Tom for a different crime. As he ran out of energy and argument, he said, "To come along at the close of all of the evidence and then to instruct on a theory that the grand jury obviously didn't return an indictment on, that being that the defendant procured another to commit this crime, would be an error."

Tom sat quietly listening to this argument, just as he had done during the entire 22 preceding days of voir dire, testimony and arguments. But this argument pushed him over the edge. "Your Honor, the defense would have been..." he started to say, but Rulon cut him off.

Symmonds, too, got caught up in the emotion and cut off the judge. "Your Honor, could I suggest that perhaps..."

Rulon cut *him* off. Though the record fails to show it, all of them may have taken a deep breath before proceeding. Rulon then explained that he conducted this exercise to present the various options. He refused to declare a mistrial. He refused to expunge Henderson's testimony. He agreed not to read the inflammatory instruction.

Furthermore, he ruled that during closing arguments, Hecht could not refer to Henderson's *four* convictions and the lies he had told during testimony when Henderson stated he had only two prior convictions. The other two, Rulon said, were not for crimes of dishonesty and the law was very clear about impeaching a witness's testimony. Reference could only be made to crimes of dishonesty.

The attorneys had two hours for closing arguments. Symmonds would go first, take an hour and sit down. Hecht would do his entire two hours. Then Symmonds would take his last hour. In between, Rulon would allow the jury to stand and stretch. They then headed into court.

Tom felt helpless and held little hope for acquittal.

Symmonds steps up

(The author has summarized the closing arguments for the reader. The entire transcript of the closing arguments can be found on the internet at http://www.cagedbird.net/excerpts.htm.)

Symmonds referenced Darrel's testimony about a meeting in "May of 1983" where Tom and Lorna tried to hire him to murder Marty. "He testified that there were two plans outlined to him pertaining to how to do away with Marty Anderson. The first involved a location south of town where there is a sharp bend in the road, a person could just drive off that roadway, plunge down an embankment 50 feet to the river and that it would look like an accident." Since Sandy died at Rocky Ford Bridge, it seems this had been the scheme used to murder Sandy.

All the experts testified they saw no disturbance of the gravel on the road south of the bridge.

Persinger and Kennedy differed on their opinion of what happened at the bridge, but the dip in the road just before the concrete abutment was too great for the wreck to have happened as Kennedy suggested. Besides, there was a bottle cap and a broken bottle on the top of the abutment. They wouldn't have been there if the car scraped over the abutment as Kennedy insisted. And where were the scrape marks on the abutment? There were none, just a small chip at the northeast corner.

The idea that the car hit the wood plank seemed impossible. A tiny little piece of broken wood was the damage Kennedy pointed to—not enough to tear a door off. He pointed to pictures of the driver's door and the damage to the rear door, claiming Kennedy had been wrong. The door could not have been torn off as he said. It had to come off later, as Persinger claimed. If Kennedy had been right, where's the glass that should have been strewn all over? Investigators found glass only in the vicinity of the door itself, lying face down on the beach seven feet from the car.

John Rule testified that a car could have been hand-pushed by one person down the road fast enough to go over the edge.

Symmonds described the Kennedy-Bridgens' theory that Sandy "separated" from the car as it went over the embankment and flew 20-30 feet. Then they said she tumbled down into the water. He used his own calculations to argue against that theory. No, Sandy would have to have flown at least 40-45 feet. Didn't happen, he said. And it doesn't explain how the blood got on the tree, five feet up on the trunk.

He reviewed Persinger's testimony of how the car turned, half-rolled and came to rest. Trooper Rule had the same opinion. Neither believed the car slid five feet as Kennedy asserted. If that had happened, why isn't there any scrape marks on the roof of the car?

He reviewed the location of blood and what appeared to be blood. On the bridge railing they found blood; on the cross member, human blood. On the tree, human blood, typed A, the same as Sandy's. Blood on the bridge deck, at least one spot, lined up with the railing and bridge cross member above the tree. They found blood on the rocks, some of which had been human blood, and in one case, it ran down the side of a rock indicating a large amount had dropped there. And the blood on the tree and rocks had been fresh.

He said Dr. Eckert found that the linear marks on Sandy's wrists came from "being struck by some kind of a blunt object. "You heard him testify concerning the head injuries being caused by a similar object. In this particular case the state would suggest that those injuries were caused on the bridge, and the state would further suggest that this smear on the tree directly below was caused by a body that was falling, one that came from the bridge going to the ground as shown by the blood.

"When you look at the injuries that she received, they were on her left side; and yet you've heard the testimony of the doctor who indicated that certainly a tree could deflect a person. If they were going in one manner, that tree could change the position that they hit in."

Even Bridgens said that a broken scapula was very uncommon. Evidence showed force had been applied to the back and the scapula.

He returned to Trooper Rule who found blood on the rocks. It led from the door up the bank to the tree. Rule knew what blood looked like and this made him suspicious. "On this particular case the state would suggest that the evidence has shown by the blood that the body was then taken from its location below the bridge over to the car door and then ultimately it was moved towards the river. You've got the two rocks down there close to the river that had blood droplets on them that were picked up, collected and did have blood."

Trooper Rule claimed he saw some kind of tissue on another rock outside the path of the bloodstains. He thought it might be skin and hair, but he failed to pick it up. The next day it was gone. Symmonds said this reinforced the idea that someone carried Sandy, wandering in a crooked path toward the car, and placed her in the water. It explains how Sandy's shoe ended up where it did, near the car—it had to have fallen off while the defendant carried the body toward the river.

No one talked about drowning until Bridgens brought it up. Gabriel specifically checked for water or debris in the lungs and found none. He sarcastically described Bridgens' theory and added, "Good heavens, folks!"

Eckert said Sandy had been rendered unconscious by a blow to the head, "and we feel that that is what happened on that bridge."

The watch lay directly under the bridge, beneath a gap in the planks, planks that had blood on them.

He reviewed Amy Swint's testimony, emphasizing that someone had been in the car with Sandy when they stopped home at 9:30 p.m. Tom told everyone that he was the one in the car. "She left with the defendant and she never came back. Just that simple."

Swint said, "that when Tom Bird came home that night, he had on a suit, a tie, a pair of slacks and shoes." Is that the kind of outfit that you would really expect somebody to go jogging in?" Tom claimed he jogged sometime between 11:15 and 11:45 p.m. Others said that Tom often came to meetings in jogging clothes, Symmonds claimed, and it seemed illogical for him to jog and then change into a suit, unless he had something to conceal. (There had been absolutely no testimony about Tom going to meetings in jogging suits in this trial.)

Swint said Tom called between 1:30 and 2:00, and came home a half-hour later—maybe 2:30. Why didn't Tom call Amy first? Why did he drive all over town and call the police first? And if Sandy found herself running late, why didn't she call home as she had on previous occasions?

"In this particular case the testimony has shown that Tom Bird and Lorna Anderson were involved in a romantic relationship. You've heard the testimony of Jan Mead about that the defendant is pretty good in bed for a minister, about the little trips to Wichita and Topeka, statements of Lorna Anderson that she and Tom Bird were in love, that they wanted to spend their lives together and they wished that something terrible would happen to Sandy and Marty Anderson."

"You've also heard the testimony of Angie Duensing. You've heard from Jane and Jerry Grismer. You've heard from Louise Hinrichs." Symmonds reviewed the "marital problems that they were having."

Sandy talked to others about the problem and her concerns always were about Lorna. Henderson said Tom told him he conspired with Lorna to have his wife killed. Darrel said the same thing.

"The events of that night have been described by Tom Bird to various people. You have heard those discrepancies…and there aren't just variances in time." Symmonds listed a number of items claimed by various members of the Grismer family.

Then Tom drove the Grismer's out to the bridge the following Sunday, though he said he had never been there before. He pointed out a house, and yes, there was confusion about which house he actually pointed out. But Tom said he'd never been there. How could he point out any house?

Everyone who testified said that during the phone calls, Tom was courteous, though nervous, until after 3:30. Then he seemed calm. "As the hours passed rather than becoming more nervous, he was becoming less nervous."

Deana Koch testified that Sandy worked late, but never past midnight. And she found no evidence on Sandy's desk the next day that she had been there the night before. But why, Symmonds asked, would a mother of three be out there driving around at 3:00 a.m.?

Symmonds said the evidence from the lights suggested the headlights had been off. Nevitt never saw them at 2:00 a.m. Glaze glanced at the river saw nothing at 3:30 a.m.

That ended the first half of his closing arguments.

Defense, argue your case

Rulon told the jury to go get a cup of coffee in the jury room. When they returned, Hecht began.

"This lawsuit in my opinion is about loss, the worst loss you can think of. Mrs. Grismer lost a daughter. It's a void in her life that can never be filled, a loss she'll live with forever.

"Ralph Bird, Mrs. Bird, lost a daughter-in-law, a son and their faith in the Biblical scripture that the Lord will impose no burden upon you that you cannot bear lest ye be sorely tested.

"Tom Bird lost a wife. He has three children who lost a mother.

"If you have never had an occasion to tell a child that they've lost a mother, you cannot possibly know the pain and the gut-wrenching emotions that Thomas Bird suffered on July the 17th and the 18th and the 19th, that period of time during which he was asked to describe with chronological order and time specification what took place during that period, a request that no human being could fulfill with total accuracy.

"And we don't suggest that Thomas Bird fulfilled those requests in total accuracy. We suggest to you that he responded to questions at a time in which he was suffering the most grievous suffering that you can have, the loss of your babies' mother."

Hecht read the indictment and Bill of Particulars to the jury. He reminded them that the state had to prove "beyond a reasonable doubt four things: that the defendant, Thomas P. Bird, intentionally killed Sandra Bird and that such killing was done maliciously, that it was done deliberately and with premeditation and that it occurred on or about the 16th day of July, 1983, in Lyon County, Kansas."

No one testified that Tom threw Sandy off the bridge, though Symmonds said in his opening remarks that he would do so. "Not one single witness testified that Thomas Bird was even near the Rocky Ford Bridge on July the 16th-July the 17th, 1983." No expert said Sandy's injuries were of the type sustained from being thrown off the bridge. No expert testified that Sandy had not remained in the car when it hit either the wood plank or concrete abutment.

"And for the state to be successful in a circumstantial evidence case it must establish beyond a reasonable doubt the circumstances establish the question of guilt and exclude the question of innocence. If the question of innocence is not excluded, then you have reasonable doubt and the circumstantial evidence is not sufficient....Sheriff Andrews testified before you that this is a case full of inconsistencies."

Hecht reviewed the numerous inconsistencies and errors in testimony, both by common folk who got caught up in the case, and by experts, many of whom testified incorrectly while holding notes and reports in their hands.

He reminded them of Mark Gibbons' testimony. He heard his dogs bark. He heard a hissing sound at 3:15 a.m. or so. He never heard such a sound before nor since. Hecht said the sound resembled a hot engine and a hot hood "in cold water." Emporia Police Officer Mark Summey met with Tom at 3:22

571

in the yard in front of the Henry Street house. Tom physically couldn't have been present at the bridge at the same time.

Gibbons had described seeing a tree about three feet from the concrete abutment. The tree limbs were damaged. Trooper Rule testified about a tree, too, he said had blood on it. Rule and Gibbons disagreed on the location of that tree. Rule said it sat farther north, but the picture Hecht showed the jury showed it where Gibbons' spotted it. It could not have been directly below the blood on the railing and the bridge. Hecht reached for a photo Rule had marked. The red "X" showed where Rule said the bloody tree sat. Hecht showed it to be no more than about a foot from the bridge abutment; it could not possibly be underneath the blood measured 35 feet from the south end of the bridge.

Yes, Nevitt and Glaze testified about driving across the bridge. Nevitt, who drove it every day, said that five miles an hour was a safe speed. Besides these two—Glaze twice—several other vehicles drove across the bridge. If the blood on the bridge deck had been Sandy's, no matter what time the state says the murder occurred, several vehicles would have driven over the blood spot. Yet, there was not one single tire track imprinted in that blood. And experts said that blood spots could be evident for as much as three months, depending on heat and moisture. That blood, if it was blood, was old blood.

As for Glaze and Nevitt not seeing the headlights, Hecht said the state never proved Sandy's car had entered the water prior to Nevitt's 2 a.m. drive. That proved nothing. Glaze testified as concentrating on her own headlights because of the eerie darkness that night. Besides, the evidence showed the car was tilted downward, its headlights pointed away from the bridge. In daylight, several witnesses said they could not even see the car from the bridge as they walked across it.

So, will the state now say Sandy's car went in the river after 3:30 a.m., following Glaze's trip across the bridge? No. Instead they rely on Persinger's unprofessional and highly disputed opinion. Mr. Dirks showed that no conclusion could be drawn from the headlights.

The prosecutor brought Dennis Arb to the stand, and Arb testified he felt sure the headlights had been on. He witnessed someone, though not sure who, turned them off. "Did the state call a witness that's not going to testify truthfully?"

Arb saw a crushed red plastic cup south of the bridge. The investigators all testified to seeing a cup in the same location, but all said it had not been crushed. But the cup shown from the evidence bag at trial had been crushed.

Hecht said the state now claimed Tom beat Sandy, threw her off the bridge and then climbed down to the rocky shore below, moving her body to the water. "Now, think how crazy that would be, in the middle of the night to commit a homicide by throwing somebody off of a bridge and then climbing down a 65-foot embankment covered with rocks, shrubs and little trees. You got to have more sense than to do that if you're going to commit a homicide by throwing her off the bridge. If you're going to throw her off the bridge, why do you have to move her?"

When Trooper Smith informed Tom that Sandy's body had been found in the river, he said Tom's reactions were what he expected. "And he was experienced at telling people that."

Tom told Smith that Sandy often drove in the country to relax. Louise Hinrichs testified to this as well, having talked to Sandy about it just days before her death.

David Cox testified that he saw that the car's ignition was off while looking at the switch on the right side of the steering column. He said it sat in the 11:00 o'clock position. But the ignition is located on the left side of the steering column on Peugeots. And the photo showed that the key sat in the 1:00 o'clock position, meaning the ignition was turned to "on," not "off."

And if Tom carried her body to the water, where were all the footprints? The only footprint found had belonged to an unknown female.

Hecht addressed the bottle cap and broken bottle that sat on the bridge abutment. He showed one set of pictures with it in view and another set without it. Clearly, he said, it had not been there at the time of the accident, but was placed there later.

He used Jim Crahan's photos to show the dangerous approach to the bridge, especially at night.

An hour had passed. Rulon interrupted him and gave the jury a short recess.

Hecht headed toward his close

"I haven't been asked and you haven't been asked in your lifetime to make any more important decision than you're going to make in this case," Hecht told the jury after resuming his closing arguments.

Hecht punctuated his closing arguments with several references to inconsistencies and admitted errors in testimony made by uniformed and trained officers. If they can do so, given their training and experience, so could the grieving husband and father, Tom Bird.

"And notwithstanding that [his fatigue] he knew he had told three different law enforcement agencies that they were at the church and that she went to the school. You can't accuse and charge Thomas Bird for such a stupid inconsistency as evidence of concealment under the circumstances that the sister-in-law said that that statement was made. And who knows what *her* emotional state was at the time she was talking to Thomas Bird."

Hecht asked that though the state contends Tom pushed his wife's car over the bank, they had not shown how he got back to church. If they say he ran, why didn't anyone see him?

Hecht said Symmonds had presented his case in three sections. "Section number one was the morning of July the 17th at the Rocky Ford Bridge. Section number two was the slander of Thomas Bird, and section number three was the laboratory testimony and expert witnesses." He addressed the expert witnesses.

Eileen Burnau testified about seven blood samples. "The state in opening statements told you they were going to prove there was human type A blood on the bridge...Not a single witness including Eileen Burnau testified as to the type of blood on the bridge. It could not be typed." The state had said there had been blood on the metal railing, but Burnau said she couldn't identify it as blood. Yes, she identified blood on the bridge, but both she and Dirks testified that blood can be verifiable up to three months. This is a location where people fish, hunt and party regularly.

The only blood they could type was on the tree and on Sandy's dress. Sandy's dress had been soaked in water for hours.

As for Persinger, he never measured a thing at the bridge, though he tried to testify as to a measurement, then mentioned he got it wrong. He never inspected the car, though he claimed that doing so met proper standards. Trooper Rule inspected the car on September 9, 1984. Persinger could have done the same. Hecht then carefully laid out his arguments to rebut Persinger's reconstruction of the wreck.

How did Tom allegedly push the car? Did he set the car in neutral and push from behind? How did it keep going in a straight line? Did he get alongside and steer it by holding open the driver's door? How did he keep from getting his legs cut off? Did he reach through the window and steer the car at 15 miles an hour, running as fast as he could? How did he avoid smashing into the concrete abutment? And if he did smash into the abutment, how could he have run eight miles home?

The door glass was auto safety glass that does not shatter, and the window had been down. Most of the glass stayed inside the door.

Hecht pointed at the scraping marks on the bottom of the car, and the folded over metal at the pinch weld on the left side. This proved the car ran over the abutment.

One fact about which everyone agreed; Sandy Bird bled to death. Look at Dr. Gabriel's marked up diagram. All the bruises, breaks and lacerations for the most part are on her left side. If you had been thrown from the driver's side of a car—the left side—your injuries would be to your left side.

The rapid progression of the onset of shock combined with unconsciousness would keep her from inhaling and exhaling. This explains the lack of water or foreign matter in her lungs.

As for the second autopsy, what did Eckert find? Everything Gabriel found plus a broken scapula. Nothing more. And Eckert never said Sandy died from being thrown off a bridge. "Now, Mr. Symmonds told you in opening statement that he was going to prove that Sandra Bird was killed by Thomas Bird by being thrown off the bridge, and I waited for three weeks for a witness to tell us that in their opinion Sandra Bird was thrown off the bridge, and no one told you that." Eckert did say he'd seen injuries like Sandy's in persons who had fallen off of five-foot tall ladders.

Eckert testified that Sandy received linear bruises as a result of defensive injuries. Eckert said that defensive injuries result in lacerations and fractures, but Sandy had none. She had no injuries to her hands which, if her injuries had been defensive, is improbable.

The state must prove how Sandy died, and they failed to do so.

Dr. Bridgens testified that Sandy's injuries were consistent with being thrown from a car. "He can't tell you that he knows as fact that that's what happened. Dr. Eckert can't tell you and doesn't tell you that he knows for a fact that it happened differently. They're both rendering their expert opinions." And Bridgens is a prosecutor's forensic pathologist. Most often, he testifies on behalf of the state in trials such as this.

Bridgens said that if Sandy had been thrown off a bridge, her upper body would have fallen first, causing "major injuries to the head, skull fracture, neck fracture, back and shoulder injuries. Weren't any." If she had been dropped feet first, "you would expect major injuries to the feet and ankles. No injuries at all there."

Hecht returned to testimony about the car wreck. Kennedy proved the door couldn't have been open when it impacted, no matter what it hit. Persinger changed his testimony about the door latch from what he said during the grand jury. Here he tried to say be meant doorpost, not door latch. "An accident reconstruction expert can't make those kinds of mistakes." Kennedy proved the door had been closed at impact.

"The state's witnesses just simply do not prove that Sandra Bird was beaten to death, and that she was thrown off a bridge. There is no evidence that Thomas Bird was in the vicinity of the Rocky Ford Bridge on July the 16th or July the17th."

Everyone who knew Tom and Sandy said she never ever criticized Tom. Rather, they said she felt depressed and had been sick, and that there had been tension in the marriage. "If there's any among you that's been married for five years or more that haven't been depressed and haven't told your spouse words to the effect, 'Don't push me,' you're most unusual." No one testified that Tom beat or threatened Sandy. No one said he drank too much or threatened a separation or divorce.

Hecht addressed the apparent discrepancies in time between Tom's recollection of events and those of Amy Swint. He showed that even using the state's timetable, backing up from 2:15 a.m., the time she may have arrived at home, you arrive at 1:15 as the time Tom called the police, and police records verify those times. Amy might have been off 15 minutes in her testimony; not a serious discrepancy.

Many witnesses testified that Tom and Sandy had gotten along well during the spring and early summer of 1983. Even Angie said Tom drove to Winfield, Kansas, looking for teaching positions for them both. "Why would a man go to a college in Winfield to look for a new job for his wife and himself if he was not intending that they remain together?"

"Follow the court's instructions, look at the evidence. Don't convict this man because the state scandalizes him. Make them show you, in the evidence where there is proof that Sandra Bird was thrown off the bridge. Make them show you in the evidence that she was beaten to death. Make them show you that Thomas Bird did it. Without that, you've got to have a reasonable doubt. You can't convict this man of murder on the state of the record in this case. Send him back to his kids."

Rulon called a recess so the jurors could snack on coffee and donuts, stretch their legs and prepare for Symmonds' final closing argument.

Symmonds sums sup

He told the jury that the bottle cap and broken bottle actually appeared in all three photos. This implied it had been there during the wreck and served as proof Sandy's car didn't go over the abutment.

Gibbons couldn't have heard a hissing sound coming from the car. Gibbons first thought about that later in the day, after Sandy's body had been found. The state never said Sandy cried out or screamed and since the exhaust pointed up away from the water and, he asserted, the engine never touched the water, the hissing sound had to come from somewhere else.

Gabriel had estimated time of death as three hours after eating. He based this on the fact he only found a tomato skin in Sandy's stomach. All other foodstuff had passed through the system. Why didn't Sandy have a higher blood alcohol level at the time of her death if they had been drinking at The Station?

As for blood, even on Sandy's clothes the only blood that could be typed had been on her dress. But Burnau typed "A" blood on the tree, and some human blood on the bridge above it. Some of the rest she typed as blood. Wasn't it interesting that it all lined up over the tree? Four people testified seeing the blood on the tree leaves as they looked down from above. And the blood changed appearance from Sunday to Monday, showing it had not been out there a long time. Then there's the blood going to the car door and the trail of blood up to the bridge.

Symmonds suggested that the taillights, parking lights and side marker lights had been on, implying that they provided enough light for Tom to climb down to the rocky river bank.

Yes, it's true that Eckert didn't testify that Sandy fell from the bridge. And it's true that she could have sustained serious injuries falling from five feet, but he also said the same about 21 feet six inches.

Hecht had referred to the state's evidence as slanderous. Symmonds said to go look at the telephone records between Tom and Lorna, running into thousands of dollars of long distance costs. Look at the letters found in Lorna's lingerie drawer.

Bridgens testified that she rolled and tumbled down the hill, but he had no idea if there were bruises on her back. There should have been. The second autopsy showed the broken scapula, and both doctors agreed that to be a very uncommon injury.

Eckert said that ejection injuries caused major bodily damage, far worse than he saw on Sandy's body.

He said the tree that Mark Gibbons described and the one that Trooper Rule and the others described were two different trees. One had to look very carefully at the photos and keep in mind various angles as they looked, but for sure, they were talking about different trees.

He couldn't explain the discrepancy over the crushed cup, but Humphrey said the cup had a "pinkish fluid" in the bottom. And Tom said he and Sandy had drunk wine. And Humphrey found the cold duck bottle. The cup lay south of the bridge, suggesting someone sat there sipping it. (Was he suggesting that Tom and Sandy sat there drinking before he took her out on the bridge and beat her to death? If so, why didn't the alcohol show up in her blood?)

Neither accident reconstructionist could explain how the body got into the water. Persinger said it should have been between the door and the car. Kennedy said it tumbled down the hill in the general direction the car had traveled. (Could Sandy have been aware enough to crawl toward the headlights and then collapse into the water?)

He questioned the idea that Sandy, having had a few drinks and finished working at the school, would go for a drive in such a remote area.

He reminded the jury that Tom told Deana Koch at 6:30 a.m. on July 17,

"I'm sorry you never got to talk to her. Then in the afternoon when he's visiting with Mr. Carlson he says something to the effect that he has ruined everything for her."

Tom claimed he had been jogging between 11:15 and 11:45. Why? Because it got him out of the church in case someone called him, "and yet he comes home and he's all cleaned up. And if he did some running on that night, he would have had good reason to have been all cleaned up when he got home, to have come in with a shirt and a tie and a pair of slacks because those jogging clothes would have been dirty, those jogging clothes if he wore those out there on that particular evening would have had blood." (Symmonds spoke totally out of order here. There had been no evidence of bloody jogging clothes, nor had he said any such thing in his opening statement.)

Saying he drove to the college explained why no car had been seen in the church parking lot for a period of time.

Symmonds suggested that the correct order of events for the evening of July 16 was that once the movie ended, Tom and Sandy went to The Station, had a drink, and headed home. There they collected the wine and bourbon bottles and went to the bridge for their last drink together.

He agreed that the state had to prove the four things Hecht mentioned. But the state did not have to prove how Tom got back to the church. Darrel Carter's testimony talked of the bridge. Other testimony indicated that Tom had been in good shape and could have run races in excess of six miles.

He pointed to photos of the undercarriage that showed no damage to the pinch welds. "Maybe those photos are too far away to be accurate and for you to be able of making a complete determination." But there was no bending of the pinch weld, if you look closely. Otherwise you would see rust in the later photos.

Rulon interrupted Symmonds. He allowed the jury to stand and stretch again.

Symmonds continued.

The injuries to Sandy's body depended on where and how she had been dropped off the bridge. She could have been dropped again on the rocks as Tom carried her to the water.

He addressed the marital problems. Yes, everyone has marital problems but these stretched on from March into June. "We're talking about a woman that had lost a considerable amount of weight. We're talking about a woman who was having trouble eating, and these are evidence of marital discord and the fact that these two people were not getting along in that particular time. In fact, the evidence has shown that the defendant was involved in an affair with Lorna Anderson through this period of time."

He reminded them again of Darrel's testimony.

Mead said Lorna worried about one of her daughters having seen Tom kiss her and Lori testified she saw them kissing.

"Ladies and gentlemen, there are certain things that the judge says the state of Kansas has to prove, and from the evidence presented it appears that those things have been proven.

"But in this particular case as the judge has instructed you, don't decide this case on sympathy for or against either side because you can be assured of one thing and that is Sandra Bird is dead, but from her grave justice cries out for conviction.

"Do not be timid at heart and don't let your fears dissuade you from doing what you think is right. The state would respectfully request that you find the defendant guilty of murder in the first degree."

Rulon sent the jurors to the jury room for lunch. He told them they could not discuss the case.

Later that afternoon, Rulon offered to let the jury go home for the evening, ordering them to return the next morning. Of course, he told them not read the news or talk about the case with anyone.

The verdict

After returning from a night at home, unsequestered, the jury resumed its deliberations. Late in the morning they arrived at a verdict.

"Mr. Barger, I believe you are the presiding juror. Is that correct?"

"Yes, Your Honor."

"Has the jury reached a verdict?"

"Yes, sir, we have."

"Is the verdict unanimous?"

"Yes, it is."

Alice Thornton retrieved the verdict form and read, "The State of Kansas versus Thomas P. Bird. We, the jury in the above entitled case, do find the defendant guilty."

Tom began to hyperventilate. The unimaginable had happened to him. A jury had found him guilty of the murder of Sandy Bird.

Judge Rulon set sentencing for August 6.

Tom turned to talk to his parents who, like him, sat stunned. Rick Fenheim, the guard assigned to Tom, suggested the Birds come to the jail around 1:30 p.m. They could talk in private. Virginia wrote, "Tom expressed his feelings saying, we know the truth, we know what's going on. We shouldn't worry about him. We should keep ourselves healthy and be concerned primarily with the children and be assured that Sandy was not crying out of the grave for justice," as Symmonds had said in his closing arguments.

The Birds returned to the jail at 1:30, but guards had already removed Tom to Lansing.

Another motion denied

Diana Spires, a young woman who worked as a clerk at the Copa Villa Motel, came to court on August 6, the day of sentencing. A few days after the trial had been completed, she realized that Charles Henderson had stayed at the Copa Villa and she talked with him about the case. She told Judge Rulon that Charles Henderson lied to the court. Hecht wanted Rulon to declare a mistrial.

Spires said the same morning Henderson testified against Tom, "He said he heard a lot about the Thomas Bird case. He said that he had heard a lot about it and he had talked to a lady in the restaurant next door that seemed to be upset about it, and he said he didn't know why he was down here. He didn't have the slightest idea who Thomas Bird was. He didn't know any of the family. He couldn't figure out how or why he had been brought down here."   The day after Henderson testified, he again spoke with Spires. "He said that he had learned why he was down here. He said that he had a couple of friends that were in Oklahoma that had left him holding the bag is what he said…That he was supposed to tell what had happened or what had been overheard or something like that…He said that these friends had told him some things, but had not paid too much to [sic] it at that time."

Symmonds told Rulon that "he didn't consider what he [Henderson] had to say was that important."

Rulon denied the motion, saying a new trial could be called only if the testimony "would be likely to produce a different result upon re-trial." Rulon felt this new evidence would not change the result. The verdict stood.

In 1989, Henderson found himself once again locked up at Lansing Correctional Facility. Tom served time there as well, and Tom had found favor with many inmates. Henderson confessed to a prisoner that he had lied in court and felt badly that he caused Tom so much trouble.

Later, the prisoner showed up with a handwritten statement and asked Henderson to write out one in his own handwriting and sign it. The statement explained that he had lied at trial.

Rather than write and sign such a statement, Henderson notified a guard. He claimed Tom threatened him if he didn't sign the statement. He stood by his testimony at trial.

But later, Henderson contracted with an attorney to try and win the reward money he felt Agent Humphrey led him to believe he would collect for testifying against Tom. Not only did he want the reward money, he wanted the State of Kansas to pay interest from the time he testified, contending they should have paid him right away.

When questioned in court about trying to file suit against the state, Henderson claimed again that Humphrey never promised him anything for his testimony. Humphrey had mentioned the reward, but never said he would help him get it. Henderson took great pains to parse his words and balance them with his lawsuit to collect the reward.

He admitted Humphrey said he would look into his parole, but insisted that did not constitute promising him anything.

How many jurors had placed weight on Henderson's testimony that Tom had Sandy killed? That Tom and Lorna had an affair? That they planned Marty's murder?

All that is known is that Rulon allowed Henderson's tainted testimony to be considered by the jury.

After ruling against the motion for a mistrial, Judge Gary Rulon sentenced Tom to life in prison. He would be eligible for parole 15 years and 10 months later, but his sentence wouldn't begin until his first sentence had been satisfied.

How did this happen?

A few days following the trial, two jury members attended a forum at Emporia State University to discuss the jury system. They talked about the Bird case, how if affected their lives and how they arrived at their decision.

Bruce Webb, who worked in the bookstore at ESU, said he had experience as an Emergency Medical Technician. He never heard of dry drowning, and he couldn't buy Dr. Bridgens' testimony. Hecht never intended for Bridgens to testify about dry drowning, and it seemed to dominate all debate once he used the words.

Perhaps the key to understanding how the jury convicted Tom, given that no evidence had been presented to tie him to the site of Sandy's death, were the words uttered by Dale Barger, the presiding juror. "It wasn't so much the blood on the bridge, it was the inconsistencies." Barger referred to stories Tom gave to investigators and relatives. A closer examination, though, reveals that Tom remained very consistent then and still does. If anything, investigators should have been censored for the dozens of errors they made in testimony, even though they had their notes in hand.

Jane Grismer's testimony about the trip to Rocky Ford Bridge should have been a warning sign to the jurors. She got it wrong. She and Jerry even failed to remember that Virginia rode with them to the bridge. She pointed out the wrong house to investigators.

Jane spent months trying to find out what happened to Sandy. Over those months she and her family talked at length about events that occurred hundreds of miles away, in Emporia. They compared notes about what Tom might have said to one and another. They pieced together a puzzle and arrived at a conclusion. But they, not Tom, created inconsistent statements.

Amy Swint's testimony that Tom came home wearing a suit and tie and then claimed he had been jogging made no sense to Barger and Webb. Testimony showed the church had no showers or tubs. No one had expressed it clearly in trial that Amy babysat for the Birds perhaps 75 times by the time of Sandy's death. Tom usually came home from church and brought her home, and he usually wore a tie, often carrying his coat over his arm. Tom knew that on the morning of the 17th he wore a brown tweed sports shirt, but Amy remembered it differently.

Barger and Webb said witnesses convinced them that Sandy was a responsible person who always wore her seatbelt. Tom's expert witnesses didn't convince them it had been an accident (but the law doesn't require Tom to prove anything—the state had to prove he committed a murder).

The men saw Robert Hecht as smooth, tenacious and very capable. They mentioned how he persisted in raising objections, so that when he failed to do so, they drew inferences from his silence. Hecht, for instance, had not refuted testimony that suggested the time of death was prior to midnight. Therefore, Webb inferred he must have agreed with the conclusion.

Webb felt strongly that Tom should have testified. "What I wanted to do, after the trial, was to go over and pull Tom Bird aside and say, 'Could you tell me the truth?'" Hecht insisted that Tom not testify and the Constitution provides every accused person that protection. Rulon even instructed the jurors not to consider this during their deliberations.

Inspect Symmonds proof

Rod Symmonds quoted Darrel Carter three times during his closing arguments. He quoted Jan Mead three times as well. Both of their testimonies were refuted during Tom's 1990 trial. Their testimony spoke to motive.

Persinger and Kennedy had completely different theories as to how Sandy's car ended up in the river. Kennedy at least presented a credible, scientific analysis. Persinger's testimony, heavily influenced by John Rule's personal theory, was laughable.

Both forensic pathologists agreed to the cause of Sandy's death. Neither could conclusively prove how the injuries occurred.

No one saw Tom at or near Rocky Ford Bridge until the day he drove out there with his mother and the Grismers.

To prove that Tom murdered Sandy, the state had to prove motive, opportunity and method. Once the testimonies of Carter and Mead had been neutralized, the state had no provable motive. They never could prove Tom had opportunity—the case had been purely circumstantial. As for method, neither side had presented conclusive proof.

The burden lay with the state to prove their case. They failed. So did the judge and the jury.

SECTION VI:

LORNA GOES PUBLIC

"A corrupt witness mocks at justice,
and the mouth of the wicked gulps down evil."

Proverbs 19:28

Lorna deals

As Tom left the Lyon County Courthouse the day of his sentencing for Sandy's death, he saw Agent Vern Humphrey. "We're not done with you yet. We're gonna get you on one more murder," Humphrey said to him as sheriff's ushered Tom away.

Tom's sentence left Lorna considering her own options. Certain to face the same kind of prejudice as Tom in a Lyon County courtroom, she expected a certain conviction.

Steven Opat saw it was his turn to take center stage in the unfolding drama, and bring closure to Marty Anderson's murder case. Investigators had long focused on Tom and Lorna as the main players in this grim drama, and with the cooperation of Rod Symmonds, Opat knew the timing was right for a deal with Lorna.

The state had played Lorna well, keeping her on a tight rope until they convicted Tom twice. Now Opat could extract the smoking gun from the lips of licentious Lorna; a confession about who had really killed Marty.

First, Symmonds needed to dispose of the two criminal charges against Lorna. The grand jury had indicted her for one count of criminal conspiracy to commit murder and one count of criminal solicitation to commit murder. In a plea agreement, Lorna confessed to two counts of criminal solicitation and agreed to give prosecutors a sworn statement naming Tom as Marty's murderer. In so doing, she agreed to tell the truth.

Lorna perceived truth very subjectively, as something that depended totally on whether or not it gained her an advantage. As it concerned Tom's fate, Judge Rulon already had sentenced him to life in prison. If she named him as Marty's killer it made no difference to her, just adding another life sentence for Tom, and a person has only one mortal life. Most importantly, by telling "all," she believed that within a few months, she would be paroled.

Susan Ewert recalled events surrounding Lorna's plea agreement. Since Marty's murder, Susan served Lorna as confidant and babysitter, provided a place for her to stay when she was in Emporia, helped collect and monitor information and acted as a go-between her and Tom. Susan counted Tom and Lorna as equal victims of the squalid sensationalism that destroyed her own confidence in the legal system. But by pleading guilty, Lorna turned on her and Tom.

"I didn't know she was going to plead guilty. I was at the church the day that she pled guilty, and the night before Tom called and said he heard that she was going to plead guilty, and I had talked to her the night before, and said to Tom, 'What are you talking about? I just talked to her last night.'

"He asked me to see what I could find out, and he would call me back later. So I started trying to get her, but I couldn't get her on the phone. [Susan regularly talked to Lorna, and not finding her available was unusual.]

"Finally I ended up getting her dad, and he said, 'what are you talking about? Let me see what I can find out.' This was about 5 in the afternoon.

"Finally, about 9 or 9-30, Lorna called me and said it was true and she couldn't go on with it any longer. When I hung up the phone with her, I thought she was doing it for one of three reasons. I was led to believe that: 1) Tom's legal expenses had been horrendous and if she went to trial she probably would have been found guilty. And in Lyon County, she would have been. Remember at this time, I still believe she's absolutely innocent. Everybody in the world thinks she is guilty, except for Susan. I thought the Carters were guilty. I had been led to believe it had to do with drugs. At that time, I thought she was going to plead guilty because of the court costs and the attorneys' fees, and she was going to be found guilty and the court costs would have been hers. Tom's were horrible."

Still wanting to help her good friend, Susan went to Lorna's plea agreement hearing. "After the plea, her dad had said to me, 'Susan, what in the hell has been going on here?' He was talking about Lorna, and I said, 'I truly don't know. I've heard some things, I've been told a little.'

"If it had gone to trial, it would have been a circus. They were threatening to bring all these names to light of the other men in town [with whom she had sex, some of whom held prominent positions in the community]. I had thought there might have been threats from some of the people in town.

"I thought maybe she didn't want to subject the children to it. The end result just like Tom, who had already been through it, was that she was going to be found guilty.

"I saw her before the hearing. We talked, hugged, and she let me go into the hearing not knowing what I was facing. I had no idea she was going to accuse Tom. None whatsoever.   "I had no recollection of even going back to my house, I was so stunned. I had not even 30 seconds of recollection of my car ending up at my house. Lorna went out of that meeting. We ended up avoiding the reporters by going out on the elevator in the back. But we got put into the same elevator. Randy [Eldridge] was with her. She smiled at me but never said one word. Not 'I'm sorry,' nothing. I was a person who walked with her daily. Why did she allow me to go in there? Why did she hug me? Why did she tell me it was going to be okay? Why did she allow the best friend she ever had walk in there?"

Susan wondered if someone had threatened to hurt Lorna or her children if she told the truth. "I was worried about it. The only thing that I can ever reason was that she thought God was going to prevail and she thought that

God was going to forgive all and forgive her if she implicated Tom, if it saved her children. What else can it be?"

Saving herself.

Lorna's tells her version of "all"

On August 30, 1985, Lorna met with Sheriff Deppish, Agent Winsor and Opat in the Reno County Law Enforcement Center in Hutchinson. Jack Focht, her attorney, advised her.

Lorna swore an oath to tell the truth.

Opat explained why everyone was in the room, and then said, "I am not going to be present during the taking of the statement inasmuch as I feel that might be improper, so I'm going to absent myself from the room. The interview will be conducted by Mr. Winsor and Sheriff Deppish."

Focht wanted clarification about the terms of Lorna's statement. "The statement is being taken and the defendant is being granted, in essence, use immunity from anything that she might tell under the terms of Kastigar versus the United States," Opat explained. The "essence" meant that nothing in her statement could be used against her provided she told the truth.

Lorna began her statement by describing the events of November 4, 1983.

Her story contained some unamazing twists. She described her getting sick from eating treats at McDonald's. "We finished eating and before we left McDonald's I started not feeling well. I went to the rest room before we left. ... at McDonald's and did throw up." Marty asked whether she could drive and she assured him that would be better than having the kids climb all over her.

She described stopping at the gas station on Highway 177, just north of I-70. One of the girls fell asleep on Marty's lap and he moved her to the couch in the back of the van. "...I sat there for a little while trying to decide if I should go into the service station or if I would be okay, and finally after, you know, just, oh, not too long, I know not more than five minutes...I thought I was feeling better and that we would go on...We didn't get very far at all and I felt very sick, and so I told Marty I needed to stop."

She said Marty told her where to stop. She took the keys because Marty taught her to do that. She described throwing up.

She claimed the keys she took with her into the ditch were actually Marty's. [Investigators must have wondered why she had his keys since she had been driving since they left McDonald's. Such a question, though, might have impugned her testimony, so they failed to ask.] When she went back to the van, she "...was getting my keys out when a man appeared from the back of the van."

"He came from behind the van, was standing right towards the back of the van, and asked for Marty's wallet.... I thought Marty reached in his back pocket to get this wallet, but then I saw him bend over, and the man had already fired a shot by that time and Marty bent over. The guy just kept shooting and, I don't know, I was standing there watching him and the gun, and... then Marty was on the ground...there was a car coming.

"The first thing he did was he went down and took Marty's wallet, and I guess he got it out of his pocket, and then there was a car coming so he came back to the van and he grabbed ahold of me. He took me down this ditch place, pushed me down on the ground, told me if I said a word that I was dead, and waited until the car was by.

"After the car went by he got back up, and I know he pulled the trigger on the gun because I heard it click, but the gun did not go off, so then he took me back up to the car, wanted my purse, but when he got in the van to get my purse, he took off.... He ran... towards the back of the van..."

The officers tried to clarify the direction that the killer ran, but Lorna feigned confusion about knowing which direction was north or south.

After the killer left, Lorna walked down to Marty "...and tried to talk to him but be never would say anything. I got in the van. My first thought was I had to get out of there before he came back, but I couldn't leave Marty there, so I got back out of the van. That's when I flagged the car down..."

"Okay. Can you describe the man, approximately, age, height, so on?"

Focht interrupted the questioning. He reminded the investigators that since that night, Lorna had learned the truth. Did they want her to describe what she thought she saw, or what she now knew?

"What he looked like that night," Deppish explained.

"Okay, that night I thought the guy was probably as tall as Marty... maybe not quite, but close. As far as age, he was not an old man, I wouldn't say he was a kid either. He had on jeans and some type of a dark jacket. He had a mask, or was black. His face was black anyway, I remember that. There was nothing in particular that stood out that—I mean, not—the sound of his voice, there was no accent, there was nothing like that. Of course, he didn't say much either."

"Did you recognize the voice at all, was the voice familiar to you?" Winsor asked.

"Not at that point, no."

Winsor moved to questions about the shooting. Lorna said she thought the killer stood about 15 feet from Marty when he pulled the trigger the first time. "Now, he moved towards Marty after Marty fell to the ground."

"Was Marty standing up when he was shot or falling down or laying down, do you know?"

"That's something that was very confusing to me because when he fired the first shot Marty was standing up, I know that, but then Marty bent over, and I was very surprised after the autopsy because, I don't know, to me it seemed like he bent over like he'd been shot in the stomach or something, but then I remember Marty was into this survival stuff for the army and I remember him talking one time to somebody else...about stuff like that, and I can remember him saying that you're better off if you're being shot at to bend over because there's less area.... Now, what did you ask me? I'm sorry, Don." [Lorna even charmed investigators. It came naturally to her.]

"Do you know if Marty was facing towards the individual, turned around, do you have any idea which direction he was facing at the time the shots were first started?"

"I know he was facing the man when the guy first shot, but then after that I watched the man shooting more than I did what Marty was—I don't know."

"How close did the person doing the shooting get to Marty, approximately?"

"Oh, he was practically right next to him because he was right there, and then he just took his wallet."

Winsor asked whether the killer struck Marty, other than with a bullet? The autopsy revealed several broken ribs. Lorna said she saw no blows.

"Last time I saw him he went just back behind the van and that was—I didn't stand there and watch where he went... I just assumed he went back—you're telling me it was north—back north."

What about the gun?

Winsor asked her about the gun. She claimed that at the time she knew nothing about it. Investigators had spent hundreds of hours trying to identify the weapon, and had gotten nowhere. [Stephen Anderson eventually told them about the Colt Woodsman his father had passed down to Marty, and later it was identified as the murder weapon.]

Deppish took over the questioning. He spent a good deal of time discussing the keys, which pocket Lorna put them in, who picked them up and what she did with them that night. He seemed to be testing her story for accuracy, but when she was vague in her answers, he coached her.

"Back at the scene again, do you ever remember Marty being on his knees for any reason, either kneeling down to look for the keys or after he was shot, or at any time do you remember Marty being on his knees?"

"Not that I can recall, no." [This left unexplained how the mud got on his knees.]

"During any conversation with the subject at the van would you have been close enough to the van for Lori to have heard a conversation?"

"Oh, when he was asking for my purse, yeah."

"Was his voice loud, was he ever hollering or were you screaming?"

"I don't know what I was doing. I was just very scared. When he asked for Marty's billfold he yelled, I mean he screamed, yelled, said that in a loud voice anyway. When he asked for my purse I don't know how loud his voice would have been. It was just more demanding than…"

"You've probably read in our reports that I think Lori said, 'I heard mommy talking to a man that wasn't daddy's voice,' or something to that effect, so you were close enough that she could distinguish…"

"She could hear."

Deppish asked her about the lights in the van. Witnesses gave varying stories about whether the van's lights were on or off, and this served as a way to check Lorna's recollection of the details.

Winsor resumed the questioning and asked about the contents of the billfold. "Did those credit cards ever show up, to your knowledge?"

"No."

He asked whether she ever cancelled the credit cards. She said they were all maxed out, and could not be used, so she had done nothing about them.

"Had you ever been out to the scene of the shooting any time prior to this for any reason?"

"No, sir."

Deppish took over again. Referring back to the morning of November 4, he sought further clarification of the call Marty placed to Faith. "When you received the telephone call, you said Tom Bird answered the phone and told you it was Marty. Did Tom have any discussion with you after that? I assume you told him you were going to be leaving."

"I asked him if I could leave at 11:30. I said, 'Marty wants to go ahead and go to Ft. Riley today and get his field jacket.'"

"Did you know about the meeting that was going to take place that night in Topeka?"

"Oh, yeah, I knew that there were several of them going to be in Topeka for a meeting because that's why our volleyball team was so short of players. That's why it was so important that we get back."

Deppish asked about the travel arrangements Tom usually made for such trips and whether or not he had been looking for a new van. Lorna knew nothing about the travel, but was aware that Tom wanted to buy a new van.

Winsor asked, "Lorna, did you ever tell anybody the route that you were going to take going to and from Junction City or Ft. Riley?"

"No, I didn't. That was a way that we didn't ordinarily go. We usually went to Herington and up to Ft. Riley, but for some reason when Marty drove up this time he went north out of Council Grove and over, and then when we were at Manhattan, that was the only way to come back. It didn't make any sense to go back to Herington."

"Do you know if Tom Bird knew that you were going that route?"

"No."

Deppish asked about her state of mind, and how she felt about going that day. Lorna claimed she wanted to put it off a week, because she planned a dinner party the next night, but Marty insisted on going.

Pastor Hit Man

With all these details now explored, Deppish began asking about Tom's involvement in the murder. "Lorna, evidently since this time you have found out that you know who was there at the scene that night?"

"Yes."

"When were you told this?"

"It was the last Monday in August of 1984. It was the Monday before Tom Bird was sentenced the first time. He was sentenced on a Thursday, I believe, and this was the Monday before that."

"How did this conversation come about?"

"Tom had been down that weekend...Hutchinson, and Monday I took him back to Wichita. That day we had gone to the university to, oh, see if he could get in some type of a Doctorate or Master's program in counseling. This was part of a probationary plan, something to present to the judge if he was given probation, that is what he was going to do.

"After we finished at the university he was going to the Lutheran Social Services office, which is just across the street from the college, and see a Don Romsa that he had spent some time counseling with, and he didn't want me to go there with him. In fact, he made me go about three or four blocks down the street and park the car and he walked back, and this made me very angry. I didn't understand that. I said, you know, 'You tell me you love me but yet you won't even let me go with you to meet this man. You don't want to be seen with me,' this type of thing.

"Well, he went ahead and went. He talked to the counselor. He came back. I had sat there in the car and really gotten angry while he was gone, and we proceeded to fight all the way out to the airport, and finally when we got there I made another comment about, 'You don't really love me so don't tell me you do,' and that's when he got out of the car and said, 'I loved you enough that I wanted to be with you and I killed your husband,' and I sort of laughed.

"I thought that was funny, but then he started outlining details that made it a little more believable than just, 'I did it because I loved you.'"

"Can you give us those details?"

"Yeah. He—you know, my first thing was, 'we don't travel that road. How did you know?' He had waited and this was—it's not funny but it's strange. He didn't realize that there was a clothing sales at Ft. Riley so he assumed that we would have to go the base exchange to get this field jacket. He thought that's where all army clothes were purchased, and so he had waited there for us, which is ironic because if it hadn't been for diapers we never would have gone there, and then we didn't end up getting the diapers there, but that's where he had been waiting.

"He said he was sitting in the parking lot waiting there, and, of course, the van is not difficult to spot... He said from there it was just a matter of following us.

"What if...I don't always get sick, what if I hadn't, what if the van hadn't stopped?

"He said actually the van stopping was not at all what he wanted. He had decided that he would pull the van over somehow on the highway between Council Grove and where you get on the turnpike at Admire. He said by doing that, 'I could be on the turnpike in just a matter of a few minutes and back in Topeka in no time.'

"He was behind the van when I stopped. There is probably four hundred, five hundred ... it's four-tenths of a mile... there is a little driveway area on the...west side of the road, right? Okay, on the east side of the road. He said when I stopped he pulled up there and pulled back in there off enough that the car could not be seen. He has seen all of these police reports, and he said there is a police report in there of a guy that lives in the house just beyond south of where I stopped, he said there was a car behind him. He pulled in his driveway but that other car never went on by."

[At that point in time, Tom had not been accused of murdering Marty. He had no access to all the police investigation reports associated with that crime, unless Lorna gave them to him. The officers failed to press her on this point, or the more obvious point that *she* had seen all the reports, and had plenty of time to concoct a story.]

"He sat there in the car so he could see the van. He said with the light— I guess the font light in the van must have come on when Marty got out of the car.

"He said at that point he decided it was getting late enough that he might as well go ahead and do it and take I-70 back to Topeka, rather than try and wait and do it on the other road. To get back for the meeting at seven o'clock he was pushing the time limit. He ran down the road, on the east side of the road, to behind the van. That's when he came up.

"Everything else is just like I told you before. After he had shot Marty and waited until the car was by, he went back behind the van again, crossed the street and ran back down the road to his car. He—he threw the billfold out somewhere along there, I don't know."

Lorna claimed Tom took the money from the billfold and threw it, plus the credit cards, on the ground somewhere. Then he got back into his car and headed north toward I-70. She identified the road he planned to turn on as "something Creek Road," i.e. MacDowell Creek Road.

"He was going to take that road and throw the gun down there somewhere, but as he was driving evidently ...there's a farm pond or some kind of a pond close enough that he was able to throw the gun out the window and it landed in the pond, so then he decided that being's he had gotten rid of the gun, it was not as important that he take this other road and it would be better just to get back on I-70 and get back to Topeka."

This claim sent electricity through the room. Deppish saw the possibility of finally recovering the murder weapon, though it required draining nearby farm ponds. The farm ponds Lorna described sit back off Highway 177 at least 75 yards. Trying to throw a gun from an open car window 75 yards into a pond seemed improbable to Deppish.

"...So he got back on Interstate 70. He had, under his jeans and this jacket he had on his suit, except for his suit coat. He had his shirt and tie and dress slacks. He had a sack in the car. While he was driving he took off the jacket and the jeans and he had a pair of tennis shoes. He put them in the sack, and there is a rest area between that entrance to I-70 and Topeka, the one that's in the middle. He pulled in there and threw the sack with his clothes and the shoes in just a trash can there, and then drove back to Topeka at about 65 or 70 miles an hour. Said there was one time when he was very nervous because there was a State car in front of him or behind him.

"But he did have on a mask. He said the jeans were bought at the Salvation Army store there in Emporia. The jacket was just an old one he had. The tennis shoes were old ones that he had run in before but had a new pair and didn't use them any more. That's why they could all be thrown away. He threw the mask away in the sack."

Focht reminded her to tell about the gun.

"Oh, the gun was one that had been Marty's. Marty had been gone to Omaha, Nebraska, the weekend of September the 23rd through the 25th, I think.... When he came back he had been in one of his moods and that Sunday night had beat me up to the point where I couldn't even go to work the next day, and so I called Tom and told him that I ... wouldn't be able to work that Monday and he came over to the house to see me and then he left, and he came back and wanted to know if Marty had a gun, and I said, yeah, I thought he had this one in the basement...

"Tom said, 'Give it to me...If he has a gun in this house, one of these times he's going to get mad enough that he's going to kill you or the girls or something,' so he went down and we found it in my cedar chest...and then he took it and kept it....

"And he had intended... to shoot me in the shoulder so that it would look more like I was injured in the robbery-type thing.

"The next morning he came to the hospital in ... Junction City to see me but he didn't drive his own car, and .... He said he had gone next door to the neighbors to see if he could borrow one of their cars, using the excuse that his wasn't running well...the neighbor drove him to Junction City and then on to Topeka, but he said he was afraid that if someone on the road had seen his car and, you know, might recognize it, he didn't want his car anywhere close to Junction City."

Again, Focht reminded Lorna of a critical detail. She explained that three weeks before making this statement, she and Randy Eldridge drove out to the murder site, and she spotted the farm ponds across the road. "He just said there was a pond there and it was close enough to the road that he could throw the gun out the window without having to get out of the car."

What about the Topeka witness?

Deppish dealt with one of the more troubling details of Lorna's unfolding statement. He reminded her that a witness spotted Tom at a Burger King in Topeka during the time of the murder. Lorna had a ready answer.

"He knew that Sheri was going to be going, or had gone, I guess, to Topeka, or she went home...that weekend and he was able to talk to her before you did, and being one of his students, he told her that he had been out looking at cars and that he, you know, couldn't really say where he was at a certain time and that's when they worked out this little thing at Burger King."

Focht jumped in again to let Lorna clarify this rather profound claim that Sheri Weinmeister perjured herself for Tom. "He actually told her, he said he was a little upset when he read her report, because he wanted it to be—I don't know what time she said, but he wanted it either earlier or later than what she actually told you, but she did that to fit in with her schedule and so on." [Actually, Sheri stated that Agent Winsor interviewed her hours before Tom told her he might come asking questions.]

Deppish knew that if Tom had such influence over a young woman like Sheri, he had to have the same control over others, and he asked about that. Lorna responded excitedly to this suggestion and blathered on about how

Tom controlled everyone who went along with him. She saw it as key to the way the church grew. "Vern Humphrey said the other day that ... 'I always knew if we could just get you away from him long enough, that you would start thinking for yourself again, you would tell us the truth, but,' he says, 'that man had you totally mesmerized.'"

Lorna included in her list of mesmerized victims, the young woman Tom started dating in October of 1983, Terry Smith. Also, Lorna cited all the inmates at Lansing who believed she was a liar just because Tom said so. "He really has a power over people and I was very susceptible to it at the time."

[Lyon County sentenced Lorna to 5-18 years in prison as a result of her plea agreement. She originally served her time at Lansing Correctional Facility, but in the unit known as The Hill. It sat east of the maximum-security portion in which Tom served his time. The Hill was a minimum security facility, and it was co-ed. Reports surfaced of Lorna's sexual involvement with male and female prisoners as well as guards before the state moved her to another facility.]

Deppish asked whether Tom ever had aspirations to become an evangelist, like a Billy Graham. Lorna bleated back a non-stop description of how Tom wanted to build a big ministry around serving families. He told her to go back to school and take family counseling courses so if they got married, she could be part of his ministry team. "He could make me into what would be a good wife for him.... I mean, he's going to change the world."

Motive is key to proving any crime. Deppish explored a financial motive, asking, "did he say he needed money to do all these things?"

Tom schemed to sue Lyon County for millions and take the money to New Mexico, "down by Albuquerque somewhere and set up some kind of a retreat center for families, where families could come in and stay, and he would solve all their problems for them." She said the discussion about money happened after both Marty and Sandy had died. [To place the discussion before Marty's death might suggest that Tom knew about the life insurance she stood to gain, thus implicating her in the conspiracy to commit the actual murder.]

"On this...last Monday in August when Tom first told you about this [murdering Marty], had you known then that he had killed Sandy?"

"Yeah."

"What was your reaction in this [sic] car on the last Monday in August when Tom started to tell you this?"

This question set Lorna off on yet another long rambling answer. She claimed Tom wanted her to name Danny as the murderer. She said Mark Bird did some checking and found holes in Danny's alibi [which is true] and it provided the opening they needed to frame Danny. She said she believed

Tom would receive probation and so, take care of her and her children. "To say nothing is one thing, but to lie is something else, so I never did anything until I finally was able to break through his mind control and think for myself again."

Questioning returned to the gun. Though Lorna claimed the Colt Woodsman was the only gun in the house, she admitted Marty also had a .38, but said he had sold it.

What about Tom's voice? He had a hard-edged, deep bass voice. Lorna said it had no hint of a southern accent, but Winsor bored in. "You say you have heard his voice so many times, how come you didn't recognize it the night of November the 4th?"

"There was not that much said. He did have a mask on which muffled it to a degree, and then I just wasn't standing around trying to pick out if I knew the voice or not. When somebody has a gun you don't stop and try to analyze things, at least I didn't."

[Lorna claimed that for more than two years she had been intimate with Tom. She worked by his side every day. He counseled her in some of her most difficult times. She claimed he had an almost mystical power over her, suggesting that if he but mentioned her name, she would react instinctively. She heard him preach, teach, counsel, love, pray, cry and scream in anger on other occasions. But on November 4, she could not recognize his voice?

In Tom's two trials, Judge Rulon allowed witnesses to testify as to what they believed Tom had said to them during his times of greatest duress, the days right after Sandy's death. Tom admitted to making confusing statements, but none unusual for one whose wife had just died. Yet, the court put no stock in Tom's explanation. Sweet seductive Lorna, though, could charm them into believing the preposterous explanation that she could not recognize his voice because she was under duress.]

Winsor let this slide and went back to questions about the murder site. He attempted to pin down the location where Lorna claimed Tom parked the car. She said it was south of the murder site, not across the road at the empty farm site. She said he ran north before crossing the road and running south. She tried to clarify her statement by saying the farm sat on the other side of the road south of the murder site. The fact that no such farm was so located did not trouble the investigators. Witnesses did spot a car in a driveway south of the murder site, but on the west side of the road. A small detail. They liked the rest of her story.

Winsor needed more clarification about Tom's alibi. "And you say Tom Bird got to Sheri Weinmeister and convinced her to tell me a certain time and date?"

"Uh-huh. He was suspecting that this was going to happen."

Winsor got her on this one. "Have you seen the other statements where the mother of Sheri Weinmeister and the boy—and two other people in the car also confirmed that—the time and the date?"

"No."

"You haven't seen that?"

"No."

He let it drop again and went to motive. "What was the ultimate reason for Tom Bird shooting Marty?"

"He had said before back when we had given Dan Carter the money that he needed a wife, he needed somebody to take care of his kids, and he was tired of me putting up with Marty and the beating and the verbal abuse of me and the children, and he was going to change all of that. That's not ... the way the Lord meant families to be, and he thought it was less wrong to kill Marty than it was for us to go ahead and live with that situation. It was the lesser of two evils, is the way he always put it. He was teaching a Christian Ethics class at the time at the University."

[This type of Christian Ethics teaching certainly should have raised eyebrows as it fell miles outside of the orthodox Lutheran teachings for which Tom was well-known. Lorna claimed that Tom taught murder was justified when a pastor needed a wife and a married woman's husband was beating her. Neither Winsor nor Deppish found anyone willing to corroborate her absurd claim.]

Winsor wanted to know more about the money motive. Lorna again claimed the insurance money never became an issue. Winsor wanted to know about the $5,000 paid to Danny. "Was that Tom Bird's—did he volunteer this or is it something—you asked him for the money?"

"No, we had talked about it. After the conversation with Darrel the second time Tom went back and talked to Darrel, Darrel told him then that the best thing to do might be just to hire somebody to kill Marty, and that Danny might be able to find someone, and so the end of August, the first part of September, he had me call Dan, and I talked to him, and then when I found out what it was going to be I told him and that was fine. He just—he went and got the money."

[This testimony suggested a deeper involvement by Darrel in the conspiracy scheme. She stated he was the one who designated Danny as the one to find a killer at Wolf Creek.]

Mapping it all out

Deppish took over, this time drawing a not-to-scale map on a sheet of paper. He helped Lorna locate the driveway where she said Tom waited, south of the murder site. She indicated where the ponds were that might hold the murder weapon. They settled on the pond that Lorna thought the most likely drop point. Deppish stated, "…neither of these ponds could you throw a gun or probably anything else from the highway to the pond; do you agree to that?"

She did not agree. She said Randy told her he could do it.

Lorna had placed a large number of phone calls to Mark Bird, and Deppish wanted to know why. Similar testimony about the high volume of calls between Lorna and Tom helped the prosecution "prove" they had a love affair. No one alleged such an affair between Mark and Lorna.

"Mark was always trying to get information from me as to anything I knew about Danny Carter while he was investigating… I talked to Mark a lot of times about Tom and if Tom would call me and want Mark to check something out—Mark's very hard to get ahold of…. I was just a go-between between the two of them."

This line of questioning created another potential fault line in Lorna's story. Deppish asked, "Did you tell Mark Bird either in any of these conversations or in person that you believed Marty was dealing in drugs?"

"Uh-huh."

"In Manhattan?"

"Uh-huh."

"Why do you believe that?"

"Just why else would he have gone outside and then—I don't know, just--Marty acted funny. When we got back in the van and he had this money, and he said, you know, 'Some day you're going to thank me because I'm going to have us totally out of debt.'"

"Did you ever believe Marty to be on drugs?"

"Oh, I know that Marty was using some drugs."

"I mean non-prescription drugs, illegal drugs."

"Oh, yeah. He would take things, you know, when he was working late at night to be able to stay awake. I mean, don't you consider that drugs?"

Deppish and Focht were confused by this answer and Lorna could not clarify it. "Do you believe Marty ever dealt with cocaine, marijuana?"

"Oh, I know he smoked a little marijuana when he would be out. He drank a lot." "Smoking a little marijuana and dealing is [sic] two different things."

"Okay, I thought you were asking me if he was using drugs."

He was. Deppish asked whether he used and sold drugs. They needed money and Lorna told Mark that Marty sold drugs in Manhattan to acquire "a bunch of money."

Lorna explained Marty had access to drugs at the pharmacy lab.

Focht could see where this line of questioning was leading, and wanted to get it back on track. "Let me ask something. Even though you told all of these things, when Marty died out there you thought he died as a result of a hit man that you had hired?"

"Right."

Lorna's different versions of her story had become entangled in a confusing tapestry and this latest version threatened to destroy what little credibility she still maintained. Winsor wanted to know more.

"If Marty was selling drugs, had he done it for a while or was he just getting started, would you say?"

"Oh, maybe a year."

"Selling drugs maybe a year?"

"Yeah. I mean he wasn't into it like Danny Carter is, but I think it was just something to get a little extra money that we desperately needed."

[Lorna labeled Danny a drug horse several times. No public record exists that investigators pursued him for these alleged felonies.]

"What would you say was the ultimate reason for your hiring someone to kill Marty Anderson?" Winsor asked, still looking for motive.

"So Tom and I could be married and have this perfect family; you know, set the example for the rest of the world."

"Okay. Is this your idea or is this Tom Bird's idea?"

"No, this was Tom's idea. I was not... the kind of a person that would be the wife that he needed, but he could make me into what I should be."

"But what was the reason for your hiring someone to shoot Marty Anderson?"

"Well, it wasn't something I did on my own. I mean, this was—Tom says, 'I've talked to Darrel and Darrel says we can hire somebody, and that would probably be the best way to go, and—you know, so call Dan and see if he can find somebody, and I've got the money.' It wasn't—I didn't go out and hire somebody to do it." [Again Lorna said Darrel formed part of a conspiracy.]

The investigators saw the preposterous nature of Lorna's explanation, and wanted a stronger motive. The conversation returned to life insurance. Lorna insisted life insurance had nothing to do with the murder.

Start at the very beginning

After a brief lunch break, they began again. Winsor asked Lorna to repeat how she and Tom met. Lorna described meeting Tom at a softball game in June of 1982, how she enrolled her children at Lord's Lambs. They became friends in the fall of 1982. She said Tom offered her the secretarial job, which she began in January of 1983, and began counseling her in February. He helped her with a hospitalization that month, and, "It was May before there was any type of a physical relationship."

"May of 1983?"

[This answer should have sent them scurrying to re-read Jan Mead's testimony. Twice Mead testified in trials that Lorna told her on April 19 that Tom was pretty good in bed for a minister. Mead stated Lorna took romantic trips with Tom in February and March.]

Winsor wanted to know when they first talked about killing Marty. Lorna said it must have followed Marty's return from summer camp in May of 1983. She fingered the third week of May as the time period. Had she talked with anyone other than Tom?

"Well, Darrell and Dan Carter." [This statement confirmed David Workman's testimony about what he and Lorna discussed on March 30, 1983—she had discussed roughing Marty up or murdering him with Danny and Darrel.]

"Why were the Carter brothers contacted? Why them as opposed to someone else?"

"I knew the Carter brothers and I knew Darrel and I knew the kind of things that he did, and the summer before that when I had been seeing Danny, Darrel had seen me one time when I had a black eye and a gash on my head and he said, 'Something needs to be done with that—about that.' He says, you know, 'People like that should be killed. You don't need to live with somebody like that,' so then after Tom and I discussed it, it was just natural to contact Darrel."

Winsor asked about contact between Danny and Tom. Both had stated several times that they never met nor talked at any time prior to Marty's murder. Lorna said otherwise. She claimed Danny met Tom at the church one time before that.

Tom never talked to either Greg Curry or Johnny Bingham.

Lorna insisted that Tom told her specifically to talk to Danny. She stated the $5,000 came from insurance settlements Tom received from Sandy's death.

They talked about whether there was a specific time and location for Marty's murder. Lorna said no, just that she did not want it at home. She described the events that followed her handing over the money to Danny, and insisted that the only reservation she had was that it not be done the following weekend while Marty would be with the girls.

Winsor wanted to know Lorna's reaction when she learned that whoever got the $5,000 failed to follow through with the murder? "Well, I did nothing, really. I mean, the money was gone; and then I assumed after he had been killed that whoever got the money went ahead and followed through with it."

Focht didn't like her answer and wanted it clarified. She stated that she did talk to Danny at some point when nothing had happened, and acknowledged that Danny promised to check it out and get back to her.

Winsor wondered about Tom's reaction when the money disappeared. "He really had no reaction," she said.

"He didn't ask you to try to get it back?" Deppish asked.

"No, no, he acted like he didn't even want it back.... I just told him that Danny said it wasn't going to work and that he was going to try to get the money back for us, and that was essentially it."

Winsor asked what various murder schemes had been discussed with Darrel? [Before this statement, Lorna had publicly remained mute about all such issues. She told Irv Shaw before Tom's first trial that murder had never been discussed. Her story changed now that Tom had been twice convicted and her own freedom was at stake.]

"Did you ever make any comments to Darrel Carter that you had a gun that could not be traced?"

"No, no, guns were never discussed with Darrel Carter. It was— poisoning Marty was discussed, and leaving him on a railroad crossing was discussed. Dropping a concrete block through the windshield was discussed, but shooting was just never discussed."

"He stopped in Augusta at a drug store—and I have no idea what drug store in Augusta—one day in June of 1983 and talked to a pharmacist about some kind of a drug. He used the excuse that he and a bunch of guys were getting together to have a party and they had one buddy that just never gets drunk like all the rest of them do, so just one time they wanted to drug him to the point where he passed out so that then they could come back and hey-ha-ha."

[Investigators failed to locate any druggist in Augusta to corroborate this story.]

Winsor asked Lorna about Alvin Tefft, a man with whom Marty had worked in the Reserves. Had she ever spoken to him about drugs or poisons?

"No, I mean, yeah, we talked about something, but that was back in, oh, what, March or something of that year, and it just wasn't like that at all. I had had this surgery in February and—my hemoglobin was very low and I was having to go to the hospital to have it checked. Well, Marty had hired a black guy that was working as an aide and he wasn't real efficient in going to draw my blood that particular day he used a syringe, and he pulled the plunger on the syringe out but he wasn't in the vein so we didn't get any blood, and he pushed the plunger back in and injected all of this air into my vein, and I got home later and my head went to working on me and I thought, 'Oh, my God, I'm having chest pains, I'm going to have a heart attack, I've got a blood clot, I'm going to die,' and Alvin called looking for Marty and we just got to talking, and I said, 'How much air would have to be injected into a person's vein to kill them?' and he said, 'Oh, you know, thirty cc's,' a significant amount, a lot more than what had been put back into mine, and he says, 'That's no way to kill somebody,' and then we were talking and he said, 'The way to really kill someone is to inject streptozyme, which would not cause a blood clot.' He said, 'That would cause someone to bleed to death.' He said streptozyme is something they use in the lab when they're checking clotting times."

[This answer typified those given when Lorna needed to flavor her stories so that they seemed plausible. Winsor interviewed Tefft in August of 1984. Tefft told him that Lorna called *him,* it was January of 1983, that she wanted to come to the motel and have sex with him, and that she asked about something that could be injected, cause death and not show up on an autopsy.]

"Did Tom Bird do any research on drugs or poisons?" Winsor asked.

"Uh-huh. He went to the library at Kansas University and got some books one day and read what he could on poisons and then Xeroxed off some pages out that book."

[The next time investigators searched Tom's files in Hardy, Arkansas, they were after these Xeroxed papers. None were found.]

"Did Tom ever tell you that he was going to kill Marty himself?" Winsor asked.

"No."

"Did he ever say anything in front of Darrel Carter, quote, 'I'm a man of God and I'm going to kill him if I have to,' or words to that effect?"

"Uh-huh." [In her immediately answer prior to this, she stated Tom never said he planned to kill Marty.]

"Where was this and what do you recall about that?"

"It was at the church the day that we met with Darrel Carter."

"Were there any other conversations made by him or any other documents made by him at that time, by Tom Bird?"

"He said that he was going to go ahead and have Marty's funeral. Other than that, nothing that I recall. They also discussed soccer and fireworks and building houses and this type of thing."

Winsor wanted to know how Tom felt about Marty. Lorna claimed he didn't much like him, even hated him, but put on a good show for others.

"Do you know if Tom Bird ever told anyone else, for example, his brother Mark, that he was going to kill Marty, or did, in fact, do so?"

"No. I would be very surprised if he had told anyone. I mean, I would be really shocked."

Winsor asked her specific questions about the gun. Did she know whether Tom ever practiced shooting it? She didn't.

"What were you and Tom's plans if this crime was never solved, if we didn't find out who did it?"

"Well, we just planned to get married and work with families." [Lorna had married Randy Eldridge that spring. Apparently she gave up on Tom.]

Who threatened you?

"After we started talking to Tom Bird, as investigators talking to Tom Bird, did Tom Bird ever counsel you about or threaten you in any way about this investigation?"

"Well, he always just told me that I should not say anything, I should keep my mouth shut about my involvement with him and Sandy's death."

"Did he threaten you that if you ever said anything that he would do this or that?"

"Well, it wasn't so much that, it was, the threats were, 'You've got to have somebody to take care of you,' and, you know. I did receive a sympathy card that was threatening that I assumed it had come from somebody. I still don't know that it did come from him because he has never said, but just that I needed to keep my mouth shut, that type of thing."

Lorna described the threatening letters, stating she could provide them to the investigators. [They carried a picture of her family that had been taken out of the Faith church directory, and they warned her to keep her mouth shut. They were written and mailed while Tom sat in Lansing Prison.]

"Are you afraid of Tom Bird?"

"Well, yeah, I guess I'm afraid of him now. I'm afraid of his brother. I'm afraid of people that he knows at Lansing that have friends out here. Yeah, we're being very careful around the house."

"Has anyone actually threatened you...either in person or by telephone?"

"I've had...a phone call shortly after I moved to Hutchinson—in fact, it was still while I was living at my folks—and I was told to keep my mouth shut and something about the girls. Then the only other thing has been Mark Bird's phone call the other day, when he just threatened me that I—really that I not talk to you, but if I did, that I not say anything that was going to hurt his brother's appeal."

[Threatening a witness is a felony. Lyon County took quick action against a female member of Faith Lutheran who confronted one of the witnesses in Tom's trial, charging her with this very crime. No one took any action against Mark Bird based on Lorna's testimony about alleged threats, indicating that investigators were selective in what part of her testimony they believed.]

"Why didn't you divorce Marty rather than hire someone to kill him?"

"Financially it was impossible. Our financial situation was such that there's no way I could have. There's no way Marty could have afforded any child support and I had four little girls to take care of, and I just don't think that divorce would have solved the problems..."

"Did you love Tom Bird?"

"Yes."

"Do you love him now?"

"No, I mean, I care about him; I mean, he's a friend. I worry about him. I wish he'd get his head together or something, but to love him as far as— like I do my husband, no."

"When you and Tom left Emporia to go somewhere, a motel or something, which cities and what motels would you stay at?"

"We went to Wichita in August of 1983 and we stayed at the Sheraton Inn out by the airport. Other than that, we were in Tulsa a couple times and stayed at a Holiday Inn there."

[Lorna placed the latter trips in 1984, long after Marty and Sandy had died. They did meet in Tulsa in July of 1984, but Lorna stayed in one room with her four daughters and Tom stayed in another with his three children. Seven young witnesses do not allow for sexual contact—there was none. Tom left Tulsa and drove on to Arkansas. As for the 1983 trip, Tom stayed with his three children that night as well, and Lorna drove to her parents' house. Tom denies any other trips with Lorna.]

"Why didn't you come forward with your statement prior to this occasion?"

"I don't know. He kept telling me I couldn't say anything and so I didn't."

"Why didn't you come forward when Tom Bird was convicted of the solicitation in Emporia and went to prison?"

"Because, you know, he kept telling me he was going to be out soon, that he would be out on appeal and everything was going to work out okay, and I believed him."

Winsor asked whether Lorna felt afraid because of giving this testimony. She claimed no one at Lansing believed her, and she had received a bizarre letter from someone named Tony Love, a former inmate, who reminded her that snitches don't last long in prison.

Sandy's murder, according to Lorna

The questioning turned to Sandy's death. Lorna claimed Tom confessed murdering Sandy to her as well. She said the confession happened the day they drove around in her van about 10 days after Sandy's death, the day she resigned as church secretary. Lorna placed the day as Wednesday or Thursday, the 27th or 28th.

[Jan Mead testified, corroborated by Kim Clark her replacement at the American Heart Association, that they met with Lorna on the 26th, and that during that meeting, Lorna made it clear that Sandy's death was no accident. If Lorna told the truth to investigators in this 1985 statement, she had no knowledge for her statements to Mead and Clark. Either she lied to them or she lied to investigators.]

"He told me that they had gone to the movie, they had gone to The Station and had a couple of drinks. When they left there they went back home and Sandy went in the house and got a bottle of wine and a bottle of Seagrams 7, and they were going for a drive in the country, said he got out to the bridge and he used the excuse, 'Let's walk out on the bridge and look at the water,' or whatever. When they got out there he hit her and tried to throw her over the bridge. She was able to grab ahold of the railing with her hands and then he kicked her. There was in the autopsy a kidney that was cut in two. He said that was why, because he kicked her, then she dropped...

"He then went down and held her under water until he thought she had quit breathing, and then he got in the car and started it, and drove it down the hill and then jumped out just before the car went over. I did see on his leg the—the scrape, I guess is what you would call it, that it left when he hit the ground; and he took the bottle of Seagrams 7 and tried to wash the blood off of the bridge. After that he started running, and I was able to tell them what road it is. It's the one that curves and goes out there.

"He took his shoes off and his socks off and threw them in a ditch somewhere along there. He had his jogging shorts on under his slacks. He took his slacks off, threw them out. He left his shirt on until he got back to town and then he threw his shirt in somebody else's trash can somewhere. He was concerned that it might be found....

"He ran on back to the church, and they told me some things that I didn't know. He had gone back to the church and evidently put on a shirt and tie and gone home. I was able to tell them that he wore his brown suit when he left Emporia to go to Little Rock for the funeral because he had no black shoes. He had thrown his black shoes away and he had to buy a pair of black shoes when he got to Little Rock."

About those Carter brothers

Deppish next asked about the Carters. Lorna described the day she alleges the Carters committed arson and she served as their alibi.

"It was actually a garage that Darrel had turned into an apartment behind the apartment house that Danny lives in, and it was in the way, they needed it for parking, and it was the weekend of the Fourth of July of 1982 that they decided to burn it down, and I was helping—they have a fireworks stand— well, in fact, that year they had two of them in Emporia, and I was helping them with one of them..."

"Danny and I were out there and Darrel came up and told Danny, 'Get that stuff out of the attic because I want to do it tomorrow,' I guess Darrel stayed there and Danny and I went back to the garage, and there were some old chairs and a trunk and some things like that in the attic that Danny took out of there and put in the basement of the apartment house, and then the next day it was set up..."

"They needed me to work at the fireworks stand that afternoon, and so I went out, and Dan left about one-thirty, and Darrel was at the other fireworks stand, and Danny says, 'Don't ask questions, but if anyone ever asks you, I never left here,' so he went back to the garage, and then we found out later that it had burned down...."

"Well, I questioned Dan about it and he said, 'Well, the trouble with arsonists is most of the time they start the fire on the floor and fires don't start on floors,' and then he told me that there was a light fixture that came out of the wall, in the bathroom and Darrel had messed with the wiring so that it would short out and Dan had put a wet wash cloth over it. By the time the fire actually got started to where it was reported, Darrel was at this fireworks stand and Dan was at this one, so they were both taken care of as far as alibis.

"I could show you where Dan Carter grows his marijuana crop. I could tell you places to look in his house where I'm sure you didn't look."

Lorna described an area behind a wall in the closet and another area up in the chimney where Danny hid his marijuana.

Deppish acknowledged the seriousness of arson crime, but wanted to know whether the Carters had ever been involved in more violent crime. Had they ever murdered anyone? Lorna knew only that Darrel made threatening remarks about Marty, but had no knowledge of anything else.

"Do you have any reason to believe that Mark Bird was involved in any way with Marty's death?"

"I have no reason to believe it, Mark has always wanted me to try and say it was Dan Carter. I mean, I just always assumed, because Mark thinks it is Dan Carter."

"Do you have any explanation for Tom Bird, or whoever it was at Marty's death scene, as being as tall or taller than Marty?"

"I do now after we were back out there. That's one of the things that I told my husband. 'Tom's not as tall as Marty,' but then when we stopped, Randy said, 'But this is an incline.' He said, 'If someone was standing here and Marty was down there, to just look across and not think about it you would think the person was as tall as Marty, and then after Tom got down to where Marty was, Marty was already on the ground,'"

[How a man with virtually no firearm experience or record of violence could have fired one shot from 15 or more feet away and hit Marty is a fact that seemed to escape all who heard Lorna's claim.]

By the time this statement concluded, investigators heard Lorna make very serious claims about Tom. She had nothing to lose by spinning yarns, and they knew it. She had much to gain if they believed her and found the same kind of sensationalized circumstantial evidence to convict him as Lyon County had done just weeks earlier. But the bizarre theories about Tom went beyond even these as indicated by Agent Winsor's final line of questioning, almost a post-script to the session.

"Does Tom Bird use drugs or talk about using drugs?"

"He's never mentioned it...He drinks—I mean, he doesn't now, I'm sure, but he drank quite a bit before."

"Does he ever talk about getting a large amount of money and buying drugs, making more money, or anything like this at all?"

"No."

[In that period of time when the media trumpeted dozens of stories about the scandals in the ministries of Jim and Tammy Baker, and Jim Schweiger, almost any allegation against a pastor seemed plausible.]

The session ended.

Sign what?

Lorna swore to make truthful statements during this testimony. Jack Focht sat alongside her while she talked, and he only corrected her or coached her on a few occasions. He had heard her story before she told it to the police.

When Lorna saw the transcript a few days later, she was asked to make corrections if there were any errors. She made none; neither did she sign the document as she told investigators she would do. Lorna thought that signing the document opened her to perjury charges, and forgot that taking an oath to tell the truth required that she, in fact, actually do so.

Armed with an eyewitness testimony that Tom had murdered Marty, the kind of proof that had eluded them from the beginning, investigators began focusing on proving their case. This meant carefully checking Lorna's statement and pursuing irritating facts that got in the way of their theory. Still, with Lorna in tow, they had far more evidence against Tom than Lyon County had, and Symmonds had twice convicted Tom.

It took many months for Tom to finally see Lorna's statement, yet within weeks, a lawyer in Little Rock had it. Months later, a CBS TV producer had it and within 21 months, America knew about it thanks to *Murder Ordained,* the four-hour miniseries that told the world that Tom Bird was a cold-blooded murderer.

Lorna spent the fall of 1985 fantasizing about her release from prison, winning people to the Lord with help from her new husband, and selling her story in the hopes that she would save others from the kind of life she had led—at least that is what she told authors David Hacker, Barbara Livingston and writer Joan Baker. She reserved her greatest public bombshell for a March, 1986 article by Scott Kraft, a writer for *The Los Angeles Times,* when she told the world what she had told Deppish and Winsor that August: that Tom murdered Marty.

Gun found

Lorna told investigators on August 30, that Tom threw the murder weapon into a pond as he made his way up the road. Deputy Deppish drew a rough map of the area near the murder site and drew in the ponds that sat across Highway 177. She pointed to one, about 200 yards from the murder site.

Geary County spent thousands of dollars procuring metal detection and other specialty equipment, and on draining the pond. A bulldozer pushed the silt around, and deputies searched each muddy lump looking for the gun. On November 1, Deputy Gary Berges spotted a gun-shaped object buried in the mud, and after photographing it, reached down and pulled it out.

Stephen Anderson had earlier picked out a picture of the gun. He said it had been his father's who gave it to Marty. He identified a Colt Woodsman that matched the description Lorna had given. On this cold November day, almost two years after the murder, Berges finally held it in his hands.

Deppish and Opat refused to publicly divulge any details about the gun, referring to it as "an instrumentality of a crime." Opat said the "instrumentality" would help them move toward solving the crime by pointing them toward a likely killer. He refused to reveal any more details.

Later that month, Deppish hinted to Joan Baker of *KS Magazine,* that they had "the" gun, but said they would withhold any further identification, hoping to keep the defense guessing as long as possible. They planned to have the gun cleaned up and test-fired to ensure it was the same weapon. Shell casings found bear Marty could be compared to those fired during tests on the gun.

Lorna breaks her silence

During the late fall of 1985, Lorna decided to break her silence about both her private life and the crimes with which she had become associated. This meant writing a book, or several books as Lorna hoped, and talking to selected reporters like Joan Baker, the editor of *KS Magazine*.

Baker wrote to Lorna and asked for an interview that fall. She planned to publish a feature story about what she believed was the soon-to-be-resolved murder case of Marty Anderson. She hoped to provide readers details of that case and tie it to Tom's conviction in Sandy's death—equal parts of the same scheme.

Like nearly every other Kansan and tens of thousands of others who followed the news stories about Tom, Baker viewed this story as extremely unusual. She labeled it a "quadrangle murder"—two married couples with two murdered spouses. She knew the court had convicted Tom based on a motive of a torrid love affair with Lorna. Baker desperately wanted to write "the" definitive story.

Lorna agreed to an interview, setting limitations on certain questions, as she did with all interviewers. She forbade Baker from asking who actually murdered Marty, and she just refused to answer certain other questions. Lorna insisted that Baker agree not to interview Tom Bird. In December 1985, Baker entered Lansing prison to meet Lorna and her husband, Randy Eldridge.

Before Baker met Lorna, she had developed lines of communication that reached deep inside the investigation and she possessed extensive knowledge of the complicated case, having already interviewed several key players. One of her investigation sources was Sheriff Bill Deppish. She grew almost chummy with him, conducting her taped phone interview in a spirit usually reserved for good friends.

Baker asked Deppish whether test bullets fired from the gun they recently unearthed matched the spent cartridges found near Marty's body. Deppish explained that he and Opat had announced only that a weapon had been found, but would not confirm it as "the" murder weapon. "It may be one of those things we want to keep from the defense as long as we can." This quote begged the question, "What else do you plan to keep from the defense?" which Baker failed to ask.

Baker worried about when arrests would be made. Her story carried a short deadline and she wanted to name the accused killer. Deppish said no arrests would be made until after January 1, 1986, based on a pragmatic prosecutorial strategy. Prosecutors expected that more than 70 friendly witnesses could be called to the trial. If the county filed charges against anyone before Christmas, it meant bringing those 70 people to Junction City during the holidays. The "friendlies" could quickly become unfriendly, and prosecutors weren't interested in taking such a risk. The defendant's "right to a speedy trial" would interfere with the prosecution's best chances of winning.

Deppish said the county was "well over our budget and this is going to take a lot more money to bring this case to final conclusion...It's thousands and thousands of dollars." He planned additional visits to West Memphis and Fayetteville, Arkansas, Springfield, Illinois and Albuquerque, New Mexico. He and others had traveled to Mississippi, Florida and Texas. The case drained the county of time, money and human resources. Deppish longed to see it over and execute a sure conviction.

"Is it fair to say that Tom Bird is a prime suspect?" Baker asked.

"Yes."

"Is there any theory that charges might be filed against anyone else as an accomplice?"

"Yes. We know for a fact that there was [sic] seven people at the crime scene." (Four children, Marty, Lorna and the hit man.) None of the children were suspects. Marty was dead. Deppish said there existed a remote possibility that an eighth person could have been involved. He implied that Lorna would be charged as an accomplice.

Baker needed photographs of the crime scene to dramatize her story. Deppish said he would talk to the Chief Investigator and they would provide them. "Give us a call ahead of time," he said, because they were busy with another murder investigation.

When Baker's articles ran in *KS Magazine,* along with numerous pictures of various individuals involved in the investigation and crime sites, they included an artist's rendition of the gun even though the gun's identity had never been public. Baker refused to tell the court how the magazine knew what kind of gun deputies had found. Someone leaked the information to her, but she wasn't tattling.

Baker begged Deppish to call her right away if anything new developed and he readily agreed. She provided him with alternative phone numbers to be sure his call got through. As she said good-bye, he stated, "I keep hoping everyday when I wake up that somebody's gonna call up and say, 'Hey, I want to confess to this or tell you all about it.'"

Ask Darrel or Lorna

Baker attempted to interview Darrel Carter, but he refused to meet. She spoke by phone to him and was startled to hear him state, "I really don't think the story's over. We don't have the person that did the killing. I mean really they don't."

Baker was caught off guard. "In both cases [Martin Anderson and Sandy Bird], you mean?" she asked.

Darrel said, "Right." At the time he stated this, Tom sat incarcerated at Lansing Correctional Facility during the first days of his life sentence for Sandy's murder. Baker failed to pursue any line of questioning to determine what prompted Darrel to make such a claim. It's too bad she didn't call Deppish immediately to report this quote.

Baker interviewed many others for her article, but the star of the piece was Lorna, with Randy Eldridge sitting faithfully alongside during the interview.

As she spoke with Lorna she expressed frustration at trying to get her arms around the details of the case. She saw Tom's guilty verdict as confounding and wondered how prosecutors ever won a conviction without any evidence. Lorna told her it was because of the gossip and sensationalism in Emporia, and stated her belief that had Tom been tried in another county, he never would have been convicted.

Lorna told the reporter that Tom had a terrible problem telling the truth, and perhaps even had gotten to the point of no longer recognizing the truth. Her conclusions sounded more like her own life as she described it to David Hacker several days later.

Book deal

David Hacker, a Pulitzer Prize-winning writer from the *Manhattan Mercury,* who later moved to the *Wichita Eagle-Beacon,* saw Lorna as a type of woman who comes along once in a century. Writing Lorna's story could provide him a ticket to prosperity and national acclaim, though he denied that was his motive, so intrigued was he about how Lorna the little girl got to be Lorna the licentious lady.

Lorna told Hacker she wanted the story written to help others. She reasoned that readers could learn from her own sad story and find a path to God. She told him she had become a "born again Christian."

Lorna signed a contract with Hacker late in 1985. They agreed to limit the story to her life prior to age 21, rationalizing that these critical years determined the crooked path that she walked as an adult.

Hacker agreed to write the book in partnership, giving Lorna wide latitude to review and edit his copy. She planned to use the proceeds from the book to benefit her girls, or to provide income once she won parole. She strongly believed that her prison time would be limited to several months, though she told Hacker that if his story required it, she would chose to stay in prison longer.

Hacker saw Lorna at Lansing three times in late 1995 for a total of about 18 hours. "I very carefully steered clear of any reference to the death of her husband. I was not interested in that then; I am not now. I was only interested, and the book was aimed, solely at the mind of Lorna Anderson," he told the court during the inquisition. "By arbitrarily choosing about the age 20...I was trying to establish the character, the persona, of Lorna Slater."

He uncovered much of her hysteria and paranoia, her abortion and how she viewed her relationship with Tom Bird. He heard Lorna describe how she habitually used lies and distortions to win attention and approval. Lorna described her penchant for realistic fantasies and drama.

Lorna gloated about her power to control and manipulate men, especially Marty, but she said Tom was the only man she never could manipulate. She said he had a mysterious control over her. (Tom laughed at this. "She was right about one thing. She couldn't manipulate me into bed with her like she did with other men. But she certainly has controlled my life putting me here in prison.")

Hacker never published the book. Instead, Lorna became very nervous about it, fearing it would expose too much of her private life. She tried to stop its publication in a series of letters to Hacker. Hacker moved ahead and wrote a proposal and submitted it to publishers and tried to win a movie contract with it, but did so without Lorna's specific approval. Once he finally shared the draft chapters with her, she demanded to be released from the contract. She didn't want the world to know the real Lorna. She also feared potential unresolved criminal charges against her.

Hacker never spoke to Tom Bird.

Another book

Kansan Barbara Livingston also started to write a book about Lorna and Tom. She interviewed Lorna in prison on December 14, 1985 During that interview, Livingston inferred from Lorna's comments that she confessed her duplicity in Marty's murder.

"All right. Now, just so I get it clear, what you're telling the court is this. You questioned her about her involvement in a conspiracy to have Martin killed?" Opat asked.

"Yes."

"And she indicated to you that she was involved in such a conspiracy."

"Yes."

"And she indicated to you that she knew before Martin was killed the day he was going to be killed on?"

"I assu—yes, I assume so. If it—by her innuendoes, uh-huh."

"And she knew about the time the murder was to occur?"

"Approximately. Uh-huh."

"And that she knew about where it was going to occur in terms of location?"

"Yes."

Opat bored in, forcing Livingston to refer to her interview notes to be sure of her answers. She could not find specific references in those notes to support her claims, yet she remained convinced that Lorna had told her these things.

"Mrs. Anderson ever tell you she wanted her husband murdered?"

"I think 'dead.' Wanted him dead."

"Okay, dead. Why did she want him dead?"

"Her life, she felt, had become so tension-filled, so bad, so ugly, that she saw it was impossible to maintain any kind of a relationship anymore."

"Why did it become so ugly?"

"The verbal and physical abuse she had taken from Mr. Anderson."

Opat wondered why Lorna just didn't get a divorce, and Livingston stated she attempted to contact an attorney a couple of times, but Marty found out.

Opat feared that Lorna might claim spousal abuse in her defense, and wondered if there were any other possible defenses of which he needed to aware? Livingston mentioned Post Menstrual Syndrome. Lorna claimed PMS caused her to experience intense mood swings. She told David Hacker the same thing.

He asked Livingston about Lorna and Tom. Lorna told the woman she had been deeply in love with Tom and committed adultery with him. "She was deeply in love—or had loved him, she was deeply dependent on him." Here her answer provided a keen insight that had been discounted by prosecutors. "He seemed to answer a lot of needs about her quest for spiritual guidance, God, and true religious feelings she had for many, many years."

Lorna never told Livingston anything about desiring to see Sandy dead—just Marty. She acknowledged being in church the Sunday morning Sandy's body was found (confirming the testimony of Susie Graf who claimed Lorna was crying and left the service a few times).

"You know, she's previously told investigators and given sworn statements that this whole thing just happened without any preplanning or without her knowledge that it was going to happen at this particular time and particular place. You know she's made those kinds of statements, don't you?" Opat became upset at this turn of events. These answers complicated his prosecution of the case.

"August, when she and her attorney made their statement to the investigators," Livingston answered, referring to the August 30 statement Lorna gave police.

Opat acknowledged the August date, but reminded her of several previous statements Lorna made as well. Opat said Lorna had always claimed ignorance of the timing of the murder, "As if she didn't know that it was going to happen."

"Yes, that's right. That's what she said."

"Well, that is a lie, isn't it?"

"Yes."

"And she told you it was a lie?"

"I saw Lorna in December, 1985 at Lansing Women's Prison," implying that the passage of time made Lorna more prone to tell the truth.

"I understand that. Did she tell you that the earlier statement she'd given about how the murder of Martin had occurred was the truth or was a lie?"

"I did not ask her if it were a truth or a lie, sir."

"Okay. When she told you it was planned, it wasn't an accident."

"That it was no accident."

Opat knew that Livingston's claims violated the use immunity agreement he fashioned with Lorna in exchange for her statement that fingered Tom as the hit man. Now he needed a new strategy to use her to get Tom convicted, but it took him until 1988 following yet another plea agreement with Lorna.

Livingston never published a book, but she tried to keep close to the investigation. She never interviewed Tom.

Welcome to Los Angeles

Lorna changed the entire prosecution strategy and destroyed any chance Tom had for a fair appeals process by telling Scott Kraft and the world that Tom murdered Marty. Kraft wrote for the *Los Angeles Times* and sought and won an interview with Lorna.

Kraft's March 17, 1986, story ran 101 paragraphs and captured the imagination of Hollywood producers, agents and movie companies. Attorney Ben Wood filed Tom's appeal of his 1985 conviction with the Kansas Supreme Court on April 8, 1986. The feeding frenzy created by Kraft's article had a perverse effect on the outcome of that appeal.

Sophisticated Californians read how Trooper John Rule thought from the start that Sandy's death was no accident. They snickered at Rule's quote; "I started to feel hinky about the whole thing."

Kraft wrote that Marty's murder intensified the investigation into Sandy's unusual death. "For nearly three years, this small Kansas town watched in uneasy fascination as the minister and his secretary were exposed as adulterers and imprisoned for using the insurance money from one murder to make a down payment on a second."

"In a town where the cleric's robe is as revered as the judicial robe, the secret affair and the murderous schemes—discussed in the church of all places—were scandalous...Said Trooper Rule, 'We don't have those type of people out here.'"

Rule could have added that neither the Birds nor the Anderson's grew up in Emporia, making them even more suspect. He could have mentioned the nearly 60 men, many of them prominent Emporians, who admitted having sex with Lorna, but he believed "those type of people" didn't live in Emporia.

"At its root were motives as old as the Bible: Love. Money. Ambition," Kraft wrote.

Had Kraft actually interviewed Tom, he could have avoided many embarrassing factual errors. Lorna, though, provided him enough fodder to write several soap opera scripts.

When Virginia Bird learned of The Times' story details, she wrote, "It contains so many quotes from Lorna which are lies she is telling about Marty and Sandy's death implicating Tom to get herself out of trouble. She appears to us to include too many details which we had no knowledge of and this makes us very suspicious of her own involvement. Was she at the scene herself? This is a question in our minds."

Kraft reported that Tom ran five miles daily—wrong, he ran once or twice a week at most.

He wrote that by spring, Lorna and Tom were lovers—wrong, that was Lorna's story and it was one she changed as time passed.

He wrote that Lorna and Tom sneaked away to other towns where they could hold hands in public without fear of discovery—wrong, no proof exists, although proof exists that Lorna and her former boss did this.

He wrote, "Bird was unhappy in his marriage too." Wrong again, according to many witnesses, especially Bird family members who saw them together days before Sandy's death. Even Jane acknowledged that Sandy told her she found peace in their relationship.

Next, Kraft's story got bound up in what Darrel claimed and what Lorna now claimed happened during the meeting at Faith. Kraft slanted the story to match Darrel's court testimony, though Lorna denied to Tom, Irv Shaw and Joan Baker many of Darrel's claims.

Kraft wrote that Sandy Bird was buried in Arkansas, but said Tom presided at her funeral—wrong, Ralph Bird spoke and presided at the funeral. Tom sat weeping with his children.

Lorna told Kraft that Tom confessed to her that he murdered Sandy, that he ran barefoot on gravel roads and dumped his clothes in trash cans along the way. This confession never happened.

Kraft wrote that the $5,000 used to lure someone to murder Marty came from Tom. This allegation had never been established in court and was, in fact, disproved eventually.

Kraft wrote a deft description of the circus atmosphere surrounding Tom's first trial. "In June, 1984, after weeks of headlines and chatter in Emporia, the show finally came to town. Tom Bird went on trial. Emporians, some carrying their own stadium cushions, stood in line for a spot on the long gallery benches. Women brought cookies and cakes for Bird."

Kraft might have described Jane's active courting of prosecution officials and witnesses, but he didn't.

"The trial boiled down to a question of motive. Was Bird or wasn't he having an affair with Marty Anderson's wife, Lorna?" (Lorna said "yes." Tom said "no." No one else knew the truth. Should the public believe the promiscuous woman or the preacher?)

"Bird's attorney argued that the romantic relationship was all in Lorna's mind." (There being no other evidence, Shaw had arrived at a rational conclusion.)

Kraft described the ethical struggles faced by the *Emporia Gazette*. His description hinted at the real issues that drove the paper's fascination with the story and its passionate pursuit of a resolution to Sandy's death. "Emporia's appetite for the scandal was growing, too. 'It was just a bottomless reservoir of gossip,' says [Ray] Call, the Gazette's managing editor. The story raised ethical questions for the Gazette...The newspaper published a series of articles about the unanswered questions in the Bird case. When local investigators still showed no interest, the Gazette editors met privately with the state attorney general to express their concerns."

[Reporters are hired to report the news, not to become prosecutorial or defense advocates. Gazette reporters Nancy Horst and Roberta Birk crossed that line by pressuring the Kansas Attorney General to become involved in the case. This placed unwanted additional pressure on local investigators to "do something," make someone pay for Sandy's mysterious death, even if there existed no proof. Investigators were chasing a string of rumors and gossip that drove their investigation with very little evidence in hand. Given Lorna's seduction of a fair number of men, whom they no doubt knew personally, they became anxious to bring closure to the story. Sheriff Andrews lost a re-election bid in part because of a perception that he was doing too little to bring Sandy's murderer to trial. This method of reporting, buoyed by "Emporia's appetite for the sandal" exploded and in its wake, had destroyed any hope that Tom Bird could find justice in Lyon County.]

Kraft wrote about Susan Ewert's "open letter" published in the Gazette. He described Susan as "a Faith Lutheran parishioner." Wrong—Susan belonged to First Presbyterian where she had served as an elder.

Kraft wrote that in August of 1985, Lorna told investigators that she and Tom plotted to murder Marty. Wrong—in that statement, Lorna told investigators that Tom confessed to murdering Marty and she had known nothing about it.

The coup de grace of Kraft's article was next. "In the recent interview with The Times, Lorna Eldridge admitted working with Bird to murder her husband the night of Nov. 4, 1983. She says that she has since told investigators that Bird was the 'masked robber' who killed her husband, and that the weapon was Marty's own gun, taken from a cedar chest in her basement months earlier."

"She says that she followed Bird's instructions that night."

In these paragraphs, Kraft wrote a startling thing, the kind of scoop that could result in a Pulitzer Prize, if true. For the first time in print anywhere, Kraft wrote that Tom murdered Marty and that Lorna served as his accomplice. For Love. For Money. For Ambition. It was a powerful tale much like Greek tragedies, Shakespeare's greatest works or "As the World Turns."

Hollywood loved this story. Within days, as many as 24 production companies chased Lorna, Tom, Jane, Ralph and Virginia, John Rule, Vern Humphrey, Don Winsor, Dan Andrews, Bill Deppish, Rod Symmonds, Stevan Opat—a cast of dozens associated with this sordid tale. A quadrangle murder meant a Hollywood smash hit.

Tom's court appeal hung in the balance during the height of the Hollywood feeding frenzy. The Kansas Supreme Court read his brief and heard his arguments at the same time CBS filmed their scurrilous soap opera, *Murder Ordained,* as a four-hour mini-series. Any hopes that Tom had that facts would overcome fancy fell dead.

Tinsel Town, Kansas

Early in 1986 several stories were published about Tom, Lorna and the deaths of their spouses. Calvin Trillin wrote a mostly factual story in the *New Yorker*. *The Kansas City Star* carried a two-part series in its magazine section (the story, titled "The Preacher and the Spider Lady" won a Ball State University National Journalism Writing Award for its author, Bill Norton). Supermarket tabloids and detective magazines published their sordid sensationalized versions.

The first edition of Joan Baker's three-part *KS Magazine* series appeared in February 1986. Virginia Bird wrote of Tom's reaction to the Baker article:

"Tom calls and is upset because he hears of the *KS Magazine* article that came out written by Baker that points him out as such a monster. This article which contains incidents told by Lorna A. [includes]... the words supposedly screamed and begged by Sandy as she came to her violent death. [Lorna claimed to have nothing to do with Sandy's death, yet she told Baker about the words Sandy shouted out while being murdered. How did she know?]

"How horrible to depict this gentle Tom as such a harsh killer, when he could never do such a thing to the Sandy he always loved.

"These character assassinations by newsprint just seem to keep on and on and we are powerless to do anything about it. Tom speaks of giving up hope for his appeal and saying he will be convicted again by the news media before anyone ever gets a chance to exonerate him in the appeals court."

Even with all this exposure, it took Scott Kraft's *Los Angeles Times* story to really catch Hollywood's attention and penchant for making merchandise of the latest real life tragedy.

So sick of the lies and distortions as he had become, Tom hoped that a movie about his life and legal travails could set the record straight. The Bird's asked Robert Hecht, Tom's attorney in the murder trial, to help them sort through all the offers that they received. In case Tom signed a contract, Hecht hoped to establish a trust fund for the children to be funded by income from the sale of Tom's story. Tom wrote furiously on his own book, thinking he was the only person who could accurately tell his side of the story.

Eleven companies contacted Tom vying for his story rights.

Responding to this Hollywood courtship and the very idea that a criminal might sell his story, two Kansas lawmakers introduced a bill to stop criminals from profiting by their crimes. Republican Representatives Martha Jenkins of Leavenworth, and Clint Acheson of Topeka, spurred on by the quick-paced tempo set by Hollywood, introduced their bill on March 24, a week after the Kraft article appeared in The Times. Congress had earlier passed a similar law when John Hinkley Jr. made public his plan to write a book about his attempt to kill President Ronald Reagan. The infamous New York murderer, Son of Sam, had published his story and gained an infamous notoriety that set off debates in state legislatures across America. Kansas decided to join 22 other states that had already passed such laws.

Governor John Carlin signed the new law on April 21, less than a month later. "The law, which goes into effect July 1, is directed at Thomas P. Bird, a former Emporia pastor convicted of murder, and former state Senator Paul Hess, who fled the country..." reports stated. The article failed to mention Lorna, who had at least one signed contract with an author, negotiated with movies companies and planned a few books of her own.

Trillin, one of the few writers Tom allowed to interview him, offered him $1,000 for the rights to his story.

David Hacker, deep into the process of marketing his book about Lorna, also dickered with some movie producers.

Dick Clark Productions sought to make an NBC movie. Clark signed an agreement with Jane Grismer. "We could not, in good conscience, tell the story from their [Tom and Lorna] point of view. And, we respect and applaud the Kansas State law which forbids a criminal from profiting from his or her crime. We are working with the Grismer family ... to depict a moving account of the tragic story which we plan to present responsibly and sensitively," Clark wrote to the *Emporia Gazette*. Clark decided Tom's point of view was without merit.

Henry "The Fonz" Winkler sought the story rights. Tom felt he presented the best case for fairness and planned to produce a movie for ABC. Winkler signed a contract with both Tom and Lorna on June 26, just days before the law became effective that banned such agreements. Tom saw in this agreement the potential to raise money from a movie to set up a trust for his children.

Before all the dust cleared, as many as three dozen companies fought for the story. CBS beat them all.

Mike Robe led the CBS effort to do a movie originally titled *Kansas Gothic,* then *Broken Commandments,* and finally *Murder Ordained.* Robe's grandfather had run an Emporia hardware store, his father attended college in Emporia and he still had relatives living there. Robe represented Interscope Communications, directed the movie and co-wrote the script. "Because it happened in an area that has always seemed like home to me, I really wanted to do the story. I wanted to try to find out how those things could happen and why they happened. Additionally, I think I wanted to make sure that it was done in a way that was fair to Kansas."

Kathleen Cromley, another Interscope employee who worked on the movie, had relatives in Emporia and the nearby town of Olpe. At the beginning of the production, CBS took great care to salve the sensitivities of Emporians, and Cromley helped ease their way. "We do not want to dwell on the early [sexual] events at all. We're interested in unraveling how it happened, who was involved in bringing these two to justice."

Robe won the support and imagination of most Emporians. He waged and lost one battle, though, trying to find a church willing to be used as the set for Faith. The public debate got ugly and Robe threatened to move the shoot out of Emporia altogether. The mere thought of losing the notoriety and the $10 million the community hoped to earn from the movie caused the Gazette to gag. Ray Call wrote a "Classified Ad" begging some understanding church to realize how important the movie was to the community's economy and release their building as a movie set. The churches united and refused to cooperate stating that their mission was to spread the Gospel, not the filthy lucre of a Hollywood movie.

Eventually a church in Lawrence signed on. Aware of the centuries old division between the Lutheran and Catholic churches, Robe snidely scripted the church as St. Mary's Lutheran.

Emporia finds life as Tinsel Town

Emporia came alive. The town's spirit was captured in an April 1, 1986, letter to the editor written by Kay Little "and unnamed cohorts."

"A bunch of us were sitting around Saturday evening discussing the major issues of our fair community…when we decided what this town needs is a movie based on the lives and loves of our most famous (infamous?) couple, Tom and Lorna.

"It seems highly probable that there will be a movie, so why not make it here where everything really happened. Our ailing economy would benefit greatly by all those movie people coming to town. Motels and restaurants and bars would be full again, and they could probably use any number of us locals as extras."

Ms. Little suggested various actors to play lead roles in the movie, picturing Jack Nicholson as Tom and Jessica Lange as Lorna. For Danny and Darrel, she debated between "Don Johnson, Burt Reynolds, Tom Sellack and Dom Deluise." Little believed such a movie could win an Emmy.

Ms. Little forgot that Tom's court appeal was, at that time, headed for the Kansas Supreme Court, and if she did know, she may not have cared. Emporia, the sleepy commercial town suffering from an economic downturn, would win money, jobs, and notoriety.

Jake Thompson wrote in the *Kansas City Star,* quoting Janis Ralston from the Emporia Chamber of Commerce. "I think it's unfortunate this whole scandal happened. But if we've already had the negative publicity, we might as well get something positive back."

The "something" she referred to meant money for Emporia's businesses. Thompson knew that the Kansas Film Board stood to make millions off such a production.

A Tom Bird movie meant an economic boost for everyone.

On August 12, 1986, *The Los Angeles Times* ran a special story about the movie's progress, but Emporians took offense at the way it pictured them. The Gazette wanted to deflect the Times' perception of Emporia as a backwoods town and in an editorial, Ray Call wrote:

> "It is clear that writers and television reporters arrive in town with a pre-conceived notion of what Emporia is like. Usually their descriptions seem to fit the old visions that city dwellers have of heartland America; a place where life is stuck in a Leave-It-to-Beaver time frame.
>
> "Emporia City Commissioner Leonore Rowe makes a good point when she is quoted... 'We're really not a backwoods town.'
>
> "A careful reporter would find that most Emporians DO NOT depend on cable television to keep in touch with the outside world. Many Emporians are well-traveled. Indeed, there is a good chance that the ratio of world-travelers is greater in Emporia than it is in Los Angeles.
>
> "Mayor William Jenks commented. 'I don't want to sound inhuman, but we do need income (from a TV production). But we need that kind of publicity like a hole in the head.'
>
> "Chamber of Commerce president Dale Stinson said, 'We wish it had never happened...but we're going to make the most of it.'"

The battle for Emporia's pride even drew barbs from other Kansas towns. The Gazette reacted to a story written in Hays. The writer warned Emporia to shed its naivete about how Hollywood would tell the story. She saw Tinsel Town as totally uninterested in accuracy, only caring about sensationalism. The Gazette acknowledged this, but chastised the writer for this quote: "Probably, Emporians won't much care. They seem more interested in the money that's to be made by cooperating with the vultures..."

The Gazette retorted, "Most of the folks who agreed to help with the film were motivated more by the desire for accuracy than by greed. These Emporians and members of Sandy Bird's family, signed on as consultants to help the filmmakers tell the story right. They will work for their money. They also will be paid for allowing the film makers to portray them in the film."

The Gazette didn't realize the bias this story revealed, or if it did, it totally discounted Tom's side of the story. Mentioning Sandy's family as consultants sent a clear signal to the Birds: Jane's version of events would set the movie's tone. Without the Birds to counter her clouded recollections, it left little hope for accuracy.

What Emporians might profit from the movie?

Trooper John Rule became the highest paid of the local consultants. While still on the Kansas Highway Patrol payroll, he signed a contract paying him $75,000, plus $1,000 a day for his work on the movie.

Dennis Arb testified in Tom's second trial and was a cousin of Sheriff Dan Andrews. He wrote to the Gazette on October 30, 1986:

> "Were you on the bridge July 17, 1983? Did you see the fine investigative work of our Highway Patrolman? Several citizens did. We found blood that he wanted to push aside as 'fish-bait blood,' the same samples that were used as evidence in the trial. And what about the other evidence—the party cups. Why were no fingerprints established? Our patrolman let the cups sit at the murder scene over half a day to be fingered by all onlookers, including himself.

> "I, myself, went back that afternoon. No one was around, but there sat those cups. It was easy to see that foul play was involved, but for some reason blood samples were filed away and another life had to be lost before our Highway Patrolman came forward and said he had it figured out all along.

> "If it took $75,000 for a lie to become a true story, what is the truth worth? A little peace of mind, a bit of satisfaction, and a little less respect for the law enforcement and reporters just doing their job."

Arb said Andrews, and later Agent Humphrey, actually kept the investigation going. It rankled Arb that Rule became the movie's hero and its highest paid consultant. Rule's big payday rankled others too, who thought Kansas law prevented these types of payments to government employees. Rule eventually received a promotion and a transfer out of town. Arb said it was the result of bad feelings by other local police toward him because of the money and credit that he received.

Gazette reporters Horst and Birk also got paid. They were portrayed in the movie as duel heroines for forcing local and state authorities to pursue the investigation into Sandy's death. Humphrey became a consultant.

The Kansas film board received $3 million from the producers for helping stage the movie.

Kansas made money. Emporia made money. Officials made money. Robe made a lie.

On June 11, Terry Smith called Ralph and Virginia about a Topeka TV news story. "Channel 13 had a news item about the people in Tom's case signing with the movie companies and in the background the TV coverage of the trial was shown again picturing Ralph and me, etc. Lorna A. has signed with HBO (ye gods!)."

Virginia wondered, since so many of the investigators, reporters, and Jane received offers from production companies, why she and Ralph were ignored. "It's funny, but no one has asked us for a contract as yet. I don't think they are interested in Tom's true story or ours."

CBS began filming on November 3, 1986. The Kansas Supreme Court heard oral arguments for Tom's appeal of his murder conviction four days earlier, on October 30.

Movie fouls appeal

Appeals attorney Ben Wood wrote what seemed like a brilliant appeal to the Kansas Supreme Court and hand-delivered it to Kansas Attorney General Robert Stephan on April 8, 1986. Wood raised nine points of contention with the Lyon County jury's decision in the Sandy Bird murder case.

Item 1. The indictment was defective and made it impossible for Tom to defend himself.

Item 2. Judge Rulon failed by not striking Billy Persinger's entire testimony, and by overruling Robert Hecht's many objections to that testimony.

Item 3. During closing arguments, Symmonds interjected as truth certain facts that never had been heard in the trial. (He said Tom wore a bloody jogging suit.)

Item. 4. Judge Rulon should never have allowed Trooper Rule's rough drawing of the murder scene admitted as evidence—or even used during testimony.

Item 5. Judge Rulon should have ordered a new trial once Diana Spires came forward to testify that Charles Henderson lied in court.

Item 6. Symmonds' presentation of evidence failed to prove the charges in the indictment or Bill of Particulars.

Item 7. Symmonds' presentation of evidence that a homicide had occurred fell far short of any reasonable doubt that Sandy died by auto accident. In addition, Symmonds failed to prove that Tom Bird was present at the death site.

Item 8. Judge Rulon failed when he denied a change of venue, violating Tom's Sixth Amendment rights to a fair trial by an impartial jury.

Item 9. One of Judge Rulon's jury instructions caused the jury to conclude that the state did not have to prove beyond reasonable doubt that Tom had intent to commit homicide. This violated his right to due process under the Fourteenth Amendment.

In May, when he visited Tom at Lansing, accompanied by private investigator James Kenney, Wood believed Tom would prevail. The three of them were upbeat. Virginia reflected on this, "They are very optimistic and feel that the state of Kansas has to take a good hard look at the appeal because if it is taken to a higher court it would embarrass the judges."

During oral argument on October 30, Supreme Court Justice Harold Herd grilled Rod Symmonds. "I think there's plenty of evidence of her death by foul play," but went on to question how the state could put her time of death and the presence of Tom together at the same site. Then he asked, "Is there or do you have any evidence to show Bird was with his wife and was available to kill her? Would you list the evidence you relied upon to connect Bird with the foul play? If you've given it already, I still haven't picked up on it." "Tom Bird was not convicted on one piece of evidence," Symmonds told the court. "Each witness added a piece to the puzzle, which we put together." He spoke of the more than 70 witnesses and hundreds of pieces of evidence he presented. Had the judges looked closely at the witness list, they would have seen that the vast majority of witnesses were involved in "chain of custody. These witnesses saw no crime, just the results of Sandy's death. The sheer number of "witnesses" suggested, Symmonds believed, that the state presented a thorough case.

Had the justices looked closely at the hundreds of pieces of evidence described by Symmonds, they would have seen that a large number of exhibits—"evidence"—were nothing but empty paper bags used to store and file rocks, blood samples and the like. Or they could have counted the more than 100 photos, many of them duplicates. "It's like the state loaded up a cannon with a lot of mud and sticks and twigs. Then they put Thomas Bird up against a barn and fired the cannon. Then they looked to see how much of the mud got on Tom Bird," Wood said.

Winkler wanted to wait until the appeal ruling was issued before moving ahead with his version of the movie. He wanted Tom's situation resolved—it made a better story line. Winkler expected the court to free Tom Bird.

The Kansas Supreme Court issued its decision on December 4, 1986. On Friday, December 5, 1986, Virginia wrote:

"This day shall live in as much infamy to our family as Pearl Harbor which is remembered this week. We receive the news in a phone call from Tom that the Supreme Court has upheld the decision to call Tom guilty. We are devastated to say the least. We had such hopes. The news stories after the oral arguments were so encouraging. It is almost sadistic to offer us and Tom this ray of hope the judges gave by asking the questions—especially the Judge Herd. Then snatching this hope away as a morsel of food from a hungry dog. We just can't believe that seven judges could be objective and yet come up with this erroneous decision."

The next day, she wrote:

"Oh, the hurt we must carry. We have so many thoughts running through our minds.

"Such unfair decisions must be politically motivated. Tom says the seven judges didn't have the guts to buck the publicity even though they know what's right. They had to think of Kansas and the economy as it is and then decide whether to reverse the decision for Tom and lose $3 million for the film commission of Kansas due to this movie which already has filmed its story of Sandy's death declaring Tom the murderer, which would have to be stopped, redone or quit altogether. This is a lot of money riding on a decision like this. The judge could not deny Kansas so they denied Tom."

On December 15, Wood talked to Ralph and Virginia.

"He says he spent a week in shock and can't believe what happened in Tom's case. He really believes in him and feels just awful. He says that at a budget meeting he overheard some reporters saying they were very surprised at the verdict too. Mr. Woods will work on a re-hearing process (30 days) and also hopes to get it all in Federal Court."

Wood filed a Writ of Certiorari with the United States Supreme Court on March 24, 1987. He informed the court of four issues:

Issue 1. The indictment for first degree murder failed to specify how Tom allegedly murdered Sandy.

Issue 2. The effect of allowing Charles Henderson to testify was to use his testimony that Tom "had his wife killed" to prove Tom's intent to commit murder; these are two different crimes. Wood asked how the state could use one alleged crime that would have exonerated Tom of murder, i.e. conspiracy, to prove that he committed a different crime?

Issue 3. The denial of a change of venue damaged Tom's ability to win a fair trial and Tom had met all the requirements to prove prejudice.

Issue 4. Allowing Charles Henderson to testify that Tom conspired to have someone kill his wife prejudiced the jury. Woods correctly claimed that Tom never was charged with conspiracy to commit Sandy's murder.

The Supreme Court refused to hear Tom's case.

Emporia becomes a movie set

Hollywood came to Emporia amidst a welcome by Gov. Carlin and a gaggle of excited Emporians. Filming started on a cold, brisk Kansas day. Mike Robe made sure to film Gov. Carlin for a cameo appearance.

The cold weather complicated matters for the filmmakers and set the tone for the movie's many factual errors. Since Sandy's death occurred in mid-July, CBS had to ignore the steam emanating from character's mouths caused by the cold November air.

Kansas newspapers were awash that fall and early winter with stories about the movie describing the crews, cast, set locations, disruption of lives and curiosity of Emporians. Stories documented the economic success brought by the movie to motels, restaurants, and all manner of stores. Even a local clothier profited when it learned that costumers prefer buying from local venders. Two local houses were rented for the movie's stars.

News stories featured Keith Carradine, hired to play Trooper Rule, the movie's hero, JoBeth Williams, the aptly chosen soap opera star who played Lorna Anderson, and Chicago playhouse actor Terry Kinney who played Tom Bird. Kinney's deep-set eyes and smirky smile perfectly fit the film's perception of Tom as a shady, charismatic and sensual man.

Robe's script took great care to protect those he saw as innocent. Danny and Darrel Carter's names were changed, as were most of those who would most likely sue CBS. No such care was taken with Tom, Sandy, Lorna and Marty. Law enforcement officials' real names were used, but their on-screen images were positive. Rumors floated about town over the names of Lorna's many lovers, and care was taken to protect them. One rumor had the Kansas City Royals threatening a lawsuit if any of their players became part of the story as Lorna's lovers.

Scores of local aspiring actors and wannabes auditioned for bit parts, and many appeared in the movie, shot mostly on-location in and around Emporia. Even Ray Call, the Gazette's editor, played a drummer in a dance scene.

National opposition

As expected, the Bird family opposed making *Murder Ordained*. Stephen Anderson, Marty's brother, also wanted it stopped.

"I'm extremely doubtful that the issue of truth will be served by the premature production and airing of this movie. In fact, what it can do is help to stifle the truth. This movie is being produced for one reason and one reason only: to exploit a particular human tragedy and to make a buck.

"There is no question my brother was murdered. We need to know the truth, not have the story told first in the newspapers or in a movie, but first and last in a court of law. We should not be a part of something that will destroy the process of justice."

Winkler and Bird sued CBS and Interscope to stop production to protect their own story. Robert Hecht saw part of the script. "It is filled not only with inaccuracies, but with a substantial number of false, totally fabricated incidents, which could not be the result of any inference at all from public records or law enforcement records."

Though they failed in their $40 million suit, eventually dropping it altogether, they were able to win release of an early copy of the first half of the script. Tom read it and knew the movie would be a disaster. It contained hundreds of factual errors and outright fictional representations. Hecht identified several instances of factual error and said the movie producers had been told several times to delete the lies, but " they have no interest in doing so."

Despite earlier assurances that the film would avoid the seedy sexual allegations of Tom's two trials, it contained several scenes, which, by 1986 standards, pushed the envelope of decency. Ralph Bird pleaded with CBS to stop the movie, fearing it would irreparably damage the Bird children. Ralph said the script relied too much on Lorna's statements. Though Lorna never was interviewed for the movie, her statements had been plastered from coast to coast in several news articles.

Sheriff Deppish wanted the movie stopped. He still had a murderer to convict.

The movie concluded filming on December 22, after 40 days.

Ray Call of the Gazette expressed nostalgia as the actors left town.

"At a 'Wrap Party' to celebrate completion of the shooting, director Michael Robe and producer Phillip Parslow had nothing but kind words to say about Emporia. At that point, they were through with the town so there was no reason for them to gloss over any hard feelings. They seemed sincere.

"Now the film makers are gone and the wait begins. For the next six or seven weeks the raw film will be edited, spliced and matched to a sound track. And come next March [it was May], Emporians will see the results.

"At this point, most townspeople expect the best."

On February 9, Winkler called Ralph and Virginia with bad news. "They will probably not make a TV mini series of Tom's story....Henry Winkler did say that he heard that CBS had their rendition of this in the cutting room at this time and yet really didn't know when it could be aired."

Tom expected the worst and so did hundreds of members of the Lutheran Church Missouri Synod. Tom mailed a newsletter to his friends and supporters, urging them to write CBS. The Gazette saw Tom's newsletter as a pathetic plea and wrote a story about it. CBS received hundreds of letters of protest and sent a response to each, stating the movie was accurate and it would air, but "thanks for writing." CBS knew that controversy meant more viewers.

LC-MS Pastor James Likens called Ralph and Virginia and said that *TV Guide* agreed to let him write a story giving Tom's view of the movie. Likens collected information from the Birds and submitted his article. On March 9, Virginia wrote, "Likens tells us *TV Guide* turned down his story for the April issue. He was so sorry—but he said they weren't ready to come out that strongly on Tom's innocence. Isn't that something—they prefer to write about guilt."

Tom watches with a few "friends"

The movie aired on May 3 and May 5, after weeks of hype and promotion. The broadcast schedule called for two, two-hour segments. CBS billed it as "based on a true story."

The first two hours of *Murder Ordained* portrayed many of the story's sleazier elements and pictured Tom as a highly charismatic man who controlled the minds, hearts and actions of Faith's members. It pictured those members as uneducated, just like it pictured most other Emporians. To everyone viewing these Kansans, they saw backwoods people living in a backwoods city.

Tom sat watching in utter horror at the lies and distortions. Especially repugnant were scenes between him, Sandy and the children. Robe fabricated them all. Sandy lay dead and he never spoke with Tom, the children or any of the Birds.

Most of the scenes involving Lorna were also fabrications, but they were based on her numerous interviews and statements. Perhaps one of Jane's Little Rock attorneys or Junction City police officials gave them a copy of Lorna's August 30 statement. Any private interaction between her and Marty was fabricated as well since, like Sandy, he lay dead and Robe never interviewed Lorna.

Tom watched the movie on a TV shared by several inmates. The others hooted, hollered and harassed him as they viewed him pinning Lorna on his church office desk in a frantic sex scene. Robe staged the frenzied lovers pushing the LC-MS blue hymnal off the desk to make room for her backside, sticking yet another needle in the church.

The first two-hour segment left a clear impression that Tom murdered Marty. Robe had Terry Kinney dressed in the black mask and tight jacket worn by the hit man as testified to by Lorna. Kinney's eyes, by then viewed numerous times, were prominent in the murder scene. Aired in 1987, Robe asserted that Tom murdered Marty, though he had not even been charged with the crime.

The following day Tom did his best to avoid the catcalls and perverse prattle of other inmates. They knew he had been a preacher and now they saw this licentious side of him. They thought it was a hoot.

On Tuesday evening, the second segment aired. Much of it dealt with Tom's two trials. His fellow inmates once again were glued to the screen only this time they were subdued. They each had been the subject of police investigations and sat through their own trials. They saw through the legal tricks and tactics of the prosecutors and investigators. Then knew about Tom's stubborn claim of innocence. Seeing him as depicted in the movie, they began to believe him—the system got Tom, not his guilt.

CBS feared being sued by Lorna who had yet to be tried for Marty's murder (she was charged May 1, just two days before the movie aired). The movie carried a disclaimer at the end stating that she had been charged but that the trial was to be held soon. No such disclaimer existed about Tom. Viewers were left with the clear impression that he not only was an adulterer who murdered his wife, but a cold-blooded assassin who murdered Marty. Almost 34 months later, Tom entered the Geary County Courthouse to face that murder charge—the second part of Judge Gradert's "equal scheme" scenario.

America knew about and had judged Tom guilty, thanks to CBS. A movie such as this, though, cannot be resigned to a library to collect dust. Turner Network Television began broadcasting it years later so that a new generation of viewers could judge and condemn him.

SECTION VII:

TRIAL IN JUNCTION CITY

"Facts are stubborn things; and whatever may be our wishes, our inclinations, or the dictates of our passions, they cannot alter the state of facts and evidence."

President John Adams, December, 1770

Jailhouse stories

Steven Opat and Bill Deppish received a curious piece of mail in early January, 1986. Postmarked in Kansas City on January 8, the anonymous letter read:

"Dear D.A. Opat and Sherif [sic] Deppish:

"I am an inmate at the Kansas Correctional Woman's Prison. I am writing you because your names keep coming up in conversations with Lorna Eldgridge [sic]. I realize I am breaking the inmate code of silence but I believe I must and have good reason to.

"I am guilty. I am being punished for what I have done. According to Lorna she is the guilty one. She mocks you and said she has lied about that preacher guy. She laughs that he is doing time for doing nothing. She said he is guilty of wanting her and now he and his goodie goodie attitude will see who has power. She says she'll show everyone that she has power and is in control. She does not seem to deal with real life at times. And I am scared of her. I'm not sure she is all there.

"I am sick of her lies and the acts she puts on. She will get us in trouble up here. She already has a nother [sic] lover—a guard and it makes it hard on us. I did not know who to write to about her lies. She said she fooled you with her statement [sic] so I thought you should know. I do not know if that preacher's lawyer should be told or the judge?

"I will testify but right now I am afraid of her. She is an evil wicked woman. She will make it hard on all of us her here. She sneaks around with that guard and I don't need no more troubles.

"I am guilty and deserve my punishment. This woman plans to get out and out of both murders she was involved in and let others suffer for what she and carter and bingham and currie [sic] has done. Will you help bring about justice?

"I will keep looking for someone to help if she keeps getting away with MURDERS and other people suffer. It's not right that, that preacher is being punished for nothing. I would have thought him to be just as guilty if I hadn't heard it myself from that woman. I do not want them to make it hard for me for being a snitch so...

"no name for now"

Deppish sent the letter to the KBI laboratory and they identified the typewriter model. Agent Winsor then spoke with John Callison, Deputy Director at the woman's prison.

Lorna claimed he had called her into his office because he heard that her life had been threatened. Callison denied such a meeting ever took place. Winsor read Lorna's prison file and found no references about any such threats. Callison knew of no threats on Lorna's life.

Winsor requested an inventory of all the typewriters in the prison and found one that matched the description given by the KBI. Another one like it sat in an office in downtown Lansing where some inmates worked during the day. Whether either of these matched the type on the anonymous letter remains unknown, but it appeared the strange letter had originated in prison.

Investigators visited Lansing Correctional Facility and talked with two more male inmates, looking for another jailhouse snitch. Humphrey had done this to win the testimony of Charles Henderson for Tom's first murder trial, and Tom feared that the same tactic would be used again for his inevitable trial for Marty's murder.

Investigators also sought a snitch or two from those who knew Lorna.

They found a snitch in Connie Wheeler. Wheeler told them in a January 23, 1986, interview that she was about the only friend Lorna had in prison— the anonymous letter suggested this to be true. "Lorna was mostly a loner. She and I were friends because we were cellmates."

Lorna had told her the entire story about Tom murdering Marty, but added some new twists. Lorna met Tom and the hit man earlier in the day of the murder, but the hit man said he needed more money. Tom decided to do the murder himself. When the murder happened, "Lorna says she was in shock then even though she and Bird planned the killing, she was shook up when she saw it happen."

"Lorna told me shortly after the murder of her husband a man she knew was in her house when she came home and he had a gun and threatened her and told her if she ever talked about what happened she would be killed. She never told me who this man was."

Investigators asked about Lorna's mental state during her incarceration. "She was very depressed, she called her husband and told him to come get her wedding rings, and divorce me because I know I won't ever get out of prison. I asked her why she felt that way and she said because I know the cops will find out the truth about what happened and charge me with it."

"Did Lorna ever discuss any other plans she had with Bird or anybody to kill her husband?"

"Yes, she told me about a plan to make it look like a burglary and about a plan to kill Marty and drive him off a bridge and make it look like an accident." This latter suggestion now matched Darrel's version of the meeting at Faith. A month earlier, she had totally and with great drama contradicted this plan while talking with Joan Baker.

"This money and hit man she told you about on the day of Marty's murder, was this different from the other one with Carter and Curry?"

"Yes, she told me about those and this was a totally different conspiracy."

Investigators asked about others who might have heard Lorna's story. There were two. Louisa Edmonson served as Lorna's bodyguard and Betty Cooper her go-between. Lorna paid Edmonson money for the commissary and gave her care packages from outside. "Why did Lorna need a protector?" they asked.

"Lorna was not well-liked, she didn't associate with anyone and put on airs like she was better than everyone else."

Deppish showed Wheeler the anonymous letter and asked her if it could have come from within the prison. Wheeler said the envelope resembled those that prisoners received from the "Seven Step Foundation" and the words sounded like something Lorna herself would write, even suggesting that some of the words "...is [sic] almost exactly like a Bible quote that Lorna was always writing on note paper and stuff." (Why would Lorna send such a letter to Opat and Deppish, or did someone who knew her well steal her words and send it?)

"Did Lorna ever say anything about her past?"

"Ya, she said she used to drink a lot and smoke pot, and had lots of sex with different guys."

"Do you think Lorna could be having an affair with one of the guards?"

"Yes, I work nights and sleep days when I was there so Lorna had the cell to herself during the night. I believe anyone could have sex with either a male or female guard if they wanted to. I know for a fact several inmates did while I was there. Lorna could have been turned out by an inmate, too, but I don't think she was."

"What do you mean turned out?"

"Sex with another inmate, by force or threat, etc."

"Would you be willing to come back to Kansas and testify in court about what you told us today?"

"Yes, if it will help keep an innocent person out of jail. I wish someone had taken as much interest in my case as you guys are with Lorna. It might have helped me."

Wheeler, twice convicted of murder, viewed Deppish and Buskey as Lorna's friends who were interested in keeping her out of prison. Was she right? Had all their years of contact with her convinced them that she was a victim?

Inquisition goes on

The inquisition into Marty Anderson's murder resumed in January of 1986. Police had leaked rumors for months that an arrest was imminent, but were unable to nail their number one suspect, Tom Bird. They saw the need for more evidence, given the inconsistencies in Lorna's previous statements now made more complicated by their conversation with Connie Wheeler and the anonymous letter.

Lorna had said Mark Bird threatened her and she implied he might have some involvement in the murder.

Mark went to James Smith, a Little Rock defense lawyer who partnered with Jim Guy Tucker. Tucker assisted Smith in preparing Mark for his testimony. (Later, Arkansans elected Tucker as the Lt. Governor to Bill Clinton, and when Clinton became president, Tucker became their governor. Eventually, Tucker fell victim to the legal problems created by Bill and Hillary Clinton and was forced to serve jail time under house arrest.)

When the Birds visited Tom at Lansing on April 21, 1986, Tom expressed worry about Opat's tactics. He wanted to make sure Mark answered carefully. Scott Kraft's article was still warm and contained so many factual errors, Tom could not afford any mistakes in his defense.

Mark's attorney began negotiating with Geary County and won a use immunity agreement to protect him during testimony. On May 1, Mark took the stand in the Geary County courtroom of Judge George Scott. Before going in, Mark and Ralph met with Tom's court-appointed attorney, Al Bandy, and James Kenney, a private investigator. Tom hired Kenney to probe leads and theories ignored by county officials. Mark learned that Charles Henderson had testified earlier at the inquisition, as well as another Lansing inmate.

Mark felt his testimony went well and it would help Tom. Virginia wrote, "When Mark talks about things they have always used it against Tom some way and don't seem inclined to investigate others' participation."

Virginia had sound reason for her skepticism. Mark had provided Lyon County Attorney Rod Symmonds with several investigative issues related to Sandy's and Marty's deaths following his testimony at the grand jury a year earlier. When Symmonds dismissed the grand jury, Mark knew the leads went cold. Virginia wrote, "I just don't trust anyone in the whole state of Kansas anymore."

Terry Smith continued to regularly visit Tom at Lansing. She became involved in a service organization, "Outside Connections," that met in a small building just across the street from the prison. During one of the group's meetings, Kansas City attorney Carl Cornwell took Terry aside to talk about Tom's case. He said Lorna's new defense strategy involved claiming spousal abuse and PMS, based on emerging cases where juries dismissed felonies against battered wives. Cornwell claimed that investigators were taking another look at Mark Bird as the hit man, since they had found no way to place Tom at the murder scene.

Virginia wrote, "It is a fact that because Lorna said so many things to Mark about the night Marty died he has become a threat to her since she has changed her story so many times. Somehow she has to discredit Mark."

Opat never charged Mark with anything.

New appeal

New information came to Tom in 1987 that provided another explanation of Sandy's mysterious death.

Tom learned of the conversations Sandy had with his good friend Charlie Smith in St. Louis a week before her death. Sandy told Charlie and his wife Carolyn that she knew exactly how she would commit suicide, should she ever consider such a thing. She knew of a bridge in a remote area outside of town where a car could plunge over the edge and no one would be able to tell whether it was an accident or intentional.

Agent Humphrey had heard about this possible suicide theory during September of 1984, and traveled to Florida to interview the Smiths. As a result, Humphrey reported that Smith felt Sandy had died by accident or suicide, but certainly not by Tom's hands.

Humphrey failed to report that Carolyn participated in the interview, though many years later under oath he acknowledged it. By omitting this significant fact, any person reading the report would lack knowledge that Carolyn knew anything about Sandy's emotional state during that St. Louis convention. Knowing of Carolyn's clear statements to Humphrey, and earlier to Pat Boysen, would have provided Tom with a second alternative explanation for Sandy's death in 1985. But Humphrey chose not to disclose this, leaving Tom wondering what else Humphrey had failed to disclose.

Ben Wood convinced Tom that raising the issue of suicide constituted "new evidence," and that winning a new trial on these grounds would allow him to air all that he had learned since the second trial. "On a scale of 1 to 10, I think the possibility of suicide is a 2 at best. I could never live with it if I felt Sandy died by suicide," Tom said. "But my attorney said my feelings didn't matter."

On July 31, 1987, Tom's new court-appointed attorney Monte Miller filed a motion for a new trial. On August 25, Miller filed an amended motion asserting that Agent Humphrey and the prosecution had failed to provide

Tom with all the investigative reports, specifically those revealing Humphrey's September, 1984 interview of the Smiths.

Humphrey called Pat Boysen on Wednesday, August 12, and asked her about her knowledge of the alleged suicide. She complained later that he intimidated her and tried to discourage her from testifying. Humphrey told her "That [suicide] was considered in 1984 by his office and discarded as being unacceptable and now it was old hat." His revelation to Boysen was the first time Tom knew of the 1984 KBI investigation. Boysen reported that Humphrey called her two more times, seemingly intent on keeping her away from court.

But Judge Rulon denied Tom's motion for a new trial, claiming that Tom knew or should have known about this possible defense back in 1985, and the fact that he never raised the possibility at trial disqualified him from a new trial. Rulon said that if Tom had presented suicide during his 1985 trial as an alternate explanation for Sandy's death, in his opinion it would not have effected the jury's verdict. During that 1985 trial, Dr. Bridgens had tried in vain to introduce "autocide" to the jury, but Symmonds objected and Rulon refused to allow it. With this 1987 filing, Rulon now saw this as old evidence, not new. Tom filed an appeal with the Kansas Supreme Court and lost once again.

The factual basis of whether Sandy might have committed suicide never was considered in a trial court. Jane Grismer, though, publicly blasted Tom for even considering such a thing.

Lorna lied

The articles in *KS Magazine, The Los Angeles Times, Kansas City Star* and elsewhere revealed some of Lorna's lies in her August 30, 1985, statement to police. Opat spotted those contradictions and subpoenaed the various writers who had interviewed her.

David Hacker and his employer fought Opat's subpoena, but lost. Hacker believed his interviews were protected information. He eventually provided Opat with the transcript of his interviews with Lorna, though they provided few insights into whether she lied in August of 1985. Opat gained insights from Hacker's notes into Lorna's personality and cunning ways.

Barbara Livingston answered the subpoena, and helped Opat understand how Lorna lied about her involvement in Marty's murder. Joan Baker testified as well.

The Times sent Scott Kraft packing off to Nairobi, Kenya, on special assignment to try and keep him away from the Kansas court. The paper fought hard to prevent him from testifying at the inquisition and by virtue of the cost of flying him to Junction City, won that battle. But he could not escape the subpoena to appear at Tom's 1990 trial.

Once Opat finished his review of Lorna's lies, he filed first degree murder charges against her on May 1, 1987, two days before CBS aired *Murder Ordained*.

Unlike Rod Symmonds and the Lyon County Grand Jury in their indictment of Tom, Opat ensured that this complaint spelled out how Lorna allegedly murdered Marty.

> "COMPLAINT/INFORMATION
>
> I, Steven L. Opat, the undersigned County Attorney of said County in the name, and by the authority and on behalf of the State of Kansas, come now here, and give the Court to understand and be informed that on or about the 4th day of November, 1983, in said County of Geary and said State of Kansas, one Lorna G. Anderson a/k/a Lorna Anderson-Eldridge then and there being present did then and there unlawfully, feloniously, willfully, maliciously, deliberately, and with premeditation, kill and murder a certain human being, to-wit: Martin K. Anderson, by shooting the said Anderson with a hand gun, more specifically described as a .22 caliber Colt Woodsman, contrary to K.S.A. 21-3401, (Murder in the First Degree), a class A felony."

Opat seemed ready to bring Lorna to justice—or was he using this charge as a ploy to get her to testify in court against Tom? Without witnesses it could have been a tough case to prove. Sheriffs had allowed Lorna to wash her hands prior to testing her for nitrate traces, and they could not prove that she had fired the gun. Their case rested on circumstantial evidence, though far more plausible than that used to convict Tom of Sandy's murder.

Lorna spared Opat the difficulty of trying her. She pled guilty to second-degree murder. Opat recharged her on November 3, 1988.

> "AMENDED COMPLAINT/INFORMATION
>
> "I, Steven L. Opat, the undersigned County Attorney of said County in the name, and by the authority and on behalf of the State of Kansas, come now here, and give the Court to understand and be informed that on or about the 4th day of November, 1983, in said County of Geary and said State of Kansas, one Lorna Anderson-Eldridge then and there being present did then and there unlawfully, feloniously, willfully, knowingly, intentionally, and maliciously, but without premeditation and deliberation, kill and murder Martin K. Anderson, a human being, and that the said Lorna Anderson-Eldridge did commit said act by aiding, abetting, advising, counseling and procuring another to commit said crime and that, specifically, she did

aid and abet by providing to another the instrumentality which was used to effect the homicide of Martin K. Anderson to-wit: a .22 caliber Colt Woodsman handgun, which was then used by another to effect the completion of the homicide of the said Martin K. Anderson, and further that she did counsel with another as to the time, location and manner of said homicide, contrary to K.S.A. 21-3402, (Murder in the Second Degree), a class B felony, and Liability for Crimes of Another, K.S.A. 21-3205."

The amended complaint contained a contradiction. It said she committed this crime "without premeditation and deliberation." It also said she aided and abetted, providing the gun to the killer. She "did counsel with another as to the time, location and manner" of the murder. How this could not indicate premeditation is confusing.

First-degree murder carried a mandatory life sentence, second-degree murder carried a reduced charge. Opat told Lorna he would petition the judge for a 10-year sentence, and ask that the time run concurrently with her solicitation convictions. He agreed to drop the mandatory sentencing requirements for use of a gun in the crime. The price for his offer would be testifying truthfully in open court against Tom. She agreed.

Lorna had lied regularly and with impunity to authorities, both in sworn statements and during numerous investigative interviews. In 1984, Irv Shaw felt that even if she had been willing to testify, he could not trust her to tell the truth on the stand. Those who interviewed her for their books and articles all heard various lies about her own complicity in Marty's murder.

Even Randy Eldridge finally admitted Lorna was a liar. After she accepted the second-degree murder agreement, Eldridge said, "She lied to me, too, at first. She didn't talk about it a whole lot, and of course, she had her story down pat. Love's blind sometimes. I know she lied to me, but I kind of see why she did it.

"But there was a point where she told me the truth. It was before she pleaded guilty to the soliciting charge in late August (1985). Maybe a week or two before.

"She never used the words 'we planned it,' but after she was in prison, we talked about it. She did admit the truth"—or at least the fall of 1985 version.

Eldridge divorced Lorna once her life sentence had been set. He had previously adopted the four Anderson girls. She eventually married, by proxy, another inmate who, reportedly, she had sex with while he remained incarcerated. He had been serving time for a sex offense.

In Lorna, Opat had the eyewitness that he felt could seal Tom's fate, and finally close the investigation into Marty's murder. He told the court that without Lorna's cooperation, the matter could have dragged on for two or three more years before anyone could have been charged with the murder. Perhaps Opat saw the conclusion of this investigation as his ticket to bigger things; a book with a movie contract, or election to higher office. Perhaps he feared that when Geary County citizens learned the investigation cost them more than $400,000, they would want his political hide. For whatever reason, that year he announced he would not seek another term as County Attorney.

Opat told Lorna that even with her willingness to help, the judge ultimately would decide the length of her prison sentence. "This court will not bargain justice," Judge George Scott said in refusing the sentencing portion of Lorna's agreement. Instead, he sentenced Lorna to 15 years to life. Still, her deal required her to testify against Tom.

Tom finally charged

On November 16, 1988, Geary County charged Tom with the first-degree murder of Marty Anderson. Bill Deppish arrested Tom and brought him to Junction City. Attorney Ron Wurtz of Shawnee County told Tom and his family that he wanted to represent him, and the judge did appoint him as Tom's public defender. The county set November 23 as the date for the preliminary hearing, giving Wurtz one week to prepare. He prevailed on the court to postpone the hearing and it was moved to December 16. As that date approached, Wurtz became incensed with the treatment he and Tom were receiving and, in a candid moment with Ralph and Virginia, stated that if the judge refused to postpone the hearing again, he planned to get very aggressive, even if it meant hurting his career.

Wurtz and Opat argued bitterly in front of the judge, but in the end, Wurtz won another delay, to January 6, 1989.

Tom liked Wurtz. Wary of attorneys and courts following his first two convictions, he had become slow to trust anyone associated with the legal system, but he saw Wurtz as the kind of aggressive attorney he wanted.

Tom heard that Opat might fly to Colorado and bring Randy Rahal back with him to testify. Rahal gave a statement to KBI agents in the spring of 1985, much like that of Charles Henderson, claiming Tom confessed to him. For agreeing to testify against Tom, Rahal found himself paroled and with $200 in his pocket. He skipped the state, leaving prosecutors looking foolish. Why would Opat threaten to bring him to Junction City? Tom's attorney would eat him alive on the witness stand. It made no sense, until Wurtz read the witness list.

The day before Tom's scheduled preliminary hearing, on January 5,

1989, Wurtz resigned from the case. He had represented Rahal in an earlier case and therefore, knew this was a potential conflict of interest. Given the evidence that Wurtz planned to aggressively pursue Tom's defense, and in light of their mid-December court argument, Tom saw this as another trick by Opat to win an advantage. Now Tom had no attorney. (Opat never did bring Rahal to Junction City to testify, but by putting his name on the witness list, managed to rid himself of having to contend with Wurtz.)

Tom asked Judge Scott to appoint Richard Ney, a public defender from Wichita, as his new attorney. "I have a concern about local representation and their strategy because of the notoriety this case might bring. The prosecution knows he (Rahal) is a liar and now he's taking my attorney away, your honor," Tom said in asking for Ney. Tom believed an attorney who lived elsewhere would give him the best representation.

Scott disagreed and appointed a young Junction City defense attorney, Mike McKone. The slender McKone, just the past summer an unsuccessful candidate for Geary County Attorney, had a young family and a budding legal practice. Quick-minded and quick-tongued, McKone jumped into the defense as fast as he could and dragged along his young partner, Roger Unruh to assist him. The court scheduled Tom's preliminary hearing for January 26, giving McKone just 21 days to prepare. He had to set aside other work to give exclusive attention to Tom's case, but vowed to involve his partners and recruit law students. McKone determined to provide Tom with an aggressive, effective defense. His determination imposed on his own family life as it sucked up his time, and it would be 14 months before he was finished.

After two criminal trials and more than five years in prison, Tom knew that he had to play a strong role in his own defense, and he planned to make no assumptions. This included reading volumes of investigative records, court transcripts, and writing letters to convince witnesses to come forward. He studied Lorna's many sworn statements and articles written from interviews with her. He read sworn statements given by others, especially Darrel and Danny Carter, Susan Ewert, the newly discovered testimony of David Workman, and Jan Mead, and compared their testimony to Lorna's, painstakingly identifying their numerous contradictions. Tom meant to take no chances with the one opportunity he finally had to get Lorna on the stand.

If he could at all, Tom intended to use the 1990 trial to introduce evidence that would prove exculpatory in his first two trials.

Junction City prepared for the kind of court circus for which Emporia had become famous. With Tom Bird on trial, the sleepy western town saw its own soap opera opportunity for notoriety unlike that since the days of Wild Bill Hickcock.

Delay followed delay

McKone threw himself into Tom's case. He filed for a motion to delay the first preliminary hearing to give himself a chance to prepare. Winning a reprieve gave him time to read thousands of pages of transcripts. He persuaded his law partner Roger Unruh to help him, eventually assigning him the responsibility to take Lorna apart on the witness stand.

McKone and Tom corresponded by letter and met at the prison on several occasions.

Tom wrote dozens of letters to McKone, many including the questions he felt the attorney needed to ask each witness. Tom estimated he wrote between 3,000 and 3,500 questions, of which 1,500 were directed at Lorna. More than four years of prison life taught him the importance of preparation and taking nothing for-granted. He prevailed on McKone and Unruh to be aggressive in their questioning of prosecution witnesses, and they agreed.

On April 6, 1989, Tom faced the preliminary hearing on his first-degree murder charge. The court heard the prosecution's case, testing it to see whether enough evidence existed to bring the case to trial.

Tom submitted a motion to dismiss the entire case based on his constitutional right to due process of law. He wrote an affidavit laying out the grounds for his motion, showing Judge Melvin Gradert that Steven Opat, along with Sheriff Deppish, had rehearsed the state's star witness, Lorna Anderson. Opat conducted this rehearsal on March 14, 1989, at the Geary County Courthouse, with Stephen Anderson present. Tom alleged that the purpose of that meeting was to go over Lorna's testimony, given the fact that Opat knew she had lied so many times previously.

Gradert said he would be surprised if the attorneys on either side didn't first meet with their witnesses to go over testimony prior to trial. He saw no prejudice in Opat's action and ruled against this motion to dismiss.

Gradert bound Tom over for a jury trial scheduled to begin on July 5, 1989. The hearing produced a glimpse of what lay ahead. Lorna admitted to dozens of lies during her time on the stand.

Motions filed

McKone filed a motion to suppress all evidence from Tom's first trials. He believed that the state had the burden to prove Tom's guilt based only on the evidence gathered as a direct result of this charge. Gradert denied this motion, stating that, "The State contends that the prior crimes committed by the defendant in this case are admissible to prove motive, intent, preparation, plan and identity."

As had Robert Hecht in Lyon County, McKone commissioned Capital Research to test public knowledge of the murder case in Geary County. The results were less startling than in Emporia, indicating something more than 55 percent knew of the case and had formed an opinion. He moved for a change of venue, but the judge denied it.

McKone moved to sequester the jurors. The judge denied it.

He asked the court to appoint Tom as co-counsel in the case. The judge agreed.

Opat had moved to demand that Tom "deliver copies of any and/or all witness statements that the defendant or his counsel possess in their files." This ran contrary to Kansas law. Though the prosecution was required to produce all its records, the defendant was not, and the judge agreed.

McKone wanted access to Lorna's psychological reports. The judge agreed, but greatly limited him. He allowed him to read her file, but not to take notes or photograph anything. McKone wanted to know what it said about her pathological lying and emotional stability.

Tom's Emporia trials had been the first in Kansas' history to be televised. Gradert accepted McKone's motion to ban TV cameras from this trial as a practical matter. He noted that the courtroom was small and that cameras would be intrusive. He allowed one photographer to attend, taking photos as a service for all the media. He also allowed one audiotape to be made by a pool reporter.

McKone wanted the jury to travel out to the crime site, to see it firsthand. The judge disagreed.

The jury pool had been drawn from a list based on driver's licenses. McKone moved to dismiss the pool, saying this did not adequately allow for a jury of Tom's peers. Gradert ruled it was a sufficient method.

McKone wanted anyone who had viewed *Murder Ordained* to be automatically excluded as a juror. The judge did not agree, and a few jurors claimed to have watched it. Those that did insisted it made no difference to them.

Lastly, given the time lag between November 4, 1983, and the spring of 1989, McKone believed Tom had been deprived of his constitutional right to a speedy trial. The last piece of evidence the prosecution produced against Tom came from Lorna's August, 1985, statement. Furthermore, several of Tom's witnesses had moved away and one KBI agent had died. The judge disagreed.

Among the motions Opat wanted accepted was one that barred Tom from introducing any alternative explanation for Marty's murder. He feared that Tom would use the trial to try and prove that someone else murdered Marty, rather than simply provide a defense. Unruh argued passionately against this motion, frustrated that Opat left it until just before opening arguments were to begin. Gradert denied Opat's motion.

McKone had asked for 30 or 60 days to prepare for trial. Gradert suggested postponing to August 14—90 days. McKone suspected that Opat wanted more time, but agreed to the date.

Though he no longer served as County Attorney the county appointed Opat as a special prosecutor. He recruited John Bork to assist him. Bork served as an Assistant Attorney General, and his specialty was difficult murder cases. They presented Tom with the charge.

"I, John Bork, Assistant Attorney General for the State of Kansas and I, Steven L. Opat, the undersigned Special Prosecutor of said County, in the name and by the authority and on behalf of the State of Kansas, come now here and give the Court to understand and be informed that on or about the 4th day of November, 1983, in said County of Geary and said State of Kansas, one Thomas Paul Bird then and there being present did then and there unlawfully, feloniously, willfully, maliciously, deliberately, and with premeditation, kill and murder a certain human being, to-wit: Martin K. Anderson, by shooting the said Martin K. Anderson with a certain gun, to-wit: a .22 caliber Colt Woodsman semi-automatic pistol, contrary to K.S.A. 21-3401, (Murder in the First Degree), a class A felony.

At least with this charge, Tom knew what it was the state said he did.

Tom discovered a decision in which a case had been thrown out because of a fraudulent arrest. On July 27, McKone filed a motion to dismiss the case. On August 10, Gradert agreed. Since Geary County officials had no jurisdiction to arrest anyone in another county, Deppish's arrest of Tom on November 16, 1988, at Lansing had been "fraudulent," as Virginia wrote it. Opat said he disagreed with the application of the law in this instance, but another problem had developed. Dr. Eckert, who had performed the autopsy on Marty, had suffered a heart attack. This made him unavailable for trial. Opat didn't mind the delay.

Geary County had to start over.

Opat and Bork re-filed the charge against Tom on August 23, 1989, and this time the judge issued an order for temporary custody. Deppish exercised the order at Lansing Correctional Facility and brought Tom back to Geary County where an arrest warrant was issued.

The court held a new preliminary hearing on October 6.

Virginia wrote about that October 6, 1989, hearing:

"At 7 p.m. Terry calls and gives us a rundown on the hearing. Lorna and 6 others testified for the prosecution. Dr. Eckert was there.

We did not have any defense witnesses there. Tom was bound over for trial and the date may be decided on October 24th along with many motions.

"During cross-examination, Lorna contradicted herself several times. She said she was never actually sick—a lie. She said she waited 5 minutes for Tom's getaway instead of 15 which she said before. Even Opat corrected her. McKone remarked during her answers whether she was looking to Opat for proper replies? She also said she and Tom drove to J. City the day before to case the place and plan this!

"PI Jim Kenny was on hand at the hearing also. In the inquiry to Dr. Eckert he remarked that the shooting was almost like an execution style. The news media picked up on this and applied it to Tom.

"Reporters also stopped Terry and asked for her comment on McKone's actions & she remarked that McKone was a smart man.

"Deppish was taking Tom (in blue jeans) back to KSP but remarked he didn't know if they would accept him. Terry interjected she would be happy to come get him."

But the trial would not begin in October, or November, or December, or January.

Finally, on February 26, 1990, more than six years after Marty's murder, jury selection began in the first-degree murder trial of Tom.

Bird #3 begins

Geary County jailed Tom in the building that sits on the south side of the courthouse. A fenced-in walkway leads from the jail to the basement of the old courthouse building. Entering the building, Tom rode the elevator to the third floor and entered the "big" courtroom. (The author viewed this room in 1999, months after it had been completely remodeled and is unable to provide a description of the room as it appeared in 1990).

Ironically, the county held Lorna in the same jail at the same time as Tom, but the two of them only saw each other in the courtroom.

Jane Grismer had enough favor with Deppish to win a tour of the jail. Ostensibly, she wanted to see what such a facility looked like, but made sure her path took her to the cell area in which Tom was held. Tom heard her coming and hid himself behind the shower curtain, pulling his feet up to make sure she did not have the pleasure of seeing him behind bars.

Jane made sure to attend every day of this trial as she had the first two. Bird family members reported that she bought donuts for the jury and, as in the earlier trials, schmoozed with the prosecution and their witnesses.

Though Tom already served one life sentence for Sandy's murder, Jane looked forward to seeing the door slam shut on him for the rest of his life.

The jury pool numbered 96. From this, the court selected 12 jurors and two alternates. The final panel consisted of Marie Burgett, Thelma Roth, LeRoy Dupere, Loren Langvardt, Marion White, Annie Horton, Bert Thomas, William Semanko, Lois Hauser, William Levinson, Margaret Dugan and James Christenson.

By now a realist, Tom knew that jury trials were a crapshoot. "I knew we would lay it out well and have a good record. I was hoping we could use this trial to bring out new evidence concerning the first two trials. But I cannot say I was confident about the verdict."

As he sat at the defendant's table, he noted once again the jammed courtroom. This trial, like the others, attracted widespread media coverage, but he had grown immune to what people said. By the time this trial began, nearly everything negative that could be said about him had been said.

Opat told the jury that he would prove "Bird planned the killing with the victim's wife. The facts will show it's all part of a great big plan between Thomas P. Bird and Lorna Anderson to do away with Martin K. Anderson."

Opat admitted that Lorna had told different versions of her story, but the fact remained that Tom shot Marty.

McKone said he would show that witnesses placed Tom in Topeka at the time of the shooting. He could not possibly have done it. He told them that Tom would testify in his own defense. About Lorna, McKone said, "She wouldn't know the truth if it jumped up and slapped her in the face."

McKone said several others could have shot Marty including Lorna herself. He named Danny and Darrel Carter, Greg Curry and Johnny Bingham all as possibilities.

Opat presented four witnesses during that first afternoon beginning with Sheriff Deppish. Deppish claimed he had been suspicious of Lorna's story from the beginning. He described executing the search warrant of her house and finding the "love letters" under the lingerie in her drawer.

Opat called Jan Mean Dykehouse to the stand (she had married since the 1985 trial). Dykehouse's testimony during the first two trials had been pivotal. Rod Symmonds referred to her three times during his closing arguments in the second trial so central was her testimony to proving Tom had a long-standing affair with Lorna.

During this testimony, very little new was added. She claimed that Lorna's affair with Danny continued into February of 1983, though Danny insisted it was over by the end of the previous summer. Lorna said Tom was pretty good in bed for a minister at their February meeting (Lorna, in various versions of her story, said her affair with Tom started in April or May).

Late in March, Lorna told her that she and Tom had gone to Wichita and she asked Dykehouse to cover for her if Marty called. She repeated her charge that Tom and Lorna had been in love and wished their spouses would be out of the way. Then they could spend their lives together. None of this was new to those who followed the first two trials, but all new to this jury (unless they had watched *Murder Ordained*).

McKone asked why her November, 1983, written statement contained no mention of Tom being good in bed for a minister. "Correct me if I'm wrong, that's sort of something that kind of jumps up and grabs you, don't you think?"

"That's right."

"How come that didn't get in there?"

"She told me lots of things, and as I began thinking about them, I remembered these things."

"Did she tell you the truth sometimes?"

"All I know is what she told me. I don't know whether it was the truth or not."

"Quite frankly, everything you testified to here today is what Lorna told you. You don't know whether that's true or not?"

"That's true."

A few questions later, McKone asked, "As a matter of fact, Lorna used you too, didn't she, Jan?"

"Uhm-hum."

"She used you to cover?"

"And she used the American Heart Association."

McKone established that though the second job caused no problems for Dykehouse, she had been upset that Lorna didn't tell her about it.

As he wound down his cross-examination of Dykehouse, he asked, "Jan, did Lorna ever mention any other affairs, other than Danny or Tom, talk about other boyfriends?"

"Yeah, she mentioned several, and I don't know names and those kinds of things, but she talked about men she was sleeping with...Probably several, three or four, that she told me about."

Mead Dykehouse stepped down.

Dr. Eckert testified that Marty died from three gunshot wounds to the head. He said they had been fired from behind and above.

Denise Baccus, one of Lorna's army of babysitters, said she saw a gun in a holster in Lorna's dresser drawer. Investigators never found the holster but they did find the gun, though they didn't ask Baccus to identify it. Baccus added that she had been concerned because Danny Carter often stayed overnight at Anderson's while Marty was away, even though the children were at home.

Angie Duensing Davis who, like Mead, had married since the 1985, came next. About Tom and Lorna, she said, "I was concerned with the closeness of their relationship because they were both married to other people." After she talked to Tom on June 24, she said he became cold toward her. She had not said this in previous testimony, but she also didn't offer the rest of the story. She had told Tom she once had a dream that Sandy and the children died in a car wreck, and he subsequently married her. This discussion, Tom said, took place three weeks before Sandy died—in a car wreck.

Pastor Kalsow had been called as a prosecution witness. Sometime before he was to testify, Opat decided his testimony would hurt his case and dismissed him. McKone jumped at the opportunity to put him on the stand. Gradert allowed him to go out of order as a defense witness because Kalsow needed to return home.

Kalsow explained that Tom reacted with shock and surprise when hearing of Marty's death. The prior night Marty had sponsored Tom as a new member of the Optimist Club. The three of them had played basketball together.

Opat questioned Kalsow about the July 27, 1983, turnpike incident, recalling the discussion he had with Tom about Lorna.

Darrel took the stand the morning of the second day. He recalled his prior testimony about the May, 1983, meeting and Tom's attempts to hire him to murder Marty. Darrel added nothing new to his testimony, but getting him on record as to the various schemes he said had been discussed set up the defense for their cross-examination of Lorna.

Danny Carter came next. He described how Lorna asked him to help find someone to murder Marty during the summer of 1983. He said he found Greg Curry and that Lorna gave him $5,000, which he gave to Curry.

Later, he tried to get out of the deal and "get the money back." He admitted to having an affair with Lorna that, he said, lasted about three months during the summer of 1982.

Greg Curry followed Danny to the stand. Greg said that Danny approached him in late August saying he had a lady friend who was being abused by her husband. Danny sought him out because Greg had bragged about knowing members of the syndicate. "He wanted somebody to beat this guy up and let him know his wife had some tough friends," Greg testified.

Greg contacted Johnny Bingham, a man about whom his dad had "told me to stay away from." When he learned the price was $5,000 and realized it was for a murder, Greg said he gave all the money to Johnny and wanted nothing else to do with it.

Danny told him to call if off and when he went to see Johnny, the man laughed at him. "He had a new satellite dish in his yard and two new horses, so he didn't have the money either."

Before being charged in November of 1983, Greg said he had never heard the names of Martin Anderson or Tom Bird.

Geary County had chased Scott Kraft, *The Los Angeles Times* reporter, to Nairobi. The Times sent him there to keep him from testifying. They even brought a legal action to quash the subpoena, but lost. Finally, in 1990, they flew Kraft in to testify. McKone had but one question for him. He had him read the paragraph from his article where Lorna named Tom as the murderer. "Did Lorna tell you that?" "Yes." That was all McKone needed the jury to hear, and Kraft was free to go. Kraft's 1986 news story slandered Tom, sparked the production of *Murder Ordained,* and probably quashed his appeal. Kraft never asked Tom weather or not Lorna lied. Too bad, he could have saved himself, the Times and investigators much embarassment.

Agents Humphrey and Winsor testified about tracing the $5,000. A bank teller, Terri Morgan from the Emporia Savings and Loan, testified that she handled a deposit for Tom on September 7, 1983. He asked for $5,000 in cash and she tried to get him to take some sort of cashier's check or money order. Tom told her he planned on buying a car and wanted cash.

Gradert ordered the weekend recess. Tom went back to the jail and the jurors headed home.

Lady Lorna steps up

This day had been long in coming. After more than six years of national and international coverage of this quadrangle murder case, Opat called the woman who played the leading role to the stand—Lorna Anderson.

Finally, Lorna faced a jury, though it was Tom's not hers. She same into the courtroom in a soft-toned multicolor dress. Someone from the prosecution team had to go shopping with her over the weekend. And her hair had been done as well. She wore heavy makeup to present a picture of a soft, feminine and demure creature.

As she testified, she looked directly at Opat and avoided eye contact with Tom, even when asked to identify him in court. She talked softly so that the judge had to ask her to speak up several times. She acted the part of a contrite woman who had been swept up by negative influences that drove her to make some bad decisions.

Unruh got the judge to agree to let Lorna hold a copy of her August 30, 1985, statement for reference as he quizzed her. For dramatic effect, Lorna would remove her reading glasses as she answered, but after a time, that began to wear on the jury.

Between Opat's softball questions and Unruh's incessant grilling, Lorna faced nearly two days of testimony. Her August 30, 1985, statement ran 126 pages. This testimony generated a 292-page transcript. Everyone, prosecution, defense, media, family and courtroom spectators wanted to hear what she had to say.

The early part of her testimony simply established the fact that she had pled guilty to two counts of solicitation and to the second-degree murder of Martin K. Anderson. She explained how she and Tom met, at a softball game. "Did you come to know him better?"

"Yes. I got to know him better through the preschool at Faith Lutheran Church. Eventually, I went to work as the secretary for the church, we became emotionally involved, and then became lovers."

She claimed the lay ministers hired her at Tom's request. (They didn't agree with that.)

She said that yes, she had talked to Jan Mead about her relationship with Tom and her frustrations with Marty. "I told her that things were bad at home, that I was not happy, but that I was really in love with a man I was working for."

"Tom, the minister?"

"Yes, sir." She claimed a sexual relationship began in April of 1983.

"Jan Mead has testified that you made a statement to the effect that sometimes you wished something would happen to Marty and his wife so that you and Tom would be together."

"That's true."

She said she told Mead that she took trips with Tom, maybe two or three, during the period of April to August, 1983. Opat showed her a motel receipt from the Sheraton Inn in Wichita dated August 9, 1983. She said they checked in together. (Lorna had her four girls, Tom had his three children. Tom checked in, but without Lorna who, after supper, drove on to Hutchinson.)

Opat told her to describe the plan to murder Marty.

"Tom and I had devised a plan where we would drive out to Highway 177 in Geary County, I would stop the van pretending to be ill, then I would get out of the van and lose my keys as a means to lure Marty out of the van. While Marty was out of the van looking for the keys, Tom was going to come up and shoot him."

She claimed they devised the plan at Faith the prior day, "late in the afternoon or early evening."

Since Marty had to buy a camouflage jacket at Ft. Riley, she said the plan would be to kill him sometime during the trip to or from the Fort. If not on November 4, then on November 11.

Tom, she said, had driven out to the murder site on November 3 and measured the distances she needed to know in order to find the right spot to stop. She carried out the plan as Tom designed it.

"Did someone with a gun come up?"

"Yes. Tom Bird."

"What happened?"

"He shot Marty and took his wallet to make it look like a robbery and then left."

After Tom shot Marty, "I told him to get out of there, and he said, 'Don't worry, you know I can run.'"

"She's going to have to speak up, because we aren't hearing her well," a juror said.

"Well, you were questioned by some investigators later that night, weren't you?"

"Yes, I was."

"You didn't tell them that the man was Tom Bird?"

"No, I didn't."

"You told them it was some unknown black man or some man wearing a lack mask, didn't you?"

"Yes."

"You lied to them, didn't you?"

"Yes, I did."

"And you lied to them three days later when they questioned you about this event, didn't you?"

"Yes."

"Who else did you lie to?"

"Besides the investigators, I lied to my father, I lied to Stephen Anderson."

She claimed she gave Tom the gun during July, just prior to his leaving on vacation. Now she claimed he planned to shoot Sandy during that trip. She identified the gun for the court.

Opat reminded her that she told a different story about the gun during her August, 1985, statement. "So you lied to them again?"

"Yes."

"Why did you lie to them?"

"In August, when I lied to them about the gun, I had been told by my attorney that he would be able to get me out of it as long as I didn't say anything that would incriminate myself."

"So you kept lying to them?"

"Yes."

"Despite the fact you wanted to tell the truth."

"Right."

Opat asked about Darrel. She said yes, during May or June they talked about killing Marty. The three of them talked about poisoning, shooting or a car accident during their meeting, and then in September, they gave $5,000 to Danny.

Lorna admitted having a sexual relationship with Darrel, and said her adultery with Danny lasted "Maybe a year, off and on."

"Tell me about the plan that was developed between you and Dan and Tom."

"After Darrel had said he was not going to help with killing Marty, he had suggested to Tom that possibly Danny knew somebody that would do it from Wolf Creek. So in August sometime, Tom told me to call Dan and talk to him and see if that was the case, if he could find someone.

"I called Dan, and we met one evening and told him what we wanted. He said he would do some checking and get back with me.

"It was a few days later that he informed me he had found someone that would do it. He would need a picture of Marty, an itinerary of where Marty was going to be the following weekend, and $,5000."

"What happened as a result of this conversation with Dan Carter?"

"The next evening, I met him at the Zip Card Machine at Emporia State Bank, in Emporia, and I gave him the itinerary and a picture that I had, and the $5,000 that Tom had given me." Lorna claimed Tom got the money from Sandy's insurance money.

Later, when nothing happened, Danny tried to get the money back. "So nothing happened then, until the first part of November, when Tom said that we would kill him ourselves."

"Well, now, how did you and Tom come to that conclusion?"

"It was obvious no one else was going to help. We weren't going to be able to hire someone to do it. There was no other alternative."

"Why did you want to kill your husband or have someone else kill him?"

"Because *I was in love with Tom and I really wanted to be with him* [emphasis added]. I thought that's the way it was supposed to be."

"Was your life with Martin that bad?"

"No, I was so much in love with Tom." (Never mind the beatings or previous requests she made to Darrel to kill Marty, now she says things had been fine.)

"Why didn't you just divorce Martin?"

"Because even though the Lutheran Church didn't condemn divorce, Tom believed that for his ministry, what he wanted, divorce would not look right. It just wouldn't be proper, and he had always said that it was the lesser of two evils for Marty and Sandy to be killed than it was for things to go on as they were." (What?)

Opat asked why she agreed to a plea agreement the first time. She said that investigators had just discovered where Tom got the $5,000, a few days before she had been scheduled for trial.

"After your plea of guilty in Emporia, you talked to investigators from the KBI in Geary County?"

"Yes, I did."

"So you were given a form of immunity, were you not?"

"Just insofar as my testimony, my statement wouldn't be used against me."

"What were you promised?

"If I told the truth at that statement..."

"Were you promised immunity from prosecution?"

"No, sir, I was not."

"Did you tell the truth in your statement?"

'Partly, not all of it was the truth."

"So you lied during the statement?"

"Yes, I did."

Opat knew that Tom's best defense would be to destroy altogether any credibility Lorna might have. Here he tried to preempt the effects of what he knew would happen when Unruh began his cross-examination. During this time, she admitted to several substantial lies in previous statements.

Once in prison, Lorna began telling her story to others, including staff and inmates. Eventually she told it to Scott Kraft of *The Los Angeles Times,* "the first time that I had ever completely told the truth."

Why did you want to tell Kraft your story?

"Because by that point I wanted it over with." But her attorney kept telling her not to talk, "that he would get me out of it as long as I didn't say anything, but I couldn't because I wanted to get it over with."

She said she hoped investigators would read the story and finally bring the case to closure. This statement defied logic since she had already told them Tom murdered Marty. All she added were some details about her complicity. She knew they wanted to convict Tom as the killer and their history showed they would negotiate with anyone who could help them. In negotiations, timing is always a key factor, and her timing was off. Eventually, Opat charged her with first-degree murder. They negotiated second-degree murder.

"From what I understand, the agreement was if I pled guilty to second-degree murder and agreed to testify against Marty's killer, then I would be sentenced for second-degree murder. Instead of going ahead and trying me for first-degree murder, the state was able to recommend a sentence of ten years to life." But the judge gave her a stricter sentence.

"You have a modification motion pending that your attorney has never argued to the court?"

"Yes. It was filed in March of 1989."

"Well, do you expect, because of your testimony here today, that you're going to get a modification or reduction of that sentence?"

"No, I don't." (But this negotiation remained open, and it is likely that by helping convict Tom Bird, she could reduce her sentence. Courts have always shown a disposition to go easier on women, especially when they claim victim status. Lorna claimed that Tom manipulated her.)

"Do you understand by your testimony here today that you're basically telling the whole room that you helped Tom Bird murder the father of your four children out there in a rural location in Geary County, Kansas, while those children were present?"

"Yes, I am."

Opat sat down.

Like the anticipation before she began, now the court sat spellbound wondering how Unruh planned to discredit "The Spider Woman," as the *Kansas City Star* had labeled her.

Gradert agreed to a recess. The courtroom crowd buzzed about what they had heard. No one wanted to leave the room that day.

Defense, ask away

Unruh stood and walked toward Lorna. The tall, thin man looked at the defiant, confident, self-confessed murderer, liar and adulteress and began his questioning. He had a precarious balancing act to maintain, convincing the jury that nothing she said could be believed, but taking care not to attack her. The last thing he wanted to do was build sympathy for her.

Lorna had been in Junction City for two weeks awaiting this day. She told several folks that she felt reluctant to testify, but "wanted to get it over with."

"In preparation for being in the court today, have you studied your proposed testimony today with Mr. Opat?"

"We've discussed it, yes. What he would ask, yes." She had also talked with Bork. Deppish attended her trial briefing sessions as well. "He has been present when we've gone over, yes, sir, what might be asked."

She had reviewed all the various versions of her story she had given to Winsor and Humphrey, Deppish and Opat. "I went over it with Mr. Opat and Mr. Bork and told them what I had lied about in that statement," she said referring to the August 30, 1985, statement.

She had also reviewed all of her testimony from the preliminary hearings.

Unruh showed Lorna the first criminal complaint against her that charged her with first-degree murder. He showed her the second complaint that had reduced the charge to second-degree murder. Jack Focht, her attorney, represented her on these charges—still did, in fact. The negotiated plea left Lorna with the hope for parole after 7-1/2 years. She could have received as little as a five-year sentence, but Judge Scott gave her 15 to life.

Unruh noted that the difference between the two murder charges centered on the issue of premeditation. "But, you in fact planned that; is that correct?"

"Yes."

"For the death of Martin Anderson?"

"Yes, we did."

He pointed to the clause setting aside a mandatory sentence for crimes committed with a gun. "No gun, no mandatory sentence," she said.

Opat had recommended a 10 to life sentence, and asked that it run concurrently with her prior convictions. All of it taken together comprised her motivation to testify against Marty's killer.

Unruh questioned her about the motion Focht filed for a sentence modification in March of 1989. At that time everyone speculated that Tom's trial would soon be getting underway. Lorna's testimony, just as in this trial, would come early. The date of filing suggested that Focht looked for another reward for Lorna's "truthful" testimony. Since then, the trial had been delayed several times. Unruh suggested by this line of questioning that the state had purposely not moved on this issue to keep Lorna on a tight string. If Tom would be found guilty, she could gain credit and, quite possibly, win an earlier release. She denied all this.

Her plea agreement also requested that she be moved from Lansing to the Topeka women's prison. The Topeka facility was minimum security as was the one in which she lived at Lansing, but a somewhat more comfortable facility. Unruh asked her why she wanted to be moved?

"Because of the men that are housed at Lansing, I felt like I would be safer in Topeka that the—a lot of the men that they have brought over have come from KSP, and they knew Tom, and I was concerned for my safety." (She had also caused at least one guard to be fired for having sex with her, and more than one inmate had been sent back to medium security for the same reason.)

Unruh reviewed her relationship with Darrel. She met him through the sorority sometime in the late 1970s. He did kitchen remodeling at her home.

She said she became sexually active with him during this time, and though she could not remember how many times, it was more than once—perhaps for a few months. Then she corrected herself and said, "Two or three weeks."

"Earlier in this trial, Darrel Carter testified to the jury he slept with you but one time. Are you telling the jury he committed perjury?"

"I'm telling the jury that, as well as I can remember, I can remember more than one occasion."

Darrel knew that she and Marty had marital problems. Her affair with him started after the one with Danny. This testimony made no sense as to the timeline that she had provided on numerous occasions touching both of the affairs.

Yes, Darrel saw her bruised and injured, "sometime in 1982."

"What was Darrel's response to seeing you bruised up?"

"He didn't like it."

"Did he make a statement to you to the effect of, 'People like that should be killed?'"

"I don't know that he necessarily said people like that should be killed. He said, 'Something needs to be done about that.'"

She denied ever asking Darrel to find someone to beat Marty up or murder him during the summer of 1982. Darrel had testified specifically that she had done this. "I don't recall flagging him down and asking him to do that specifically. There might have been an occasion when we were together that I made a comment, just almost joking, that I wished somebody would kill him."

"Last week Darrel testified that on at least two occasions you asked him to find someone to kill Marty before the meeting with Tom Bird at the church. Was he lying?"

"I don't remember them. I can't say he was lying, but I don't remember specifically asking him to find someone to kill Marty." She failed to remember they had even discussed divorce, though Darrel said they did.

Unruh asked whether prosecutors or investigators had told her to answer such questions with, "I don't remember,"

"No, sir, I was not."

She insisted the first time she ever talked to Darrel about killing Marty was at the church meeting with Tom present. Unruh asked her why she felt comfortable asking him to participate in a murder? "Because Darrel knew that Marty was beating me, I knew that he didn't approve of that, and he was someone I felt like I could trust."

"You weren't concerned with him going to the police?"

"No, sir."

"Why not?"

"We had been lovers. We had been friends for a long time." (She had just testified that they had a two-three week affair, hardly qualifying them as lovers. Did she ask every man she slept with to murder Marty?)

She said she introduced Darrel to Tom at the church and said "that Tom and I were wanting to kill Marty and we were looking for someone to help."

"If you would, what were the ways, once again, that you talked about killing him?"

"We discussed poisoning, we discussed a car accident, and we discussed shooting and making it look like a robbery."

"In a statement that you gave to Vern Humphrey on August 28, 1985, you told Agent Humphrey that you talked about poisoning him, throwing a concrete block through his windshield while he was driving on the turnpike, and getting him drunk and parking his car on a railroad track. Do you recall that?"

"Yes, I do." She hadn't said anything to Humphrey about shooting Marty.

"If Darrel Carter testified a couple of days ago that the only things that were discussed at this meeting at the church were homicide, possibly by shooting or running the car off the road by a bridge, and nothing else, was he lying?"

"I can't say he was lying. He probably remembered what he remembered from the meeting, and I've remembered what I can remember."

"Was Darrel Carter an active participant in the conservation at the church?"

"Yes, he was."

"What ideas did he come up with at the church?"

"It was his idea to throw the concrete block through the windshield of the car. He suggested looking out west of town for a railroad crossing where the car could be left."

"Now if Darrel says he never said those things at that meeting, was he lying?"

"I remember him saying that."

"And if he says he didn't was he lying?"

"Possibly, he didn't remember."

"If he testified he remembered, but he didn't say those things, was he lying?"

"I would say yes."

Humphrey's report said that Lorna insisted that running a car off the bridge had never been part of the plan. He asked, did you tell him this? "I can't recall exactly what I did tell Mr. Humphrey. I think that we discussed a traffic accident."

She agreed they talked about getting Marty drunk and leaving his car on a railroad track. She said they talked about shooting Marty in a phony robbery attempt at her grandmothers.

Unruh showed her the August 30, 1985, statement and asked her to read what it said on page 88 of that testimony. "No, no guns were ever discussed with Darrel Carter. It was—poisoning Marty was discussed, and leaving him on a railroad crossing was discussed. Dropping a concrete block through the windshield was discussed, but shooting was just never discussed with Darrel Carter."

Lorna said Darrel agreed to look "for a railroad crossing…West of town." Darrel testified differently earlier in the trial. Unruh asked if he had lied. Not necessarily a lie. Maybe he doesn't remember it, and that doesn't make it a lie. But, "I'm just saying I can remember it was discussed."

No, she had not offered Darrel any of the insurance money to help murder Marty. She didn't even talk about insurance at that meeting. She thought she had told him about the unregistered gun, though. That, of course, directly contradicted what she had told investigators in August, 1985. "I've already stated that I lied during that time."

She had just asserted that Darrel agreed to go look for a place to leave a drunk Marty in his car on some railroad tracks west of town. Unruh asked whether or not she believed at the time that Darrel planned to help murder Marty. No, "He said he would think about it." (Looking for a place to murder Marty seemed more than just thinking about it.)

In 1985, she had told investigators the meeting took place on June 7. She had told several interviewers the same thing. At this trial, she said it was in late May or early June, and said she could not be sure of the date.

Unruh had Lorna describe her office. He asked about people coming and going in the church the day of their meeting. She couldn't remember. "So from the best you can recall, you, Darrel Carter and Tom Bird sat around in your office, probably with the door open, maybe with other people in the church, openly discussing the demise of your husband?"

"I don't remember. There were not other people walking around church. If there had been other people in the church, they were strictly in the preschool classroom."

Yes, there had been some small talk about soccer and fireworks.

Following that church meeting, Lorna said she never again talked to Darrel about killing Marty. Tom did, and Darrel told Tom to talk with Dan about it. (Darrel denied this. Dan said he never heard the name Tom Bird until long after Marty's murder.)

"Prior to the summer of 1983, had you been aware of the Carter brothers engaging in illegal activities of any kind?"

"Yes."

"What type of illegal activities were you aware that they engaged in?"

"I knew that Danny had sold drugs occasionally, and I knew that they had a garage apartment that they were going to burn down." She said that this fact is why she felt she could trust them not to go to police.

Unruh walked her through her relationship with Danny. They met in the spring of 1981, at Mr. and Ms. Place where he worked as a hairdresser. He also cut the children's hair. "Did you, at some point in time, lead Dan Carter into a sexual relationship with yourself?"

"I can't say that I led him, but I know we were lovers." She said the sex with Danny started during the spring or summer of 1982 through the end of 1982.

"If Dan Carter testified that the sexual relationship with you lasted only a period of two to three months, would he have been lying?"

"It really only lasted two or three months. There was maybe, under a very rare occasion after that, when we would be together."

She saw Danny nearly every day that Marty was at guard camp. Yes, he stayed overnight at the Andersons. Yes, the children had been present. Yes, they went to the Paragon Pub and other public places together. Did you ever talk about this to Marty? No. Did he know about it? I don't know.

"Was there ever an occasion where you were together with Dan Carter and you were naked, and Marty came home?"

"Yes, that's true...in November. October or November of 1982."

She never talked to Danny about marriage, she claimed.

She got pretty close to Danny, and talked more with him than she ever had with Darrel.

"Did Danny ever have occasion to see you when you were bruised up?"

"Yes, he did."

"What was his response to seeing you bruised up?"

"He didn't like it, either." No, she never told Danny that Marty beat the children and no, Danny never said anything about having his friends beat up Marty.

Danny had testified that he broke off the sexual relationship because Lorna had gotten too serious. "Maybe that's the way he perceived it. I don't know."

"Following December of 1982, did you have any other sexual encounters with Dan Carter?"

"No, I didn't." (Jan Mead testified that Lorna told her in February that she had been sexually active with her hairdresser.)

Unruh reviewed Opat's line of questioning about when she called Danny Carter to help find someone to murder Marty. She said it had been late

August or early September. They met at Village School and drove around the country talking about it.

"So your testimony is that after the intimate portion of your relationship had been gone from eight months, you called Mr. Carter up pretty much out of the blue to talk with him about killing your husband?"

"Yes, I did." She claimed she had not talked with him earlier that spring about this and neither had she discussed killing Marty with him in 1982. She called Danny, she said, because Darrel had told Tom to do so. Danny might know someone at Wolf Creek who could do such a thing. (Darrel certainly never testified in this manner.)

She and Danny talked about how "things had gotten worse at home, and that I was in love with Tom and I wanted to be with him."

"Did you also talk about how you were still being abused?"

"Yes."

"Did you tell him that the children were also being beaten at this time?"

"I don't remember telling him that, no."

"Did you ask him if he would personally kill Marty?" (In 1983, Danny told Deppish that Lorna asked if he wouldn't personally do it, would he help her find someone who would?)

She said that at this time she told Danny about Tom's involvement in the murder scheme. "He knew that not only from me, but also from his brother." (This testimony totally contradicted Darrel, Dan and Tom, as well as her earlier testimony.)

"So your testimony is that Dan and Darrel had talked about killing Marty; is that correct?"

"From what Dan indicated to me, yes." (This made Darrel a co-conspirator, a crime for which he had never been charged.) Both men had denied this in their testimony during this trial. He asked whether that made them liars?

"I can't say whether they were lying or not. I don't know what they remember and what they don't remember. All I can testify to is what I remember."

"Did you tell him that you wanted it to look like an accident?"

"I told him it couldn't look like an accident; it needed to look like a killing, like a robbery or something. Because of Sandy's car accident, we could no longer just pretend it was an accident."

Unruh asked who called whom after the car meeting occurred. She said they called each other. Danny called her at home on more than one occasion. "If Dan Carter has previously testified that he never called you at your house to this jury last week, would that be a lie?"

"I know that while Marty was gone to summer camp, he did

call...Maybe Dan never remembered calling me at my house."

(By continually asked these questions about what Lorna remembered and comparing it to the testimony of others, Unruh cast doubt on all the testimony. Who lied here? Darrel? Danny? Lorna? All of them? Somebody had to be lying.)

Unruh asked her about how and when Danny informed her that he had found someone, and how the hand off of the money had occurred. He asked her to describe in detail the contents of the envelope she handed over to him. The itinerary contained several locations where the shooter could find Marty the following weekend, all of them public areas. He asked whether or not she had worried about others being hurt in a murder attempt?

"I hadn't thought about that."

"As a matter of fact, your children were going to be present at most of these places, weren't they?"

"Yes, they were." That's why she said that particular weekend would not be a good time for a murder.

Unruh told the judge he had reached a place where it would made sense to break for lunch. Gradert agreed. This gave everyone a chance to mull over the sensationalized testimony they just had heard from the state's star witness, a woman who thought so much of herself and so little of her own children that she helped plan their father's murder in their plain sight, perhaps where they could also be hurt.

Following lunch

Lorna knew her testimony would be difficult. Following lunch, she may have hoped the ordeal would end shortly, but Unruh had hundreds of more questions to ask.

When the murder didn't occur the following weekend, Lorna contacted Danny. She told Danny on the phone more of Marty's itinerary for the weeks to follow.

Lorna sat back and waited for something to happen. She called him a few times wondering why nothing had happened, but denied calling Danny at 4:00 a.m. on October 24th. During the last conversation, "He indicated to me that it was not going to be done and that he would try to get the money back, and that was the end of it."

Dan didn't seem to care whether or not he got the money back. She said she couldn't remember Tom's reaction to not getting the money back, neither could she remember telling Humphrey about it on August 30, 1985.

Unruh referred both to her February, 1985, indictment in Lyon County and to her plea agreements made in mid-August, 1985. "At the time you entered your pleas in Lyon county, you said publicly that you desired to purge your soul; is that correct?"

"That's true."

"And basically, did that mean you intended to tell the truth, or wanted to tell the truth at that time?"

"I wanted to tell the truth, yes."

She resisted agreeing with Unruh that by offering her statement that August she received protection against prosecution. The deal said that nothing in her statement could be used against her unless it contained lies. (It did. Many of them.)

She acknowledged that prior to making the statement she had taken an oath to tell the truth. During her time on the stand, Lorna admitted to more than 80 lies in previous statement.

This remaining testimony runs nearly 180 pages, and the bulk of it recorded Unruh setting up numerous situations where asked her, "Was that a lie or was that the truth," to which she usually responded, "That was a lie." The dialogue sounded like an antiphonal choir where one choir sings a phrase and the other choir answers, "That was a lie!"

The author has selected several exchanges as examples, leaving out dozens of others.

"I'd ask you to turn to Page 9, and on Page 9, at line 10 of your sworn statement, you said, '...I went to the restroom at McDonald's and did throw up.' Was that the truth, or was that a lie?"

"That was a lie."

"I'd ask you to go to Page 10 of that statement, and I would refer you to Line 3 therein. You said, '...I sat there for a little while trying to decide if I should go into the service station or if I would be okay...' That is referring to a service station close to the interstate, isn't it."

"Yes."

"Is that statement the truth or a lie?"

"I did sit there for a little while, but it was not because I was feeling ill and trying to decide if I should go in."

"Would you agree with me that that was a partial lie?"

"Yes."

"Same page, Lines 13 through 14, you said, '...I felt very sick, and so I told Marty I was—I needed to stop...' Did you feel sick?"

"I wasn't sick, no."

"That was a lie?"

"Yes."

"On Page 12 of the statement, Lines 23 through 24, you said, of Marty, 'He took me down this ditch place, pushed me down on the ground, told me if I said a word that I was dead...' Was that the truth or a lie?"

"I was not saying that of Marty. I was saying that of the killer."

"Okay."

"And, yes..."

"Did the shooter say that to you?"

"No, sir."

"So that was a lie?"

"Yes."

Unruh punctuated his questions and responses with dramatic changes in inflection, to communicate an increasing incredulity over Lorna's answers.

"On Page 20 of your sworn statement, at Lines 11 through 12, and Lines 24 and 25, you were asked, '...do you have any idea what type of weapon it was, handgun,' and you answered, '...at that time, I couldn't have told you what that one was.' Were you telling the truth or lying?"

"That was a lie."

"On Page 34, Lines 2 through 5 of that sworn statement, you were asked, 'Lorna, did you ever tell anybody the route that you were going to take going to and from Junction City or Ft. Riley,' and you answered, 'No, I didn't.' Was that the truth or a lie?"

"That was a lie," she added defiantly. "Tom knew,".

"On Page 39, Lines 11 through 14, you said, 'What if—you know, I don't always get sick...what if the van hadn't stopped. He said actually the van stopping was not at all what he wanted.' Mrs. Anderson, were these quotes from Tom Bird the truth or a lie?"

"They were lies."

"On Page 39, Line 18 through 20 of your sworn statement, you quote Tom Bird as saying, 'I could be on the turnpike in, you know, just a matter of a few minutes and back to Topeka in no time.' Was that the truth or a lie?"

"That was a lie."

"On Page 41, at Lines 19 through 20 of your sworn statement, you said he just threw Marty's billfold and the credit cards along the east side of the field or ditch, or something like that. Was that the truth or a lie?"

"I was told that."

"Pardon me?"

"I was told that that's what he did with the billfold and credit cards."

"So you're saying that was the truth there?"

"Yes."

"On Page 45, Lines 24, you said, 'He just said there was a pond there and it was close enough to the road that he could throw the gun out the window without having to get out of the car.' Are you telling us today you were telling the truth or lying?"

"The gun was thrown in a pond, but it was not thrown out of the car."

"Another half-truth; is that correct?"

"Yes."

After this long list of questions, one wonders whether the jury still listened.

"Going back to 68...I believe at that point you were pointing to the map that had been drawn and pointing to a ditch that was east of 177 and south of the van, and you said, '...I think in there is where he threw the billfold...' Was that the truth or a lie at that time to the law enforcement officers."

"That was a lie, because the billfold was thrown north of the scene."

"I couldn't hear the answer," a juror said. (They *were* listening.)

"I'm sorry. That was a lie, because the billfold was thrown out north of the scene."

He asked her about the statement that Marty had perhaps done a drug deal in the parking lot. No, that was a lie, too. He asked whether Marty did, in fact, use drugs? "That was the truth. I knew that Marty was taking some drugs to stay awake when he was working late at night." They were over-the-counter drugs. She lied to Mark Bird about Marty selling drugs, too.

"At this time, Agent Winsor asked you, commencing on Line 10, 'And you say Tom Bird got to Sheri Weinmeister and convinced her to tell me a certain time and date,' and your response was, Huh-uh. Was that the truth or a lie?"

"I think that he talked to Sheri about the time that she saw him in Topeka."

Gradert exercised mercy on the courtroom and called the afternoon recess. Lorna still had hundreds more questions to answer.

Afternoon, lies continue

Before Unruh began again, Opat asked Gradert, "Your Honor, because of the way this is proceeding, can I turn my other witnesses loose?" The judge suggested they come back at 9:00 a.m. the next day.

Unruh referred to another of Lorna's quotes about Sheri. "At that time in your sworn statement, you responded to a question, 'He knew that Sheri was going to be going, or had gone, I guess, to Topeka, or she went home, which is, what, St. Marys or Marysville, somewhere, I don't know. She had gone home that weekend and he was able to talk to her before you did, and being one of his students, you know, anything to—because his comment was—you know, he told her that he had been out looking at cars and that he, you know, couldn't really say where he was at a certain time and that's when they worked out this little thing at Burger King.' Did you make that statement?"

"Yes, I did."

"Was that the truth or a lie?"

"It was the truth in that he had been out looking for cars, he had talked to Sheri, he had seen her at Burger King, but there was some discrepancy about the time, and yes, he had talked to her."

"Once again, you would say this is a partial truth; is that correct?"

"Yes." And she admitted that Tom never told Sheri to lie. This admission became very important later on when McKone called Sheri to the stand.

"Are you saying that here today, in 1990, five years later, you're finally telling the truth?"

"Yes, I am."

Unruh asked whether she came forward to Mr. Opat following that statement and admitted she had lied? "No, I didn't."

"Am I correct in saying that you never intended to cooperate with Mr. Opat?"

"I can't say that I never intended to cooperate. I was proceeding on the advice of my attorney."

"Did Mr. Focht tell you to lie?"

"No, but he told me as long as I didn't say anything to incriminate myself, he could get me out of that."

Unruh referenced the gun. She, of course, had known about it all along and now admitted it. She never fired it and no one ever showed her how to do so. She never carried it in her purse. She couldn't remember ever owning a .38 caliber handgun, and as far as she knew, there had been no ammunition for either in the house.

Unruh turned to the events of November 4, 1985. She claimed that it had been Marty's decision to go to Ft. Riley that day. Earlier she testified that the plan was to murder him on that Friday or a week later, depending on when they took this trip. She had planned a social event at her home for Saturday evening, but "I knew ahead of time that Marty was going to be killed so there would be no social function at my house."

She said that Tom cased the murder site and he drew her a map. She never had the map in her possession, though.

Unruh asked her to try and be specific about the time of the November 3 meeting at Faith. She felt it still was light out, but sometime after Marty got home from work. Marty got home anytime between 3:30 and 5:00 p.m.

Unruh continued to lead her through a discussion of the plan as Marty knew it for Friday, November 4. They would go to the PX, have a picnic lunch, go to Wal-Mart and be sure to head back in time for a 7:15 or 7:30 volleyball game.

Marty drove to Ft. Riley, but she asked him to take a different route than normal, telling him that she wanted to "Just have a ride." She had never gone that way before, but Tom had laid out the map, she said. Though the road was new to her, she watched for the road marker at McDowell Creek Road as they drove north toward I-70.

Arriving at Ft. Riley, they went to the Clothing Exchange Store and Marty bought his jacket. Then they ate their picnic lunch in the van. Marty then drove to the Post Exchange, intending to buy diapers, but she had been refused entry. She left her ID in the van.

"Was there any reason why you left your purse in the van?"

"No. I just forgot it and didn't think about needing it, needing my identification to get in."

"You had been in the Exchange before, hadn't you?"

"Yes."

"Hadn't they always checked your identification?"

"I don't remember."

They drove to Wal-Mart, bought the diapers and then went to McDonalds.

"Is McDonalds where you started with your acting?"

"Yes."

"What did you do?"

"I went to the bathroom, and told Marty that I was sick."

"And when you came out of the bathroom, did you say anything to Marty?"

"I told him that I wasn't feeling well."

"Did you tell him that you had thrown-up?"

"I believe so, yes."

"At that time, were you telling the truth to Marty, or were you lying?"

"I was lying." And she lied to Agent Winsor later, when she told him her story.

She took over the driving and headed south toward I-70. She stopped at the gas station just north of I-70. Marty held Jennifer in his lap. Lorna took her and laid her on the back seat. No one got out of the van.

"Did you meet Tom Bird at the restaurant that's adjacent to that filling station?"

"No, I didn't."

"Did you see Tom Bird there?"

"No."

"Did you see Darrel Carter there?"

"No."

"Dan Carter?"

"No."

Unruh asked the judge to announce a short recess. Opat had agitated for the break saying he needed to make a phone call. (Did he see his case falling apart on the stand? Did he need to call one of the investigators to get something to bail out his case?)

More Lorna

After the short recess, Unruh continued questioning Lorna. She had lost some of her self-confidence and defiance, but she had a long way to go before Unruh finished with her.

She headed the van south, down 177. She drove the speed limit, she thought, and could not recall whether it was still light out. No, she didn't remember if her headlights had been on.

"Did you see anything on McDowell Creek Road?"

"I saw a blue Toyota that looked like Tom Bird, parked on McDowell Creek Road."

Tom's car sat on the left side of the road facing north, she claimed. He told her to stop a certain number of tenths of a mile south of the road, but during this testimony, she couldn't recall that distance. She claimed she had only been to the murder scene twice since the murder took place and still didn't know the distance.

Unruh wondered if it had been light enough to see where she was to pull off the road. She couldn't remember, but she felt sure she saw Tom's car when she drove past. "Was Tom's car lighted by your headlights as you drove past McDowell Creek Road?"

"No, sir." (Unruh tried to establish the time as precisely as possible. This fact loomed large for Tom's defense.)

She eventually pulled off at the prescribed spot, faking illness. She asked Marty whether it would be a good place to stop. (This seemed like an odd assertion, since she also said Tom told her stop there. What if Marty had told her to continue driving toward the farm that sat less than a half-mile south?)

Once stopped, she got out of the van. She couldn't remember where the kids had been sitting, but presumed they all laid on the back bench seat. It had been pulled out into a bed.

"Back on November 7, 1983, you indicated to Agent Winsor you left your headlights on when you stopped the van and left the van; is that true or not?"

"I assume it was, yes."

She went to the ditch and pretended to throw up. She had taken the keys out of the ignition. They were Marty's.

"Was it light enough for him to see you at that time?"

"Yes." (This was a good answer for Tom's sake. The earlier they could show the murder took place, the better for him.)

She saw the shooter when he stood directly behind the van. She couldn't describe exactly where, but just somewhere behind the van. Marty still sat in the van and she stood in the ditch. During the preliminary hearing in April, 1989, she said Marty had been in the ditch when the shooter came up. She told Agent Winsor the same thing in November of 1983, and again on August 30, 1985.

"My question, then, would be, are you lying to us today, or did you lie under oath, as well as lie to Sheriff Deppish and Winsor in your prior testimony in this action and prior sworn statements?"

"I've already admitted that I lied to Mr. Deppish and Mr. Winsor. I'm not lying here today. The arrangement was for me to wait until I saw Tom and then lure Marty out of the van."

Unruh showed she had given several different versions of exactly when Marty got out of the van to help search for the keys. Now she said Marty got out and went down to the ditch and started searching. In perhaps two or three minutes, Tom began firing.

In earlier statements, she testified that cars had slowed down as they drove south past the van. She and Marty had been down in the ditch looking for the keys. "So these cars would have been able to see the shooter who was behind the van; is that correct?" She didn't know because she wasn't at all sure where the shooter was as they looked for the keys. She had just said he stood behind the van, but now she wasn't sure.

"Was there anything there for the shooter to hide behind?"

"There was the van."

Marty told her to go to the van and get her keys out of her purse, start the van and turn it around to shine light down into the ditch. She went to the van and opened the passenger door. Reaching in, she grabbed her purse. "Did you have any kind of weapon in your purse that evening?"

"No, sir." (She could have simply gone back, gotten the gun and, walking down behind Marty, pulled the trigger.)

The girls turned the light on in the back of the van as she reached in to get her purse. With the light on, it would be hard for them to see what was going on outside.

"Was it totally dark out at this time?"

"It was dark. You could still see. I was able to see Tom. I was able to see Marty."

"When you were getting your purse, where was the shooter?"

"When I was up to the van to get my purse, that's when he moved out into the field and started shooting."

Unruh tried to get her to be specific about exactly where Tom stood before going down in to the field. The back of the van, she said, but couldn't differentiate between the actual back and the side of the van toward the back. She also couldn't describe how far from the van Tom stood. She testified three different ways in prior testimony. Finally, with the aid of Opat, she said maybe 8-10 feet from the van (clearly far enough away to be visible to someone driving down the road).

She said Marty turned and faced Tom when he asked for the wallet, "and that's when he started firing." (Very interesting. Dr. Eckert said Marty died from three wounds inflicted from behind and above. It would take quite a trick-shot artist to shoot from the front and hit someone in the back.)

In early statements, she said Marty staggered backwards. Later she said he fell forward. "I really couldn't tell you today whether he fell forward or backward."

She had told investigators that the gun shots sounded like a machine gun, but had no idea how many rounds had been fired. Unruh reminded her that the police found four spent cartridges. "Okay. Three or four. I don't remember what I've read, but yes...I'm sure it was fired more than that."

After Marty fell, "Tom went up, he took Marty's wallet, there was a car coming, he and I went down a ways, and he pushed me down so that the car lights couldn't see me." She had stood up near the van as all this happened. Tom came up and brought her down to the ditch, she said.

"Were your children awake at this time?"

"Yes."

"What were they doing at this point?"

"I don't remember. I couldn't tell you if they were screaming or what they were doing. Crying, I'm sure they were crying."

Tom motioned to Unruh to come over to the table. After a brief discussion, Unruh turned back to the judge. "Your Honor, my co-counsel suggests that this might be an appropriate time to break for the day. I will leave that up to the court's discretion."

Gradert ordered the recess until 9:00 a.m. the next day. The jury left the courthouse with a vision of crying or screaming kids playing across their minds, while the father of those children lay dead in the ditch, with their mother standing nearby.

A different Lorna this morning

On March 5, 1990, Lorna re-entered the courtroom. All eyes followed her as she took the stand. She looked completely different than the woman who had sat smug and defiant in the same chair the day before. She pulled her hair back, wore little makeup and looked defeated. Her answers were robotic and without energy.

Mulling over images of screaming children since the night before, during this day's testimony the jury scowled at her. Unruh had accomplished his task—impeaching every word she uttered while keeping the jury from treating her as a victim. He planned to continue the process during the morning's questioning.

She changed yesterday's story slightly. Tom didn't come up to the van and get her, she walked down to him. A car drove by and they got down on the ground to avoid being seen. Earlier she testified that the day had been cold and damp, but here she said it had not been raining. "Where we were there was still grass, so it was soft, but as far as just being dirt and mud, it was not." (Marty's knees were covered with mud, but witnesses saw no mud on Lorna, though they had been in the same ditch at the same time.)

"On the evening of the shooting, in your conversation with Mr. Deppish, you stated, 'He pointed the gun right at my head and said he was going to kill me.' Was that a misrepresentation to Sheriff Deppish?"

"It was a misrepresentation. It was what we had agreed on as a story to make it seem like a robbery." She had also told Agent Winsor that the shooter pushed her down in the mud. "I was not physically pushed, no. We went down and got out."

"So at no time were you shoved into the mud; is that correct?"

"That's correct."

"So your statement, once again, to Agent Winsor was a lie; is that correct?"

"Yes."

Unruh began to ask the question about the mud in a different way, but Opat objected. He said Lorna had already answered the question and this had become repetitive. Gradert agreed, but added, "There have been a number of questions that have been repetitive, but I've tried not to limit you too much in your cross." He allowed Unruh to continue. Gradert's handling of Tom's 1990 trial differed greatly from the way Judge Rulon handled the Emporia trials. There, Rulon worked closely with the prosecutor, almost always sustaining his objections while overruling those of Irv Shaw and Robert Hecht. Gradert seemed intent on refereeing between the attorneys, not coaching one at the expense of the other.

While they lay in the ditch, Tom allegedly told her that there were no bullets left in the gun. "The plan was I would be shot in the shoulder to make it look as though it was a robbery. The gun didn't fire." She claimed Tom promised her that it wouldn't bleed much nor cause permanent damage. Within several minutes someone would stop and she would be whisked off to the hospital.

They planned this shooting the day before, she said, including her getting shot in the shoulder. Unruh suggested that Tom could have missed, hitting a vital nerve and she could have bled to death. Wasn't she worried? "Tom told me that if I was shot in the shoulder, there would be no permanent damage and I wouldn't bleed that much, and in those 24 hours, I was thinking more of Marty's death than I was concerned for myself." (As poorly as Tom would have been as a gunman, she should have worried mightily about endangering herself, if this story had been true.)

She and Tom walked toward the van. The children were crying. No, he never asked for her purse or her keys. "In your sworn statement of 1985, you testified, 'When he asked for my purse, I don't know how loud his voice would have been. It was just more demanding.' Is that another incident where you lied under oath?"

"Yes."

Lorna told him to "get out of there," and he ran "toward Manhattan," on the west side of the road. "I didn't stand there and watch until he disappeared. Once Tom took off running, I got back in the van with the girls."

She gave statements to Deppish that night in which she claimed the shooter had a black mask, or had black on his face. But she intentionally tried to avoid saying he was a black man. She told Deppish the man was taller than Marty (6' 2"). In her statements to Winsor, she said he was Marty's height and had black hands. "That was part of the plan."

Unruh continued to compare the various reports Lorna gave to police just after the shooting. They contained many contradictions, to which she agreed.

After the shooter ran away, she planned to stay in the van until he had a chance to get onto I-70. She couldn't be sure how long she actually waited before flagging down traffic. In previous statements she said she first went down to Marty before getting into the van. She didn't touch or talk to him, and she couldn't remember whether he lay face down or up. She thought perhaps she had been away from the van a minute, but she couldn't be sure.

"You weren't away from the van long enough to, say, hide a gun?"

"No, sir."

"You weren't away from the van long enough to go down to a pond?"

"No, sir."

She went to the van and tried to calm the girls down, but didn't remember whether she specifically talked to Lori. In a prior statement, she said she got out of the van and went back down to Marty. "That was a lie."

She couldn't remember whether or not cars passed by while they sat inside the van. At the planned time, "I got out back out of the van, I went to the side of the road in front of the van and tired to stop a car that was coming.

Um, the car went on, so when the next car came along, I walked clear out to the highway."

She remembered that the occupants of the first car had been a young couple with a baby. She thought the man went down to the body, but couldn't be sure. She didn't recall specifically the next car that stopped, nor the one that directed its headlights down into the ditch.

She remembered a lady had gotten off the school bus that stopped, and helped settle her and the children down. The police then took Lorna to the hospital.

He returned to her statements about Tom at the murder site. Tom ran north in the ditch, but she couldn't recall whether there even were ditches there. Yes, she had been to the murder site later on, but not for five years. She couldn't remember a thing about the topography or distances or any environmental evidence.

"And your description today is that Tom had on jeans, a jean jacket, and a ski mask; is that correct?"

"Yes."

"Do you recall what he was wearing on his feet?"

"Yes. He had on an old pair of tennis shoes. They were ones that he knew he could throw away."

Yes, she knew Tom had a meeting in Topeka and that's where he went after the shooting. "Would it be unusual for Tom to go to a meeting such as this conference you're describing dressed in blue jeans, a jean jacket, and a ski mask?"

"But he didn't wear those clothes to the meeting."

"You're saying he changed clothes?"

"Yes."

"In your sworn statement of '85, you testified he had—under his jeans and this jacket, he had his suit, except for the coat, at that point in time. Were you saying that the jeans and the jean jacket were placed on over his suit?"

"They were over his shirt and tie, and the jeans were over his suit pants, yes."

"So he has two pair of pants on, a shirt and a tie, and jean jacket and a ski mask; is that right?"

"Well, I don't know that he had the tie on, I shouldn't say that, but yes." Tom told her he stopped at the turnpike rest stop and disposed of the clothes in a trashcan. She had no idea when he changed clothes.

She told investigators that Tom threw the credit cards away with the billfold, yet she didn't worry about them. They all were maxed out and no one could have used them anyway. She had no credit cards of her own because Marty took them away from her. "Were those accounts ever paid off?

"I couldn't tell you when." (They had been joint accounts. She remained liable for the balances, but had no idea of their disposition.)

"In '85, you testified that you received a sympathy card that was threatening; is that not true?"

"I testified to that, yes, but that was not true; again, to make it look like there was some other motive."

"In '84, you told Mark Bird you received a card that said, 'If you don't keep your mouth shut, the same thing will happen to you and your children.' That was a lie?"

"That was a lie. That was again to make it look like Marty was involved in something that resulted in his death." (She had told Tom that Marty sold drugs and Tom believed her. The threatening cards added weight to her story.)

"Did you ever tell Susan Ewert that you received threatening cards and phone calls?"

"Yes. Again, that was something that Tom and I did to make it seem like there was some other motive."

She denied lying to her attorney and her parents about cards, though she had told investigators a different story. "Was that a lie in your sworn statement?" Unruh emphasized the word "sworn."

"Yes, it was."

Unruh showed her photocopies of the cards. "They were mailed to my home in Hutchinson...The postmark on the envelope is '85. I don't know if they're threatening. One is asking if my phone was still tapped; one says, 'It's not over yet,' and the other says, 'What did you tell the children?' I did give these to my attorney. I had forgotten."

"Do you know who posted [the cards] to you in Hutchinson?"

"I have no idea....I don't know whether this was something that Tom did, or had someone do, or not. It was nothing that I ever knew about ahead of time." (Tom sat in prison when these were mailed. They bore no prison postmark.)

Unruh showed that Lorna stood to gain in excess of $350,000 in death benefits from Marty's murder. She agreed. That day in May, when Chris Kimble added $100,000 to the coverage, she now claimed it was just to bring the coverage back up to where it had previously been. It had been Marty's idea to do this, she said. (But the Andersons let the $100,000 lapse right after Marty returned alive from Reserves that May.)

"Did you want Martin Anderson dead in order to obtain the insurance money?"

"No, sir."

"If you considered divorcing Marty as financially impossible, did you consider killing him as a possible financial alternative?"

"No, sir, I didn't. The only reason for Marty's death was because I was in love with Tom and I wanted to be with him." (Again, the affection was directed toward Tom. She made no claim that he returned that affection.)

"Your testimony is that you never took into consideration the over a third of a million dollars' worth of insurance?"

"That was for the girls." (The same girls she had exposed to the execution of her husband.)

"Who was the beneficiary?"

"I was the beneficiary, but Marty provided the life insurance for my daughters." She called Kimble less than 24 hours after Marty's death, asking when the insurance money could be expected. Here she denied asking that question.

She no longer recalled Esther Aldrete talking about the phone call where Lorna said she couldn't wait to get all that green stuff. Yes, she remembered talking to Agent Humphrey on August 28, 1985, but not about Aldrete. She just didn't remember. Then she did remember. She told Humphrey she had been talking about spilled green jello.

No, she never had a man over who she embraced while lying on a coffee table. No, Aldrete never saw her with another man. She denied having sex with anyone other than Danny, Darrel and Tom from June, 1982, on. (Investigators had statements from dozens of men testifying to sexual encounters and offers of the same with her during that time period.) All ears in the courtroom perked up. Writers got their pens ready. Finally, Lorna's list would become public. But no, by prior agreement, this had been barred from the courtroom. Only specific instances could be questioned.

Lorna admitted asking Alvin Tefft about injecting air or chemicals into someone's veins.

Still more Lorna grilling

Each answer now seemed to dig Lorna's hole deeper. Opat knew he had a lot of ground to make up once this ordeal ended, but Unruh had more. One thing was for sure about Lorna; the stories never ended.

Lorna agreed she had had a book contract with David Hacker. She also granted an interview to Joan Baker. "Was part of your agreement with Mrs. Baker that Tom Bird not be interviewed for that article?"

"Yes, it was." Scott Kraft, too, had testified. And Barbara Livingston.

"During the course of that interview, Barbara Livingston asked you, 'In his trial testimony about the meeting in the church office with you and

Tom...' — I think the exact date is in question, whether May or June — '...was Darrel's testimony about that conversation accurate, as you recall it,' and you responded, 'Some of it. Darrel is a liar. He never liked Marty. He told me I should get rid of him, leave him. Darrel Carter is no angel. He broke up at least one marriage in the sorority. Sure, he'd like to save Danny's skin.' Was that your response to her on that date?"

"Yes, it was."

"Later on in the same response, did you testify, or did you tell Barbara Livingston, 'I can tell you one thing. No bridge was ever mentioned, or pushing the car down the bank, and Tom never asked him to be a pallbearer at the funeral, Darrel just thought that sounded good, I guess...because he hated Marty, and he was the type" — and she said, 'Ruthless,' and you said, 'Yeah,' Do you recall telling her those things?"

"It's down here, so I'm sure I did."

Unruh quizzed her about how she had been hired as the church secretary. Yes, the three lay ministers hired her after an interview process. She said Tom had been involved, too. Yes, Tom and Marty became friends during the fall of 1982 and, yes, both Andersons joined the church. Marty attended irregularly.

She and Marty finished taking instructions in the Lutheran faith, taught by Tom, and the lessons were conducted in the Anderson's home.

She claimed that though Tom provided counseling to her, it never occurred at set times. "The only counseling that would take place would be while I was at work." She felt comfortable taking her problems to him.

Marty and Tom played several different team sports together. They all attended various church activities together, including "a couple's club at the church."

"In your sworn statement of August, '85, you testified it was May before there was any type of physical relationship; you said that?"

"Yes, I did. That was a lie."

"Do you know an individual by the name of Irv Shaw?"

"Yes, I do."

"You told him that the physical relationship didn't start until January of '84, didn't you?"

"I don't recall."

He asked her about various statements concerning going to motels. She now swore they had done so in June of 1983, plus the time in August. (Jan Mead had thrice testified that Lorna told her they began going to motels during February and March, 1983.)

"Believe it or not, I'm just about to get my hat and sit down," Unruh said. "Who is Susan Ewert?"

"Susan Ewert was a friend of mine."

They became closer following the homicide and you "stayed at her house for awhile; is that correct?"

"Yes, I did." Susan helped care for the children. She had lied to Susan about the murder.

"And once in Hutchinson, you developed another relationship with another church; is that correct?"

"Yes."

"You became acquainted with a reverend by the name of Tom Mendenhal?"

"Yes, I did."

"And he could counsel with you about problems you were having in your life; is that correct?"

"Yes."

"Would it be a fair statement that you lied to him also about your involvement in the homicide?"

"Yes, I did." (Investigators had kept watch on Lorna's house. One night they recorded that a car registered to Pastor Mendenhal came late in the evening and left early in the morning. Mendenhal's first name was "Tom." It just seems too much of a coincidence that he, just like Tom Bird, had begun to counsel her and by coming to her home late at night, he had unwittingly set himself up for rumors similar to those leveled against Tom Bird.)

Unruh asked whether it was true that Lorna lied repeatedly to Mark Bird. "Yes, I did."

Stephen Anderson sat in the back of the courtroom watching all this. Unruh began to quiz her about their relationship. "Shortly after the homicide itself, did you become angry at Stephen Anderson?"

"Not really, no."

"Did you convey to Stephen Anderson that you were angry with him?"

"Yes, I did."

"I hand you something which was previously marked as Defendant's exhibit T and ask if you recognize that document?"

"Yes, I do. It was a letter that I wrote to Stephen Anderson." She claimed Tom told her to write it. She expressed anger that Stephen had been working with the investigators and she returned gifts she had received from him on behalf of the children. Her attorney recommended her to do this, she said.

"Did you indicate in that letter to Stephen that you truly loved Marty and cared about him?"

"Yes, I did."

"That was a lie?"

"I don't know. I really can't say right now." Yes, she agreed that she told

678

Stephen that Marty had been involved in drug dealing and yes, that, too was a lie.

He asked about Randy Eldridge, the man she married in June of 1985. "You lied to him about your involvement in Marty's death, didn't you?"

"Yes, I did."

"You have repeatedly lied to members of your own family about this incident, haven't you?"

"Yes, I have."

Unruh finished his cross-examination. Those in the courtroom breathed a sigh of relief.

Bork tries to resurrect something

John Bork had a tough job. He began trying to resurrect Opat's case.

Who told you to call the insurance agent? Stephen Anderson, she answered. Stephen told her to call the funeral home, call someone in Wellington and notify the agent. She did everything he had told her when she returned to Emporia. (Stephen had recounted this conversation for investigators and said he took care of the Wellington contacts.)

Aldrete, she said, had a poor grasp of the English language, and was very hard to understand. "It was impossible for me to talk to her on the phone." What Lorna really said about green stuff was more like, "Marty's going to die when he gets home and sees this green Jello on the floor."

Tom told her he threw the billfold along the road and the gun into he pond, she said. Her affair with Danny lasted from May to, perhaps August, 1982, when it began to fade. She saw him occasionally through the end of 1982. "And would you have sex with him when you saw him on some of those occasions?"

"On some of those occasions, yes." But the affair she now defined as "a few months," apparently referring to the quantity of sexual encounters.

Bork used her to remind the jury that the result of her plea agreement was a sentence of 15 years to life, implying she had nothing to gain by testifying in this case.

The purpose of the handwritten letter she sent to Stephen, she said, was to get investigators to change the direction of their inquiry—start looking at drugs and such, and away from her and Tom. "Tom Bird not only suggested that I write the letter, but he essentially told me what to say in the letter."

On August 30, 1985, when you told investigators that you never talked to anyone about the shooting, that was to protect yourself against incrimination. Yes, and my attorney told me he could get me out of it if I didn't incriminate myself.

Bork asked when Lorna had visited the murder scene with Tom? Following his conviction for solicitation, during August of 1984. "Have you ever discussed with Tom Bird the murder of Sandy Bird?"

"Yes, I have."

"And what did he have to say about that?"

McKone objected strongly. "That's out of the scope of our cross-examination." He had previously moved to strike all evidence from the first two convictions and he renewed that objection. Gradert overruled him.

Lorna reviewed her entire version of how Tom killed Sandy, in a sense, trying that case in front of *this* jury.

"After you had pled guilty to solicitation to commit murder in 1985, but prior to the statement you gave on August 30, 1985, did Mark Bird talk to you?"

"Yes, he called me at my home in Hutchinson."

"What did he say then?"

"He told me that if I said anything in that statement to investigators that would hurt his brother, that I would be sorry I had done that." (She had accused Mark of a felony crime—intimidating a witness. If Bork and Opat believed this to be true, they would have filed charges against Mark. Rod Symmonds did this to Dee Wagoner in Lyon County when she got in Susie Graf's face following Graf's testimony. But Geary County never charged Mark with anything.)

"Mrs. Anderson, did you ever name anyone other than Tom Bird as the killer of Martin Anderson?"

"No, I have not."

Bork stood down and McKone approached Lorna.

"Let me get this straight. Sometime after the murder of your husband, which you've admitted to the jury and all these people in this room you helped plan and conceive, you wrote a letter to your brother-in-law, Stephen, right?"

"Yes."

"And you're telling this jury, basically, your intention was to taint your husband as a drug dealer?"

"Yes."

"And shift the focus of the investigation away from you, isn't that right?"

"Yes."

"And you did that for your own self-interest and your own protection?"

"For mine and Tom's, yes."

He asked whether everything she had just testified to had been actions she took under Tom's direction. Yes, she said that was true. "Did he have some kind of magical hold over you, Mrs. Anderson?"

"No, I was just in love with the man."

She agreed that Tom had known nothing about Darrel and Danny, except what she had told him. "And you considered them to be the kind of people — if you want to have somebody roughed up or killed, those were the kind of people you go talk to?"

"I felt like I could trust them yes."

"You could trust people you thought would go out and beat somebody up or kill them?"

"I knew that they were not happy that Marty was beating me, and yes." She had offered nothing to them and their sexual affairs had already ended, she said.

"Do you have any other friends like that, Mrs. Anderson?"

"No, sir."

"I'm glad to hear that."

As for her August, 1985, statement, she said once again that her attorney told her to tell the truth, but to be careful not to incriminate herself. (Jack Focht must have been squirming in his chair. No attorney can advise his client to lie, and that was what Lorna kept implying.) So she made a conscious effort to lie all on her own.

He turned to her comments about Sheri Weinmeister. Lorna had earlier said that day that Tom got Sheri to lie to investigators by making up a story. Though she knew that investigators had talked to Sheri, she had no idea what she had said. Yes, she lied about that, too.

"You're not trying to tell us today that your recollection is that it was a preconceived plan to get Sheri to be there [at the Burger King]; is that right?"

"No, sir. No, sir. There was no preconceived plan for her to be there."

McKone focussed on the November 3, alleged meeting she had with Tom at Faith. He needed to firmly establish her timelines in the minds of the jurors. Later he would show that Tom had ironclad alibis for that time, including playing basketball with Marty.

He asked her to repeat the things she claimed Stephen had told her to do that Saturday at the hospital. She rattled them off precisely. Yet, McKone said, you can't recall other details that pertain to your meeting with Tom or many precise details about the commission of the murder?

He once again reviewed Lorna's claims about what she expected from giving her sworn statement on August 30, 1985. She expected nothing, she said, despite the letter Jack Focht had sent to Opat stating otherwise.

Finally, her time on the stand ended.

Author's aside

Lorna's testimony had been unavailable to Tom during his 1984 and 1985 trials. It contained much exculpatory evidence. Irv Shaw knew that, but worried that even had she testified, what she actually would say on the stand was a crapshoot.

Her timelines in this testimony completely refuted those given by Jan Mead. Soon, jurors would hear further impeachment of Mead's testimony from Susan Ewert. Judge Gary Rulon had allowed Jan Mead's hearsay evidence to be heard by two Lyon County juries. Without the ability to examine Lorna on the stand in these earlier trials, Mead's testimony stood unchallenged.

Without Mead's testimony in 1984 and 1985, the state had no motive. Without motive, they had no case.

In this testimony, Lorna agreed with statements made by Shaw that her sexual relationship with Tom began in January of 1984. This testimony changed all the claims made by Mead, Workman, Danny or any others that implicated Tom in adultery while Sandy and Marty lived. Interestingly, neither Sandy nor Marty ever told anyone that Tom and Lorna were lovers.

Lorna's testimony also constantly contradicted that of Darrel and Danny Carter. And many of her answers impeached Darrel's testimony.

She repeatedly said she was in love with Tom, and not once said he loved her. Though several times during this day-and-a-half testimony she said Tom murdered Marty, all her lies—more than 80—and different versions of her story left her totally without credibility. The state saw her as their star witness. When she finished, Opat and Bork knew their case was in deep trouble.

Continuing the prosecution

On Monday, Judge Gradert had allowed the defense to call David Workman to the stand, giving Lorna a 25-minute break. Workman had moved to Texas and wanted to return home.

Workman said he saw Lorna bruised and battered late in March or early April, 1983. She told him of a plot to rough up or shoot Marty and it had been in the context of a discussion about Darrel and Danny Carter.

He spotted a gun in her purse that day. He identified it as the Colt Woodsman, now entered as evidence in this trial. Ballistics tests proved it to be the weapon that was used to murder Marty.

Workman said that Lorna's sexual affairs were common knowledge at Newman, and that frustrated her. He said that in August, 1983, Lorna told him she was in love with Tom. Yes, people at Newman believed they, too, had an affair.

Workman's testimony served to impeach both Lorna and Darrel, though it didn't necessarily exclude Tom from some later conspiracy. Later on, after Susan Ewert's testimony, Workman's words formed a strong defense against any involvement in any of the crimes, especially in Marty's murder.

Opat called Rod Symmonds to the stand following Lorna's testimony. Symmonds described details surrounding the first two convictions and stepped down. His testimony meant to show Tom was a twice-convicted felon who was capable of murdering Marty. It spoke to the motive from those two trials that Tom and Lorna had a long-standing affair.

Most of the balance of the state's case consisted of investigative reports on evidence, chain of custody and their versions of Tom's statements. The men and women who viewed the murder scene that night testified as to what they saw, none of which particularly spoke to guilt or innocence. Witnesses recalled that Lorna seemed to be acting or overdoing it a bit, but those observations had little to do with the charges against Tom.

The state rested its case. McHone took control.

Joan Johnson, testified that she drove past the van and saw two men standing in front of it, talking. She described one as wearing a tight jacket and a mask. She felt sure he wore wire-rimmed glasses because the light reflected off of them. She described what the other man wore as well, and neither description sounded like Marty. This left open the possibility that the second man served as the driver for the shooter—more people had been involved in this than the police either knew or cared about.

Dennis Bayless said that when he arrived at the scene, he saw fresh tire tracks that looked as though someone drove away fast. By the time police arrived, those tracks had been trampled by gawkers. He said police didn't do enough to protect evidence at the site.

One very important hamburger

Sheri Weinmeister Galliart had married since November 4, 1983. That November day she, along with Kristen Speaks, Doug Carlson, Susan Perich and her mother Jeanette, left Emporia around 4:30 p.m. They planned on attending a football game in Atchison that evening.

On the way, they stopped at a Burger King in Topeka. As they got out of the car, Sheri spotted Tom. She had belonged to the Faith youth group and was a student in the ethics course Tom taught at ESU. They hugged and chatted for several minutes.

Galliart could not be exactly sure of the time of day, but felt it had to be

5:30 or so. Tom told her he had been looking for a van and that he planned to attend the church growth seminar at Washburn University that evening. Tom had acted very normal — warm and friendly, not nervous.

Before they left that night, the others saw Sheri with Tom for about 10 minutes. When she rejoined them, she told them his identity. Leaving the Burger King they arrived at Atchison long after dark.

Galliart's testimony firmly set Tom's presence in Topeka at 5:30, perhaps as late as 5:45. Marty's murder most likely occurred sometime between 6:00 and 6:15. Topeka is 52 miles from the murder scene. Tom could not possibly be there and at the Burger King at the same time.

Steve Hanschu said he saw Tom arrive at Washburn sometime around 7:10 p.m., late for the start of the seminar.

Bart Laib said he noticed that Tom came late into the meeting. He thought they were supposed to ride together to the meeting, but Tom left early. Laib went with someone else. He saw Tom get upset upon hearing of Marty's murder. Tom wanted to go right over to Junction City, but instead, drove home with him.

Prosecutors asked him about his concerns over Tom's relationship with Lorna. He, along with one of the lay ministers, had confronted Tom about it, but Tom became defensive and denied it.

Joyce Rosenboom said that she attended Tom's ethics class on Thursday, November 3, 1983, and had her notes to prove it. The class met from 2:30 to 4:30. Lorna testified earlier that Tom had been at the murder scene during that time period.

Mike Pruisner said Tom played basketball with the Optimists, and their game started at about 5:00 on the night of November 3. Marty played, too. They played until 7:00 p.m. During this time, Lorna insisted Tom had been with her, going over the murder plans.

Stephanie said Lorna picked her up at home at about 6:30 p.m. that night. They went to a sorority dinner together. On the way, Lorna stopped at Messiah and either made some copies of something, or made a phone call. When Lorna came out of the church, she got very upset because she couldn't find her purse, the one that carried the gun David Workman had seen during March.

Rev. Al Burroughs said that Tom met with the Family Life Committee from 9:00 a.m. until past Noon on November 3. They all had lunch together. He felt sure that Tom stayed until 1:00 p.m. or so.

With the testimony of these individuals, Tom could account for all of Thursday, November 3, and the most critical times on Friday, November 4, during the time someone shot Marty.

Connie Wheeler had been subpoenaed by the prosecution and brought from prison in Arizona to testify at trial. Wheeler, serving a life sentence for murder, had been Lorna's cellmate. Lorna told her all the details of Marty's murder and implicated Tom. But McKone used Wheeler's testimony to further impeach Lorna, showing several inconsistencies with Lorna's testimony earlier in the trial.

John MacMahon said he worked as a para-legal at Lansing prison. He knew Tom from the time the two of them had previously served together before Kansas transferred MacMahon to the "Hill" where Lorna also lived. He and Lorna became friends.

Following Lorna's second-degree guilty plea, during December of 1988, she approached him asking for legal and ethical advice. Lorna asked if she had committed perjury by agreeing to the reduced charge in exchange for testifying against Tom?

MacMahon asked what the state had offered her? She said the deal, if accepted, would allow her to be released within a few years. He asked specifically what the state wanted her to say? "That Tom was the person that killed Marty."

He told her that he and Lorna both knew Tom very well and they both knew he never murdered Marty. He asked her, "Do you want to tell me who did?"

"Johnny, I want to get out of here to be with my children and Tom's already doing a life sentence. I'm tired of going to court. I want it over with."

MacMahon asked her again who it was that killed Marty? She didn't respond. He asked, "It wasn't Tom, was it?" She shook her head, "no."

"Am I to understand this to mean that the state wants you to perjure your testimony to implicate Tom as the murderer?"

"They want to get the case over with. So do I. Hey, let's face it. The news people have put the pressure on, and Tom's the one they want. It's not my fault."

Susan Ewert, take the stand

Susan explained how she came to know Tom—at Lord's Lambs preschool—and Lorna in 1977 or 1978 at First Presbyterian Church. She and Lorna became close friends. After Marty's death, their bond grew closer because most of Lorna's friends fell away.

Lorna described in detail the events of November 4, 1983, to her on the following Sunday. Susan laid them out at length as she remembered them. Her story contradicted several details of Lorna's 1990 version. Lorna had expended quite a bit of effort trying to convince Susan that Marty dealt in drugs, even asking her to help identify some pills Lorna said she found in

Marty's briefcase.

Lorna stayed with Susan the weekend of Danny Carter's arrest. Susan asked her, "Do you think Danny would have been the one that killed Marty? And she said, 'I suppose so.' She said, 'He was about the same size.'"

Lorna told her on two occasions that someone had threatened her. She appeared genuinely frightened.

"Mrs. Ewert, you know Jan Mead, don't you?"

"I do not know her. I have seen her on the stand."

"You've heard her testify before?"

"Yes, I have."

"Did Mrs. Anderson ever relate any information to you about this Jan Mead information?"

"Yes, she did. Lorna was staying at my house during Tom's trial. Darrell Meyer, her attorney, had wanted her there in Emporia, and I believe Lori was to testify in the trial. And Darrell called her during the noon recess, after Jan Mead had testified, and told her Jan Mead's testimony."

"This is what she's telling you now?" referring to that July, 1984, day.

"Uhm-hum...I answered the phone and handed it to Lorna, and Darrell told her of the testimony, and her face began to drop as she was listening to Darrell, and she went upstairs and—in the room that she was in, my son's room, where she was sleeping, and got between the bed and the wall on the floor on her knees and sobbed and sobbed and sobbed."

"Why was she doing that?"

"I left her alone for a little bit, then I went upstairs and put my hands on her shoulder, on her head, and I said, can I help? And she related to me what Darrell [Meyer] had said on the phone, and then what the true story was."

"Did she tell you that Jan had confused Mr. Bird with someone else?"

"Yes, she did." Susan knew the name of the person, but was not allowed to say it at trial. (Willie Porter, her former boss, was the man Lorna had actually described to Jan Mead.)

"She said that Jan had misunderstood her conversation, that she had never mentioned Tom's name to Jan, that she had talked to Jan about an affair that she had had with a hospital supply salesman or district manager...She related the story to me about being in Herington with this man, and walking down the street hand in hand, and walking into a jewelry store, and the woman at the jewelry store commented because they seemed so much in love. And Lorna said, this was not Tom I was talking to Jan about...this man was bald-headed...somewhat older than Lorna...' And I may have remarked for an older, bald-headed man he was good in bed.'"

Susan said that she had believed that Lorna was innocent of all charges until her plea agreement in August, 1985. Once Lorna pled guilty, Susan quit believing her, because all along Lorna had maintained her innocence.

McKone established that Susan also considered Tom to be a close friend, but she had never been to a church service at Faith. She never heard him preach. She didn't know anything about his teachings. She continued to write to Tom at prison and visit him there. The letters he sent to her resembled the kind that had earlier been entered into testimony—the so-called "love letters."

John Bork began his cross-examination.

He asked whether Susan knew that since the day Lorna broke up in sobs at her house that she had testified that she had, in fact, told Jan Mead about Tom? Yes, she knew that. And that "certain parishioners" had gone to Tom about his relationship with Lorna? Yes, she knew that, too. She said that after January of 1984, the bond between Tom and Lorna had grown stronger. Susan stepped down after McKone clarified that Tom and Lorna grew close following Marty's death.

Chris Kimble testified that Lorna called him within 24 hours of Marty's death to discuss the insurance settlements. He thought she sounded differently than others whose spouse had died. It bothered him.

Terry Bird testified as well. Tom wanted to keep her out of the spotlight during the 1984 and 1985 trials. Now he needed her.

Terry explained that she and Tom started dating in early October, 1983. She told about the pastor's conference in November where they spent a lot of time together. This time period was the same as when Tom delivered the "love letters" to Lorna. She and Tom married in 1988. Prosecutors asked her whether she knew about the 600 or so phone calls between Tom and Lorna during 1984 and that Tom was also seeing Lorna during this time. No, at the time she didn't know about that.

Virginia Bird testified that investigators had twice visited their house in Hardy, warrants in hand, looking for evidence. She had totally cooperated with them.

They searched in vain for one critical piece of evidence. An excellent plaster cast of the killer's footprint had been made at the scene of Marty's murder. To ensure that it indeed belonged to the killer, investigators had checked every accident scene witnesses' shoes—none matched. They traveled to prison and checked Tom's foot size and shoes—no match. At the Bird's Hardy home they found nothing.

Since the casting failed to match Tom's shoe and foot size and they had settled on him as Marty's killer, and despite the monetary and time expense they had invested in it, they decided to ignore it instead of pursing any one of several others implicated in the murder. They let their real "Cinderfella" get away.

Sheriff Deppish made a brief appearance as a defense witness. He had interviewed Casey Carter early in the investigation. Danny said he and Casey were together all day on November 4, but Casey couldn't be sure whether it had been that day or a week earlier. He had been off of school both days.

McKone also called Agent Winsor to the stand. Winsor had driven from the murder scene to Washburn, measuring it as almost 51 miles. It took him an hour and five minutes. He also drove from the murder scene to the Burger King. That measured just over 52 miles and took 58 minutes.

Two Birds testify next

On Monday morning, March 12, 1990, both Tom and Mark Bird testified, as did Jim Kenney, a private investigator that helped McKone prepare Tom's defense.

Before they came to the stand, McKone's secretary read a deposition taken of Margaret Wyatt. She suffered an emergency appendectomy the previous Thursday and could not testify in person. She saw a blue-gray car parked the wrong way on McDowell Creek Road sometime just before 6:00 p.m. on November 4, 1983. Wyatt had looked at several different cars in books shown to her by investigators. None of them matched Tom's Toyota.

Mark said he became involved in Tom's case during August of 1984, when he visited the murder scene following Tom's first conviction. But his most important testimony dealt with loans Tom made to him in the fall of 1983. During September, Tom loaned him $1,100, money that came from the $5,000 check Tom cashed on September 7. Tom loaned him an additional $700 later on that fall.

Mark said he asked Tom whether or not he and Lorna had a physical relationship during 1983. Tom told him no, they had had one sexual experience, and that occurred on January 1, 1984.

McKone spent 30 minutes questioning Tom, and Opat took 40 minutes with him. Tom said he did not murder Marty. He wasn't even in Geary County at the time of the murder. He had been at the White Lakes Mall in Topeka. Earlier he had shopped for vans in Topeka and arrived late—perhaps at 7:15 p.m.—at Washburn University for the seminar.

Tom laid out his schedule from the prior day, showing he could not possibly have met with Lorna as she claimed, nor could he have visited the murder scene that day. He confessed to having a sexual relationship with Lorna during 1984, but denied any physical contact with her in 1983.

He denied being involved in a conspiracy to solicit a murderer. He denied murdering Sandy.

He acknowledged cashing a check for $5,000 on September 7, 1983, but said he gave $1,000 to Lorna. He had loaned some to his brother and used the rest to live on. He had written very few checks that fall, paying most of his expenses in cash. He paid a medical bill for Terry during October. Tom accounted for all the money. Opat challenged him on the unlikely coincidence that his cash withdrawal happened on the same day Lorna gave $5,000 to Danny. Tom could only say that Lorna conned him even on this.

Unlike the scowling faces Lorna saw during her testimony, the jury paid close and respectful attention to Tom. At one place he struggled for a word during an answer. The jury box sat very close to the witness stand and a juror spoke up, providing the word he had forgotten. Judge Gradert admonished the juror.

Tom handled this 1990 testimony very well. So did McKone, who took great care to limit his questions to Tom. Tom knew the stakes and he had learned much about juries.

The defense rested.

Opat, in what jurors later labeled a desperation attempt, called Deputy Garry Berges to the stand as a rebuttal witness. Berges and other officers on the past weekend had staged a reenactment of the murder. An official from the attorney general's staff ran from McDowell Creek Road to the murder scene, waited five minutes, and ran back to McDowell Creek Road. Officers added this time to what it took them to drive a car to Topeka and back. They showed it could be done in two hours, four minutes and ten seconds. Opat claimed that, despite Sheri Galliart's testimony, Tom still could have done the murder. This meant, of course, that he got to Washburn later than the 7:10 p.m. time that Hanschu's said they saw him, or that Galliart had been wrong about the time she saw him at Burger King.

Closing arguments

During the morning of March 13, 1990, Ralph and Virginia Bird arrived at the courthouse early. After passing through tightened security, they were led to a room where they could talk with Tom for a few minutes. "Tom leads us in prayer this morning as we go for the morning session," Virginia wrote later that day.

The day before, several observers noted that Opat looked white as a sheet. They believed he knew his case had failed. Before going in for closing arguments, Judge Gradert commented that if the case ever made it to an appeal, he would be retired. Tom believed Gradert also knew the state had failed.

"I submit to you, ladies and gentlemen, that despite all his protestations of innocence, despite all his disavowals of a romantic and sexual relationship with Lorna Anderson, despite his purported alibi, despite the fact that he is a self-described knight in shining armor, that Tom Bird was part of the plan," Opat said. "He engaged in the preparation, there was a motive, there was the intent and that these prior convictions coupled with the other evidence that you have heard establish the identify of the killer of Martin K. Anderson. That person is not a victim of circumstances and coincidences, lies, distortions and conspiracies, but that the identity of that person is Thomas Paul Bird."

McKone said there had been more than reasonable doubt established. He attacked Lorna. "There's nothing and no person that woman wouldn't lie to. She lied to everyone in the world and now they want to say 'let's disregard those lies because she's conveniently named Tom Bird as the murderer."

No one could place Tom at the murder scene (thought that made little difference in Emporia) except Lorna. She admitted to more than 50 lies just in the first morning of her testimony.

Lorna said Tom shot Marty from 50 feet away and that's not consistent with Dr. Eckert's testimony. Eckert said Marty had been shot from behind and above.

McKone said the evidence pointed more at Darrel or Danny Carter, Greg Curry or Johnny Bingham. Tom had produced five witnesses who put him in Topeka at the time of the murder.

At 12:45., the judge gave the case to the jury.

Jury deliberates and gives a verdict

Before beginning their deliberations, the jurors had a prayer. Then James Christenson, the foreman, called for a vote. They thought it made sense to find out right away where everyone stood. The first vote was 11 to 1 for acquittal.

The one vote came from a woman who said she thought Tom had done something and, besides, he had been convicted before. "We talked to her about how the two crimes had to be separated and how to look at the evidence in this crime only...She was finally able to see," jurist Marie Burgett wrote to the author. Bert Thomas, another jurist, said the woman just wanted to say how she felt.

They took a second vote—12-0, not guilty.

Thomas and Burgett both agreed: they didn't believe the prosecution witnesses, especially the Carters, and they found Sheri Galliart's testimony very compelling. The state couldn't put Tom at the scene, thanks to her testimony.

Burgett wrote concerning Lorna, "We actually rather giggled at her. She was totally not believable and her attempts at trying were rather pathetic. She made quite a show of pulling her glasses out of a handmade glasses case that said, 'Mom'."

Thomas said about Tom, "He was a good witness for himself. I believe he told what he thought was true. Sometimes we believed a lot he said. His witnesses proved him out. Anybody that knew him liked him. He was setting convicted of another murder and that probably weighed on our minds. He was very articulate." (This was in sharp contrast to his first trial when he often stumbled over words. And when the 1984 jury heard the tape of the meeting with Carter, Tom had been anything but articulate.)

When the jury returned to the courtroom, just as in the first two trials, tension ran high. The bailiff read the not guilty verdict and a cry of joy came from the Birds and their friends. Tom saw McKone nearly collapse from exhaustion and relief. Sitting down next to him at the defense table, Tom draped his arm over the young attorney's shoulders and thanked him for all he had done.

Terry Bird read a statement the family had prepared. "There's no question that today's verdict will open the door for a complete review of Tom's previous convictions. We're hoping to continue the appeal process and we feel today's verdict will have a domino effect in a positive way for Tom. It's our hope that the truth, the whole truth, will come out now."

As Ralph Bird walked down the front steps of the courthouse that day, James Christenson stopped him and said, "You certainly have a wonderful son, Mr. Bird." Then he moved on.

Jane attended the entire trial as well. She also had a statement for the press. "I'm disappointed, I'm very disappointed, because I think differently...Thank goodness he's not out of jail over this.

"We have a different way of seeing things, but we've learned to accept things, and I learned *that* when I found out there was nothing I could do to bring my child back.

"I think of Sandy every day. If the sun shines or the moon or if something funny happens, any small thing might make me think of her."

So does Tom, everyday he rises behind bars and goes to bed behind bars. He loved her, too.

A day later, Opat saw Bert Thomas somewhere in town. Thomas worked as a mail carrier. Opat asked him why they found Tom not guilty. "Didn't put him at the scene." No one could put Tom at Rocky Ford Bridge, either, but it made no difference to that jury.

Tom said, "By the end of the trial I knew we won. I talked to Terry about it." When he heard the verdict, "I was depressed. They led me back to a jail cell, not to freedom. Too many people see trials as ball games. Like, this time

I won. To me I stopped the losing at that point."

Before being taken back to Lansing prison to continue his life sentence, Tom predicted that within a short time—months, perhaps, at least not much more—he would win exoneration from his first two convictions. To establish motive, Opat had used the same evidence against him as had Symmonds in the first two trials. McKone said the state's case in Junction City had been far stronger than in Emporia; here they had two eyewitness in Lorna and Lori. Tom's witnesses had provided exculpatory evidence that could now be used to win his freedom.

SECTION VIII:

CONCLUSION AND POST SCRIPT

"The Kansas Court system has got him and they refuse
to let him go."

Michael McKone, Junction City attorney

Whodunit

"The present crimes and the prior crimes are but *equal parts in a scheme.* The crimes are so closely connected that their probative value overwhelms their prejudicial effect. This crime did not occur in a vacuum and proof of its commission and the identity of the actor should not be tried in a vacuum."

Judge Gradert wrote these words in a decision that denied a motion to suppress testimony from Tom's first two trials. He meant that Sandy's murder and Marty's were coupled. He said "the identity of the actor" in the first murder shouldn't be hidden from the second jury. But Tom didn't murder Marty; the Junction City jury said so. Was Gradert right in his assertion that the actor in Marty's murder was the same person as in Sandy's death?

You want to know "whodunit," don't you? You think that after working on this book for more than 2,200 hours, I have the answer to the puzzle. You want to know, if Tom Bird didn't kill Sandy, how *did* she die? Did anyone kill her or was her death a tragic, single car accident?

You're itching to know who shot Marty.

You want to know why, if Tom is innocent, is he still in prison?

And you want me to tell you these answers.

Be patient.

It is a great temptation to want to write a stinging editorial about the Kansas—and American—criminal justice system. I shall resist that notion. If you want to hear this stinging editorial, you'll have to invite me to visit your group and give me a platform. Such a lecture will surely indict the courts in Emporia and Topeka, and the role of the news writers in the sordid, scandalous, soap-opera story line they overplayed.

Tom still sits at Lansing Prison because Kansas' court system refuses to consider newly found facts and allow him to be re-tried. They continue to deny his appeals motions because of legal tricks and technicalities. A common phrase in their rulings is, "He either knew or should have known." Even with exculpatory evidence such as Charles Henderson's perjury, refutation of Jan Mead Dykehouse's hearsay testimony and David Workman's powerful testimony about Lorna's on-going attempts to have Marty murdered, the appeals court turns a deaf ear.

On the stand in 1990, Lorna provided numerous contradictions of Darrel Carter's testimony. Granted, her stories have changed so often as to be nearly impossible to follow. Yet, they cast far more than reasonable doubt on almost all of Darrel's testimony.

The pathetically deficient indictment of the 1985 grand jury should be overturned in a federal habeas corpus suit. Attorneys debate this action, but

I don't. You can follow this debate, as well as the developments in Tom Bird's attempts to win freedom, on the internet at http://www.tombird.net.

Mike McKone said it best. "The Kansas court system has got him and they refuse to let him go." Careers and reputations were built on putting Tom Bird in prison. Much is at stake setting aright his convictions.

American citizens count on the court system to reign in and punish criminals and protect law abiding citizens. To accomplish this, our justice system rests on more than a thousand years of common law and the codification of that law that began in the Seventeenth Century and continues to this day. Kansas's justice system violated at least ten well-established principles of jurisprudence in Tom Bird's cases.

1. The accused has the right to know exactly of what he has been accused.
2. No one can be convicted of a crime based on hearsay evidence.
3. The accused has the right to a trial by a fair and unbiased jury.
4. The state must prove guilt, not force the defendant to prove his innocence.
5. Guilt must be determined only on facts, not on implications or speculations.
6. The state must be prohibited from buying testimony from anyone to help win a conviction.
7. No matter how heinous the crime, investigators cannot justify illegal and unethical means to collect evidence.
8. Punishment of a convicted criminal should fit the crime. The Bill of Rights prohibits cruel and unusual punishments, but it does not require allowing self-confessed felons to walk free (Danny Carter, one day in jail; Greg Curry, about 40 days in jail; Lorna Anderson, second-degree murder with 15 years to life.)
9. Media and public sentiment should play no role in the trying of a felony.
10. Just as there is no statute of limitations on a prosecution for murder, there should be no limitation on the presentation of new evidence that tends to exonerate a convicted murderer.

Had these long-held legal traditions been strictly observed in Tom's cases, he never would have seen the inside of a prison.

Lorna at the center

You want me to tell you about Lorna, don't you?

I think David Hacker should finish writing the book he started. He met her face-to-face and managed to come out morally whole. I agree with him, or at least pray that he is right—there is but one woman like her in a century.

Without Lorna, none of these events would have happened. Sandy Bird might still be alive. Marty Anderson would still be alive, enjoying the first of his grandchildren. The Birds and the Stringer/Grismer families would be friends. Tom Bird's church ministry would have flourished. Perhaps he and Sandy would be teaching together at a prestigious college. They, too, might already be enjoying the first of several grandchildren.

If you haven't yet figured it out, let me tell you plainly. In this sad story, Lorna is the center of the universe. Everything starts, finishes and turns on the hub of her hellish heart. She fooled investigators, prosecutors, parents, and what friends she had left—and dozens of men.

Consider how Lorna's actions left dozens of lives devastated.

Four young girls, who witnessed their father's execution, aided by the hand of their mother, grew up separated from parental care. Adopted by Randy Eldridge, they have struggled with their own demons. Randy divorced Lorna and in the late 1990s, a court convicted him of embezzling money from the girls' insurance settlement.

Loren and Alta Slater, God-fearing parents and upstanding citizens, were deprived of the joys of growing old with the companionship of their daughter.

Stephen Anderson, separated from the friendship of his own brother, spent many long years trying to bring closure to his brother's death. He still waits for justice.

A long list of men—and women, once she went to prison—live in fear that their names would someday surface and threaten their own marriages and families. Maybe some who read this book, wondered whether I would publish "the list" (Darrel Carter told Joan Baker he had "the list").

The world would never have heard about Julie Palmer's secret shame. Even Darrel and Danny Carter might have been spared their public flogging. Greg Curry would have been nothing but an entry on a payroll ledger, among hundreds of other men who passed each other every day at Wolf Creek.

Lyon County Sheriff Dan Andrews might have kept his job.

Deputy Bill Deppish might never have become Geary County Sheriff.

Gary Rulon might never have become an Appeal's Court Judge.

CBS would never have broadcast *Murder Ordained*.

Jane Grismer has spent years in bitterness and anger directed at Tom Bird. Without Lorna, she could have grown close to her remarkable daughter and her beautiful children, perhaps even have come to grips with Sandy's unflappable faith in God. She might have grown to love Tom.

Ralph and Virginia Bird would have grown old loving and guiding their pastor son and his pastor's wife. They would have experienced the full joy of three adult children maturing and building their lives around the Lutheran faith they held to so tightly. Tom would have seen his mother's death.

Mark Bird and Gloria Cates, always close to Tom, Sandy and their children, have had to watch from hundreds of miles away, powerless to do anything and frustrated by the mulish Kansas court system, instead of enjoying the love of their brother and his family. They visit Tom at Lansing quite often, and they watch his physical body grow old before its time.

Andrea, Paul and Aaron lost their mother. And though Tom remarried Terry Lyn Smith, the children grew up never exposed to the witness of the bonds of this new marriage as it would have grown ever closer, or knowing the wonderment of a new baby that this new marriage might have borne. Terry Smith might never have become Terry Bird, had Lorna left Sandy alone.

And, of course, I would have had no reason to meet Tom and write this book. I do not thank Lorna for this.

But Lorna did do her devilish deeds and because of these, many lives were devastated.

Who murdered Marty?

An unknown man shot four bullets at Marty; three of them hit him in the back of the head. Marty died instantly.

At least three people know the identity of the shooter. Perhaps two more do as well.

It has never been my purpose to solve this murder case. Perhaps Sheriff Deppish will try to resurrect the case some day, but I keep in mind that Marty's murderer has never been brought to justice. I am also aware of the libel and slander laws that protect private citizens, and I have no interest in defending myself in court.

In the fall of 1985, Darrel Carter told Joan Baker that investigators had not yet caught the murderer in either Sandy or Marty's case (Tom had been convicted of Sandy's murder just a few months earlier). I feel certain that Darrel, Danny and Lorna all know the identity of the murderer. I do not intend to finger either of the Carter brothers, though Mike McKone certainly did several times during the 1990 jury trial.

Weighty evidence exists that Lorna asked Darrel to help murder Marty on at least two occasions prior to May, 1983. Is it possible that Darrel steered her toward yet another unknown man, the man who actually did the murder?

What about the charge that Tom met with Darrel and Lorna, and the three of them planned Marty's murder? This charge led to his first conviction. This simply didn't happen. In 1984, Lorna insisted it never happened. Only after she pled guilty herself did her story change. Yet, evidence from Darrel himself, and David Workman, prove that Lorna talked about various plans to murder Marty with Danny and Darrel Carter; perhaps even during May, 1983. Why else did she take the initiative to add $100,000 to Marty's life insurance before he left for Reserves?

Take all their versions of plans to murder Marty into account and they sound more like ideas that evolved over time. Perhaps the first ideas emerged in 1982, when Lorna flagged Darrel down and they talked on the street. By the end of March, 1983, they talked again and then in May. Darrel Carter told Darrell Warren that someone wanted him to kill someone, and that someone might have been Lorna who had visited him at the building site.

Darrel had many levers on Lorna, especially as it concerned her solicitation of him to either murder or find someone to murder Marty. And she had levers on him. He had sex with her. He could easily have gone to Marty and caused a divorce. She could have gone to Darrel's wife, or told authorities about her charge that he burned down his garage.

Darrel may never have done anything about Lorna's ideas to murder Marty, except to discuss them in a light-hearted fashion. Maybe he never took her seriously, but she was dead serious. Danny certainly took her seriously and, as Lorna testified, those two brothers were very close to each other.

Mike Patton only heard what Darrel told him. Patton felt his job was to win the best deal possible for Danny. He had no knowledge of Tom Bird's involvement, but he added weight to Darrel's claims when they met with Vern Humphrey. Patton called Humphrey his friend and said they trusted each other. Humphrey had chased rumors about Lorna and Tom ever since Sandy's death. Darrel's story made sense, especially when he spiced it up with the idea of running Marty off a bridge Southeast of Emporia. "He made that up," Lorna said later, to give his story credibility.

Marty's murder

I don't know whodunit in Marty's case, but this is what I believe happened:

Lorna staged the murder with the help of two men. After she pulled off the road at the preconceived spot—the mailbox served as her marker—a large, light colored late model car pulled up behind the van and stopped. The shooter got out. Lorna handed him the gun that she carried in her purse, and he went down behind Marty and killed him.

The driver got out of the car and the two men talked briefly while standing in front of the van. Leaving peel marks in the dirt as they left, they turned around in the tractor path that sat in front of the van, and drove north to McDowell Creek Road. The driver let the shooter out and drove away.

The shooter took off his mask, jacket and shoes, and stuffed them into a garbage bag. Putting them into the car, he drove north to I-70 and then east toward Topeka. Stopping at the turnpike rest-stop, he dropped the garbage bag into a trashcan he drove home—or to a bar to get smashed. The gun sat under his seat and sometime later (it could have been months later), Lorna or an accomplice drove out to an area just north of the murder scene and threw it into a farm pond.

While the driver and shooter got away, Lorna climbed into the van and talked to the children. She calmed them down and told them her version of what happened, making sure by this that they didn't say anything incriminating.

Once she had waited long enough, she got out of the van and flagged down the first car. Later, before police arrived, someone moved her van backwards allowing John Leonard to position his Blazer to shine light down in to the ditch. This obliterated the tire tracks of the getaway car.

From that point on, it became a matter of how the story and investigation developed. Though investigators suspected from the start that Lorna was complicit in Marty's murder, she manipulated them time and again, convincing them that someone else did it. She never planned to name Tom— she planned to marry him. When that plan failed, she pointed the finger at him to save herself.

Investigators built their case against Tom on gossip. Given Lorna's well-earned reputation, Tom easily got slandered just by being associated with her. "She's dirty. Everyone knows that. No matter what he says, he's gotta be dirty, too."

Women didn't like Lorna. They spotted her cunning and conniving ways and kept a close eye on their own husbands and lovers. For sure, Sandy wasn't the only wife who complained about Lorna Anderson.

But what about Sandy? How did she die?

Sandy Bird's death

Someday, when I enter heaven, after I chat briefly with my family members who have preceded me, I am going to find Sandy Bird. She, along with God, knows exactly what happened at Rocky Ford Bridge during the evening of July 16 and 17, 1983. If Sandy was murdered, the two people who did it also know the details—Tom Bird does not.

Though I do not know what happened to Sandy, I will offer an explanation that I believe is the closest anyone can come to the truth, save a confession by the guilty parties. It certainly makes far more sense than the case against Tom Bird.

First, some foundation, as lawyers and judges love to say.

During the 1985 trial, William Kennedy did a terrific job of explaining how Sandy's car ended up in the river. I totally agree with him, save on one point—the door had been open before the car went over the embankment. Kennedy didn't offer a very convincing argument of how Sandy ended up in the river.

Dr. Eckert, Bridgens and Gabriel all had the cause of death right—she bled to death from blunt trauma. Neither of them could explain conclusively what caused the blunt trauma. Bridgens' theory that Sandy fell in the water and currents carried her body to its final resting place seems unlikely to me.

Rod Symmonds and John Rule might have been right about her being thrown off the bridge. Lorna said Sandy got kicked in the back and kicked off the bridge, and she, too, might have been right. But no one at Tom's 1985 trial really knew how Sandy died. (Lorna never attended that trial.)

Every theory of how Sandy died has its strengths and weaknesses, as does my theory. But given all the events and discoveries that followed Lorna during the next days, months and years, mine is a good theory.

During 1972, Lorna aborted her first child. The father's name was Tom. Pastor Bird's name was Tom. Pastor Bird had a son named Thomas Aaron Bird—called Aaron. Lorna believed God had punished her for aborting her baby and He kept her from having sons. Following her abortion, she became extremely promiscuous.

Tom Bird had everything Lorna wanted in a marriage. Sandy and Tom were quite possibly the most stable and successful couple Lorna ever knew, save her own father and mother. Tom was strong, self-assured, very caring and a professional with a great future. He showed genuine interest in her spirit, not her body. Tom had two sons. She fixated on Aaron and that fact greatly irritated Sandy, as did her attempts to seduce Tom.

Lorna had been beaten, though it's not certain to me that Marty was the one who beat her. Given the number of sexual encounters she had, it is just as likely that some of her sex partners beat her. But Marty had severe financial problems and, not only never gave a son to replace the aborted child, forced her to have her tubes tied.

Lorna wanted Tom's family, not her own.

When Jan Mead testified that Lorna said she and Tom were in love and that she wished something would happen to Marty and Sandy so they could be together, I believe Mead testified truthfully. Lorna often fantasized about being married to Tom and having Marty out of the way.

Lorna knew about Rocky Ford Bridge. Given its popularity as a party spot, it lent itself well to sexual trysts. I believe she discussed killing Marty at that site. She mentioned to Darrel and, most likely Danny, her idea to get Marty drugged or drunk and run him off a bridge. Perhaps she used the bridge site to bring Danny or Darrel sexual pleasure.

She told David Workman about getting Marty drugged or drunk and leaving him on a railroad crossing. Workman told her that no one would believe such a story because Marty hated drugs. But he had no knowledge of the research she had done.

Lorna talked with Alvin Tefft, an Army friend of Marty's. Besides asking him to have sex with her, which he refused, "three to four months" before Marty died, she asked him about some kind of a drug that could be injected into a person that would cause bleeding. She wanted a drug that could not be identified in an emergency room or in an autopsy. Though she denied in this conversation that she referred to herself, she could easily inject such a drug into Marty—or Sandy—and no one would ever know.

Her plan to murder Marty during May, 1983, fell through, but it left her several options for Sandy's murder.

July 16, 1983—I speculate

Late in the morning of July 16, 1983, Tom walked out of the Wal-Mart northwest of town. As he drove south down Industrial Boulevard, he saw Lorna's van parked at the Holiday Inn. She had a meeting with the Optimisses that day. He found her and told her to call home; Lori had been looking for her. She asked him what he planned to do that day, and he told her about celebrating Sandy's promotion by going to see *Return of the Jedi*.

Marty left for Reserves on Friday night and wouldn't return until Sunday evening. Lorna saw a deadly opportunity in this timing.

Lorna knew Tom's car sat in the church parking lot, so at some point, Sandy would be alone in her car. She and an accomplice sat in the parking lot waiting for Tom and Sandy to come out of the movie. They followed them to their Henry street house and waited for them to come out. They followed them to church and, once again, waited out of view. They had to use a different car because Lorna's van was so recognizable.

They saw them leave the church and go to The Station. The accomplice, a man unknown to the Birds, went in to keep an eye on them.

They followed the Birds when they left The Station and saw them drive back to the church. Lorna hadn't counted on Sandy going to ESU, but that made her plan even more workable.

Once Sandy left the church, Lorna followed her to ESU and confronted her when she got out of the car. Hit with a blunt object by Lorna's accomplice, Sandy fell unconscious. They bound her arms and legs tight with rubber hose, the kind Marty often brought home from Newman, and took her back to the Anderson house. The rubber hoses caused linear bruises on her arms. Lorna injected her with the kind of drug that Tefft had recommended. She lay weak and tied up. It was around 10:50 p.m.

Around 2:45 a.m., Lorna and her accomplice loaded the bound woman into the van, taking care to put a plastic tarp on the carpet. They drove to Rocky Ford Bridge. Lorna parked in the field opening south of the bridge, back as far as she could. She took a sip of the champagne she had found in Sandy's car and threw the red plastic cup out the window.

The man carried Sandy down to the bridge. She had awakened slightly and he hit her in the face to knock her unconscious, causing a laceration and bleeding. He held her horizontal to the bridge railing and, using all his strength, lifted her high, blood dripping down onto the rail and the cross member below. The body fell and hit the tree and rocks. The contact with the rocks caused her kidney to tear and broke her scapula. Her watch flew off from the impact. She lay there rapidly bleeding to death. But the plan wasn't done yet.

The man, who had driven the Peugeot to the bridge, lined it up on the gravel road to head it straight toward the embankment. Turning the lights on, he put the car in gear, got it rolling and, 10 feet short of the bank, rolled out of the driver's door. He took care not to leave any kind of "peel" marks and wore gloves to leave no finger prints. He planned to have the car fall on Sandy, making it look as though she got crushed when thrown from the car, but it missed her. It ended up in the water, upside down. It was around 3:10 a.m. Mark Gibbons' dogs barked and he heard a hissing sound as the radiator came in contact with the water.

Since the car had missed her, the man suggested they should put the body into the water. He climbed down the steep rocky embankment, but could barely stand up trying to walk on the rocks. And he couldn't see where he was going. He told Lorna to get a flashlight, climb down and give him some light. She feared falling on the rocks or tumbling down the embankment and, instead, walked east of the bridge, found a less steep bank, and climbed down there. She left a footprint in the mud on the beach as she walked back west toward the bridge.

She shined the flashlight on his path down to the water where he placed Sandy's body. They climbed back up the embankment and walked to the van, but heard a car coming. They got in the van and laid down as Linda Glaze drove past. They quickly drove away south, leaving a "skid mark" in the road.

After the murder

When church started on July 17, 1983, Don Froelich announced that Tom would not be there. Sandy had not come home the night before.

Susie Graf looked over at Lorna and saw her begin to cry and then she left the service, returning a few minutes later. Graf noticed she did this a couple of times that morning.

Lorna didn't come to the Bird's house until quite late in the afternoon, unlike her normal mother-hen treatment of Tom. She acted grief-stricken and remorseful, just as one would expect. She was an experienced actress.

The Birds left Monday to travel to Little Rock for Sandy's funeral.

Susan Ewert drove to Lorna's on Monday and, upon arriving, found her dressed in a party dress. Don Froelich was there talking about Tom and church business that needed attention, so Susan didn't stay. As she stepped off the porch, Susan said out loud to herself, "Did you have something to do with this?" She had a strong sense that Lorna knew something.

Dr. Gabriel performed the autopsy early that day at Newman Memorial. Marty worked there and Lorna knew about the autopsy. On Tuesday, she drove to Newman and found David Workman. Workman opened up the lab for her and later, saw her reading Sandy's autopsy report. She looked for any evidence of drugs and for the determination of the cause of death. What she saw pleased her. "Auto accident."

While Tom mourned his wife's loss in Arkansas, Lorna called him at Jane Grismer's house. Even while there, she could not leave him alone. But they needed to plan for the following Sunday service and the Monday memorial service.

That following Saturday, Angie Duensing came and talked with Tom for a long time. She again warned him of Lorna.

The memorial service was Monday. Tuesday, Jan Mead stopped at Lorna's house with Kim Clark in tow. They wanted to talk about American Heart Association business. Neither knew about Sandy's death, so Lorna told them. But both women later testified that they saw her with a strange look on her face when she said these things, a smile or smirk, like she knew something. Whatever she knew didn't seem to be unsettling. Lorna said that everyone thought it was an accident, and implied that she knew differently.

Wednesday, Tom called Lorna into his office. He told her that he could not afford any more distractions or the perception that something might be going on between them. He had been cautioned again. People in the church were talking. She needed to resign. She blew up and stomped out of the church.

Tom followed her to the van and they drove off. Tom convinced her to offer a well-reasoned resignation letter. The next day Tom visited Larry Kalsow and they talked about the incident. Kalsow talked with the lay ministers on Friday, and a tearful Lorna talked to Kalsow as well.

She did resign, as Tom suggested, but when the lay ministers met with her, she manipulated them into not accepting her resignation.

She stepped up her pressure on Tom, but he refused to counsel her anymore, offering instead to lend her $1,000 to pay for an out-of-town counselor. While continuing to try and win Tom's romantic favor, she asked Danny Carter to find someone to murder Marty.

When Danny named the dollar amount, Lorna told Tom she needed the $1,000 on September 7. He gave her the money. Where she got the balance of the money is unknown, but given Danny's drug dealings, she may have conned him into lending it to her. After all, she would soon have more than $300,000 in death benefits from Marty's insurance.

After Marty's murder, Tom, who had begun dating Terry Smith, told Lorna he'd be gone for a couple of days. She broke down. How could he leave her? Her husband had died. She loved Tom. She had murdered Sandy and Marty just so they could be together. He wanted to run off to Wichita to be with "that little teacher from Kansas City," as she snidely labeled Terry.

Tom gave her two cards and, after reading them, she put them in her lingerie drawer. She started to write him a love letter, but failed to complete it.

In all her testimony about Tom, Lorna continued to say, "I was in love with Tom and I wanted to be with him." This became her fixation, her fantasy, and it drove her to murder.

"Lorna Anderson" is the identity of the actor" Judge Gradert saw in these two murders.

So what of Tom Bird?

Kansas twice convicted Tom without evidence. What they claimed as evidence has since been repudiated.

Tom asks for a re-trial to prove his innocence. Kansas should grant that request, either by trying him again in a county far away from Emporia, or by asking the federal government to intervene.

Meanwhile, the state can parole him during his re-trial. If he loses during this re-trial, he will spend the rest of his life in prison, but he is willing to risk it. If he wins acquittal at the re-trial, he should be exonerated.

(If you want to keep current with events surrounding Tom Bird, or want to contact him, his friends operate a website at http://www.tombird.net. Visit it. Do what you can to help.)

Rev. Kothe's Post Script

Now that we have read Tom Bird's story and have examined the circumstantial evidence, what do we see? We see violations of common sense and the rule of law in ways that were immensely harmful to Tom Bird and dangerous to our society. Tom's wrongful conviction rested on gossip to establish the motive for murder. The prosecutor and judge dishonored the judicial system when they willfully introduced and allowed unverifiable gossip (hearsay testimony) to be heard by the jurors. This violates both the spirit and the letter of the law.

Like me, you have seen that the judge and the prosecutor in these trials were wrong in introducing and allowing the jurors to hear the unverifiable gossip about Tom; gossip that was latter proved false, but nonetheless fueled his convictions.

Whether Jan Mead knew it or not, by her testimony she caused great harm to Tom and to justice itself. She told the jurors what she "heard" from Lorna Anderson—for a minister Tom was good in bed. This gossip helped cement the motive to commit murder. There are two big problems here: First, Lorna said moments latter that she never meant Tom; she was referring to another man. Second, since Lorna hid behind her protection against self-incrimination, Rod Symmonds knew that she could not be cross-examined so as to verify or deny Mead's gossip.

Allowing Mead to testify was a clear and dishonorable act. Judge Rulon's tortured reasoning under the guise of a "declaration against interest" fails the test. Lorna had a well-founded and well-known reputation for promiscuity among dozens of men and their wives. To suggest that she would not make false statements to Mead that might sully her reputation is, simply, preposterous.

But as you read you may have thought, "I don't agree with what the prosecutor did or the fact that the judge allowed it. They *were* wrong in introducing hearsay testimony and Symmonds got by with it, but 'he was just doing his job.'"

I have often wondered where that little phrase, "he was just doing his job," came from. You and I regularly quote this vulgarity. Did someone like you coin the phrase or did you hear it from someone else? Probably from a lawyer. And in what context have you heard it? You certainly did not hear it in the context of a lawyer's job description, but more likely when a lawyer has performed an unethical or immoral act while representing a client. You question him and he responds, "I was just doing my job."

Years ago, when character and integrity were still important, we believed that a lawyer's job was to make sure that a defendant's constitutional rights were protected; that a person should get a fair and impartial trail, free of prejudice, lies, deception and manufactured evidence—free of hearsay. We believed that lies and gossip should never be allowed to either convict an innocent person or acquit a guilty one. We knew this to be a travesty of justice.

Once again, some lawyers tell us that they are just doing their job when they ignore evidence and introduce equivocation, and we buy it! We should not.

Justice fails because some lawyers hide behind their plea, "I was just doing my job."

What should we do?

First of all, we should demand that our judicial system protect individual rights and hold the government to the strictures of the constitution and the law. We should demand that those who lie and gossip in court, and those who introduce and allow such lies and gossip, be punished. For when the constitution is trashed by arbitrary judicial tampering, individuals' protection under the law is gravely threatened and injustice for one turns quickly into tyranny for all. Society is put at risk, leaving us all unsure of the rightness of any law or the impartiality of its application. We become vulnerable to the whims of the state. If we allow this judicial jaundice to go uncorrected, then we all shall in the end, become subject to it, be persecuted, and the nation itself will fall.

Before closing arguments, Judge Rulon threatened to give the following instruction to the jury. "A person who either before or during its commission intentionally aids, abets, advises, hires, counsels or procures another to commit a crime with the intent to promote or assist in its commission is criminally responsible for the crime regardless of the extent of the defendants' participation if any in the actual commission of the crime."

He repented of this threat, but the principle he stated in the instruction needs to be applied as well to judges and lawyers. It might be stated this way: "If a judge or lawyer either before or during trial intentionally aids, abets, advises, hires, counsels or procures another to lie, deceive, introduce hearsay testimony (gossip), manufacture evidence or allow such in court with the intent to promote or assist in a conviction or acquittal, he is criminally responsible for the crime regardless of the extent of the lawyer's or judge's participation, if any, in the actual commission of the crime."

When the people of the United States experience such courtroom travesties as occurred in Tom's trial, they ought to rise up and demand impeachment of the judges and lawyers. They ought to work diligently for the release of the wrongfully convicted, like Tom Bird. They ought to write letters to the Chief Justice of the Kansas Supreme Court demanding him to grant Tom a new trial. And they ought to write and call Kansas lawmakers and ask them to do the same.

Finally, "A judge ought, above all, to be a man of integrity, and not only honest but also a wise, sagacious, brave, and fearless man."* A lawyer ought, likewise, to have the same qualities.

"He who is to administer justice equitable in all cases will often offend good friends, relatives, neighbors, and the rich and powerful who are in a position to help or harm him. He must therefore be quite blind, shutting his eyes and ears to everything but the evidence presented, and make his decision accordingly."* A witness and a juror should be fearless and honest.

Had all this been done, inmate Tom Bird would never have been caged—he would be a free Bird. Instead, Kansas caged him in a sort of vicarious punishment for the crimes committed by Lorna Anderson, Danny Carter and Greg Curry. Perhaps the jurors wanted to punish Darrel Carter for his adultery with Lorna and Julie, and his self-confession to at least three attempts by Lorna to help him find a murderer, but Lyon County never charged him. Or maybe the jurors wanted to try Johnny Bingham, but Mississippi law enforcement fouled up that possibility, eventually driving Geary County to drop all charges.

Whatever lays behind the complicated reasoning of two juries, it's time to set the caged Bird free.

*Book of Concord, Tappert Edition, p. 400

Acheson, Clint
Kansas Republican State Representative

Aldrete, Esther
One of Lorna's babysitters

Anderson, Lorna G.
Promiscuous church secretary, who participated in murdering her husband, played the central role in destroying Tom Bird's life. Serving a 15-year to life sentence for a second degree conviction in the murder of Marty Anderson

Anderson, Martin K.
Murdered husband of Lorna Anderson

Anderson, Stephen
Marty's brother

Anderson, Lori
Marty and Lorna's oldest daughter

Andrews, Dan
Lyon County Sheriff at the time of Sandy Bird's death

Arb, Dennis
A witness at Rocky Ford Bridge and cousin to Sheriff Dan Andrews

Baccus, Denise
One of Lorna's many babysitters

Baker, Joan
Writer of a series of 1986 articles about Tom and Lorna for KS Magazine

Barger, Dale
Presiding juror in Tom's 1985 murder trial

Barnhart, Peggy
Member of Faith Lutheran Church who lived near Rocky Ford Bridge

Bayless, Dennis and Deborah
Two of the first to arrive on the murder scene the night of Marty's death

Bell, Bob
Tow truck driver who helped pull Sandy's car out of the river

Berges, Gary
Geary County Deputy Sheriff who found the murder weapon

Bingham, Jimmy
Brother to Johnny Bingham

Bingham, Johnny
Implicated by Greg Curry as Marty's killer—Later, all charges were dropped against him

Bird Family
Rev. Ralph and Virginia: Tom's parents
Mark: Tom's brother
Gloria (Cates): Tom's sister
Andrea, Paul and Aaron: Tom's children
Sandy: Tom's wife, who died at Rocky Ford Bridge

Bird, Thomas P.
Former pastor at Faith Lutheran Church, Emporia, Kansas, convicted of criminal solicitation to hire someone to murder Mary Anderson; convicted of murdering Sandy Bird; acquitted of murdering Marty Anderson; Serving a life sentence at Lansing Correctional Facility in Lansing, KS

Birk, Roberta
Reporter for the Emporia Gazette

Blomenkamp, Larry
Emporia Chief of Police

Bohlken, Dan, Rev.
Seminary classmate of Tom's

Bork, John
Assistant Kansas Attorney General who helped prosecute Tom in 1990

Boysen, Al and Pat, Rev.
Pastor and wife who were close friends of Sandy and Tom, and spent time with Sandy a week prior to her death

Bridgens, James, M.D.
Forensic Pathologist who testified on Tom's behalf in the 1985 murder trial

Bryant, Earl
    An ambulance driver who helped remove
    Sandy's body from the river

Bryant, Jody
    Member of the joint youth board of Faith
    and Messiah Lutheran churches

Burgett, Marie
    Member of the 1990 Junction City jury

Burnau, Eileen
    Scientist from the KBI labs

Burroughs, Al, Rev.
    Tom worked with his committee to put
    on family life seminars all around
    Kansas

Buskey, Al
    Geary County Deputy Sheriff who
    investigated Marty's murder

Butcher, Thomas, M.D.
    Pathologist who served as Lyon County
    coroner

Cales, Charron
    Stayed and helped calm the Anderson
    girls after Marty's murder

Call, Ray
    Editor of the Emporia Gazette

Callison, John
    Assistant Warden at Kansas Correctional
    Institution at the co-ed facility where
    Lorna first lived

Carlin, John
    Kansas Governor in 1986 who had a
    cameo appearance in *Murder Ordained*

Carlson, John
    Sandy's supervisor at Emporia State
    University and a friend of the Bird's

Carlson, Doug and Susan
    Both saw Tom at the Burger King in
    Topeka on November 4, 1983

Carradine, Keith
    Actor who played John Rule in *Murder
    Ordained*

Carter, Casey
    Danny Carter's son

Carter, Darrel
    Emporia builder who accused Tom of
    trying to hire him to murder Marty;
    brother of Danny

Carter, Danny
    Confessed to giving $5,000 to Greg
    Curry to hire Marty's murderer; brother
    of Darrel

Carter, Ron
    Younger brother of Darrel and Danny
    Carter

Cates, Gloria and Felix
    Tom's sister and brother-in-law

Christenson, James
    Presiding juror in Tom's 1990 Junction
    City trial

Clark, Dick
    Hollywood personality who signed a
    contract with Jane Grismer to do a movie
    about Sandy's death

Clark, Kim
    Employee of American Heart
    Association who became Lorna's
    supervisor in the summer of 1983

Coleman, David
    Corinth, Mississippi for Johnny Bingham

Cotharn, Nancy
    Sandy's aunt, Jane Grismer's sister

Cox, David
    Paramedic who helped take Sandy's
    body out of the river

Crahan, James
    Auto insurance adjuster who investigated
    Sandy's death

Cromley, Kathleen
    Emporia native and advance staff person
    for Interscope productions, the company
    that produced *Murder Ordained*

Cronk, Scott
Emporia police officer

Curry, Gerald
Greg's father and resident of Corinth, MS

Curry, Greg
Received $5,000 from Danny Carter to give to the person who would kill Marty; claimed he gave the money to Johnny Bingham

Curry, Harold
Brother of Gerald and uncle of Greg, resident of Corinth, MS

De Boer, Mertin
Lyon County Undersheriff who arrested Tom at Lansing Correctional Facility

De Zago, Ralph
Greg Curry's attorney

Dehaemers, David
Owner/operator of I-35 Auto Parts who bought Sandy's Peugeot

Delmont, Dennis
Emporia police officer

Deppish, Bill
Geary County Sheriff

Dirks, Gary
Forensic scientist who testified in Tom's 1985 trial

Duensing, Angie (Davis)
Director of Lord's Lambs preschool at Faith Lutheran Church and former friend of Sandy and Tom, who testified against Tom three times

Eckert, William, M.D.
Forensic Pathologist who performed a second autopsy on Sandy's body and testified for the state in Tom's 1985 trial

Eggeman, Ken
Friend of Tom and Sandy's from Faith Lutheran Church

Eichorn, Gary
Lyon County Deputy Sheriff who participated in aspects of the investigation of Sandy's death

Eldridge, Randy
Married Lorna in June of 1985, adopted her children and divorced her after she received a life sentence

Enoch, Mark
Reporter from Hutchinson, KS

Estes, Larry
Owner/operator of towing company that pulled Sandy's car out of the river

Ewert, Susan
Close friend of both Tom and Lorna

Faust, Scott
Reporter for the Wichita Eagle Bulletin

Fenheim, Rick
Security officer at Lyon County court

Fletcher, Brian
Canoeist who first saw Sandy Bird's body in the river

Focht, Jack
Kansas defense attorney for Lorna Anderson

Ford, Robert, M.D.
Sandy's West Memphis OB-GYN doctor

Froelich, Don
Chief Lay Minister at Faith Lutheran Church

Gabriel, Juan, M.D.
Pathologist who performed the first autopsy on Sandy's body

Geller, Fred
Arkansas friend of Mark Bird, who acted as his driver in 1984

Gerits, John
ESU professor who worked with Sandy Bird

Gibbons, Mark
Lived in mobile home 300 feet south of Rocky Ford Bridge on the night that Sandy died

Glaze, Linda
Emporia attorney and horse trainer who testified at the 1985 trial

Gradert, Melvin
Judge who presided at Tom's 1990 Junction City trial

Graf, Susan
Member of Faith Lutheran Church who testified against Tom in his 1984 trial

Green, Dannell
Missouri Highway Patrolman who stopped Danny Carter for speeding and discovered a loaded handgun on his front seat.

Grismer, Jane Stringer
Sandy Stringer Bird's mother who divorced Randall and married Dr. Jerry Grismer

Grismer, Jerry, M.D.
Jane's second husband and a Little Rock physician

Grother, Kermit
Member of Messiah Lutheran Church, friend of Tom Bird's, who bought fireworks from Darrel Carter

Hacker, Cliff
Lyon County Sheriff who followed Dan Andrews into office in 1985

Hacker, David
Pulitzer Prize winning writer who had a contract to write a book about Lorna's first 20 years of life

Hackett, Rev. Tom and Sue
Seminary friends of Tom and Sandy Bird

Hanschu, Steven and Beth
Members of Faith Lutheran Church who saw Tom at a Washburn University based seminar on November 4, 1983

Hecht, Robert
Defense attorney who represented Tom at his 1985 murder trial and in several other subsequent legal matters

Heffley, Stanley
KBI chemist who tested bottle contents and plastic cups

Henderson, Charles
Four-time convicted inmate who testified against Tom in his 1985 trial

Henderson, Scott
A security officer at ESU

Herd, Harold
Kansas State Supreme Court Justice who heard Tom's 1986 appeal

Hinrichs, Louise
Friend of Sandy and Tom, a co-worker at ESU

Hoffman, Brian
Witness to crime scene at Marty's murder

Hoffman, Sheryll
Bus-riding witness who helped with the children following Marty's murder

Horst, Nancy
Emporia Gazette reporter who covered Tom Bird's trials and the interim between them

Hughs, Donna
Rod Symmonds secretary who read Julie Palmer's testimony to the court in the 1985 trial

Humphrey, J. Vernon (Vern)
Lyon County based KBI agent who investigated Tom and Lorna

Jenkins, Martha
Kansas Republican State Representative who co-authored the bill preventing felons from profiting from the sale of their books

Johnson, Joan
> Driver who witnessed two men talking while standing in front of the Anderson van the night of Marty's murder

Kalsow, Larry, Rev.
> Pastor of Messiah Lutheran Church, seminary classmate of Tom's and his friend

Kaufman, Charles
> Handwriting expert who testified in Tom's first trial

Kemp, Kenneth, DDS
> Dentist who was a witness at the murder scene of Marty Anderson

Kennedy, William
> Engineer and accident reconstructionist who testified for Tom in his 1985 trial

Kidd, Guy
> Director of Security at ESU in 1983

Kimble, Chris
> Lorna and Marty's life insurance agent

King, Eugene
> Corinth, Mississippi, resident who claimed Johnny Bingham was with him on November 4, 1983.

Kinney, Terry
> Chicago stage actor who played the role of Tom Bird in *Murder Ordained*

Klamm, David
> Junction City police officer

Koch, Deana
> Sandy's friend from ESU

Kothe, Kenneth, Rev.
> Seminary classmate of Tom's who caused this book to be written

Kraft, Scott
> Wrote a major article on Tom Bird and Lorna Anderson published in The Los Angeles Times in 1987 that caused a bidding war for the TV rights to the murder story

Kramer, Terry
> Ambulance driver who helped remove Sandy's body from the river

Laib, Bart
> Member of Faith Lutheran Church who rode with Tom back from Topeka on November 4, 1983

Lapping, Joe
> Darrel Carter's neighbor who said Darrel told him about someone wanting him to hire a murderer

Larson, Ray, Rev.
> LC-MS pastor who served as a chaplain at Fort Riley on November 4, 1983

Lassiter, Jack
> Little Rock attorney of Jane Grismer who investigated Sandy's death

Leonard, John and Becky
> Witnesses at the murder scene of Marty Anderson

Lesher, Tom
> Junction City police officer who collected evidence at the Marty murder scene

Livingston, Barbara
> Planned to write a book about Lorna and the murders, interviewed her late in 1985

Lofgren, Mike
> Lead the Minnesota Highway Patrol's school for accident reconstructionist training

Long, Mack
> Lyon County Deputy Sheriff

McKone, Mike
> Attorney who represented Tom in his 1990 murder trial

Mead, Jan (Dykehouse)
> Lorna's supervisor at the American Heart Association. Testified against Tom three times.

Mendenhal, Tom, Rev.
Lorna's pastor after she moved back to
Hutchinson.

Meyer, Darrell
Lorna's first attorney, attorney for Faith,
and friend of Tom's

Meyer, Sharon and Howard
Howard served as a lay minister at Faith.
Sharon was active in church ministries.
Both testified for the state in the 1984
and 1985 trials.

Miguelino, "Mike", M.D.
Emporia doctor who assisted in Sandy's
first autopsy, and belonged to the
Optimist Club with Tom and Marty.

Miller, Monte
Served for a short time in 1987 as Tom's
court-appointed attorney

Mohan, Rakesh
Chemist who tested Sandy's blood for
toxins and poisons

Moore, Steven and Stephanie
Friends and next door neighbors of the
Birds. Members of Faith Lutheran
Church.

Morgan, Terry
Emporia bank teller who cashed Tom's
September 7, 1983, check

Nevitt, Robert
Lived south of Rocky Ford Bridge and
drove across it the night Sandy died

Ney, Richard
Kansas attorney whom Tom preferred to
handle his Junction City case

Olson, Raymond
In charge of roads and sign for the
Kansas Department of Transportation

Opat, Steven
Geary County Attorney who prosecuted
Tom and Lorna for Marty's murder

Otten, Herman, Rev.
Publisher of Christian News, the weekly
Lutheran newspaper that kept Tom's
story alive

Palmer, Julie
A pseudonym for an Emporia home
maker who had a long-standing affair
with Darrel Carter

Patton, Mike
Emporia attorney who represented
Danny and Darrel Carter, and consulted
with Lorna at least once

Peck, Doug
Highway patrolman who witnessed and
took pictures at Sandy's first autopsy

Perich, Jeanette
Susan Carlson's mother and a witness to
Tom's presence in Topeka on November
4, 1983

Persinger, William
The state's accident reconstructionist
who testified at Tom's 1985 trial

Pierce, Richard
Analyzed Sandy's blood samples for
evidence of alcohol

Pruisner, Mike
An elder at Messiah Lutheran Church,
fellow member of the Optimists and
friend of Tom's and Marty's

Rahal, Randolph "Randy"
Inmate who claimed Tom confessed to
him. Received parole and then skipped
town. He never did testify in court.

Rath, John, Rev.
An LC-MS pastor who served as the
district counselor while Tom pastored at
Faith

Rees, Alan
A member of the youth board at Faith
Lutheran Church

Richardson, Joe
> Owner of Rich Industries, the company that eventually bought Sandy's car

Robe, Mike
> Producer and writer of *Murder Ordained*, the CBS four-hour mini-series about Tom and Lorna

Robinson, Michael
> An Army Guard sergeant who traveled to Reserve camp with Marty

Roelfs, Lorie
> Police official who briefly testified in one of Tom's Emporia trials

Rohrig, Timothy, M.D.
> A forensic toxicologist for the KBI who testified at Tom's 1985 trial

Romsa, Don, Rev.
> LC-MS pastor who also served as a counselor to Tom the summer of 1984

Rosenboom, Joyce
> Member of Faith Lutheran, friend of Tom's who testified at the 1984 and 1985 trials

Rosenboom, Reka
> Daughter of Joyce, active in youth group at Faith and a babysitter for Lorna

Rule, John
> Kansas Highway patrolman assigned as an accident specialist to Sandy's wreck. Headed the police investigation into the accident. Portrayed as a hero in *Murder Ordained*.

Rulon, Gary, Judge
> The presiding judge at Tom's 1984 and 1985 trials, friend of Marty and Lorna's. Eventually appointed to the Kansas Appeals Court.

Sadowski, Tom
> A security guard at ESU who had been on duty the night of Sandy's death

Samuels, David
> Lyon County Sheriff who watched Danny Carter's apartment while deputies questioned him at the sheriff's office

Say, Ron
> One of the witnesses at Marty's murder site

Schreck, Charles
> Lyon County Undersheriff in 1983

Schwinn, Harold
> One of the three lay ministers at Faith Lutheran Church during 1982-1983

Scott, George, Judge
> One of the Geary County judges who heard part of the inquisition into Marty's murder

Shaw, Irv
> Emporia attorney who represented Tom during his 1984 trial

Shipley, Jeff
> Worked with the young people at Faith Lutheran and heard Tom talk about firecrackers

Simmons, Gladys
> Lorna's grandmother who lived in Topeka

Slater, Loren and Alta
> Lorna's parents

Smith, Charles and Carolyn, Rev.
> Tom's best friend from seminary days and his wife, who spent time with Sandy a week before she died

Smith, Charles
> Kansas Highway Patrolman who told broke the news of Sandy's death to Tom

Speaks, Kristin
> One of the five witnesses who saw Tom in Topeka at 5:30 on November 4, 1983

Speltz, Teresa
One of the women who helped care for
the Anderson children the night of
Marty's murder

Spires, Diana
Member of Faith Lutheran who heard
Charles Henderson confess he knew
nothing about Tom's case

Sprick, Donavan, Rev.
LC-MS pastor who served a church in
Junction City

Stackhouse, Earl
Kansas Highway Patrolman who helped
investigate Marty's murder site

Stephen, Robert
Kansas Attorney General

Stephens, Jeffrey, Rev.
LC-MS Pastor in whom Rev. Charles
Smith confided about counseling Sandy

Stringer, Laura
Tom and Sandy's sister-in-law

Summey, Mark
Emporia Police Officer who visited Tom
around 3:30 a.m. on July 17, 1983

Swint, Amy, Brenda and Carol
Carol is the mother of the other two who
served as babysitters for the Birds. Amy
babysat the night of Sandy's death.

Symmonds, Rod
Lyon County Attorney who prosecuted
Tom in 1984 and 1985

Teeselink, Scott
Junction City police officer who assisted
in the investigation of Marty's murder

Tefft, Alvin
Fellow member of the Army Reserve
with Marty who talked several times
with Lorna

Thomas, Kenton
Mortician who embalmed Sandy's body

Thomas, Bert
One of the Junction City jurors

Thompson, Tommy
Bank officer at Lyon County Bank

Thornton, Alice
Lyon County Bailiff

Trillin, Calvin
Writer for New Yorker magazine who
wrote a feature about Tom and Lorna

Tucker, Jim Guy
Former Governor of Arkansas who
served as an advisor to Mark Bird's
Little Rock attorney

Tuner, Jeanne
Chief Clerk for the Lyon County court

Unruh, Roger
Co-counsel to Mike McKone at the 1990
Junction City trial that questioned Lorna

Wagoner, Dee
Member of Faith Lutheran Church who
testified for Tom in 1984

Warren, Darrell
Sheetrock taper who worked for Darrel
Carter who testified against Tom in 1984

Waters, John
Bread truck driver who spotted two cars,
one that resembled Lorna's, near Marty's
murder site a couple of weeks before he
was murdered

Webb, Bruce
One of the Lyon County jurors during
Tom's 1985 trial

Weinmeister, Sherry (Galliart)
Friend and student of Tom's who talked
with him at 5:30 p.m. on November 4,
1983, in Topeka

Wheeler, Connie
Inmate confidant of Lorna's from the
Kansas Correctional Facility

White, Donald
> Peugeot mechanic who testified at the
> 1985 trial

Williams, JoBeth
> Soap opera actress who played the role
> of Lorna Anderson in *Murder Ordained*

Wilson, Gail
> Former girlfriend of Danny Carter who
> notified the KBI of his involvement in
> Marty's murder

Winkler, Henry "The Fonz"
> Signed a 1986 contract with Tom to do a
> movie about his life